Documents Office Classification

Fifth Edition

Volume I
A - GS

DOCUMENTS OFFICE CLASSIFICATION

Fifth Edition
June, 1976

compiled by
Mary Elizabeth Poole

including

An explanation of the Superintendent

of Documents Classification System

and an

Alphabetical Index of U.S. Government Author Organizations

VOLUME I
A - GS

The United States Historical Documents Institute, Inc.
Arlington, Virginia

Copyright © 1977 by United States Historical Documents Institute, Inc.
1911 Ft. Myer Drive, Arlington, Virginia 22209

All rights reserved, including those to reproduce this book or any parts thereof in any form.

Library of Congress Catalog Card Number: 77-87107   ISBN 0-88222-022-5 (Vol. I)

CONTENTS

Preface to the Fifth Edition
  by Mary Elizabeth Poole vii

An Explanation of the Superintendent
  of Documents Classification System xi

The Documents Office Classification, as of June, 1976 1

Major Segments:

VOLUME I

A	Agriculture Dept.	1
C	Commerce Dept.	217
D	Defense Dept.	439
EP	Environmental Protection Agency	591
FAA	Federal Aviation Agency	615

  Alphabetical Index A-1

VOLUME II

HE	Health, Education and Welfare Dept.	773
I	Interior Dept.	915
N	Navy Dept.	1227
NAS	National Aeronautics and Space Administration	1261
P	United States Postal Service	1291
Pr	President of the United States	1327

  Alphabetical Index A-1

VOLUME III

S	State Dept.	1429
T	Treasury Dept.	1499
TD	Transportation Dept.	1569
W	War Dept.	1613
Y	Congress	1727

  Alphabetical Index A-1

    KEY: Volume One includes the entries from A through GS
           Volume Two includes the entries from HE through RR
           Volume Three includes the entries from S through Z

Preface

The Documents Office Classification compilation was made because we needed it. In 1939, when I was reclassifying documents in Duke University Library and collecting needed numbers from invoices, Dr. G. A. Nuermberger discovered that Mr. Ralph M. Brown at Virginia Polytechnic Institute Library, had a compilation of numbers, and they let us borrow it to copy. They had not copied the number beyond the colon and the compilation was incomplete. I added to it from all the sources available to me. Mr. Alton P. Tisdell, Superintendent of Documents, lent us depository invoices for 1910-24 which supplied many numbers.

In 1943/44 I was in Virginia Polytechnic Institute Library where I saw some original pages in Mr. Brown's handwriting. They had not kept up their compilation; so I borrowed the one from Duke University and typed in the additions. At this time I typed a copy for myself.

I arrived in Raleigh to begin work for North Carolina State College with three notebooks (now I have 8) of the classification and a typewriter. Mrs. Reba Davis Clevenger, who had organized the document collection at North Carolina State and was then Acting Librarian, wanted me to type a copy for the Library, and she encouraged me to go to Washington where Miss Mona H. McGregor, Chief of the Library, Division of Public Documents, let me use their shelflist to look for titles of skipped numbers. It was the copy I made for North Carolina State College that was photographed for the lithoprint edition produced by Edwards Brothers, Ann Arbor, Michigan. This was done because Mrs. Clevenger said I had something that other libraries needed and should share it with them. That was 1945.

In 1958 I asked University Microfilms about filming it because I knew people who wanted copies. Mr. Stevens Rice said he had examined the compilation and it was not the sort of thing people should have to use on microfilm. He proposed publishing it by Xerography. That edition was also from the Library copy, but the 1967 edition was from my original copy with much retyping. For the 4th all pages not previously retyped were so the print would be the same. For the 5th much retyping was done to clean up pages after the addition of many inserted classes.

For the second edition, Mr. Joseph A. King, Chief of the Library, supplied some titles for a list of classes I sent him. I had used their shelflist to obtain listings for numbers that showed up as skips. For the third edition, Mrs. Margaret B. Wilson, Chief of the Library, supplied titles for several pages of skipped classes.

The fourth edition contained unpublished, inserted and added-on classes as well as more skips. New classes could be inserted or added at the end without showing up as skips and there was no practical way to obtain this information until Checklist of U.S. Public Documents 1789-1970, the microfilm of the card catalog of the Public Documents Department. I had a list of skips waiting, and after they had been searched, began, what we had never been able to do before, to compare the classification compilation with all the guide cards in the catalog. Thus it was possible to find numbers previously inaccessible. I read through the first half (current classes) just looking for new numbers, and the second half (noncurrent classes) more slowly checking all cross references. When Mr. William Buchanan said he would publish it, I knew the first half of the film should be rechecked. Susan Rose did that and also checked the Third Supplement to <u>Checklist 1970</u>.

The 4th edition was through 1973. Mrs. Mae Collins, Chief of the Library, Public Documents Department, answered questions about later skips, titles not legible on the film, and provided advance copies of December 1973 and February 1974 "New Classification Numbers" in order that entries through 1973, including 1973 periodical publications, could be included.

The 5th edition is through June 1976. This is rather soon after the 4th, but <u>Checklist of United States Public Documents, 1789-1976</u> offered a unique chance to acquire the subsequent unpublished numbers. The film is as of about March 1976 and Mrs. Mae Collins assured me that they are now putting all additions to the classification in "New Classification Numbers".

The time of the change in format of the Monthly Catalog is an appropriate time for the classification compilation to be published.

Checking my, already updated from the <u>Monthly Catalog</u>, compilation with the microfilm produced pages of new (inserted and added on) classes and cross references.

A listing in this compilation does not necessarily indicate publications have been issued. Formerly classes .1: through .4: were always established for new agencies and these classes of publications were not always issued. Later only classes .1: and .2: were routinely published in "New Classification Numbers". Classes 1 through 8 are saved for specific form classes and space is left for them even if none were issued. This is in accordance with all previous editions.

When FS became HE many existing numbers were continued with the HE prefix and were not relisted in "New Classification Numbers". I had been adding these to my copy of the classification as I cataloged publications issued since the change, depository copies and non-depository Microprints. But some are listed on the January 1973 Classified List, and these I included even if I had no evidence of publication.

Mary Elizabeth Poole
Document Librarian

The D. H. Hill Library
North Carolina State University
Raleigh, North Carolina
February 1977

On Supplementing the Classification

To maintain the classification compilation in sheet form (my copy is loose-leaf) requires much retyping because of inserted classes. A card format would avoid the retyping, but I have never made a classification compilation that way.

I made a loose-leaf supplement to the 4th edition on 9 1/2 x 6" paper so it would more nearly match in size the bound volumes; my original was on 8 1/2 x 11" paper. Each size has its advantages and disadvantages. A line was left between entries to make it easier to read and so an inserted class can be added without having to retype the page. On the larger pages additional inserts in the same place could even go in the margin. On the smaller paper one line is often not long enough for an entry and there is practically no margin to write in. There is more retyping of pages, but the pages are smaller and I planned to retype only enough to keep the numbers in correct sequence. If a page is not full and the agency is continued on the next page I draw a little down-pointing arrow in the lower left hand corner.

And there are more symbols. It is important that the supplement be tied to the compilation. One way, of course, is the Earlier and Later references that are a part of so many entries. There is enough space in the compilation to write in Later notes.

I used many little-lines, really no more than a hyphen. A little-line drawn following the last entry for an agency indicates continued in the supplement. In the supplement after the agency name, (continued) indicates earlier classes are in the compilation. An inserted class (or classes) is indicated by a little-line drawn in the classification between the two numbers it falls between. In the supplement a hyphen typed before the class number indicates this is an insert and for references to surrounding classes see the compilation. The hyphen also shows that, since the entry is an insert, numerical skips before and after it are meaningless.

There should be no skips between the last number of a class in the compilation and the first (not an insert) in the supplement. If the number I am adding is not the next one I hold space for it, writing in the unknown number and spacing down to the one I do have a title for.

Inserts come first and then higher numbers. If inserts are numerous to the point of being a nuisance I may make the first page(s) inserts only and start the added numbers on another page. This is a time to use the down-pointing arrow.

Sometimes in the supplement I repeated an isolated entry from the classification to avoid an apparent skip and marked it # in the supplement.

In the case of a new agency I have put a double little-line in the compilation, probably not necessary. Little-lines in the index could mean new index entries in the supplement, but I have not done this because there were 3 of the indexes in the compilation.

M.E.P.

AN EXPLANATION OF THE SUPERINTENDENT OF DOCUMENTS CLASSIFICATION SYSTEM

....as currently used in the Library of the Division of Public Documents, United States Government Printing Office, and as catalog numbers for the stocks of Government publications sold by the Superintendent of Documents.

The following section has been reproduced in its entirety from a pamphlet which was prepared originally by the late Superintendent of Documents, Mr. Joseph A. King, to answer frequent inquiries received by his office, and to provide an aid in the training of new personnel in the Division of Public Documents. The original edition was first published in March 1963. This revised edition was prepared by Norman N. Barbee, classification specialist, under the supervision of Mrs. Mae S. Collins, Chief of Library, and issued in July, 1970.

THE SUPERINTENDENT OF DOCUMENTS CLASSIFICATION SYSTEM

This system was formed in the Library of the Division of Public Documents sometime between 1895 and 1903. The first explanation of it was given in October 1903 by William Leander Post, then in charge of the Library, in the preface to List of Publications of the Agriculture Department 1862-1902, Department List No. 1, issued by the Superintendent of Documents in 1904.

Mr. Post gives credit for the basis of the system (classification by governmental author) to Miss Adelaide R. Hasse, who used this basis in assigning classification numbers to a List of Publications of the U.S. Department of Agriculture from 1841 to June 30, 1895, inclusive. Miss Hasse prepared the list while assistant librarian in the Los Angeles Public Library but it was published by the Department of Agriculture in 1896 as its Library Bulletin No. 9.

Like other classification systems in use for many years, this one has expanded as the Federal Government has grown, and has changed in some details and methods of use, though still retaining the principles upon which it is based.

It has one fundamental weakness — the position in the scheme, of the publications of any Government author (i.e. department, bureau, office, etc.), is determined by the current organizational status of the author. Thus it is at the mercy of any Government reorganization which may be directed by the President, by Congress, or by the head of a department or agency, with the result that the publications of some authors may be located in as many as three different places in the scheme.*

*Publisher's Note:

As explained in the Introduction, Index Volume Number II (U.S. Government Author-Organization Index, 1789-1970) contains the names of over 8,300 government author-organizations. As the names are listed alphabetically, all SDC numbers ever used by any government author are grouped together in this Index, regardless of its organizational history.

Despite this fundamental weakness, it has stood the test of time as a workable arrangement for publications of the United States Government, having been used for over 50 years by the Library of the Division of Public Documents (the Office of the Superintendent of Documents in earlier years) for the collection of public documents which has accumulated as a by-product of the Division's cataloging and publishing functions, and as a catalog system for the stocks of Government publications sold by the Superintendent of Documents.

PRINCIPLES OF THE SYSTEM

The basis of the classification is the grouping together of the publications of any Government author — the various departments, bureaus, and agencies being considered the authors. In the grouping, the organizational structure of the United States Government is followed, that is, subordinate bureaus and divisions are grouped with the parent organization.

Author Symbols

Each executive department and agency, the Judiciary, Congress, and other major independent establishments are assigned a place in the scheme. The place is determined by the alphabetical designation assigned to each, as "A" for Agriculture Department, "Ju" for Judiciary, and "NS" for National Science Foundation, the designation usually being based on the name of the organization. (See attached Table I for symbols currently in use.)

Subordinate Offices

To set off the subordinate bureaus and offices, numbers are added to the symbols with figure "1" being used for the parent organization and the secretary's or administrator's office.

Beginning with the figure "2" the numbers are applied in numerical order to the subordinate bureaus and offices, these having been arranged alphabetically when the system was established, and new subordinate bureaus or offices having been given the next highest number. A period follows the combination of letters and numbers representing the bureau or office. For example:

Agriculture Department (including Secretary's Office)	A 1.
Forest Service	A 13.
Information Office	A 21.
Rural Electrification Administration	A 68.

Series Designations

The second breakdown in the scheme is for the various series of publications issued by a particular bureau or office. A number is assigned to each series and this number is followed by a colon.

In the beginning the following numbers were assigned for the types of publications common to most Government offices:

1: Annual reports
2: General publications (unnumbered publications of a miscellaneous nature)
3: Bulletins
4: Circulars

In setting up classes for new agencies or bureaus, these numbers were reserved for those types of publications. Later, new types common to most offices evolved and the following additional numbers were set aside in the classes of new agencies for particular types of series:

5: Laws (administered by the agency and published by it)
6: Regulations, rules, and instructions
7: Releases
8: Handbooks, manuals, guides

Any additional series issued by an office are given the next highest numbers in order of issuance — that is, as an office begins publication of a series the next highest number not already assigned to a series is assigned to the new series of the particular office.

Related Series

New series which are closely related to already existing series are now tied-in to the existing series so as to file side by side on the shelf. Originally no provision was made for this except in the case of separates from publications in a series. Tie-in is provided by use of the shilling mark after the number assigned to the existing series, followed by a digit for each related series starting with "2". (The "1" is not generally used in this connection since the existing series is the first.) Separates are distinguished by use of a lower case letter beginning with "a" rather than by numbers.

A theoretical example of these "tie-in" classes is as follows:

4: Circulars
4/a: Separates from Circulars (numbered)
4/b: Separates from Circulars (unnumbered)
4/2: Administrative Circulars
4/3: Technical Circulars

Class Stem

Thus by combining the designations for authors and those for the series published by the authors, we obtain the class stems for the various series of publications issued by the United States Government. For example:

A 1.10: Agriculture Yearbook
A 13.1: Annual Report of Chief of Forest Service
A 57.38: Soil Survey Reports

Book Numbers

The individual book number follows the colon. For numbered series the original edition of a publication gets simply the number of the book. For example, Department of Agriculture Leaflet 381 would be a 1.35:381. For revisions of numbered publications, the shilling mark and additional figures beginning with 2 are added, as: A 1.35:381/2, A 1.35:381/3, etc.

In the case of annuals, the last three digits of the year are used for the book number, e.g., Annual Report of Secretary of Agriculture, A

1.1:954. For reports or publications covering more than one year, a combination of the dates is used, e.g., Annual Register of the U.S. Naval Academy, 1954-1955 is D 208.107: 954-55.

Unnumbered publications (other than continuations) are given a book number based on the principal subject word of the title, using a 2-figure Cutter table. An example is "Radioactive Heating of Vehicles Entering the Earth's Atmosphere, NAS 1.2:R 11", 'Radioactive" being the key subject word and the Cutter designation being R 11. Another publication, "Measurements of Radiation from Flow Fields of Bodies Flying Speeds up to 13.4 Kilometers per Second," issued by the same agency, falling in the same series class (NAS 1.2:), and having the same Cutter number for the principal subject word, **is individualized by adding the shilling** mark and the figure 2, as NAS 1.2:R 11/2. Subsequent different publications in the same subject group which take the same Cutter designation would be identified as R 11/3, R 11/4, etc.

In assigning book numbers to unnumbered separates or reprints from whole publications, the 3-figure Cutter table is used. This is done for the purpose of providing for finer distinctions in class between publications whose principal subject words begin with the same syllable. The 3-figure table is also sometimes used in regular unnumbered series for the same purpose.

Another use of the 3-figure Cutter table is for non-Government publications which although not officially authored by a particular Government bureau or agency, may have been written by some of its personnel, or may be about it and its work, and it is desirable to have them filed on the shelf with the organization's own publications. The book numbers assigned to the non-Government publications are treated as decimals so as to file with the same subject groups but yet not disturb the sequence of book numbers of publications actually authored by the organization.

Revisions of unnumbered publications are identified by addition of the shilling mark and the last three digits of the year of revision. For example, if the first publication mentioned in the preceding paragraph was revised in 1964, the complete classification would read NAS 1.2:R 11/964. Subsequent revisions in the same year would be identified as 964-2, 964-3, etc.

Periodicals and other continuations are identified by number, or volume and number as the case may be. Volume and number are separated by use of the shilling mark. Some examples are:

Current Export Bulletin, No. 732,
C 42.11/2:732
Marketing Information Guide, Vol 17, No. 1,
C 41.11:17/1

Unnumbered periodical and continuations are identified by the year of issuance and order of issuance throughout the year. The last three digits of the year are used, and a number corresponding to the order of issuance within the year is added, the two being separated by the shilling mark. An example is:

United States Savings Bonds Issued and Redeemed, January 31, 1954, T 63.7:954/1

SPECIAL TREATMENT OF PUBLICATIONS OF CERTAIN AUTHORS

While the foregoing principles and rules govern the classification of the publications and documents of most Government authors, special treatments are employed for those of certain Government agencies. These consist of classes assigned to:

(1) Some series issued by the Interstate Commerce Commission

(2) Boards, Commissions, and Committees established by act of Congress or under authority of act of Congress, not specifically designated in the Executive Branch of the Government nor as completely independent agencies

(3) Congress and its working committees

(4) Multilateral international organizations in which the United States participates

(5) Publications of the President and the Executive Office of the President including Committees and Commissions established by executive order and reporting directly to the President

Interstate Commerce Commission

The classes assigned to publications of this agency were revised in December 1914 to provide better groupings of material than could formerly be given due to the lack of bureau breakdowns within the Commission at that time. Accordingly, those publications of the Commission as a whole, such as annual reports, general publications, bulletins, circulars, etc., continued to follow the regular form of classification, while all others were grouped by subject. This subject grouping took the place of bureau breakdowns and was designated by adding the first three or four letters of the subject word to the main agency designation of IC 1. Thus those publications relating to "accidents" were grouped under IC 1 acci., those relating to "express companies" were under IC 1 exp., and similarly for other subjects. The series designations and individual book numbers were then assigned under each subject grouping as though it were a regular bureau. For example, Accident Bulletin Number 3 is classed as IC 1 acci.3:3. A list of current subject breakdowns is contained in Table II attached.

Boards, Commissions, and Committees

Those agencies established by act of Congress or under authority of act of Congress, not specifically designated in the Executive Branch of the Government nor as completely independent agencies, are grouped under one of the agency symbols assigned to Congressional publications – namely, Y 3. This place in the scheme is reserved for all such agencies. The classification numbers of the publications of these agencies are then literally pushed over to the right so that instead of the series designation following the period, the individual agency designation follows it. This agency designation is the Cutter author number from the 2-figure table for the first main word of the agency name, followed by the colon. Thus the agency designation for Atomic Energy Commission is Y 3.At 7: and that of Selective Service System is Y 3.Se 4:. The shilling mark and numbers are used to distinguish between author designations of agencies having the same or similar first principal word in their names as Y 3.F 31/8: for Federal Deposit Insurance Corp. and Y 3.F 31/13: for Federal Inter-Agency River Basin Committee.

Series designations for publications of these agencies then follow the colon instead of preceding it. These series designations are assigned in the regular way.

Individual book numbers are then added to the series designations with no separation if the individual book numbers begin with letters, and are separated by the shilling mark if they begin with numbers. Thus the Annual Report of the Atomic Energy Commission for the year 1961 is Y 3.At 7:1/961 while the unnumbered AEC Report on Status Centrifuge Technology is classed as Y 3.At 7:2G 21.

Table III attached gives a list of current Boards, Commissions, and Committees with their class symbols.

Congress and its Working Committees

The working committees of Congress such as Appropriations, Judiciary, etc., are grouped under one of the agency symbols assigned to Congress— namely, Y4. As in the case of the Y 3. classifications outlined above, an author designation based on the name of the Committee follows the period and is followed by the colon. Thus the House Committee on Judiciary is Y 4.J 89/1: and the Senate Committee on Judiciary is Y 4.J 89/2:, the shilling mark and the figures 1 and 2 being used to distinguish between the two committees. If other committees were to be appointed having the word "judiciary" as the principal subject work of their name, J 89/3:, J 89/4:, etc., would be used as the author designations. (See Table IV attached for symbols of current committees.)

No regular **numbered** series designations are normally used after the colon for the publications of Congressional Committees since they are for the most part simply unnumbered hearings or committee prints. These are given book numbers by use of the two-figure Cutter tables based on the principal subject word of the title of each as for unnumbered publications in the regular classification treatment.

Where series do occur within the publications of a Committee they have been treated in various ways. Some examples follow.

Congressional Directory. This has been given a series designation or "1" following the colon, as Y 4.P93/1:1. Individual book numbers are then marked off by use of the shilling mark following the series designation, as Y 4.P93/1: with the particular issue being designated by Congress and session, as Y 4.P93/1: 1/84-1.

Economic Indicators. This monthly periodical issued by the Joint Economic Committee has been assigned a place in the group of publications issued by this Committee by use of the Cutter designation following the colon (instead of the regular numerical series designation), based on the subject word "Economic" as Y 4.Ec7:Ec7. The book numbers for individual issues are then designated by year of issue and number corresponding to the month of issue as 954-1 for January 1954, 954-2 for February 1954, etc. These are added to the series designation of "Ec7" following the colon and separated by the shilling mark, as: June 1954 issue, Y 4.Ec7/954-6.

Serially Numbered Hearings and Committee Prints. Hearings and the committee prints of some Congressional Committees are numbered as serials within each Congress. These are designated by Congress and number (separated by the shilling mark) immediately following the colon, as: House Judiciary Committee Serial 13, 83d Congress would be Y 4.J89/1:83/13, the number of the Congress taking the place of the usual numerical series designation. These are filed behind the hearings and committee prints bearing letter and number Cutter designation — that is, to the right on the shelf.

Congressional Bills, Documents, and Reports. These numbered series of publications issued by Congress are not given a place in the scheme by use of lettered symbols but are simply filed at the end of all other classifications by Congress, session, and individual number with abbreviations being used for the series titles. The order of filing and the manner of designation is as follows: (The examples given were chosen at random.)

Series	Individual examples
Senate Bills	91-2:S.528
House Bills	91-2:H.R.15961
Senate Joint Resolutions	91-2:S.J.Res.172
House Joint Resoltuions	91-2:H.J.Res.1098
Senate Concurrent Resolutions	91-2:S.Con.Res.70
House Concurrent Resolutions	91-2:H.Con.Res.578
Senate Resolutions	91-2:S.Res.304
House Resolutions	91-2:H.Res.108
Senate Reports	91-2:S.rp.885
House Reports	91-2:H.rp.983
Senate Documents	91-2:S.doc.82
House Documents	91-2:H.doc.342

Other Congressional Publications. Attached as Table Y is a list of currently published Congressional series not explained above with notes as to methods of assigning book numbers.

Multilateral International Organizations in which the United States Participates

Many of the publications of these organizations are published simultaneously by the United States and other countries. The United States portions of these organizations may also publish separately, for example, the United States National Commission for UNESCO. Since participation by the United States is in the realm of foreign relations, such publications are classed under the State Department with two main class designations assigned as follows:

S 3.   Arbitrations and Mixed Commissions to Settle International Disputes

S 5.   International Congresses, Conferences and Commissions

The individual organizations are then treated as subordinate bureaus or offices, a number being assigned to each as it begins to publish, but following the period rather than preceding it as in regular class construction. Individual book numbers are assigned after the colon, using the

2-figure Cutter table and based on the principal subject word of the title.

If the organization proves to be a prolific publisher, however, issuing several definite series of publications, each is distinquished by adding the shilling mark and digits beginning with 2 to the number assigned to the organization as a bureau designation, as in the case of related series in regular class construction. For example some of the series issued by the U.S. National Commission for UNESCO are classed as follows:

S 5.48/9:   Addresses
S 5.48/10:   Maps and posters
S 5.48/11:   Executive committee, summary of notice of meetings

Individual book numbers are then assigned in the regular way.

Publications of the President and the Executive Office of the President including Committees and Commissions Established by Executive Order and reporting directly to the President

The agency symbol assigned to the President of the United States in Pr followed by the number corresponding to the ordinal number of succession to the presidency as Pr 37, Richard M. Nixon, 37th president of the United States. Breakdowns under the agency symbol follow normal methods of classification expansion. However, in recent years, presidents have appointed many special committees and commissions to study particular problems and to report their findings directly to the Chief executives. These organizations usually cease to exist after making their report. Since their publications are usually few in number, normal bureau treatment is not practical and special treatment is therefore indicated to prevent establishment of classes which will not be used, and in addition to keep together the publications of all such organizations appointed by one president.

Therefore, beginning with those appointed by President Eisenhower, one series class (Pr –.8:) has been assigned for all such committees and commissions. A Cutter designation using the 2-figure table is then assigned to each based on the principal subject word of its name as Pr 34.8:H81, President's Advisory Committee on Government Housing Policies and Programs. Publications of the committee are distinguished by addition of the shilling mark and Cutter numbers based on the principal subject word of the title as in normal classification.

Beginning with the administration of President Kennedy, the continuing offices assigned to the President, which make up the Executive Office of the President, have been given permanent classes under the symbol PrEx. Thus with a change in administration it will no longer be necessary to change the classes for such offices as Bureau of the Budget, National Security Council, Office of Emergency Planning, etc. These have been given breakdowns as subordinate offices of the Executive Office of the President, the Bureau of the Budget for example, being assigned PrEx2. Series and book numbers are then assigned in the usual manner.

Table I

Department and Agency Symbols Currently in Use

A	Agriculture Department	D	Defense Department
AC	Arms Control and Disarmament Agency	DC	District of Columbia
		FA	Fine Arts Commission
C	Commerce Department	FCA	Farm Credit Administration
CC	Federal Communications Commission	FHL	Federal Home Loan Bank Board
		FM	Federal Mediation and Conciliation Service
CR	Civil Rights Commission		
CS	Civil Service Commission	FMC	Federal Maritime Commission
		FP	Federal Power Commission
CZ	Panama Canal Company and Canal Zone Government	FR	Federal Reserve System Board of Governors

TABLE I (Cont'd)

FT	Federal Trade Commission	NC	National Capital Planning Commission
FTZ	Foreign Trade Zones Board		
GA	General Accounting Office	NCU	National Credit Union Administration
GP	Government Printing Office		
GS	General Services Administration	NF	National Foundation on the Arts and the Humanities
HE	Health, Education, and Welfare Department	NMB	National Mediation Board
HH	Housing and Urban Development Department (Formerly Housing and Home Finance Agency)	NS	National Science Foundation
		P	Post Office Department
		Pr	President of United States
		PrEx	Executive Office of the President
I	Interior Department	RA	National Railroad Adjustment Board
IA	United States Information Agency	RnB	Renegotiation Board
IC	Interstate Commerce Commission	RR	Railroad Retirement Board
		S	State Department
J	Justice Department	SBA	Small Business Administration
Ju	Judiciary (Courts of the United States)	SE	Securities and Exchange Commission
L	Labor Department	SI	Smithsonian Institution
LC	Library of Congress	T	Treasury Department
LR	National Labor Relations Board	TC	Tariff Commission
NA	National Academy of Sciences	TD	Transportation Department
NAS	National Aeronautics and Space Administration	VA	Veterans Administration
		X and Y	Congress

Table II

Current Subject Breakdowns of the Interstate Commerce Commission

Symbol	Publications relating to:	Symbol	Publications relating to:
IC 1 acci.	Accidents	IC 1 mot.	Motor carriers
IC 1 act.	Acts to regulate commerce	IC 1 pip.	Pipe line companies
IC 1 blo.	Block signals	IC 1 rat.	Rates
IC 1 def.	Defense Transport Administration	IC 1 saf.	Safety
IC 1 elec.	Electric Railways	IC 1 sle.	Sleeping car companies
IC 1 exp.	Express companies	IC 1 ste.	Steam roads
IC 1 hou.	Hours of service	IC 1 val.	Valuation of property
IC 1 loc.	Locomotive inspection	IC 1 wat.	Water carriers

Table III

Agency Symbols of Boards, Commissions, and Committees Established by Act of Congress or under Authority of Act of Congress
(not specifically designated in the Executive Branch of the Government nor as completely independent agencies.)

Y 3.Ad9/7:	Advisory Commission on Information
Y 3.Ad9/8:	Advisory Commission on Intergovernmental Relations
Y 3.Am3:	American Battle Monuments Commission
Y 3.At7:	Atomic Energy Commission
Y 3.B61:	Committee on Purchase of Blind-Made Products
Y 3.C49/2:	Civil War Centennial Commission
Y 3.C63/2:	Coastal Plains Regional Commission
Y 3.C66:	Coinage Joint Commission
Y 3.D37/2:	Delaware River Basin Commission
Y 3.Ed8/2:	National Advisory Council on Education of Disadvantaged Children
Y 3.Eq2:	Equal Employment Opportunity Commission
Y 3.Ex7/3:	Export-Import Bank of United States
Y 3.F31/8:	Federal Deposit Insurance Corporation
Y 3.F31/13:	Federal Inter-Agency River Basin Committee
Y 3.F31/14:	Federal Inter-Agency Committee on Recreation
Y 3.F31/17:	Federal Radiation Council
Y 3.F76/3:	Foreign Claims Settlement Commission
Y 3.F82:	Four Corners Regional Commission
Y 3.G79/3:	Great Lakes Basin Commission
Y 3.H73:	Permanent Committee for the Oliver Wendall Holmes Devise
Y 3.In2/6:	Indian Claims Commission
Y 3.In8/6:	Interdepartmental Committee on Children and Youth
Y 3.In8/8:	Inter-Agency Committee on Water Resources
Y 3.In8/13:	Interdepartmental Committee on Nutrition for National Defense
Y 3.In8/15:	Commission on International Rules of Judicial Procedure
Y 3.In8/16:	Interagency Committee on Automatic Data Processing
Y 3.In8/17:	Interdepartmental Committee to Coordinate Federal Urban Area Assistance Programs
Y 3.In8/21:	Interdepartmental Committee on Status of Women
Y 3.J66:	Joint Publications Research Service
Y 3.L58:	Lewis and Clark Trail Commission
Y 3.M33:	Maritime Advisory Committee
Y 3.M69:	Missouri Basin Inter-Agency Committee
Y 3.M84:	Mortgage Interest Rates Commission
Y 3.N21/16:	National Advisory Council on International Monetary and Financial Problems
Y 3.N21/21:	National Capital Transportation Agency
Y 3.N21/23:	National Visitors Center Study Commission
Y 3.N21/24:	National Water Commission
Y 3.N21/25:	National Commission on Product Safety
Y 3.N42/2:	New England Regional Commission
Y 3.N42/3:	New England River Basins Commission
Y 3.Oz1:	Ozarks Regional Commission
Y 3.P11/2:	Pacific Southwest Inter-agency Committee
Y 3.P96/u:	Public Land Law Review Commission
Y 3.Se4:	Selective Service System
Y 3.Sh6:	Ship Structure Committee

TABLE III (Cont'd)

Y 3.Sp2/7:	Cabinet Committee on Opportunity for Spanish Speaking	Y 3.T25:	Tennessee Valley Authority
Y 3.Sul:	Subversive Activities Control Board	Y 3.Up6:	Upper Great Lakes Regional Commission
Y 3.T22:	National Commission on Technology, Automation, and Economic Progress	Y 3.W29:	Water Resources Council

Table IV

Agency Symbols of Current Congressional Committees
(Temporary select and special committees not included)

Y 4.Ae8:	Aeronautical and Space Sciences (Senate)	Y 4.In8/13:	Interior and Insular Affairs (Senate)
Y 4.Ag4:	Special Committee on Aging (Senate)	Y 4.In8/14:	Interior and Insular Affairs (House)
Y 4.Ag8/1:	Agriculture (House)	Y 4.In8/15:	Internal Security Committee (House)
Y 4.Ag8/2:	Agriculture and Forestry (Senate)	Y 4.J89/1:	Judiciary (House)
Y 4.Ap6/1:	Appropriations (House)	Y 4.J89/2:	Judiciary (Senate)
Y 4.Ap6/2:	Appropriations (Senate)	Y 4.L11/2:	Labor and Public Welfare (Senate)
Y 4.Ar5/2:	Armed Services (House)	Y 4.L61/2:	Joint Committee on the Library
Y 4.Ar5/3:	Armed Services (Senate)	Y 4.M53:	Merchant Marine and Fisheries (House)
Y 4.At7/2:	Joint Committee on Atomic Energy	Y 4.N22/4:	Joint Committee on Navajo-Hopi Indian Administration
Y 4.B22/1:	Banking and Currency (House)		
Y 4.B22/3:	Banking and Currency (Senate)	Y 4.P84/10:	Post Office and Civil Service (House)
Y 4.C73/2:	Commerce (Senate)		
Y 4.D36:	Joint Committee on Defense Production	Y 4.P84/11:	Post Office and Civil Service (Senate)
Y 4.D63/1:	District of Columbia (House)	Y 4.P93/1:	Joint Committee on Printing
Y 4.D63/2:	District of Columbia (Senate)	Y 4.P96/10:	Public Works (Senate)
Y 4.Ec7:	Joint Economic Committee		Public Works (House)
Y 4.Ed8/1:	Education and Labor (House)	Y 4.R24/4:	Joint Committee on Reduction of Federal Expenditures
Y 4.F49:	Finance (Senate)		
Y 4.F76/1:	Foreign Affairs (House)	Y 4.R86/1:	Rules (House)
Y 4.F76/2:	Foreign Relations (Senate)	Y 4.R86/2:	Rules and Administration (Senate)
Y 4.G74/6:	Government Operations (Senate)		
Y 4.G74/7:	Government Operations (House)	Y 4.Sci2:	Science and Astronautics (House)
Y 4.H81/3:	House Administration (House)		
Y 4.In8/4:	Interstate and Foreign Commerce (House)	Y 4.Sml:	Small Business Select Committee (House)
Y 4.In8/11:	Joint Committee on Internal Revenue Taxation		

TABLE IV (Cont'd)

Y 4.Sml/2:	Small Business Select Committee (Senate)	Y 4.V64/3:	Veterans' Affairs (House)
		Y 4.W36:	Ways and Means (House)

Table V

Classification of Congressional Publications
(other than bills, deocuments, and reports)

X.	Congressional Record (bound). Congress and session form the series designation with individual book numbers made up of volume and part. For example: 83d Congress, 2d session, volume 100, part 2, classified X.83/2:100/pt.2.
X/a.	Congressional Record (daily). These are numbered throughout each session with no volume numbers. For example: 83d Congress, 2d session, number 32 is classified X/a.83/2:32.
XJH:	Journal of House of Representatives. These are simply designated by Congress and session as XJH:83-2.
XJS:	Journal of the Senate. Designated by Congress and session as XJS:83-2.
Y 1.1:	Here are classified joint miscellaneous publications pertaining to both House and Senate, individual book numbers being formed by 2-figure Cutter designations based on the principal subject word of the title. This class may also be used by libraries desiring to file them serially for reports of organizations chartered by Congress such as the Boy Scouts of America, Disabled American Veterans, etc., with dates of the reports being added to the 3-figure Cutter designations for the titles of the organizations. For example, the 1954 report of the Boy Scouts of America would be classified Y 1.1:B691/954.
Y 1.2:	House of Representatives miscellaneous publications. Individual book numbers are assigned in the usual manner for unnumbered publications.
Y 1.2/2:	Calendars of the United States House of Representatives and history of legislation. Book numbers are assigned by Congress, session, and individual number as Y 1.2/2:84-1-13.
Y 1.3:	Senate miscellaneous publications. Individual book numbers are assigned in the usual manner for unnumbered publications. The volumes of the Journal of executive proceedings are given the Cutter designation Ex3 with the volume numbers added as: Y 1.3:Ex3/v.91,pt.2.
Y 1.3/3:	Executive calendar [relating to nominations and treaties]. Book numbers are assigned by date and number as: Y 1.3/2:955/1.
Y 1.3/3:	Calendar of business. Book numbers are assigned by Congress and individual number as Y 1.3/3:84-16.
Y 1.Cong.sess:	Senate Executive documents and reports. Congress and session

TABLE V (Cont'd)

	numbers form the series designations for these two series with the individual document letters or report numbers (preceded by the letters "rp") forming the individual book numbers as: Y 1.83/2:A (Senate Executive Document A) and Y 1.83/2:rp.5 (Senate Exeucitve Report 5).		Senate bills, H.R. for House bills, S. con. res. for Senate concurrent resolutions, H. res. for House resolutions, etc.
		Y 3.	Boards, Commissions, and Committees. (See main text.)
		Y 4.	Congressional Committees. (See main text.)
		Y 5.	Contested elections. Not used in recent years.
Y 2.	This class was originally assigned for Congressional bills and resolutions and may be so used in libraries desiring to keep such material in one group. Classification is completed by use of Congress and session, and individual bill or resolution numbers preceded by the abbreviations S. for	Y 6.	Impeachments. Not used in recent years.
		Y 7.1:	Memorial Addresses on life and character of deceased members of Congress. Individual book numbers are assigned by use of the 3-figure Cutter table based on the name of the deceased member.

A AGRICULTURE DEPARTMENT

May 15, 1882 an agricultural section of the Patent Office was made a separate Department.

A1 Office of the Secretary

A1.1:date	Annual reports
A1.1/a:CT	___ separates
A1.1/2:date	Information and technical assistance delivered by the Department of Agriculture in fiscal year (annual report)
A1.2:CT	General publications
A1.2/a:CT	___ separates
A1.3:nos	Department bulletins. Superseded by Technical bulletins A1.36:
A1.3/a:CT	___ separates
A1.3/2:nos	Management bulletins
A1.4:nos	Circulars
A1.4/2:nos	Circulars. Superseded Department circulars A1.14/2:
A1.5/1:nos	Miscellaneous circulars [1st series, 1897-
A1.5/2:nos	Miscellaneous circulars [2d series, 1923-
A1.6:nos	Special reports
A1.7:nos	Miscellaneous, special reports
A1.8:nos	[Department] reports. Old series
A1.8/a:CT	___ separates
A1.9:nos	Farmers bulletins
A1.9/a:CT	___ separates
A1.10:date	Yearbook
A1.10/a:nos	Yearbook separates
A1.11:CT	Regulations

A1.11/2:nos	Import regulations
A1.11/3:CT	Handbooks, manuals, guides
A1.12:nos	General orders
A1.13:CT	Special orders
A1.14:dt/nos	Department circulars
A1.14/2:nos	Department circulars. Superseded by Circulars A1.4/2:
A1.15:nos	Food inspection decisions
A1.16:nos	Notices of judgment, food and drug act
A1.17:date	Insecticide decisions
A1.18:nos	Notices of insecticide act judgment. Later included in A34.6:
A1.19:date	Regulations of Department of Agriculture
A1.20:v.nos	Departmental circulars
A1.21:	Farm management office. Circulars. Changed to A37.4:
A1.22:v./nos	Weekly news letter. Superseded by A1.33:
A1.22/a:CT	___ separates
A1.23:v./nos	Journal of agricultural research (semimonthly)
A1.23/a:CT	___ separates
A1.24:nos	Food thrift series
A1.25:CT	Specifications
A1.26:nos	United States food leaflets
A1.27:nos	Joint orders
A1.28:nos	Joint circulars (Issued by the Treasury Department and Department of Agriculture)
A1.29:nos	Library leaflets. Thrift leaflets.
A1.30:CT	Atlas of American agriculture

A1.30/a:nos	Atlas of American agriculture. Advance sheets
A1.30/a:CT	___ separates
A1.31:dt. or nos.	Press notices
A1.32:CT	Posters
A1.33:v./nos	Official record, Department of Agriculture (wkly) Supersedes A1.22:
A1.33/a:CT	___ separates
A1.34:nos	Statistical bulletins
A1.35:nos	Leaflets
A1.36:nos	Technical bulletins. Supersede Department bulletins A1.3:
A1.36/a:CT	___ separates
A1.37:nos	With the corn borer. Wkly. Mim.
A1.38:nos	Miscellaneous publications
A1.38/a:CT	___ separates
A1.39:nos	National Land-use Planning Committee. Publications
A1.40:CT	Addresses. (usually mimeographed)
A1.41:nos	Memorandum. Mim. (for use of Departments and Bureaus)
A1.42:CT	Agriculture Department Graduate School [publications]. Mim.
A1.43:nos	Budget and finance circulars. Mim.
A1.44:nos	Personnel circulars. Mim.
A1.45:nos	Operation Division circulars. Mim. Later A60.4:
A1.46:nos	Discussion group topics. Mim.
A1.47:date	Agricultural statistics
A1.47/a:nos	___ separates
A1.48:CT	World's poultry congress and exposition, Cleveland, Ohio, July 28-August 7, 1939, 7th.

A1.49:nos	Interbureau forage committee [publications] I.F.C. Proc.
A1.50:vol.nos.	Cotton literature, selected references. Monthly. Proc. Earlier A36.76:
A1.51:date	Extent of aerial photography by Agriculture Dept., completed, in progress and approved (maps; monthly)
A1.52:vol	Crops and markets. Monthly. Prior to July 1939, A36.11/3:
A1.52/a:CT	___ separates. Earlier A36.11/3a:
A1.53:nos	Notes on graduate studies and research in home economics and home economics education. Proc. Slightly varying titles.
A1.54:CT	Farm handbooks (by States)
A1.55:nos	Hydrologic bulletins
A1.56:vol	Agricultural labor situation (monthly)
A1.57:vol.	U.S.D.A. Administrative information
A1.58:v. nos	Agriculture decisions.
A1.58/a:v./nos	___ separates. monthly.
A1.59:nos	[Agriculture war information series] Pubs. desig. AWI-no. Superseded by A1.64:
A1.60:nos	Bibliographical bulletins
A1.60/2:CT	Bibliographies and lists of publications
A1.61:nos	Administrative series
A1.62:nos	General departmental circulars. Proc.
A1.63:CT	Interbureau Committee on Post-War Programs [publications] Proc.
A1.64:nos	[Agriculture information series] Supersedes A1.59:
A1.65:nos	[Nutrition and food conservation series] Earlier A80.123:
A1.66:nos	[Discussion series] Earlier A36.126:
A1.67:v.nos	Consumers' guide (monthly) Earlier A80.808:

A1.67/a:CT	___ separates
A1.68:nos	Program aids
A1.69:nos	War records monographs. Proc.
A1.70:CT	Famine Emergency Committee publications
A1.71:CT	Fact sheets. Printed and Proc.
A1.72:CT	Agricultural research and marketing act publications. Proc.
A1.73:nos	[Commodity statistics] Earlier A82.18:
A1.74:nos	Management improvement
A1.75:nos	Agriculture information bulletin
A1.76:nos	Agriculture handbooks
A1.76/a:nos.&sep.nos.	___ separates
A1.77:nos	Home and garden bulletins
A1.77/a:nos	___ separates
A1.78:nos	Agriculture monographs
A1.79:	Memorandum to heads of Department of Agriculture Agencies
A1.80:date	Office of the Secretary: Releases. Proc.
A1.80/2:date	Outlook for agricultural exports
A1.81:nos	Defense food delegations. Proc.
A1.82:nos	Marketing research reports
A1.83:nos	Agriculture in national defense (weekly)
A1.84:nos	Production research reports
A1.85:date	Progress in rural development program, annual reports. Proc.
A1.85/2:date	Rural development goals, annual report to Congress
A1.86:nos	Household food consumption survey reports
A1.87:nos	Home economics research reports

A1.88:nos	Utilization research reports
A1.89:date	Telephone directory. Earlier A1.2:T23 and A60.2:T23
A1.89/2:date	Officials of Department of Agriculture. Earlier A1.2:Of2/2
A1.89/3:CT	Directories
A1.90:CT	Plant disease, decay, etc., control activities of Department of Agriculture, reports. Proc.
A1.91:CT	Breeding research and improvement activities of Department of Agriculture, reports. Proc.
A1.92:date	National Fire Prevention Week. Earlier A1.2:F51/945 and A1.2:F51/2/957
A1.93:date	Budget estimates for United States Department of Agriculture, separate from Budget of United States Government. Earlier A1.2:B85
A1.94:CT	Reports of technical study groups on Soviet Agriculture
A1.95:nos	Marketing bulletins
A1.96:date	National farm safety week. Earlier A1.2:Sa1/960 and A21.2:F22/2
A1.97:nos	Checklist of reports issued by Economics Research Service and Statistical Reporting Service, AE-CL- (series)
A1.98:date	Agricultural outlook chartbook (annual) Issued by Economics Research Service, Foreign Agricultural Service, **Agricultural** Research Service, Earlier A88.8/3:, A67.24:
A1.99:date	Periodic reports of Agricultural Economics, Economic Research Service, Statistical Reporting Service (annual)
A1.99/2:v.nos./nos	Digest of world agriculture
A1.100:nos	Picture story (series)
A1.100/2:nos	Photo series
A1.101:date	CCC monthly sales list
A1.102:date	Orderly liquidation of stocks of agricultural commodities held by Commodity Credit Corporation and expansion of markets for surplus agricultural commodities, annual report by Secretary of Agriculture in response to sec. 201(b), Public law 540, 84th Congress. Later A99.9:

A1.103:date	Report and recommendations of the Farm Resources and Facilities Research Advisory Committee
A1.104:nos	Science study aids (numbered)
A1.105:CT	Water and related land resources [by area] Earlier A1.2:G95
A1.106:nos	Reference reports working materials for Southeast Wisconsin rivers basin
A1.107:nos	Agricultural economic reports. Earlier A93.28:
A1.108:date	USAA/AID News digest
A1.109:date	Meat and poultry inspection, Report of the Secretary of Agriculture (annual)
A1.109/2:date	Foreign meat inspection report of Secretary of Agriculture (annual)
A1.110:nos	Agricultural supply & demand estimates
A1.111:date	Annual report on location of new Federal offices and other facilities
A1.112:	[not used]
A1.113:date	Financial and technical assistance provided by the Department of Agriculture (annual)
A1.114:nos	Conservation research reports. Earlier A77.23:
A1.115:nos	Sugar and sweetener report Replaces A93.31/2: and A88.54:

A 2   Accounts and Disbursements Division

1889

A2.1:date	Annual reports
A2.2:CT	General publications
A2.3:	Bulletins
A2.4:	Circulars
A2.5:date	Expenditures of Department of Agriculture

A 3   Agrostology Division

Originally a part of the Division of Botany (A6). Established as an independent division, July 1, 1895.

A3.1:date	Annual reports
A3.2:	General publications
A3.3:nos	Bulletins
A3.4:nos	Circulars

Merged into Bureau of plant industry July 1, 1901 (A19)

A 4   Animal Industry Bureau

Organized 1884. Stat L. 23:31

A4.1:date	Annual reports. Later A77.201:
A4.2:CT	General publications. Later A77.202:
A4.3:nos	Bulletins
A4.4:nos	Circulars
A4.5:nos	B.A.I. orders. Later A77.218:
A4.5/a:CT	___ separates
A4.6:date	Map of districts infected with splenetic fever

A4.7:nos	Rules
A4.8:date	Regulations. Later A77.206:
A4.9:nos	Press bulletins
A4.10:date	Meat inspection directory
A4.11:date	Address list of (meat) inspectors
A4.12:nos	Meat inspection rulings
A4.13:nos	Service and regulatory announcements (monthly) Later A77.208:
A4.14:date	Directory of Bureau of Animal Industry. Later A77.221:
A4.15:CT	Animals imported for breeding purposes, etc.
A4.16:CT	Posters. Later A77.220:
A4.16/2:CT	Livestock health series (Posters)
A4.17:nos	Milk plant letters. Monthly. Mim. Later A44.17:
A4.18:pt.nos.	Index-catalogue of medical and veterinary zoology. Later A77.219:
A4.19:date	International veterinary congresses Proceedings
A4.19/a:CT	___ separates
A4.19/a:nos	___ separates
A4.20:nos	Declarations. Proc.
A4.21:date	Summary of Bang's disease work in cooperation with various States. Monthly. Proc. Later A77.212:
A4.22:date	Summary of tuberculosis eradication in cooperation with various States. Monthly. Proc. Later A77.216:
A4.23:date	Summary of Bang's disease control program conducted by Bureau of animal industry in cooperation with various States. Monthly. Proc. Later A77.213:
A4.24:nos	Extension poultry husbandman. Annual. Proc. Earlier A53.5/12:
A4.25:nos	Extension animal husbandman. Quarterly. Proc. Later A77.214:
A4.26:nos	Animal husbandry division mimeographs. A.H.D. Proc. Later A77.209:

A4. 27:nos   Animal nutrition division publications, A.N.D. Proc. Later A77. 210:

A4. 28:vol.   Monthly record, administration of packers and stockyards act. Proc. Earlier A39. 5: Superseded by A66.18:

A4. 29:date   Statement of indemnity claims and averages in cooperative Bang's disease work (monthly) Proc. Later A77. 211:

A4. 30:date   Statement of indemnity claims and averages in cooperative tuberculosis eradication (monthly) Later A77. 215:

A4. 31:nos   Notices, activities of licensed establishments supervised by Virus-Serum Control Division (monthly) Proc.

A4. 32:nos   Administrative notices.

A4. 33:date   Names of counties declared to be modified accredited Bang's disease-free areas. Proc.

A4. 34:CT   Addresses.

Transferred to Agricultural Research Administration February 23, 1942, Executive order 9069.

A5   Biological Survey Bureau

Established July 1, 1885 under the Division of Entomology (A9). Became an independent division July 1, 1886.

A5. 1:date   Annual reports. Later I47.1:

A5. 2:CT   General publications. Later I47. 2:

A5. 3:nos   Bulletins

A5. 4:nos   Circulars

A5. 5:nos   North American fauna. Later I49. 30:

A5. 6:nos   Service and regulatory announcements.

A5. 6/a: ___ separates

A5. 7:date   Annual reports of Governor of Alaska on Alaska game law

A5. 8:date   Directory of officers and organizations concerned with protection of birds and game. This has been issued annually since 1900 as circulars (A5. 4:) no. 94 being the one for 1912.

A5.9:nos	Open season for game. Later I47.8:
A5.9/2:CT	Posters.
A5.10:	Alaska Game Commission
A5.10/1:date	Annual reports
A5.10/2:CT	General publications
A5.10/3:	Bulletins
A5.10/4:nos	Circulars. Later I49.12:
A5.10/5:nos	Service and regulatory announcements
A5.11:nos	Wildlife research and management leaflets. Proc. Later I47.7:
A5.12:nos	Wildlife review. Proc. Later I47.9:
A5.13:CT	Lists of publications. Proc. Later I47.12:
A5.14:CT	Addresses. Proc. Later I47.13:
A5.15:vol.	Bird banding notes. Proc. Later I47.10:
A5.16:nos	Bird migration memorandum. Proc. Later I49.31:

Transferred to Dept. of the Interior, July 1939.

A6   Botany Division

Organized March 1869.

A6.1:date	Annual reports
A6.2:CT	General publications
A6.3:nos	Bulletins
A6.4:nos	Circulars
A6.5:v.nos	Contributions from U.S. National herbarium Later SI3.8:
A6.5/a:CT	___ separates
A6.6:nos	Inventories

Merged into Bureau of plant industry (A19) July 1, 1901.

A7 Chemistry Bureau

Established 1862.

A7.1:date	Annual reports
A7.2:CT	General publications
A7.3:nos	Bulletins
A7.3/a:CT	___ separates
A7.4:nos	Circulars
A7.5:nos	Food inspection decisions
A7.6:nos	Service and regulatory announcements
A7.6/2:nos	___ supplements
A7.6/2a:	___ separates.
A7.6/3:	Indexes
A7.7:date	Tea inspection service, Annual reports
A7.8:date	Food and drug review (monthly) Mimeo. [Confidential] Later A46.5: Food and drug review. Changed to A47.7:
A7.9:date	Review of U.S. patents relating to insecticides and fungicides. Quarterly. Later A47.7:

Merged into Chemistry and Soils Bureau 1928.

A8 Entomological Commission

Transferred from Interior Department June 16, 1880 - Stat. L 21:276.

A8.1:nos	Annual reports
A8.2:	General publications [none issued]
A8.3:nos	Bulletins
A8.4:nos	Circulars [None issued under Agriculture Department]

Discontinued June 30, 1882.

A9 Entomology Bureau

Established 1863.

A9.1: date	Annual reports
A9.1/a: CT	___ separates
A9.2: CT	General publications
A9.3: nos	Bulletins
A9.4: nos	Circulars (1st series)
A9.5: nos	Circulars (2d series)
A9.6: nos	Bulletins (new series)
A9.7: v.nos	Insect life
A9.7/a: CT	___ separates
A9.8: nos	Technical series
A9.9: CT	Posters Later A77.319:
A9.10: vol	Insect pest survey bulletin (monthly, March to November) Mim. Later A56.18:
A9.11: nos	Forest entomology briefs. Mim.
A9.12: nos	Monthly letters. Later A56.12:
A9.13: date	Publications of Bureau of Entomology available for free distribution. Mim.
A9.14: vol	Entomology current literature. Bi-monthly. Mim. Later A56.10:
A9.15: vol	Blister rust news. Monthly. Mim. Earlier issues A19.21:
A9.16: E-nos	E [series] Later A56.19:

Consolidated into Entomology and Plant Quarantine Bureau July 1, 1934.

A10 Experiment Stations Office

Established July 1, 1888.

A10.1/1:date	Annual reports. Later A77.401:
A10.1/2:date	Report on agricultural experiment stations. Later A77.401/2:
A10.1/2a:CT	___ separates
A10.2:CT	General publications
A10.3:nos	Bulletins
A10.4:nos	Circulars
A10.5:nos	Miscellaneous bulletins
A10.6:v.nos	Experiment station record. Later A77.408:
A10.6/2:incl.n.	General index to Experiment station record
A10.7:nos	Food and diet charts
A10.8:nos	Irrigation and investigation schedules

A10.9: Hawaii Agricultural Experiment Station

A10.9/1:date	Annual reports. Later A77.481:
A10.9/1a:CT	___ separates
A10.9/2:CT	General publications. Later A77.482:
A10.9/3:nos	Bulletins. Later A77.483:
A10.9/4:nos	Circulars. Later A77.484:
A10.9/5:nos	Press bulletins

A10.10: Alaska Agricultural Experiment Station

A10.10/1:date	Annual reports. Later A77.441:
A10.10/1a:CT	___ separates
A10.10/2:CT	General publications. Later A77.442:
A10.10/3:nos	Bulletins. Later A77.443:

A10.10/4:nos	Circulars Later A77.444:
A10.11:v.nos	Experiment station work
A10.12:	Porto Rico Agricultural Experiment Station
A10.12/1:date	Annual reports. Later A77.461:
A10.12/1a:CT	___ separates
A10.12/2:CT	General publications. Later A77.462:
A10.12/3:nos	Bulletins. Later A77.463:
A10.12/4:nos	Circulars. Later A77.464:
A10.13:nos	Farmers' institute lectures
A10.14:date	List of publications of Office of Experiment Stations on agricultural education
A10.15:date	List of publications of Office of Experiment Stations on food and nutrition of man
A10.16:date	List of publications of Office of Experiment Stations on irrigation and drainage
A10.17:date	List of publications received by Office of Experiment Stations
A10.18:date	Institutions in United States giving instruction in agriculture
A10.19:date	Address list of agricultural experiment stations
A10.20:date	Address list of agricultural and mechanical colleges
A10.21:nos	(Food) charts, composition of food materials
A10.21/2:nos	Food selection and meal planning charts
A10.22:	Guam Agricultural Experiment Station
A10.22/1:date	Annual reports
A10.22/2:CT	General publications
A10.22/3:nos	Bulletins
A10.22/4:nos	Circulars
A10.22/5:nos	Extension circulars

A10.23:date   States Relations Service. List of workers in subjects pertaining to agriculture

A10.24:CT   Cooperative extension work in agriculture and home economics

A10.25:date   Address list of State Institutions and officers in charge of agricultural extension work under Smith-Lever Act (to provide for cooperative agricultural extension work between agricultural colleges and Department of Agriculture.)

A10.26:   Virgin Islands Agricultural Experiment Station

A10.26/1:date   Annual reports

A10.26/2:CT   General publications

A10.26/3:nos   Bulletins

A10.26/4:nos   Circulars

A10.27:CT   Addresses

Consolidated into Agricultural Research Administration by Executive Order 9069 of February 23, 1942.

A11   Fiber Investigations Office

Jan. 1, 1891

A11.1:date   Annual reports

A11.2:CT   General publications

A11.3:nos   Bulletins

A11.4:nos   Circulars

A11.5:nos   Reports

June 30, 1898 its work was assigned to the Division of Botany

A12   Foreign Markets Division

1894

A12.1:date   Annual reports

16

A12. 2:CT   General publications

A12. 3:nos   Bulletins

A12. 4:nos   Circulars

Placed under Bureau of Statistics, Agriculture Dept. July 1, 1903.

A13 Forest Service

1880

A13.1:date	Annual report
A13.1/a:CT	___ separates
A13.1/2:date	California Region, progress reports
A13.2:CT	General publications
A13.2/a:CT	___ separates
A13.3:nos	Bulletins
A13.4:nos	Circulars
A13.5:v.	Report on forestry
A13.6:	Press bulletins
A13.7:CT	Notes on forest trees suitable for planting in the United States
A13.8:date	Field program (and service notes). Monthly.
A13.8/2:date	Service directory
A13.9:nos	Forest planting leaflets
A13.10:date	National forest areas
A13.11:date	List of publications
A13.11/2:CT	Lists of publications (misc.) Proc.
A13.12:nos	Silvical leaflets
A13.13:CT	Information pamphlets relating to national forests
A13.13/2:CT/date	[National forests, reports of activities during year]
A13.13/3:date	National forests, lands of many uses, report. Issued by California region
A13.14:nos	Amendments to 1911 edition of Use book and National forest manual
A13.14/1:date	Use book. Changed from A13.2:
A13.14/2:CT	Use book. Sections. Changed from A13.2:

A13.14/3:date	National forest manual. Changed from A13.2:
A13.14/4:CT	National forest manual. Sections. Changed from A13.2:
A13.14/5:nos	Amendments to use book and National Forest manual. Changed from A13.14:
A13.15:date	Wholesale prices of lumber, based on actual sales made f.o.b. mill. Quarterly
A13.16:date	Wholesale prices of lumber, based on actual sales made f.o.b. each market. Quarterly.
A13.17:nos	Forest atlas
A13.18:CT	Forestry laws
A13.19:date	Forest worker. Bi-monthly. Mim.
A13.20/1:CT	Posters
A13.20/2:nos	Standard posters
A13.20/3:CT	**Posters (miscellaneous)**
A13.20/4:dt.&nos	Cooperative forest fire prevention program
A13.21:nos	Progress report of forest taxation inquiry. Mim.
A13.21/2:date	State forest tax law digest. Proc.
A13.22:date	Information regarding employment on national forests. Changed from A13.2:
A13.23:date	Index of standard forms
A13.24:date	Fire handbook. Region 7. Changed from A13.2:
A13.25:date	Forestry current literature. Mim. Superseded by A17.18:E
A13.26:vol	National plan for American forestry
A13.26/a:CT	___ separates
A13.27:	Forest Products Laboratory, Madison, Wisconsin
A13.27/1:date	Annual reports
A13.27/2:CT	General publications

A13.27/3:   Bulletins

A13.27/4:   Circulars

A13.27/5:   Laws

A13.27/6:CT   Regulations, rules and instructions. Includes handbooks and manuals.

A13.27/7:CT   Lists of publications (by subject) Mim.

A13.27/8:date   Lists of publications

A13.27/9:nos   Technical notes

A13.27/10:date   Log of the laboratory, items of current interest

A13.27/11:date   Research in forest products

A13.27/12:CT   Addresses. Proc.

A13.27/13:nos   Reports to aid Nation's defense effort

A13.27/14:nos   [Research reports] Proc. Earlier in A13.27/2:CT, A13.27/7:CT, A13.27/12:CT, and A13.27/13:CT

A13.28:CT   Maps. Maps originally assigned to A13.13:

A13.28/2:CT   Sheets of National Atlas of United States

A13.29:nos   Western range

A13.30:   Northern Rocky Mountain Forest and Range Experiment Station

A13.30/1:date   Annual reports. Proc.

A13.30/2:CT   General publications. Proc.

A13.30/3:

A13.30/4:

A13.30/5:nos   Forest survey releases; progress reports. Proc.

A13.30/6:nos   Progress reports. Proc.

A13.30/7:nos   Research notes. Proc.

A13.30/8:nos   Station papers. Proc.

A13.30/9:v.nos   Selected bibliography of range management literature

A13.30/10:v./nos Range research hi-lites. (monthly) Proc.

A13.30/11:nos   Miscellaneous publications

A13.31:CT   American woods pamphlets. Proc.

A13.31/2:CT   Foreign woods series. Proc.

A13.32:nos   Fire control notes. Later title: Fire management

A13.32/a:CT   ___ separates

A13.32/2:date   Forest fire statistics (annual) Earlier A13.2:F51/38

A13.32/3:date   National forest fire report, Calendar year. Proc. Earlier A13.2: F51/39

A13.33:vol   Constructive hints. Bi-weekly. Proc.

A13.34:CT   Farm woodlands of States (charts) Proc. (by States)

A13.35:CT   Addresses

A13.36:CT   Regulations, rules and instructions (miscellaneous) Includes handbooks and manuals.

A13.36/2:CT   Handbooks, manuals, guides. Formerly in A13.36:

A13.36/3:nos   Managing your woodland, how to do it guides

A13.36/4:nos   TT [Training text]

A13.37:nos   General survey of forest situation. Proc.

A13.38:nos   Club series. Proc. Pubs. desig. CS-no.

A13.39:nos   Legislation relating to town and community forests. Proc. Pubs. desig. LG-no.

A13.40:   Southern Forest Experiment Station, New Orleans

A13.40/1:date   Annual reports

A13.40/2:CT		General publications

A13.40/3:

A13.40/4:

A13.40/5:nos		Forest survey releases. Proc.

A13.40/6:nos		Occasional papers. Proc.

A13.40/7:nos		Southern forestry notes. Proc.

A13.40/8:CT		Bibliographies. Proc.

A13.40/8-2:date		Recent publications of Southern Forest Experiment Station (irregular) Title varies. Earlier A13.40/8:P96

A13.40/8-3:date		Publications of the Southern Forest Experiment Station [list] (annual)

A13.40/9:nos		Southern forest insect reporter. Proc.

A13.40/10:v.nos.&nos.	Southern forest research (irregular)

A13.40/11:date		Forest research news for the Midsouth [irregular]

A13.41:nos		Forest research project reports

A13.42:		Northeastern (formerly Allegheny) Forest Experiment Station, Philadelphia

A13.42/1:date		Annual reports

A13.42/2:CT		General publications

A13.42/6:CT		Regulations, rules and instructions

A13.42/6-2:CT		Handbooks, manuals, guides

A13.42/7:nos		Technical notes. Proc.

A13.42/8:nos	Occasional papers. Proc.
A13.42/8-2:nos	Occasional papers. Allegheny Forest Experiment Station
A13.42/9:nos	Anthracite survey papers. Proc.
A13.42/10:nos	Forest survey notes. Proc.
A13.42/11:nos	Forest management notes. Proc.
A13.42/12:nos	Forest management papers. Proc.
A13.42/13:nos	Forest economic notes. Proc.
A13.42/14:nos	Forest products papers. Proc.
A13.42/15:nos	Station notes. Proc.
A13.42/16:nos	Station papers. Proc. Changed from A13.67/8:
A13.42/17:nos	Forest survey releases. Proc. Changed from A13.67/7:
A13.42/18:nos	Forest products notes
A13.42/19:nos	Beech utilization series. Proc.
A13.42/20:nos	Northeastern research notes. Proc.
A13.42/21:CT	Forest statistics series (by States) Proc.
A13.42/22:dt/nos	Northeastern forest pest reporter
A13.42/23:date	New publications available

A13.43:	Southwestern Forest and Range Experiment Station, Tucson, Arizona.
A13.43/1:date	Annual reports
A13.43/2:CT	General publications

A13.43/7:nos	Research notes. Proc.
A13.43/8:nos	Research report
A13.44:CT	Charts. Proc.
A13.45:nos	Tables (statistical) Proc. Pubs. desig. T-nos.
A13.46:nos	Useful trees of United States. Proc.
A13.47:date	Why did it happen? Proc.
A13.48:date	Life line. Proc. Quarterly.
A13.49:nos	[Equipment development] reports. Proc.
A13.49/2:nos	Equipment development report R.M. (series)
A13.49/3:nos	Technical equipment report F-(series)
A13.49/4:nos	ED&T reports
A13.49/4-2:CT	Equip tips. Earlier in A13.9/4:
A13.49/5:date	Equipment development and test program, progress, plans, fiscal year
A13.50:nos	Forest resource reports
A13.51:nos	Tree planters' notes. Proc.
A13.51/a:CT	___ separates
A13.51/2:date	Forest and windbarrier planting and seeding in the United States, report (annual) Formerly issued as part of A13.51:
A13.52:nos	Forest pest leaflets (numbered)
A13.52/2:date	Forest insect conditions status report (annual) Earlier A13.2:In7/4
A13.52/3:nos	Northeastern forest pest reporter. Issued by Region 7
A13.52/4:nos	Southern forest pest reporter. Issued by Southern region
A13.52/5:nos	Bug business. Published by Division of Timber Management, Denver.
A13.52/6:date	Forest insect conditions in Pacific Northwest (annual) Earlier A13.66/2:In7/4
A13.52/7:date	Forest insect conditions in Northern Region

A13.52/8:les-nos	Northeastern Area State and Private Forestry [publications]
A13.52/9:date	Forest pest conditions in the North East
A13.53:nos	Interim technical reports
A13.54:date	Blister rust control in California, cooperative project of State and Federal agencies and private owners, annual reports. Proc.
A13.55:date	Forest Service films available on loan for educational purposes (annual) Earlier A13.2:F48
A13.56:date	Southern Region report (annual)
A13.57:date	Intermountain region yearbooks
A13.58:date	National forest timber sale activities for calendar year
A13.58/2:date	Stumpage prices for sawtimber sold from National forests, by selected species and region (quarterly)
A13.59:date	White pine blister rust control annual report
A13.60:nos	State law for soil conservation districts
A13.61:	Lake States Forest Experiment Station, St.Paul, Minnesota 1924
A13.61/1:date	Annual reports
A13.61/2:CT	General publications
A13.61/7:nos	Lake States aspen reports. Proc.
A13.61/8:nos	Station papers. Proc.
A13.61/9:nos	Miscellaneous reports. Proc.
A13.61/10:nos	Lake States Forest Experiment Station: Technical notes. Proc.
A13.61/11:nos	Economic notes. Proc.

A13.61/12:date   Publications by Lake States Forest Experiment Station [List] (annual)

        1966 - Joined with Central States to form North Central Forest Experiment Station, St.Paul, Minn.

A13.62:   California Forest and Range Experiment Station, Berkeley, California. Later Pacific Southwest Forest and Range Experiment Station

A13.62/1:date   Annual reports

A13.62/2:CT   General publications

A13.62/7:nos   Forest research notes. Proc.

A13.62/8:nos   Forest survey releases. Proc.

A13.62/9:nos   Miscellaneous papers. Proc.

A13.62/10:nos   Technical papers. Proc.

A13.62/11:date   Publications [list] Formerly entitled Staff publications.   Earlier A13.62:P96/date

A13.62/11-2:CT   Bibliographies and lists of publications

A13.62/11-3:date   List of available publications

A13.62/12:CT   Handbooks, manuals, guides

A13.62/13:date   What's new in research

A13.63:   Appalachian Forest Experiment Station, Asheville, North Carolina 1921. Southeastern Forest Experiment Station, 1946-

A13.63/1:date   Annual reports

A13.63/2:CT   General publications

A13.63/7:nos	Forest survey releases. Proc.
A13.63/8:nos	Technical notes. Proc.
A13.63/9:nos	Station papers
A13.63/10:nos	Research news. Proc.
A13.63/11:nos	Research notes. Proc.
A13.63/12:nos	Hickory task force reports. Proc.
A13.63/13:date	Research information digest, recent publications of the Southeastern Forest Experiment Station. Formerly Bibliography of Southeastern Forest Experiment Station, calendar year. Earlier A13.62/2:B47
A13.63/13-2:CT	Bibliographies and lists of publications
A13.63/14:nos	Southeastern forest insect & disease newsletters. Proc.
A13.63/15:CT	Handbooks, manuals, guides
A13.64:	Tropical Forest Experiment Station, Rip Piedras, P.R., 1941. Institute of Tropical Forestry, 1961-
A13.64/1:date	Annual reports
A13.64/2:CT	General publications
A13.64/7:v.nos	Caribbean forester (quarterly) Proc.
A13.64/8:nos	Tropical forest notes
A13.64/9:date	List of publications currently available

A13.65:   Intermountain Forest and Range Experiment Station, Ogden, Utah

A13.65/1:date   Annual reports

A13.65/2:CT   General publications

A13.65/3:nos   Bulletins. Proc.

A13.65/7:nos   Research papers

A13.65/8:nos   Research notes. Proc.

A13.65/9:nos   Misc. pub. (series)

A13.65/10:nos   Forest survey releases. Proc.

A13.65/11:v.nos. &nos. Range improvement notes (quarterly)

A13.65/12:CT   Handbooks, manuals, guides

A13.65/13:CT   Addresses

A13.65/14:date   Publications by staff and cooperators [list] (annual)

A13.65/14-2:CT   Bibliographies and lists of publications

A13.65/14-3:nos Recent reports

A13.65/15:date   Intercom

A13.66:   Pacific Northwest Forest and Range Experiment Station, Portland, Oregon, 1937-

A13.66/1:date   Annual reports

A13.66/2:CT   General publications

A13.66/6:CT   Regulations, rules, and instructions

A13.66/7:nos   Forest research notes. Proc.

A13.66/8:nos   Forest survey reports. Proc.

A13.66/9:nos   Range research reports. Proc.

A13.66/10:nos Research papers. Proc.

A13.66/11:nos Silvical series. Proc.

A13.66/12:CT   Handbooks, manuals, guides

A13.66/12a:CT ___ separates

A13.66/13:date Production, prices, employment, and trade in Pacific Northwest Forest industries

A13.66/14:date List of available publications (quarterly)

A13.66/15:CT   Bibliographies and lists of publications

A13.66/16:nos Wood outdoor structures: general information

A13.67:   Northeastern Forest Experiment Station, 1929-1945

A13.67/1:date Annual reports

A13.67/2:CT   General publications

A13.67/7:nos   Forest survey release. Proc. Changed to A13.42/17:

A13.67/8:nos   Station papers. Proc. Changed to A13.42/16:

A13.67/9:nos   Technical notes

A13.67/10:nos Forest products papers

A13.68:   Central States Forest Experiment Station, 1926-1965.
                (Later see North Central Forest Experiment Station)

A13.68/1:date   Annual reports

A13.68/2:CT   General publications

A13.68/7:nos   Technical papers. Proc.

A13.68/8:nos   Miscellaneous releases

A13.68/9:nos   Forest survey releases

A13.68/10:nos   Station notes. Proc.

A13.68/11:v.nos Forest pest observer (irregular) Proc.

A13.68/12:CT   Bibliographies and lists of publications

A13.68/12-2:date Publications [list] (annual)

A13.69:   Rocky Mountain Forest and Range Experiment Station, 1950-

A13.69/1:date   Annual reports

A13.69/2:CT   General publications

A13.69/7:nos   Station papers. Proc.

A13.69/8:nos   Research notes. Proc.

A13.69/9:nos	Forest survey releases
A13.69/10:date	List of publications (quarterly)
A13.69/10-2:date	Publications for [year] (annual)
A13.69/10-3:CT	Bibliographies and lists of publications
A13.69/11:nos	Eisenhower consortium bulletins
A13.70:CT	Releases. Proc.
A13.71:	Report of Forest Service training activities, Civilian Conservation Corps.
A13.72:CT	Conservation teaching aids. Proc.
A13.72/2:nos	Conservation vistas, regional conservation education newsletter serving Oregon and Washington
A13.73:	Alaska Forest Experiment Station, Later Alaska Forest Research Center. **Northern Forest Exp. Sta., 1960-**
A13.73/1:date	Annual reports
A13.73/2:CT	General publications
A13.73/8:nos	Station papers. Proc.
A13.73/9:nos	Technical notes. Proc.
A13.73/10:nos	Miscellaneous publications

A13.74:date   Forest tree nurseries of United States (annual) Proc.

A13.75:date   Forest and shelterbelt planting in United States (annual) Proc.

A13.76:date   Demand and price situation for forest products (annual) Proc. Earlier A13.2:D39

A13.77:date   Lumber manufacturing, wood using and allied associations. Earlier A13.2:L97/9 and A13.2:L97/15

A13.78:letters-nos Research papers

A13.79:letters-nos Research notes

A13.80:letters-nos Resource bulletins

A13.81:nos   [Forest Service translations] FS-

A13.82:   North Central Forest Experiment Station, 1965

A13.82/1:date   Annual reports

A13.82/2:CT   General publications

A13.82/9:date   List of publications

A13.83:date	Annual grazing statistical report
A13.84:nos	Engineering technical information system: Technical report ETR (series)
A13.84/2:nos	Engineering technical information system: EM (series)
A13.84/3:	Engineering technical information system, field notes
A13.85:nos	Training texts (numbered)
A13.86:date	Forest Service comments on resolutions relating to National Forest System. Earlier A13.2:F76/72
A13.87:date	Watershed management research, semiannual report
A13.88:letters-nos	General technical report
A13.89:date	Forest-gram South, dispatch of current technical information for direct use by practicing forest resource manager in the South
A13.90:date	Resource decisions in the national forests of the Eastern Region (quarterly)
A13.91:nos	Current information reports
A13.92:CT	Final environmental statements
A13.92/2:CT	Draft environmental statements
A13.93:CT	Forest insect and disease management/evaluation reports
A13.93/2:nos	Forest insect and disease management/survey reports

A14 Garden and Grounds Division

1862

A14.1:date   Annual reports

A14.2:CT   General publications [none issued]

A14.3:nos   Bulletins [none issued]

A14.4:nos   Circulars [none issued]

Merged into Bureau of Plant Industry (A19) July 1, 1901.

A15 Irrigation Inquiry Office

Established April 15, 1890

A15.1:date   Annual reports

A15.2:CT   General publications

A15.3:nos   Bulletins

A15.4:nos   Circulars [none issued]

Discontinued June 30, 1896.

A16 Labor Employment Board

Appointed July 2, 1902.

A16.1:date   Annual reports

A16.2:CT   General publications

A16.3:nos   Bulletins [none issued]

A16.4:nos   Circulars [none issued]

Discontinued at some time after Mar. 21, 1904 and work taken over by Civil Service Commission

National Agricultural Library 1962-
A17   Library

1864

A17.1:date   Annual report

A17.2:CT   General publications

A17.3:nos   Bulletins

A17.4:nos   Circulars   Admin.

A17.5:nos   List of duplicates offered as exchanges

A17.6:v.nos   Monthly bulletins

A17.6/a:CT   ___ separates

A17.7:nos   Library leaflets - changed from A1.29: (May 5,1919)

A17.8:nos   Bibliographical contributions

A17.9:vol   Agricultural Library notes. Monthly. Mim.

A17.10:vol   Agricultural economics literature. Proc. Earlier A36.20: Later A17.18:A

A17.11:vol   Plant science literature, selected references (weekly) Later A17.18:D

A17.12:date   Agricultural Experiment Station publications received by Library, Lists of (monthly) Earlier A10.7: Later A77.409:

A17.13:vol   Cotton literature, selected references (monthly) Proc. Earlier A1.50:

A17.14:vol   Entomology current literature, selected references (bimonthly) Proc. Earlier A56.10:   Later A17.18:C

A17.15:vol   Soil conservation literature, selected current references (bimonthly) Earlier A57.20:

A17.16:vol   Agriculture in defense (weekly)

A17.17:nos   Library lists. Proc.

A17.18:sec.nos., later v.nos.&nos. Bibliography of agriculture (by sections; monthly) Section A supersedes, July 1942, A17.10:; section B supersedes July 1942, A70.7:; section C supersedes, July 1942, A17.14:; section D supersedes July 1942, A17.11: Section E supersedes A13.25:

35

A17.18/2:CT   Bibliographies and lists of publications

A17.18/3:date   Catalog Food and Nutrition Information and Educational Materials Center

A17.19:v.nos.&nos Daily digest. Administrative

A17.20:v.nos   Pesticides documentation bulletin (biweekly)

A17.21:CT   Press releases

A17.22:CT   Handbooks, manuals, guides.

A17.23:v.nos.&nos. Agricultural libraries information notes (monthly)

A18 Microscopy Division

Established 1871, became a division 1885.

A18.1:date	Annual reports
A18.2:CT	General publications
A18.3:nos	Bulletins
A18.4:nos	Circulars
A18.5:nos	Food products.

Abolished 1895.

A19 Plant Industry Bureau

Organized July 1, 1901 by the consolidation of A3, A6, A14, A20, A23, A24, A28.

A19.1:date	Annual reports. Later A77.501:
A19.2:CT	General publications. Later A77.502:
A19.3:nos	Bulletins
A19.4:nos	Circulars
A19.4/a:CT	___ separates
A19.5:sec.nos.	Food products
A19.6:CT	Seed and plant introduction and distribution
A19.7:CT	Horticultural investigations
A19.8:date	(List of) bulletins of Bureau of Plant Industry
A19.9:CT	Hints to settlers (on irrigation projects)
A19.10:date	List of publications of the Bureau of Plant Industry
A19.11:CT	Grain standardization
A19.12:nos	Inventories of seeds and plants imported by Office of Foreign Seed and Plant Introduction. Later A77.515:
A19.13:nos	Service and regulatory announcements.

A19.14:CT/date	Work of reclamation project experiment farm (by name of project)
A19.15:date	New plant introductions (annual lists)
A19.16:nos	Plant immigrants. Monthly. Mim.
A19.17:nos	Cotton, truck, and forage crop disease circulars.
A19.18:v.nos	Plant disease bulletins (later Plant Disease Reporter) Mim. Later A77.511:
A19.18/a:CT	___ separates Later A77.511/a:
A19.19:nos	___ Supplements. Mim.
A19.19/a:	___ ___ separates
A19.20:nos	Agricultural technology circulars
A19.21:vol	Blister rust news. Monthly. Mim.
A19.22:vol	Botany, current literature. Fortnightly. Mim. Later included in A19.22/2:
A19.22/2:vol	Plant science literature, selected references. Wkly. Later A17.11:
A19.23:vol	Agronomy, current literature. Fortnightly. Mim. Later included in A19.22/2:
A19.24:date	Weekly station reports of Office of Dry Land Agriculture Investigations. Mim. Later A77.508:
A19.25:vol	Weekly reports of Office of Western Irrigation Agriculture. Mim.
A19.26:nos	Plant disease posters. Later A77.517:
A19.27:vol	Horticultural crops and diseases division. Semi-monthly news letter. Mim. Later A77.510:
A19.28:CT	Papers in re. Later A77.513:
A19.29:vol	Forage crop gazette; news letter for staff workers, Division of forage crops and diseases. Monthly. Proc. Later A77.509:
A19.30:date	Alfalfa improvement conferences, Reports. Proc.
A19.31:CT	Soil survey reports (lists of by States) Proc. Earlier A47.5/a:
A19.32:date/nos	Soil survey [reports] Earlier A47.5:
A19.33:CT	Addresses. Proc. Later A77.507:

A19.34:nos   [Dry-land] agriculture. Pubs.desig. D.L.A.-no. Changed from A19.2:CT

A19.35:nos   Contributions toward a flora of Nevada. Proc. Later A77.527:

A19.36:nos   H.T.&S. office reports. Proc. Later A77.523:

Transferred to Agricultural Research Administration by Executive Order 9060 of February 23,1942.

A20   Pomology Division

Established July 1,1886.

A20.1:date   Annual reports

A20.2:CT   General publications

A20.3:nos   Bulletins

A20.4:nos   Circulars

Merged into Bureau of Plant Industry, July 1,1901.

Communication Office
Information Office, (Aug. 1, 1923)
A 21 Publications Division

A Division of Records and Editing was organized July 1, 1890, under act making appropriations for Department of Agriculture, 1891, approved July 14, 1890. This division was absorbed and succeeded by the Division of Publications, which was established July 1, 1895, under the appropriations act for 1896, approved Mar. 2, 1895.

A 21.1:date	Annual reports
A 21.2:CT	General publications
A 21.3:nos	Bulletins
A 21.4:nos	Circulars
A 21.5:ed. nos.	List of bulletins and circulars issued by Department of Agriculture for distribution
A 21.6/1:date	Monthly list of publications (of Department of Agriculture)
A 21.6/2:date	Monthly list of publications (of Department of Agriculture) for foreign distribution
A 21.6/3:nos	New publications
A 21.6/4:date	Publications of Department of Agriculture available for distribution
A 21.6/5:date	Monthly list of publications. Supersedes A 21.6/3:
A 21.7:CT	Press notices
A 21.8:ed. nos	Price list of publications of Department of Agriculture for sale by Superintendent of Documents.
A 21.9/1:date	Farmers' bulletins (available for distribution)
A 21.9/2:date	**Farmers' bulletins** of interest to persons residing in cities or towns
A 21.9/3:date	**Farmers' bulletins.** Complete list.
A 21.9/4:date	Farmers' bulletins. Subject list.
A 21.9/5:b. nos	Farmers' bulletins. Indexes.
A 21.9/6:date	Subject list of Farmers' bulletins (front space)
A 21.9/7:date	Farmers' bulletins (subject list) (back space)
A 21.9/8:nos	List (series). Formerly List of Farmers' bulletins, [etc.]
A 21.9/9:date	List of available **Farmers' bulletins** and leaflets.

A 21.10:	Publications of Department of Agriculture available for distribution.
A 21.11:CT	Maps
A 21.12;date	Indexes to Yearbooks of Department of agriculture. Earlier A 21.3:7, 9, 10
A 21.13:nos	Livestock short course
A 21.13/1:nos	Radio service, Livestock short course
A 21.13/2:nos	Radio service, Dairy short course
A 21.13/3:nos	Radio service, Poultry short course
A 21.13/4:nos	Radio service, Farm economics series
A 21.13/5:CT	Radio records
A 21.13/6:date	Radio service, Consumer facts. Weekly. Mim.
A 21.13/7:date	Radio service, Farm flashes. Mim.
A 21.13/8:date	Radio service, Housekeepers' chats. Daily. Proc.
A 21.13/9:nos	Radio service, Agriculture in defense. Proc.
A 21.14:vol.nos.	Daily digest. Mim.
A 21.15:nos	Clip sheets. Wkly.
A 21.16:CT	National farm data program, 1932-40 (by States)
A 21.17:nos	Food for freedom program, background information series. Proc.
A 21.18:nos	Food information series.
A 21.19:nos	Food fights for freedom round-up. Wkly. Proc.
A 21.20:CT	Posters
A 21.21:dt. &nos.	Farm mobilization fact sheets. Proc.
A 21.22:	Homemaker news.
A 21.23:	Releases. Proc.
A 21.24:CT	Addresses. Proc.

A 21.25:nos	Rural development program news. Irregular. Proc. Later Y3.R88/2:9 Replaced by A 21.25/3:
A 21.25/2:nos	Rural resource leaflets. Proc. CANCELLED by Y3.R88/2:8
A 21.25/3:nos	Rural areas development newsletter. Earlier entitled Rural Development Program News and classified A 21.25: and Y3.R88/2:9
A 21.26:nos	Picture story (series) Changed to A1.100:
A 21.27:nos	Consumer information TV program packages, suggested scripts
A 21.28:CT	Handbooks, manuals, guides
A 21.29:nos	Service, USDA's report to consumers (monthly)
A 21.30:nos	Response, report on actions for a better environment
A 21.31:date	Catalyst for rural development
A 21.32:nos	FPL, farm paper letter
A 21.33:date	Food and home notes (weekly)
A 21.34:letters & nos.	Farm broadcasters letters (weekly)

A22   Public Roads Bureau

October 3, 1892 (Stat. L. v. 27, p. 743)

A22.1:date	Annual reports. Later FW2.1:
A22.2:CT	General publications. Later FW2.2:
A22.3:nos	Bulletins
A22.4:nos	Circulars
A22.5:date	Publications
A22.6:v.nos	Public Roads. Monthly. Later FW2.7:
A22.6/a:CT	___ separates
A22.7:CT	Specifications
A22.8:CT	Highway transportation surveys (by States)
A22.9:CT	Maps and atlases. Later FW2.12:
A22.9/2:CT	Transportation maps. Later FW2.13:
A22.10:vol.	Highways, current literature. Wkly. Mim. Later FW2.8:
A22.11:CT	Addresses. Proc.
A22.12:nos	Planning survey memorandum. Proc. Later FW2.9:
A22.13:nos	State-wide highway planning surveys; new bulletins for bureau managers. Proc. Later FW2.10:
A22.14:nos	Information series. Proc. Later A53.10:
A22.15:CT	Addresses. Later FW2.11:

Transferred to Federal Works Agency July 1, 1939.

A23   Seed and Plant Introduction Section

Organized July 1, 1898 - Stat. L30:337.

A23.1:date	Annual reports
A23.2:CT	General publications
A23.3:nos	Bulletins

A23.4:nos   Circulars

Merged into Plant Industry Bureau July 1, 1901 (A19)

A24   Seed Division

Organized 1868.

A24.1:date   Annual reports

A24.2:CT   General publications [none issued]

A24.3:nos   Bulletins [none issued]

A24.4:nos   Circulars [none issued]

A24.5:date   Reports of special agent for purchase and distribution of seeds

Merged into Plant Industry Bureau July 1, 1901.

A25   Silk Section

1889

A25.1:date   Annual reports

A25.2:CT   General publications [none issued]

A25.3:nos   Bulletins

A25.4:nos   Circulars [none issued]

Discontinued June 30, 1891.

A26   Soils Bureau

Established February 15, 1898

A26.1:date   Annual reports

A26.2:CT   General publications

A26.3:nos   Bulletins

A26.3/a:CT   ___ separates

A 26.4:nos   Circulars

A 26.5:date   Field operations of Bureau of soils. Later A47.5:

A 26.5/a:CT   ___ separates. Later A47.5/a:

A 26.6/1:date   List of publications

A 26.6/2:date   Classified list of publications

A 26.7:nos   Service and regulatory announcements

Merged into Chemistry and Soils Bureau 1928.

A 27   Crop Estimates Bureau

Formerly Statistics Bureau. Organized 1863.

A 27.1:date   Annual reports

A 27.2:CT   General publications

A 27.3:nos   Bulletins

A 27.4:nos   Circulars

A 27.5:date   Crop circulars

A 27.6:vol   Crop reporter. Monthly.

A 27.6/2:vol   Monthly crop reports. Later A36.10:

A 27.7:date   Monthly crop synopsis

A 27.8:nos   Miscellaneous series, bulletin

A 27.9:vol   Statistical reports

A 27.9/a:CT   ___ separates

A 27.10:CT   Maps of States

A 27.11:nos   Foreign crop and livestock reports. Semi-monthly. Mim. Later A36.19:

1922 Consolidated into Bureau of agricultural economics.

A28   Vegetable Physiology and Pathology Division

1886

A28.1:date   Annual reports

A28.2:CT   General publications

A28.3:nos   Bulletins

A28.4:nos   Circulars

A28.5:v.nos   Journal of mycology

Merged into Bureau of Paint Industry, July 1, 1901.

A29   Weather Bureau

Oct. 1, 1890 (Stat. L 26:653)

A29.1:date   Annual reports. Later C30.1:

A29.1/a1:date   ___ separates. Administrative report of chief

A29.1/a2:date   ___ separates. Miscellaneous separates

A29.2:CT   General publications. Later A30.2:

A29.3:nos   Bulletins

A29.3/a:CT   ___ separates

A29.4:nos   Circulars

A29.5:letters   Bulletins

A29.5/a:sec.nos.&date   ___ reprints. Climatic summary of United States

A29.5/a:CT   ___ separates. Later C30.3/2:

A29.6:vol   Monthly weather review. Later C30.14:

A29.6/a1:distract.no.date & no. Climatological services of bureau, district no. ___

A29.6/a2:CT   ___ separates. Misc. Later C30.14/a:

A29.6/a3:date   ___ separates. Measurement of solar constant of radiations at Calama, Chile.

46

A 29.6/a4:date	___ separates; Weather of the oceans. Monthly. Later C30.14/a2:
A 29.6/2:nos	___ supplements Later C30.15:
A 29.6/2a:CT	___ ___ separates. Later C30.15:
A 29.7:dt.&nos	National weather bulletin. Earlier W42.27: Superseded by A36.11:
A 29.7/2:date	Weekly weather and crop bulletin. Earlier W42.27: Later C30.11:
A 29.8:vol	Climate and health
A 29.9:nos	Cold wave bulletin
A 29.10:pt.nos	Daily river stages. Begins with part 4.pt.1-3, see W42.19: Later C30.24:
A 29.10/a:CT	___ separates
A 29.11:letter	Instrument room [or division] circulars. Later C30.4:
A 29.11/a:CT	___ separates
A 29.12:CT	Instructions. Later C30.6:
A 29.12/a:CT	___ separates
A 29.13:date	Meteorological chart of Great Lakes
A 29.13/2:date	Meteorological chart of Great Lakes [2d series 1911-13]
A 29.14:date	Monthly report of river and flood service
A 29.15:nos	Sanitary climatology circulars
A 29.16:date	Snow and ice bulletin
A 29.17:date	Storm bulletin
A 29.18:date	Daily weather map. Later C30.12:
A 29.19:date	Special river bulletins
A 29.20:nos	Cotton region weather crop bulletin. See also A29.39:
A 29.21:v.nos	Bulletin of Mountain Weather Observatory
A 29.21/a:CT	___ separates
A 29.22:CT	Specifications

A 29. 23:date	Meteorological chart of North Atlantic Ocean. Monthly.
A 29. 24:date	Meteorological chart of North Pacific Ocean. Monthly.
A 29. 25:date	Meteorological chart of South Atlantic Ocean. Quarterly.
A 29. 26:date	Meteorological chart of South Pacific Ocean. Monthly. Later C30. 20:
A 29. 27:date	Meteorological chart of Indian Ocean. Monthly.
A 29. 28:date	Roster of commissioned officers and employees
A 29. 29:vol	Climatological data (by sections) Later C30.18:
A 29. 29/ 2:vol	Climatological data, by sections. Monthly. Bound. Later C30.18/2:
A 29. 30:date	Monthly meteorological summary, Washington, D.C.
A 29. 30/ 2:date	Annual meteorological summary, Washington, D.C. Later C30.10:
A 29. 30/ 3:date	___ Honolulu, Hawaii
A 29. 30/ 4:date	___ Erie, Pa.
A 29. 30/ 5:date	___ Ft. Worth, Texas
A 29. 30/ 6:date	___ Miami, Florida
A 29. 30/ 7:date	___ Hatteras, North Carolina
A 29. 30/ 8:date	___ Charlotte, North Carolina
A 29. 30/ 9:date	___ Miles City, Montana
A 29. 30/10:date	___ Oswego, New York
A 29. 30/11:date	___ Walla Walla, Washington
A 29. 30/12:date	___ Dubuque, Iowa
A 29. 30/13:date	___ Lander, Wyoming
A 29. 30/14:date	___ Port Arthur, Texas
A 29. 30/15:date	___ Pueblo, Colorado
A 29. 30/16:date	___ El Paso, Texas
A 29. 30/17:date	___ Albuquerque, N. Mexico

Later C30.17: (brace grouping A29.30/3 through A29.30/11)

A29.30/18:date	___ Asheville, North Carolina
A29.30/19:date	___ Baker, Oregon
A29.30/20:date	___ Escambia, Michigan
A29.30/21:date	___ Roseburg, Oregon
A29.30/22:date	___ Mobile, Alabama
A29.30/23:date	___ Corpus Christi, Texas
A29.30/24:date	___ Green Bay, Wisconsin
A29.30/25:date	___ Rapid City, South Dakota
A29.30/26:date	___ Greensboro, North Carolina
A29.30/27:date	___ Lynchburg, Virginia
A29.30/28:date	___ Brownsville, Texas
A29.30/29:date	___ Portland, Maine
A29.30/30:date	___ Tatoosh Island, Washington
A29.30/31:date	___ Seattle, Washington
A29.30/32:date	___ Palestine, Texas
A29.30/33:date	___Kalispell, Montana
A29.30/34:date	___ Medford, Oregon
A29.30/35:date	___ Yakima, Washington
A29.30/36:date	___ Concord, New Hampshire
A29.30/37:date	___ Chattanooga, Tennessee
A29.30/38:date	___ Cape Henry, Virginia
A29.31:date	Publications of Weather Bureau available for distribution
A29.31/2:CT	List of publications (miscellaneous)
A29.31/3:date	Price list of publications. Later C30.17:
A29.32:date	New England highway weather bulletin

A 29. 33:date   Climatological data, Alaska section. Later C30. 21:

A 29. 34:date   Climatological data, Hawaii section. Later C30.19:

A 29. 35:date   Climatological data, Porto Rico section. Superseded by A 29. 36:

A 29. 36:date   Climatological data, West Indies and Caribbean Service. Later C30. 20:

A 29. 37:nos   Forecast Division circulars.   Later C 20. 23:

A 29. 38:date   Weather outlook. Wkly. Later C30.13:

A 29. 39:dt. &nos   Weekly cotton region bulletins. Wkly during cotton season. Later C30.13:

A 29. 40:vol. nos   Monthly bulletins of Hawaiian volcano observatory. Later I19. 28:

A 29. 41:date   Marine calendar, Atlantic

A 29. 42:date   Marine calendar, Pacific

A 29. 43:date   Weekly corn and wheat region bulletin. Later C30. 7:

A 29. 43/ 2:date   Weekly corn and wheat region bulletin. Daily except Sundays and holidays during crop season. Later C30. 8:

A 29. 44:nos   Climatic charts for U.S.

A 29. 45:date   United States meteorological yearbook. Formerly issued as part of A 29.1: Later C30. 25:

A 29. 46:CT   Addresses. Proc.

Transferred to Commerce Department by the President's Reorganization Plan 4, effective June 30,1940.

A 30   Appointment Clerk

A 30. 1:date   Annual reports

A 30. 2:CT   General publications [none issued]

A 30. 3:nos   Bulletins [none issued]

A 30. 4:nos   Circulars [none issued]

A31 Chief Clerk

Office established 1862.

A31.1:date   Annual reports

A31.2:CT   General publications

A31.3:nos   Bulletins [none issued]

A31.4:nos   Circulars [none issued]

A32 Food and Drug Inspection Board

Organized May 1907.

A32.1:date   Annual reports

A32.2:CT   General publications

A32.3:nos   Bulletins [none issued]

A32.4:nos   Circulars [none issued]

A32.5:nos   Food inspection decisions

A32.6:nos   Notices of judgment, food and drug act.

Abolished Feb.1, 1914 by order of Secretary of Agriculture.

General Counsel of Dept. of Agriculture
A33 Solicitor of Department of Agriculture

A33.1:date   Annual reports

A33.2:CT   General publications

A33.3:nos   Bulletins

A33.4:nos   Circulars

A33.5:CT   Papers in re

A33.6:CT   Regulations, rules, and instructions.

A33.7:date   Laws applicable to Department of Agriculture. Changed from A33.2:L44 to L44/8

51

A34 Insecticide and Fungicide Board

Established by General order 143 of the Secretary of Agriculture Dec. 22, 1910.

A34.1:date   Annual reports

A34.2:CT   General publications

A34.3:nos   Bulletins

A34.4:nos   Circulars

A34.5:nos   Insecticide decisions

A34.6:nos   Service and regulatory announcements. Includes Notices of Judgment. Earlier A1.18: Later A46.7:

A34.6/a:CT   ___ separates.

Abolished and functions transferred to the Food, drug and insecticide administration, June 30, 1927.

A35 Federal Horticultural Board

Established 1912 in accordance with Plant quarantine act.

A35.1:date   Annual reports. Later A56.1:

A35.2:CT   General publications. Later A56.2:

A35.3:nos   Bulletins

A35.4:nos   Circulars

A35.5:nos   Notices of quarantine   Later A48.5:

A35.6:nos   Plant quarantine decisions

A35.7:date   Circular of information   Later A48.11:

A35.8:CT   Regulations, plant. Later A56.6:

A35.9:nos   Service and regulatory announcements. Later A48.7:

A35.9/a:CT   ___ separates

A35.10:nos   Annual letter of information. (Later published as a supplement or addition to Service and regulatory announcements).

Absorbed by Plant Quarantine and Control Administration in 1928.

A36 Bureau of Agricultural Economics

May 11, 1922 (42 Stat. 532)

A36.1:date	Annual reports
A36.2:CT	General publications
A36.3:	Bulletins
A36.4:	Circulars
A36.5:nos	Service and regulatory announcements. Later A66.27:
A36.5/a:CT	___ separates
A36.6:vol	Seed reporter. Superseded by A36.9:
A36.7:vol.	Food surveys. Superseded by A36.9:
A36.8:nos	Reports on foreign markets for agricultural products. Mim.
A36.9:vol	Market reporter. Supersedes the Seed reporter (A36.6:) and Food surveys (A36.7:)
A36.10:vol	Monthly crop reporter. Earlier A27.6/2:
A36.11:vol	Weather, crops, and markets. Wkly. Supersedes A29.7:
A36.11/2:vol	Crops and markets. Wkly.
A36.11/3:vol	Crops and markets. Monthly. Later A1.52:
A36.11/3a:CT	___ separates. Later A1.52/a:
A36.12:v.nos	Agricultural cooperation. Fortnightly. Mim. Later FF1.12:
A36.12/a:nos	___ separates. Summary of cases and decisions on legal phases of cooperation
A36.13:nos	Agricultural economics bibliographies. Mim.
A36.14:vol	Foreign crops and markets. Wkly. Mim. Later A64.8:
A36.14/a:CT	___ separates. Mim.
A36.15:vol	Agricultural situation. Monthly. Later A88.81
A36.15/a:CT	___ separates.

A36.15/2:v.nos	Agricultural situation. Special edition for crop and price reporters (monthly. Earlier A36.15/a:
A36.16:vol	B.A.E.News. Wkly. Mim.
A36.17:nos	___ Library supplements. Monthly. Superseded by A36.20:
A36.18:CT	Charts
A36.19:nos	Markets and crop estimates bureau. Foreign crop and live stock reports Semi-monthly. Mim. Earlier A27.11: Later included in A36.14:
A36.20:v.nos	Agricultural economics literature. Monthly. Mim. Supersedes BAE News, Library supplements (A36.17:) Later A17.10:
A36.20/a:CT	___ separates
A36.21:v.nos	State and federal marketing activities and other economic work. Wkly. Mim. Later A66.14:
A36.21/a:CT	___ separates. Mim.
A36.22:CT	Posters. Later A66.21:
A36.23:vol	Farm population and rural life activities. Quarterly.
A36.24:nos	Egg Standardization leaflets
A36.25:CT	Handbooks and manuals. Changed from A36.2:
A36.25/2:CT	Regulations, rules, and instruction. Includes Handbooks and manuals
A36.26:date	Crop and market news radio broadcast schedules. Mim.
A36.27/1:date	Cotton grade and staple reports. Georgia (monthly during the height of the ginning season.) Mimeographed
A36.27/2:date	Cotton grade and staple reports, Texas and Oklahoma. (monthly during the height of the ginning season.) Mimeographed.
A36.28:date	Price situation. Monthly. Mim. Later Demand & price situation. Later A88.9:
A36.29:date	Mimeographed material: Crop reports. See A66.11: Later A88.24:
A36.29/2:date	Milk production (monthly) Proc.
A36.29/3:date	Fruit (monthly) Proc.
A36.29/4:	Sugar production crop report as of. Proc.

A36.29/5:	Tobacco, crop report as of
A36.30:date	Mimeographed material: Cotton reports. Later A66.9:
A36.31:date	Mimeographed material: Estimates of cotton crops. Revised.
A36.32:date	Fruit crop prospects. Mim. (Includes nut crops). Later A66.39:
A36.33:date	Livestock reports. Mim. Later A66.42:
A36.34:date	Potato and sweet potato crop prospects. Mim.
A36.35:CT	United States standards for fruits and vegetables. Later A66.16:
A36.35/2:CT	United States standards. Later A66.16:
A36.36:nos	World wool situation.
A36.37:CT	Outline maps.
A36.37/2:CT	Maps (miscellaneous)
A36.38:date	Planting intentions. Later A66.33:, A88.24/4:
A36.39:nos	Foreign service reports. Later A67.11:
A36.40:nos	World cotton prospects. Monthly.
A36.40/2:nos	Cotton situation. Monthly. Proc. Later A88.11/8:
A36.41:nos	World dairy prospects. Monthly.
A36.42:nos	World flaxseed prospects. Monthly.
A36.43:nos	World hog and pork prospects. Monthly.
A36.44:nos	World wheat prospects. Monthly.
A36.45:nos	Foreign news on tobacco
A36.46:nos	Foreign news on vegetables. Later A64.13:
A36.47:nos	World dry bean prospects. Mim.
A36.48:CT	Market news service on fruits and vegetables
A36.49:CT	Papers in re
A36.50:CT	Outlook charts. Rotoprinted

A36.51:CT	Addresses. Mim.
A36.52:CT	Estimated nos. of apple trees by varieties and ages in commercial and farm orchards. (slightly varying title) (by States)
A36.53:nos	Folders. Grain standards.
A36.54:date	Dairy and poultry market statistics annual summaries. Later A66.35:
A36.55:date	State agricultural and marketing orders. Later A66.45:
A36.56:nos	Smutty wheat reports. Multigraphed. Later A66.30:
A36.57:date	Directory of teachers giving courses in rural sociology and rural life.
A36.58:date	Agricultural economic reports and services. Later A66.19:
A36.59:date	Check list of standards for farm products. Later A66.26:
A36.60:date	List of manufacturers and jobbers of fruit and vegetable containers
A36.61:date	Production and carry over of fruit and vegetable containers
A36.62:CT	Bibliographies
A36.63:CT	Farm real estate taxes. Later in A77.15:, A83.9/6:
A36.64:nos	Utilization of American cotton studies
A36.65:date	Dairy situation. Monthly. Later A88.14/4:
A36.66:date	Weekly European citrus fruit market cable. Later A64.12:
A36.67:date	Weekly European fruit market cable. Later A64.13:
A36.68:date	Cash income from farm marketings. Monthly.
A36.69:date	Employment on farms of crop reporters. Monthly. Later A66.10:
A36.70:CT	List of publications. Changed from A36.Z/2:
A36.70/2:date	Check list of printed and processed publications (monthly) Superseded by A88.33:
A36.71:date	Dairy outlook. Annual.
A36.72:date	Poultry and egg outlook. Annual.
A36.73:date	Cotton market review. Wkly. Later A66.8:

A36.74:date	United States winter wheat and rye reports. Annual. Later A66.48:, A88.18/11:
A36.75:nos	Prices paid by farmers
A36.76:vol	Cotton literature, selected references. Monthly. Later A1.50:
A36.77:date	Farm wage rates and related data. Quarterly. Mim. Later A66.10:
A36.78:CT	Tax delinquency of rural real estate
A36.79:nos	Foreign news on apples. Mim. Issued by Foreign Agricultural Service. Later A64.9:
A36.80:nos	Foreign news on citrus fruits. Mim.
A36.81/1:date	Receipts from sale of principal farm products by States. Monthly. Mim.
A36.81/2:date	Monthly receipts from sale of principal farm products by States. Monthly. Mim.
A36.81/2:date	___ (compilations) Mim.
A36.82:date	Capacity of elevators, reporting grain stocks. Wkly.
A36.83:CT	Agricultural outlooks (individual) Proc.
A36.84/1:nos	World feed grain prospects. Mim.
A36.84/2:nos	Feed prospects. Pubs. desig. F-no. Mim.
A36.85:nos	Hog situation. Monthly. Proc.
A36.86:nos	Wheat situation. Monthly. Proc. Later A88.18/8:
A36.87:nos	Feed grain situation. Monthly. Proc. Superseded by A36.117:
A36.88:vol	Foreign agriculture, review of foreign farm policy, production, and trade. Monthly. Proc. Later A64.7:
A36.88/a:CT	___ separates. Proc.
A36.89:nos	Wool situation. Monthly. Proc. Later Livestock and wool situation, A36.141:
A36.90:nos	Beef cattle situation. Monthly. Proc.
A36.91:nos	Sheep and lamb situation. Monthly. Proc.
A36.92:nos	Crop reporting procedure. Proc. Later A66.22: Pubs. desig. C.R.P.
A36.93:nos	Grain investigations [publications] Proc. Pubs. desig. U.S.G.S.A.-G.I.

A36.94:nos	Tobacco situation. Proc. Pubs. desig. TS Later A88.34/2:
A36.95:nos	Fruit and vegetable situation. Proc. Pubs. desig. FVS
A36.96:nos	Poultry and egg situation. Monthly. Proc. Pubs.desig.PES Later A88.15/3:
A36.97:nos	Fats and oils situation. Monthly. Proc. Later A88.32:
A36.98:vol	Market reviews and statistical summaries of livestock, meats and wool. Wkly. Proc. Later A66.13:
A36.99:nos	Fruit situation. Monthly. Proc. Pubs.desig.TFS Later A88.12/7:
A36.100:nos	Vegetable situation. Monthly. Proc. Pubs.desig. TVS Later A88.12/8:
A36.101:date	Truck crop estimate reports. Proc. Pubs. desig. TC- Later A66.17:, A36.101:, A88.12/6:
A36.102:date	Poultry and egg production reports. Monthly. Proc. Slightly varying titles.
A36.103:date	Land policy circulars. Monthly. Proc. Supersedes A61.9:
A36.103/a:CT	___ separates
A36.104:nos	Land economics reports. Proc. Supersedes A61.8:
A36.105:nos	Semi-monthly honey reports. Proc. Later A66.12:
A36.106:nos	Weekly peanut reports. Proc. Later A66.15:
A36.107:date	Cold storage reports. Proc. Monthly. Later A66.7:
A36.108:CT	Land use projects (by States)
A36.109:CT	Farm-mortgage recordings (by States) Proc.
A36.110:date	Research-reference accessions. Earlier A61.15:
A36.111:vol	Agricultural finance review. Proc. Semi-annual & annual. Later A77.14:
A36.111/a:CT	___ separates
A36.112:nos	Land economics division. Bulletins. Proc.
A36.113:nos	Economic library lists. Proc.
A36.114:CT	Cotton estimated acreage, yield, and production (by States) Proc.
A36.115:date	Quarterly flax market review. Proc. Later A66.25:

A36.116:nos	Livestock situation. Monthly. Proc. A consolidation of Beef cattle situation (A36.90:), Hog situation (A36.85:) and Sheep and lamb situation (A36.91:). Later includes Livestock and wool situation (A36.141:) also.
A36.117:nos	Feed situation. Proc. Supersedes A36.87: Later A88.18/2:
A36.118:nos	Farm management reports. Proc.
A36.119:CT	World war [1914-18] and 1939 European war (by commodities) Proc.
A36.120:nos	County planning series.
A36.121:nos	Land Economics Division, Bulletins. Proc.
A36.122:nos	Farm income situation (monthly) Proc. Pubs.desig. FIS-nos. Later A88.9/2:
A36.123:date	Farm population estimates (annual) Changed from A36.2:CT Later A88.21:
A36.124:date	**Farm returns, summary of reports of farm operators (annual) Changed from A36.2:**
A36.125:CT	Farm value, gross income, and cash income from farm production. Changed from A36.2:
A36.126:nos	[Discussion series] Pubs.desig.DS-nos. Earlier A43.13: Later A1.66:
A36.127:nos	Editorial reference series. Proc.
A36.128:nos	Fliers. Issued in cooperation with Extension service.
A36.129:vol	Agricultural situation in relation to banking (quarterly)
A36.130:nos	Rice situation. Proc. Pubs.desig.RS- Later A88.18/18:
A36.131:nos	Migration and settlement on Pacific Coast, reports. Proc.
A36.132:CT	Agricultural loans by States; semi-annual.
A36.133:nos	Agricultural history series
A36.134:nos	Statistics and agriculture
A36.135:CT	Truck crop farms, Adjustments on (by States) Proc.
A36.136:nos	Rural life studies. Proc.
A36.137/1:CT	Agricultural census analyses: Changes in land in farms by size of farm.
A36.137/2:CT	Agricultural census analyses: Changes in number of farms by size of farm
A36.138:date	Farm-retail price spreads (monthly) Proc.

A36.139:nos	Dairy production (monthly) Proc. Later A66.44:, A88.14/2:
A36.140:date	Farm labor reports (monthly) Proc. Earlier A66.10: Later A88.25:
A36.141:nos	Livestock and wool situation. Proc. Earlier Wool situation (A36.89:) and Livestock situation (A35.116:) Later A36.158: and A36.159:
A36.142:nos	Post-war plans. Proc.
A36.143:nos	Marketing and transportation situation. Monthly. Proc. Desig. MTS-no. Later A88.26/2:
A36.143/a:CT	___ separates. Later A88.26/2a:
A36.144:CT	Radio talks. Proc.
A36.145:nos	Farmer and the war
A36.146:nos	Discussion [leaflets] Proc. and printed. Desig. D-no. Earlier A43.9:
A36.147:nos	National food situation. Desig. NFS- Earlier A36.2:F73/2 Later A88.37:
A36.148:CT	Water facilities area plans (by States)
A36.149:CT	Water utilization section, Land economics Division, Publications. Proc. See also A36.148:
A36.150:nos	War records project, reports. Proc.
A36.151:nos	Statistical summary (monthly) Proc. Later A88.28:
A36.152:date	Fluid milk prices in city markets (monthly) Proc. Later A88.14/3:
A36.153:date	Evaporated, condensed, and dried milk reports (monthly) Proc. Later A88.14:
A36.154:date	Hatchery production (monthly) Proc. Later A88.15/5:
A36.155:date	Liquid, frozen and dried egg production (monthly) Proc. Later A88.15:
A36.156:nos	Surveys of wages and wage rates in agriculture, reports. Proc.
A36.157:nos	Farm cost situation. Proc. Later A77.14/2:
A36.158:nos	Livestock and meat situation (monthly) Proc. Formerly IN A36.141: Later A88.16/8:
A36.159:nos	Wool situation (quarterly) Proc. Formerly in A36.151: Later A88.35:
A36.160:date	Agricultural outlook digest (monthly) Proc. Later A88.8/2:

A36.161:date	Stocks of evaporated and condensed milk held by wholesale grocers (quarterly) Proc. Later A88.14/5:
A36.162:date	Livestock slaughter, by States (monthly) Proc. Later A88.16/2:
A36.163:date	Agricultural prices (monthly) Proc. Later A88.9/3:
A36.164:date	Peanuts, stocks and processing (monthly) Proc. Later A88.10/2:
A36.165:date	Milk sugar (monthly) Proc.
A36.166:date	Dry casein, estimated production and stocks, United States (monthly) Proc.
A36.167:v.nos	Agricultural economics research (quarterly) Later A88.27:
A36.167/a:CT	___ separates. Proc. Later A88.27/a:
A36.168:nos	Current developments in farm real estate market. Proc. Earlier A36.2:R22/8 Later A77.13:
A36.169:nos	Harvard studies in marketing farm products
A36.170:date	Canned poultry (monthly) Proc. Later A88.15/2:
A36.171:date	Consumer purchases of selected fresh fruits, canned and frozen juices, and dried fruits (monthly) Proc. Later A88.12/4:
A36.171/2:date	Consumer purchases of fruits and juices by regions and retail outlets (quarterly) Formerly A36.172: Later A88.12/4-2:
A36.172:date	Regional distribution and types of stores where consumers buy selected fresh fruits, canned and frozen juices, and dried fruits (quarterly) Proc.
A36.173:date	Consumer buying practices for selected fresh fruits, canned and frozen juices, and dried fruits, related to family characteristics, region and city size. Proc.
A36.174:date	Stocks of feed grains (quarterly) Proc.
A36.174/2:date	Stocks of wheat and rye (quarterly) Proc.
A36.175:date	Marketing margins for Florida oranges in 10 major cities (monthly during the season). Proc.
A36.176:date	Seed crops. Irregular. Proc. Later A88.30:
A36.177:date	Naval stores report (monthly) Proc. Changed from A36.2:N22 Later A88.29:
A36.177/2:date	Naval stores report (quarterly) Proc. Changed from A36.2:N22
A36.178:	Special news letters

A36.179:	Average semi-monthly retail meat prices at New York, Chicago and Kansas City
A36.180:	Dry milk reports
A36.181:	Cattle and calves: Weekly average price per 100 pounds (by localities)
A36.182:	Warehouses licensed under United States Warehouse act.
A36.183:	Sheep and lambs: Weekly average price per 100 pounds (by localities)
A36.184:	Farm product prices, Monthly.
A36.185:	Southern rice stocks and movement reports
A36.186:	California rice stocks and movement reports
A36.187:	Unloads of tomatoes in 66 cities by States of origin.
A36.188:	Season tobacco market news reports type 12
A36.189:	Tobacco market reviews
A36.190:	Meat graded by Bureau of Agricultural Economics
A36.191:	Summary of cold storage stocks
A36.192:	Grain inspector's letters
A36.193:	Fruit and vegetable inspection service. Inspectors guides
A36.194:	Reports on hatchery sales in California
A36.195:	Export and import reports, Monthly.
A36.196:	Creamery butter and American cheese production estimates
A36.197:	Cold storage holdings by States
A36.198:	Address lists
A36.199:	Animals slaughtered under Federal meat inspection in districts represented by cities
A36.200:date	Mohair production and income
A36.201:	Shipping point inspection circulars.
A36.202:	Livestock movement at 12 markets

A36.203:	Receipts and disposition of livestock at public stockyards
A36.204:	Hogs weekly average price per 100 pounds
A36.205:	Hatchery reports Later A88.15/6:
A36.206:	Quality of grain crops based on inspected receipts at representative markets.
A36.207:	Cattle, calves, and vealers: Top prices and bulk of sales, Chicago
A36.208:	Nebraska weekly weather and crop report
A36.209:date	Cattle on feed Later A88.16/6:
A36.209/2:	Cattle on feed, Illinois, Iowa, Nebraska
A36.209/3:	Cattle on feed, Illinois
A36.209/4:	Cattle on feed, Iowa. Quarterly.
A36.209/5:	Cattle on feed, Nebraska
A36.209/6:	Cattle on feed, Idaho

A36.210:v.nos.&nos. Virginia crops and livestock (monthly) Proc. Later A88.31:

Under authority of Reorganization plan no. 2 of 1953, as implemented by Memorandum 1320, supp. 4, of the Secretary of Agriculture, Nov. 2, 1953, the Bureau of Agricultural Economics ceased to operate and its functions were transferred to other services of the Department of Agriculture.

A37   Farm Management and Farm Economics Office

Transferred from the Plant Industry Bureau to the Office of the Secretary of Agriculture, July 1, 1915.

A37.1:date	Annual reports
A37.2:CT	General publications
A37.3:nos	Bulletins
A37.4:nos	Circulars. Changed from A1.21:
A37.5:CT	Maps
A37.6:date	Directory of American agricultural organizations.

Combined with Markets and Crop Estimates Bureau to form Agricultural Economics Bureau (A36) 1922.

A38 Fixed Nitrogen Research Laboratory

July 1, 1921 transferred by Executive order from the War Dept.

A38.1:date	Annual reports
A38.2:CT	General publications
A38.3:	Bulletins
A38.4:	Circulars

In 1926 it became the Fertilizer Research Division of the Bureau of Chemistry and Soils.

A39 Packers and Stockyards Administration

August 15, 1921, 67 C. Public 51.

A39.1:date	Annual reports
A39.2:CT	General publications
A39.3:	Bulletins
A39.4:	Circulars
A39.5:v.nos	Monthly record. Later A4.28:

Abolished 1928 and functions transferred to Bureau of Animal Industry.

A40 Exhibits Office

Nov. 16, 1921 attached to office of the Assistant Secretary

A40.1:date	Annual reports
A40.2:CT	General publications
A40.3:	Bulletins
A40.4:	Circulars

1922 placed under the Director of Extension Work.

A41   Grain Futures Administration

Created September 21, 1922 (42 Stat. 998)

A41.1:date	Annual reports
A41.2:CT	General publications
A41.3:	Bulletins
A41.4:	Circulars
A41.5:CT	Laws
A41.6:CT	Regulations
A41.7:vol	Trade in grain futures. Monthly. Mimeo. Later A59.7:

Superseded by Commodity Exchange Administration, July 1, 1936.

Human Nutrition and Home Economics (February 1943-)
A42   Bureau of Home Economics

Created July 1, 1923

A42.1:date	Annual reports. Later A77.701:
A42.2:CT	General publications
A42.3:	Bulletins
A42.4:	Circulars
A42.5:nos	Home Economics publications. Mim.
A42.6:nos	Home Economics bibliographies. Mim.
A42.7:nos	Nutrition charts.
A42.7/2:nos	Household refrigeration charts
A42.7/3:nos	Child feeding charts
A42.7/4:nos	Meat cooking charts
A42.7/5:nos	Clothing selection charts
A42.7/6:nos	Poultry cooking charts

A42.8:CT   Study of consumer purchases. (prelim. releases) Proc.

A42.9:CT   Addresses. Proc.

Transferred to Agricultural Research Administration by Executive Order 9069 of Feb. 23, 1942.

Federal Extension Service

A43   Extension Service

Agricultural appropriation act of 1924, (42 Stat. 1289)

A43.1:date	Annual reports. Later A80.301: Later A43.1:
A43.2:CT	General publications. Later A80.302:
A43.3:	Bulletins
A43.4:nos	Circulars. Extension service circulars. Proc. Earlier A43.5/6: Later A80.304: Later A43.4:
A43.5:	Cooperative Extension Work Office
A43.5/1:date	Annual reports
A43.5/2:CT	General publications
A43.5/3:nos	Bulletins
A43.5/4:	Circulars
A43.5/5:v.nos	Boys and Girls 4-H Club Leader. Monthly. Mim. Superseded by A43.7:
A43.5/6:nos	Timely extension information. Later A43.4:
A43.5/7:vol	Extension pathologist. Later A43.20:
A43.5/8:nos	Lantern slide series. Later A43.19:
A43.5/9:date	List of extension publications of State Agricultural Colleges received by Office of Experiment Stations Library. Monthly. Mim.
A43.5/10:CT	Series of educational illustrations. (charts) Later A43.22:
A43.5/11:nos	Extension forester. Mim. Later A43.17:
A43.5/12:date	Extension poultry husbandman. Mim. Later A4.24:
A43.5/13:nos	Here and there with home demonstration workers. Mim.
A43.5/14:vol.	Home demonstration review. Monthly. Mim. Superseded by A43.7:
A43.5/15:nos	Southern economic extension. Mim.
A43.5/16:date	Wheat production adjustment. Mim.
A43.5/17:nos	Agricultural economics extension

A43.5/18:nos	Miscellaneous extension publications. Mim.
A43.5/19:CT	Addresses. Mim.
A43.5/20:nos	Wildlife conservation and restoration notes. Proc.
A43.5/21:nos	Extension marketing news. Monthly. Proc. Later A43.18:
A43.6:nos	Timely extension information. Mim.
A43.7:vol.	Extension Service Review. Monthly. Supersedes A43.5/2: and A43.5/14: Later A80.307: Later A43.7:
A43.7/a:CT	___ separates
A43.8:CT	Posters. Later A80.308:
A43.9:nos	Discussion [leaflets] Pubs.desig. D-no. Later A36.146:
A43.9/2:date	Garden facts for garden leaders (monthly) Formerly Garden and home food preservation facts.
A43.10:nos	Discussion services. A [Leaflets] Pubs.desig. DA-no.
A43.11:nos	Discussion series. B. [Leaflets] Pubs.desig. DB-no.
A43.12:nos	Discussion series C. Proc.
A43.13:DS-nos	[Discussion series, 1936-37.]
A43.14:nos	Parent education messenger. Proc.
A43.15:vol	4-H forage (daily, except Sunday, during week of National 4-H club camp held annually during June.)Proc.
A43.15/2:vol	4-H record, National 4-H club camp, Washington, D.C., 1938- Proc.
A43.16:CT	Regulations, rules, and instructions. Includes handbooks and manuals.
A43.16/2:CT	Handbooks, manuals, guides
A43.17:date	Extension forester. Proc. Earlier A43.5/11:
A43.18:nos	Extension marketing news. Monthly. Proc. Earlier A43.5/21:
A43.19:nos	Lecture notes for filmstrip series. Proc. Earlier A43.5/8: Later A80.309:
A43.20:ser.nos	Extension pathologist; news letter for extension workers interested in plant disease control. Proc. Earlier A43.5/7:

A43.21:CT	Addresses. Proc. Later A80.310: Later A43.21:
A43.22:gr.no.	Series of educational illustrations (charts) Earlier A43.5/10:
A43.23:date	Film strips of U.S.D.A., Price lists. Earlier A43.5/2:F48/2
A43.24:date	Motion pictures of Department of Agriculture. Proc.
A43.25:program nos.	National 4-H music hour [monthly, national 4-H club radio program: descriptive notes] Proc.
A43.Z/2:date	Negro extension news [an original classification]

Consolidated within the War Food Administration by Executive Order 9334 of April 19, 1943. On June 29, 1945, when the War Food Administration was discontinued, the Extension Service reverted to its previous role of staff agency.

A43.26:nos	Extension farm labor circulars. Earlier A80.311:
A43.27:	Weekly news series
A43.28:	Random forestry notes for extension foresters.
A43.29:nos	Garden and home food preservation facts (monthly) Replaced by A43.29/2:
A43.29/2:date	Garden facts for garden leaders. Monthly. Proc. Earlier A43.29:
A43.30:nos	Clean grain notes for cooperators in clean grain program (irregular) Proc.
A43.31:CT	Folder suggestions. Proc.
A43.32:date	List of State extension entomologists and extension apiculturists
A43.33:date	Trends in forage crop varieties (annual) Earlier A43.2:T72/2/959
A43.33/2:nos	New crop varieties
A43.34:date	Annual inventory of available USDA popular publications, for use of State and county Extension Offices in ordering USDA publications
A43.34/2:CT	Bibliographies and lists of publications
A43.35:nos	You can survive, rural defense fact sheets
A43.35/2:nos	Knowledge for survival, you can survive! newsletter to State extension program leaders, rural defense (monthly)
A43.36:nos	Ideas, 4-H and youth development (series)

A43.37:CT   [State publications issued in cooperation with Federal Extension Service] Note:- use CT for State, for subject, and date

A43.38:date   Statistical summary, rural areas development and area redevelopment, quarterly progress report.

A43.39:CT   Note to agents (series)

A43.40:nos   FES aid: Sanitation series

Bureau of Dairy Industry
A44   Dairying Bureau

Established May 29, 1924 (43 Stat. 243; 7 U.S.C. 401)

A44.1:date	Annual reports. Later A77.601:
A44.2:CT	General publications. Later A77.602:
A44.3:	Bulletins [none issued]
A44.4:	Circulars [none issued]
A44.5:nos	Service and regulatory announcements
A44.6:v.nos	Cow testing association letter. Monthly. Mim. Later A77.608:
A44.7:nos	Milk plant letters. Monthly. Mim. Earlier A4.17:
A44.8:nos	Milk inspector letters. Monthly. Mim.
A44.9:nos	Dairy library list. Mim.
A44.10:nos	Orders
A44.11:date	Publications relating to dairy industry (twice a year) Proc.
A44.12:CT	Addresses. Proc. Later A77.607:

Consolidated into Agricultural Research Administration by Executive order 9060 of Feb. 23, 1942.

A45   Agricultural Instruction Office

A division of Office of cooperative extension work since July 1, 1927.

A45.1:CT	Annual reports
A45.2:CT	General publications
A45.3:	Bulletins
A45.4:	
A45.5:CT	Series of educational illustrations for schools (posters)

A46 Food, Drug and Insecticide Administration

Jan. 18, 1927 (44 Stat. 1002)

A46.1:date   Annual reports. Later FS7.1:

A46.2:CT   General publications. Later FS7.2:

A46.3:   Bulletins

A46.4:   Circulars

A46.5:nos   Service and regulatory announcements, import milk. Changed to A46.11:
A46.5:v.nos. &nos. Food and drug review
A46.5/2:nos   Service and regulatory announcements, food and drug. Changed to A46.12:

A46.5/3:nos   Service and regulatory announcements, caustic poison. Changed to A46.13:

A46.6:incl.nos   Notice of judgment under food and drug act (irregular) Later FS7.11:

A46.7:incl.nos   Notice of judgment under insecticide act (irregular) Earlier included in
                   A34.6: Later A66.46:

A46.8:nos   Notice of judgment under regulations of naval stores (irregular)

A46.9:nos   Notice of judgment under caustic poison act (irregular) Later FS7.9:

A46.10:   Vacant

A46.11:nos   Service and regulatory announcements, import milk (irregular) Changed from
                   A46.5/1: Earlier A7.8: Later FS13.114:

A46.12:nos   Service and regulatory announcements, food and drug (irregular) Changed
                   from A46.5/2:

A46.12/a:CT   ___ separates

A46.13:nos   Service and regulatory announcements, caustic poison (irregular) Changed
                   from A46.5/3: Later FS13.110:

A46.14:nos   Service and regulatory announcements, tea (irregular) Later FS7.14:

A46.15:nos   Service and regulatory announcements, insecticide and fungicide (irregular)

A46.16:CT   Papers in re

A46.17:nos   Microanalytical division publications. Proc. Later FS7.16:

A46.18:nos   Service and regulatory announcements, Naval stores.

A46.19:nos   Service and regulatory announcements, Food, drug and cosmetic. Later FS7.8:

A46.20:nos   Notices of judgment under Federal food, drug, and cosmetic act: Foods. Later FS7.10:

A46.21:nos   Notices of judgment under Federal food, drug, and cosmetic act: Cosmetics. Later FS7.13:

A46.22:nos   Notices of judgment under Federal food, drug and cosmetic act: Drugs and devices. Later FS7.12:

Transferred to Federal Security Agency by Reorganization Plan IV, section 12, effective June 30, 1940.

A47 Chemistry and Soils Bureau

July 1, 1927 (44 Stat. 976)

A47.1:date   Annual report

A47.2:CT   General publications

A47.3:   Bulletins

A47.4:   Circulars

A47.5:dt. &nos   Soil survey reports. Earlier A1.64/1, 2: and A26.5: Later A19.32:

A47.5/a:CT   ___ separates. Earlier A26.5/a:

A47.5/2:CT   Soil survey (of states) Later A19.31: See, for separates from Field operations, 1899-1922, A26.5/2: Individual reports classified as A26.5/a: and A47.5:

A47.6:CT   Papers in re

A47.7:vol   Review of U.S. patents relating to pest control. Monthly. Earlier A7.9: Later A56.17:

A47.8:date   Insecticide division publications (lists) Mim. Later A56.15:

A47.9:nos   Mimeographed circulars. Proc. Superseded by A70.4:

A47.10:CT   Addresses. Proc.

Superseded by Bureau of Agricultural Chemistry and Engineering

A48   Plant Quarantine and Control Administration

Established 1928 taking over functions of Federal horticultural board, Bureau of entomology, and to a limited extent, Bureau of plant industry.

A48.1:date	Annual reports.
A48.2:CT	General publications.
A48.3:	Bulletins
A48.4:nos	Circulars
A48.5:nos	Notice of quarantine. Earlier A35.5: Later A56.14:
A48.6:nos	Memorandum. Mim.
A48.7:nos	Service and regulatory announcements. Earlier A35.9: Later A56.14:
A48.7/a:CT	___ separates
A48.7/2:CT	___ separates. List of intercepted plant pests. Later A56.14/2:date
A48.8:CT	Rules and regulations (Supersedes A36.8:) Later A56.6:
A48.9:CT	Posters
A48.10:nos	Administrative memorandum. Mim. Later A56.16:
A48.11:nos	Circular of information. Earlier A35.7: Later A56.9:

Consolidated with Bureau of entomology to form Bureau of entomology and plant quarantine, July 1, 1934 (A56.)

Personnel Office (June 1, 1934-
A49   Personnel and Business Administration Office

In 1925 the Secretary of Agriculture consolidated nine separate independent business and personnel offices into the centralized Office of Personnel and business administration.

A49.1:date	Annual reports
A49.2:CT	General publications
A49.3:nos	Bulletins of personnel administration. Later A49.3/2:
A49.3/2:vol	Personnel bulletins. Proc. Earlier A49.3:

74

A49.4:nos	P.B.A. Circulars. Mim. See also A1.43:, A1.44:, A1.45:
A49.4/2:nos	Personnel circulars, Sept.12,1934-
A49.5:CT	Laws
A49.6:	
A49.7:nos	Memorandum for chiefs of Bureaus and offices. Pubs.desig. P-nos.
A49.8:CT	Handbooks, manuals, guides
A49.9:nos	Personnel research series

A50   Alaska Commissioner for Department of Agriculture

Created Feb. 10, 1927 (Stat. L 44, pt. 2:1068)

A50.1:date	Annual reports
A50.2:CT	General publications
A50.3:	Bulletins
A50.4:	Circulars

A51   Farmers' Seed Loan Office

Organized by authority of letters from President to Secretary of Agriculture, July 26, 1918 and 26, 1919

A51.1:date	Annual reports
A51.2:CT	General publications
A51.3:	Bulletins
A51.4:	Circulars
A51.5:	Laws
A51.6:CT	Regulations

Transferred to Farm Credit Administration by sec. 5(d) of Executive order 6084 of March 27, 1933, effective May 27, 1933.

A52   National Advisory Loan Committee - Agricultural
               Credits Division

Appointed by Secretary of Agriculture 1931

A52.1:date   Annual reports

A52.2:CT   General publications

A52.3:   Bulletins

A52.4:   Circulars

A52.5:   Laws

A52.6:   Regulations

A53   Agricultural Engineering Bureau

July 1, 1931 (46 Stat. 1266)

A53.1:date   Annual report

A53.2:CT   General publications

A53.3:   Bulletins

A53.4:   Circulars

A53.5:   Laws

A53.6:   Regulations

A53.7:   Maps

A53.8:   Posters

A53.9:vol   Agricultural engineering, current literature. Monthly. Mim. Later A70.7:

A53.10:nos   Information series. proc.   Earlier A22.14: Later A70.11:

A53.11:CT   Lists of publications

A53.12:CT   Addresses

77

A53.13:CT   Bibliographies. Proc. Changed from A53.2:

Superseded by Bureau of Agricultural Chemistry and Engineering (A70.) October 16,1938.

A54   Crop Production Loan Office

1918 and 1919 (41 Stat.1347) March 3,1921

A54.1:date   Annual reports

A54.2:CT   General publications

A54.3:   Bulletins

A54.4:   Circulars

Transferred to Farm Credit Administration by section 5(d) of Executive order 6084 of March 27,1933, effective May 27,1933.

A55   Agricultural Adjustment Administration

48 Stat.31, May 12,1933.

A55.1:date   Annual reports. Later A76.401:

A55.1/a:nos   ___ separates

A55.2:CT   General publications. Later A76.402:

A55.3:   Bulletins

A55.4:

A55.5:CT   Laws

A55.6:CT   Regulations. See for sugar regulations A36.6:   Later A76.406:

A55.7:CT   Posters

A55.7/2:nos   Regional contact charts. Pubs.desig. RC

A55.7/3:nos   ___, 2d series.

A55.7/4:nos   ___, 3d series

A55.8:nos	License series
A55.9:nos	Marketing agreement series. Changed to A65.9:
A55.10:T-nos	Cigar tobacco adjustment program. Includes cigar tobacco acreage adjustment program
A55.11:vol	News digest. Wkly. Mim.
A55.12:vol	Consumers' guide. Bi-weekly. Mim. Later A75.108:
A55.12/a:CT	___ separates.
A55.12/a:nos	___ separates (numbered)
A55.13:nos	Code of fair competition series
A55.14:CH-3	Corn hog charts
A55.15:CT	Addresses. Later A80.609:
A55.16:nos	Administrative orders
A55.17:nos	Continental U.S. beet sugar orders
A55.18:nos	Puerto Rico sugar orders. Later A63.8:
A55.18/2:nos	Puerto Rico tax fund orders
A55.18/3:nos	Puerto Rico administrative rulings
A55.19:nos	General sugar orders
A55.20:nos	Rice administrative orders
A55.21:nos	Dockets (usually mimeographed) Later A65.8:
A55.22:nos	To farm journal editors. Wkly. Mim.
A55.23:nos	Cotton production adjustments. Mim.
A55.24:CT	Papers in re
A55.25:nos	Commodity information series: Cotton leaflets
A55.25/2:nos	___: Tobacco
A55.25/3:nos	___: Milk leaflets

A55.25/4:nos	Commodity information series: Wheat circulars
A55.25/5:nos	___: Wheat leaflets
A55.25/6:nos	___: Potato leaflets
A55.25/7:nos	___: Corn-hog leaflets
A55.25/8:nos	___: Rye leaflets
A55.25/9:CT	___ (miscellaneous)
A55.26:vol	Land policy review. Monthly. Mim. Later Land policy Circular, Bureau of Agricultural Economics A36.103:
A55.27:vol	Summary of press comments. Wkly. Mim.
A55.28:nos	Hawaii tax fund orders.
A55.29:nos	Discussion statements. Mim.
A55.30:nos	[Corn-hog board of review publications] Mim.
A55.31:nos	[Tobacco letters] Mim. Pubs. desig. TL-
A55.32:CT	Committeemen's letters. Proc. (by commodity)
A55.33:nos	Current information statements
A55.34:nos	Circular letters, corn-hog work. Proc. Earlier nos. issued by Director of extension work, later ones usually by Agricultural Adjustment Admin. and Extension Service cooperating. All are classified in A55.34:
A55.34/2:dt.&nos	Circular letters. Corn-hog work. Proc.
A55.34/3:CA-nos	Corn-hog circular letters. Proc.
A55.35:nos	Circular letters: wheat work
A55.36:nos	Order series. Later A65.7:
A55.37:nos	Sugar determination. Proc. Pubs. desig. S.D. no. Later A63.7:, A55.37:, A63.7:, A76.307:
A55.38:nos	[Peanut letters] Proc. Pubs. desig. Form PL-no.
A55.39:nos	Cotton educational meetings. Proc.

A55.40:CT	State summary series. Proc.
A55.41:v.nos	Better marketing. Bi-weekly.
A55.42:	Agricultural Conservation Program, East Central Region
A55.42/1:	
A55.42/2:CT	General publications
A55.42/3:nos	Bulletins. Later A55.42/9:
A55.42/4:	
A55.42/5:nos	Regional information series
A55.42/6:nos	[Joint letters] Proc.
A55.42/7:nos	Committeemen's letters. Proc.
A55.42/8:nos	Administrative letters. Proc.
A55.42/9:CT	Programs by States. Preceded by A55.42/3: Later A80.613:
A55.42/10:CT	Regulations, rules and instructions. Includes handbooks and manuals
A55.42/11:vol	A.A.A. flashes, facts for committeemen. Proc. Later A76.410:
A55.43:	Agricultural Conservation Program, North Central Region
A55.43/1:	
A55.43/2:CT	General publications. Later A79.452:
A55.43/3:nos	Bulletins
A55.43/4:	
A55.43/5:nos	Regional information series leaflets.
A55.43/6:CT	Regulations, rules, and instructions
A55.43/7:nos	Committeemen's letters
A55.43/8:nos	[Miscellaneous series] Proc.
A55.43/9:nos	State committee [letters] Proc.

A55.43/10:nos	Cotton marketing quotas letters. Proc.
A55.43/11:CT	A.A.A.N.C.R. Agricultural conservation program by States. NCR. 501-

A55.44: Agricultural Conservation Program, Northeast Region

A55.44/1:	
A55.44/2:CT	General publications. Later A76.462:
A55.44/3:nos	Bulletins
A55.44/4:	
A55.44/5:CT	Regional information series
A55.44/6:nos	[Joint letters] Proc.
A55.44/7:nos	Committeemen's letters. Proc.
A55.44/8:nos	[Administrative letters] Proc.
A55.44/9:nos	News letters. Proc.
A55.44/10:CT	Soil-building practices applicable in States. Proc. & printed.
A55.44/11:CT	Regulations, rules, and instructions. Includes handbooks and manuals. Later A76.466:
A55.44/12:CT	Outline of agricultural conservation program (by States)
A55.44/13:v.	Facts for northeast committeemen. Proc.
A55.44/14:CT	Agricultural conservation program (by States) Proc.

A55.45: Agricultural Conservation Program, Southern Region

A55.45/1:	
A55.45/2:CT	General publications Later A76.472:
A55.45/3:nos	Bulletins
A55.45/4:	
A55.45/5:nos	Regional information series leaflets
A55.45/6:nos	Southern region miscellaneous series, Items.

A55.45/7:nos   Committeemen letters

A55.45/8:nos   Southern region agricultural conservation

A55.45/9:nos   Announcements. Proc.

A55.45/10:nos   [Procedure relative to claims] Proc.

A55.45/11:nos   Handbooks, agricultural and range conservation programs (by States) ACP, Southern region. Cotton market quota letters. Proc.

A55.45/12:CT   Handbooks, agricultural conservation programs. Later A76.476:

A55.46:   Agricultural Conservation Program, Western Region

A55.46/1:

A55.46/2:CT   General publications. Later A76.482:

A55.46/3:nos   Bulletins

A55.46/4:

A55.46/5:nos   Regional information series leaflets

A55.46/6:nos   State committee letters. Proc.

A55.46/7:nos   Committeemen's letters

A55.46/8:nos   [Administrative letters] Proc.

A55.46/9:nos   County committee memorandum. Proc.

A55.46/10:nos   State office memorandum. Proc.

A55.46/11:CT   Handbooks, agricultural and range conservation program (by States)

A55.46/12:CT   Procedure (by States)

A55.46/13:CT   County office procedure (by States) Proc.

A55.46/14:   Committee procedure. Proc.

A55.46/15:   Regulations, rules, and instructions. Later A76.486:CT

A55.47:nos   Marketing information series. Leaflets. Proc.

A55.48:   Agricultural Conservation Program, Insular Region

A55.48/1:

A55.48/2:CT   General publications

A55.48/3:nos(also CT)   Bulletins

A55.48/4:

A55.48/5:nos   Announcements

A55.49:nos   Consumers' counsel series, Publications. Later A75.111:

A55.50:nos   Community discussion papers

A55.51:nos   [Agricultural adjustment administration] Information file, inserts

A55.52:vol   Consumers market service. Proc. Later A75.109:

A55.53:nos   Consumer study outline

A55.54:le.no   Marketing information series. Letters-nos. Later A65.12:

A55.55:CT   Number of farms participating in 1934 AAA voluntary control programs (by States)

A55.56:date   Consumer notes. Proc. Later A75.110:

A55.57:CT   Schedules of payments to holders of cotton options and participation trust certificates by Congressional districts of States. Proc.

A55.58:nos   Briefly speaking

A55.59:nos   Marketing and marketing agreements division [Marketing section publications] Proc. Later A65.10:

A55.60:nos   Statistical publications

A55.61:nos   Technical charts. Pubs.desig. TC

A55.62:date   Statements of expenditures. Proc. Later A76.409:

A55.63:CT   Consumers' counsel division. General publications. Later A75.102:

A55.64:vol   Weekly summary: AAA press releases

A55.65:nos	P.C. Producer-consumer series.
A55.66:nos	Sugar beet sugar orders.
A55.67:nos	Mainland cane sugar orders
A55.68:nos	Flue-cured tobacco letters. Proc.
A55.69:CT	Rules, rulings and instructions. Later A76.406:
A55.70:nos	[Sugar beet program, Instructions relative to] Proc. Pubs.desig. SB-no. Changed from A55.2: See also A63.11:
A55.71:nos	General information series. Pubs.desig. G-no. Changed from A55.2:CT, A55.7:CT, A55.15:CT. Later A76.408:
A55.72:nos	[Consumers' Service] Proc. Pubs.desig. CS-no.
A55.73:nos	[Miscellaneous series] Earlier A63.10:

Consolidated into Agricultural Conservation and Adjustment Administration as Agricultural Adjustment Agency of the Department of Agriculture by Executive order 9069 of February 23, 1942.

A56 Entomology and Plant Quarantine Bureau

Consolidation of Entomology Bureau (A9.) and Plant Quarantine Bureau (A48.) July 1, 1934.

A56.1:date	Annual reports. Earlier A35.1: Later A77.301:
A56.2:CT	General publications. Earlier A35.2: Later A77.302:
A56.3:	Bulletins
A56.4:	Circulars
A56.5:	Laws
A56.6:CT	Regulations, rules and instructions. Earlier A35.8: and A48.8: Later A77.306:
A56.7:CT	Maps
A56.8:	Posters
A56.9:nos	[Circulars of information] Earlier A48.11: Later A77.308/3:
A56.10:vol	Entomology current literature. Bi-monthly. Mim. Earlier A9.14: Later A17.14:

A56.11:nos	[Entomology technic series] Multigraphed with rotaprinted illustrations. Pubs.desig. ET-
A56.12:vol	News letter. Monthly. Earlier A9.12:
A56.13:nos	Notices of quarantine. Earlier A48.5: Later A77.317:
A56.14:nos	Service and regulatory announcements. Earlier A48.7:
A56.14/a:CT	___ separates. Later A77.308/a:
A56.14/2:date	List of intercepted plant pests. Earlier A48.7/2: Later A77.308/2:
A56.15:date	Insecticide Division publications. Quarterly. Multigraphed. Earlier A47.8:
A56.16:nos	Administrative memorandum. Mim. Pubs.desig. EQ-nos. Earlier A48.10:
A56.17:vol	Review of United States patents relating to pest control. Monthly. Mim. Issued by Insecticide division. Earlier A47.7: Later A77.311:
A56.18:vol	Insect pest survey bulletin. Monthly. Mim. Earlier A9.10: Later A77.310:
A56.19:E-nos	E [series] Proc. Earlier A9.16: Later A77.312:
A56.20:nos	Picture sheets. Later A77.320:
A56.21:vol	Extension entomologist. Proc. Later A77.309:
A56.22:CT	Addresses. Proc. Later A77.321:
A56.23:CT	Papers in re. Later A77.315:
A56.24:nos	Insects in relation to National defense, circulars. Proc. Later A77.316:
A56.25:nos	Foreign plant quarantines in-service training series
A56.26:	Foreign plant quarantine memorandum

Transferred to Agricultural Research Administration by executive order 9069 of Feb. 23, 1942.

A57　Soil Conservation Service

April 27, 1935 (49 Stat. 163) Prior to March 27, 1935, see Soil Erosion Service (I30.).

A57.1:date	Annual reports. Later A76.201:, A79.201:, A80.2001:, A80.501:, A57.1:
A57.1/2:date	Conservation highlights, digest of annual report of Soil Conservation Service
A57.1/3:CT	Soil Conservation Service [State reports]
A57.2:CT	General publications. Later A76.202:, A79.202:, A80.2002:, A80.502:, A57.2:
A57.2/a:CT	___ separates
A57.3:nos	Bulletins. Proc.
A57.4:	Circulars
A57.5:CT	Laws
A57.6:CT	Regulations, rules and instructions. Includes handbooks and manuals.
A57.6/2:CT	Handbooks, manuals, guides
A57.6/3:CT	Irrigation guides [for areas] Earlier A57.6/2:
A57.6/4:nos	Conservation guide sheets (numbered)
A57.7:CT	Maps (by States) Reconnaissance erosion survey
A57.7/2:CT	Maps (by subjects)
A57.8:CT	Posters
A57.8/2:CT	America the beautiful (posters)
A57.9:vol.nos.&nos.	Soil conservation. Monthly. Later A76.208:, A79.207:, A80.2007:, A80.507: A57.9:
A57.9/a:CT	___ separates. Later A76.208/a:, A79.207/a:, A80.2007/a:, A80.507/a:, A57.9/a:
A57.10:nos	[Administrative publications] Proc.
A57.11:nos	[Administrative reports] Proc. Pubs.desig. SCS-AR-nos.
A57.12:nos	[Engineering publications] Pubs.desig. SCS-EP-nos.
A57.13:nos	[Miscellaneous publications] Pubs.desig. SCS-MP Later A76.213:, A57.13:

A57.14:nos	[Sedimentation studies] Proc. Pubs.desig. SCS-SS
A57.15:nos	[Technical publications] Proc. Pubs.desig. SCS-TP Later A76.211:, A80.2011:, A80.509:, A57.15:
A57.16:nos	[Regional bulletins] Proc. Pubs.desig. SCS-RB
A57.17:nos	Procedure for making soil conservation surveys, outlines
A57.18:nos	Upper Mississippi valley region. Publications. Proc. Pubs.desig. R5-Ms-no.
A57.19:nos	[Experiment Station reports] Proc. Pubs.desig. SCS-ESR
A57.20:vol	Soil conservation literature, selected current references. Bimonthly. Proc. Later A17.15:
A57.21:nos., later dates.	[Technical tables] Proc. Pubs.desig. SCS-TT. Precipitation in Muskingum River basin. Later A76.209:
A57.21/2:date	Precipitation in Muskingum River watershed, Ohio, by 30 minute periods. Proc. Monthly.
A57.22:nos.& letters.	[Regional handbooks] Pubs.desig. SCS-RH
A57.23:nos	Charts
A57.23/2:CT	Sheets on National atlas of United States
A57.24:CT	Erosion and related land use conditions (by projects)
A57.24:nos	Erosion surveys. Later A76.212:, A80.2012:, A80.510:, A57.24:
A57.25:CT	Addresses. Proc.
A57.26:CT	Land use and soil conservation, informational materials available to public, leaflets (by regions)
A57.27:nos	Bibliographies. Proc. Pubs.desig.SCS-B-no.
A57.27/2:nos	Soil conservation bibliographies
A57.28:nos	Engineering Division publications. Proc. Earlier A36.55: Pubs.desig. SCS-ED
A57.29:nos	Economic costs. Pubs.desig. SCS-EC-nos.
A57.30:nos	Conservation folders. Later A76.210:

A57.31:nos   Hourly precipitation on Upper Ohio and Susquehanna drainage basins (monthly) Proc. Pubs. desig. SCS-PC-no. PC stands for precipitation charts.

A57.32:date   Soil conservation districts (monthly) Later A76.214:, A80.2009:, A80.508:, A57.32:

Transferred to Agricultural Conservation and Adjustment Administration by Executive order 9069 of Feb. 23, 1942. Placed under control of the Secretary of Agriculture by Executive Order 9577 of June 29, 1945, effective June 30, 1945.

A57.33:nos   Conservation education reports. Proc.

A57.34:v.nos.& nos. Summary of research projects monthly reports; Quarterly. Proc.

A57.35:nos   Technical letter Sed-nos. Proc.

A57.36:date   Abstracts of recent published material on soil and water conservation Later IN A77.15:41

A57.37:nos   Woodland management plan, Agreements and Farm codes

A57.38:dt.&nos, later CT Soil survey reports. Earlier A77.514:

A57.38:list   List of soil survey reports

A57.39:CT   [Mechanical analyses data for soil types by county] loose-leaf.

A57.40:nos   Region 5, Northern Great Plains: SCS aids. Proc.

A57.40/2:nos   ___ Job sheets. Proc.

A57.40/3:nos   ___ SCS flood reports

A57.41:date   Work and management improvement (irregular)

A57.42:date   Soil survey field letter. Earlier A77.524:

A57.43:nos   Soil survey laboratory memorandums. Irregular. Earlier A77.525: Replaced by A57.52:

A57.44:nos   [Conservation information] SCS-CI (series)

A57.45:nos   [Conservation aid] SCS-CA (series)

A57.46:date   Water supply outlook and Federal-State-private cooperative snow surveys and water supply forecasts for Arizona (semimonthly Jan. 15-Apr. 1)

A57.46/2:date   Federal-State cooperative snow surveys and water supply forecasts for Idaho and Columbia Basin (monthly) Jan.-May) Proc.   Later in A57.46/12:

A57.46/3:date   Federal-State cooperative snow surveys and water supply forecasts for Montana and northern Wyoming (monthly Feb.-May) Proc.

A57.46/3-2:date   Water supply outlook for Montana and Federal-State-private cooperative snow surveys: Snow pillow records.

A57.46/4:date   Federal-State cooperative snow surveys and water supply forecasts for Nevada (monthly Feb.-Apr.) Proc. Later title Water supply outlook and...

A57.46/5:date   Federal-State cooperative snow surveys and water supply forecasts for Oregon (monthly) Jan.-May. Proc. Later title Water supply outlook...

A57.46/5-2:date   Water supply summary and outlook for Oregon and Federal-State-private cooperative snow surveys

A57.46/6:date   Federal-State cooperative snow surveys and water supply forecasts for Utah (monthly Jan.-May) Proc. Later title Water supply outlook...

A57.46/6-2:date   Fall water supply summary for Utah and Federal-State-private cooperative snow surveys

A57.46/7:date   Federal-State cooperative snow surveys and water supply forecasts for Washington (monthly Feb.-May) Proc. Later title Water supply outlook...

A57.46/8:date   [Snow surveys and water supply forecasts, western United States] (semi-annual) Proc.

A57.46/9:date   Federal-State [private] cooperative snow surveys and water supply forecasts for Colorado River, Platte River, Arkansas River, and Rio Grande drainage basins. Later title - Colorado and New Mexico. (monthly Feb.-May)

A57.46/9-2:date   Federal-State cooperative snow surveys and water supply forecasts for Colorado, Rio Grande, Platte, and Arkansas drainage basins; list and location of snow courses and soil moisture stations, season.

A57.46/10:date   Federal-State[private] cooperative snow surveys and water supply forecasts for Wyoming (monthly Feb.-May) Proc. Later title Water supply outlook...

A57.46/11:date   Water supply outlook and Federal-State-private cooperative snow surveys for Idaho (monthly) Jan.-June.

A57.46/12:date   Water supply outlook and Federal-State-private cooperative snow surveys for Western United States, including Columbia River drainage in Canada (monthly Feb.-May)

A57.46/13:date   Snow surveys for Alaska (monthly) Mar.-May

A57.46/13-2:date   Summary of snow measurements for Alaska

A57.46/14:date   Fall water supply summary for Nevada (annual) Earlier A57.2:N41

A57.46/15:CT/date	Water supply outlook [various local areas]
A57.46/16:date	Snow survey phase of Project Skywater, Colorado, annual report, fiscal year
A57.47:date	Wind erosion conditions, Great Plains, summary of local estimates (irregular) Proc. Admin.
A57.48:nos	Soils memorandum. Admin.
A57.49:date/CT	Congress of International Society of Soil Science. Publications
A57.50:CT	Technical memorandum... to the United States Study Commission. Southeast River Basins.
A57.51:nos	Technical releases
A57.52:nos	Soil survey investigations reports. Replaces A57.43:
A57.53:les/nos	Conservation planning memorandum
A57.54:CT/date	Plant Materials Centers annual reports
A57.55:CT	Plant materials annual progress reports
A57.56:CT	Habitat management for [various animals]
A57.57:CT	Appraisal of potentials for outdoor recreational development [by area]
A57.58:nos	Soil survey interpretations for woodlands, progress reports W-(series)
A57.59:CT	Watershed work plans [by area] Earlier in A57.2:
A57.60:date	Observational study of agricultural aspects of Arkansas River multiple purpose project, annual report
A57.61:CT	Classification and correlation of soils [by area]
A57.62:CT	Resource conservation and development project plans
A57.63:nos	Conservation agronomy technical notes (numbered) Issued by Western Region, Portland, Oregon.
A57.64:CT	Flood plain report [various locations]
A57.65:CT	Draft environmental impact statements
A57.65/2:CT	Final environmental impact statement

A57.66:date   Annual plan, Columbia Blue Mountain Resource Conservation and Development Project.

A58 Budget and Finance Office

Formerly a part of the Personnel and Business Administration Office (A49). Established June 1, 1934 as a separate branch of Office of Secretary.

A58.1:date	Annual reports
A58.2:CT	General publications
A58.3:	Bulletins
A58.4:nos	Budget and finance circulars
A58.7:nos	Budget and finance memorandums. Proc.
A58.8:	Bulletin for information of budget, fiscal, procurement and administrative personnel

A59 Commodity Exchange Administration

Created July 1, 1936, superseding Grain Futures Administration

A59.1:date	Annual reports. Later A75.201:
A59.2:CT	General publications. Later A75.202:
A59.3:	
A59.4:	
A59.5:CT	Laws
A59.6:CT	Regulations, rules, and instructions
A59.7:vol	Trade in grain futures. Monthly. Proc. Earlier A41.7: Later A75.209:
A59.8:vol	Commodity exchange administration literature, selected references catalogued in the library. Monthly. Proc.
A59.9:CT	Addresses
A59.10:date	Bales of cotton delivered in settlement of future on New York and New Orleans cotton exchanges. Proc.
A59.11:vol	Trade in cotton futures. Monthly. Proc. Later A75.208:
A59.12:vol	Trade in wool top futures. Monthly. Proc. Later A75.210:
A59.13:	Futures commission merchants registered under commodity exchange act, etc. alphabetical list. Proc.
A59.14:	Floor brokers registered under commodity exchange act, with addresses of each registrant, alphabetical list of. Proc.
A59.15:	Directory of principal and branch offices of registered futures commission merchants, arranged geographically. Proc.
A59.16:	Directory of item 10 correspondents and solicitors, etc., soliciting or accepting commodity futures orders on behalf of future commission merchants.

Incorporated in Agricultural Marketing Administration (A75) Feb. 25, 1942.

A60 Plant and Operations Office

1934 Division of Operations. Plant and Operations Office, Mar. 1, 1939 Agriculture Department memo. 809, Feb. 27, 1939.

A60.1:date	Annual reports
A60.2:CT	General publications
A60.4:nos	Circulars (Oct. 1, 1934-July 9, 1936) Proc. Earlier A1.45:
A60.4/2:nos	Circulars (July 31, 1936-) Proc.
A60.4/3:nos	Plant and operations circulars
A60.5:	
A60.6:CT	Regulations, rules, and instructions. Miscellaneous.
A60.7:nos	Memorandum. Proc.
A60.7/2:nos	Plant and operations memorandum
A60.8:nos	O.P.O. publications. Proc.
A60.9:CT	Addresses
A60.10:date	Organization Directory, U.S. Department of Agriculture

A61 Farm Security Administration

Changed from A61 Resettlement Administration. Earlier Y3.R31:

A61.1:date	Annual reports. Later A80.701:
A61.2:CT	General publications. Later A80.702:
A61.3:	
A61.4:	
A61.5:	
A61.6:	
A61.7:CT	Regulations, rules, and instructions. Includes handbooks and manuals. Later A80.706:
A61.8:nos	Land use planning publication. Proc. Earlier Y3.R31:23 Superseded by A36.104:
A61.9:nos	Land policy circulars. Monthly. Proc. Earlier Y3.R31:9 Superseded by A36.103:
A61.10:nos	Social research reports
A61.11:CT	Surveys of agricultural labor conditions. Proc.
A61.12:CT	Project summaries (by subject)
A61.13:CT	Maps (by subject)
A61.14:nos	Research reports. Proc.
A61.15:date	Research-reference accessions (usually semi-monthly) Proc. Earlier Y3.R31:29 Later A36.110:
A61.16:CT	Addresses. Proc. Later A80.707:CT
A61.17:CT	Posters
A61.18:nos	Leaflets-for-action. Later A80.708:
A61.19:nos	Status and progress reports, releases. Proc. Earlier A80.709:

Transferred to War food administration. Executive order 9322 March 26,1943, amended by Executive order 9334 April 19,1943.
Returned to control of the Secretary of Agriculture by Executive order 9577 of June 29, 1945.
Abolished by act of August 14, 1946 (Public 731, 79C.) which established the Farmers home Admin.

A62 Federal Crop Insurance Corporation

February 16, 1938 (52 Stat. 72, 835)

A62.1:date	Annual reports. Later A76.101:
A62.2:CT	General publications. Later A76.102:
A62.3:	
A62.4:	
A62.5:	
A62.6:nos	Regulations (numbered)
A62.6/2:CT	Regulations, rules, and instructions. Includes handbooks and manuals. Later A79.306:
A62.7:nos	General information series
A62.8:CT	Addresses. Proc.
A62.9:nos	Information [series] Later A76.108:
A62.10:nos	Kansas leaflets
A62.11:nos	General procedure. Proc. and printed.
A62.12:nos	North Dakota leaflets.

Transferred to Agricultural Conservation and Adjustment Administration by Executive order 9069 of February 23, 1942.

A63 Sugar Division

Created under the A.A.A. Became an independent division Oct. 16, 1938.

A63.1:date	Annual reports.
A63.2:CT	General publications
A63.3:	Bulletins [none issued]
A63.4:	Circulars [none issued]
A63.5:	Laws [none issued]
A63.6:CT	Regulations. Earlier A55.6:
A63.7:nos	Sugar determination. Pubs. desig. SD-nos. Earlier A55.37: Later A55.37:
A63.8:nos	Puerto Rico orders. Earlier A55.18:
A63.9:nos	Sugar information series, Publications
A63.10:nos	Miscellaneous series. Proc. Later A55.73:
A63.11:nos	Sugar beet program, Instructions relative to. Changed from A63.2: See also A55.70:

Agriculture department memorandum 849 dated Jan. 19, 1940 transferred the personnel and functions of the Sugar Division to the Agricultural Adjustment Administration, effective Feb. 1, 1940

A64 Foreign Agriculture Service

Prior to Dec. 1, 1938 under Agricultural Economics Bureau

A64.1:date	Annual reports
A64.2:CT	General publications
A64.3:	
A64.4:	
A64.5:	
A64.6:	

A64.7:vol	Foreign agriculture, review of foreign farm policy, production, and trade. Monthly. Proc. Earlier A36.88: Later A67.7:
A64.8:vol	Foreign crops and markets. Wkly. Proc. Earlier A36.14: Later A67.8:
A64.9:nos	F.S.A. [series] Proc. Earlier A36.79: Later A67.12:
A64.10:CT	Addresses. Proc.
A64.11:nos	Fruit flashes, foreign news on fruits by cable and radio: Citrus fruits. Wkly. Proc. Earlier A36.66: Later A67.9:
A64.12:nos	Fruit flashes, foreign news on fruits by cable and radio: Deciduous fruits. Wkly. Proc. Earlier A36.67: Later A67.10:
A64.13:nos	[Foreign service on vegetables] Proc. Earlier A36.46:

Abolished July 1939 and functions transferred to Foreign Agricultural Relations Office (A67)

A65 Marketing and Marketing Agreements Division

Effective Oct. 16, 1938, Marketing and Marketing Agreements Division (AAA) is responsible directly to Secretary of Agriculture.

A65.1:date	Annual reports Later A73.1:
A65.2:CT	General publications Later A73.2:
A65.3:	
A65.4:	
A65.5:CT	Laws
A65.6:	
A65.7:nos	Marketing orders. Earlier A55.36: Later A73.8:
A65.8:nos	Dockets. Proc. Earlier A55.21:
A65.9:nos	Marketing Agreement series. Earlier A55.9: Later A73.7:
A65.10:nos	Marketing section publications. Earlier A55.59:
A65.11:CT	Addresses. Proc.

A65.12:letters-nos. [Marketing information series] Earlier A55.54:

1940 consolidated with Federal Surplus Commodities Corporation (A69) to form Surplus Marketing Administration (A73)

A66   Agricultural Marketing Service

June 30, 1939 (53 Stat. 939)

A66.1:date	Annual reports
A66.2:CT	General publications
A66.3:	
A66.4:	
A66.5:	
A66.6:CT	Regulations, rules, and instructions (includes handbooks and manuals)
A66.7:date	Cold storage reports. Monthly. Proc. Earlier A36.107: Later A75.8:
A66.8:date	Cotton market review; Weekly. Proc. Earlier A36.73: Later A75.9:
A66.9:date	Cotton reports. Monthly, July-Dec. Proc. Earlier A36.30:
A66.10:date	Farm labor reports (monthly) varying title. Earlier A36.69:,
A66.10:date	Farm wage rates and related data. Quarterly. Proc. Earlier A36.77:
A66.11:date	General crop reports. (Monthly except Feb. and Mar.) Proc. Earlier A36.29:
A66.12:nos	Honey reports; Semimonthly. Proc. Earlier A36.105: Later A75.11:
A66.13:vol	Livestock, meats, and wool; market reviews and statistics. Wkly. Proc. Earlier A36.98: See for annual compilation A66.36: Later A75.10:
A66.14:vol	Marketing activities. Monthly. Proc. Earlier A36.21: Later A75.13:
A66.15:nos	Peanut reports. Wkly. Proc. Earlier A36.106: Later A75.12:
A66.16:CT	U.S. standards for fruits and vegetables. Proc. Earlier A36.35: Later A75.19:
A66.17:dt.&nos	[Truck crop estimate reports]. Pubs. desig. TC-nos. Proc. Earlier A36.101: Later (beg. Feb. 24, 1942) A36.101:
A66.18:vol	P. and S. docket, monthly report of action taken on cases arising under packers and stockyards act. Proc. Supersedes A4.28: Later A74.14:
A66.19:date	Reports issued by Agricultural Marketing Service. Proc. Earlier A36.58:
A66.20:date	Truck receipts of fresh fruits and vegetables. Proc. Earlier A36.48:F94/2

A66.21:CT	Posters. Earlier A36.22:
A66.22:nos	[Crop reporting procedure] Proc. Earlier A36.92:
A66.23:CT	Addresses. Proc.
A66.24:date	Car-lot shipments of fruits and vegetables, by commodities, States, and months. Proc. Earlier A36.2:F94/10
A66.24/2:date	Carlot shipments of ... from stations in United States. Proc. Earlier A36.2:F94/21
A66.25:date	Flax market review. Quarterly. Proc. Earlier A36.115:
A66.26:date	Check list of standards for farm products. Proc. Earlier A36.59:
A66.27:nos	Service and regulatory announcements. Earlier A36.5: Later A75.16:
A66.28:date	Driven-in receipts of livestock. Proc. Earlier A36.2:L75/5 Later A78.2: L75/date
A66.29:date	Crop reports to be issued by Crop Reporting Board. Proc. Earlier A36.2:C88/7
A66.30:nos	Smutty wheat reports. Proc. Earlier A36.56:
A66.31:vol	A.M.S. news (semi-monthly) Proc.
A66.32:CT	Publications, Lists of. Proc.
A66.33:date	Prospective plantings. Proc. Earlier A36.38:
A66.34:date	Farm production and income from meat animals. Proc. Earlier A36.2: M46/5(date)
A66.35:date	Dairy and poultry market statistics, annual summaries. Proc. Earlier A36.54:
A66.36:date	Livestock, meats, and wool, market statistics and related data (annual compilation) Earlier A36.2:L75/8(date) See for weekly issues A66.13:
A66.37:date	Quality and prices of cotton linters produced in United States. Proc. Earlier A36.2:C82/56
A66.38:date	Directory [of] market news broadcasts. Earlier A36.2:M34/3(date)
A66.39:date	Fruit and nut crop prospects. Earlier A36.32:

A66.40:date   Car-lot unloads of certain fruits and vegetables (annual) Proc. Earlier A36.48: F94/date

A66.41:CT   Cotton, estimated acreage, yield and production

A66.42:date   Livestock reports. Proc. Earlier A36.33:

A66.43:date   Poultry and egg production (monthly)

A66.44:nos   Dairy production (monthly) Proc. Later A36.139:

A66.45:date   State agricultural departments and marketing agencies, with names of officials. Proc. Earlier A36.55:

A66.46:incl.nos Notices of judgment under insecticide act. Earlier A46.7: Later A77.15:

A66.47:CT   Corn, estimated planted acreage, yield, and production by States. Proc.

A66.48:date   Winter wheat and rye reports. Proc. Earlier A36.74:

A66.49:date   Tobacco statistics; Annual reports on

Agricultural Marketing Service incorporated in Agricultural Marketing Administration (A75) February 23, 1942.

Foreign Agricultural Service, 1953-
A67 Foreign Agricultural Relations Office

Established July 1939. Took over some of the functions of Foreign Agricultural Service (A64.).

A67.1:date   Annual reports

A67.2:CT   General publications

A67.3:nos   Foreign agricultural bulletins

A67.4:

A67.5:

A67.6:CT   Regulations, rules, and instructions

A67.7:v.nos.&nos Foreign agriculture, review of **foreign farm policy, production, and trade.** Monthly. Proc. Earlier A64.7:

A67.7/a:CT   ___ separates

A67.7/2:v.nos.&nos. Foreign agriculture, included in Foreign crops and markets (weekly) Combines A67.7: and A67.8:

A67.8:v.nos.&nos Foreign crops and markets. Wkly. Proc. Earlier A64.8:

A67.8/a:CT   ___ separates

A67.8/2:date   ___, monthly supplement. Superseded by A67.19:

A67.8/3:date   ___, world summaries, crops and livestock (monthly) Proc. later title, World agriculture production and trade, statistical report

A67.9:nos   Fruit flashes, foreign news on fruits by cable and radio; Citrus [fruits] Wkly. Proc. Earlier A64.11:

A67.10:nos   Fruit flashes, foreign news on fruits by cable and radio: Deciduous [fruits] Wkly. Proc. Earlier A64.12:

A67.11:nos   [Foreign service reports] Proc. Earlier A36.39:

A67.12:nos   [Foreign statistics on apples and other deciduous fruits] Proc. Earlier A64.9:

A67.13:CT   Addresses. Proc.

A67.14:nos   [Foreign service on vegetables] Proc. Earlier A64.13: Pubs.desig. FSV-

A67.15:vol   Agriculture in the Americas

A67.15/a:CT   ___ separates

A67.16:nos   Foreign agriculture reports

A67.17:CT   Economic plans of interest to the Americas. Proc.

A67.18:le-nos   Foreign agriculture circulars. Proc.

A67.19:date   Foreign agricultural trade (monthly) Proc. Supersedes Foreign crops and markets monthly supplement A67.8/2: Later A93.17:

A67.19/2:date   ___ statistical report for calendar year. Later A93.17/3:

A67.19/3:date   ___ fiscal year with comparisons. Earlier in A67.19: Later A93.17/6:

A67.19/4:date   ___ by commodity and by country. Earlier in A67.19: (annual fiscal year) Later in A93.17/4:

A67.19/5:date   ___ value by countries, calendar year with comparisons. Earlier in A67.19: Later A93.17/4:

A67.19/6:CT&date	Foreign agricultural trade, United States trade in agricultural products with individual countries by calendar year. Earlier A67.19:
A67.19/7:date	Foreign agricultural trade, United States imports of fruits and vegetables under quarantine by countries of origin and ports of entry, annual fiscal year. Earlier A67.2:F94/date Later A93.17/5:
A67.19/8:date	Foreign agricultural trade digest of United States (monthly) Contains material formerly included in A67.19: and A67.8: Later A93.17/2:
A67.20:nos	International agricultural collaboration series
A67.21:date	Foreign trade in farm machinery and supplies (monthly) Proc.
A67.22:	British-American Agricultural news service
A67.23:date	World cotton prices (weekly) Proc.
A67.24:date	Foreign agricultural situation, maps and charts (annual). Previously classified A67.2:C38/date and A67.2:C38/2/date Later A1.98:
A67.25:nos	World tobacco analysis (quarterly). Designated Circular FT-nos
A67.26:nos	[Foreign Agricultural Service, miscellaneous] FAS-M-series
A67.27:date	World agricultural situation (annual) Earlier A67.2:Ag8/9 Later A93.29:
A67.28:date	Competitive position of United States farm products abroad (annual) Earlier A67.2:F22
A67.29:date	Developing foreign markets for U.S. farm products, summary of promotional activity (annual)
A67.30:CT	Prospects for foreign trade in [various commodities]
A67.31:nos	Foreign training letter, to foreign agricultural contacts at land-grant colleges
A67.31/2:	FAS letter to attaches and offices
A67.31/3:	Foreign training letter
A67.32:date	U.S. Agricultural exports (annual) Earlier A67.2:Ex7/2 Later A93.30:
A67.32/2:date	U.S. Agricultural imports, fact sheet (annual) Proc. Later A93.30/2:
A67.33:CT	Bibliographies and lists of publications
A67.34:CT	International animal feed symposium reports

A67.35:date	Report of Government of United States to Food and Agriculture Organization of United Nations (triennial)
A67.36:CT	Indices of agricultural production in [various] countries. Later A93.32:
A67.37:date	Annual summary of foreign agricultural training
A67.38:date	Document retrieval subject index (monthly)
A67.39:nos	Agricultural trade policy, ATP (series)
A67.40:date	U.S. export sales (weekly)

A68   Rural Electrification Administration

Formerly an independent agency; transferred to the Agriculture Department by Reorganization Plan II, part 1, section 5, effective July 1, 1939.

A68.1:date	Annual reports. Earlier Y3.R88:1
A68.1/2:date	Annual statistical reports. Changed from A68.2:St2
A68.1/3:date	Annual statistical report, rural telephone program
A68.2:CT	General publications. Earlier Y3.R88:2
A68.3:nos	REA bulletins
A68.5:CT	Laws
A68.6:CT	Regulations, rules, and instructions
A68.6/2:date	List of materials acceptable for use on systems of REA
A68.6/3:sec.nos	Telephone operators' manual
A68.6/4:sec.nos	Telephone engineering and construction manual
A68.6/5:date	List of materials acceptable for use on telephone system of REA borrowers
A68.7:nos	Construction reports. Proc. Earlier Y3.R88:13
A68.8:nos	Progress bulletins, general. Proc. Earlier Y3.R88:12
A68.9:vol	Rural electrification news. Monthly. Earlier Y3.R88:9
A68.9/a:CT	___ separates. Earlier Y3.R88:9/a:
A68.10:date	[Library list of pamphlets, books, etc.] Wkly. Proc. Earlier Y3.R88:17
A68.11:nos	Electro-economy supplements
A68.12:CT	Posters
A68.13:nos	Statistical bulletins (monthly) Later See also A68.13/2, 3
A68.13/2:nos	Monthly statistical bulletin, electric program. Earlier in A68.13:
A68.13/3:nos	Monthly statistical bulletin, telephone program. Earlier in A68.13:

A68.14:CT   Addresses. Proc.

A68.15:v.nos.&nos. The lineman (monthly) Proc.

A68.16:nos   Suggested co-op electrification adviser training outline. Proc.

A68.17:   Engineering memorandum

A68.18:v.nos.&nos. Rural lines (monthly)

A68.18/a:CT   ___ separates

A68.19:date   Electric farming news exchange of Inter-Industry Farm Electric Utilization Council. irregular. Proc. Changed from A68.2:Eℓ2/9

A68.20:date   Number and percentage of farms electrified with central station service, by States (annual) Proc. Earlier A68.2:F22/6/date

A68.21:nos   Staff instructions. Admin.

A69 Federal Surplus Commodities Corporation

(50 Stat. 323; sec. 204 of the Agricultural Adjustment Act of 1938, 52 Stat. 38)

A69.1:date	Annual reports Earlier Y3.F31/9:1
A69.2:CT	General publications. Earlier Y3.F31/9:2
A69.7:CT	Addresses. Proc.
A69.8:CT	Facts on surplus foods. Proc. (Issuing agency omitted from publications.)
A69.9:nos	[General information series] Pubs. desig. GI-nos.

Federal Surplus Commodities Corporation incorporated in Agricultural Marketing Administration (A75) February 25, 1942.

and Industrial Chemistry Bureau
A70 Agricultural Chemistry and Engineering Bureau

October 16, 1938 - combination of Bureau of Chemistry and Soils and Bureau of Agricultural Engineering.

A70.1:date	Annual reports. Later A77.101:
A70.2:CT	General publications. Later A77.102:
A70.3:	
A70.4:nos	[Circular series] Proc. Supersedes A47.9: Later A77.104:
A70.5:	
A70.6:	
A70.7:vol	Current literature in agricultural engineering. Monthly. Proc. Earlier A53.9: Later A17.18:B
A70.8:CT	Addresses

A70.9:CT   Bibliographies. Proc.

A70.10:CT   Publications, Lists of. Proc.

A70.11:nos   Information series. Earlier A53.10: Later A77.518:

Transferred to Agricultural Research Administration (A77.) by Executive order 9069 of February 23, 1942.

A71 Commodity Credit Corporation

Formerly an independent agency (Y3.C73:) Transferred to Agriculture Department by the President's Reorganization plan 1, effective July 1, 1939.

A71.1:date   Annual reports. Earlier Y3.C73:1   Later A80.401:

A71.2:CT   General publications. Earlier Y3.C73:2   Later A80.402:

A71.3:   Bulletins

A71.4:

A71.5:

A71.6:CT   Regulations, rules and instructions. Earlier Y3.C73:6   Later A80.406:

A71.7:date   Statement of loans and commodities owned. Semimonthly. Proc. Earlier Y3.C73:12   Later A80.407:

A71.8:CT   Addresses. Proc.

Consolidated within the War Food Administration by Executive order 9322 of March 26, 1943 as amended by Executive Order 9334 of April 19, 1943.
Placed under control of the Secretary of Agriculture by Executive order 9577 of June 29, 1945, effective June 30, 1945.

A71.9:nos   Food trade letters. Wkly. Proc. Later A80.410:

A71.10:CT   Fact sheets. Proc.

By Departmental Memorandum 1118, dated Aug. 18, 1945, effective Aug. 20, 1945, it became a part of the Production and Marketing Administration.

A72   Farm Credit Administration

Formerly an independent agency (FCA) Transferred to Department of Agriculture by the President's Reorganization Plan 1, effective July 1, 1939.

A72.1:date	Annual reports. Earlier FCA1.1: Later A79.101: Later FCA1.1:
A72.2:CT	General publications. Earlier FCA1.2: Later A79.102: Later FCA1.2:
A72.3:nos	Bulletins. Earlier FCA1.3: Later FCA1.3:
A72.4:nos	Circulars (numbered) Earlier FCA1.4: Later A89.4:, FCA1.4:
A72.4:le.-nos	Circulars (lettered-numbered) Earlier FCA1.4/2:, FCA1.4/3:
A72.5:	
A72.6:CT	Regulations, rules, and instructions
A72.7:nos	[Leaflets] Pubs.desig. L-nos.
A72.8:nos	Miscellaneous reports. Earlier FCA1.13:
A72.9:nos	Special reports. Proc. Earlier FCA1.21:
A72.10:vol	News for farmer cooperatives (monthly) Earlier FCA1.10: Later A79.107: Later A89.8:
A72.10/a:CT	___ separates. Earlier FCA1.10/a:CT
A72.10/a2:nos	___ reprints. Later A89.8/a:
A72.11:CT	Addresses. Proc. Earlier FCA1.9:
A72.12:date	Loans and discounts, quarterly reports on. Proc. Earlier FCA1.12: Later A79.108:, FCA1.12/2:
A72.13:vol	Cooperative savings with Federal credit unions (bimonthly) Earlier FCA1.14/2: Later Y3.F31/8:12
A72.14:date	Federal credit unions, monthly reports of organization and operations. Proc. Earlier FCA1.15:, Later Y3.F31/8:13
A72.15:vol	Farm credit quarterly. Earlier FCA1.7:
A72.16:date	Joint stock land banks, progress in liquidation including statements of condition (quarterly) Earlier FCA1.7/2:

A72.17:CT	Farmer co-ops (by States) Earlier FCA1.19:
A72.18:nos	Summary of cases relating to farmers' cooperative associations. Proc. Earlier FCA1.18: Later A89.9:
A72.19:date	Federal credit unions, annual reports on operations. Earlier FCA1.16: Later Y3.F31/8:14
A72.20:CT	Cooperative-creamery routes (by States). [Preliminary summaries] Proc.
A72.21:CT	Lists of publications Earlier FCA1.20:
A72.22:date	Cooperative Research Service Division, Quarterly reports. Proc.
A72.23:nos	War circulars
A72.24:nos	Confidential reports.
A72.25:date	Production credit associations, summary of operations (annual) Proc. Later FCA1.22:

The act approved August 6, 1953 (67 Stat. 390; 12 U.S.C. 636a note), provided that the Farm Credit Administration become independent of the Department of Agriculture effective December 4, 1953.

A73 Surplus Marketing Administration

A consolidation, in 1940, of Marketing and Marketing Agreements Division (A65) and Federal Surplus Commodities Corporation (A69).

A73.1:date	Annual reports. Earlier A65.1:
A73.2:CT	General publications. Earlier A65.2:
A73.3:	
A73.4:	
A73.5:	
A73.6:	
A73.7:nos	Marketing agreement series. Earlier A65.9:
A73.8:nos	Marketing orders. Earlier A65.7: Later A75.20:

A73.9:CT   Addresses. Proc.

A73.10:CT   Publications, Lists of. Proc.

A73.11:nos   [Food stamp series] Pubs. desig. FS-no.

A73.12:nos   [Supplementary cotton program series] Pubs. desig. SC-no.

A73.13:nos   [School lunch series] Pubs. desig. SL-no.

A73.14:CT   Papers in re.

Surplus Marketing Administration incorporated in Agricultural Marketing Administration (A75) February 25, 1942.

A74 Agricultural Defense Relations Office

May 5, 1941 letter of request by President.

A74.1:date   Annual reports

A74.2:CT   General publications

A74.7:series nos. Farm defense program. Proc.

A74.8:CT   Addresses. Proc.

Executive order 9280 of December 5, 1942 transferred all functions concerned with food production to the Food production administration and all functions concerned with food distribution to the Food distribution administration.

A 75 Agricultural Marketing Administration

Agricultural Marketing Service (except Agricultural Statistics Division, which is transferred to Agricultural Economics Bureau) (A66); Commodity Exchange Administration (A59); Federal Surplus Commodities Corporation (A69.),(A73.); Surplus Marketing Administration (A73); are consolidated into an agency to be known as Agricultural Marketing Administration.

A75.1:date	Annual reports
A75.2:CT	General publications
A75.7:CT	Addresses. Proc.
A75.8:date	Cold storage reports (monthly) Proc. Earlier A66.7:, Later A78.7:
A75.9:date	Cotton market review; Weekly. Earlier A66.8:, Later A78.9:
A75.10:vol	Livestock, meat and wool; market reviews and statistics (wkly.) Earlier A66.13: Later A78.11:
A75.11:nos	Honey reports; semi-monthly. Earlier A66.12: Later A78.10:
A75.12:nos	Peanut reports; weekly. Earlier A66.15: Later A78.12:
A75.13:vol	Marketing activities (monthly) Earlier A66.14: Later A78.14:
A75.14:vol	P. and S. docket, monthly report of action taken on cases arising under Packers and Stockyards Act. Earlier A66.18: Later A78.15:
A75.15:nos	Notices of judgment under insecticide act. Earlier A66.46: Later A78.13:
A75.16:nos	Service and regulatory announcements. Earlier A66.27: Later A80.118:
A75.17:CT	Posters
A75.18:nos	[School lunch series] Pubs.desig. SL-no. Earlier A73.13:
A75.19:CT	United States standards for fruits and vegetables. Earlier A36.35/1:, A36.35/2:, and A66.16: Later A80.221:

A75. 20:nos   Marketing orders. Earlier A65.7: and A73.8: Later A80.116:

Consolidated into Food Distribution Administration by Executive order 9280 of December 5,1942. Food Distribution Administration consolidated into War Food Administration by Executive order 9322 of March 26,1943, as amended by Executive order 9334 of April 19,1943.

      A75.101:   Agricultural Marketing Administration - Consumers' Counsel Division

A75.101:date   Annual reports. Earlier A55.63:R 29(date)

A75.102:CT   General publications. Earlier A55.63:

A75.108:vol   Consumers' Guide (monthly from June through Sept., semimonthly from Oct. through May) Earlier A55.12: Later A78.8:

A75.109:vol   Consumers' market service (semi-monthly) Proc. Earlier A55.52:

A75.110:v. nos. &nos. Consumer notes clipsheet. Weekly. Earlier A55.56:

A75.111:nos   Consumers Counsel Division, Consumers' counsel series publications. Earlier A55.49:

      A75.201:   Agricultural Marketing Administration - Commodity Exchange Administration

A75.201:date   Annual reports. Earlier A59.1:

A75.202:CT   General publications. Earlier A59.2:

A75.208:vol   Trade in cotton futures (monthly) Proc. Earlier A59.11: Later A82.30:

A75.209:vol   Trade in grain futures (monthly) Proc. Earlier A59.7: Later A82.29:

A75.210:vol   Trade in wool top futures (monthly) Earlier A59.12:

A76   Agricultural Conservation and Adjustment Administration

Agricultural Adjustment Administration (A55), Soil Conservation Service (A57) Federal Crop Insurance Corporation (A62), Sugar Division of Department of Agriculture (various classes under A55 and A63) are consolidated into an agency to be known as Agricultural Conservation and Adjustment Administration. Information from Executive order 9060 of Feb. 23, 1942 in Federal Register v. 7, no. 38, Feb. 25, 1942, p. 1409.

A76.1:date   Annual reports

A76.2:CT   General publications

Consolidated into Food Production Administration by Executive order 9280 of December 5, 1942.

A76.101:   Agricultural Conservation and Adjustment Administration
Federal Crop Insurance Corporation

A76.101:date   Annual reports. Earlier A62.1: Later A79.301:

A76.102:CT   General publications. Earlier A62.2: Later A79.302:

A76.106:CT   Regulations, rules, and instructions. Earlier A62.6/2: Later A79.306:

A76.107:   Addresses

A76.108:nos   F.C.I. Information [series] Earlier A62.9: Later A80.907:

A76.201:   Agricultural Conservation and Adjustment Administration
              Soil Conservation Service

A76.201:date   Annual reports. Earlier A57.1: Later A79.201:

A76.202:CT   General publications. Earlier A57.2: Later A79.202:

A76.208:vol   Soil conservation; official organ (monthly) Earlier A57.9: Later A79.207:

A76.208/a:CT   ___ separates. Earlier A57.9/a: Later A79.207/a:

A76.209:date   Precipitation in Muskingum River basin (monthly) Earlier A57.21: Later A80.2010:

A76.210:nos   Conservation folders. Earlier A57.30:

A76.211:nos   Technical publications. Earlier A57.15: Later A80.2011:

A76.212:nos   Physical land surveys. Earlier A57.24: Later A80.2012:

A76.213:nos   [Miscellaneous publications] Proc. Earlier A57.13: Later A57.13:

A76.214:date   Soil conservation districts (monthly) Proc. Earlier A57.32: Later A80.2009:

A76.215:nos   Special reports of Sedimentation Section, Office of Research. Later A80.2013:

A76.301:   Agricultural Conservation and Adjustment Administration
              Sugar Agency

A76.301:date   Annual reports

A76.302:CT   General publications

116

A76.307:nos   Sugar determination. Earlier A55.37: Pubs.desig. S.D.no. Later
                  A80.117:

A76.401:   Agricultural Conservation and Adjustment Administration
           Agricultural Adjustment Agency

A76.401:date   Annual reports. Earlier A55.1: Later A79.401:

A76.402:CT   General publications. Earlier A55.2: Later A79.402:

A76.403:

A76.404:

A76.405:

A76.406:CT   Regulations, rules, and instructions. Proc. Earlier A55.6: and A55.69:

A76.408:nos   [General information series] Pubs.desig. G-no. Earlier A55.71:
                  Later A80.614:

A76.409:date   Statement of expenditures (monthly) Earlier A55.62:

A76.410:vol   AAA flashes, facts for committeemen (monthly) Proc. Earlier A55.42/11:

A76.441:   East Central Region Publications

A76.451:   North Central Region Publications

A76.461:   Northeast Region Publications
A76.462:CT   General publications. Earlier A55.44/2:

A76.466:CT   Regulations, rules, and instructions. Earlier A55.44/11: Later A80.2166:

A76.471:   Southern Region Publications

A76.472:CT   General publications. Earlier A55.46/2: LaterA80.2172:

A76.476:CT   Regulations, rules and instructions. Earlier A55.45/12:

A76.481:   Western Region Publications

A76.482:CT   General publications. Earlier A55.46/2: Later A80.2182:

A76.486:CT   Regulations, rules, and instructions. Earlier A55.46/15: Later A80.2186:

A 77   Agricultural Research Administration

Agricultural Chemistry and Engineering Bureau (A70), Animal Industry Bureau (A4), Beltsville Research Center, Dairy Industry Bureau (A44.), Entomology and Plant Quarantine Bureau (A56), Experiment Stations Office (A10.), Home Economics Bureau (A42), Plant Industry Bureau (A19) are consolidated into an agency to be known as Agricultural Research Administration. Information from Executive order 9060 of Feb. 23, 1942.

A 77   Agricultural Research Service

Under authority of Reorganization plan no. 2 of 1953, the various research bureaus of the Agricultural Research Administration have been regrouped into an integrated Agricultural Research Service, by Memorandum 1320, supplement 4 of the Secretary of Agriculture dated Nov. 2, 1953.

A77.1:date	Annual reports
A77.1/a:CT	___ separates
A77.2:CT	General publications
A77.6/2:nos	Service and regulatory announcements. Earlier A82.23:
A77.6/3:CT	Handbooks, manuals, guides
A77.7:nos	Research achievement sheets
A77.8:date	Report of activities under Research and Marketing act (annual) Earlier A87.1:
A77.9:CT	Releases. Proc.
A77.10:CT	Addresses
A77.11:	Administrator's memorandum
A77.12:v.nos	Agricultural research (bimonthly)
A77.12/a:CT	___ separates
A77.13:nos	Current developments in farm real estate market. Proc. Earlier A36.168: Later in A77.15: Later A93.9/4:

A77.14:nos	Agricultural finance review. Earlier A36.111: Later A93.9/10:
A77.14/a:CT	___ separates. Earlier A36.111/a:
A77.14/2:nos	Farm cost situation. [Issued irregularly] Earlier A36.157: Later in A77.15: Later A93.9/3:
A77.14/3:date	Deposits of country banks: Index numbers of total, demand and time deposits selected groups of States, specified periods (monthly) Proc. Earlier A36.2:B22/7/925-53 Later A93.9/7:
A77.15:nos	ARS (series) This series replaces the various lettered-numbered series of research bureaus of ARA.
A77.16:nos	Publications PE (series) Proc.
A77.16/2:nos	Publications issued. Proc. Later A93.18:
A77.17:CT	Lists of publications and bibliographies
A77.17/2:nos	Semiannual list of publications and patents with abstracts, Western Division. Earlier A77.2:P96/2/date
A77.17/3:date	List of publications and patents of Southern Utilization Research Branch (semiannual) Earlier A77.2:P96/3/date
A77.17/4:date	Publications and patents of Eastern **Utilization Research and Development** Division (semiannual) Proc. Earlier in ARS series (A77.14:)
A77.17/5:date	Publications and patents of Northern Utilization Research and Development Division (semiannual) Formerly in A77.15:
A77.18:le-nos	Correspondence aids CA (series)
A77.19:CT	Sheets of National Atlas of United States
A77.20:fascile no. &pt.no.	General catalogue of Homoptera
A77.21:date	Manuscripts approved by divisions for publication
A77.22:nos	USDA consumer expenditure survey reports
A77.23:nos	Conservation research reports Later A1.114:
A77.24:date	Southwest Branch annual report
A77.25:v.nos.&nos.	Notes from Washington, International Programs Division

Agricultural and Industrial Chemistry Bureau
A77.100   Agricultural Chemistry and Engineering Bureau

A77.101:date   Annual reports. Earlier A70.1:

A77.102:CT   General publications. Earlier A70.2:

A77.104:nos   [Circular series] Proc. Pubs. desig. ACE-no. Earlier A70.4:

A77.104/2:nos   [Circular series] Supersedes A77.104: Pubs. desig. AIC

A77.108:CT   Addresses. Proc.

A77.109:nos   Progress in candy research, reports

A77.200 Animal Industry Bureau

A77.201:date	Annual reports. Earlier A4.1:
A77.201/2:date	Meat Inspection Branch, summary of activities (annual) Earlier A77.202:M46
A77.202:CT	General publications. Earlier A4.2: Later A101.2:
A77.206:CT	Regulations, rules, and instructions. Earlier A4.8:
A77.206/2:CT	Handbooks, manuals, guides [relating to animal industry]
A77.208:nos	Service and regulatory announcements (monthly) Earlier A4.13:
A77.209:nos	Animal husbandry division [publications] Proc. Pubs.desig.A.H.D.no. Earlier A4.26:
A77.210:nos	Animal nutrition division [publications] Proc. Pubs.desig.A.N.D.no. Earlier A4.27:
A77.211:date	Bang's disease work; Statement of indemnity claims and averages in cooperative (monthly) Earlier A4.29: Later combined in A77.216/2:
A77.212:date	Brucellosis (Bang's disease) work in cooperation with various States: Summary of (monthly) Proc. Earlier A4.21: Later combined in A77.216/2:
A77.212/2:date	Summary of bovine brucellosis eradication in cooperation with various States (annual) Proc. Earlier A77.202:B83
A77.212/3:date	Statistical tables showing progress of eradication of brucellosis and tuberculosis in livestock in United States and territories for fiscal year. Proc. Earlier A77.202:B83/9 Later A77.212/5:
A77.212/4:date	Cooperative State-Federal brucellosis eradication program, statistical tables, fiscal year. Earlier A77.212/3:
A77.212/5:date	Cooperative State-Federal tuberculosis eradication program statistical tables, fiscal year. Earlier A77.212/3: Later A101.18:
A77.212/6:date	Cooperative State-Federal brucellosis eradication program [maps] (quarterly) Proc.
A77.212/6-2:date	Cooperative State-Federal brucellosis eradication program, charts and maps. fiscal year.

A77.212/7:date	Summary of brucellosis eradication activities in cooperation with various States under cull and dry cow testing program (monthly)
A77.212/8:date	Summary of brucellosis eradication activities in cooperation with various States under market cattle testing program
A77.212/9:date	Disease control services activities (quarterly)
A77.213:date	Brucellosis (Bang's disease) control program conducted by Bureau of Animal Industry in cooperation with various States; Summary of (monthly) Proc. Earlier A4.23:
A77.214:nos	Extension animal husbandman (quarterly) Proc. Earlier A4.25:
A77.215:date	Tuberculosis eradication; Statement of indemnity claims and averages in cooperative (monthly) Earlier A4.30:
A77.216:date	Tuberculosis eradication in cooperation with various States; Summary of (monthly) Earlier A4.22: Later in A77.216/2:
A77.216/2:date	Summary of bovine tuberculosis eradication in cooperation with various States, statement of indemnity claims and averages in cooperative bovine brucellosis work (monthly) Proc. Combines A77.216:, A77.212:, A77.211:
A77.217:nos	Notices: Activities of licensed establishments supervised by Virus Serum Control Division (monthly) Earlier A4.31: Replaced by A77.226/2:
A77.218:nos	Orders. Earlier A4.5:
A77.219:pt.nos	Index-catalogue of medical and veterinary zoology. Earlier A4.18:
A77.219/2:supp.nos.	___ supplements
A77.219/3:CT	Index-catalogue of medical and veterinary zoology [by subjects]
A77.219/4:nos	Index-catalogue of medical and veterinary zoology, Special publications
A77.220:CT	Posters. Earlier A4.16/1:
A77.221:date	Directory of Bureau of Animal Industry. Earlier A4.14:
A77.221/2:date	Working reference of livestock regulatory establishments. Replaces A77.221:
A77.222:CT	Livestock health series (posters)
A77.223:CT	Addresses. Proc.
A77.224:nos	Report of developments on eradication of vesicular exanthema

A77.225:date	Report on incidence of anthrax in animals in United States (monthly)
A77.226:nos	Biological products notices. Proc.
A77.226/2:nos	Biological products memo. Irregular. Proc. Replaces VSC notices (A77.217:) and VSC letters
A77.226/3:nos	Veterinary Biologics Division notices Later A101.14:
A77.227:date	National status on control of garbage-feeding (monthly) Proc.
A77.228:nos	APH-correspondence aid (series) Proc. Later AHCorrespondence aids.
A77.228/2:nos	[Correspondence aids] CA (series) Animal Disease Eradication Division. Later in A77.18:
A77.229:date	Animal morbidity report. Proc. (monthly) Later A101.12:
A77.229/2:date	Animal morbidity report (annual) Proc. Later A101.12/2:
A77.230:date	ADE Branch notice, reported incidence of infectious equine encephalomyelitis in United States (annual) Earlier A77.202:Enl
A77.230/2:date	Reported incidence of arthropod borne encephalitis of equine in United States in calendar year
A77.231:date	Incidence of bluetongue as reported in United States (annual) Proc. Earlier A77.202:B62
A77.232:date	Reported incidence of rabies in United States (annual) Proc. Earlier A77.202:R11/4
A77.233:date	Annual report of cooperative State-Federal sheep and cattle scabies eradication fiscal year. Proc. Earlier A77.202:Sh3/8 Later A77.233/3:
A77.233/2:date	Annual report of cooperative State-Federal sheep scabies eradication activities. Earlier A77.233:
A77.233/3:date	Annual report of cooperative psoroptic cattle scabies eradication activities. Earlier A77.233:
A77.233/4:date	Cooperative State-Federal sheep and cattle scabies epidemiology and related activities, fiscal year. Earlier A77.202:Sh3/13
A77.234:date	Northeastern States Regional Poultry Breeding Project. Annual report.
A77.235:date	Western States regional turkey breeding project. Annual report.
A77.236:date	North Central States Regional Poultry breeding project. Annual report

A77.237:date	Report of cooperative cattle fever tick eradication activities, fiscal year
A77.237/2:date	National tick surveillance program, calendar year. Earlier A77.202: T43/2
A77.238:CT	Maps [concerning animal industry]
A77.239:nos	Facilities and equipment fact sheet MID-FE (series) Issued by Meat Inspection Division
A77.239/2:nos	Chemical evaluation and control fact sheet MID-CEC (series)
A77.240:CT	Psoroptic sheep scabies outbreaks in [various States], fiscal year
A77.241:date	Cooperative State-Federal hog cholera eradication program progress report (annual)
A77.242:date	Equine proplasmosis report, fiscal year Later A101.16:
A77.243:CT	Bibliographies and lists of publications
A77.244:date	Equine infectious anemia progress report and history in United States, fiscal year

A77.300 Entomology and Plant Quarantine Bureau

A77.301:date	Annual reports. Earlier A56.1:
A77.302:CT	General publications. Earlier A56.2: Later A101.2:
A77.306:CT	Regulations, rules and instructions. Earlier A56.6:
A77.306/2:nos	Administrative instructions under [sections of Plant quarantine act] Reprints from Federal Register]
A77.306/3:CT	Handbooks, manuals, guides [relating to entomology and plant quarantine]
A77.308:nos	Service and regulatory announcements (quarterly) Earlier A56.14:
A77.308/a:CT	___ separates. Earlier A56.14/a:
A77.308/2:date	___: List of intercepted plant pests. Earlier A56.14/2: later title List of intercepted plant pests.
A77.308/3:nos	BEPQ series. Proc. Earlier A56.9:
A77.308/4:nos	P.P.C. series. Proc. Formerly issued in B.E.P.Q. series, A77.308/3:
A77.308/5:date	Plant regulatory announcements
A77.309:vol	Extension entomologist. Proc. Earlier A56.21:
A77.310:vol	Insect pest survey bulletins (monthly) Proc. Earlier A56.18:
A77.310/2:date	The more important insect records (monthly) Proc.
A77.310/3:dt.&nos	Insect pest survey, special supplements. Proc. Earlier A77.310:22/sp. supp.1-13
A77.311:v.nos.&nos.	Pest control; review of United States patents related to (monthly) Proc. Earlier A56.17:
A77.312:nos	E [series] Proc. Earlier A56.19:
A77.313:nos	ET [series] [Entomological technical] Earlier A56.11:

A77.314:nos	Administrative memorandum. Proc. Pubs.desig. EQ-no. Earlier A56.16:
A77.314/2:nos	Plant quarantine memorandum. Admin.
A77.315:CT	Papers in re. Earlier A56.23:
A77.316:nos	Insects in relation to national **defense circulars.** Earlier A56.24:
A77.317:nos	Entomology and Plant Quarantine Bureau, Notices of quarantine. Earlier A56.13:
A77.317/2:nos	Plant quarantine P.P.C. (series) Proc. Formerly included in BEPQ-Q series, A77.317:
A77.318:date	Publications and patents of Division of Insecticide Investigations, Lists of. Earlier A56.15:
A77.318/2:date	List of U.S. Patents granted members of Division of Insecticide Investigations. Earlier in A77.318:
A77.319:CT	Posters. Earlier A9.9:
A77.320:nos	Picture sheets. Earlier A56.20:
A77.321:CT	Addresses. Proc. Earlier A56.22:
A77.322:dt.&nos	Cotton insect conditions. Proc.
A77.323:nos	[Entomological control series] Proc.
A77.324:v.nos.&nos	Cooperative economic insect report (biweekly) Proc. Later A101.9:
A77.324/a:CT	___ separates
A77.324/2:v.nos.&nos	___ special reports
A77.324/3:CT	___ [unnumbered miscellaneous reports]
A77.325:nos	Notices of judgment under Federal insecticide, fungicide and rodenticide act. Earlier A82.56:
A77.326:date	Japanese beetle-European chafer control program, annual report. Proc.
A77.327:date	Cooperative pest control programs. Irregular. Proc.
A77.327/2:date	Plant pest control, **cooperative programs,** western region, fiscal year

A77.328:date   Conference report on cotton insect research and control (annual) Earlier A77.302:C82

A77.329:CT   Plant quarantine import requirements [of various countries] Later A101.11:

A77.330:CT   Posters

A77.400 Experiment Stations Office

A77.401:date   Annual reports. Earlier A10.1:

A77.401/2:date   Report on agricultural experiment stations. Earlier A10.1/2:

A77.401/2a:CT   ___ separates

A77.402:CT   General publications. Earlier A10.2:

A77.406:CT   Regulations, rules, and instructions

A77.407:CT   Addresses. Proc. Earlier A10.27:

A77.408:vol   Experiment station record (monthly) Earlier A10.6:

A77.409:date   Agricultural experiment station publications received by the office; Lists of (monthly) Proc. Earlier A17.12:

A77.410:nos   OES circular letters. Admin.

A77.411:v.nos   Bibliography on poultry industry, chickens, turkeys, aquatic fowl, gamebirds. Annual. Admin.

A77.440 Alaska Agricultural Experiment Station

A77.441:date   Annual reports   Earlier A10.10/1:

A77.442:CT   General publications   Earlier A10.10/2:

A77.443:nos   Bulletins. Earlier A10.10/3:

A77.444:nos   Circulars   Earlier A10.10/4:

A77.461: Puerto Rico Agricultural Experiment Station, Mayaguez

A77.461:date   Annual report   Earlier A10.12/1:

A77.462:CT   General publications. Earlier A10.12/2:

A77.463:nos   Bulletins. Earlier A10.12/3:

A77.464:nos   Circulars. Earlier A10.12/4:

A77.481 Hawaii Agricultural Experiment Station

A77.481:date   Annual reports. Earlier A10.9/1:

A77.482:CT   General publications. Earlier A10.9/2:

A77.483:nos   Bulletins. Earlier A10.9/3:

A77.484:nos   Circulars. Earlier A10.9/4:

A77.487:nos   Technical bulletins.

A77.490:   Virgin Islands Agricultural Experiment Station

A77.491:date   Report of Virgin Islands Agricultural research and extension program

A77.492:CT   General publications

A77.500: Plant Industry, Soils, and Agricultural
          Engineering Bureau

Functions transferred to Agricultural Research Service under Secretary's memorandum 1320, supp. 4, of Nov. 2, 1953.

A77.501:date   Annual report. Earlier A19.1:

A77.501/a:CT   ___ separates

A77.502:CT   General publications. Earlier A19.2:

A77.507:CT   Addresses. Proc. Earlier A19.33:

A77.508:date   Dry Land Agriculture Division, weekly station reports. Proc. Earlier A19.24:

A77.509:vol.   Forage crop gazette, news letter for staff workers, Division of Forage Crops and diseases (monthly) Proc. Earlier A19.29:

A77.510:vol.   Fruit and Vegetable Crops and Diseases Division, semi-monthly news letters. Proc. Earlier A19.27:

A77.511:vol.   Plant disease reporter (semi-monthly) (later monthly) Proc. Earlier A19.18:

A77.511/a:CT   ___ separates Earlier A19.18/a:

A77.512:nos   Plant disease reporter supplements. Earlier A19.19:

A77.513:CT   Papers in re. Earlier A56.23:

A77.514:date   Soil survey reports. Earlier A19.32: Later A57.38:

A77.515:nos   Plant material introduced by Division of plant exploration and introduction; inventories. Earlier A19.12:

A77.516:nos   Forest pathology special releases. Proc.

A77.517:nos   Plant disease posters. Earlier A19.26:

A77.518:nos   Information series. Proc. Earlier A70.11:

A77.519:CT	Cooperative inter-American plantation rubber development. Proc.
A77.520:nos	Plant Disease Survey special publications. Proc.
A77.521:date	Bibliography of weed investigations (quarterly)
A77.522:nos	Research reports. Proc.
A77.523:nos	H.T.&S. office reports. Proc. Earlier A19.36: Later A88.39:
A77.524:date	Soil survey field letters. Irregular. Proc. Later A57.42:
A77.525:nos	Soil survey laboratory memorandums. Later A57.43:
A77.526:nos	National arboretum contributions
A77.526/2:nos	National arboretum leaflets
A77.527:nos	Contributions toward a flora of Nevada. Proc. Earlier A19.35:
A77.528:nos	Progress in soil and water conservation research, quarterly reports
A77.529:nos	RSIM-(series)
A77.530:date	Progress report, annual varietal and environmental study of fiber and spinning properties of cottons (annual) Proc. Earlier A77.502:and A77.2:
A77.531:date	Report of Alfalfa Improvement Conference (biennial)
A77.532:date	Annual report of vegetable breeding in Southeastern United States, Hawaii, and Puerto Rico.
A77.533:nos	Series I, Evaluation of foreign fruits and nuts
A77.534:nos	CR (series) Issued by Crops Research Division.

A77.600 Dairy Industry Bureau

E.O.9060, Feb. 23,1942.

A77.601:date Annual reports. Earlier A44.1:

A77.602:CT General publications. Earlier A44.2:

A77.607:CT Addresses. Proc. Earlier A44.12:

A77.608:vol. Dairy herd-improvement association letters (monthly) Proc. Earlier A44.6:

A77.609:nos BDI-Inf (series) Proc. Changed from A77.602: and A77.607:

Human Nutrition and Home Economics Bureau

A77.700   Home Economics Bureau

E.O. 9060, Feb. 23,1942.

A77.701:date	Annual reports. Earlier A32.1:
A77.702:CT	General publications. Earlier A42.2:
A77.706:CT	Regulations, rules, and instructions issued by Home Economics Research Branch and Human Nutrition Research Branch
A77.707:CT	Posters
A77.708:nos	(Agriculture war information series) Pubs. desig. AWI-no. CHANGED TO A1.59:
A77.708:date	Wartime family living (monthly) Proc. Later title: Family economics review.
A77.709:nos	Commodity summary. Proc.
A77.710:nos	Nutrition news letter (monthly) Earlier A82.48: Later title: Nutrition program news
A77.710/a:CT	___ separates
A77.711:nos	Special reports (1948 food consumption surveys) Proc.
A77.712:nos	Studies of family clothing supplies, preliminary reports
A77.713:CT	Addresses. Proc.
A77.714:CT	Bibliographies and lists of publications, Human Nutrition Research Branch. Proc. Earlier in A77.702:

A78 Food Distribution Administration

Executive order 9280, December 5, 1942.

A78.1:date	Annual reports. Later A80.101:
A78.2:CT	General publications. Later A80.102:
A78.6:CT	Regulations, rules, and instructions. Later A80.106:
A78.7:date	Cold storage reports (monthly) Proc. Earlier A75.8: Later A80.107:
A78.8:vol	Consumers' guide (monthly) Earlier A75.8: Later A80.108:
A78.9:date	Cotton market review: Weekly. Proc. Earlier A75.9: Later A80.109:
A78.10:nos	Honey reports; Semimonthly. Proc. Earlier A75.11: Later A80.110:
A78.11:vol	Livestock, meats and wool; market reviews and statistics (wkly) Proc. Earlier A75.10: Later A80.111:
A78.12:nos	Peanut reports; Wkly. Proc. Earlier A75.12: Later A80.112:
A78.13:incl.nos.	Notices of judgment under insecticide act. Earlier A75.15: Later A80.113:
A78.14:vol	Marketing activities (monthly) Proc. Earlier A75.13: Later A80.114:
A78.15:v.nos	P. and S. docket, monthly reports of action taken on cases arising under Packers and stockyards act. Proc. Earlier A75.14: Later A80.115:
A78.16:nos	Meat Inspection Division memorandums. (Proc. & print.)

By Executive order 9322 of March 26, 1943 as amended by Executive order 9334 of April 19, 1943, the Food Distribution Administration was consolidated within the War Food Administration.

A79 Food Production Administration

Under the Food Production Administration, established by Executive order 9280 of December 5, 1942, were grouped the Agricultural Adjustment Agency; the Farm Credit Administration; the Farm Security Administration; the Federal Crop Insurance Corporation; the Soil Conservation Service; those functions of the War Production Board concerned primarily with the production of food; and the Division of Farm Management and costs of the Bureau of Agricultural Economics.

A79.1:date   Annual reports. Later A80.201:

A79.2:CT   General publications. Later A80.202:

A79.7:nos   Food production memorandum. Proc. Later A80.208:

On March 26, 1943, by Executive order 9322, as amended by Executive order 9334, of April 19, 1943, the Food Production Administration was consolidated within the War Food Administration.

A79. 100   Farm Credit Administration

A79.101:date   Annualre port. Earlier A72.1:

A79.202:CT   General publications. Earlier A72. 2:

A79.107:v./nos   News for farmer cooperatives (monthly)

A79.108:date   Semiannual reports on loans and discounts. Proc. Earlier A72.12:

<u>All these classes cancelled</u>. Farm Credit Administration was made subordinate to Food Production Administration (A79.) by Executive order 9280 of Dec. 5, 1942. Status as an agency directly subordinate to Agriculture Department was regained by Executive order 9322 of Mar. 26, 1943. Since very few publications were issued by Farm Credit Administration while subordinate to Food Production Administration (A79) all publications are to be changed to their respective classes in A72. set-up, so that all issues of a series may be filed together.

A79. 200   Soil Conservation Service

A79.201:date   Annual reports. Earlier A76. 201: Later A80. 2001:

A79.202:CT   General publications. Earlier A76. 202: Later A80. 2002:

A79.207:v.nos   Soil conservation; official organ (monthly) Earlier A76. 208: Later A80. 2007:

A79.208/a:CT   ___ separates. Later A80. 2007/a:CT

A79.300 Federal Crop Insurance Corporation

A79.301:date   Annual reports. Earlier A76.101: Later A80.901:

A79.302:CT   General publications. Earlier A76.102: Later A80.902:

A79.306:CT   Regulations, rules, and instructions. Earlier A62.6/2: and A76.106: Later A80.906:

A79.400 Agricultural Adjustment Agency

A79.401:date   Annual reports. Earlier A76.401: Later A80.2101:

A79.402:CT   General publications. Earlier A76.402: Later A80.2102:

A79.406:CT   Regulations, rules, and instructions. Earlier A76.406: Later A80.2106:

A79.441:   East Central Region publications

A79.451:   North Central Region publications

A79.452:CT   General publications. Earlier A55.43/2: Later A80.2152:

A79.458:CT   Production practices, 1943 farm program. Proc.

A79.461:   Northeast Region publications

A79.471:   Southern Region publications

A79.481:   Western Region publications

A80   War Food Administration

Executive order 9322 of March 26, 1943, amended by E.O. 9334 Apr. 19, 1943.

A80.1:date   Annual reports

A80.2:CT   General publications

A80.6:CT   Regulations, rules, and instructions.

A80.7:CT   Addresses

A80.8:CT   Posters

The War Food Administration was terminated by authority of Executive order 9577 of June 29, 1945 effective June 30, 1945, and the records, property, personnel, funds and agencies of the Administration were placed under the jurisdiction and control of the Secretary of Agriculture.

A80.100   Food Distribution Administration

A80.101:date   Annual reports. Earlier A78.1:

A80.101/a:CT   ___ separates.

A80.102:CT   General publications. Earlier A78.2:

A80.106:CT   Regulations, rules, and instructions. Earlier A78.6:

A80.107:date   Cold storage reports. Earlier A78.7: Later A80.807:

A80.108:vol   Consumers' guide (monthly) Earlier A78.8: Later A80.808:

A80.109:date   Cotton market review (weekly) Earlier A78.9: Later A80.809:

A80.110:nos   Honey reports (semimonthly) Proc. Earlier A78.10: Later A80.810:

A80.111:v.nos   Livestock, meats and wool; market reviews and statistics (wkly) Proc. Earlier A78.11 Later A80.811:

A80.112:nos   Peanut reports (wkly) Proc. Earlier A78.12: Later A80.812:

A80.113:incl.nos.   Notices of judgment under insecticide act. Earlier A78.13: Later A80.8: Later A80.823:

A80.114:v.nos   Marketing activities (monthly) Earlier A78.14: Later A80.813:

A80.114/a:CT   ___ separates.

A80.115:v.nos   P. and S. docket, monthly reports of action taken on cases arising under packers and stockyards act. Earlier A78.15: Later A80.814:

A80.116:nos   Marketing orders. Earlier A75.20: Later A80.825:

A80.116:CT   Marketing orders (miscellaneous)

A80.117:nos   Sugar determination. Earlier A55.37: and A76.307: Later A80.817:

A80.118:nos   Service and regulatory announcements. Earlier A75.16: Later A82.23:

A80.119:nos   Commodity statistics. Later A80.826:

A80.120:CT   Addresses. Proc.

A80.121:CT   United States standards for fruits, etc., earlier A75.19: Later A80.822:

A80.122:CT   Posters

A80.122:nos   Posters (numbered)

A80.123:nos   Nutrition and Food Conservation Branch publications. Later A1.65:

A80.124:date   Stocks of leaf tobacco owned by dealers and manufacturers (quarterly) Proc. Earlier A75.2:T55/3   Later A80.821:

A80.125:nos   Food trade letters (wkly) Proc. Later A80.410:

A80.126:nos   Container notes. Proc.

A80.127:date   Industrial nutrition service (monthly) Proc.

A80.128:v.nos   Cotton price statistics, monthly averages. Proc. Later A80.815:

A80.129:date   Quarterly soybean market review. Proc. Later A80.818:

A80.130:date   Margarine production (monthly) Proc. Later A80.820:

A80.131:CT   Fact sheets. Proc.

A80.132:date   Food supply reports (monthly) Proc. Later A80.816:

A80.133:vol.   Cotton linters review; Wkly. Later A80.819:

A80.134:v.nos.   U.S. cotton quality report for ginnings. Later A80.824: Later A82.28:

A80.135:nos   Nutrition news letter (monthly) Earlier Pr32.4502:N95/7 Later A80.830:

A80.136:   Federal food reporter

A80.137:   Nutrition kit

A80.138:   School lunch kit

Abolished by Administrator's memorandum 27, revision 1, Dec.13,1944, effective Jan.1,1945. Certain functions transferred to Office of Marketing Services created by the same memorandum.

A80.200   Food Production Administration

A80.201:date   Annual reports. Earlier A79.1:

A80.202:CT   General publications. Earlier A79.2:

A80.206:CT   Regulations, rules, and instructions.

A80.207:CT   Addresses

A80.208:nos   Food production memorandums. Earlier A79.9:

Abolished by Administrator's memorandum 27, revision 1, Dec.13,1944, effective Jan.1,1945. The functions, etc., of the Office of Production dealing with feed management and crop production were transferred to the Agricultural Adjustment Agency, while its land conservation functions were transferred to the Soil Conservation Service.

A80.301   Extension Service

A80.301:date   Annual reports. Earlier A43.1: Later A43.1:

A80.302:CT   General publications. Earlier A43.2: Later A43.2:

A80.304:nos   Extension service circulars. Earlier A43.5/6: Later A43.4:

A80.306:CT   Regulations, rules, and instructions

A80.307:v.nos   Extension service review (monthly) Earlier A43.7: Later A43.7:

A80.307/a:CT   ___ separates

A80.308:CT   Posters. Earlier A43.8:

A80.309:nos   Lectures for slidefilms. Proc. Earlier A43.19:

A80.310:CT   Addresses. Earlier A43.21: Later A43.21:

A80.311:nos   Extension farm labor circulars. Later A43.26:

The Extension Service, formerly subordinate to the War Food Administration was placed under the jurisdiction and control of the Secretary of Agriculture by Executive order 9577 of June 29, 1945, effective June 30, 1945.

A80.400   Commodity Credit Corporation

A80.401:date   Annual reports. Earlier A71.1: Later A82.301:

A80.402:CT   General publications. Earlier A71.2: Later A82.302:

A80.406:CT   Regulations, rules, and instructions. Earlier A71.6: Later A82.306:

A80.407:date   Loans and commodities owned, Statements of (monthly) Earlier A71.7: Later A82.307:

A80.408:CT   Addresses

A80.410:nos   Food trade letters. (wkly.) (Supply Office) Earlier A71.9:

Placed under control of the Secretary of Agriculture by Executive order 9577 of June 29, 1945, effective June 30, 1945.

A80.501: Soil Conservation Service

A80.501:date   Annual reports. Earlier A80.2001: Later A57.1:

A80.502:CT   General publications. Earlier A80.2002: Later A57.2:

A80.507:v.nos   Soil conservation (monthly) Earlier A80.2007: Later A57.9:

A80.507/a:CT   ___ separates. Earlier A80.2007: Later A57.9/a:

A80.508:date   Soil conservation districts (monthly) Proc. Earlier A80.2009: Later A57.32:

A80.509:nos   [Technical publications] Proc. Earlier A80.2011: Later 57.15:

A80.510:nos   Physical land surveys. Earlier A80.2012: Later A57.24:

Placed under control of the Secretary of Agriculture by Executive Order 9577 of June 29, 1945, effective June 30, 1945.

A80.601: Agricultural Adjustment Agency

A80.601:date   Annual reports. Earlier A80.2101: Later A83.1:

A80.602:CT   General publications. Earlier A80.2102: Later A83.2:

A80.606:CT   Regulations, rules, and instructions. Includes handbooks and manuals. Earlier A80.2101: Later A83.1:

A80.602:CT   General publications. Earlier A80.2102: Later A83.2:

A80.606:CT   Regulations, rules, and instructions. Includes handbooks and manuals. Earlier A80.2106: Later A83.6:

A80.607:CT   Posters. Conservation practices

A80.608:CT   Agricultural conservation practices (by States) Later A82.111:

A80.609:CT   Addresses. Proc. Earlier A55.15: Later A82.113:

A80.610:nos   Special services memorandums. Proc. Later A83.7:

A80.611:CT   Committeemen's practice handbooks (by States) Later A82.107:

A80.612:CT   Instructions for completing farm plans (by States)

A80.613:CT   **Agricultural conservation program (by States) Earlier for ECR A55.42:9: Later A82.110:**

A80.614:nos   General information series. Earlier A76.408:

The Agricultural Adjustment Agency, formerly subordinate to the War Food Administration, was placed under the jurisdiction and control of the Secretary of Agriculture by Executive order 9577 of June 29, 1945, effective June 30, 1945.

A80.701: Farm Security Administration

A80.701:date   Annual reports. Earlier A61.1:

A80.702:CT   General publications. Earlier A61.2:

A80.706:CT   Regulations, rules, and instructions. Earlier A61.7:

A80.707:CT   Addresses. Earlier A61.16:

A80.708:nos   Leaflets for action. Earlier A61.18:

A80.709:dt.&nos. Family progress report, releases. Earlier A61.19:

Returned to control of the Secretary of Agriculture by E.O. 9577 of June 29, 1945.

A80.801 Marketing Services Office

Established Jan. 1, 1945 by Administrator's memorandum 27, revision 1, Dec. 13, 1944. Certain functions of the Office of Distribution are transferred to Marketing Services Office.

A80.801:date   Annual reports. Later A81.1:

A80.802:CT   General publications. Later A81.2:

A80.807:v.nos   Cold storage reports (monthly) Proc. Earlier A80.107: Later A81.7:

A80.808:v.nos   Consumers' guide (monthly) Earlier A80.108: Later A1.67:

A80.809:v.nos   Cotton market review; Wkly. Proc. Earlier A80.109: Later A81.9:

A80.810:v.nos   Honey reports; Semimonthly. Proc. Earlier A80.110: Later A81.10:

A80.811:v.nos   Livestock, meats and wool, market reviews and statistics (weekly) Proc. Earlier A80.111: Later A81.11:

A80.812:v.nos   Peanut reports. Wkly. Earlier A80.112: Later A81.12:

A80.813:v.nos   Marketing activities (monthly) Earlier A80.114: Later A81.13:

A80.814:v.nos   P. and S. docket, monthly reports of action taken on cases arising under Packers and stockyards act. Earlier A80.115: Later A81.14:

A80.815:v.nos   Cotton price statistics (monthly) Proc. Earlier A80.128: Later A81.17:

A80.816:date   Food supply reports; Monthly. Earlier A80.132: Later A82.16:

A80.817:nos   [Sugar determination] Earlier A80.117: Later A81.16:

A80.818:date   Soybean market summary (quarterly) Proc. Earlier A80.129: Later A81.18:

A80.819:vol   Cotton linters review; Wkly. Proc. Earlier A80.133: Later A81.8:

A80.820:date   Margarine production (monthly) Proc. Earlier A80.130: Later A82.26:

A80.821:date   Tobacco stocks reports (quarterly) Proc. Earlier A80.124: Later A82.11:

A80.822:CT   United States standards [for fruits, etc.] Proc. Earlier A80.121: Later A81.15:

A80.823:nos   Notices of judgment under insecticide act. Earlier A80.113: Later A81.15:

A80.824:v.nos   U.S. cotton quality report for ginnings. Proc. Earlier A80.134: Later A82.28:

A80.825:nos   Marketing orders. Earlier A80.116: Later A82.22:

A80.826:nos   [Commodity statistics] Earlier A80.119: Later A82.18:

A80.827:v.nos   Commercial grain stocks reports (weekly) Proc. Later A81.9:

A80.828:v.nos   Feed market review; Weekly. Proc.

A80.829:v.nos   Rice market review; Weekly. Later A81.21:

A80.830:nos   Nutrition news letters (monthly) Earlier A80.135: Later A81.2:N95

A80.831:   Spot cotton quotations

The Marketing Services Office was placed under the jurisdiction and control of the Secretary of Agriculture by Executive order 9577 of June 29, 1945, effective June 30, 1945.

A80.901: Federal Crop Insurance Corporation

Transferred from Food Production Administration April 19, 1943.

A80.901:date   Annual reports. Earlier A79.301: Later A82.201:

A80.902:CT   General publications. Earlier A79.302: Later A82.202:

A80.906:CT   Regulations, rules and instructions. Earlier A79.306:

A80.907:nos   Information [series] Earlier A76.108: Later A82.207:

The Federal Crop Insurance Corporation was established as a bureau within the Production and Marketing Administration of the Department of Agriculture by supp.1 to Memorandum 1118 of the Secretary of Agriculture dated Oct. 8, 1945.

A80.2001: Soil Conservation Service

A80.2001:date   Annual reports. Earlier A79.201: Later A80.501:

A80.2002:CT   General publications. Earlier A79.202: Later A80.502:

A80.2007:v.nos   Soil conservation. Earlier A79.207: Later A80.507:

A80.2007/a:CT   ___ separates. Earlier A79.207/a:CT Later A80.507/a:

A80.2008:CT   Addresses. Proc.

A80.2009:date   Soil conservation districts. Proc. (monthly) Earlier A76.214: Later A80.508:

A80.2010:date   Daily totals of precipitation in Muskingum River basin (monthly) Proc. Earlier A76.209:

A80.2011:nos   [Technical publications] Proc. Earlier A76.211: Later A80.509:

A80.2012:nos   Physical land surveys. Earlier A76.212: Later A80.510:

A80.2013:nos   Special reports of Sedimentation Section, Office of Research. Earlier A76.215:

A80.2101: Agricultural Adjustment Agency

A80.2101:date   Annual reports. Earlier A79.401: Later A80.601:

A80.2102:CT   General publications Earlier A79.402: Later A80.602:

A80.2106:CT   Regulations, rules and instructions. Earlier A79.406: Later A80.606:

A80.2141:   East Central Region

A80.2142:CT   General publications. Earlier A55.42/2:

A80.2151:   North Central Region

A80.2152:CT   General publications. Earlier A79.452:

A80.2158:CT   Production-conservation program, committeemen's handbooks.

A80.2161:   Northeast Region

A80.2162:CT   General publications

A80.2166:CT   Regulations, rules and instructions. Proc. Earlier A76.466:

A80.2171:   Southern Region

A80.2172:CT   General publications. Earlier A76.472:

A80.2181:   Western Region

A80.2182:CT   General publications. Earlier A76.482:

A80.2186:CT   Regulations, rules, and instructions. Proc. Earlier A76.486:

The War Food Administration was terminated by authority of Executive order 9577 of June 29, 1945, effective June 30, 1945, and the records, property, personnel, funds and agencies of the Administration were placed under the jurisdiction and control of the Secretary of Agriculture.

A81 Marketing Services Office

The Marketing Services Office was placed under the jurisdiction and control of the Secretary of Agriculture by Executive order 9577 of June 29, 1945, effective June 30, 1945.

A81.1:date   Annual reports. Earlier A80.801:

A81.1/a:CT   ___ separates.

A81.2:CT   General publications. Earlier A80.802:

A81.7:vol   Cold storage reports (monthly) Proc. Earlier A80.807: Later A82.15:

A81.8:vol   Cotton linters review; Wkly. Earlier A80.819: Later A82.8:

A81.9:vol   Cotton market review; Wkly. Proc. Earlier A80.809: Later A92.9:

A81.10:vol   Honey reports; Semimonthly. Earlier A80.810: Later A82.12:

A81.11:vol   Livestock, meats and wool, market reviews and statistics. Wkly. Earlier A80.811: Later A82.7:

A81.12:vol   Peanut reports; Wkly. Earlier A80.812: Later A82.10:

A81.13:vol   Marketing activities (monthly) Earlier A80.813: Later A82.17:

A81.14:vol   P. and S. docket, monthly report of action taken on cases arising under packers and stockyards act. Earlier A80.814: Later A82.14:

A81.15:CT   United States standards for grades of [fruits, **vegetables,** etc.] Proc. Earlier A80.822 Later A82.20:

A81.16:nos   [Sugar determination] Earlier A80.817: Later A82.19:

A81.17:vol   Cotton price statistics (monthly) Earlier A80.815: Later A82.13:

A81.18:date   Soybean market summary (quarterly) Proc. Earlier A80.818: Later A82.21:

A81.19:v.nos   Commercial grain stocks reports (weekly) Proc. Earlier A80.827: Later A82.31:

A81.20:v.nos   Feed market review; Weekly. Proc. Earlier A80.828: Later A82.32:

A81.21:v.nos   Rice market review; Weekly.   Earlier A80.829:   Later A82.33:

The Office was consolidated into the Production and Marketing Administration by authority of Memorandum 1118 of the Secretary of Agriculture dated Aug. 18, 1945, effective Aug. 20, 1945.

A82   Production and Marketing Administration

The Production and Marketing Administration was established within the Department of Agriculture by authority of Memorandum 1118 of the Secretary of Agriculture, dated Aug.18,1945, effective Aug. 20,1945. The Agricultural Adjustment Agency, the Office of Marketing Services ... were consolidated into the newly established board.

A82   Commodity Stabilization Service

Under authority of Reorganization plan #2 of 1953, the Production and Marketing Administration was designated Commodity Stabilization Service, by Memorandum 1320, supp. 4, of the Secretary of Agriculture, dated November 2,1953. The marketing research and marketing services work was reassigned to the Agricultural Marketing Service.

A82   Agricultural Stabilization and Conservation Service

Name changed to Agricultural Stabilization and Conservation Service by Secretary's memorandum 1458 of June 14,1961, effective June 5,1961.

A82.1:date	Annual reports
A82.1/2:CT/date	Annual reports (by States)
A82.2:CT	General publications
A82.3:	
A82.3/2:date	Export corn meal bulletin
A82.3/3:date	Domestic corn meal bulletin Later in A82.3/7: and A83.3/8:
A82.3/4:date	Domestic corn (hominy) grits bulletin
A82.3/5:date	Export wheat flour bulletin
A82.3/6:date	Domestic wheat flour bulletin
A82.3/7:date	Export corn meal price bulletin. Formerly included in A82.3/3:
A82.3/8:date	Export corn meal port bulletin. Formerly included in A82.3/3:
A82.3/9:date	Export wheat flour price bulletin. Formerly included in A82.3/5:
A82.3/10:date	Export wheat flour port bulletin. Formerly included in A82.3/5:
A82.5:CT	Laws

A82.6:CT	Regulations, rules and instructions. Later A85.6:
A82.6/2:nos	S.R. [Sugar requirements]
A82.6/3:nos	Soil bank handbooks. Administrative.
A82.6/4:CT	Handbooks, manuals, guides Earlier in A82.6:
A82.7:v.nos	Livestock, meats and wool, market reviews and statistics. Wkly. Earlier A81.11: Later A88.16/4:
A82.8:v.nos	Cotton linters review; Wkly. Proc. Earlier A81.8: Later A88.11/3:
A82.9:v.nos	Cotton market review. Wkly. Proc. Earlier A81.9: Later A88.11/2:
A82.10:v.nos	Peanut reports. Wkly. Proc. Earlier A81.12: Later A88.10:
A82.11:date	Tobacco stocks reports. Quarterly. Proc. Earlier A80.821: Later A88.34:
A82.12:v.nos	Honey reports; Semimonthly. Proc. Earlier A81.10: Later A88.19:
A82.13:v.nos	Cotton price statistics. Monthly. Earlier A81.17: Later A88.11/9:
A82.14:v.nos	P. and S. docket, monthly report of action taken on cases arising under packers and stockyards act. Proc. Earlier A81.14: Later A88.16/5:
A82.15:v.nos	Cold storage reports. Monthly. Proc. Earlier A81.7: Later A88.20:
A82.16:date	Food supply reports; Monthly. Restricted. Proc. Earlier A80.816:
A82.17:v.nos	Marketing activities (monthly) Proc. Earlier A81.13: Later A88.26:
A82.17/a:CT	___ reprints. Proc.
A82.18:nos	[Commodity statistics] Earlier A80.826: Later A1.73:
A82.19:nos	[Sugar determination] Earlier A81.16:
A82.20:CT	United States standards for grades of [fruits, vegetables, etc.] Proc. Earlier A81.15: Later A88.6/2:
A82.21:date	Soybean market summary (quarterly) Proc. Earlier A81.18:
A82.22:nos	Marketing orders. Earlier A80.825:
A82.23:nos	Service and regulatory announcements. Earlier A80.118: Later A88.6/3:, A77.6/2:

A82.24:CT	Addresses. Proc.
A82.25:CT	Posters. Later A88.38:
A82.26:date	Margarine production (monthly) Proc. Earlier A80.820:
A82.27:nos	Serving many (monthly) Proc.
A82.28:v.nos	United States cotton quality report for ginnings. Proc. Earlier A80.824: and A80.134: Later A88.11:
A82.29:v.nos	Trade in grain futures (monthly) Proc. Earlier A75.209: Later A85.8:
A82.30:v.nos	Trade in cotton futures (monthly) Earlier A75.208: Later A85.7:
A82.31:v.nos	Commercial grain stocks reports (weekly) Proc. Earlier A81.19: Later A88.18/2:
A82.31/2:CT	Commercial grain stocks revised figures for calendar year. Proc. Later A88.18/2-2:
A82.32:v.nos	Feed market review; Weekly. Proc. Earlier A81.20: Later A88.18/4:
A82.33:v.nos	Rice market review; Weekly. Earlier A81.21: Later A88.18/9:
A82.34:nos	Notices of judgment under insecticide act. Earlier A80.823: Later A82.56:
A82.35:date	Feed market summary (quarterly) Proc. Later A88.18/3:
A82.36:date	Cold storage stocks of frozen fruits and vegetables by container size (monthly) Proc.
A82.37:CT	Agricultural conservation program (by States); Handbooks. Earlier A82.112 Later A90.8:
A82.37/2:CT	Agricultural conservation program service publications. Later A90.2:
A82.37/3:CT	Statistical summaries [various commodity programs]
A82.38:date	Domestic dairy markets review; Monthly. Proc. Later A88.13:
A82.38/2:date	___ Statistical supplement. (monthly) Proc. Later A88.13/2:
A82.39:date	Egg and poultry markets review; Monthly. Proc. Later A88.13: , A88.13/3:
A82.39/2:date	___ Statistical supplement (monthly); Proc. Later A88.13/4:
A82.40:CT	Fact sheets

A82.41:date	Receipts and disposition of livestock at 66 public markets (monthly) Proc. Later A88.16:
A82.42:date	Estimated refrigerator car movement of domestic fresh fruits and vegetables by regions (monthly) Proc.
A82.43:date	USDA food deliveries (monthly) Proc.
A82.44:date	Purchase report (monthly) Proc. Later A82.60:
A82.45:date	Summary of carlot shipments; weekly. Proc. Later A88.12:
A82.46:date	Carlot unloads of fruits and vegetables at Washington, D.C. (monthly) Proc. Later A88.12/5:
A82.47:nos	Sugar reports. Proc.
A82.48:nos	Nutrition news letters (monthly) Proc. Earlier A81.2:N95 Later A77.710:
A82.49:date	Rice, stocks and movement, California mills (monthly) Proc. Later A88.18/11:
A82.50:date	Rice, stocks and movement, southern mills (monthly) Proc.
A82.51:date	Unfinished cotton cloth prices, cotton prices, and mill margins (monthly) Proc. Later A88.11/6:
A82.52:date	Wholesale prices of fruits and vegetables at New York City and Chicago; Weekly summary of. Proc. Later A88.12/3:
A82.53:date	F.O.B. prices of fresh fruits and vegetables in representative shipping districts; Weekly summary of. Proc. Later A88.12/2:
A82.54:date	USDA meat production report (weekly) Proc. Later A88.17:
A82.55:date	Digest of decisions of Secretary of Agriculture under perishable agricultural commodities act
A82.56:nos	Notices of judgment under Federal insecticide, fungicide, and rodenticide act. Earlier A82.34: Later A77.325:
A82.57:date	Releases
A82.58:v.nos	Survey of capacity of refrigerated storage warehouses in United States (biennial) Proc.
A82.59:	Production and inspection reports. Proc.

A82.59/2:date   Alfalfa meal production (monthly) Later A88.18/5:

A82.59/3:date   Brewers' dried grain production (monthly) Later A88.18/6:

A82.59/4:date   Distillers' dried grain production (monthly) Later A88.17/7:

A82.59/5:date   Soybean inspection report (monthly)

A82.60:date   Purchase reports. Earlier A82.44:

A82.61:date   Sales reports

A82.61/2:date   Purchase and sales reports. Irregular. Proc.

A82.62:v.nos.&nos. Weekly molasses market reports. Proc. Later A88.23:

A82.63:nos   PMA procedure check list. Irregular.

A82.64:nos   DFO [Defense food orders]

A82.65:v.nos.&nos. Cottonseed review, South Central area

A82.65/2:v.nos.&nos. ___ Southeastern area

A82.65/3:v.nos.&nos. ___ Southwestern area

A82.66:   Industrial nutrition service

A82.67:v.nos.&nos. Farmers weekly cotton price quotations

A82.68:   Cotton quality report for ginnings, Western upland cotton

A82.69:CT   Estimated grade and staple length of upland cotton ginned (by States)

A82.70:CT   Cotton quality reports for ginnings (by States)

A82.71:v.nos   Grain market news and statistical report (weekly) Proc. Later A88.18:

A82.72:date   Primary sugar distribution for week. Proc. Later title, Distribution of sugar by refiners, importers and domestic beet processors for week ended.

A82.72/2:nos   Monthly deliveries of sugar by States. Proc.

A82.72/3:date   Sugar production and movement report (monthly) This release was incorporated into sugar reports (A82.47:).

A82.73:v.nos.&nos. Spot cotton quotations, designated markets. Daily except Saturdays, Sundays, and holidays. Proc. Later A88.11/4:

A82.74:le-n os	Announcements [of sales]. Proc.
A82.75:	Dissemination of research results [on poultry and egg marketing subjects] (issued 5 or 6 times a year). Later A88.15/8:
A82.76:date	Pesticide situation (annual) Proc. Earlier A82.2:P43
A82.77:date	Fertilizer situation (annual) Proc. Earlier A82.2:F41 Later title, Fertilizer supply
A82.78:date	Acquisition and disposal of CCC price-support inventory (annual) Proc. Earlier A82.2:P93/2
A82.79:CT	Soil bank summaries. Proc.
A82.79/2:date	Conservation reserve program of soil bank, statistical summaries
A82.80:date	What we are doing about agricultural surpluses (irregular) Proc. Earlier A82.2:Su7
A82.81:nos	Federal milk order market statistics, summary (monthly) Earlier A88.14/11: Later title Federal milk order statistics FMOS-(series)
A82.81/2:date	Bulk cooling tanks on farms supplying Federal milk order markets (annual) Earlier A88.40:261/date
A82.82:nos	ASCS background information BI (series)
A82.82/2:CT	ASCS Commodity fact sheet
A82.83:date	Information releases
A82.84:CT	Maps, charts, posters

A82.101 Field Service Branch

The Field Service Branch was established as a bureau within the Production and Marketing Administration by authority of Memorandum 1118 of the Secretary of Agriculture, dated Aug. 18, 1945, effective Aug. 20, 1945.

A82.101: date   Annual reports. Earlier A83.1:

A82.102: CT   General publications. Earlier A83.2:

A82.106: CT   Regulations, rules, and instructions. Earlier A83.6:

A82.107: CT   Committeeman's practice handbooks (by States) Earlier A80.611:

A82.108: CT   Posters

A82.109: nos   Special services memorandums. Proc. Earlier A83.7:

A82.110: CT   Agricultural conservation program (by States) Earlier A80.613:

A82.111: CT   Handbook of conservation practices (by States) Earlier A80.608:

A82.112: CT   Agricultural conservation program (by States) Later A82.37:

A82.113: CT   Addresses. Earlier A80.609:

A82.114:   Grain memorandums. Admin.

A82.115:   Reports memorandum

A82.200: Federal Crop Insurance Corporation

The Federal Crop Insurance Corporation was established as a bureau within the Production and Marketing Administration of the Department of Agriculture by supp.1 to Memorandum 1118 of the Secretary of Agriculture dated Oct. 8, 1945.

A82.201: date   Annual reports. Earlier A80.901:

A82.202: CT   General publications. Earlier A80.902:

A82.207: nos   Information [series] Earlier A80.907:

A82.301: Commodity Credit Corporation

The administration of the program of the Commodity Credit Corporation, transferred to the Secretary of Agriculture under Reorganization Plan no. 3, was vested in the Production and Marketing Administration by supp. 9 to Memorandum 1118 of the Secretary of Agriculture, dated July 15, 1946, effective July 16, 1946.

A82.301:date	Annual reports. Earlier A80.401:
A82.302:CT	General publications. Earlier A80.402:
A82.305:CT	Laws
A82.306:CT	Regulations, rules, and instructions. Earlier A80.406:
A82.307:date	Loans and commodities owned, Statement of (quarterly) Proc. Earlier A80.407:
A82.308:date	Report of financial condition and operations (monthly) Proc.
A82.309:date	CCC loans on cotton (weekly) Proc.
A82.310:date	Active and announced price support programs approved by Board of Directors (monthly) Proc. Replaced by A82.310/3:
A82.310/2:date	Price support program, chart and tables, selected activities (quarterly) Proc.
A82.310/3:date	CCC price support program data. Replaces A82.310:
A82.311:date	Commodity Credit Corporation charts providing graphic summary of operations (annual) Proc. Earlier A82.302:C38

A83 Agricultural Adjustment Agency

The Agricultural Adjustment Agency, formerly subordinate to the War Food Administration, was placed under the jurisdiction and control of the Secretary of Agriculture by Executive order 9577 of June 29, 1945, effective June 30, 1945.

A83.1:date	Annual reports. Earlier A80.601: Later A82.101:
A83.2:CT	General publications. Earlier A80.602: Later A82.102:
A83.6:CT	Regulations, rules, and instructions. Earlier A80.606: Later A82.106:
A83.7:nos	Special services memorandums. Proc. Earlier A80.610: Later A82.109:

The Agency was consolidated into the Production and Marketing Administration by authority of Memorandum 1118 of the Secretary of Agriculture, dated Aug. 18, 1945, effective Aug. 20, 1945.

A84 Farmers' Home Administration

The Farmers' Home Administration was established in the Department of Agriculture in accordance with Public law 731, 79th Congress, approved Aug. 14, 1946. The same law abolished the Farm Security Administration whose functions, etc., were merged into the Farmers Home Administration on Nov. 1, 1946.

A84.1:date	Annual reports
A84.2:CT	General publications
A84.6:CT	Regulations, rules, and instructions.
A84.6/2:CT	Handbooks, manuals, guides
A84.7:date	Monthly report of Farmers Home Administration. Proc.
A84.8:CT	Addresses. Proc.

A84.9:nos   Farmers Home Administration features

A85   Commodity Exchange Authority

The Commodity Exchange Authority was established in the Department of Agriculture by Memorandum 1185 of the Secretary of Agriculture, dated Jan. 21, 1947, effective Feb. 1, 1947.

A85.1:date　　　　Annual reports

A85.2:CT　　　　 General publications

A85.6:CT　　　　 Regulations, rules and instructions.   Earlier A82.6:

A85.7:v.nos　　　 Trade in cotton futures (monthly) Proc.   Earlier A82.30:

A85.8:v.nos　　　 Trade in grain futures (monthly)   Earlier A82.29:

A85.9:nos　　　　Commitments of large traders in cotton futures (monthly) Proc.   Later Y3.C73/5:9/dt. &nos.

A85.9/2:nos　　　Commitments of traders in wheat futures and in soybean futures (monthly) Proc.   Later Y3.C73/5:9/2/dt. &nos.

A85.9/3:nos　　　Commitments of traders in wool and wool top futures, N.Y. Cotton exchange.   Later combined with A85.9:

A85.10:CT　　　　Addresses

A85.11:nos　　　　Futures trading and open contracts in potatoes, eggs, butter, and rice. Proc.

A85.11/2:nos　　　Futures trading and open contracts in cotton and wool tops (daily except Saturdays, Sundays, and holidays). Proc.

A85.11/3:nos　　　Futures trading and open contracts in potatoes (daily except Saturdays, Sundays, and holidays). Proc.

A85.11/4:nos　　　Futures trading and open contracts in butter, eggs and potatoes, [Chicago Mercantile Exchange](daily except Saturdays, Sundays & legal holidays). Proc.

A85.11/5:nos　　　Futures trading and open contracts in cotton and cottonseed oil [New Orleans Cotton Exchange]. (daily) Proc.

A85.11/6:nos　　　Futures trading and open contracts in soybean meal and cottonseed meal [Memphis Board of Trade Clearing Association] (daily) Proc.

A85.11/7:nos	Futures trading and open contracts [wheat, corn, oats, etc.] on Chicago Board of Trade (daily except Saturdays, Sundays and legal holidays).
A85.11/8:nos	Futures trading and open contracts in frozen concentraded orange juice [on Citrus Associates of New York Cotton Exchange]
A85.12:nos	Weekly report [cotton] Proc.
A85.13:date	List of publications of Commodity Exchange Authority. Earlier A85.2:P96
A85.14:date	Stocks of grain in deliverable position at Chicago, Ill., represented by outstanding warehouse receipts, as reported by licensed warehouses (weekly) Later Y3.C73/5:10/date
A85.15:v.nos.&nos.	Monthly summary of commodity futures statistics
A85.15/2:date	Monthly commodity futures statistics, on futures trading in commodities regulated under commodity exchange act.
A85.16:nos	Market survey reports
A85.17:nos	Weekly reports (numbered)

Functions transferred to the Commodity Futures Trading Commission by act of Oct. 23, 1974 (88 Stat.1414; 7 U.S.C. 4a note).

A86 Food and Feed Conservation Office

The Office for Food and Feed Conservation was established by Agriculture Department Memorandum 1204, dated Jan. 27, 1948.

A86.1: date   Annual reports

A86.2: CT   General publications

A86.7: nos   [Office for Food and Feed Conservation numbered publications]

A86.8: nos   Posters

A87 Research and Marketing Act, Administrator of

A87.1: date   Annual reports   Later A77.8:

A87.2: CT   General publications

A87.7: CT   Addresses. Proc.

Responsibility for administering the RMA was assigned to the Agricultural Research Administrator July 29, 1949.

A88 Agricultural Marketing Service, April 2, 1972-

A88 Consumer and Marketing Service, Feb. 8,1965-Apr. 2, 1972

A88 Agricultural Marketing Service

Under authority of Reorganization plan no. 2 of 1953 the Agricultural Marketing Service was established by Memorandum 1320, supplement 4, of the Secretary of Agriculture dated Nov. 2, 1953.

A88.1:date	Annual reports
A88.2:CT	General publications
A88.3:	
A88.3/2:nos	Recruiting bulletins. Proc.
A88.4:	
A88.5:CT	Laws
A88.6:CT	Regulations, rules, and instructions
A88.6/2:CT	United States standards for grades of fruits, vegetables, etc. Proc. Earlier A82.20:
A88.6/3:nos	Service and regulatory announcements. Earlier A82.23:
A88.6/4:CT	Handbooks, manuals, guides.
A88.6/5:nos	USDA-C&MS visual aids (series)
A88.7:	Releases
A88.8:v.nos	Agricultural situation (monthly) Earlier A36.15: Later A92.23:
A88.8/a:CT	___ separates
A88.8/2:date	Agricultural outlook digest (monthly) Earlier A36.160: Later A93.10:
A88.8/3:date	Agricultural outlook charts (annual) Earlier A36.50:C38/3 Later A1.98:
A88.9:date	Demand and price situation (monthly) Proc. Earlier A36.28: Later A93.9/2:
A88.9/2:nos	Farm income situation (bimonthly) Earlier A36.122: Later A93.9:
A88.9/3:date	Agricultural prices (monthly) Proc. Earlier A36.163:
A88.9/4:date	Agricultural prices, Louisiana Crop Reporting Service

A88.9/5:date	Agricultural prices, annual summary. Desig.Pr 1-3. Later A92.16/2:
A88.10:v.nos	Weekly peanut report. Proc. Earlier A82.10:
A88.10/2:date	Peanuts, stocks and processing (monthly) Proc. Earlier A36.164: Later A92.14:
A88.10/2-2:date	___ (annual) Proc. Later A92.14/2:
A88.10/3:date	List, Peanut shellers and crushers (annual) Later A92.14/3:
A88.10/4:date	Tree nuts by States (annual) Proc. Earlier A88.2:N95 Later A92.27:
A88.10/5:date	Pecan report, Louisiana Crop Reporting Service
A88.10/5-2:date	Annual pecan summary, Louisiana Crop Reporting Service
A88.10/6:date	List, peanut processors (users of raw peanuts) Later A92.14/4:
A88.11:v.nos	United States cotton quality report for ginnings. Proc. Earlier A82.28:
A88.11/2:v.nos	Weekly cotton market review. Proc. Earlier A82.9:
A88.11/3:v.nos	Weekly cotton linters review. Proc. Earlier A82.8:
A88.11/4:v.nos	Spot cotton quotations, designated markets. Proc. Earlier A82.73:
A88.11/5:date	Cotton production (monthly June-Dec.) Proc. Earlier A36.30: Later A92.20:
A88.11/6:date	Unfinished cotton cloth prices, cotton prices, and mill margins (monthly) Proc. Earlier A82.51:
A88.11/7:v.nos	Estimated grade and staple length of upland cotton ginned in United States
A88.11/8:nos	Cotton situation. Issued 6 times a year. Earlier A36.40/2: Later A93.24:
A88.11/9:v.nos	Cotton price statistics (monthly) Proc. Earlier A82.13:
A88.11/10:date	Prices of cotton cloth and raw cotton, and mill margins for certain constructions of unfinished cloth (monthly) Proc.
A88.11/10-2:date	Prices of cotton cloth and raw cotton, and mill margins for certain constructions of unfinished cloth (annual) Proc. Earlier A88.2:C82/6
A88.11/10-3:date	Mill margins report [new series] (monthly)
A88.11/11:date	Cotton varieties planted in early producing areas of Texas (annual)Proc. Earlier A88.2:C82/3

A88.11/12:date	Charges for ginning cotton, costs of selected services incident to marketing, and related information, season. Proc. Earlier A88.2:C82/10
A88.11/13:date	Cotton varieties planted (annual) Proc. Earlier A88.2:C82/11
A88.11/14:date	Quality of cotton in carry-over (annual) Proc. Earlier A88.2:C82/7
A88.11/15:date	Cottonseed quality crops (annual) Earlier A88.2:C82
A88.11/16:date	Cotton production: Cotton and cottonseed production (annual) Earlier A88.2:C82/2
A88.11/17:date	Cotton fiber and processing test results. Semimonthly during harvest season. Earlier in AMS-nos (A88.40:).
A88.11/17-2:date	Summary of cotton fiber and processing test results, crop of [year]
A88.11/18:nos	Futures trading and open contracts [Wheat, corn, oats, etc.] on Chicago Board of Trade (daily except Saturdays, Sundays and legal holidays).
A88.11/19:date	Cotton gin equipment (annual) Earlier A88.2:C82/14
A88.11/20:v.nos.&nos.	Long staple cotton review
A88.11/21:date	Average premiums and discounts for CCC settlement purposes for offers received, grade and staple differences.
A88.12:date	Weekly summary of fruit and vegetable carlot shipments. Proc. Earlier A82.45:
A88.12/2:date	Weekly summary of F.O.B. prices and fresh fruits and vegetables in representative shipping districts. Proc. Earlier A82.53:
A88.12/3:date	Weekly summary of wholesale prices of fresh fruits and vegetables at New York City and Chicago. Proc. Earlier A82.52:
A88.12/4:date	Consumer purchases of fruits and juices (monthly) Later title, Consumer purchases of citrus and other juices. Proc. Earlier A36.171:, A88.12/4-2: and A88.2:F94/4 Later A93.12:
A88.12/4-2:date	Consumer purchases of fruits and juices by region and retail outlet. Earlier A36.171/2: Later A88.12/4:
A88.12/5:date	Carlot unloads of fruits and vegetables by commodities (monthly) Earlier A82.46:
A88.12/6:dt.&nos	Commercial vegetables TC (series) Proc. Earlier A36.101: Later A92.11:
A88.12/6-2:CT	[Truck crops] TC-series (annual) Earlier A88.2:V52 and V52/2. Later title Vegetables, fresh market [and processing] Later A92.11/10: and A92.11/10-2:

A88.12/7:nos	Fruit situation. Earlier A36.99: Later A93.12/3:
A88.12/8:nos	Vegetable situation. Proc. Earlier A36.100: Later A93.12/2:
A88.12/9:date	Merchantable potato stocks, with comparisons (monthly) Proc. Later title, Total potato stocks. Later A92.11/11:
A88.12/10:date	State carlot shipments of fruits and vegetables, by commodities, counties, and billing stations (annual)
A88.12/11:date	Sour cherry reports (annual) Proc. Earlier A88.2: Later A92.11/3:
A88.12/12:date	Cranberries (annual) Proc. Earlier A88.2:C85 Later A92.11/6:
A88.12/13:date	Hybrid corn (annual) Proc. Earlier A88.2:C81/2
A88.12/14:date	Popcorn production (annual) Proc. Earlier A88.2:P81 Later A92.11/7:
A88.12/15:date	Apples, production by varieties, with comparisons (annual) Proc. Earlier A88.2:Ap5 Later A92.11/9:
A88.12/16:date	Production, farm disposition, and value of principal fruits and tree nuts (annual) Proc. Earlier A88.2:F94
A88.12/17:date	Washington, D.C. unloads of fresh fruits and vegetables (annual) Proc. Earlier A88.2:F94/2
A88.12/18:date	Fruit and vegetable market news, weekly arrival summary. Replaced by A88.12/22:
A88.12/19:date	Potatoes and sweetpotatoes, estimates by States and seasonal groups (annual) Earlier A1.34:190 Later A92.11/4:
A88.12/20:date	Fruits, noncitrus, by State, production, use, value (annual) Proc. Earlier A88.2:F94/9 Later A92.11/2:
A88.12/21:date	Citrus fruits by States, production, use, value (annual) Proc. Earlier A88.2:C49 Later A92.11/8:
A88.12/22:nos	Fresh fruit and vegetable market news, shipments, unloads, weekly summary. WS (series) Proc. Replaces A88.12: and A88.12/18:
A88.12/22-2:date	Fresh fruit and vegetable market news, wholesale market prices summary (annual)
A88.12/23:date	Louisiana annual vegetable summary, Louisiana Crop Reporting Service. Proc.

A88.12/24:date   Annual sweet potato summary; Louisiana Crop Reporting Service. Proc.

A88.12/24-2:date   Sweet potato report, Louisiana Crop Reporting Service

A88.12/25:date   Onion stocks (annual) Earlier A88.2:On4   Later A92.11/12:

A88.12/26:date   Vegetable report, Louisiana Crop Reporting Service

A88.12/27:date   Prospective strawberry acreage, Louisiana Crop Reporting Service

A88.12/28:date   Fresh Products Standardization and Inspection Branch, annual progress report

A88.12/29:date   Marketing of South Carolina peaches, summary of season. Later A88.12/30:CT/dt

A88.12/30:CT/date Market news service on fruits and vegetables. Earlier A36.48: and A88.2:P31

A88.12/31:nos   Fresh fruit and vegetable unloads FVUS(series) Earlier in A88.40/2:

A88.13:date   Monthly domestic dairy markets review. Proc. Earlier A82.38:

A88.13/2:date   Statistical supplement to Monthly domestic dairy markets review. Proc. Earlier A82.38/2:

A88.13/3:date   Monthly egg and poultry markets review. Proc. Earlier A82.39:

A88.13/4:date   Statistical supplement to Monthly egg and poultry market review. Proc. Earlier A82.39/2:

A88.14:date   Evaporated, condensed, and dry milk report (monthly) Proc. Earlier A36.153: Later A92.10/4:

A88.14/2:date   Dairy production (monthly) Proc. Earlier A36.139: Later A92.10:

A88.14/3:date   Fluid milk and cream report (monthly) Proc. Earlier A36.152: Later A92.10/3:

A88.14/4:nos   Dairy situation (bimonthly) Proc. Earlier A36.65: Later A93.13:

A88.14/4a:date   ___ separates

A88.14/5:date   Stocks of evaporated and condensed milk held by wholesale grocers [Later "stocks of" omitted from title] (quarterly) Proc. Earlier A36.161:

A88.14/6:date   Household purchases of butter, cheese, nonfat dry milk solids and margarine (monthly) [Later title Household purchases of butter, fluid whole milk, and other fluid milk.] Proc.

A88.14/7:date   Milk production on farms and statistics of dairy plant products (annual) Earlier A88.2:M59   Later A92.10/6

A88.14/8:date   Milk, farm production, disposition, and income. Proc. Earlier A88.2:M59/2   Later A92.10/2:

A88.14/9:nos   Milk distrubutors, sales and costs MDSC (series) (quarterly) Proc. Later A93.13/2:

A88.14/10:date   Production of manufactured dairy products (annual) Earlier A88.2:D14/5 Later A92.10/5:

A88.14/11:nos   Federal milk order market statistics, summary (monthly) Desig. FMOS- Later A82.81:

A88.14/12:date   Dairy plants surveyed and approved for USDA grading service (semiannual)

A88.15:date   Liquid, frozen, and dried egg production (monthly) Proc. Earlier A36.155: Later A92.9/4:

A88.15/2:date   Canned poultry (monthly) Proc. Earlier A36.170: See, for later information A88.15/9:

A88.15/3:nos   Poultry and egg situation. Proc. Earlier A36.196: Later A93.20:

A88.15/3a:CT   ___ separates. Proc.

A88.15/4:date   Turkeys (and chickens) tested by official State agencies (monthly) Proc. Later A92.9/2:

A88.15/5:date   Hatchery production (monthly) Proc. Earlier A36.154: Later A92.9/6:

A88.15/6:date   Commercial hatchery report. Proc. Earlier A36.205:

A88.15/7:date   Weekly poultry slaughter report. Later titles, Dairy and poultry market news, Commercial poultry/slaughter report. Proc.

A88.15/8:   Dissemination of research results [on poultry & egg marketing subjects] (issued 5 or 6 times a year) Earlier A82.75:

A88.15/9:date   Poultry used in canning and other processed foods. Later title Poultry, canned and processed food, eviscerated, Federal inspection. Later A92.9/5: Monthly.

A88.15/9-2:date   Poultry slaughtered under Federal inspection and poultry used in canning and processed foods (annual)

A88.15/10:date   Chickens raised on farms (annual) Proc. Earlier A88.2:C43/4 Later A92.9/7:

A88.15/10-2:date   Chickens raised, Louisiana Crop Reporting Service

A88.15/11:date	Turkeys raised on farms (annual) Proc. Earlier A88.2:T84/2 Later A92.9/8:
A88.15/11-2:date	Turkeys raised, Louisiana Crop Reporting Service
A88.15/12:date	Turkey breeder hens on farms (annual) Earlier A88.2:T84 Later A92.9/11:
A88.15/13:date	Commercial broiler production (annual) Earlier A88.2:B78 Later A92.9/10:
A88.15/14:date	Chickens and eggs, layers and egg production, monthly (annual) Earlier A88.2:Eg3 Later A92.9/13:
A88.15/15:date	Broiler chicks placed (annual) Earlier A88.2:C43 Later A92.9/14:
A88.15/16:date	Farm production, disposition, cash receipts and gross income, turkeys (annual) Proc. Earlier A88.2:T84/3 Later A92.9/15:
A88.15/17:date	Chickens and eggs, layers and rate of lay, first of each month (annual) Earlier A88.2:C43/2 Later A92.9/12:
A88.15/18:date	Chickens and eggs, farm production, disposition, cash receipts, gross income, chickens on farms, commercial broilers, by States (annual) Proc. Earlier A88.2:C43/3 Later A92.9/3:
A88.15/9:date	Pullet chick replacements for broiler hatchery supply flocks (annual) Later A92.9:
A88.15/20:date	Commercial egg movement report (weekly) Proc.
A88.15/21:date	Broiler chick report, Louisiana Crop Reporting Service
A88.15/22:date	Hatchery production, Louisiana Crop Reporting Service
A88.15/23:date	List of plants operating under USDA poultry and egg inspection and grading programs. Earlier A88.2:P86/2
A88.15/24:date	Broiler marketing facts (quarterly)
A88.15/25:date	Turkey marketing facts
A88.16:date	Receipts and disposition of livestock at public markets (monthly) Proc. Earlier A82.41:
A88.16/2:date	Livestock slaughter by States (monthly) Proc. Earlier A36.162: Superseded by A88.16/9:
A88.16/2-2:date	Livestock slaughter, Louisiana Crop Reporting Service
A88.16/3:date	Pig crop report (semiannual) Earlier A36.2:P62 Later A92.18/7:
A88.16/3-2:date	Pig crop report, Louisiana Crop Reporting Service

A88.16/4:v.nos.&nos. Market news, Livestock Division, Market reviews and statistics (weekly) Proc. Earlier A82.7:

A88.16/5:date P. & S. docket, monthly report of action taken on cases arising under Packers and stockyards act. Earlier A82.14:

A88.16/5-2:v.nos.&nos. Packers and stockyards resumé (monthly) Replaces A88.16/5: Later A96.9:

A88.16/6:date Cattle on feed. Proc. Earlier A36.209: Later A92.18/6:

A88.16/7:date Cattle on feed, Illinois, Iowa, Nebraska, Idaho, and California. Proc.

A88.16/8:nos Livestock and meat situation. Proc. Earlier A36.158: Later A93.15:

A88.16/8a:CT ___ separates

A88.16/9:date Livestock slaughter and meat production (monthly) Proc. Later title, Commercial livestock slaughter and meat production. Supersedes A88.16/2: Later A92.18/3:

A88.16/10:date Calf crop report. Proc. Earlier A88.2:C12 Later A92.18/5:

A88.16/10-2:date Calf crop, Louisiana Crop Reporting Service.

A88.16/11:date Lamb crop report. Proc. Earlier A88.2:C12 Later A92.18/4:

A88.16/12:date Lamb feeding situation (annual) Proc. Earlier A88.2:L16/2:

A88.16/13:date Sheep and lambs on feed (annual) Proc. Earlier A88.2:Sh3 Later A92.18/9:

A88.16/14:date Livestock and poultry inventory (annual) Earlier A88.2:L75/8 Later A92.18/8:

A88.16/15:date Salable [and total] receipts of livestock at public markets in order of volume (annual) Proc. Earlier A88.2:L75

A88.16/16:date Total livestock slaughter, meat and lard production (annual) Proc. Earlier A88.2:L75/3

A88.16/17:date Commercial livestock slaughter, number and live weight, by States, meat and lard production, United States, by months (annual) Later A92.18:

A88.16/18:date Shipments of stocker and feeder cattle and sheep (monthly) Proc. Later A92.18/2:

A88.16/18-2:date Cattle and sheep, shipments of stocker and feeder cattle and sheep into selected North Central States (annual) Earlier A88.2:C29/5

A88.16/19:date Lamb crop and wool production, Louisiana Crop Reporting Service

A88.16/20:date   Working reference of livestock regulatory establishments, stations and officials (monthly) Earlier A77.221/2:   Later A101.15:

A88.17:date   USDA meat production report (weekly) Proc.   Earlier A82.54:

A88.17/2:date   Meat scraps and tankage production (semiannual) Proc.   Later title, Meat, meal and tankage production.   Earlier A88.2:M46   Later A92.17/2:

A88.17/3:date   Meat animals, farm production, disposition, and income by States (annual) Later A92.17:

A88.17/4:CT   Institutional meat purchase specifications

A88.17/5:v.nos.&nos.   Meat hygiene abstracts

A88.17/6:nos   MIP guidelines

A88.17/7:date   Federal meat and poultry inspection statistical summary (annual) Supersedes C & MS-54.   Later A101.6/3:

A88.17/8:nos   C&MS meat and poultry inspection programs: Publications   Later A101.6/2-2:

A88.18:v.nos.&nos.   Grain market news and statistical report (wkly) Proc.   Earlier A82.71:

A88.18/2:v.nos.&nos.   Commercial grain stocks reports (wkly) Proc.   Earlier A82.31:

A88.18/2-2:CT   Commercial grain stocks [revised figures for calendar year] Proc.   Earlier A82.31/2:

A88.18/3:date   Feed market summary (quarterly) Proc.   Earlier A82.35:

A88.18/4:v.nos.&nos.   Weekly feed review.   Proc.   Later title: Feed market news, weekly summary and statistics.   Earlier A82.32:

A88.18/5:date   Alfalfa meal production (monthly) Proc.   Earlier A82.59/2:

A88.18/6:date   Brewers' dried grains production (monthly) Proc.   Earlier A82.59/3:

A88.18/6-2:date   Brewers' dried grains, United States, production and stocks in hands of producers (annual) Proc.   Earlier A88.2:B75

A88.18/7:date   Distillers' dried grains production (monthly) Proc.   Earlier A82.59/3:

A88.18/7-2:date   Distillers' dried grains, United States, production by kinds by months (annual) Proc.   Earlier A88.2:D63

A88.18/8:nos   Wheat situation.   Proc.   Earlier A36.86:   Later A93.11:

A88.18/9:v.nos.&nos.   Weekly rice market review.   Later title Rice market news.   Proc.   Earlier A82.33:

A88.18/10:date   Rice, stocks and **movement: California** mills (monthly) Proc. Earlier
                    A82.49:

A88.18/11:date   Crop production, winter wheat and rye (annual) Proc. Earlier A36.74:
                    Later A92.15/4:

A88.18/12:nos   Feed situation. Earlier A36.117: Later A93.11/2:

A88.18/13:date   Stocks of flaxseed, stocks of soybeans. Proc.

A88.18/13-2:date   Soybeans and flaxseed summary, crop year. Proc.

A88.18/14:date   Stocks of grain in all positions (quarterly) Proc. Earlier A88.2:G76
                    Later A92.15:

A88.18/15:date   Storage capacity of elevators reporting commercial grain stocks (annual)
                    Proc. Earlier A88.2:G76/2

A88.18/16:date   Wheat and rye summary, crop year. Proc.

A88.18/17:date   Rough and milled rice stocks. Proc. Later A92.15/2:

A88.18/18:nos   Rice situation. Earlier A36.130: Later A93.11/3:

A88.18/19:date   Soybeans harvested for beans by countries, acreage, yield production
                    (annual) Earlier A88.2:So9/2 Later A92.15/3:

A88.18/20:v.nos.&nos. Rice market news supplement, rough rice receipts. Wkly. Proc.

A88.18/21:v.nos.&nos. Grain market news, quarterly summary and statistics. Consolidation
                    of separate quarterly reports for wheat, oats, barley, rye, flaxseed,
                    corn, grain sorghums, and soybeans, which were classed A88.42:CT

A88.18/22:date   Crop production: Quarterly grain stocks in farms, revised estimates

A88.18/23:date   Annual rice summary, Louisiana Crop Reporting Service. Proc.

A88.18/24:date   Winter wheat report, Louisiana Crop Reporting Service

A88.18/25:date   Louisiana soybeans for beans, acreage, yield and production

A88.18/26:date   Rice production, Louisiana Crop Reporting Service

A88.18/27:v.nos.&nos. Grain Division news. Administrative.

A88.18/28:v.nos.&nos. Southern rice inspected for export

A88.19:v.nos.&nos Semi-monthly honey report. Later Title Honey market news, semi-monthly **report Proc. Earlier A82.12:**

A88.19/2:date   Honey report (annual) Proc. Earlier A88.2:H75/3   Later A92.28:

A88.19/2-2:date Honey report, Louisiana Crop Reporting Service.

A88.19/2-3:date Honey production

A88.19/3:date   Honey, annual summary. Proc. Earlier A88.2:H75   Later A92.28/2:

A88.20:v.nos.&nos Cold storage report (monthly) Proc. Earlier A82.15:   Later A92.21:

A88.20/2:date   Summary of regional cold storage holdings (annual) Earlier A88.2:C67   Later A92.21/2:

A88.20/3:date   Capacity of refrigerated warehouses in United States. Earlier in A1.34:   Later A92.21/3:

A88.21:date   Farm population, annual estimates by States, major geographical divisions, and regions. Proc. Earlier A36.123:

A88.21/2:date   Number of farms by States. Proc. Earlier A88.2:F22/2

A88.22:CT   Addresses

A88.23:v.nos.&nos. Weekly molasses market report. Later title, Molasses market review. Proc. Earlier A82.62:

A88.24:date   Crop production (monthly) Proc. Earlier A36.39:   Later A92.24:

A88.24/2:CT   Crop report as of ... various crops. Proc. Note: Information appears in Crop production (A88.24:)

A88.24/3:v.nos   Crops and markets (annual) Earlier A36.11/3:   Replaced by A88.26/3:

A88.24/4:date   Crop production, prospective plantings (annual) Earlier A36.38: (This class replaces and cancels A88.30/2:) Later A92.24/2:

A88.24/5:date   Crop values (annual) Earlier A88.2:C88/5   Later A92.24/3:

A88.24/6:date   Louisiana annual crop summary, Louisiana Crop Reporting Service. Proc.

A88.24/7:date   General crop report, Louisiana Crop Reporting Service.

A88.25:date   Farm labor (monthly) Proc. Earlier A36.140:   Later A92.12:

A88.26:date	Marketing activities (monthly) Earlier A82.17: Replaced by A88.26/3:
A88.26/a:CT	___ separates. Proc.
A88.26/2:nos	Marketing and transportation situation (quarterly) Proc. Desig. MTS-nos. Earlier A36.143: Later A93.14:
A88.26/2a:CT	___ separates. Earlier A36.143/a:
A88.26/3:v.nos.&nos.	Agricultural marketing (monthly) Replaces Marketing Activities A88.26:, and Crops and Markets A88.24/3:
A88.26/3a:CT	___ separates
A88.26/4:nos	Acreage-marketing guides (irregular) Earlier A88.2:M34 & some in AMS
A88.26/5:nos	PMG (series)
A88.27:v.nos.&nos.	Agricultural economics research (quarterly) Earlier A36.167: Later A93.26:
A88.27/a:CT	___ separates. Earlier A36.167/a:
A88.28:nos	Statistical summary (monthly) Proc. Earlier A36.151: Later A92.13:
A88.29:date	Naval stores report (monthly) Proc. Earlier A36.177: Later A92.25:
A88.29/2:date	Naval stores report (annual) Earlier A88.2:N22 Later A92.25/2:
A88.30:date	Seed crops. Proc. Earlier A36.176: Later A92.16/a: , A92.19/2:, A92.19/3:
A88.30/2:	Crop production, prospective plantings (annual) Earlier A36.38: Class cancelled. See A88.24/4:
A88.30/3:date	Seed crops annual summary. Proc. Earlier A88.2:Se3/3 Later A92.19/4:
A88.30/4:date	Field and seed crops, farm production, farm disposition, value, by States (annual) Later A92.19:
A88.30/5:date	Vegetable-seed stocks. Proc.
A88.30/6:date	Seed crops, certified seed potato report. Designated Pot 3. Later A92.19/6:
A88.30/7:date	Prosecutions and seizures under the Federal seed act

A88.31:v.nos	Virginia crops and livestock (monthly) Proc. Earlier A36.210: Later A92.22:
A88.32:nos	Fats and oils situation (monthly) Proc. Earlier A36.97: Later A93.23:
A88.33:date	Checklist of reports and charts issued by Agricultural Marketing Service. Supersedes A36.70/2:
A88.33/2:CT	Bibliographies and lists of publications
A88.33/3:CT	[Checklist of reports issued by Agricultural Marketing Service] supplements. Formerly classified as supplements to individual numbers in A88.33: Designated CL-(letters) supplement.
A88.34:date	Tobacco stocks report (quarterly) Proc. Earlier A82.11:
A88.34/2:nos	Tobacco situation (issued 4 times a year). Proc. Earlier A36.94: Later A93.25:
A88.34/3:date	Dark air-cured tobacco market review (annual) Proc. Earlier A88.2:T55/3 Later A88.34/8:
A88.34/4:date	Fire-cured tobacco market review (annual) Proc. Earlier A88.2:T55/6 Later A88.34/8:
A88.34/5:date	Light air-cured tobacco market review (annual) Earlier A88.2:T55/2
A88.34/6:date	Flue-cured tobacco market review (annual) Earlier A88.2:T55
A88.34/7:nos	Weekly tobacco market news summary. Proc.
A88.34/8:date	Fire-cured and dark air-cured tobacco market review (annual) Earlier A88.34/3: and A88.34/4:
A88.34/9:date	Tobacco crop summary
A88.34/10:date	Tobacco market news summary (annual)
A88.35:nos	Wool situation (quarterly) Proc. Earlier A36.159: Later A93.19:
A88.35/a:CT	___ separates
A88.35/2:date	Shorn wool production (annual) Proc. Earlier A88.2:W88/2 Later A92.29:
A88.35/3:date	Wool production and value of sales (annual) Proc. Earlier A88.2:W88/4 Later A92.29/3:
A88.35/4:date	Mohair production and value of sales (annual) Proc. Earlier A88.2:M72 Later A92.29/4:
A88.35/5:date	Wool and mohair prices, marketing year. Later A92.29/2:

A88.36:date	Sugar situation (annual) Proc. Formerly World sugar situation, A36.2:Su3 Later A93.31:
A88.37:nos	National food situation (quarterly) Proc. Earlier A36.147: Later A93.16:
A88.37/a:CT	___ separates
A88.37/2:nos	Plentiful foods. PF-series
A88.38:CT	Posters. Earlier A82.25:
A88.39:nos	H.T.&S. Office reports. Proc. Earlier A77.523:
A88.40:nos	AMS (series)
A88.40/a:CT	___ separates
A88.40/2:nos	C&MS (series) Interim classification Reverted to A88.40:
A88.41:	Special news letter (monthly)
A88.42:CT	Field releases of Agricultural Marketing Service
A88.42/2:CT	State publications issued in cooperation with the Agricultural Marketing Service
A88.43:date	Offices of Processed Products Standardization and Inspection Branch (annual) Earlier A88.2:P94/3
A88.43/2:date	Plants under agreement for plant inspection-pack certification (irregular) Proc. Earlier A88.2:P69. Later title, Plants under USDA continuous inspection, processed fruits and vegetables and related products
A88.44:date	Stocks of hops (semiannual) Proc. Earlier A88.2:H77 Later A92.30:
A88.45:date	Farm telephones (annual) Proc. Earlier A88.2:P56, A88.2:T23
A88.45/2:date	Farm telephone & electricity combined report. Proc. See for separate reports A88.45: and A88.46:
A88.46:date	Farm electricity report (annual) Proc. Earlier A88.2:Eℓ2/3
A88.47:date	Cut flowers, production and sales. Proc. Later A92.32:
A88.48:date	Nursery products, production and sales. Proc. Later A92.31:
A88.49:nos	Mississippi weekly weather-crops bulletin

A88.49/2:date	Louisiana weekly weather and crop bulletin. Proc.
A88.50:date	Type A topics, National school lunch program. Earlier A77.202:Sh3/13 Later A98.10:
A88.51:date	Molasses market news, market summary (annual) Earlier A88.40/2:2/date
A88.52:v./nos.	Official journal of Plant Variety Protection Office
A88.53:date	Egg marketing facts
A88.54:v./nos.	Sugar market news (monthly) Later in A1.115:

A89 Farmer Cooperative Service

The Farmer Cooperative Service was created by Memorandum 1320, supplement 4, of the Secretary of Agriculture, dated Nov. 2, 1953, under authority of Reorganization plan no. 2 of 1953. It was assigned functions of the Cooperative Research and Service Division of the Farm Credit Administration which became an independent agency on Dec. 4, 1953.

A89.1:date	Annual reports
A89.2:CT	General publications
A89.3:nos	FCS bulletins
A89.3/a:nos	Bulletin reprints
A89.4:nos	FCS circulars. Earlier A72.4:
A89.4/2:nos	FCS educational circulars. Formerly in A72.4:
A89.8:v.nos/nos	News for farmer cooperatives (monthly) Earlier A72.10:
A89.8/a:nos	___ reprints. Proc. Earlier A72.10/a2:
A89.9:nos	Summary of cooperative cases. Proc. Earlier A72.18: Replaced by A89.9/2:
A89.9/2:nos	___, legal series (irregular) Proc. Replaces A89.9:
A89.10:CT	Addresses
A89.11:nos	General reports. Proc.
A89.12:nos	Service reports. Proc.
A89.13:CT	Bibliographies and lists of publications
A89.14:nos	Educational aids
A89.15:nos	Information (series)
A89.16:date	Highlights of annual workshop of Farmer Cooperative Service. Earlier A89.2:F2
A89.17:date	Midwest regional member relations conference sponsored by American Institute of Cooperation and Farmer Cooperative Service

A89.17/2:date	North Central Membership Relations Conference
A89.18:date	National research and teaching conference in agricultural cooperation
A89.19:nos	FCS research reports
A89.20:nos	Special report series

A90 Agricultural Conservation Program Service

The Agricultural Conservation Program Branch was taken out of the Production and Marketing Administration and given agency status Jan. 22, 1953. This agency was officially designated Agricultural Conservation Program Serve Nov. 2, 1953.

A90.1:date   Annual reports

A90.2:CT   General publications   Earlier A82.37/2:

A90.8:CT   Agricultural conservation program (by States) handbooks. Earlier A82.37:

A90.9:CT   Addresses

A90.10:date   Agricultural conservation program, statistical summary (annual) Earlier A90.2:St2

A90.10/2:date   Agricultural conservation program, summary (annual)   Earlier A90.2:Su6

Merged with Commodity Stabilization Service by Secretary's memorandum 1446, Supp. 2, dated Apr. 19, 1961, effective Apr. 24, 1961.

A91 Administrative Management Office

A91.1:date   Annual reports

A91.2:C T   General publications

A91.8:nos   OAM publications.

A92 Statistical Reporting Service

The Statistical Reporting Service was established as a program agency within the Department of Agriculture by Memorandum 1446, Supplement 1, of the Secretary of Agriculture, dated April 3, 1961.

A92.1:date   Annual reports

A92.2:CT   General publications

A92.8:CT   Handbooks, manuals, guides.

A92.9:date   Pullet chicks for broiler hatchery supply flocks, Pou 2-7 (series) (monthly) Earlier A88.15/9: Replaced by A92.9/16:

A92.9/2:date   Turkeys and chickens tested, Pou 1-2 (series) (monthly) Earlier A88.15/4: Replaced by A92.9/16:

A92.9/3:date   Chickens and eggs, farm production, disposition, cash receipts and gross income. Designated Pou 2-3. Earlier A88.15/18:

A92.9/4:date   Egg products, liquid, frozen, solids, production, Pou 2-5 (series) (monthly) Earlier A88.15:

A92.9/5:date   Poultry slaughtered under federal inspection and poultry used in canning and other processed foods, Pou 2-1 (series) (monthly) Earlier A88.15/9:

A92.9/6:date   Hatchery production, Pou 1-1 (series) Monthly. Earlier A88.15/5: Replaced by A92.9/16:

A92.9/7:date   Chickens, number raised, preliminary estimates (annual) Desig. Pou 2-2/ Earlier A88.15/10:

A92.9/8:date   Turkeys raised (annual) Earlier A88.15/11:

A92.9/9:date   Turkey breeder hens hatching season intentions. Designated Pou 3-4

A92.9/10:date   Commercial broilers production in 22 States (annual) Designated Pou 2-7 Earlier A88.15/3:

A92.9/11:date	Turkey breeder hens [on farms] (annual) Designated Pou 3-3. Earlier A88.15/12:
A92.9/12:date	Layers, potential layers and rate of lay first of month (annual) Desig. Pou 2-8. Earlier A88.15/17:
A92.9/13:date	Chickens and eggs, layers and egg production (annual) Desig. Pou 2-4. Earlier A88.15/4:
A92.9/14:date	Broiler chicks placed in 22 States. Desig. Pou 2-7. Earlier A88.15/15
A92.9/15:date	Farm production, disposition and gross income, turkeys ... (annual) Desig. Pou 3-1-1. Earlier A88.15/16:
A92.9/16:date	Eggs, chickens and turkeys (monthly) Replaces A92.9/6:, A92.9/2:, A92.9:
A92.9/17:date	Turkeys. Pubs.desig. (Pou 3) Includes material previously in A92.9/9:, A92.9/8:, and A92.9/15:
A92.10:date	Milk production, DA 1-1 (series) Earlier A88.14/2:
A92.10/2:date	Milk production, disposition, and income. Designated DA 1-2(date) Earlier A88.14/8:
A92.10/3:date	Fluid milk and cream report, DA 1-3(series) (monthly) Earlier A88.14/3:
A92.10/4:date	Evaporated, condensed, and dry milk report, Da 2-6 (series) (monthly) Earlier A88.14:
A92.10/5:date	Production of manufactured dairy products (annual) Designated Da 2-1. Earlier A88.14/10:
A92.10/6:date	Milk production and dairy products, annual statistical summary. Designated Da 3. Earlier A88.14/7:
A92.10/7:date	Dairy products weekly. Desig. Da 2-4
A92.11:date	Vegetables, fresh market [and] processing, Vg 2-1 (series) and Vg 3-1 (series) Earlier A88.12/6:
A92.11/2:date	Fruits, noncitrus, by States, production, use, value. Designated FrNt 2-1 Earlier A88.12/20:
A92.11/2-2:date	Noncitrus fruits and nuts (annual) Desig. FrNC 1-3.
A92.11/3:date	Sour cherry report (annual) Designated FrNt 2-4. Earlier A88.12/11:

A92.11/4:date	Potatoes and sweetpotatoes, estimates by States and seasonal groups (annual) Desig. Pot -6. Earlier A88.12/19
A92.11/5:date	Irish potatoes, utilization of crop with comparisons (annual) Desig. Pot 1-3. Earlier A88. 2:P84/6
A92.11/6:date	Cranberries, indicated production (annual) Desig. SpCr 1. Earlier A88.12/12:
A92.11/7:date	Popcorn acreage for harvest (annual) Earlier A88.12/14:
A92.11/7-2:date	Popcorn production
A92.11/8:date	Citrus fruits by States, production, use, value (annual) Desig. FrNt3-1. Earlier A88.12/21:
A92.11/9:date	Commercial apples, production by varieties, with comparisons (annual) Desig. FrNt 2-2-2. Earlier A88.12/15:
A92.11/10:date	Vegetables, processing, annual summary, acreage production, etc. Vg3-2. (series) Earlier A88.12/6-2:V52/2/date
A92.11/10-2:date	Vegetables, fresh market, annual summary, acreage, production, etc., Vg 2-2 (series) Earlier A88.12/6-2:V52/date
A92.11/10-3:date	Total commercial production of all vegetables and melons for fresh market and processing (annual) Earlier A92. 2:V52
A92.11/10-4:date	Celery, Vg 2-1-1 series (monthly)
A92.11/11:date	Total potato stocks, Pot 1-2 (series) (monthly) Earlier A88.12/9:
A92.11/12:date	Onion stocks (annual) Desig. Vg 4. Earlier A88.12/25:
A92.11/13:date	Bush berries production. Desig. FrNt5. Title varies
A92.12:date	Farm labor, La 1 (series) (monthly) Earlier A88. 25:
A92.13:nos	Statistical summary. Earlier A88. 28:
A92.14:date	Peanut stocks and processing (monthly) Earlier A88.10/2:
A92.14/2:date	Peanut stocks and processing, seasonal report, GrLg 11-2-1 (series) Earlier A88.10/2-2:
A92.14/3:date	List, peanut millers (shellers and crushers) Earlier A88.10/3:
A92.14/4:date	List, peanut processors. Earlier A88.10/6:

A92.15:date	**Stocks of grains** in all positions, GrLg 11-1 (series) (quarterly) Earlier A88.18/14:
A92.15/2:date	Rice stocks, rough and milled. Earlier A88.18/17:
A92.15/3:date	Soybeans harvested for beans by countries (annual) Designated GrLg9-1. Earlier A88.18/19:
A92.15/4:date	Crop production, winter wheat and rye (annual) Designated CrPr 2-3 Earlier A88.18/11:
A92.15/5:date	Stocks of soybeans in all positions (annual)
A92.16:date	Agricultural prices. Monthly. Earlier A88.9/3:
A92.16/a:date	Seed crops, reprinted from Agricultural prices. Earlier A88.30:
A92.16/2:date	Agricultural prices, annual summary. Designated Pr1-3. Earlier A88.9/5:
A92.16/3:date	Prices received by farmers for manufacturing grade milk in Minnesota and Wisconsin (annual) Pr 1-4
A92.17:date	Meat animals, farm production, disposition, and income, by States. (annual) Designated MtAn 1-1. Earlier A88.17/3:
A92.17/2:date	Meat meal and tankage production, semiannual report. Desig. MtAn3. Earlier A88.17/2:
A92.18:date	Livestock slaughter (annual) Desig. MtAn 1-2-1 Earlier A88.16/7:
A92.18/2:date	Shipments of stocker and feeder cattle and sheep, MtAn 5-3-3 (series) (monthly) Earlier A88.16/18:
A92.18/3:date	Commercial livestock slaughter and meat production, MtAn 1-3 (series) (monthly) Earlier A88.16/9:
A92.18/4:date	Lamb crop (annual) Desig. MtAn 5-1. Earlier A88.16/11:
A92.18/5:date	Calf crop (annual) Desig. MtAn 2-2. Earlier A88.16/10:
A92.18/6:date	Cattle and calves on feed, cattle sold for slaughter, selected markets, MtAn 2-1 (series) (monthly) Earlier A88.16/6:
A92.18/6-2:date	Cattle inventory, special report on number of cattle and calves on farms by sex and weight (Lv Gn 3-)

A92.18/7:date   Pig crop report. Designated Mt An 4. Earlier A88.16/3:

A92.18/8:date   Livestock and poultry inventory, January 1, number, value and classes. Desig. LvGn 1. Earlier A88.16/1:4:

A92.18/9:date   Sheep and lambs on feed (semiannual) Desig. MtAn 5-2. Earlier A88.16/3:

A92.18/10:date   Western range and livestock report. Desig. MtAn 2-3

A92.18/11:date   **Mink production,** pelts produced in [calendar year] Desig. Mt An 6-

A92.19:date   Field and seed crops, production, farm use, sales, value by States (annual) Designated CrPr 1. Earlier A88.30/4:

A92.19/2:CT   Seed crops forecasts (irregular) Designated Se Hy 1-1. Earlier A88.30:

A92.19/3:CT   Seed crops stock reports (irregular) Designated Se Hy 1-4. Earlier A88.30:

A92.19/4:date   Seed crops, annual summary. Designated Se Hy 1-3. Earlier A88.30/3:

A92.19/5:date   Field seeds, supply and disappearance (annual) Earlier A88.2:Se3/6/date

A92.19/6:date   Seed crops, certified potato report (annual) Desig. Pot 3. Earlier A88.30/6:

A92.20:date   Cotton production, Cn 1 (series) (monthly) Earlier A88.11/5:

A92.21:v.nos.&nos.   Cold storage report, Co St 1 (series) (monthly) Earlier A88.20:

A92.21/2:date   Summary of regional cold storage holdings (annual) Designated CoSt 3-(date) Earlier A88.20/2:

A92.21/3:date   Capacity of refrigerated warehouses in United States. Designated CoSt 2. Earlier A88.20/3:

A92.22:v./nos   Virginia crops and livestock (monthly) Earlier A88.31:

A92.23:v./nos   Agricultural situation (monthly) Earlier A88.8:

A92.24:date   Crop production, CrPr 2-2 (series) (monthly) Earlier A88.24:

A92.24/a:CT   ___ separates

A92.24/2:date   Crop production, prospective plantings (annual) Desig. CrPr 2-4. Earlier A88.24/4:

A92.24/3:date   Crop values, season average prices received by farmers and value of production (annual) Desig. CrPr 2-1-1. Earlier A88.24/5:

A92.25:date	Naval stores (monthly) Earlier A88.29:
A92.25/2:date	Naval stores (annual) Designated SpCr3. Earlier A88.29/2:
A92.26:CT	Addresses
A92.27:date	Tree nuts by States (annual) Designated FrNt 4-1. Earlier A88.10/4:
A92.28:date	Honey report (annual) Designated Hny-7. Earlier A88.19/2:
A92.28/2:date	Honey, annual summary. Designated Hny-1. Earlier A88.19/3:
A92.29:date	Shorn wool production (annual) Designated MtAn 5-3. Earlier A88.35/2:
A92.29/2:date	Wool and mohair prices (annual) Desig. Prl-2. Earlier A88.35/5: Later in A92.29/5:
A92.29/3:date	Wool production and value (annual) Desig. MtAn 5-3. Earlier A88.35/3: Later in A92.29/5:
A92.29/4:date	Mohair production and value (annual) Desig. MtAn 5-3. Earlier A88.35/4: Later in A92.29/5:
A92.29/5:date	Wool and mohair production, price and value (annual) Earlier A92.29/2:, A92.29/3:, A92.29/5:
A92.30:date	Stocks of hops (semiannual) Earlier A88.44: Designated SpCr 6-2.
A92.31:date	Nursery products, production and sales (annual) Desig. SpCr 6-2. Earlier A88.48:
A92.32:date	Cut flowers, production and sales (annual) Desig. SpCr 6-1. Earlier A88.47: Later title, Flowers and foliage plants, production and sale.
A92.33:date	Wheat pasture report (monthly) Desig. MtAn 2-5.
A92.34:nos	SRS (series)
A92.35:CT	Bibliographies and lists of publications
A92.37:date	Consumption of commercial fertilizers and primary plant nutrients in United States (annual) Desig. SpCr 7.
A92.38:date	Exports, outstanding export sales (weekly)
A92.39:date	Acreage. Designated Crpr 2-2

A93 Economic Research Service

The Economic Research Service was established as a program agency within the Department of Agriculture by Memorandum 1446, Supplement 1 of the Secretary of Agriculture dated April 3, 1961.

A93.1:date   Annual reports

A93.2:CT   General publications

A93.8:CT   Handbooks, manuals, guides

A93.9:nos   Farm income situation. Earlier A88.9/2:

A93.9/2:nos   Demand and price situation (monthly) Earlier A88.9:

A93.9/3:nos   Farm cost situation, FCS (series) Earlier A77.14/2: and A77.15:

A93.9/4:nos   Current developments in farm real estate market, CD (series) Earlier A77.13: and A77.15:

A93.9/5:nos   Farm-mortgage lending experience of life insurance companies, Federal land banks, and Farmers Home Administration, FML (series) Earlier in ARS series

A93.9/6:nos   Farm real estate taxes, recent trends and developments, RET-(series)

A93.9/7:date   Deposits of country banks: Index numbers of total, demand, and time deposits, selected groups of States, specified periods (monthly) Earlier A77.14/3:

A93.9/8:nos   Agricultural finance outlook, AFO (series) Formerly in A77.15:

A93.9/9:nos   Farm real estate debt, RED (series)

A93.9/10:nos   Agricultural finance review. Earlier A77.14:

A93.9/10-2:nos   Agricultural finance statistics, AFS (series) Formerly supplement to A93.9/10:

A93.9/11:nos   Costs and returns, FCR (series)

A93.9/12:nos   Farm mortgate debt FMD (series)

A93.10:nos	Agricultural outlook digest (monthly) Earlier A88.8/2:
A93.10/2:nos	Agricultural outlook (11 times annually, Jan.-Feb. issue combined)
A93.11:nos	Wheat situation. Earlier A88.18/8:
A93.11/2:nos	Feed situation (bimonthly) Earlier A88.18/2:
A93.11/3:nos	Rice situation (annual) Earlier A88.18/18:
A93.12:nos	Consumer purchases of citrus and other juices, CPFJ (series) Earlier A88.12/4:
A93.12/2:nos	Vegetable situation (quarterly) Earlier A88.12/8:
A93.12/2a:CT	___ Reprint
A93.12/3:nos	Fruit situation (quarterly) Earlier A88.12/7:
A93.13:nos	Dairy situation (bimonthly) Earlier A88.14/4:
A93.13/2:nos	Milk distributors, sales and costs (quarterly) Earlier A88.14/9:
A93.14:nos	Marketing and transportation situation (quarterly) Earlier A88.26/2:
A93.15:nos	Livestock and meat situation, LMS-nos (bimonthly) Earlier A88.16/8:
A93.15/a:CT	___ separates
A93.16:nos	National food situation, NFS-nos (quarterly) Earlier A88.37:
A93.17:date	Foreign agricultural trade of United States, statistical report (monthly) Earlier A67.19:
A93.17/2:date	Foreign agricultural trade of United States, digest (monthly) Earlier A67.19/8:
A93.17/3:date	Foreign agricultural trade of United States, statistical report for calendar year. Earlier A67.19/2:
A93.17/4:date	Foreign agricultural trade of United states, trade by countries for calendar year. Earlier A67.19/5: and A67.19/4:
A93.17/5:date	Foreign agricultural trade of United States, imports of fruits and vegetables under quarantine by countries of origin and ports of entry, fiscal year. Earlier A67.19/7:
A93.17/6:date	Foreign agricultural trade of United States, fiscal year. Earlier A67.19/3:

A93.17/7:date	Foreign agricultural trade of United States (monthly) Incorporates now discontinued A13.17/2: and A93.17:
A93.17/7a:CT	___ separates
A93.17/8:date	Foreign agricultural trade of United States, annual supplement, trade by commodities, fiscal year
A93.18:nos	Publications received. Earlier A77.16/2:
A93.18/2:CT	Bibliographies and lists of publications
A93.19:nos	Wool situation (quarterly) Earlier A88.35: Later in A93.24/2:
A93.20:nos	Poultry and egg situation (bimonthly) Earlier A88.15/3:
A93.21:nos	ERS (series)
A93.21/2:nos	ERS-foreign (series)
A93.22:CT	Addresses
A93.23:nos	Fats and oils situation, FOS (series) Earlier A88.32:
A93.24:nos	Cotton situation (bimonthly) Earlier A88.11/8: Later in A93.24/2:
A93.24/2:nos	Cotton and wool situation (quarterly) Replaces A93.19: and A93.24:
A93.25:nos	Tobacco situation, TS (series) Earlier A88.34/2:
A93.26:v.nos.&nos.	Agricultural economics research (quarterly) Earlier A88.27:
A93.26/a:CT	___ separates
A93.27:nos	Foreign agricultural economic reports
A93.28:nos	Agricultural economic reports. Later A1.107:
A93.29:date	World agricultural situation (annual) Earlier A67.27:
A93.29/2:nos	World agricultural situation, WAS (series)
A93.30:date	U.S. agricultural exports, fact sheet (annual) Earlier A67.32:
A93.30/2:date	U.S. agricultural imports, fact sheets. Earlier A67.32/2:
A93.31:nos	Sugar situation. Earlier A88.36:
A93.31/2:nos	Sugar and sweetener situation (SSS series) Replaced by A1.115:

A93.32:CT	Indices of agricultural production in [various] countries. Earlier A67.36:
A93.33:v.nos	Farm index (monthly)
A93.33/a:CT	___ separates
A93.34:date	Foreign gold & dollar reserves (semiannual) Earlier A93.2:G57
A93.34/2:nos	WMC - [World Monetary Conditions] Later title, World economic conditions in relation to agricultural trade.
A93.35:v.nos	Net migration of the population, by age, sex, and color
A93.36:nos	Fertilizer situation. See also A82.77:
A93.37:date	FDD field reports
A93.37/2:nos	ERS field reports
A93.38:nos	Foreign economic development reports (numbered) Earlier A100.9:

Cooperative State Research Service, 1964-
A94   Cooperative State Experiment Stations Service

The Cooperative State Experiment Station Service was established in the Department of Agriculture by Secretary's memorandum no. 1462, Supplement 1, dated August 30, 1961.

A94.1:date   Annual reports

A94.2:CT   General publications

A94.9:CT   Addresses

A94.10:nos   CSESS-(series), CSRS series

A94.11:v.nos.&nos. Agricultural science review

A94.11/a:CT   ___ separates

A94.12:nos   Experiment station letters. Admin.

A95 International Agricultural Development Service

The International Agricultural Development Service was established in the Department of Agriculture by Secretary's memorandum no. 1541 of July 12, 1936.

A95.1:date   Annual reports

A95.2:CT   General publications

A95.9:nos   International agricultural development, monthly newsletter to cooperators in agricultural technical assistance and training programs around the world

A95.10:nos   IADS-S (series)

A95.10/2:nos   IADS-C (series)

A95.10/3:nos   IADS-T (series)

A95.11:CT   Addresses

Functions and delegations of authority transferred to Foreign Agricultural Service by Secretary's memorandum of Mar. 28, 1969.

A96 Packers and Stockyards Administration

The Packers and Stockyards Administration was established within the Department of Agriculture by Secretary's memorandum 1613, supplement 1, effective May 8, 1967.

A96.1:date   Annual report

A96.2:CT   General publications

A96.5:CT   Laws

A96.9:v.nos.&nos. Packers and stockyards resumé (biweekly)   Earlier A88.16/5-2:

A96.10:nos   P&SA (series)

A97 Rural Community Development Service

The Rural Community Development Service maintains a working liaison with non-USDA agencies to determine what programs and services would be useful to rural people and communities.

A97.1:date   Annual report

A97.2:CT   General publications

Abolished Feb. 2, 1970, by Secretary's Memorandum 1670 of Jan. 30, 1970, and functions transferred to other agencies within the Department.

A98 Food and Nutrition Service

The Food and Nutrition Service was established by Secretary of Agriculture's Memorandum no. 1695, Supplement 1, August 8, 1969.

A98.1:date   Annual report

A98.2:CT   General publications

A98.8:CT   Handbooks, manuals, guides

A98.9:nos   FNS-(series)

A98.10:date   Type A topics, National school lunch program. Earlier A88.50:

A98.11:v.nos.&nos. Food and nutrition (bimonthly)

A98.11/2:nos   Food and nutrition newsletter

A98.12:date   Reaching people, review of field activities

A99 Export Marketing Service

The Export Marketing Service was established Mar. 28, 1969, by the Secretary of Agriculture under authority of revised statutes (5 U.S.C. 301), and Reorganizztion Plan 2 of 1953.

A99.1:date   Annual report

A99.2:CT   General publications

A99.6:CT   Regulations, rules, and instructions

A99.9:date   Orderly liquidation of stocks of agricultural commodities... annual report by Secretary of Agriculture. Earlier A1.102:

A100 Foreign Economic Development Service

The Secretary of Agriculture established the Foreign Economic Development Service within the Department of Agriculture, Dec.1, 1969.

A100.1:date   Annual report

A100.1/2:date   Annual summary

A100.2:CT   General publications

A100.9:nos   Foreign economic development reports (numbered) Later A93.38:

A100.10:nos   FEDS staff papers (numbered)

Abolished by order of the Secretary on Feb. 6, 1972, and functions and authorities transferred to the Economic Research Service.

A101 Animal and Plant Health Service

The Animal and Plant Health Service was established by Secretary of Agriculture's Memorandum no.1744, Supplement 1, October 29, 1971.

A101.1:date	Annual report
A101.2:CT	General publications. Earlier A77.202:, A77.302:
A101.6:CT	Regulations, rules, and instructions
A101.6/2:date	Meat and poultry inspection regulations
A101.6/2-2:date	Issuances of meat and poultry inspection program Earlier A88.17/8:
A101.6/3:date	Federal meat and poultry inspection statistical series. Earlier A88.17/7:
A101.8:CT	Handbooks, manuals, guides
A101.9:v.nos.&nos.	Cooperative economic insect report (weekly) Earlier A77.324:
A101.9/2:v.nos.&nos.	Cooperative plant pest report (weekly)
A101.10:nos	APHS (series)
A101.10/2:nos	APHIS (series)
A101.11:CT	Plant quarantine import requirements of [various countries]. Earlier A77.329:
A101.12:date	Animal morbidity report (monthly) Earlier A77.229:
A101.12/2:date	Animal morbidity report, calendar year. Earlier A77.229/2:
A101.13:date	Directory of animal disease diagnostic laboratories (annual)
A101.14:nos	Veterinary biologics notices. Earlier A77.226/3:
A101.15:date	Directory of meat and poultry inspection program establishments, circuits and officials. Earlier A88.16/20:
A101.16:date	Equine proplasmosis (EP) progress report, fiscal year Earlier A77.242:

A101.17:date   Foreign animal diseases report

A101.18:date   Cooperative State-Federal tuberculosis eradication program, statistical tables, fiscal year. Earlier in A77.212/5:

A101.19:CT   Bibliographies and lists of publications

A102 Rural Development Service

A102.1:date   Annual report

A102.2:CT   General publications

A102.8:CT   Handbooks, manuals, guides

AA1　ACTION

ACTION was established as an independent agency in the executive branch by Reorganization Plan 1 of 1971, effective July 1, 1971.

AA1.1:date　　　　Annual report

AA1.2:CT　　　　General publications

AA1.8/2:nos　　　Handbooks (numbered)

AA1.9:date　　　　VISTA fact book (monthly)　Earlier PrEx10.21:

AA1.9/2:date　　　Domestic programs fact book.

AA1.10:v.nos.&nos.　Transition, a magazine for former ACTION volunteers (monthly)

AA1.11:nos　　　　ACTION pamphlets

AA1.11/2:nos　　　ACTION flyers

AA1.12:date　　　Bi-annual statistical summary

AA1.13:v.nos.&nos. InterACTION

AA1.14:date & nos. ACTION news digest

AA 2.1: Older Americans Volunteer Programs

Older Americans Volunteer Programs, which consists of a series of programs, was appointed by the President and merged with Action on July 1, 1971.

AA2.1:date   Annual report

AA2.2:CT   General publications

AA2.9:nos   Older Americans in ACTION

AA3 National Student Volunteer Program

National Student Volunteer Program, transferred from the Office of Economic Opportunity, is a part of ACTION established July 1, 1971.

AA3.1:date   Annual reports

AA3.2:CT   General publications

AA3.8:CT   Handbooks, manuals, guides

AA3.9:v.nos.&nos.   Synergist.

AA4 Peace Corps

The Peace Corps functions, powers, and responsibilities were transferred from State Department to ACTION by Reorganization Plan 1 of 1971, effective July 1, 1971.

AA4.1:date   Annual report. Earlier S19.1:

AA4.2:CT   General publications. Earlier S19.2:

AA4.9:date   Bibliographies and lists of publications. Earlier S19.14:

AC Arms Control And Disarmament Agency

The United States Arms Control and Disarmament Agency was established by Public Law 297 of the 87th Congress, 1st session, approved Sept. 26, 1961.

AC1.1:date   Annual reports

AC1.2:CT   General publications

AC1.9:nos   General series

AC1.10:nos   Economic series

AC1.11:nos   Disarmament document series.   Earlier Sl.117/3:

AC1.11/2:date   Documents on disarmament.   Earlier Sl.117:

AC1.12:CT   Addresses

AC1.13:CT   Bibliographies and lists of publications.

AC1.14:date   Report on U.S. Government research and studies in field of arms control and disarmament matters.

AC1.15:nos   Research reports.

AC1.16:date   World military expenditures

AE National Archives Establishment

June 19, 1934 (48 Stat. 1122-24)

AE1.1: date	Annual reports Later GS4.1:
AE1.2: CT	General publications Later GS4.2:
AE1.3: nos	Bulletins Later GS4.3:
AE1.4:	Circulars
AE1.5:	
AE1.6:CT	Regulations, rules, and instructions. Later GS4.6:
AE1.7:nos	National Archives accessions (quarterly) Proc. Later GS4.8:
AE1.8:date	Franklin D. Roosevelt Library, Annual reports of archivist of Later GS4.9:
AE1.9:nos	Staff information circulars. Proc. Later GS4.12:
AE1.10:nos	Preliminary inventories. Later GS4.10:
AE1.11:nos	Special lists. Proc. Later GS4.7:
AE1.12:nos	Reference information circulars. Proc. Later GS4.15:
AE1.13:nos	Miscellaneous processed documents
AE1.14:nos	Records administration studies
AE1.15:nos	Preliminary checklists. Proc.
AE1.16:CT	Addresses
AE1.17:nos	Indexes. Proc.
AE1.18:nos	[Special reports] Proc. Pubs. desig. SR-nos.
AE1.19:nos	Inventories of World War II. Proc.
AE1.20:dt. &nos	Circular letters. Proc.
AE1.21:nos	National Archives facsimiles. Later GS4.11:

Under provisions of Public law 152, 81st Congress, 1st session, effective July 1, 1949, the National Archives Establishment and its functions, personnel, etc., were transferred to the General Services **Administration.**

AE2   Federal Register Division

AE2.1: date	Annual reports. Later GS4.101:
AE2.2:CT	General publications Later GS4.102:
AE2.5:CT	Laws
AE2.6:CT	Regulations, rules, and instructions. Includes handbooks and manuals
AE2.7:vol	Federal register Later GS4.107:
AE2.8:vol	Code of regulations of United States of America
AE2.9:date	Code of Federal regulations of United States of America, Supplements
AE2.10:incl.dts.	Code of Federal regulations of United States, cumulative supplements
AE2.11:date	United States Government manual. Earlier Pr33.407: Later GS4.109:
AE2.12:title nos	Code of Federal regulations, 1949 edition. Earlier AE2.8: Later GS4.108:

AR American Republics Bureau

July 14, 1890 (Stat. L. 26: 275)

AR1.1: date	Annual reports. Later PA1.1:
AR1.2:CT	General publications. Later PA1.2:
AR1.3:nos	Bulletins. Later PA1.3:
AR1.4:nos	Circulars Later PA1.4:
AR1.5:vol	Bulletins
AR1.6:vol	(Monthly) Bulletins Later PA1.6:
AR1.6/a:CT	___ separates
AR1.7:nos	Additions to Columbus Memorial Library
AR1.8:CT	Maps Later PA1.8:
AR1.9:date	International Sanitary Conference of American Republics. Later PA1.9:
AR1.10:v.nos	American constitutions Later PA1.10:
AR1.11:nos	Educational series monographs Later PA1.11: Changed to PA1.11:
AR1.12:dt.&nos	Agriculture. Monthly. Also P. & S. Later PA1.12: Changed to PA1.12:
AR1.13:dt.&nos	Education. Monthly. Also P. & S. Later PA1.13: Changed to PA1.13:
AR1.14:dt.&nos	Finance, industry and commerce. Monthly. Also P. & S. Later PA1.14: Changed to PA1.14:
AR1.15:dt.&nos	Public health and child welfare. Monthly. Also P. & S. Later PA1.15: Changed to PA1.15:
AR1.16:nos	Forestry. Later PA1.16: Changed to PA1.16:
AR1.17:nos	Silvicultura Pan Americana. Later PA1.17: Changed to PA1.17:

NOTE: Classes AR1.18: through AR1.34: changed to PA1.18: through PA1.34:

1907 Bureau Reorganized and name changed to Pan American Union. Many publications originally classed AR have been changed to PA.

C COMMERCE DEPARTMENT

February 14, 1903 (Stat. L32:825)

C1 Office of the Secretary

C1.1:date	Annual reports
C1.1/a:CT	___ separates
C1.2:CT	General publications
C1.2/a:CT	___ separates
C1.3:	Bulletins [none issued]
C1.4:nos	Circulars. See for compilation of circulars in effect July 1911, C16.2:C49
C1.4/2:letters & nos	Department circulars. Lettered.
C1.5:date	Estimates of appropriations for Department of Commerce
C1.6:nos	Decisions
C1.7:CT	Reports on trade conditions
C1.8:CT	Rules and regulations
C1.8/2:nos	Defense Air Transportation administrative orders. Official use. Reprinted from Federal Register
C1.8/3:CT	Handbooks, manuals, guides
C1.8/4:nos	Federal meteorological handbooks
C1.9/1:date	National Council of Commerce, proceedings of annual meetings
C1.9/2:date	___ Proceedings of quarterly meetings of executive committee
C1.10:CT	International conference on safety at sea, Reports
C1.10/2:CT	International conference on safety of life at sea, London, 1929. Later S5.29:
C1.11:CT	Tables to convert [foreign moneys, weights and measures into U.S. standards]
C1.12:CT	Posters
C1.13:CT	Elimination of waste series

C1.14:CT	National Committee on Wood Utilization
C1.15:CT	President's organization on unemployment relief. See also Y3.P92:
C1.16:date	Catalogue of books and blanks furnished by Dept. of Commerce to customs officers
C1.17:CT	Accident prevention conference
C1.18:CT	Addresses
C1.18/2:CT	[Addresses issued as press releases] Irregular. Proc.
C1.19:date	Weekly business survey of key cities. Proc. Varying titles. No. of cities varies.
C1.20:nos	Stories of American industry. Proc.
C1.21:CT	National Conference on Street & Highway Safety, 1st Washington, D.C., Dec.15-16,1924; 4th May 23-25,1934. [Not a Govt. body]
C1.22:pt.nos	St. Lawrence Survey [reports]
C1.23:nos	Banking institutions owned and operated by Negroes; Annual reports. Proc.
C1.24:date (later v.nos)	Business service check list (weekly) Proc.
C1.25:v.nos	Domestic Commerce (monthly) Earlier C18.32:
C1.25/a:CT	___ separates
C1.26:nos	Second decontrol act of 1947; Quarterly report under. Later title, Export control, quarterly reports Later C57.411:
C1.27:nos	World War II history of Department of Commerce. Proc.
C1.28:date	Rubber, annual report
C1.29:v.nos.&nos.	Meritorious suggestions digest. Proc.
C1.30:	Quarterly report of budgetary operations
C1.31:date	Library reference list, selected list of current acquisitions (monthly)
C1.32:CT	Releases. Proc.
C1.32/2:nos	Science and technology news features. Proc.
C1.32/3:nos	Century 21 U.S. science exhibit releases (irregular) Proc.

C1.32/4:date	Department of Commerce trade tips on world markets
C1.32/5:date	Commercial news letter. Administrative.
C1.32/6:date	Domestic and international business news to use for trade association periodicals
C1.32/7:nos	Telecommunications Office: Press releases
C1.33:nos	Patent abstract series. Proc.
C1.34:nos	Employee survival bulletin. [Admin.]
C1.35:nos	Supervision series. Proc. [Admin.]
C1.36:nos	Department orders. Proc. [Admin.]
C1.37:date	Telephone directory. Earlier C1.2:T23 [Admin.]
C1.38:nos	Commerce log. [official use]
C1.39:date	Commerce budget in brief, fiscal year. [official use only] [Some issues entitled Commerce operating budget in brief.
C1.40:nos	Commerce news digest. [for official distribution]
C1.41:date	Outlook and year-end economic review. Earlier C1.2:Ec7/2
C1.42:v./nos	Export expansion tidings. Issued by National Export Expansion Council Official use.
C1.42/2:v/nos	Export Expansion Council news. Administrative.
C1.42/3:CT	National Export Expansion Council publications.
C1.43:v./nos	Field services newsletter
C1.44:date	List of export licenses approved
C1.45:nos	Statistical profile, redevelopment area series. Replaces C3.228:
C1.45/2:nos	Statistical profiles, rural redevelopment areas, Sp (series)
C1.46:CT	Export origin studies [by State]
C1.47:CT	Great Lakes Pilotage Administration publications
C1.48:nos	Staff reports. Issued by Office of Assistant Secretary of Commerce for Science and Technology

C1.49:nos	TDC employee news bulletin. Published for employees of Technical Documentation Center.
C1.50:nos	Overseas business reports OBR (series) Earlier C42.20: Later C57.11:
C1.51:date	Trade center announcements
C1.52:nos	Northeast Corridor Transportation Project technical papers
C1.53:nos	State Technical Services newsletter. Issued by Office of State Technical Services.
C1.53/2:date	Office of State Technical Services annual report
C1.53/3:date	List of State designated agencies, official and working contacts. Earlier C1.2:St2/6
C1.53/4:nos	Office of State Technical Services press releases
C1.54:CT	Bibliographies and lists of publications
C1.54/2:date	United States Department of Commerce publications, a catalog and index. Earlier C1.2:P96
C1.55:nos	DIB computer news
C1.56:date	Directory of private programs for minority business enterprise
C1.57:nos	Minority business Enterprise Office: Press releases
C1.57/2:date	OMBE [Office of Minority Business Enterprise] outlook. Later C1.57/4:
C1.57/3:date	National roster of minority professional consulting services
C1.57/4:date	Access. Formerly entitled OMBE Outlook and classified C1.57/2:
C1.57/5:date	Marketing and procurement briefs
C1.58:v.nos.&nos	Commerce today (biweekly) Replaces C42.8:
C1.58/a:CT	___ separates
C1.58/2:v./nos	Commerce America (bimonthly)
C1.59:nos	Ionospheric predictions (monthly) Earlier C52.10:

Cl. 60:nos	OT/ITS research reports. Issued by Office of Telecommunications. Institute of Telecommunications Sciences
Cl. 60/2:nos	OT special publication, OT-SP- (series)
Cl. 60/3:dt-nos	OT report (series) Office of Telecommunications
Cl. 60/4:nos	OT bulletin
Cl. 60/5:date	IRAC gazetter (annual)
Cl. 60/6:nos	TELE-IRAC (series) Office of Telecommunications
Cl. 60/7:nos	OT contractor report. Telecommunications Office
Cl. 61:date	Interagency Auditor Training Center bulletin
Cl. 62:CT	Technology assessment and forecast publications. Earlier Cl. 2:T22/5 and Cl. 62:T22 Later C21. 24:
Cl. 63:CT	Posters
Cl. 64:CT	Country commercial program for [various countries]
Cl. 65:date	Nevada today, development in business, technology and international trade

C2 Alaska Fisheries Division

July 1, 1903 - certain functions of Special Agents Division of Treasury Dept. (T35)

C2.1:date   Annual reports on salmon fisheries. Earlier T35.6:

C2.2:CT   General publications

C2.3:   Bulletins [none issued]

C2.4:   Circulars [none issued]

Division abolished December 28, 1909. Functions transferred to Fisheries Bureau (C6)

C3   Census Bureau

On July 1, 1903, the Census Office was transferred from the Department of the Interior to the Department of Commerce and Labor under the name Bureau of the Census. January 1, 1972 the Bureau of the Census became a part of the Social and Economic Statistics Administration. Bureau of the Census restored as a primary operating unit of Department of Commerce, effective Aug. 4, 1975.

C3.1:date	Annual reports Later C56.201:, C3.1:
C3.2:CT	General publications Later C56.202:, C3.2:
C3.2/a:CT	___ separates
C3.3:nos	Bulletins
C3.3/a:CT	___ separates
C3.3/2:v./nos	Census bulletins, official information for census employees
C3.4:nos	Circulars
C3.4/2:nos	Circular letter
C3.5:CT	Special reports
C3.5/a:CT	___ separates
C3.6:CT	Instructions Later C56.206:, C3.6:
C3.6/2:CT	Handbooks, manuals, guides. Later C56.208:, C3.6/2:
C3.7:nos	Manufactures division. Special bulletins
C3.8/1:vol	Philippine Islands census, 1903. Reports
C3.8/2:nos	Philippine Island census, 1903. Bulletins
C3.9:date	Cotton ginning reports. Later C3.20:
C3.10:date	Official register of the United States. Earlier I1.25: Later CS1.31:
C3.10/a:CT	___ separates
C3.11:CT	Heads of families at 1st census, 1790
C3.12:nos	Forest products [series 1907]

C3.12/2:nos	Forest products, 1908
C3.12/3:nos	Forest products, 1909
C3.12/4:nos	Forest products, 1910
C3.12/5:nos	Forest products, 1911
C3.12/6:nos	Forest products, 1912
C3.12/7:CT and date	Manufactures division. Special bulletins
C3.13:CT	List of publications (by subject)
C3.14/1:CT	13th census, 1910. Bulletins, Population (by States)
C3.14/2:CT	13th census, 1910. Bulletins, Agriculture (by States)
C3.14/3:CT	13th census, 1910. Bulletins, Manufactures (by States)
C3.14/4:CT	13th census, 1910. Bulletins, Mines (by States)
C3.14/5:CT	13th census, 1910, Bulletins [Misc.] (by States)
C3.14/6:CT	13th census, 1910, General bulletins
C3.14/7:CT	13th census, 1910. Special bulletins
C3.14/8:CT	13th census, 1910. Bulletins, Irrigation (by States)
C3.15:CT	Abstracts, 13th census, 1910, with supplements only for individual States (by States)
C3.15/a:CT	___ supplements only for individual States (by States)
C3.16:vol	Census reports (final volumes) 13th census, 1910
C3.16/a:CT	___ separates
C3.17:CT	Press summaries, 13th census, 1910.
C3.18/1:nos	Tobacco reports, Semi-annual
C3.18/2:latest date covered.	Tobacco reports (advance information)
C3.19:nos	Circulars of information
C3.20:date	Report on cotton ginned (preliminary report on postal cards) Earlier C3.9: Later C3.239/3:, C3.20:

C3.20/2:CT&date   Cotton ginned (by States) Proc.

C3.20/3:nos   Cotton ginnings: Report on cotton ginnings by countries. Proc. Desig. A20:nos Later C56.239:, C3.20/3:

C3.20/4:date   Cotton ginnings: Consolidated cotton report. Proc.

C3.21:date   Report of cotton consumed, on hand, imported, and exported, and active spindles (preliminary report)

C3.22:date   Cotton seed crushed and linters obtained

C3.23:CT   Special census, 1923, High Point, N.C.; Virgin Islands 1917

C3.24/1:date   Biennial census of manufactures (final volumes) Later C56.244:

C3.24/1a:CT   ___ separates

C3.24/2:CT   ___ Final volumes. separates. Later C56.244/2:

C3.24/3:date and CT ___ Bulletins (by States) Later C56.244/7:

C3.24/4:date and CT ___ Bulletins (by principal industries) Later C56.244/6:

C3.24/5:   ___ Press summaries

C3.24/6:CT   Rules, regulations and instructions

C3.24/6a:CT   ___ separates

C3.24/7:CT   Census of manufactures. Maps.

C3.24/8:ser.nos   ___, preliminary reports. Proc. Later C56.244/5:

C3.24/8-2:dt./le&nos ___. Industry and product reports

C3.24/8-3:dt/nos ___: Preliminary general statistics

C3.24/8-4:dt/le-nos ___: Area report MC(P)-S series (irregular) Proc.

C3.24/9:le-nos   Annual survey of manufactures series MAS-nos. Later Desig. M(date)(AS)-nos

C3.24/9-2:date   Annual survey of manufactures. Later C56.221/2:, C3.24/9-2:

C3.24/9-3:CT   Annual survey of manufactures reports

C3.24/9-4:CT   Annual survey of manufactures, miscellaneous publications

C3.24/9-5:date   Publication announcement and order form, Annual survey of manufactures.

C3.24/10:date   Announcements, Census of manufactures. Later C56.244/4:

C3.24/11:date-nos Census of manufactures, Puerto Rico. Earlier C3.24/2:P96 Later in C56.259:

C3.24/12:date/MC-nos Census of manufactures: Subject bulletin MC-(series) Later C56.244/8:

C3.24/13:dt.&nos   Census of manufactures: [Special reports] bulletin MC- (series)

C3.24/13-2:dt/nos ___ : Special report MC58(1)-D11 (series)

C3.24/14:pt.nos   Location of manufacturing plants by industry, county, and employment size. Later in C3.24/15:

C3.24/15:dt./nos   Census of manufactures: Supplementary reports, Special reports, Mc58(S)-series. Series title varies, but designation is always MC(date)(S) Later C56.244/3:

C3.25:date   Cottonseed received, crushed, and on hand, etc. Preliminary report

C3.26:date   Birth, still-birth and infant mortality statistics, Annual report

C3.27:CT   Census of war commodities

C3.28:   14th Census, 1920

C3.28/1:date   Annual reports

C3.28/2:CT   General publications

C3.28/3:   Bulletins

C3.28/4:   Circulars

C3.28/5:vol   Final reports

C3.28/5a: ___ separates

C3.28/6:CT   Rules, regulations and instructions

C3.28/7:date   Abstracts and compendium

C3.28/7a:CT   ___ separates

C3.28/8:CT	Bulletins. Population (by States)
C3.28/9:CT	Bulletins. Population (misc.) [including occupations]
C3.28/10:CT	Bulletins. Agriculture (by States)
C3.28/11:CT	Bulletins. Agriculture (misc.)
C3.28/12:CT	Bulletins. Irrigation
C3.28/13:CT	Bulletins. Drainage
C3.28/14:CT	Bulletins. Manufactures (by States)
C3.28/15:CT	Bulletins. Manufactures (by industries)
C3.28/16:CT	Bulletins. Forest products
C3.28/17:CT	Bulletins. Mines and quarries (by States)
C3.28/18:CT	Bulletins. Mines and quarries (by industries)
C3.28/19:CT	State compendiums
C3.29:CT	Press notices
C3.30:nos	Census monographs
C3.30/a:CT	___separates
C3.31a:CT	___summary statistics
C3.31/1:date	Census of agriculture, 1925, Final volumes. (referred to at times as Farm Census)
C3.31/1a:CT	___ separates.
C3.31/2:CT	Census of agriculture, 1935- (by States)
C3.31/3:CT	Census of agriculture, 1935- 2d series (statistics by counties)
C3.31/4:CT	Census of agriculture, 1935- Miscellaneous. Later C56.227:
C3.31/4:vol/pt	Census of agriculture: Final volumes - area reports. Later C56.227:
C3.31/5:CT	Agriculture, census of ... Special reports. Later C56.227/2:date
C3.31/6:CT	___ sample census of agriculture
C3.31/7:nos	___ farms, farm characteristics, farm products, preliminary reports, Series AC54-1. Proc. Later C56.227/4:

C3.31/8:dt.&nos	Announcements, Census of agriculture.
C3.31/9:date	Census of agriculture, v. 2. General report Later C56.227/3a:
C3.31/9a:dt/CT	___ separates
C3.31/10:dt./CT	Sheets of National atlas of United States. For other sheets and later editions, C3.62/3:
C3.31/11:dt./nos	Census of agriculture, statistics by subjects, Series AC54-3 (irregular) Proc.
C3.31/12:dt/v.nos___:	Final volumes [other than area reports, general reports, and special reports]. Later C56.227/3:
C3.31/13:CT	Census of agriculture, County data, [by county]
C3.32:date	Cotton production, crop of. Changed from C3.2:C82/3 Later C56.239/2:
C3.33/1:date	Survey of current business. Monthly. Later C18.35:
C3.33/2:CT	Record book of business statistics
C3.34:date	Survey of current business, weekly supplements. Later C18.36:
C3.35:date	Census of religious bodies. Changed from C3.2:
C3.35/a:CT	___ separates
C3.36:date	Supply and distribution of cotton in United States
C3.37:	15th Census, 1930
C3.37/1:date	Annual reports
C3.37/2:CT	___ separates
C3.37/3:	Bulletins
C3.37/4:	Circulars
C3.37/5:CT	Final volumes
C3.37/5a:CT	___ separates
C3.37/5a/2:	___ separates from Agriculture volumes
C3.37/6:CT	Rules, regulations and instructions

C3.37/7:date	Abstract
C3.37/8:CT	Population bulletins, 1st series (by States)
C3.37/9:CT	Population bulletins, 2d series (by States)
C3.37/10:CT	Population bulletins. Families
C3.37/11:CT	Agriculture (by States)
C3.37/12:CT	Agriculture, 1st series (by States)
C3.37/13:CT	Agriculture, 2d series (by States)
C3.37/14:CT	Agriculture, 3d series (by States)
C3.37/15:CT	Agriculture (miscellaneous reports)
C3.37/16:CT	Unemployment bulletins (by States)
C3.37/17:CT	Census of distribution (by place names) Preliminary
C3.37/17a:CT	___ separates
C3.37/18:CT	Census of distribution, merchandising series
C3.37/19:CT	Census of distribution. Preliminary reports, States summary series (by States)
C3.37/20:CT	Census of distribution. County series, preliminary (by States)
C3.37/21:CT	Census of distribution. Construction industry, State series
C3.37/22:CT	Census of distribution. Retail distribution (by States)
C3.37/23:CT	Census of distribution. Wholesale trade bulletins, State series
C3.37/24:CT	Irrigation, agricultural lands (by States)
C3.37/25:CT	Drainage of agricultural lands (by States)
C3.37/26:CT	Manufactures. Industry series
C3.37/27:CT	Manufactures (miscellaneous)
C3.37/28:CT	Manufactures. State series
C3.37/30:CT	Final bulletins (U.S. Territorial possessions)

C3.37/31:CT	Occupational statistics
C3.37/32:CT	Census of mines and quarries
C3.37/33:CT	Census of mines and quarries (by States)
C3.37/34:CT	Census of distribution. Distribution of agricultural commodities
C3.37/35:CT	Census of distribution. Wholesale distribution. Trade series
C3.37/36:CT	Census of distribution. Hotels. Preliminary report
C3.37/37:CT	Census of distribution. Wholesale distribution. Special series
C3.37/38:CT	Census of distribution. Small city and rural trade series
C3.37/39:CT	Census of distribution. Retail distribution. Trade series
C3.37/40:CT	Census of distribution. Retail distribution. Special series
C3.38:dt.&CT	Census of electrical industries
C3.38/2:CT	___ Instructions for preparing reports
C3.38/2:dt.&nos	___ Electric light and power plants
C3.39:dt.(later v.)	Summary of mortality from automobile accidents. Monthly
C3.40:date	Mortality statistics
C3.41:vol	Weekly health index. Later FS2.107:
C3.41/2:date	Weekly health index, annual mortality summaries. Proc.
C3.42:date	Leather gloves and mittens. Monthly. **Multigraphed**
C3.43:date	Production of boots and shoes. Monthly.
C3.44:date	Harness leather and skivers, Preliminary report on. Monthly
C3.45:date	Report on hides, skins and leather. Monthly.
C3.46:date	Marriage and divorce. Annual reports
C3.47:date	Financial statistics of cities having a population of over 30,000
C3.47/2:date	Financial statistics of cities having a population of over 100,000. Later C3.142:

C3.48:date	Financial statistics of States. Later C3.141:
C3.49:CT	Financial statistics of State and local government (Compilation) Earlier C3.2:W37/2-3
C3.49/2:date	Financial statistics of State and local government
C3.50:CT	Digest of State laws relating to taxation and revenue
C3.51:date	Activity of machinery in wool manufactures. Monthly. Mimeo.
C3.52:date	Wool consumption reports. Monthly. Mimeographed
C3.52/2:date	Wool stocks reports. Quarterly. **Rotoprinted.** Superseded by C3.52/3:
C3.52/3:date	Commercial stocks of wool and related fibers, tops, noils, waste clips and rags in U.S. (quarterly) Supersedes C3.52/2:
C3.52/4:date	Wool manufactures (monthly) Proc.
C3.53:date	Activity in cotton spinning industry. Monthly. Mim.
C3.54:date	Physician's pocket reference to international list of causes of death. Changed from C3.2:
C3.55:date	Manufacture and sale of farm equipment. Changed from C3.2:
C3.56:date	Animal and vegetable fats and oils. Changed from C3.2:
C3.57:nos	Distribution of sales (Rotoprint) Pubs.desig. IG- (Industry group) nos.
C3.58:date	Current industrial reports (Multigraphed) Changed from C3.2:
C3.59:date	Mental patients in State hospitals. Changed from C3.2: Later FS2.59:
C3.59/2:date	Patients in hospitals for mental disease
C3.60:date	Mental defectives and epileptics in State institutions. Changed from C3.2:
C3.61:CT	Maps (Minor civil divisions)
C3.62:CT	Maps (county outline)
C3.62/2:CT	Maps (miscellaneous) Includes U.S. outline maps. Later C56.242/3:
C3.62/3:CT	Sheets of National Atlas of United States. See also C3.31/10:
C3.62/4:nos	United States maps, GE-50 (series) Later C56.242:, C3.62/4:

C3.62/5:date	Congressional district atlas. Earlier C3.62/2:C76/2 Later C56.213/2:
C3.62/6:CT	State county subdivision maps
C3.62/7:nos	Urban atlas, tract data for standard metropolitan statistical areas, GE80 (series) Earlier C56.242/4:
C3.62/8:nos	GE-70 Map series. Earlier C56.242/2:
C3.63:date	Knit wool gloves and mittens
C3.64:date	Work clothing (garments cut) Monthly.
C3.65:CT	Census of American business, 1933. Proc.
C3.66:date	Weekly business survey of 33 cities. Proc. Varying titles. Number of cities varies.
C3.67:vol	Vital statistics, Special reports. Proc. Later FS2.109:
C3.67/a:CT	___ separates
C3.67/2:CT	___ abstracts
C3.68:date	Air conditioning systems and equipment. Proc. Monthly. Title varies slightly.
C3.69:date	Automobile financing. Monthly. Proc.
C3.70:date	Automobiles. Monthly. Proc.
C3.71:date	Babbitt metal. Monthly. Proc. Beginning Jan.1936, title reads White-base antifriction bearing metals.
C3.72:date	Bathroom accessories (recessed and attachable, all clay) monthly. Proc.
C3.73:date	Cellulose plastic products (nitro-cellulose and cellulose acetate sheets, rods and tubes). Monthly. Proc.
C3.74:date	Commercial steel castings. Monthly. Proc.
C3.75:date	Convection-type radiators. Monthly. Proc.
C3.76:date	Distillate oil burners. Monthly. Proc.
C3.77:date	Domestic pumps, water systems, and windmills, Shipments of. Monthly. Proc.

C3.78:date	Domestic water softening apparatus, Shipments of. Monthly. Proc.
C3.79:date	Edible gelatin. Quarterly. Proc.
C3.80:date	Electrical industrial trucks and tractors. Monthly. Proc.
C3.81:date	Electric locomotives (mining and industrial) Quarterly. Proc.
C3.82:date	Electrical goods. Quarterly. Proc.
C3.83:date	Fabricated steel plate. Monthly. Proc.
C3.84:date	Fire extinguishing equipment, Report of shipments. Monthly. Proc.
C3.85:date	Floor and wall tile (except quarry tile) Monthly. Proc.
C3.86:date	Galvanized range boilers and tanks for hot water heaters. Monthly. Proc. Earlier title Range boilers
C3.87:date	Hosiery. Monthly. Proc.
C3.88:date	Lacquers, Sales of. Quarterly. Proc.
C3.89:date	Malleable iron castings. Monthly. Proc.
C3.90:date	Measuring and dispensing pumps, gasoline, oil, etc. Shipments of. Monthly. Proc. Title varies slightly.
C3.91:date	Mechanical stokers. Monthly. Proc.
C3.92:date	Men's, youth's and boys' clothing cut. Monthly. Proc. Title varies slightly.
C3.93:date	Oil burners. Monthly. Proc.
C3.94:date	Paint, varnish, lacquer, and fillers. Monthly. Proc. Title varies.
C3.95:date	Paperboard. Monthly. Proc.
C3.96:date	Plastic paints, cold water paints, and calcimines. Monthly. Proc.
C3.97:date	Plumbing brass. Monthly. Proc.
C3.98:date	Porcelain enameled flat ware. Monthly. Proc.
C3.99:date	Porcelain plumbing fixtures (all clay) Monthly. Proc.
C3.100:date	Prepared roofing. Monthly. Proc.

C3.101:date   Production of methanol. Monthly. Proc.

C3.102:date   Public merchandise warehousing. Monthly. Proc.

C3.103:date   Pulverizers, for pulverized fuel installations, New orders for. Monthly. Proc.

C3.104:date   Pyroxylin-coated textiles. Monthly. Proc.

C3.105:date   Railroad locomotives. Monthly. Proc.

C3.106:date   Steel barrels and drums. Monthly. Proc. Title varies slightly.

C3.107:date   Steel boilers. New orders. Monthly. Proc.

C3.108:date   Steel office furniture, shelving, and lockers, and fireproff safes. Monthly. Proc.

C3.109:date   Structural clay products (common brick, face brick, vitrified paving brick, hollow building tile) Monthly. Proc.

C3.110:date   Sulphuric acid, production, stocks, etc. Reported by fertilizer manufacturers. Monthly. Proc.

C3.111:date   Superphosphates, production, etc., reported by fertilizer manufacturers. monthly. Proc.

C3.112:date   Terra cotta. Monthly. Proc.

C3.113:date   Underwear and allied products. Monthly. Proc.

C3.114:date   Vitreous-china plumbing fixtures. Monthly. Proc.

C3.115:date   Wheat and wheat-flour stocks held by mills. Quarterly. Proc.

C3.116:date   Wheat ground and wheat-milling products. Monthly. Proc.

C3.117:date   Wheat ground and wheat-milling products, by States. Monthly. Proc.

C3.118:date   Wheat ground and wheat-milling products, merchants and other mills. (quarterly) Proc.

C3.119:date   Red cedar shingles. Quarterly.

C3.120/1:CT   Census of business, 1935. Final reports. Proc.

C3.120/1a:CT   ___ separates. Retail reports. Proc.

C3.120/2:CT	Census survey of business, 1937-38. [Reports] Proc.
C3.121:date	Soybean crush products. Quarterly. Proc. Preliminary report
C3.122:date	Production of linseed oil. Quarterly. Proc. Preliminary report
C3.123:date	Production, consumption, and stocks of fats and oils. Quarterly. Proc. Preliminary report
C3.124:date	Fats and oils subjected to supphonation. Quarterly. Proc.
C3.125:date	Cottonseed products manufactured and on hand at oil mills by States
C3.126:date	The Registrar. Monthly. Proc. Later FS2.11:
C3.127:date	Monthly vital statistics bulletins. Proc. Later FS2.110:
C3.128:vol	Weekly accident bulletins. Proc.
C3.128/2:date	Weekly accident bulletins, annual summaries. Proc.
C3.128/3:date	Motor vehicle accident fatalities; Summary of (quarterly)
C3.129:date	Knit fabric gloves. Monthly. Proc.
C3.130:date	Imported dates packed and shipped. Monthly. Proc.
C3.131:nos	Negro statistics bulletin. Proc. Transferred from C18.19:
C3.132:CT	Addresses. Proc. Later C56.257:
C3.133:date	Wholesale trade. Monthly. Proc. Earlier C18.196: Later C56.219:, C3.133:
C3.134:date	Statistical abstract of United States. Earlier C18.14: Later C56.243:, C3.134:
C3.134/a:CT	___ separates. Later C56.243/a:, C3.134/a:
C3.134/2:CT	Supplements to Statistical Abstract of United States. Later C56.243/2:, C3.134/2:
C3.134/2a:CT	___ separates
C3.134/3:date	Pocket data book (biennial) Later C56.243/3:, C3.134/3:
C3.134/4:nos	Congressional district data, CDD-(series) Later C56.213:, C3.134/4:
C3.135:date	Monthly comparative sales of confectionery and competitive chocolate products. Earlier C18.72/11:

C3.136:date	Quarterly canned foods stocks reports. Proc. Earlier C18.72/12:
C3.137:date	List of reports and publications relating to vital statistics
C3.138:date	Retail sales, independent stores, summary for States. Monthly. Proc.
C3.138/2:date	Retail trade report, United States summary; Monthly. Proc.
C3.138/3:date	Monthly retail trade report, United States and selected areas and cities. Proc. **Supersedes C3.173-181: Later C56.219/4:, C3.138/3:**
C3.138/3-2:date	Retail trade annual report. Earlier in C3.138/3: Later C56.219/4-2:
C3.138/4:date	Advance retail sales report (monthly) Proc. Later C56.219/6:
C3.138/5:date	Weekly sales of retail stores Later C56.219/7:
C3.139:date	Vital statistics of the United States. Prior to 1937, vital statistics data compiled by Census Bureau were published annually in two volumes, Mortality statistics (C3.40:) and Birth, stillbirth and infant mortality statistics (C3.26:) Later FS2.112:
C3.140:dt.&nos	State and local government quarterly employment survey. Proc. Later title Government employment
C3.140/2:nos	Government employment, GE-(series) Later C56.209/2:, C3.140/2:
C3.141:vol(later dt.&nos.)	Financial statistics of States. Earlier C3.48: Later title State finances. Later in C3.191/2:
C3.142:vol	Financial statistics of Cities. Earlier C3.47: Later title City finances. Later in C3.191/2:
C3.143:date	Blowers, fans, unit heaters, and accessory equipment (quarterly) Proc. Prior to Jan.1940 data included in C3.68:
C3.144:date	Warm-air furnaces, winter-air-conditioning systems, and accessory equipment (quarterly) Proc. Prior to Jan.1940 included in C3.68:
C3.145:nos	State and local government special studies. Proc. Later C56.231: Later C3.145:
C3.145/2:dt.&nos	Census of governments advance release CGA (series) Proc.
C3.145/3:date	Census of governments, announcement
C3.145/4:dt./v.nos.&nos.	Census of **governments** Later C56.247/2:
C3.145/4a:CT	___ separates

C3.145/5:dt./nos	Census of governments: Preliminary reports Later C56.247:
C3.145/6:dt./nos	Quarterly tax reports G-TR (series) Later C56.231/2:, C3.145/6:
C3.146:date	Illuminating glassware manufactures, sales and credits. Monthly.
C3.147:date	Monthly (later Quarterly) summary of foreign commerce of United States. Earlier C18.7:
C3.148:date	Cotton linters produced and on hand at oil mills by type of cut, by States (monthly) Preliminary. Superseded by C3.149:
C3.149:date	Cottonseed received, crushed and on hand; cotton linters produced; and linters on hand at oil mills (monthly) Preliminary reports. Supersedes C3.25: and C3.148:
C3.150:letters	Schedules. Earlier C18.18/1: Later C56.210/3:, C3.150:
C3.150/2:nos	___ changes. Proc.
C3.150/3:nos	[Collectors' bulletin] Proc. Pubs.desig. C.B. nos.
C3.150/4:date	United States import duties annotated for statistical reporting. Later TC1.35/2:
C3.150/5:nos	United States import duties annotated, public bulletins. Later TC1.35/2:
C3.150/6:date	U.S. imports for consumption & general imports, tariff schedules annotated by country (annual)
C3.151:dates	Sales finance companies (monthly) Proc. Replaces C3.69:
C3.152:vol	Current mortality analysis (monthly) Later FS2.108:
C3.153:date	Elections
C3.154:date	Animal and vegetable fats and oils by classes of products, Factory consumption of (quarterly)
C3.155:nos	Labor force, Monthly reports on. Proc.
C3.156:nos	Labor force bulletin
C3.157:date	United States exports of domestic merchandise to Latin American republics. Proc.
C3.157/2:date	United States exports of foreign merchandise to Latin American republics
C3.157/3:date	United States general imports from Latin American republics. Proc.

C3.157/4:date	United States exports of domestic and foreign merchandise to Canada (including lend-lease exports) Proc.
C3.157/5:date	United States general imports from Canada, excluding strategic and critical materials and military equipment
C3.158:series nos.	Facts for industry. Later title, Current industrial reports. Later C56.216:, C3.158:
C3.159:date	Foreign commerce and navigation of United States. Earlier C18.19:
C3.160:series CA-nos.&nos.	Population [congested areas] Proc.
C3.161:dt.&nos	Population, special reports. Proc.
C3.162:nos	State documents. Proc.
C3.163:v.nos.-pt.nos.&nos.	Census publications. Proc. See for other lists of census publications C3.2:P96/3, C3.2:P96/4, C3.13:CT&date and C3.19: Later C3.163/2:, C3.163/3:
C3.163/2:date	Census publications, list of publications issued (monthly) Formerly C3.163:2 Later C56.222/2:, C3.163/2:
C3.163/3:date	Census publications, catalog and subject guide (annual) Earlier in C3.163: Later C56.222:
C3.163/3a:CT	___ separates
C3.163/4:CT	___ miscellaneous lists. Later C56.222/3:, C3.163/4:
C3.163/5:nos	Foreign social science bibliographies, series P-92
C3.164:nos.&dt.	[Foreign trade] reports. Proc. Desig. FT-nos.&nos. Later C56.210:, C3.164:
C3.164/2:CT	Foreign trade reports, special
C3.164/2-2:date	United States general imports of cotton manufactures, TQ2002, Country of origin by agreement category arrangement. Later C56.210/4:
C3.164/2-3:date	United States general imports of cotton manufactures, TQ2004 combined country totals..., TQ2005, Agreement category totals... TQ2002, Selected agreement category. Later C56.210/4:
C3.164/2-4:date	United States general imports of wool manufactures except floor coverings, wool grouping by country of origin and schedule of commodity by country of origin, TQ2201 Later C56.210/4:

C3.164/2-5:date   United States general imports of wool manufactures except floor coverings, country of origin by wool groupings, TQ2202   Later C56.210/4:

C3.164/2-6:date   United States general imports of wool manufactures except floor coverings, Quantity totals in terms of equivalent square yards in country of origin by commodity grouping arrangement, TQ2203.   Later C56.210/4:

C3.164/2-7:date   United States general imports of textile manufactures except cotton and wool, grouping by country of origin and Schedule A Commodity by country of origin, TQ2501.   Later C56.210/4:

C3.164/2-8:date   United States general imports of cotton manufactures: TQ2190 Schedule A by country of origin totals... which became effective in Jan.1962; TC-2191, Schedule A by country of origin totals... which became effective in Oct.1962.   Later C56.210/4:

C3.165:CT   Summary of biostatistics. Proc.

C3.166:date   United States foreign trade statistical publications (monthly) Proc.

C3.167:date   Foreign trade statistics notes (monthly) Proc.

C3.167/a:CT   ___ separates

C3.168:date   Canned fruits and vegetables, production and wholesale distribution (monthly) Proc. Superseded by C3.189:

C3.169:date   Coffee inventories and roastings (monthly) Proc.

C3.170:nos   City documents. Proc.

C3.171:nos   Government organizations. Proc.

C3.172:date   Trends in electrical goods trade (monthly) Proc.

C3.173:date   Retail trade report, New England (monthly) Proc. Superseded by C3.138/3:

C3.174:date   Retail trade report, Middle Atlantic region (monthly) Proc. Superseded by C3.138/3:

C3.175:date   Retail taade report, South Atlantic region (monthly) Proc. Superseded by C3.138/3:

C3.176:date   Retail trade report, East North Central (monthly) Proc. Superseded by C3.138/3:

C3.177:date   Retail trade report, East South Central (monthly) Proc. Superseded by C3.138/3:

C3.178:date	Retail trade report, West North Central (monthly) Proc. Superseded by C3.138/3:
C3.179:date	Retail trade report, West South Central (monthly) Proc. Superseded by C3.138/3:
C3.180:date	Retail trade report, Mountain region (monthly) Proc. Superseded by C3.138/3:
C3.181:date	Retail trade report, Pacific region (monthly) Superseded by C3.138/3:
C3.182:date	Trends in drug trade (monthly) Proc.
C3.183:date	Trends in grocery trade (monthly) Proc.
C3.184:date	Trends in tobacco trade (monthly) Proc.
C3.185:date	Service trade reports. Monthly. Proc.
C3.186:P-nos. &nos.	Current population reports. Proc. Later C56.218:, C56.112/2:, C3.186:
C3.187:nos	Labor force memorandums. Proc.
C3.188:CT	Committee on 1950 Census of the Americas. Proc.
C3.189:date	Canned food report; Monthly. Proc. Replaces Canned fruits and vegetables C3.168: Later C56.219/8:, C3.189:
C3.190:date	Trends in jewelry trade (monthly) Proc.
C3.191:dt.&nos	Government finances in United States. Proc. Later in C3.191/2:
C3.191/2:nos	[Government finances] GF (series) Consolidation of C3.141:, C3.142:, and C3.191: Later C56.209:, C3.191/2:
C3.191/3:date	Government finances and employment at a glance
C3.192:dt.&nos	County finances. Proc.
C3.193:nos	Farms of nonwhite farm operators, number of farms, land in farms, cropland harvested and value of land and buildings, by tenure, censuses of 1945 and 1940 (by States) Proc.
C3.194:nos	Survey of World War II veterans and dwelling unit vacancy and occupancy (in specified areas) Proc. Later C3.186:HVet-nos
C3.195:date	Gold and silver exports and imports; Weekly statement of, United States. Proc. Earlier C18.185:2401

C3.196:date	Gold and silver movements: United States (monthly) Proc. Earlier C18.185:2402
C3.196/2:date	Summary of U.S. exports & imports of gold and silver, fiscal year. Proc.
C3.196/3:date	Summary of U.S. exports & imports of gold and silver, calendar year. Proc.
C3.197:date	Trends in dry goods trade (monthly)
C3.198:v.nos	List of acquisitions of municipal reference service; Semimonthly. Proc.
C3.199:date	Publications of foreign countries, annotated accession list (quarterly) Later title, Foreign statistical publications, accession list. Later C56.238:
C3.200:date	Trends in wholesale wines and spirits trade (monthly) Proc.
C3.201:nos	Farm population. Proc.
C3.202:CT	Census of business. [Printed and processed] Earlier C3.65:, C3.120:, C3.940-21 to 28: Later C56.251:
C3.202/2:CT	___ Retail trade bulletins (by States) Later C56.251/2:
C3.202/3:CT	___ Wholesale trade bulletins (by States) Later C56.252/3:
C3.202/4:CT	___ Service trades bulletins (by States) Later C56.253/3:
C3.202/5:nos	___ Final volumes. Later C56.251/6:, C56.252/5:, C56.253/5:
C3.202/6:CT	___ Subject bulletins, retail trade Later C56.251/3:
C3.202/7:CT	___ Subject bulletins, service trades Later C56.253/4:
C3.202/8:CT	___ Subject bulletins, wholesale trades Later C56.252/4:
C3.202/9:CT	___ Retail, wholesale, service trades, subject bulletin RWS (series)
C3.202/10:CT	___ Trade series, Bulletins
C3.202/11:CT	___ Census monographs
C3.202/12:1e-nos	___ Preliminary reports
C3.202/12-2:1e&nos	___ Preliminary area reports. Later C56.251/7:, C56.252/2:, C56.253/2:
C3.202/13:dt.&nos	___ Central business district statistics bulletin CBD (series) Later title Major retail centers Later C56.251/5:
C3.202/14:date	___ Announcements

241

C3.202/15:date   ___ Puerto Rico   Later in C56.259:

C3.202/16:dt/EC-nos ___ Manufactures, Mineral industries, EC (series)

C3.202/17:nos   ___ Advance reports

C3.202/18:le-nos   ___ Special reports

C3.202/19:date   ___ Merchandise line sales, BC-MLS (series)   Later C56.251/4:

C3.203:nos   Special statistical reports on United States water-borne commerce (monthly) Proc. Earlier C3.2:W29/2

C3.204:date   County business patterns.   Earlier C18.270:   Later C56.233:, C3.204:

C3.204/2:dt/pt.nos ___ [bound volumes]

C3.205:CT   International population statistics reports, series P-90   Later C56.112:

C3.205/2:nos   Statistical briefs from around the world (irregular)

C3.205/3:series no. &nos.   ISPO [International Statistical Programs Office] (series)   Later C56.226:, C3.205/3:

C3.205/4:nos   ISP [International Statistical Programs] supplemental course series

C3.205/5:nos   Demographic reports for foreign countries, P96-(series)

C3.205/6:nos   International research documents, ISP-RD-(series)   Earlier C56.226/2:

C3.206:nos   Census supervisor (monthly)

C3.207:   Library notes (monthly)   Later C56.9:

C3.208:nos   Geographic reports, series GEO.   Proc.

C3.208/2:nos   Area measurement reports.   GE-20 (series)

C3.209:CT   Releases CGS (series)   Proc.   Later C56.207:

C3.209/2:nos   Industry [releases]   Proc.   Later C56.207:

C3.210:nos   TIPS

C3.211:nos   Census of the Americas, population census, urban area data.   Proc.

C3.211/2:date   Business information service.   United States foreign water-borne commerce. Earlier C3.2:W29/4

C3.211/3:CT	Business information service: General publications. Proc.
C3.211/4:les-nos	Current business reports
C3.211/5:les-nos	Special current business reports: Monthly department store sales in selected areas. Later C56.219/3:
C3.212:nos	Technical papers Later C56.215/2:, C3.212:
C3.212/2:nos	Technical notes Later C56.215:
C3.213:date	Petroleum products, secondary inventories and storage capacity. Proc. Included in C3.158:
C3.214:nos	Working papers. Proc. Later C56.229:, C2.314:
C3.215:le-nos	Housing and construction reports (series) Later C56.214:, C3.215:
C3.215/2:le-nos	Construction reports: housing starts, C20-(series) Replaces L2.51/4:, Later C56.211/8:, C3.215/2:
C3.215/3:nos	Construction reports: Construction activity, C30-(series) Replaces L2.22/2: Later C56.211/5:, C3.215/3:
C3.215/4:nos	Construction reports: Building permits, C-40 (series) Replaces L2.51/5: Later C56.211/4:
C3.215/5:nos	Construction reports: Authorized construction Washington, D.C., area C41- (series) Later C56.211/6:
C3.215/6:nos	Construction reports: Building permits: C42-(series). New residential construction authorized in permit issuing places, C42- Later title Current housing reports. Later C3.215/11:
C3.215/7:le-nos	Construction reports: Building permits, C49- (series)
C3.215/8:nos	Construction reports: Residential alterations and repairs, C50- (series) Later C56.211/7:
C3.215/9:nos	Construction reports: Housing sales, preliminary report, C25-(series) Later C56.211/2:, C3.215/9:
C3.215/9-2:nos	Construction reports: Price index of new one-family houses sold C27- (series) Earlier C56.211/2:
C3.215/10:nos	Quarterly public construction reports, G-C (series) Later C56.233:
C3.215/11:nos	Construction reports C40/42, Housing authorized by building permits and public contracts. Earlier C3.215/6:

C3.215/12:date   Construction reports: Permits issued for demolition of residential structures in selected cities, 045 series.   Later C56.211/3:

C3.215/13:letters-nos   Construction reports: Housing completions C22(series) Monthly. Later C56.211:

C3.215/14:nos   Current housing reports, series H-150. Annual Housing Survey. Earlier C56.214/2:   CLASS CANCELLED   See C3.215:H-150

C3.215/5:nos   New residential construction in selected standard metropolitan statistical areas, C21- (series) (quarterly)

C3.216:dt/CT or nos Census of mineral industries: [Industry] bulletins MI- (series) Later C56.236/3:

C3.216/2:dt./nos   ___ [State] bulletin MI-(series)   Later C56.236/4:

C3.216/3:dt/no   ___ Preliminary reports

C3.216/3-2:dt./le&nos ___ Industry and product reports

C3.216/4:dt./le   ___ [Subject] bulletin MI-(series)   Later C56.236/5:

C3.216/5:date   ___ Final volumes.   Later C56.236/2:

C3.216/6:date   ___ Announcements

C3.217:date/nos   International news letter. [admin.]

C3.218:date   Reconditioned steel barrels and drums report (quarterly) Proc. Earlier C3.211/3:B27/date

C3.219:date   Puerto Rico censuses, announcements

C3.220:date   Census telephone listing of Bureau activities.   Proc.   Admin.

C3.221:dt./v.no.pt.no.   National housing inventory

C3.222:dt.&nos   Company statistics bulletins, Census of business, manufactures, and mineral industries

C3.223:CT   Census of population: General publications.   Earlier C3.950-2:

C3.223/2:dt./le.nos.   Census of population: Preliminary reports

C3.223/3:dt./no   Census of population and housing: Announcements

C3.223/4:dt./le-nos Census of population: Advance reports. Note - Includes:
    PC(A1)-nos. Final population counts
    PC(A2)-nos General population characteristics
    PC(A3)-nos General social and economic characteristics

C3.223/5:dt./nos U.S. census of population: Number of inhabitants PC(1)-A (series)

C3.223/6:dt./nos Census of population: General population characteristics, PC(1)-B (series)

C3.223/7:dt./nos **Census of population: General social and economic characteristics, PC(1)-C (series)**

C3.223/8:dt./nos Census of population: Detailed characteristics, PC(1)-D (series)

C3.223/9:dt./pt.nos Census of population: Characteristics of the population (bound volumes)

C3.223/10:dt./v.nos Census of population: Final volumes (other than by States)

C3.223/11:dt./nos Censuses of population and housing: Census tract reports

C3.223/12:dt./nos Census of population: Supplementary reports

C3.223/13:dt./nos United States censuses of population and housing: Geographic identification code scheme, PHC(2) (series)

C3.223/13-2:Reg. Geographic identification code scheme (by regions)

C3.223/14:nos   Graphic pamphlets GP (series)

C3.223/15:dt./nos Censuses of population and housing: Census county division boundary descriptions, PHC(3) series

C3.223/16:nos   Evaluation and research reports ER (series)

C3.223/17:dt./nos Employment profiles for selected low-income areas, PHC(3) series

C3.224:dt./le-nos Census of housing: Advance reports. Includes housing characteristics, States, HC(A1) (series)

C3.224/2:dt./le-nos Census of housing: Preliminary reports

C3.224/3:dt./nos U.S. census of housing: State and small areas, final report HC(1) (series)

C3.224/4:dt./nos Census of housing - Metropolitan housing series HC(2)

C3.224/5:dt./nos Census of housing: City blocks, series HC(3)

C3.224/6:dt/nos   Census of housing: Components of inventory change, final report HC(4) (series)

C3.224/7:dt./pt.nos Census of housing. Residential finance

C3.224/8:dt./nos Census of housing: Special reports for local housing authorities, HC(S 1) (series)

C3.224/9:dt./v.nos Census of housing: Final volumes

C3.224/10:date Census of housing: Subject reports HC(7)- (series)

C3.225: Procedural studies of censuses. Earlier C3.950-10:

C3.226:nos Business cycle developments. Later title: Business conditions digest. Later C56.111:

C3.226/a:CT ___ separates

C3.226/2:nos BCD technical papers

C3.226/3:date Advance BDC [Business conditions digest] (monthly) Later C56.111/2:

C3.227:nos Census tract memo. Later C56.235/2:, C3.227:

C3.227/2:nos Census tract papers GE-40 (series) Later C56.235:, C3.227/2:

C3.228:nos Statistical profile series SP. Prepared for Area Redevelopment Administration. Replaced by C1.45:

C3.229:nos U.S. commodity exports and imports as related to output, series ES2, Later C56.232:, C3.229:

C3.230:nos Enterprise statistics, series ES3 Later C56.228:

C3.230/2:1e.-no Enterprise statistics, preliminary reports

C3.231:nos Manufacturers' shipments, inventories, and orders, series M3-1. Formerly Industry survey. Later C56.245:, C3.231:

C3.232:nos Research documentation lists. Official use.

C3.233:CT Census of transportation, publications. Later C56.246:

C3.233/2:nos ___ Advance and/or preliminary reports Later C56.246/2:, C56.246/3:

C3.233/3:dt/v.nos ___ Final volumes. Later C56.246/2:

C3.233/4:date ___ Announcement and order forms. Census of transportation

C3.233/4-2:dt./nos ___ Publication program. Earlier C3.233:P96

C3.234:date	Census of commercial fisheries: Final volumes
C3.234/2:date	Census of commercial fisheries. Preliminary reports
C3.235:date	U.S. exports and imports, working day and seasonal adjustment factors and months for cyclical dominance (MCD) (annual) Earlier C3.2:Ex7
C3.236:date	Green coffee inventories and roastings (quarterly) Later C56.219/2:, C3.236:
C3.237:v./nos	Census bureau statistical daily
C3.238:v./nos	Small-area data activities (irregular) Later title, Small-area data notes. Later C56.217:, C3.238:
C3.238/2:nos	Small-area statistical papers, Series GE-41 Earlier C56.217/2:
C3.239:letters & nos.	Current selected services reports: Monthly selected services receipts. Later C56.219/5:, C3.239:
C3.240:nos	Data access descriptions: Matching studies series MS
C3.240/2:nos	Data access descriptions: Automated address coding guide and data retrieval series AAC
C3.240/3:nos	Data access descriptions: Census tabulations available on computer tape, series CT Later C56.212/3:, C3.240/3:
C3.240/4:nos	Data access descriptions: Policy and administration series PA
C3.250/5:nos	Data access descriptions: Collection, evaluation, and processing series CEP Later C56.212:, C3.240/5:
C3.240/6:nos	Data access description: Census geography series, CG-(nos) Later C56.212/5:, C3.240/6:
C3.241:date	Defense indicators (monthly) Supersedes Selected economic indicators D1.43:nos Later C56.110:
C3.242:dt./nos	Holdings for selected public-employee retirement systems, quarterly report, GR (series) Later C56.224:
C3.243:nos	Financial management systems series, FMSS
C3.244:nos	Census use study reports. Later C56.220:, C3.244:
C3.245:letters-nos	Census of construction industries: Advance industry reports
C3.245/2:date	Census of construction industries: Announcements and order forms

C3.245/3:dt./nos	Census of construction industries: Final reports Later C56.245/3:, C56.245/4:
C3.245/4:dt./v.nos	Census of construction industries: Bound volumes
C3.245/5:nos	Census of construction industries: Special report Later C56.254/5:
C3.246:nos	Computerized geographic coding series GE60 Later C56.237:, C3.246:
C3.247:nos	DAUList (series) Later C56.241:
C3.248:nos	SCRIS reports
C3.249:les.&nos	GBF/DIME system (GEO-nos) Earlier C56.255:
C3.249/2:CT	Geographic base (DIME file, CUE, correction-update-extension publications. Earlier C56.255:
C3.250:date	Women owned businesses, WB (series)
C3.251:nos	Status, a monthly chartbook of social and economic trends

C3.940   16th Census, 1940

C3.940-2:CT   General publications

C3.940-5:CT   Final volumes
C3.940-5/a:CT   ___ separates
C3.940-6:CT   Regulations, rules, and instructions
C3.940-6/a:CT   ___ separates
C3.940-7:CT   Posters
C3.940-8:CT   Narratives
C3.940-9:CT   Irrigation of agricultural lands (by States)
C3.940-10:CT   Retail trade (by States)
C3.940-11:CT   Service establishments (by States)
C3.940-12:CT   Mineral industries, 1939
C3.940-13:CT   Population, 1st series (by States)
C3.940-13/2:CT   Population, 2d series (by States)
C3.940-14:CT   Agriculture, 1st series (by States)
C3.940-15:CT   Agriculture, 2d series (by States)
C3.940-16:CT   Agriculture, 3d series (by States)
C3.940-17:CT   Territories and possessions reports (individual reports)
C3.940-18:CT   Manufactures (by industries)
C3.940-19:CT   Manufactures, 1939: State series
C3.940-20:   [not used]

C3.940-21:CT	Census of business, 1939. See for earlier censuses:- C3.65:, C3.120/1: and C3.120/2: Later C3.202:
C3.940-22:CT	Census of business, 1939: Retail trade (miscellaneous)
C3.940-23:CT	Census of business, 1939: Retail trade (by States)
C3.940-24:CT	Census of business, 1939, Retail trade, Commodity sales (by commodities)
C3.940-25:CT	Census of business, 1939: Wholesale trade (by States)
C3.940-26:CT	Census of business, 1939: Wholesale trade (miscellaneous)
C3.940-27:	[Not used]
C3.940-28:CT	Census of business, 1939: Construction (by States)
C3.940-29:	[Not used]
C3.940-30:CT	Housing, 1st series (by States)
C3.940-31:CT	Housing, supplement to 1st series: Housing bulletins (by States)
C3.940-32:CT	Housing, 2d series (by States)
C3.940-33:CT	Housing, 3d series (by States)
C3.940-34:CT	Housing, 4th series (by States)
C3.940-35:	[not used]
C3.940-36:	[not used]
C3.940-37:CT	Population, 3d series (by States)
C3.940-37/2:CT	Population, 4th series (by States)
C3.940-38:CT	Population and housing, (by States)
C3.940-39:CT	Population, Outlying possessions

C3.950   17th Census, 1950

C3.950-2:CT   General publications

C3.950-2/a:CT   ___ separates

C3.950-4:PC-nos.&nos. Series PC reports. Proc.

C3.950-4/2:HC-nos.&nos. Series HC reports. Proc.

C3.950-4/3:nos or le. 1950 Census of population & housing announcements

C3.950-6:CT   Regulations, rules, and instructions

C3.950-6/a:CT   ___ separates

C3.950-7:CT   United States census of population 1950: Number of inhabitants (by States)

C3.950-7/2:CT   ___ Census tracts

C3.950-7/3:CT   ___ General characteristics (by States)

C3.950-7/4:CT   ___ Detailed characteristics (by States)   P-C (series)

C3.950-7/5:v.nos   ___ (final volumes)

C3.950-7/6:nos.-les   ___ Special reports, P-E (series)

C3.950-8:CT   United States census of population, 1950: Block statistics reports

C3.950-8/2:CT   ___ General characteristics (by States), report H-A (series)

C3.950-8/3:nos   ___ Nonfarm housing characteristics [of standard metropolitan areas] H-B (series)

C3.950-8/4:   Housing census separate reports and bulletins

C3.950-8/5:v.nos   Census of housing, 1950; (final volumes)

C3.950-9:v.nos   United States census of agriculture, 1950 (final volumes)

C3.950-9/2:CT   ___ v.1. Counties and State economic areas. Separates.

C3.950-9/3:CT   ___ Irrigation of agricultural lands (by States)

C3.950-9/4:CT   Location of irrigated land, maps (by States)

C3.950-9/5:chap.nos   United States census of agriculture, 1950: v. 2. General report
       (separates)

C3.950-9/6:nos   United States census of agriculture, 1950: Announcements

C3.950-10:nos   Procedural studies of 1950 censuses. Later see C3.225:

January 1, 1972 the Bureau of the Census became a part of the Social and Economic Statistics Administration.

C4   Coast and Geodetic Survey

July 1, 1903 transferred from Treasury Department.

C4.1:date	Annual report of the director. Earlier T11.1:
C4.1/a:date	___ separates
C4.2:CT	General publications
C4.2/a:CT	___ separates
C4.3:nos	Bulletins See also C4.20:
C4.4:nos	Circulars. Earlier T11.4:
C4.4/2:nos	Circulars. 2d series, 1913-1917.
C4.4/3:nos	Circulars. 3d series, 1919-
C4.4/4:	P & A circulars
C4.4/5:nos	C & GS General circular
C4.5:date	Catalogs of charts, coast pilots and tide tables Later C55.418:
C4.5/a:CT	___ separates
C4.5/2:nos	Nautical charts and other publications recently issued. Some read Nautical charts recently issued.

252

C4.6/1:pt.nos.(later Letters/date)	U.S. Coast pilot. Atlantic Coast. Earlier T11.6: Later C55.422:
C4.6/2:CT	U.S. Coast pilot. West Indies Later C55.422:,
C4.6/3:CT	Inside route pilot (Atlantic and Gulf coasts) Later C55.422:
C4.6/4:date	U.S. Coast pilot. Gulf coast. Later C55.422:
C4.7/1:date	U.S. Coast pilot. Pacific Coast., Cal., Ore., and Wash. Earlier T11.7/1: Later C55.422:
C4.7/2:date	U.S. Coast pilot. Pacific Coast. Alaska. Earlier T11.7/2: Later C55.422:
C4.7/3:nos	Coast pilot notes. Pacific Coast. Alaska, pt. 2. Later C55.422:
C4.7/4:CT	Coast pilot notes. Hawaiian Islands.
C4.7/5:date	U.S. Coast pilot. Hawaiian Islands.
C4.7/6:date	Wartime information to mariners supplementing U.S. Coast pilots
C4.7/7:date	U.S. Coast pilot, Alaska, Aleutian islands
C4.8:date	Laws relating to Coast and Geodetic Survey
C4.9:nos	Maps and charts. Earlier T11.9:
C4.9/2:CT	Maps and charts (unnumbered)
C4.9/3:R-nos	Radio charts
C4.9/4:CT	Aeronautical charts. Formerly C23.10/3:
C4.9/5:nos	Regional aeronautical charts. Formerly C23.10/4:
C4.9/6:date	Aeronautical charts; lists of published charts, etc. Proc. Changed from C4.2: Ae8
C4.9/7:nos	Chart correction notices. Proc.
C4.9/8:nos	World aeronautical charts. Restricted.
C4.9/9:nos	Route charts
C4.9/10:nos	Instrument approach and landing charts
C4.9/11:nos	Airport obstruction plans
C4.9/11-2:	Airport obstruction plans, monthly bulletin

C4.9/11-3:nos	Airport obstruction charts (bimonthly bulletin)
C4.9/12:date	Radio facility charts. Later title, Dates of latest prints, flight information publications of U.S.
C4.9/13:date	Aeronautical charts, dates of latest prints. Proc. Earlier C3.2:C38/5 Later C55.409:
C4.9/13-2:date	Latest editions of U.S. Air Force aeronautical charts (quarterly) Later C55.418/3:
C4.9/14:nos	Instrument approach charts. I.L.S.
C4.9/15:area	Danger area charts
C4.9/16:nos	Instrument approach chart, radio beacon
C4.9/17:nos	Route charts
C4.9/18:date	Dates of latest prints, instrument flight charts (monthly) Proc. Earlier C4.9/10: Title varies. Later C55.411:
C4.9/18-2:date	Instrument approach procedure charts [Alaska, Hawaii, U.S. Pacific Islands]. Later C55.411/2:
C4.9/19:date	Eastern United States, dates of latest prints, instrument approach procedure charts and airport obstruction plans (OP) monthly. Proc. Earlier C4.9/18:
C4.9/20:date	Western United States, dates of latest prints, instrument approach procedure charts and airport obstruction plans (OP) (monthly) Proc. Earlier C4.9/18:
C4.9/21:CT	Sheets of National Atlas of United States
C4.9/22:date	Military fields United States, dates of latest editions, instrument approach procedure charts (quarterly) Later C55.418/4:
C4.10:nos	Leaflets for distribution from survey's exhibition at Louisiana Purchase Exposition, St. Louis, Mo., 1904.
C4.11:nos	Notice to mariners. Earlier T11.11: Later C9.26:
C4.12:CT	Rules, regulations and instructions. Earlier T11.12:
C4.12/2:	Bureau personnel manual. Administrative
C4.12/3:	Bureau finance manual. Administrative
C4.12/4:CT	Handbooks, manuals, guides

C4.12/5:nos	C&GS technical manuals Later C55.408;, C55.408/2:
C4.13:date	Tide tables, Atlantic Coast for (calendar year) Earlier T11.13: Later C4.15/3:
C4.14:date	Tide tables, Pacific Coast for (calendar year) Earlier T11.14: Replaced by C4.15/2:
C4.15:date	Tide tables for calendar year. Earlier T11.15: Later C5.15/2:, 3:
C4.15/2:date	Tide tables, Pacific Ocean and Indian Ocean. Replaces C4.15: & C4.14: Replaced by C4.15/5: and C4.15/6:
C4.15/3:date	Tide tables, Atlantic Ocean. Replaces C4.15: & C4.13: Replaced by C4.15/4: and C4.15/7:
C4.15/3a:date	___ separates
C4.15/4:date	Tide tables, east coast, North and South America. Replaces C4.15/3: Later C55.421/2:
C4.15/5:date	Tide tables, west coast, North and South America. Replaces C4.15/2: Later C55.421:
C4.15/6:date	Tide tables, central and western Pacific Ocean and Indian ocean. Replaces C4.15/2: Later C55.421/4:
C4.15/7:date	Tide tables, Europe and West Coast of Africa (including Mediterranean Sea) Replaces C4.15/3: Later C55.421/3:
C4.15/8:CT	Special tide tables
C4.16:nos	Results of observations made at C. & G. Survey magnetic observatories. Proc. Pubs. desig. MO-nos
C4.17:CT	Specifications
C4.18/1:date	Coast and Geodetic Survey suboffice, Manila. Catalog of charts, sailing directions and tide tables. Earlier T11.19/1:
C4.18/2:date	Notice to mariners. Earlier T11.19/2:
C4.18/3:sec.nos	Sailing directions. Earlier T11.19/3:
C4.18/4:date	General instructions for surveys in Philippine Islands
C4.18/5:pt.nos	Coast and Geodetic Survey suboffice, Manila, U.S. Coast pilot, Philippine Islands

C4.19:nos	Special publications
C4.19/a:CT	___ separates
C4.19/2:nos	Publications. Supersedes C4.19: Later C55.419:
C4.19/2a:CT	___ separates
C4.20:date	Bulletin. Monthly - Coast survey bulletin
C4.21:CT	Digest of geodetic publications
C4.22:date	Current tables, Atlantic Coast. Later C55.425:
C4.22/a:date	___ separates
C4.23:date	Current tables, Pacific coast Later C55.425/2:
C4.24:CT	Magnetic declinations (by States)
C4.24:nos	Magnetic declinations (by nos.) Proc. pubs.desig.MD-nos.
C4.25:date	Seismological reports. Quarterly
C4.25/a:date	___ separates
C4.25/2:date	U.S. Earthquakes. Later C55.417/2:
C4.25/3:	Progress during ... strong-motion earthquake in California and elsewhere. Official use. See for inf. on this subject C4.25/2:
C4.25/4:nos	Quarterly seismology bulletin MSP (series) Proc.
C4.26:date	Magnetic observations
C4.27:CT	Tide tables (individual harbors)
C4.28:nos	Current diagrams
C4.29:CT	Tidal current charts Later C55.424:
C4.30:vol	Geodetic letters. Quarterly. Proc.
C4.31:nos	Field engineers bulletins. Annual. Proc.
C4.32:CT	Tidal bench marks. Proc. (by States)
C4.32/2:CT	Index maps, tidal bench marks

C4.32/3:	Tidal bench marks (loose-leaf, by individual stations)
C4.33:nos	Density of sea water (D.W.)
C4.34:nos	Water temperatures, Coast and Geodetic Survey tide stations. Pubs.desig. TW-nos
C4.35:nos	Tidal harmonic constants. Proc. Pubs.desig. TH-no.
C4.36:nos	Seismological bulletins (monthly) Proc. Later C55.414:
C4.36/2:nos	Preliminary determination of epicenters
C4.36/2-2:date	Preliminary determination of epicenters, monthly listing. Later C44.412:
C4.37:CT	Geographic names in Coastal areas (by States)
C4.38:nos	Magnetograms. Proc. See for old series C4.16:
C4.39:	Second-order leveling, list of standard elevations
C4.40:le-nos	Magnetic hourly values HV (series) Proc.
C4.40/2:nos	Magnetograms and hourly values MHV (series) Proc.
C4.41:nos	Journal [issued irregularly, about once a year.] Superseded by C4.41/2:
C4.41/2:nos	Technical bulletins. Supersedes the Journal, C4.41:
C4.41/3:letters	Technical bulletins, special
C4.42:nos	MSA-nos Later C55.417:
C4.43:nos	MSS-nos
C4.44:nos	Information leaflet MM-nos
C4.45:	Buzzard
C4.46:	Personal panorama
C4.47:nos	Releases CGS (series) Proc.
C4.48:nos	Photogrammetric instructions
C4.49:nos	Publication notice PN series (irregular) Proc.
C4.50:CT	Bibliographies and lists of publications

C4.51:v.nos.&nos. Survey with safety. Administrative.

C4.52:CT   Posters

C4.53:CT   Addresses

C4.54:v.nos.&nos. Earthquake information bulletin   Later C55.410:

C4.55:nos   Digest of science and engineering presentations

C4.56:nos   Antarctic traverses

Transferred to the Environmental Science Services Administration by Reorganization Plan no. 2 of 1965, effective July 13, 1965. Abolished by Reorganization Plan no. 4 of 1970 effective Oct. 3, 1970 and functions transferred to the National Ocean Survey.

C5   Corporations Bureau

Created under act approved February 14, 1903

C5.1:date   Annual reports

C5.2:CT   General publications

C5.2/a:CT   ___ separates

C5.3:   Bulletins [none issued]

C5.4:   Circulars [none issued]

Discontinued. The act approved Sept. 25, 1914 creating the Federal Trade Commission provided that upon its organization the Corporations Bureau should cease to exist.

C6   Fisheries Bureau

July 1903. Formerly Fish Commission (FC).

C6.1:date   Annual reports. Later I45.1:

C6.1/a:date   ___ separates. Commissioner's report

C6.1/a:CT   ___ separates. Miscellaneous

C6.2:CT   General publications. Later I45.2:

C6.3:v.nos	Bulletins. Earlier FC1.3:
C6.3/a:CT	___ separates
C6.3/2:nos	Bulletins. Numbered. Later I45.3:
C6.4:nos	Circulars
C6.5:nos	Statistical bulletins. Earlier FC1.5: Later I45.8:
C6.6:date	List of publications of the Bureau of Fisheries available for distribution. Later I45.16:
C6.7:nos	Econonic circulars
C6.8:	Alaska Fisheries Service
C6.8/1:date	Annual reports
C6.8/2:CT	General publications
C6.8/3:nos	Bulletins
C6.8/4:nos	Circulars
C6.9:date	Fisheries service bulletin. Monthly. Later I45.7:
C6.10:CT	Posters
C6.11:date	Pacific coast salmon pack. Later I45.15:
C6.12:nos	Investigational reports. Later I45.19:
C6.13:nos	Fishery circulars. Superseded by I49.4:
C6.14:nos	Inquiry memoranda. Mim. Later I45.12:
C6.14/a:CT	___ separates. Proc.
C6.15:nos	Scientific inquiry memoranda. Mim. Later I45.13:
C6.16:nos	Library bulletins, recent accessions. Monthly. Proc. Later I45.10:
C6.17:nos	Black bass and anglers division publications. Proc. Later I45.17:
C6.18:vol	Fishery market news. Monthly. Proc. Later I45.9:

Transferred to Interior Department (I45) by authority of Reorganization plan II, pt.1.sec.4, 1939.

C 7   Immigration and Naturalization Service

Transferred from Treasury Department (T 21) July 1, 1903.

C7.1:date	Annual reports. Earlier T21.1: Later L3.1:
C7.2:CT	General publications. Earlier T21.2: Later L3.2:
C7.3:nos	Bulletins [none issued]
C7.4:nos	Circulars. Earlier T21.4: Later L3.4:
C7.5:date	Chinese exclusion treaties, laws and regulations. Earlier T21.5: Later L3.7:
C7.6:date	Immigration laws and regulations. Earlier T21.5: Later L3.5:
C7.7:CT	Decisions
C7.8:date	Immigration bulletin. Monthly.
C7.9:CT	Terms, conditions and limitations, with form proposal
C7.10:	Naturalization Division
C7.10/1:date	Annual reports. Later L6.1:
C7.10/2:CT	General publications. Later L6.2:
C7.10/3:nos	Bulletins. Later L6.3:
C7.10/4:nos	Circulars [none issued]
C7.10/5:date	Naturalization laws and regulations. Later L6.5:
C7.11:	Information Division Later L3.6:
C7.11/1:date	Annual reports
C7.11/2:CT	General publications
C7.11/3:nos	Bulletins [none issued]
C7.11/4:nos	Circulars [none issued]
C7.11/5:nos	Agricultural opportunities Later L3.6/5:

Transferred to Labor Department March 4, 1913, as Immigration Bureau (L3) and Naturalization Bureau (L6).

C 8   Labor Bureau

Formerly independent Labor Dept. (La), Transferred to Commerce Dept. July 1, 1903.

C8.1:date	Annual reports. Earlier Lal.1: Later L2.1:
C8.1/a:CT	___ separates
C8.2:CT	General publications. Earlier Lal.2: Later L2.2:
C8.3:v. nos	Bulletins. Bimonthly. Earlier Lal.3:
C8.3/a:CT	___ separates
C8.3/2:whole nos	Bulletins. Irregular.
C8.4:nos	Circulars [none issued]
C8.5:nos	Special reports. Earlier Lal.5:
C8.6:date	Report on Hawaii. Earlier Lal.7:

Transferred to Labor Department March 4, 1913, under the name of Labor Statistics Bureau (L2).

C 9   Lighthouse Bureau

Transferred from Treasury Dept. (T25) July 1, 1903.

C9.1:date	Annual reports. Earlier T25.1:
C9.1/a:CT	___ separates
C9.2:CT	General publications. Earlier T25.2:
C9.3:nos	Bulletins. Earlier T25.3: Superseded by C9.26:
C9.4:nos	Circulars. Earlier T25.4:
C9.5:date	Lights, buoys, and day marks, 1st district. Earlier T25.5: Superseded by C9.42:
C9.6:date	___, 2d district. Earlier T25.6: Superseded by C9.42:
C9.7:date	___, 3d district. Earlier T25.7: Superseded by C9.43:
C9.8:date	___, 4th district. Earlier T25.8: Superseded by C9.44:

C9.9:date	Lights, buoys, and day marks, 5th district. Earlier T25.9:
C9.10:date	___ 6th district. Earlier T25.10: Superseded by C9.48:
C9.11:date	___, 7th district. Earlier T25.11:
C9.12:date	___, 8th district. Earlier T25.12:
C9.13:date	___, 9th district. Earlier T25.13:
C9.14:date	___, 10th district. Earlier T25.14:
C9.14/2:date	List of buoys, 19th district, Hawaiian and Samoan Islands
C9.15:Cong.&Sess.	Laws relative to Light House Establishment passed at ___ session ___ Congress. Earlier T25.15:
C9.16:date	Laws and regulations relating to lighthouse establishment. Earlier T25.15:
C9.16/a:CT	___ separates
C9.17:date	Lights, buoys and day marks, 1st-9th districts. Earlier T25.16:
C9.18:date	Lights and fog signals, northern lakes and rivers and Canada [3d and 9th-11th districts]. Earlier T25.17:
C9.19:date	Lights, buoys and daymarks, 16th-19th district.
C9.20:date	Notice to mariners (issued irregularly) Earlier T25.19: Superseded by C9.26:
C9.21:date	Lights on western rivers. Earlier T25.20: Later C9.27:, C9.28:, C9.29:
C9.22:CT	Specifications. Earlier T25.21:
C9.23:date	Instructions to lightkeepers. Earlier T25.22:
C9.24:date	Lights, buoys and daymarks, 3d division. Earlier T25.23:
C9.25:CT	Regulations, Miscellaneous. Earlier T25.24:
C9.26:date	Notice to mariners. Wkly. Supersedes notice to mariners, issued irregularly (C9.20:) and Bulletins (C9.3:) Earlier C4.11: Later T47.19:
C9.26/a:CT	___ separates

C9.27:date	Lights, buoys and daymarks, 13th district Earlier C9.21:
C9.28:date	Lights, buoys and daymarks, 14th district Earlier C9.21:
C9.29:date	Aids to navigation, 15th district Earlier C9.21:
C9.29/2:date	Light list, lights, buoys, and day marks, Mississippi and Ohio rivers, 15th lighthouse district. Combines publications which have been classed as C9.27:, C9.28: and C9.29:
C9.30:date	Light and fog signals of United States and Canada on Northern Lakes and rivers (3d and 10th-12th districts)
C9.31:nos	Lighthouse service bulletin. Monthly. Changed to Coast Guard bulletin T47.21:
C9.32:date	Buoy list, 10th lighthouse district Later C9.39:
C9.33:date	___, 11th lighthouse district Later C9.39:
C9.34:date	___, 12th lighthouse district Later C9.39:
C9.35:date	___, 16th lighthouse district Superseded by C9.46:
C9.36:date	___, 17th lighthouse district Superseded by C9.46: and C9.47:
C9.37:date	___, 18th lighthouse district Superseded by C9.47:
C9.38:CT	Notice to mariners
C9.38/1:nos	Poster notice to mariners. Atlantic Coast
C9.38/2:nos	Poster notice to mariners. Pacific Coast
C9.38/3:nos	Poster notice to mariners. Great Lakes
C9.39:date	Buoy list, 10th to 12th lighthouse districts
C9.40:nos	Circular letter
C9.41:dt.&nos	Notice to mariners, Great Lakes. Wkly. Later T47.20:
C9.42:date	Local light list, 1st and 2d districts Supersedes C9.5: and C9.6:
C9.43:date	Local light list, 3d district. Supersedes C9.7:
C9.44:date	Local light list, 4th and 5th districts Supersedes C9.9:
C9.45:date	Local light list, 7th and 8th districts.

C9.46:date   Local light list, 16th and 17th districts   Supersedes C9.35: and portion of C9.36:

C9.47:date   Local light list, 17th and 18th districts   Supersedes portion of C9.36: and C9.37:

C9.48:date   Local light list, 6th district   Supersedes C9.10:

C9.49:date   Local light list, 6th and 7th districts.   Later T47.23:

C9.50:date   Light list, 1st-5th districts. (North Atlantic coast of U.S. Annual. Later T47.24: Replaces C9.4/2:, C9.4/3: and parts of C9.44:

C9.51:date   Light list, 5th-9th districts. (South Atlantic and Gulf coasts of U.S.) Annual. Replaces parts of C9.17:, C9.44:, C9.45:

C9.52:date   Light list, 5th-8th districts (Atlantic coast of U.S., intracoastal waterway Hampton Roads to Rio Grande including inside waters. Annual. Replaces parts of C9.17:, C9.44:, C9.45:, C9.49:

C9.53:CT   Maps. The radio beacon system maps transferred to T47.22: from C9.53:R11, R11/2, R11/3

Lighthouse Bureau (C9) and its functions are transferred to and shall be consolidated with and administered as a part of the Coast Guard (T47), effective July 1, 1939.

C10   Manufactures Bureau

Created July 1, 1903.

C10.1:date   Annual reports

C10.2:CT   General publications

C10.2/a:CT   ___ separates

C10.3:nos   Bulletins [none issued]

C10.4:nos   Circulars [none issued]

C10.5/1:nos   Daily consular and trade reports (old series) Monthly. Earlier C14.6:

C10.5/2:dt.&nos   Daily consular and trade reports, series July 5, 1910-June 29, 1912.

C10.5/2a:CT   ___ separates

C10.6:nos	Daily consular and trade reports. Earlier C14.8: Later C18.5:
C10.6/a:CT	___ separates
C10.7:v.nos	Special consular reports. Earlier C14.10: Later C18.9:
C10.8:date	Commercial relations. Earlier C14.15: Later C18.16:
C10.9:date	Review of world's commerce. Earlier C14.15:
C10.10:nos	Tariff series. Later C18.12:
C10.11:	Report on trade conditions. Changed to C10.13:
C10.12:nos	Consular reports, annual series. Later C18.11:
C10.13:nos	Special agents series
C10.13/a:CT	___ separates
C10.14:v.nos	Weekly consular and trade reports. Later C18.5/1:
C10.15:nos	Confidential bulletins
C10.16:nos	Foreign tariff note. Later C18.13:
C10.17:nos	Miscellaneous series. Later C18.15:

Consolidated with Statistics Bureau (C14) August 23, 1912 as Foreign and Domestic Commerce Bureau (C18.)

C11   Navigation Bureau

Transferred from Treasury Department July 1, 1903 (T30).

C11.1:date	Annual reports. Earlier T30.1:
C11.1/a:CT	___ separates
C11.2:CT	General publications. Earlier T30.2:
C11.3:nos	Bulletins [none issued]
C11.4:nos	Circulars [none issued]
C11.5:date	Annual list of merchant vessels. Earlier T30.5: Later C25.11:

C11.6:date	Navigation laws. Earlier T30.6: Later C25.5/2:
C11.6/a:CT	___ separates
C11.7:	Radio Service. Later Radio Division C24
C11.7/1:date	Annual reports. Issued as part of Annual report of Commissioner of navigation
C11.7/2:CT	General publications
C11.7/3:nos	Bulletins - Radio service bulletins. Later C24.3:
C11.7/4:	Circulars [none issued]
C11.7/5:date	Radio communication laws and regulations
C11.7/6:date	Radio stations of United States, list of. Later C24.5:
C11.8:date	American documented seagoing merchant vessels of 500 gross tons and over, 4 degree. Monthly.
C11.9:nos	General letter
C11.10:date	Merchant marine statistics. Later C25.10:

In 1933 combined with Bureau of Steamboat Inspection to form Bureau of Navigation and Steamboat Inspection (C25).

C12 Shipping Commissioners

July 1, 1903 transferred from Treasury Department.

C12.1:date	Annual reports
C12.2:CT	General publications [none issued]
C12.3:	Bulletins [none issued]
C12.4:nos	Circulars [none issued]

C13 National Bureau of Standards

Transferred from Treasury Department July 1, 1903.

C13.1:date	Annual reports. Earlier T41.1:
C13.1/a:CT	___ separates
C13.1/2:date	Center for Radiation Research, technical highlights, fiscal year.
C13.1/3:date	Institute for Applied Technology, technical highlights, fiscal year
C13.1/4:date	Institute for Basic Standards, technical highlights, fiscal year
C13.1/5:date	Institute for Materials Research, technical highlights, fiscal year
C13.1/5-2:date	Institute for Materials Research, Metallurgy Division, technical highlights, fiscal year.
C13.1/6:date	Center for Computer Sciences and Technology technical highlights, fiscal year
C13.2:CT	General publications
C13.3:vol	Bulletins
C13.3/a:nos	___ separates
C13.3/a:CT	___ separates
C13.3/2:vol	Decennial index to bulletins
C13.3/3:nos	Administrative bulletins
C13.4:nos	Circulars. Superseded by C13.44:
C13.4/a:CT	___ separates
C13.5:nos	Circular of information. Earlier T41.5:
C13.6:CT	Rules, regulations, and instructions
C13.6/2:CT	Handbooks, manuals, guides (unnumbered)
C13.6/3:nos	Cyrogenic materials data handbook. Earlier C13.6/2:C88/nos Later D301.45/41:
C13.7:date	Conference on weights and measures
C13.7/a:CT	___ separates

C13.8:nos	Technologic papers
C13.8/2:vol	Technologic papers. Bound volumes.
C13.9:serial nos.	Specifications. International aircraft standards
C13.10:nos	Miscellaneous publications, later title Special publications
C13.10/a:CT	___ separates
C13.10/2:dt/nos	Measurement users bulletin, supplement to NBS special publication 250
C13.11:nos	Handbook series, later title **Handbooks**
C13.11/a:CT	___ separates
C13.12/1:nos	Simplified practice recommendations. Later C18.277:, C41.20:, C13.12: Replaced by C13.20/2:
C13.12/2:nos	Limitation of variety recommendations
C13.13:nos	Technical news bulletins. Monthly. Later title, Dimensions
C13.13/a:CT	___ separates
C13.13/b:	Technical reports, also called Summary technical reports (STR's) [Preprints from Technical News Bulletin]
C13.14:date	Wholesale prices of building materials. Monthly.
C13.15:nos	News publications. Monthly list.
C13.16:nos	Letter circulars. Mim.
C13.17:nos	Certificate of analyses of standard samples
C13.18:CT	Press notices
C13.19:nos	American Marine Standards Committee
C13.20:nos	Commercial standards. Later C18.276:, C41.25:, C13.20: Replaced by C13.20/2:
C13.20/2:nos	Product standards. Replaces C13.20: and C13.12:
C13.21:vol	Commercial standards. Monthly.
C13.22:v.nos.&nos.	Journal of research. Monthly

C13.22/sect.A:v.nos.&nos.	Journal of research. Sec.A. Physics and chemistry (bimonthly)
C13.22/sect.A/a:CT	___ separates
C13.22/sec.B:v.nos.&nos.	___ Sec.B. Mathematics and mathematical physics (quarterly)
C13.22:sec.C: v.nos.&nos.	___ Sec.C. Engineering and instrumentation (quarterly)
C13.22/sec.Ca:CT	___ ___ separates
C13.22/sec.D:v.nos.&nos.	___Sec.D. Radio propagation (bimonthly) Later C52.9:
C13.22/sec.Da:CT	___ ___ separates
C13.22/a:CT	Research papers. Separates from the Journal of research
C13.22/2:vol	Journal of Research. Bound volumes.
C13.23:nos	National screw thread commission. Mimeographed
C13.24:nos	Federal specifications board, United States Government master specifications
C13.25:nos	Building and housing publications
C13.26:vol	Report on current hydraulic laboratory research in U.S. Mim.
C13.26/2:date	Hydraulic laboratory bulletin, series B
C13.27:nos	Technical information on building materials for use in design of low cost housing. Proc.
C13.28:date	News bulletin of paper section. Monthly. Proc.
C13.29:nos	Building materials and structures report. Superseded by C13.44:
C13.29/2:nos	Building science series
C13.30:nos	[Mathematical tables]
C13.31:nos	Basic radio propagation predictions (monthly) Continued by C13.31/.3:
C13.31/2:	Radio propagation forecasts
C13.31/2a:CT	___ separates
C13.31/3:nos	Central Radio Propagation Laboratory Ionospheric predictions (monthly) Continuation of C13.31: Later C52.10:
C13.32:nos	Applied mathematics series

C13.32/a:CT	___ separates
C13.33:nos	Central Radio Propagation Laboratory reports. Proc. Desig.CRPL
C13.33/2:	Quarterly report of Central Propagation Laboratory. Admin.
C13.33/3:	List of reports received in library. Central Propagation Laboratory. Admin.
C13.33/4:nos	List of unclassified reports received from Department of Army Signal Corps. Pubs. desig. SC list no. Admin.
C13.34:nos	Thermal properties of gases [tables]
C13.35:CT	Addresses. Proc.
C13.36:nos	[Releases of general information] TRG (series) Proc.
C13.36/2:nos	Announcements of new publication TRA (series)
C13.36/3:nos	[Releases pertaining to personnel] TRP (series) Proc.
C13.36/4:date	Releases [miscellaneous]
C13.36/5:nos	NBS publications newsletter
C13.36/6:date	Technical news from Department of Commerce, National Bureau of Standards
C13.37:nos	List of publications, LP (series) Proc.
C13.37/2:v.,dt/nos.	Bibliography on the high temperature chemistry and physics of materials in the condensed state (quarterly)
C13.37/3:nos	Bibliography on the high temperature chemistry and physics of gases and gas-condensed phase reactions
C13.37/4:CT	Bibliographies and lists of publications
C13.37/5:nos	Superconducting devices, literature survey (quarterly)
C13.37/6:nos	Liquefied natural gas, literature survey (quarterly)
C13.38:nos or CT	Reports [on projects]
C13.39:nos	Technical memorandum (Applied Mathematics Division) Proc. Admin.
C13.40:nos	Building research, summary reports. Proc. Official use only
C13.41:date	Graduate School announcement of courses. Annual. Earlier C13.2: G75/date. Admin.

C13.42:v.nos.&nos.	NBS standard. Official use.
C13.43:date	National Applied Mathematics Laboratories. Projects and publications, quarterly report.
C13.44:nos	Monographs. Supersedes C13.4: and C13.29:
C13.45:nos	National Bureau of Standards certificate of calibration
C13.46:nos	NBS technical notes
C13.47:date	Resident research associateships, postdoctoral, tenable at National Bureau of Standards (annual) Earlier C13.2:R 31/3
C13.48:nos	National standard reference data series, NSRDS NBS (series)
C13.48/2:CT	NBS standard reference materials [announcements]
C13.49:nos	Review of selected U.S. Government research and development reports OTR (series)
C13.50:nos	News for users of NBS standard reference materials
C13.51:nos	Cryogenic Data Center current awareness service list (biweekly)
C13.52:nos	Federal information processing standards publications
C13.53:nos	NBS consumer information series
C13.53/a:CT	___ separates
C13.54:date	Electromagnetic metrology, current awareness service (monthly)
C13.55:date	Model weights and measures ordinance
C13.55/2:date	Model State weights and measures law
C13.55/3:date	Model State regulations [on various subjects]
C13.56:nos	Overlap, measurement agreement through process evaluation
C13.57:CT	Experimental technology incentives program, program area descriptions
C13.58:nos	NBSIR (series)
C13.59:date	Center for Building Technolgoy, project summaries, fiscal year
C13.60:date	NBS time & frequency broadcast services

C14 Statistics Bureau

Formed by consolidation of Foreign Commerce Bureau, State Dept. (S4) and Statistics Bureau, Treasury Dept. (T37), July 1, 1903.

C14.1:date	Annual reports. Earlier T37.1: Later C18.19:
C14.1/a:CT	___ separates.
C14.2:CT	General publications
C14.3:date	Bulletins, Exports of domestic bread stuffs. Earlier T37.3/1: and T37.3/4: Later C18.3:
C14.4:nos	Circulars [none issued]
C14.5:date	Commercial relations. Earlier S4.1: Later C10.8:
C14.6:nos	Daily consular reports. Earlier S4.5: Later C10.5/1:
C14.7:date	Index to Daily consular reports. Earlier S4.6:
C14.8:v.nos. (later nos.)	Monthly consular reports. Earlier S4.7: Later C10.6:
C14.9:date	Index to monthly consular reports. Earlier S4.8:
C14.10:v.nos	Special consular reports. Earlier S4.9: Later C10.7:
C14.11:date	List of publications
C14.12:date	Total values of imports and exports. Monthly. Earlier T37.7: Later C18.6:
C14.13:date	Advance sheets from Monthly summary of commerce and finance. Earlier T37.9: Later C18.8:
C14.14:date	Monthly summary of commerce and finance. Earlier T37.8: Later C18.7:
C14.14/a:CT	___ separates
C14.15:date	Review of the world's commerce. Earlier S4.12: Later C10.9:
C14.16:date	Statistical abstracts of the United States. Earlier T37.10: Later C18.14:
C14.16/a:CT	___ separates. Later C18.14/a:
C14.17:le.nos	Classification schedules. Later C18.18:
C14.18:date	Imported merchandise entered for consumption in United States, etc. Later C18.17:

C14.19:date   Sailing dates of steamships from the principal ports of the United States to ports in foreign countries. Monthly. Later C18.10:

Consolidated August 23, 1912, with Manufactures Bureau (C10) as Foreign and Domestic Commerce Bureau (C18).

C15   Steamboat Inspection Service

Transferred from Treasury Department, July 1, 1903 (T38.).

C15.1:date   Annual reports. Earlier T38.1:

C15.2:CT   General publications

C15.3:nos   Bulletins [none issued]

C15.4:nos   Circulars. Earlier T38.4:

C15.5:date   Laws governing Steamboat Inspection Service. Earlier T38.5/1: Later C35.5:

C15.6:ed.nos.   Steamboat Inspectors' Manual. Earlier T38.6:

C15.7:date   List of officers of merchant steam, motor and sail vessels licensed during (calendar) year. Earlier T38.7:

C15.8:date   Pilot rules. Earlier T38.8: Later C25.8: and C25.9: C25.10:

C15.9:date   General rules and regulations. Earlier T38.9: Later C25.6/2:

C15.9/2:date   Supplement to General rules and regulations

C15.9/3:dt.&rule no.   Revision of rules (all classes)

C15.10:nos   Steamboat-inspection Service bulletin. Later C24.3:

June 1932 consolidated with Navigation Bureau (C11) to form Navigation and Steamboat Inspection Bureau.

C16   Printing and Publications Division

Established July 1, 1903

C16.1:date   Annual reports

C16.2:CT   General publications

C16.3:nos   Bulletins [none issued]

C16.4:nos   Circulars [none issued]

C16.5:edition no. (later date)   List of publications of the Department of Commerce and Labor available for distribution

C16.6:date   Monthly list of publications

C16.7:CT   List of publications (miscellaneous)

C17 Appointment Division

Organized Feb. 1904

C17.1:date   Annual reports

C17.2:CT   General publications [none issued]

C17.3:nos   Bulletins [none issued]

C17.4:nos   Circulars [none issued]

C18 Foreign and Domestic Commerce Bureau

Created August 23, 1912 by consolidation of Manufactures Bureau (C10.) and Statistics Bureau (C14.)

C18.1:date   Annual reports

C18.1/a:CT   ___ separates.

C18.2:CT   General publications

C18.3:dt.&nos   Bulletins. Exports of domestic breadstuffs, etc. Monthly bulletins. Earlier C14.3:

C18.3/2:nos   National industrial recovery act. Mim.

C18.3/3:   International bulletins. Admin.

C18.4:nos   Circulars

C18.5/1: dt. &nos.(later vol.) Daily Consular and trade reports. later Commerce Reports (wkly) 1927-1940; Foreign commerce weekly 1940- Earlier C10.6:, C10.14: Later C42.8:

C18/5/1a:CT (later date) ___ separates   Later C42.8/a:

C18.5/2:dt. &nos or dt. &CT Supplements to commerce reports.

C18.5/3:date   Monthly supplements to commerce reports

C18.6:date   Total values of imports and exports. Monthly. Earlier C14.12:

C18.6/2:date   Value of exports, including reexports.. by grand divisions and principal countries. Monthly. Proc.

C18.6/3:date   Analysis of economic groups of domestic exports from and imports into U.S. Monthly. Proc. Early nos. read "Analysis of domestic ...

C18.7:date   Monthly summary of foreign commerce of United States. Earlier C14.14:

C18.7/a:CT   ___ separates

C18.8:date   Advance sheets from Monthly summary of the foreign commerce of the United States. Monthly. Earlier C14.13:

C18.9:nos   Special consular reports. Earlier C10.7: Displaced by C18.27:

C18.10:date   Sailing dates of steamships from the principal ports of the United States to ports in foreign countries. Monthly. Earlier C14.19:

C18.11:nos   Special agents series. Earlier C10.13: Displaced by C18.27:

C18.12:nos   [Foreign] tariff series. Earlier C10.10:

C18.13:nos   Foreign tariff notes. Earlier C10.16:

C18.14:date   Statistical abstract of the United States. Earlier C14.16: Later C3.134:

C18.14/a:CT   ___ separates. Earlier C14.16/a:

C18.15:nos   Miscellaneous series. Earlier C10.17: Displaced by C18.27:

C18.15/a:CT   ___ separates

C18.16:date   Commercial relations. Earlier C10.8:

C18.17:date   Imported merchandise entered for consumption in United States, and duties collected thereon during the quarter ending... Earlier C14.18:

275

C18.18:letters	Classification schedules. Earlier C14.17: Later C3.150:
C18.18/1a:CT	___ separates
C18.18/2:CT	Classification of imports and exports.
C18.19:date	Foreign commerce and navigation. Earlier C14.1: Later C3.159:
C18.19/a:CT	___ separates
C18.20:nos	Confidential bulletin
C18.21:nos	Monthly letter, review of bureau's activities at home and abroad
C18.22/1:date	List of publications for sale by the Superintendent of Documents, etc.
C18.22/2:date	Catalogue of bureau publications. Issued about once a year.
C18.22/3:CT	Lists of publications
C18.23:nos	Confidential circulars
C18.24:nos	Industrial standards
C18.25:nos	Trade information bulletins
C18.26:date	Commerce yearbooks
C18.26/a:CT	___ separates
C18.26/2:date	Foreign commerce yearbooks. Earlier C18.26:1926/v.2-1932/v.2 Later C42.12:
C18.26/2a:CT	___ separates
C18.27:nos	Trade promotion series. Displaces C18.9:, C18.11:, C18.15:
C18.28:nos	Domestic commerce series. See also C18.271:
C18.29:CT	Conversion tables
C18.30:nos	Electrical standards
C18.31:CT	Press notices
C18.32:nos	Domestic commerce (irregular) Mim. and printed. Later C1.25:
C18.32/a:CT	___ separates
C18.32/2:nos	Domestic commerce news letter. Monthly. Proc.

C18.33:nos	Distribution cost studies
C18.34:nos	Foreign port series
C18.35:vol	Survey of current business. Monthly. Earlier C18.5/3:C33 Later C43.8:
C18.35/a:CT	___ separates. Later C43.8/a:
C18.35/2:CT	___ Special supplements. Earlier C18.2:In2/2 Later C43.8/3:
C18.36:date	Survey of current business. Weekly supplement. Earlier C3.34: Later C43.8/2:
C18.37:date	Survey of current business. Annual supplement. Later C43.8/4:
C18.38:CT	Aid for analyzing markets. (by States) Changed from C18.2:
C18.39:CT	Bibliographies (including reading lists) Mim. Changed from C18.Z/1:
C18.40:CT	Radio talks. Mim. Changed from C18.Z/2:
C18.41:nos	Market research series. Multigraphed.
C18.42:nos.&CT	Real property inventory. Proc.
C18.43:nos	Advertising abroad. Monthly. Proc.
C18.44:CT	Advertising media in certain foreign countries
C18.45:nos(later v.nos.&nos)	Aeronautical world news
C18.46:vol	Aeronautics export news (wkly) Proc. [Confidential]
C18.47:nos	Agricultural implements & farm equipment, monthly export and import bulletin
C18.48:	[vacant]
C18.49:nos	Automotive world news
C18.50:vol	Bimonthly review of medicinal preparation exports. Proc.
C18.51:vol	Bimonthly review of toilet preparations exports. Proc.
C18.52:nos-les.	Box series. Proc.
C18.52/2:nos-les.	Cigar box series. Proc.
C18.53:date	British exports of electrical apparatus. Monthly. Proc.

C18.54:nos	Building abroad. Fortnightly. Proc.
C18.54/2:date	Business situation at home and abroad. Wkly. Proc.
C18.55:date	Chemicals & allied products entered for consumption. Monthly. Proc.
C18.56:	[vacant]
C18.57:date	Commercial notes on Canada. Wkly. Proc.
C18.58:	[vacant]
C18.59/1:nos-les	Comparisons of international gray cloth prices. Proc. Quarterly.
C18.59/2:nos	Construction abroad, construction circular no.
C18.60:nos	Cooperage series. Proc.
C18.61:letters	Cost of current series. Proc. Electrical Equipment Division.
C18.62:nos-le, later nos.	Cotton goods in world markets. Wkly. Proc.
C18.63:le-nos. Later v.nos.	Current release of non theatrical film.
C18.64:nos	District office releases. Wkly. Proc. [Confidential]
C18.65:nos	Door series. Proc. Issued by Lumber Division.
C18.66:nos-le	Dry goods merchants world news letter. Proc.
C18.67:nos, later v.nos. &nos.	Electrical and radio world trade news
C18.68:nos	End-matched softwood lumber series. Proc.
C18.69:nos	Essential oil production and trade. Proc.
C18.70:nos., later v.nos.	European financial notes. Semi-monthly. Proc.
C18.71:nos	Far eastern financial notes. Semi-monthly. Proc.
C18.72/1:v.nos	Food stuffs round the world: Canned and dried foods. biweekly. Proc.
C18.72/2:date, later v.nos.	___ Fishery news. Bi-weekly. Proc.
C18.72/3:v.nos	___ Fresh fruits and vegetables
C18.72/4:v.nos	___ Grain and grain products. Proc. bi-weekly
C18.72/5:v.nos	___ Meats, livestock, fats and oils. Fortnightly. Proc.

C18.72/6:v.nos	Food stuffs round the world: Sugar, confectionery, nuts. Fortnightly. Proc.
C18.72/7:v.nos	___ Tropical products. Fortnightly. Proc.
C18.72/8:v.nos	___ World dairy and poultry news section. Fortnightly. Proc.
C18.72/9:v.nos	___ World news on rice. Fortnightly. Proc.
C18.72/10:date	___ Foreign bean market information. Monthly. Proc.
C18.72/11:date	___ Monthly comparative sales of confectionery. Later C3.135:
C18.72/12:date(later nos.)	___ Quarterly canned foods stock reports. Proc. Later C3.136:
C18.72/13:date	___ Weekly fruit exports. Proc.
C18.73:nos., later v.nos.	Foreign communication news. Semi-monthly. Proc.
C18.74:date	Foreign construction news. Proc. wkly. [Confidential]
C18.75:date	Foreign exchange rates. Proc. monthly.
C18.76:letters-nos. later v.nos.	Hardware trade bulletin
C18.77:nos	Foreign highway news. Proc. Wkly.
C18.78:nos.-le	Foreign knit goods letter; special bulletins. Proc. Later C18.101:
C18.79:v.nos	Comparative law series, monthly world review
C18.79/a:CT	___ separates
C18.80:letters & nos.-le.	Foreign lumber tariff series.
C18.81:nos	Foreign market bulletin. Proc.
C18.82:nos	Foreign markets for builders' hardware. Proc. [Confidential]
C18.83:nos	Foreign markets for hand tools. Proc. [Confidential]
C18.84:nos	Foreign markets for heating and cooking appliances. Proc. [Confidential]
C18.85:nos	Foreign markets for scales and other weighing devices. Proc.
C18.85/2:nos	Foreign markets for metals & minerals circulars. Earlier C18.91/2:
C18.86/1:nos-les.	Foreign petroleum statistics. Proc.
C18.86/2:nos	Foreign petroleum statistics (monthly) Proc.

C18.87:CT	Foreign radio broadcasting services
C18.88:v.nos	Foreign railway news
C18.88/2:nos.-le. later v.nos. &nos.	___ Wkly. [Confidential] Proc.
C18.88/3:nos	___ supplements. [Confidential] Proc.
C18.88/4:nos	___ special circulars. [Confidential] Proc.
C18.89:nos., later v.nos.	Foreign shipping news. weekly. Proc.
C18.90:nos	Foreign trade mark application service. Proc. pubs.desig. FTA-nos.
C18.91:nos	Foreign trade notes, Minerals and metals [and] petroleum. Proc. Each commodity biweekly.
C18.91/2:v.nos	Foreign trade notes, Minerals and metals. Monthly. Proc. Later C18.85/2:
C18.91/3:v.nos	Foreign trade notes, petroleum. Proc. Bi-weekly.
C18.92:nos.-le	Foreign yarn trade notes. Proc.
C18.92/2:nos	Forest products division circulars. Proc. Confidential and semi-confidential.
C18.92/3:nos-le	Forest products division Paper circulars. Proc. [Confidential]
C18.93:nos	Fur bearing animals abroad, news jottings from field for American breeders. Bulletins. Proc.
C18.94:nos-le	Fur trade developments. monthly. Proc.
C18.95:nos	General legal bulletin, foreign laws affecting American business. Proc.
C18.96/1:nos	Geographic section - statistical research division. Special circulars. Proc.
C18.96/2:v.nos	Geographic news. Proc.
C18.97:nos	Implements & tractor notes
C18.98:nos	Industrial machinery letters. Proc. Semi-monthly.
C18.99:nos	Industrial property bulletin. Proc.
C18.99/2:nos	Insurance and labor law series. Proc.
C18.100:dt., later v.nos.	International coal trade. Monthly. Proc. Later I28.42:
C18.101:nos-le	International knit goods news. Monthly. Proc. Earlier C18.78:

C18.102:v.nos   International petroleum trade. Proc. Monthly. Later I28.43:

C18.103:nos   Irish Free State tractor exports. Proc.

C18.104:nos, later v.nos.&nos. Iron and steel fortnightly. Proc.

C18.104/2:v.nos.&supp.nos. ___ supplements. Proc.

C18.105:   [vacant]

C18.106:nos   Latin American circulars. Proc.

C18.107:nos., later v.nos.&nos. Latin American financial notes. semi-monthly.

C18.108:nos   Leather advertising circulars. Proc. Monthly.

C18.109:nos   Leather foreign markets bulletins. Proc.

C18.109/2:nos   Foreign markets bulletins for raw materials. Proc.

C18.110:nos, later v.nos.&nos. Leather fortnightly. Proc.

C18.111:nos   Leather manufacturers advertising circulars. Monthly.

C18.112:nos   Leather manufactures in foreign markets. Proc.

C18.113:nos.-le   Linens and laces. Proc. Monthly.

C18.114:nos.&nos.-le. Lumber tariff manuals. Proc.

C18.114/2:nos   Manual of foreign lumber tariffs. Proc.

C18.115:nos.-le, later v.nos. Motion pictures abroad. Biweekly. See for supplement C18.180:

C18.116:nos.-le & le-nos. Motion pictures educational [and] industrial. Proc.

C18.116/2:date   Motion picture theaters throughout the world. Annual.

C18.117:nos and nos.-les. New uses for cotton series. Proc.

C18.118:nos   Plumbing supplies reports. Proc. [Confidential]

C18.119:nos-le   Pole series. Proc. [Confidential] Issued by Lumber Division.

C18.120:CT   World radio markets. Proc. Later C18.220/2:

C18.120/2:CT   World radio markets [series] Proc.

C18.120/3:date   Radio markets check list of circulars. Proc.

C18.120/4:date	World radio markets, index. Proc.
C18.121:date	Rayon and other synthetic textile fiber imports. monthly. Proc.
C18.122:nos	Rug and floor covering material notes. Proc. Quarterly.
C18.123:nos, later v.nos.&nos.	Russian economic notes. Semi-monthly. Proc.
C18.124:v.nos	Side runs of paper trade
C18.125:nos-le	Silk and rayon and other synthetic textile fibers. Monthly
C18.126:nos-le	Sisal, hemp, jute and miscellaneous fibers. Proc. Monthly.
C18.127:nos	Special bulletins. Textile division
C18.128:v.nos	Special cement bulletins. Proc.
C18.129:	[vacant]
C18.130/1:nos	Special circulars: Agricultural implements division. Proc.
C18.130/2:nos	___: Exports of harvesters & binders & combines from the United States. Proc. monthly.
C18.131:nos	___: Automotive division. [Confidential] Proc.
C18.131/2:nos	___: Automotive-aeronautics trade division. Irregular. Proc.
C18.132:nos	___: Chemical division. Proc.
C18.133:nos	___: Commercial laces division. Proc.
C18.134:nos	___: Electrical equipment division. Proc.
C18.135:nos	___: Finance division. Proc.
C18.136:nos	___: Foodstuffs division
C18.137:nos	___: Foreign construction division. Proc.
C18.138:nos	___: Industrial machinery division. Proc.
C18.139:nos	___: Iron & steel division. Proc. Later C18.141/2:
C18.140/1:nos	___: Leather & rubber division.
C18.140/2:nos	Rubber news letter. Proc. Semi-monthly. Earlier C18.143:

C18.141:nos	Special circulars. Lumber division. Proc.
C18.141/2:nos	Iron and steel fortnightly, intermediate issue. Earlier C18.139:
C18.142:nos	Special circular. Regional information division. Proc.
C18.143:nos	Special circulars. Rubber division. Later C18.140/2:
C18.144:	[vacant]
C18.145:nos	Special circulars. Transportation division. Proc. [Confidential]
C18.146:nos	Special series, Paper division. Proc.
C18.147:nos	Tariff correction circular. Proc.
C18.148:nos-le	Textile maintenance notes. Proc. Monthly.
C18.149:nos	Textile raw materials. Weekly. Proc.
C18.150:nos (later v.nos.&nos.)	Textiles and allied products. Weekly. Proc.
C18.151:nos & nos.-les.	Tie series. Proc.
C18.152:nos(later v.nos.&nos.)	Tobacco markets and conditions abroad. Weekly.
C18.152/2:date	U.S. export & import trade in leaf & manufactured tobacco. Annual.
C18.153:CT	Trade lists. Proc. Later C42.10:
C18.154:date	Monthly trade report, China.
C18.155:date(later v.nos.&nos.)	Monthly trade report, Japan. Proc.
C18.156:date(later v.nos.&nos.)	Trade review; quarterly trade review of Southeastern Asia. Proc.
C18.158:date	Values of German exports of electrical apparatus & equipment. Monthly. Proc.
C18.159:nos.-les&nos.	Veneer and plywood series. Proc.
C18.160:nos	Vital statistics of Latin America. Proc.
C18.161:nos-le	Wearing apparel in world markets. Monthly. Proc.
C18.162:nos-le	Weekly cotton service bulletins. Proc.
C18.163:nos, later v.nos.&nos.	World lumber digest. Early titles: World lumber news letter and World lumber press information.

C18.164:nos	World electrical markets. Later C18.220/3:
C18.165:vol	World retail prices and taxes on gasoline, kerosene and motor lubricating oils. Quarterly. Proc. Later I28.44:
C18.166:date	World survey of foreign railways
C18.167:le-nos	World trade in coal tar dies. Proc. [Confidential]
C18.168:nos	World trade in dental preparations, WTDP-nos
C18.169:nos	World trade in explosives
C18.170:nos	World trade in insecticides. W.I.I.-nos. Proc.
C18.171:nos	World trade in paints and varnishes.
C18.172:nos	World trade in plastic paints. Proc. WTPP-nos
C18.173:nos	World trade in plastics. Proc. [Confidential]
C18.174:nos	World trade in prepared medicines. Proc. WTPM-nos
C18.175:nos	World trade in synthetic aromatics. Proc. WTSA-nos
C18.176:nos	World trade in toilet preparations. Proc. WTTP-nos
C18.177:nos	World trade in veterinary preparations. Proc. WTVP-nos
C18.178:nos	World trade in wood, furniture, floor, metal and automobile polishes. PWT pol-
C18.179:v.nos	World trade notes on chemicals and allied products. Weekly. Proc.
C18.179/a:CT	___ separates. Proc.
C18.180:date(later vol)	World wide motion picture developments. Proc. Supplements C18.11:5
C18.181:nos-le	World's wool digest. Wkly. Proc.
C18.182:	Business information service. Basic information sources. Superseded by C18.228:CT
C18.183:	Business information service. Abstracts.
C18.184:CT	Basic data on import trade and trade barriers. Proc.
C18.185:nos and date	United States foreign trade statistics (monthly and weekly **statements) Proc.**

C18.186:nos	Leather and raw materials bulletin (monthly)
C18.186/2:nos	International trade in goatskins
C18.186/3:nos	International trade in sheepskins
C18.187:v.nos	World machinery news (monthly) Proc.
C18.188:CT	Financial data on housing. Proc. Preliminary
C18.189:date, later v.nos	Monthly trade review of France. Early title: Survey of French economic conditions.
C18.190:date	Trend of U.S. foreign trade. Proc. Monthly.
C18.191:vol	Home and abroad with Bureau of foreign and domestic **commerce. Proc.** Fortnightly.
C18.192:nos	[Foreign tariffs] Proc. Publications designated F.T.nos.
C18.193:nos	Negro Affairs Division, Bulletins. usually proc. Later C3.131:
C18.194:vol	Digest of trade hints for paint and varnish merchants (monthly)
C18.195:date	Manufacturers sales and collections on accounts receivable. (monthly) Later included in C18.196:
C18.196:date	Wholesale trade. Proc. Monthly.
C18.197:date	Manchurian soy bean trade. Monthly. Proc.
C18.198:date	U.S. foreign trade in pulp and paper. Proc. Monthly.
C18.199:date	Philippine copra market. Monthly.
C18.199/2:dt.&nos	Philippine copra market. Weekly. Proc. Pubs.desig. FS-6-nos. Earlier C18.185:3043
C18.200:CT	List of State and local trade associations (by States)
C18.200/2:CT	State-local businessmen's organizations. Proc.
C18.201:vol	Rubber products trade news.
C18.202:nos	Export market series. Proc. Issued by Machinery Division
C18.203:vol	Foodstuffs round the world, weekly publication containing Foreign food trade news

C18.204:CT	[Trade of the United States with foreign countries]
C18.205:v.nos.&nos	Tariff items. Monthly. Proc.
C18.206:nos	Economic series
C18.207:date	Trade of U.S. with Japan, China, Hong Kong, and Kwantung. Monthly. Proc.
C18.208:v.nos	Foreign inland waterway news, intracoastal waterways, rivers, lakes, canals, equipment. Monthly. Proc.
C18.209:date	Tung oil monthly. Production in America, foreign trade, etc. Proc. Earlier C18.185:2890
C18.210:CT	Addresses
C18.211:CT	U.S. Foreign trade (by commodities) Proc. Title varies. Changed from C18.2:
C18.212:date	Current developments in drug distribution. Monthly. Proc.
C18.213:date	Current developments in electrical trade. Monthly. Proc.
C18.214:date	Current developments in food distribution. Monthly. Proc.
C18.215:date	Current distribution developments in hardware and allied trades. Monthly. Proc.
C18.216:vol	Automotive foreign trade manual. Proc.
C18.217:CT	Regulations, rules and instructions. Proc. Includes handbooks and manuals.
C18.218:date	Food exports and imports (monthly) Proc.
C18.219:date	Industrial banking companies, installment loans to consumers (monthly) Proc.
C18.220:pt.nos	Industrial reference service. Later title, World trade in commodities. Later C34.10:
C18.220/2:CT	Radio, telephone, telegraph. Earlier C18.120:
C18.220/3:nos	World electrical markets. Earlier C18.164:
C18.221:nos	Industrial reference service. Business service. Proc.
C18.222:date	Personal finance companies, installment loans to consumers. (monthly) Proc.
C18.223:vol	International reference service. Later C34.11:
C18.223/2:nos	Reports on Geneva tariff concessions.

C18.224:date	Industry survey: Manufacturers' inventories, shipments, incoming business [and unfilled orders (monthly) Proc. Later C43.9:
C18.225:nos	Industrial series
C18.226:date	Credit unions, installment loans to consumers (monthly)
C18.227:CT	Marketing laws survey publications. Proc.
C18.228:CT	Inquiry reference service: Supersedes C18.182: Later title Business information service. Later C41.8:CT, C42.9: C41.8/2:
C18.228/2:CT	Inquiry reference service: County basic data sheets, selected counties by States. Proc.
C18.229:date	Pulp and paper industry reports (monthly) Proc. Later C40.11:
C18.229/a:CT	___ separates
C18.230:date, later v.nos. &nos.	Industry reports: Lumber (quarterly) Proc.
C18.230/a:CT	___ separates
C18.231:date	Industry reports: Sugar, molasses and confectionery (quarterly) Proc.
C18.232:date	Industry reports: Domestic transportation (bimonthly) Proc. Replaced by C18.274:
C18.233:date	Industry report: Construction and construction materials (monthly) Proc. Later C40.10:
C18.234:date	Industry report: Canned fruits and vegetables, production and wholesale distribution. Proc. Bimonthly. later Quarterly
C18.235:date	Industry report: Chemicals and allied products (monthly) Proc.
C18.236:date	Industry report: Crude drugs, gums, balsams, and essential oils (monthly)
C18.237:date	Industry report: Drugs and pharmaceuticals (monthly) Proc. Later in C18.235:
C18.238:date	Industry report: Fats and oils (monthly) Later bimonthly. Proc.
C18.239:date	Industry report: Leather (monthly) Proc.
C18.240:date	Industry report: Coffee, tea and spices (quarterly)
C18.241:date	Industry report: Rubber (bimonthly)

C18.242:date   Containers and packaging (quarterly) Later C40.12:

C18.242/a:CT   ___ separates

C18.243:

C18.244:

C18.245:

C18.246:

C18.247:

C18.248:

C18.249:

C18.250:

C18.251;   Reserved for industry reports

C18.252:

C18.253:

C18.254:

C18.255:

C18.256:

C18.257:

C18.258:

C18.259:

C18.260:

C18.261:

C18.262:

C18.263:

C18.264:

C18.265:

C18.266:nos	Current export bulletins. Printed and processed. Earlier Pr32.5807: Later C42.11/2:
C18.267:nos	Comprehensive export schedules. Earlier Pr32.5808: Later C42.11:
C18.267/a:CT	___ separates
C18.268:nos	Small business aids. Proc. Later C40.7/2:
C18.269:v.nos.&nos.	Bulletin of commerce. Proc. Later C41.10:
C18.270:date	Business establishment, employment and taxable pay rolls under old-age and survivors insurance program. Printed and Proc. Later C3.204:
C18.271:nos	[Domestic commerce series] See also C18.28:
C18.271/a:CT	___ separates
C18.272:date	Association conventions (quarterly) Proc.
C18.273:nos	[International trade series] Pubs.desig. IT-nos.
C18.274:nos	Transportation series. Replaces C18.232:
C18.275:nos	[Business economics series] Pubs.desig. BE-nos.
C18.276:nos	Commercial standards. Earlier C13.20: Later C41.25:
C18.277:nos	Simplified practice recommendations. Earlier C13.12/1: Later C41.20:
C18.278:date	Foreign transactions of U.S. Government (quarterly)
C18.279:date	Foreign aid by the U.S. Government (quarterly) Later C43.11:
C18.280:	World trade directory reports
C18.281:nos	Business news reports OBE [releases] Later C43.7:
C18.281/2:nos	Office of Industry and Commerce releases OIC (series) Proc.
C18.281/3:nos	Office of International Trade releases OIT (series) Proc.
C18.282:	World economic notes
C18.283:	Domestic trade digest
C18.284:nos	Synopsis of U.S. Government proposed procurement and contract awards (daily Mon. thru Fri. except Federal legal holidays) Later C41.9:

C18.285:date   Domestic economic developments, weekly business indicators. Proc.

C18.285/2:date   Domestic economic developments, monthly business indicators (weekly)

Through internal reorganizations, functions of the Bureau have been reassigned to other offices of the Department - no date given. This information from 1954-55 U.S. Government Manual.

C19   Children's Bureau

April 9, 1912 (37 Stat. 79)

C19.1:date   Annual reports. Later L5.1:

C19.2:CT   General publications. Later L5.2:

C19.3:nos   Bulletins

C19.4:nos   Circulars

C19.5:nos   Monographs. Later L5.8:

1913 transferred to Department of Labor (37 Stat. 736)

C20   Waste Reclamation Service

January 1, 1919, authorized by President.

C20.1:date   Annual reports

C20.2:CT   General publications

C20.3:   Bulletins

C20.4:   Circulars

Ceased to function on June 30, 1919.

Patent and Trademark Office

C 21 Patent Office

Transferred from Interior Department by Executive order on April 1, 1925.

C21.1/1:date	Annual reports to Congress (calendar year) Earlier I23.1/1:
C21.1/1a:date	___ separates. Reports of commissioner. Calendar year. Earlier I23.1/1a:
C21.1/2:date	Annual reports to Secretary of Commerce. Earlier I23.1/2:
C21.2:CT	General publications. Earlier I23.2:
C21.2/a:CT	___ separates
C21.3:nos	Bulletins. Earlier I23.3: Later C21.3/2:
C21.3/2:nos	Classification definitions. Formerly Classification bulletin C21.3:
C21.4:	Circulars
C21.5:vol.nos	Official gazette. Wkly. Earlier I23.8:
C21.5/a1:v.nos	___ separates. Classification of patents. Wkly. Changed from I28.8/a3:
C21.5/a2:v.nos	___ separates. Decisions of commissioner of patents. Wkly. Changed from I23.8/a4:
C21.5/a3:v.nos	___ separates. Trademarks published. Wkly. Changed from I23.8/a5:
C21.5/a4:v.nos	___ index. Wkly. Changed from I23.8/a7:
C21.5/a5:CT	___ separates, miscellaneous. Changed from I23.8/a6:
C21.5/a6:date	___ separates. Changes in classification of inventions (irregular) Changed from I23.8/a2:
C21.5/a7:v.nos	___ separates. Applications vested in Alien Property Custodian
C21.5/a8:date	Patent abstracts section (separate from Official Gazette)
C21.5/2:date	Index of patents Earlier I23.1/1:date/2
C21.5/3:date	Index of trade marks
C21.5/4:v.nos.&nos.	Official gazette of United States Patent Office: Trademarks
C21.6:date	Decisions of commissioner of patents (Calendar year)

C21.7/1:date	Patent laws (general) Earlier I23.11/1:
C21.7/2:date	U.S. statutes concerning the registration of trade marks. Earlier I23.11/2:
C21.7/3:date	U.S. statutes concerning the registration of prints and labels. Earlier I23.11/3:
C21.7/4:date	Trademark laws
C21.8:date	Rules of practice. Earlier I23.13:
C21.8/a:CT	___ separates
C21.9:date	Roster of registered attorneys. Earlier I23.12:
C21.9/2:date	Patent attorneys and agents available to represent inventors before U.S. Patent Office, arranged by States and counties
C21.10:CT	Briefs. Earlier I23.15:
C21.11:date	Specifications and drawings of patents. Earlier I23.14:
C21.12:date	Manual of classification of patents. Earlier I23.2:C56/4/date
C21.12/2:date	Index to classification
C21.13:date	Patent Office news letter (monthly) Proc.
C21.14:CT	Regulations, rules, and instructions
C21.14/a:CT	___ separates
C21.14/2:CT	Handbooks, manuals, guides
C21.14/3:nos	Supervisor and personnel administration (numbered)
C21.15:date	Manual of patent examining procedure
C21.15/2:nos	Trademark examining procedure directive (numbered)
C21.16:nos	Releases
C21.17:CT	Bibliographies and lists of publications
C21.18:nos	Research and development reports
C21.19:nos	Notes on patent matters. Official use.

C21.20:CT	Addresses	
C21.21:nos	Employee bulletin	
C21.22:CT	Translations of [foreign] patents	
C21.23:CT	Patents	
C21.24:CT	Technology Assessment and Forecast Office: Publications Cl. 2:T22/5	Earlier Cl.62: and

C 22   Mines Bureau

Transferred from Interior Department by Executive order 4239 of June 4, 1925, change effective July 1, 1925.

C22.1:date	Annual reports. Earlier I28.1:, Later I28.1:
C22.2:CT	General publications. Earlier I28.2:, Later I28.2:
C22.3:nos	Bulletins. Earlier I28.3:, Later I28.3:
C22.4:	Circulars [none issued]
C22.5:nos	Technical papers. Earlier I28.7:, Later I28.7:
C22.6:nos	Miners' circulars. Earlier I28.6:, Later I28.6:
C22.7/1:date	Publications of Bureau of Mines. Earlier I28.5/1:, Later I28.5/1:
C22.7/2:date	Index to Bureau of Mines publications. Earlier I28.5/4:, Later I28.5/4:
C22.7/3:nos	New publications. Earlier I28.5/2:, Later I28.5/2:
C22.8:date	Mineral resources of United States (calendar years) Earlier I19.8:, Later I28.37:
C22.8/a:CT	___ separates. Earlier I19.8/a: Later I28.37/a:
C22.8/2:date	Minerals yearbook. Earlier I19,8: and C22.8: Later I28.37:
C22.8/2a:CT	___ separates. Earlier I19.8/a: and C22.8/a:, Later I28.37/a:
C22.9:date	Petroleum statistics, later Monthly petroleum statement. Earlier I28.18:1923/1-1925/4 Later I28.18/2:
C22.9/2:date	Petroleum statistics. Annual. Mim. later Annual petroleum statement. Earlier I28.17:
C22.10:nos	Schedules. Earlier I28.8: Later I28.8:
C22.11:nos	Information circulars. Later I28.27:
C22.12:nos	Reports of investigation Earlier I28.23:, Later I28.23:
C22.13:nos	Economic papers. Later I28.38:
C22.14:nos	Weekly coal report. Mim. Earlier I19.30: Later I28.33:
C22.15:nos	Monthly coke report. Mim. Later I28.30:
C22.16:date	Commercial stocks of coal. Quarterly. Mim. First published intermittently. Earlier I19.31:

C22.17:date	Preliminary estimates of production of coal and beehive coke. Later I28.31:
C22.18:CT	Rules, regulations and instructions handbooks. Later I28.16:
C22.19:nos	Coal mine fatalities. Monthly. Mim. Later I28.101:
C22.19/2:date	Coal mine fatalities. Monthly. Supersedes C22.19: Later I28.10/2:
C22.20:CT	Maps
C22.21:nos	General survey of conditions in coal industry. Monthly. Mim. Succeeded by C22.22:
C22.22:dt.&nos.	Monthly coal market survey. Mim. Succeeds C22.21:
C22.23:nos	Monthly coal distribution report. Mim. Later I28.24:
C22.24:nos	Monographs. Later I28.40:
C22.25:date	Recent articles on petroleum and allied substances. Monthly. Earlier I28.22:
C22.26/1:CT	Motion-picture films (Miscellaneous list)
C22.26/2:date	Motion-picture films (semi-annual list) Later I28.35:
C22.27:nos	Bibliography of fire hazards and prevention and safety in petroleum industry. Semi-annual. Proc.
C22.28:nos	Mineral market reports. Mim. Later I28.28:
C22.29:nos	Monthly cement statement. Later I28.29:
C22.30:nos	Consumption of explosives. Monthly.
C22.31:nos	Health and safety statistics. Later I28.26:
C22.32:nos	Geophysical abstracts. Monthly. Mim. Later I28.25:
C22.33:nos	Quarterly gypsum reports. Mim. Later I28.32:
C22.34:date	Statistics of bituminous coal loaded for shipment on railroads and waterways as reported by operators. Annual. Mim. Later I28.34:
C22.35:nos	Question and answer handbooks. Later I28.48:
C22.Z:CT	Mimeographed material.

Transferred back to the Department of the Interior, April 24, 1934 (I28), by Executive order 6611, of Feb. 22, 1934.

C23   Air Commerce Bureau. Aeronautics Branch

May 20, 1926 (44 Stat. 568)

C23.1:date	Annual reports
C23.2:CT	General publications
C23.3:	Bulletins [none issued]
C23.4:	Bureau circulars. Proc. Admin.
C23.5:nos	Aeronautical bulletins, State series. Earlier W87.21/1: Replaced by C23.7:
C23.6:date	Regulations (general)
C23.6/2:CT	Civil air regulations - Handbooks, regulations & manuals, Misc. (individual)
C23.6/3:nos	Regulations. Later CA1.6:(Sept.1939) CA1.9: (April 1940)
C23.6/3:date	Civil air regulations (compilations)
C23.6/4:nos	Air commerce manuals
C23.6/5:chap. &pt. nos.	Manual of operations. Later CA1.15:
C23.7:nos	Airway bulletin **(loose leaf) (irregularly)** Replaces C23.5:
C23.7/2:nos	Airway bulletins. nos.1 and 2 supersede C23.7:
C23.7/3:nos	Airport bulletins.
C23.8:nos	Information bulletins. Mim. Superseded by C23.11:
C23.9:v. nos. &nos.	later serial nos. Domestic airnews. Mim. Superseded by C23.12:
C23.10/1:nos	Airway maps. See for index N6.25:1932/21, map. See also N6.27: and W87.22/2:
C23.10/2:CT	Maps. Miscellaneous.
C23.10/3:letters	Aeronautical charts, sectional. Later C4.9/4:
C23.10/4:nos. & letters	Regional aeronautical charts. Later C4.9/5:
C23.11:nos	Aeronautics bulletin (Supersedes Information bulletin C23.8:) See for Civil aeronautics bulletins CA1.3:
C23.12:vol	Air commerce bulletin. Monthly. Later CA1.8: Supersedes C23.9:

C23.13:date   Liaison Committee on Aeronautics Radio Research

C23.14:nos   Inspection Service memorandum

C23.15:date   Weekly notices to airmen. Proc. Later CA1.7:

C23.16:le.nos.   Instruction bulletins. Proc. Superseded by Manuals, CA1.10:

C23.17:nos   Army Navy Commerce Committee on Aircraft-Requirements-(publications) desig. ANC-no. Later C31.113:nos. Cancel. <u>Transfer publications to Y3.Ar5/3:7(nos)</u>

C23.18:date   Tabulation of air navigation radio aids. Monthly. Proc. Early issues quarterly. Later CA1.9:

C23.19:nos   Safety and Planning Division reports. Proc. Later CA1.11:

C23.20:date   Domestic scheduled air line operation statistics (monthly) Proc. Earlier CA1.22: and C31.112:

C23.21:   720 hour check. Monthly. Proc.

August 22, 1938 transferred by Executive order 7959 to Civil Aeronautics Authority.

C24   Radio Division

Earlier - prior to Mar. 31, 1927 - Radio Service C11.7:

C24.1:date   Annual reports

C24.2:CT   General publications

C24.3:nos   Radio service bulletins. Monthly. Earlier C11.7/3:

C24.4:   Circulars

C24.5:date   Radio stations of the U.S. (issued annually in two separate pamphlets: Commercial and government radio stations; Amateur radio stations. Earlier C11.7/6:

Superseded July 20, 1932 by the Federal Radio Commission. (RC)

C25 Navigation and Steamboat Inspection Bureau

Consolidation and coordination of Navigation Bureau (C11) and Steamboat Inspection Service (C15) June 1932.

C25 Marine Inspection and Navigation Bureau

Name changed by act of May 27, 1936 (49 Stat. 1380)

C25.1:date	Annual reports
C25.2:CT	General publications
C25.3:nos	Bulletins. Monthly. Mim. Earlier C15.10:
C25.4:	Circulars
C25.5:date	Laws governing steamboat inspection. Earlier C15.5:, C25.6/3:CT
C25.5/2:date	Navigation laws of U.S. Issued every 4 years. Earlier C11.6:
C25.6/1:date	General rules and regulations. Earlier T38.9: and C15.9:
C25.6/2:nos	___ supplements. Earlier C15.9/2:
C25.6/3:CT	Regulations. Miscellaneous. Earlier C15.9:
C25.7:vol	Current shipping data. Monthly. Mim.
C25.8:date	Pilot rules for rivers whose waters flow into Gulf of Mexico and their tributaries and Red River of the North. Earlier C15.8:
C25.9:date	Pilot rules for certain inland waters of Atlantic and Pacific coasts and of coast of Gulf of Mexico. Earlier T38.8:In3/1-4 and C15.8:In5/1-29
C25.10:date	Merchant marine statistics. Earlier C11.10: Later C25.15:6, 9, 12
C25.11:date	Merchant vessels of U.S. Earlier T37.11:, T30.5:, C11.5: Later in C25.15:
C25.12:vol	Merchant marine bulletin. Monthly. Later N24.24:
C25.13:nos	Circular letters. Proc. Superseded by N24.27:
C25.14:nos	Rules and regulations series
C25.15:nos	Report series
C25.16:nos	Educational series

C25.17:CT   Posters

February 27, 1942 transferred by Executive Order 9083 to Bureau of Customs (Treasury) and United States Coast Guard (Navy) effective March 1, 1942.

C26   Federal Employment Stabilization Board

February 10, 1931 (46 Stat. 1085)

C26   Federal Employment Stabilization Office

Established May 1934, by Executive order 6623 of Mar. 1, 1934.

C26.1: date   Annual reports. Later Pr32.301:

C26.2:CT   General publications

C26.3:   Bulletins

C26.4:   Circulars

Reorganization plan no. 1 of 1939, effective July 1, 1939 abolished the Office and transferred its functions to the National Resources Planning Board.

C27   Shipping Board Bureau

Formerly an independent agency (SB) transferred to Commerce Department August 1934, by Executive order 6166 dated June 10, 1933.

C27.1:date   Annual reports. Earlier SB1.1:

C27.2:CT   General publications. Earlier SB1.2:

C27.3:   Bulletins

C27.4:   Circulars

C27.5:   Laws

C27.6:date   Regulations (Includes rules)

C27.7:   Maps

C27.8:   Posters

C27.9:   Shipping Board Bureau. Research Division Reports:

299

C27.9/1:date   American flag services in foreign trade with U.S.   Earlier SB7.2:Am3/2   Later MC1.12:

C27.9/2:CT   Comparative statement of foreign commerce of U.S. ports by States.   Earlier SB7.5/298:   Later MC1.10:

C27.9/3:date   Comparative summary of water borne foreign commerce (Calendar and fiscal years)   Earlier SB7.5/399:   Later MC1.19:

C27.9/4:q-date and a-date.   Imports and exports of commodities by U.S. coastal districts and foreign trade regions (quarterly, fiscal and calendar years).   Report D.R. 275.   Earlier SB7.5/275:   Later MC1.11:

C27.9/5:date   Merchant fleet in service on Great Lakes.   Semi-annual.   Report D.R.1111

C27.9/6:date   Ocean going merchant fleets of principal maritime nations, vessels of 2,000 gross tons and over.   Semi-annual.   Report D.R.100.   Earlier SB7.5/100:   Later MC1.16:

C27.9/7:date   Quarterly report on employment of American merchant vessels.   Mim.   Report DR 300.   Earlier SB7.5/300:   Later MC1.8:

C27.9/8:date   Status of vessel construction and reconditioning under merchant marine acts of 1920 and 1928.   Monthly.   Mim.   Report D.R.1105.   Earlier SB7.5/1105:

C27.9/9:date   U.S. Water borne intercoastal traffic by ports of origin and destination and principal commodities.   Fiscal and calendar years.   Report D.R. 317.   Earlier SB7.5/317:   Later MC1.9:

C27.9/10:date   Report on volume of water borne foreign commerce of U.S. by ports of origin and destination (fiscal years)   Earlier SB7.2:C73   Later MC1.17:

C27.9/11:date   Water borne foreign and domestic commerce of U.S. (calendar years) Report D.R. 295.   Earlier SB7.5/295:   Later MC1.20:

C27.9/12:date   Water borne passenger traffic of U.S. (fiscal and calendar years) Report D.R. 157.   Earlier SB7.5/157:   Later MC1.15:

C27.9/13:CT   Research Division maps.   Earlier SB7.6:   Later MC1.14:

C27.10:CT   Papers in re.   Earlier SB1.13:

C27.11:date   Annual report and general financial statement.   Earlier SB10.7:

In 1936 functions transferred to Maritime Commission (MC)

C28 Business Advisory Council

Established June 26,1933; Business Advisory and Planning Council. Name changed to Business Advisory Council, April 11,1935.

C28.1:date   Annual reports

C28.2:CT   General publications

C29 Inland Waterways Corporation

Transferred from War Department (W103) July 1,1939.

C29.1:date   Annual reports. Earlier W103.1:

C29.2:CT   General publications. Earlier W103.2:

Corporation sold to Federal Waterways Corporation of Delaware on September 19,1953.

C30 Weather Bureau

Transferred from Agriculture Department (A29) by the President's Reorganization Plan 4, effective June 30, 1940.

C30.1:date	Annual reports. Earlier A29.1:
C30.2:CT	General publications. Earlier A29.2:
C30.3:	
C30.3/2:nos	Climatic summary of United States. Earlier A29.5/a:sec.nos
C30.4:letters	Circulars (lettered) Earlier A29.11:
C30.6:CT	Regulations, rules and instructions. Earlier A29.12: Later C55.106:
C30.6/2:CT	Handbooks, manuals, guides. Earlier in C30.6: Later C55.108:
C30.6/3:nos	Forecasting guide
C30.6/4:nos	Weather Bureau forecasters handbooks Later C55.108/3:
C30.6/5:nos	Weather Bureau engineering handbooks
C30.6/6:nos	Weather Bureau observing handbooks Later C55.108/2:
C30.7:dt.&nos	Corn and wheat region bulletins, Weekly during season, April-September. Issued at Chicago. Earlier A29.43:
C30.8:date	Corn and wheat region bulletins (daily except Sundays and holidays during season, April-September). Issued at Region Center of Weather Bureau, Chicago, Ill. Earlier A29.43/2:
C30.9:dt.&nos	Cotton region bulletin, Weekly (during season April-October). Issued at New Orleans, La. Earlier A29.39:
C30.9/2:	(Crop bulletin)
C30.10:date	Meteorological summary, Washington, D.C. Monthly. Earlier A29.30/2: Later C30.10:1
C30.10:1/date	Station meteorological summary, Washington. Earlier C30.10: Later C30.56/1:
C30.10:2/date	Station meteorological summary, San Juan, P.R. (monthly) Earlier C30.45:
C30.10:3/date	Station meteorological summary, Los Angeles, Calif. (monthly)

302

C30.10/2:1/date	Special meteorological summaries, Washington National Airport, Washington, D.C. (monthly)
C30.10/2:2/date	Special meteorological summaries, San Juan, P.R. (monthly) Later C30.56/2:
C30.10/2:3/date	Special meteorological summaries, Los Angeles WB Airport, Calif. (monthly)
C30.10/2:4/date	Special meteorological summaries, Burbank WB Airport, Calif. (monthly)
C30.10/2:5/date	Special meteorological summaries, Detroit, Mich., WB Airport (monthly)
C30.10/3:CT	Local climatological summary with comparative data
C30.11:dt.&nos	Weather and crop bulletins: Wkly. Earlier A29.7/2: Later C55.209:
C30.11/2:date	Utah weather, crops and livestock
C30.12:date	Weather maps, Daily. Earlier A29.18: Later C52.11/2:
C30.13:date-nos	Weather outlook (weekly) Proc. Earlier A29.38: name changed to Weather forecast .Later Extended forecast
C30.14:vol	Monthly weather review. Earlier A29.6/1: Later C55.11:
C30.14/a:CT	___ separates. Miscellaneous. Earlier A29.6/a2: Later C55.11/a:
C30.14/a2:date	___ separates: Weather of oceans. Monthly. Earlier A29.6/a4:
C30.14/a3:date	Weather and circulation (monthly)
C30.15:nos	___ Supplements. Earlier A29.6/2:
C30.16:CT/dt	Meteorological summaries, Annual (CT by States) Earlier A29.30/2: to A29.30/38:
C30.17:date	Price list of publications. Earlier A29.31/3:
C30.17/2:pt.nos	Weather Bureau publications. Proc.
C30.17/3:CT	Bibliographies and lists of publications
C30.18:vol	Climatological data for United States by sections (monthly) Earlier A29.29:
C30.18/2:v.nos	___ bound edition. Earlier A29.29/2:

C30.18/3:v.nos   Climatological data for United States by sections (monthly) Alabama. Later C55. 214/2:

C30.18/4:v.nos   ___Arizona   Later C55. 214/4:

C30.18/5:v.nos   ___Arkansas   Later C55. 214/5:

C30.18/6:v.nos   ___California   Later C55. 214/6:

C30.18/7:v.nos   ___Colorado   Later C55. 214/7:

C30.18/8:v.nos   ___Florida   Later C55. 214/8:

C30.18/9:v.nos   ___Georgia   Later C55. 214/9:

C30.18/10:v.nos   ___Idaho   Later C55. 214/11:

C30.18/11:v.nos   ___Illinois   Later C55. 214/12:

C30.18/12:v.nos   ___Indiana   Later C55. 214/13:

C30.18/13:v.nos   ___Iowa   Later C55. 214/14:

C30.18/14:v.nos   ___Kansas   Later C55. 214/15:

C30.18/15:v.nos   ___Kentucky   Later C55. 214/16:

C30.18/16:v.nos   ___Louisiana   Later C55. 214/17:

C30.18/17:v.nos   ___Maryland and Delaware   Later C55. 214/18:

C30.18/18:v.nos   ___Michigan   Later C55. 214/19:

C30.18/19:v.nos   ___Minnesota   Later C55. 214/20:

C30.18/20:v.nos   ___Mississippi   Later C55. 214/21:

C30.18/21:v.nos   ___Missouri   Later C55. 214/22:

C30.18/22:v.nos   ___Montana   Later C55. 214/23:

C30.18/23:v.nos   ___Nebraska   Later C55. 214/24:

C30.18/24:v.nos   ___Nevada   Later C55. 214/25:

C30.18/25:v.nos   ___New England   Later C55. 214/26:

C30.18/26:v.nos   ___New Jersey   Later C55. 214/27:

C30.18/27:v.nos   ___New Mexico   Later C55. 214/28:

C30.18/28:v.nos	Climatological data for United States by sections (monthly) New York Later C55.214/29:
C30.18/29:v.nos	___ North Carolina Later C55.214/30:
C30.18/30:v.nos	___ North Dakota Later C55.214/31:
C30.18/31:v.nos	___ Ohio Later C55.214/32:
C30.18/32:v.nos	___ Oklahoma Later C55.214/33:
C30.18/33:v.nos	___ Oregon Later C55.214/34:
C30.18/34:v.nos	___ Pennsylvania Later C55.214/36:
C30.18/35:v.nos	___ South Carolina Later C55.214/38:
C30.18/36:v.nos	___ South Dakota Later C55.214/39:
C30.18/37:v.nos	___ Tennessee Later C55.214/40:
C30.18/38:v.nos	___ Texas Later C55.214/41:
C30.18/39:v.nos	___ Utah Later C55.214/42:
C30.18/40:v.nos	___ Virginia Later C55.214/43:
C30.18/41:v.nos	___ Washington Later C55.214/44:
C30.18/42:v.nos	___ West Virginia Later C55.214/45:
C30.18/43:v.nos	___ Wisconsin Later C55.214/46:
C30.18/44:v.nos	___ Wyoming Later C55.214/47:
C30.18/45:date	[Climatological data map] (monthly)
C30.19:vol	Climatological data, Hawaii section (monthly) Earlier A29.34: Later C55.214/10:
C30.19/2:v.nos	Climatological data, Pacific (monthly) Proc. Later C55.214/35:
C30.20:v.nos.&nos	Climatological data, West Indies and Caribbean service (monthly) Earlier A29.26:date and nos
C30.20/2:v.nos	Climatological data: Puerto Rico and Virgin Islands. Later C55.214/37:
C30.21:v.nos.&nos.	Climatological data, Alaska Section. Earlier A29.33: Later C55.214/3:

C30.21/2:nos	Climatological data for Arctic stations Later C55.214/49:
C30.21/3:nos	Climatological data for Antarctic stations Later C55.214/50:
C30.22:CT	Maps and charts Later C55.122:
C30.22/2:CT	Maps and charts (sets)
C30.22/3:CT	Storm warning facilities charts
C30.22/4:CT	Sheets of National atlas of United States
C30.22/5:dt/pt.nos	International Geophysical Year world weather maps (monthly) July 1957-Dec. 1958
C30.22/6:CT	Weather Bureau marine service charts Later C55.112:
C30.23:nos	Radio circulars. Earlier A29.37:
C30.24:vol.nos	Daily river stages at river gage stations on principal rivers of United States. Earlier A29.10: Later C55.117:
C30.25:date	United States meteorological year book Earlier A29.45:
C30.26:date	Correspondence course, elements of surface weather observations. Lessons. Proc.
C30.27:date	Daily synoptic series, historical weather maps, Northern Hemisphere sea level (monthly) For official use only.
C30.28:nos	Technical papers. no.1 is restricted
C30.29:nos	Research papers. Proc.
C30.30:date	Hydrologic bulletin, hourly and daily precipitation, north Atlantic district (monthly) Proc.
C30.31:date	Hydrologic bulletin, hourly and daily precipitation, southeast district (monthly) Proc.
C30.32:date	Hydrologic bulletin, hourly and daily precipitation, Ohio river district (monthly) Proc.
C30.33:date	Hydrologic bulletin, hourly and daily precipitation, Upper Mississippi district (monthly) Proc.
C30.34:date	Hydrologic bulletin, hourly and daily precipitation, Missouri River district (monthly) Proc.

C30.35:date	Hydrologic bulletin, hourly and daily precipitation, lower Mississippi-West Gulf district (monthly) Proc.
C30.36:date	Hydrologic bulletin, hourly and daily precipitation, Pacific district (monthly) Proc.
C30.37:date	Hydrologic bulletin, hourly and daily precipitation, South Pacific district (monthly)
C30.37/2:date	Daily and hourly precipitation data, hydrologic network region 7, Southwestern district, Weather Bureau Office, Albuquerque, N.Mex.
C30.38:date	Daily synoptic series, historical weather maps, Northern Hemisphere 3,000 dynamic meters (monthly)
C30.39:date	Daily synoptic series, historical weather maps, southwest Pacific, sea level (monthly)
C30.40:date	Daily synoptic series, historical weather maps, North America, 10 kilometers (monthly)
C30.41:date	Daily synoptic series, historical weather maps, North America, 13 kilometers (monthly)
C30.42:date	Daily synoptic series, historical weather maps, North America, 16 kilometers (monthly)
C30.43:date	Daily weather bulletin
C30.43/2:	___ Norfolk, Va.
C30.43/3:	___ New York City
C30.43/4:	___ Bismark, N.Dak.
C30.43/5:	___ Houston, Tex.
C30.43/6:	___ Dallas, Tex.
C30.44:nos	Hydrometeorological reports. Proc. Later C55.28:
C30.44/2:nos	Hydrometeorological Section technical papers
C30.45:date	Climatological summary; Monthly, San Juan, P.R. Proc. Later C30.10:2
C30.46:date	Average monthly weather resumé and outlook (semimontnly) Later C55.109:

C30.47:dt. &nos, later v.nos. &nos. Heating degree day bulletin

C30.48:nos   Weather bureau training papers

C30.49:date   Synoptic weather maps, Northern Hemisphere, sea level and 500 millibar charts with synoptic data tabulations; Daily series (monthly) See for 1899 to June 1939 maps, C30.27:   Later C55.213/2:

C30.49/2:date   Daily series, synoptic weather maps, part 2, Northern Hemisphere data tabulations, daily bulletin. Formerly monthly and classed C30.49:date/pt.2

C30.49/3:date   ___ Northern Hemisphere, 100 millibar and 50 millibar charts

C30.50:v.nos.&nos Climatic data for world by continents; Monthly. Proc. Later C55.211:

C30.50/2:date   Monthly climatic data for world, supplements (annual)

C30.51:v.nos.&nos. Climatological data, national summary (monthly) Later C55.214:

C30.52:CT   Terminal forecasting reference manual (by terminals) Proc. or ptd.

C30.53:v.nos.&nos Library circular (monthly) Proc.

C30.54:   Daily weather and river bulletins: St.Louis, Mo. Later title, Daily Mississippi river stages and forecast bulletin. Later C55.110/3:

C30.54/2:   ___ Columbia, S.C.

C30.54/3:   ___ Houston, Tex.

C30.54/4:nos   ___ Albuquerque, N.Mex. Later C55.110/4:

C30.54/5:   ___ Jackson, Miss.

C30.54/6:   ___ Little Rock, Ark.

C30.54/7:   ___ Memphis, Tenn. Later C55.110/2:

C30.54/8:   ___ Mobile, Ala.

C30.54/9:   ___ Montgomery, Ala. area.

C30.54/10:   ___ New Orleans, La. District Forecast Center   Later C55.110/5:

C30.54/11:   ___ Sacramento, Calif

C30.54/12:   ___ Shreveport, La.   Later C55.110/6:

C30.54/13:   ___ Vicksburg, Miss.

C30.54/14:   ___ La Crosse, Wis

C30.54/15:   Daily weather and river bulletin, Cairo, Ill.

C30.54/16:   ___ Charleston, S.C.

C30.54/17:date   Ohio river summary and forecasts. Later C55.110:

C30.54/18:   Daily weather and river bulletin, Portland, Oregon

C30.55:   Daily river bulletin, Davenport, Iowa

C30.55/2:   ___ Atlanta, Ga.

C30.55/3:   ___ Evansville, Ind.

C30.55/4:   ___ Pittsburgh, Pa.

C30.56/1:date   Local climatological data, Washington, D.C. (monthly) Formerly Station meteorological summary C30.10:1   Later C55.217:

C30.56/2:date   ___ San Juan, P.R. (monthly) Formerly Station meteorological summary C30.10:2

C30.56/3:date   ___ Chicago, Illinois

C30.56/4:date   ___ Roanoke, Virginia

C30.56/5:date   ___ Raleigh, North Carolina

C30.56/6:date   ___ Minneapolis, Minnesota

C30.56/7 to C30.56/295: Reserved for local climatological data. Numbers not assigned.

C30.57:nos   Daily upper air bulletin   Later D210.10:

C30.58:   Water supply forecasts

C30.59:v.nos.&nos. Hourly precipitation data (monthly with annual summary): Alabama Later C55.216:

C30.59/2:v.nos.&nos. ___ Alaska

C30.59/3:v.nos.&nos. ___ Arizona   Later C55.216/2:

C30.59/4:v.nos.&nos. ___ Arkansas Later C56.216/3:

C30.59/5:v.nos.&nos. ___ California Later C55.216/4:

C30.59/5-2:date   California, monthly and seasonal precipitation (fiscal year)

C30. 59/6:v. nos. &nos. Hourly precipitation data (monthly with annual summary): Colorado. Later C55. 216/5:

C30. 59/7:v. nos. &nos. ___ Florida   Later C55. 216/6:

C30. 59/8:v. nos. &nos. ___ Georgia   Later C55. 216/7:

C30. 59/9:v. nos. &nos. ___ Idaho   Later C55. 216/9:

C30. 59/10:v. nos. &nos. ___ Illinois   Later C55. 216/10:

C30. 59/11:v. nos. &nos. ___ Indiana.   Later C55. 216/11:

C30. 59/12:v. nos. &nos. ___ Iowa.   Later C55. 216/12:

C30. 59/13:v. nos. &nos ___ Kansas.   Later C55. 216/3:

C30. 59/14:v. nos. &nos. ___ Kentucky   Later C55. 216/14:

C30. 59/15:v. nos. &nos. ___ Louisiana   Later C55. 216/15:

C30. 59/16:v. nos. &nos. ___ **Maryland and** Delaware   Later C55. 216/16:

C30. 59/17:v. nos. &nos. ___ Michigan   Later C55. 216/17:

C30. 59/18:v. nos. &nos. ___ Minnesota   Later C55. 216/18:

C30. 59/19:v. nos. &nos. ___ Mississippi   Later C55. 216/19:

C30. 59/20:v. nos. &nos. ___ Missouri   Later C55. 216/20:

C30. 59/21:v. nos. &nos. ___ Montana   Later C55. 216/21:

C30. 59/22:v. nos. &nos. ___ Nebraska   Later C55. 216/22:

C30. 59/23:v. nos. &nos. ___ Nevada.   Later C55. 216/23:

C30. 59/24:v. nos. &nos. ___ New England.   Later C55. 216/24:

C30. 59/25:v. nos. &nos ___ New Jersey.   Later C55. 216/25:

C30. 59/26:v. nos. &nos. ___ New Mexico.   Later C55. 216/26:

C30. 59/27:v. nos. &nos. ___ New York   Later C55. 216/27:

C30. 59/28:v. nos. &nos. ___ **North Carolina**   Later C55. 216/28:

C30. 59/29:v. nos. &nos. ___ North Dakota   Later C55. 216/29:

C30.59/30:v.nos.&nos. Hourly precipitation data. Ohio. Later C55.216/30:

C30.59/31:v.nos.&nos. ___ Oklahoma. Later C55.216/31:

C30.59/32:v.nos.&nos. ___ Oregon. Later C55.216/32:

C30.59/33:v.nos.&nos. ___ Pennsylvania. Later C55.216/33:

C30.59/34:v.nos.&nos. ___ South Carolina. Later C55.216/34:

C30.59/35:v.nos.&nos. ___ South Dakota. Later C55.216/35:

C30.59/36:v.nos.&nos. ___ Tennessee. Later C55.216/36:

C30.59/37:v.nos.&nos. ___ Texas. Later C55.216/37:

C30.59/38:v.nos.&nos. ___ Utah. Later C55.216/38:

C30.59/39:v.nos.&nos. ___ Virginia. Later C55.216/39:

C30.59/40:v.nos.&nos. ___ Washington. Later C55.216/40:

C30.59/41:v.nos.&nos. ___ West Virginia. Later C55.216/41:

C30.59/42:v.nos.&nos. ___ Wisconsin. Later C55.216/42:

C30.59/43:v.nos.&nos. ___ Wyoming. Later C55.216/43:

C30.59/44:nos Climatography series 70-nos., Precipitation data from storage-gage stations

C30.59/45:v.nos Storage-gage precipitation data for Western United States

C30.59/46:v.nos.&nos. Hourly precipitation data: Hawaii Later C55.216/8:

C30.60: Releases. Proc.

C30.61:nos Cooperative studies reports

C30.62: Daily temperature, degree data and precipitation normals

C30.62/2: Monthly normal temperatures, precipitation and degree days CLASS CANCELLED. See C30.2:T24/3

C30.62/3:date Monthly precipitation and temperature [Columbia River basin in Pacific Northwest] Later C55.114:

C30.63:nos Training papers

C30.64:sec.nos	Inventory of unpublished climatological tabulations
C30.65:nos	Aviation series
C30.66:CT	Key to meteorological records documentation [State series]
C30.66/2:nos	___ [miscellaneous reports] Later C55.219:
C30.66/3:CT	___ 6.11, Decadal census of weather stations by States
C30.67:nos	Climatic guides (Climatography of the United States No. 40-nos.)
C30.68:nos/CT	Summary of hourly observations (Climatography of the United States no. 30-nos.)
C30.69:nos	[Letter supplements] L.S. series
C30.70:nos	National Hurricane Research Project reports. Proc.
C30.70/2:nos	National Severe Storms Project reports
C30.71:nos. &CT	Climatography of United States 20-nos. Climatological summary [by States]
C30.71/2:nos	Climatography of United States 10-nos. Climatic summary [by regions] Earlier A29.5/a:sec.
C30.71/3:nos	Climatography of United States, 60-nos. Climates of the States. Later C55.221:
C30.71/4:nos	Decennial census of United States climate; Monthly normals of temperature, precipitation, and heating degree days, Climatography of United States no. 81-
C30.71/5:nos	Decennial census of United States climate. Summary of hourly observations, 75th meridian time zone, Climatography of United States 82 (series) Later C55.221/2:
C30.71/6:nos	Climatography of United States 21- (series) Climatic summaries of resort areas
C30.71/7:nos	Decennial census of United States climate: Climatography of United States [miscellaneous series]
C30.71/8:nos	Decennial census of United States climate, Climatic summary of United States, supplement 1951-60, Climatography of United States, no. 86- (series)
C30.72:v.nos./nos	Mariners weather log (bimonthly) Later C55.210:
C30.73:date	Directory of weather broadcasts (annual) Earlier C30.2:B78
C30.74:v./nos	Storm data (monthly) Information formerly published in Climatological data national summary, C30.51: Later C55.212:

C30.75:date	Research progress and plans of the Weather Bureau, fiscal year
C30.75/2:date	Current Federal meteorological research and development activities (annual)
C30.76:date	Daily aerological cross-section pole to pole along meridian 75°W for the IGY period, July 1957-Dec.1958 (monthly) Note: 18 in series
C30.77:date	Summer student trainee report. Earlier C30.2:T68
C30.78:CT	Study kits
C30.79:date	Weather service for merchant shipping Later C55.119:
C30.80:nos	National Meteorological Center technical memorandums
C30.81:CT	Addresses
C30.82:nos	Technical notes
C30.83:date	Operations of the Weather Bureau (semi-annual) Later C55.111:
C30.84:nos	Eastern Region Radar progress report
C30.85:v./nos	Water supply outlook for western United States (monthly) Prior to v. 21, no.1, entitled Water supply forecasts for western United States. Later C55.113:
C30.86:date	Observers quarterly
C30.87:nos	System Development Office reports (numbered)
C30.88:date	Cooperative observer, regional newsletter, Western Region, Salt Lake City, Utah.

By Department Organization order 25A, effective Oct. 9, 1970 the Bureau was redesignated National Weather Service and placed under the National Oceanic and Atmospheric Administration.

C31 Civil Aeronautics Authority

The Civil Aeronautics Authority (CA) and its functions and the functions of the Air Safety Board are transferred to Commerce Department. The functions of the Air Safety Board are consolidated with the functions of the Civil Aeronautics Authority, which shall hereafter be known as Civil Aeronautics Board. Transferred to Commerce Department by the President's Reorganization plan 4, effective June 30, 1940.

C31.1:date	Annual reports. Earlier CA1.1:date
C31.2:CT	General publications. Earlier CA1.2:CT
C31.5:CT	Laws
C31.6:CT	Regulations, rules and instructions. Includes handbooks and manuals.
C31.7:vol	Civil aeronautics journal (twice monthly) Earlier CA1.17: Later C31.118:
C31.8:date	Air navigation radio aids, Tabulation of (monthly) Earlier CA1.9: Later C31.108:
C31.9:vol	Airmen, Weekly notices to. Proc. Earlier CA1.7: Later C31.109:
C31.10:dt.&nos	Airmen, Special notices to. Proc. Earlier CA1.7/2: Later C31.110:
C31.11:nos	Technical development reports. Earlier CA1.20: Later C31.119:
C31.12:nos	Technical development notes. Proc. & printed. Later C31.125:

C31 Civil Aeronautics Administration

That part of Civil Aeronautics Authority the functions of which are administered by Administrator of Civil Aeronautics shall be known as Civil Aeronautics Administration.

C31.101:date	Annual reports
C31.102:CT	General publications
C31.103:nos	Civil aeronautics bulletins. Earlier CA1.3:
C31.103/a:CT	___ separates
C31.103/2:nos	Airport engineering bulletins. Proc. Admin.

C31.103/4:nos	Maintenance Engineering Branch training bulletin, OJT nos. Admin.
C31.104/2:	Air traffic control performance standards circulars. Proc. Admin.
C31.104/3:	Air traffic control training circular. Proc. Admin.
C31.105:CT	Laws
C31.106:CT	Regulations, rules, and instructions
C31.106/2:date	ANC procedures for control of air traffic. Earlier C31.106:T67/3 Later FAA3.9:
C31.106/3:nos	ATC manual. Official use.
C31.106/4:nos	Maintenance Operations Division instructions. Administrative. Later FAA1.6/3:
C31.106/5:CT	Handbooks, manuals, guides (unnumbered) Earlier C31.106:
C31.107:nos	Manuals (numbered) Proc. Earlier CA1.10:
C31.107/2:v.nos	Civil aeronautics manuals [by volume number] Earlier C31.107: Later FAA1.34:
C31.108:date	Air navigation radio aids, Tabulation of (monthly) Earlier C31.8:
C31.109:vol	Weekly notices to airmen. Earlier C31.9: Superseded by C31.127:
C31.110:date	Special notices to airmen. Earlier C31.10:
C31.111:nos	Certificates and Inspection Division releases. Proc. Earlier CA1.21: Later FAA5.7:
C31.112:date	Domestic air carrier operation statistics (monthly) Proc. Earlier CA1.22:
C31.113:nos	Army Navy Civil Committee on Aircraft Requirements publications. Desig. ANC Earlier C23.17: Cancel. Transfer publications to Y3.Ar5/3:7/nos
C31.114:nos	Flight engineering reports. Proc.
C31.115:CT	Civil aeronautics Administration, Maps. Earlier CA1.13: Later FAA3.12:

C31.116:chap.&pt.nos. Manual of operations. Proc. Earlier CA1.15: Superseded by C31.116/2:

C31.116/2:v.Chap.&pt. nos. Federal airways manual of operations. Proc. Supersedes C31.116: Superseded by C31.116/3:

C31.116/3:nos.-les Federal airway manual of operations. Supersedes C31.116/2: Later FAA4.9:

C31.117:chap.nos Inspection handbook

C31.118:vol Civil aeronautics journal (twice monthly) later title, CAA journal. Earlier C31.7:

C31.119:nos Technical development reports. Earlier C31.11: Later FAA2.8:

C31.120:nos Specifications. Proc. pubs.desig.CAA-nos. Later FAA1.13:

C31.120/2: Aircraft specifications (subscription) Consists of Specifications, Alphabetical index, Aircraft listing and Monthly supplementary service, Aircraft listing formerly C31.102:Ai7/37 Later FAA1.29:

C31.120/3: Engine & propeller specifications (subscription) Consists of Specifications, Alphabetical indexes, Engine listing, Propeller listing, and monthly supplements. Aircraft engine listing and propeller listing formerly C31.102:Ai7/39 and C31.102:R94. Later FAA1.29/2:

C31.121:nos Flight information bulletins. Proc. Aircraft listing formerly C31.102:Ai7/37

C31.122:CT Posters

C31.123:nos Study of air traffic control, Reports. Proc.

C31.124:CT Addresses

C31.125:nos Technical development notes. Proc. Earlier C31.13:

C31.126:date Directory of airfields, U.S. Army & Navy (bimonthly) Proc. [Restricted] Superseded by C31.127:

C31.127:vol Airman's guide (biweekly) Proc. Supersedes C31.126:, C31.109: and C31.121:3/dt Later FAA1.23:

C31.128:v.nos Flight information manual (semiannual) Proc. [Companion publication to Airman's guide, C31.127:] Later FAA1.20:

C31.129:CT [Technical papers] Proc.

C31.130:date Military and civil aircraft and aircraft engine production, Monthly production report. Restricted. Proc.

C31.131:nos	Reports of Division of Research. Proc.
C31.131/2:nos	Special series reports of Division of Research. Proc.
C31.132:date	Civil aircraft by States and by counties within States (monthly) (quarterly beginning July 1, 1948)
C31.132/2:date	United States active civil aircraft by State and county. Earlier C31.102: Ai7/50 Later FAA1.35:
C31.133:v.nos	International notams (daily) Proc. Later FAA1.26:
C31.134:v.nos	Alaska flight information manual. Proc. Later FAA1.21:
C31.135:v.nos	Alaska airman's guide. Proc. Later FAA1.24: Supplemented by C31.133:
C31.136:v.nos	Airman's guide, 9th region supplement [Pacific Ocean area] (monthly) Proc. Supplements C31.127: Later FAA1.25:
C31.137:CT	Airport management series
C31.138:nos	Technical manuals. Later FAA5.8:
C31.139:v.nos	International flight information manual (quarterly) Proc. Later FAA1.22:
C31.140:pt.nos	Regulations of administrator. Later FAA1.6/4:
C31.141:nos	Airways operating and training series bulletins
C31.142:date	Annual reports of Air Navigation Development Board
C31.142/2:	Air Navigation Development Board releases
C31.142/3:nos	Air Navigation Development Board reports. Proc.
C31.142/4:nos	Air Navigation Development Board technical specifications
C31.143:le-nos	Technical standards orders. Proc. Later FAA1.38:
C31.143/2:date	Technical standards register (annual) Proc. or ptd.
C31.144:date	Statistical handbook of civil aviation. Later FAA1.32:
C31.145:CT	Airport planning. Proc.
C31.145/2:date	National airport plan. Proc. Earlier C31.102:Ai7/16 Later FAA4.8:
C31.145/3:date	Annual report of operations under Federal airport act. Earlier C31.105: M31 Later FAA1.30: Later TD4.22:

C31.146:nos	Releases. Proc.
C31.146/2:nos	[Profiles] P series. Proc.
C31.147:date	Airworthiness directive summary. Earlier C31.102:Ai7/34
C31.147/2:nos	CAA airworthiness directive (biweekly) Proc. Later FAA1.28:
C31.148:	Federal-air airport program, Summary of. [Monthly]
C31.149:	Office of Federal airways maintenance engineering division newsletter (Bi-monthly)
C31.150:nos	Aircraft emergency evacuation reports
C31.151:date	Status of CAA releases, manuals, and regulations (quarterly) Later FAA1.18:
C31.152:	Monthly comment on aviation trends
C31.153:date	Air commerce traffic patterns. Later FAA4.11:
C31.153/2:date	International air commerce traffic pattern, U.S. flag carriers, calendar year. Earlier C31.102:T67/4
C31.154:	CAA memo
C31.155:unit nos	Basic supervision
C31.156:nos	Airframe and equipment engineering reports. Proc.
C31.157:date	Location identifiers. Earlier C31.102:L78 Later FAA3.10:
C31.158:date	Federal airways air traffic activity (semi-annual) Later FAA1.27:
C31.159:	CAA news digest
C31.160:date	Statistical study of U.S. civil aircraft (annual) Proc. Earlier C31.102:Ac2/2 Later FAA1.15:
C31.160/2:date	General aviation accidents (non-air carrier), statistical analysis (annual) Proc. Earlier C31.102:St2 Later FAA1.32/2:
C31.161:nos	Electronic equipment modification. Admin.
C31.161/2:nos	Airborne electronics modification. Admin.
C31.162:date	List of publications. Earlier C31.102:P96/2 Later FAA1.10:
C31.163:date	General maintenance inspection aids (annual with monthly supplements) Later FAA1.31:

C31.163/2:nos	General maintenance alert bulletins. Later FAA1.31/2:
C31.163/3:date	United States standard flight inspection manual. Later FAA5.9:
C31.164:nos	Power plant engineering reports. Proc. Official use only.
C31.165:date	Enroute IFR air traffic survey (annual) Proc. Later FAA3.11:
C31.166:nos	Quality control digests. Later FAA5.11:
C31.167:date	Federal airway plan. Earlier C31.102:Ai7/52/date Later FAA1.37:
C31.168:nos	Jet age planning, progress reports. Later FAA1.36:
C31.169:nos	Administrator's notice. Admin.

Civil Aeronautics Administration transferred to Federal Aviation Agency by act of August 23, 1958. (72 Stat. 810).

C 31. 200 Civil Aeronautics Board

Formerly Air Safety Board, subordinate to Civil Aeronautics Authority (CA). Name changed and transferred to Commerce Department, effective June 30, 1940.

C31. 201:date	Annual reports
C31. 202:CT	General publications
C31. 203/2:nos	Accident prevention bulletin, U.S. general aviation
C31. 205:CT	Laws
C31. 206:serial nos.	Regulations. Proc. Earlier CA1.6:
C31. 206/2:CT	Regulations, rules, and instructions
C31. 206/3:nos	Special civil air regulations. Proc. Later FAA1.6/2:
C31. 206/4:nos	Safety investigation regulations, SIR (series)
C31. 206/5:date	Uniform system of accounts and reports for certificated route air carriers in accordance with sec. 407 of Federal aviation act
C31. 206/6:nos	Organization regulations OR (series)
C31. 206/7:date	Regulations of Civil Aeronautics Board
C31. 206/8:pt. nos	Special regulations
C31. 206/9:CT	Handbooks, manuals, guides. Formerly in C31.206/2:
C31. 207:serial nos.	Orders. Proc. Earlier CA1.12:
C31. 208:dt. &nos.	Weekly summary of orders and regulations. Proc. Earlier CA1.18:
C31. 209:pt. nos	Civil air regulations. Earlier CA1.19: and C23.6/3: Later FAA1.6/6:
C31. 209/2:nos	Civil air regulations draft release. Later FAA1.6/5:
C31. 210:nos	Special tariff permission under section 224.1 of Economic regulations. Proc.
C31. 211:vol	Civil Aeronautics Board reports. Earlier CA1.23:

C31.211/a:CT	___ separates
C31.211/2:	Dockets. Preliminary
C31.211/3:v.nos	Civil Aeronautics Board reports: Cumulative index-digest
C31.212:CT	Papers in re
C31.213:CT	Accidents involving civil aircraft; Reports of investigations of. Later TD1.112:
C31.214:CT	Safety bulletins. Proc. (later numbered)
C31.215:CT	Addresses
C31.216:v.nos	Foreign air news digest (fortnightly) Proc.
C31.217:CT	Maps. Proc.
C31.218:date	Air traffic survey [maps] Proc.
C31.219:date	Report of formal economic proceedings. Monthly. Proc.
C31.220:pt.nos	Economic regulations. Formerly published in processed regulations C31.206:
C31.220/2:date	Economic regulations (compilations)
C31.221:date	Applications and/or amendments thereto filed with Civil Aeronautics Board (weekly) Proc.
C31.222:date	Airline manual
C31.223:nos	Safety studies
C31.224:pt.nos	Procedural regulations
C31.224/2:nos	Regulations and policy statements
C31.225:dt.&nos	Airline traffic survey (semiannual) Changed from C31.202:Ai7/5
C31.226:dt.&nos	Releases. Proc.
C31.227:	Calendar of prehearing conferences hearings, and arguments conferences
C31.228:	Agreements filed with CAB under 412(a) during week ending...

C31.229:date	Recurrent report of mileage and traffic data: Proc. Domestic local service carriers (monthly) Later C31.241: Title varies, sometimes Certificated air carrier mileage
C31.229/2:date	___ ___ quarters [comparisons] Later C31.241:
C31.229/3:date	___ ___ 12 months ending [comparisons] Later C31.241:
C31.229/4:date	Domestic helicopter service, certificated air-mail carriers, (monthly) Proc. Later C31.241:
C31.229/5:date	___ quarters [comparisons] Proc. Later C31.241:
C31.230:date	Recurrent report of mileage and traffic data: Proc. Domestic air mail trunk carriers (monthly) Later C31.241:
C31.230/2:date	___ ___ quarters [comparisons] Later C31.241:
C31.230/3:date	___ ___ 12 months ending [comparisons] Later C31.241:
C31.231:date	___ Foreign, overseas & territorial air mail carriers (monthly) Later C31.241:
C31.231/2:date	___ ___ quarters [comparisons] Later C31.241:
C31.231/3:date	___ ___ 12 months ending [comparisons] Later C31.241:
C31.232:date	___ All certificated air cargo carriers (monthly) Later C31.241:
C31.232/2:date	___ ___ quarters [comparisons] Later C31.241:
C31.232/3:date	___ ___ 12 months ending [comparisons] Later C31.241:
C31.233:date	___ Recapitulation by carrier groups, certificated air carriers (monthly) Later C31.241:
C31.233/2:date	___ ___ quarters [comparisons]
C31.233/3:date	___ ___ 12 months ending [comparisons]
C31.234:date	Recurrent report of financial data: Proc. Domestic air mail trunk carriers, quarters [comparisons] Included in C31.240:
C31.234/2:date	___ ___ 12 months ending [comparisons] Included in C31.240:
C31.235:date	Certificated air carrier financial data: [Some of the following class numbers were formerly assigned to Recurrent report of financial data series. The title has been changed from Recurrent report of financial data to Certificated air carrier financial data]. Domestic local service [quarterly comparisons]. Proc. Included in C31.240:

322

C31.235/2:date	Certificated air carrier financial data: Domestic local service 12-month comparisons (quarterly) Proc. Included in C31.240:
C31.236:date	Certificated air carrier financial data: Foreign or overseas [quarterly comparisons]. Proc. Included in C31.240:
C31.236/2:date	Certificated air carrier financial data: Foreign or overseas [12-month comparisons] (quarterly) Proc. Included in C31.240:
C31.237:date	Recurrent report of financial data: Proc. All certificated air cargo carriers, quarters [comparisons] Included in C31.240:
C31.237/2:date	___ ___ 12 months ending [comparisons]
C31.238:date	Certificated air carrier financial data: Recapitulation by carrier groups [quarterly comparisons] Proc. Included in C31.240:
C31.238/2:date	Certificated air carrier financial data: Recapitulation by carrier groups [12 month comparisons] (quarterly) Proc. Included in C31.240:
C31.239:date	Domestic air carriers (trunk lines), comparative statement of balance sheet data (semiannual) Proc.
C31.240:date	Quarterly report of air carrier operating factors (financial statistics)
C31.240/2:	Summary of air carrier traffic statistics (quarterly)
C31.241:date	Certificated air carrier traffic statistics (monthly) Proc. Formerly Recurrent reports of airline mileage and traffic and financial data C31.229-232(release classes) Later title, Monthly report of air carrier traffic statistics
C31.241/2:date	Supplement to Monthly report of air carrier (financial and) traffic statistics (quarterly)
C31.241/3:v.nos.&nos.	Air carrier analytical charts and summaries including supplemental air carrier statistics (quarterly)
C31.242:date	Certificated air carrier financial data: Domestic helicopter service [quarterly comparisons] Proc. Included in C31.240:
C31.242/2:date	Certificated air carrier financial data: Domestic helicopter service [12-month comparisons] Quarterly. Proc. Included in C31.240:
C31.243:date	Certificated air carrier financial data: Territorial intra-Alaska & other Alaska [quarterly comparisons]. Proc. Included in C31.240:

C31.243/2:date	Certificated air carrier financial data: Territorial intra-Alaska & other than Alaska [12-month comparisons] (quarterly) Proc. Included in C31.240:
C31.244:date	Resumé of U.S. civil air carrier and general aviation aircraft accidents, calendar year. Proc. Earlier C31.202:Ac8
C31.244/2:date	Aerial crop control accidents (annual) Proc. Earlier C31.202:Ac2/12
C31.244/3:date	Accidents in U.S. Civil air carrier and general aviation operations (annual) Proc. Earlier C31.202:Ac2/13
C31.244/4:date	Summary reports of accidents, U.S. civil aviation (semimonthly)
C31.244/5:date	Briefs of accidents, U.S. general aviation (semimonthly)
C31.244/6:date	Briefs of accidents, U.S. civil aviation (monthly) Later TD1.109:
C31.245:date	Annual review - airworthiness civil air regulations meeting. Proc. Admin.
C31.246:date	All-cargo carriers [quarterly comparisons] Proc. Included in C31.240:
C31.246/2:date	All-cargo carriers [12 month comparisons] Proc. Included in C31.240:
C31.247:date	Other carriers [quarterly comparisons] Proc. Included in C31.240:
C31.247/2:date	Other carriers [12 month comparisons] Proc. Included in C31.240:
C31.248:date	Telephone directory. Earlier C31.202:T23
C31.249:date	Handbook of airline statistics, United States certificated air carriers, calendar year. Earlier C31.202:Ai7/date and C31.202:Ai7/6
C31.250:nos	Air transport economics in jet age, staff research reports
C31.251:date	Airport activity statistics of certificated route air carriers (semiannual) Issued jointly by CAB and Federal Aviation Agency. Combination of former Air commerce traffic pattern (FAA8.9:) of FAA and Airport activity statistics of certificated route air carriers of CAB. Later TD4.14:
C31.252:nos	Bureau of Safety pamphlet BOSP (series)
C31.252/2:nos	Bureau of Safety reports, BOSR (series) Later TD1.113:
C31.253:date	Local service air carriers' unit costs (semiannual)
C31.253/2:date	Local service by air carriers, selected flight load data by city pair, by frequency grouping, by aircraft type (annual)

C31.254:date	List of U.S. air carriers (semiannual)
C31.255:date	List of publications (annual)
C31.256:date	To mayor of each city with local airline service
C31.257:date	Subsidy for United States certificated air carriers (annual)
C31.258:nos	Regional air cargo workshop
C31.259:v.nos	Aircraft operating cost and performance report (annual)

C32   National Inventors Council

August 1940.   The National Inventors Council was established by the Secretary of Commerce with the full concurrence of the President.

C32.1:date   Annual reports

C32.2:CT   General publications

C32.7:nos   Information bulletins.

C32.8:dt.&nos   Technical problems affecting national defense. Proc.

C33   Reconstruction Finance Corporation

February 24, 1942, transferred from Federal Loan Agency by Executive order 9071.

C33.1:date   Annual reports.   Earlier FL5.1:   Later FL5.1:

C33.2:CT   General publications.   Earlier FL5.2:   Later FL5.2:

C33.3:

C33.4:nos   Circulars.   Earlier FL5.4:   Later FL5.4:

C33.5:CT   Laws.   Earlier FL5.5:   Later FL5.5:

C33.6:

C33.7:date   Quarterly reports.   Earlier FL5.7:   Later FL5.7:

C33.8:CT   Papers in re.   Earlier FL5.10:   Later FL5.10:

C33.9:letters   Regulations - War Damage Corporation.

C33.10:CT   Addresses.   Earlier FL5.9:CT

C33.11:date   Summary of surplus property (semimonthly) Proc.   Later FL5.11:

Reconstruction Finance Corporation returned to Federal Loan Agency by Public law 4, 79th Congress, approved Feb. 24, 1945.

C34   International Trade Operations Office

Established by Department (Commerce) Order 6 of Oct. 21, 1945 to administer functions transferred from Foreign Economic Administration by E.O. 9630, Sept. 27, 1945.

C34 CLASSES CANCELLED Oct. 1947 AND PUBLICATIONS CHANGED TO C18 CLASSES.

C34.1:date   Annual reports

C34.2:CT   General publications

C34.9:date   Trade relations bulletin. Proc.

C34.10:v.nos   Industrial reference service.   Earlier C18.220:

C34.11:v.nos   International reference service.   Earlier C18.223:

1953, The Bureau of Foreign Commerce was established and transferred to it were the functions of the Office of International Trade.

C35 Technical Services Office

The Office of Technical Services was established by the Secretary of Commerce on July 1, 1946, and assumed the functions formerly performed by the Office of the Publication Board.

C35.1:date   Annual report

C35.2:CT   General publications

C35.7:v.nos   Bibliography of scientific and industrial reports. Wkly. Earlier Y3.P96/6:9 Later C41.21:

C35.7/2:nos   Newsletter (monthly) Proc. Later C41.21/2:

C35.7/3:nos   Numerical index supplement to Bibliography of technical reports.

C35.8:nos   Technical services. Proc.

C35.9:v.nos   Federal science progress (monthly)

C35.10:nos   Office of Technical Services reports suitable for commercial publications, bulletins. Proc.

C35.11:CT   Bibliography of reports. Proc. Later C41.23/2:, C41.23/3:

C35.11/2:nos   Bibliography of motion pictures and film strips, FB(series) Later C41.23:

C35.11/3:nos   Bibliography of reports SB (series) Proc.

C35.12:nos   OTS technology guide circulars. Proc.

C35.13:nos   **Technical Division reports. Proc.**

C35.13/2:nos   Technical Division reports IR (series) Later C41.26/2:

C35.14:   Questions & answer service.

C35.15:nos   Releases OTS (series) Proc.
C35.16:v.nos.&nos.   Current industrial methods
October 1, 1953 included in organization of Business and Defense Services Administration.

C36 Domestic Commerce Office

The Office of Domestic Commerce was established in the Department of Commerce by Department order no. 10 of Dec. 18, 1945, by consolidating functions formerly carried on by certain organizational units of the Bureau of Foreign and Domestic Commerce.

<u>C36 CLASSES CANCELLED Oct. 1947</u> AND PUBLICATIONS CHANGED TO C18 CLASSES.

C36.1:date	Annual reports
C36.2:CT	General publications
C36.7:nos	Industrial series. Earlier C18.225:
C36.8:CT	Inquiry reference service. Proc. Earlier C18.228:

1950. The Office of Industry and Commerce was established; the Office of Domestic Commerce was abolished and its functions transferred to the new office.

C37 Public Roads Bureau

By provisions of Public law 152, 81st Congress, 1st session, effective July 1, 1949, the Public Roads Administration was transferred from the Federal Works Agency to the General Services Administration and its name changed to the Bureau of Public Roads. It was transferred to the Department of Commerce by Reorganization plan no. 7 of 1949, effective Aug. 20, 1949.

C37.1:date	Annual reports. Earlier GS3.1: Later TD2.101:
C37.2:CT	General publications. Earlier GS3.2: Later TD2.102:
C37.4/2:nos	Hydraulic engineering circulars. Later TD2.104:
C37.5:CT	Laws. Earlier FW2.5: Later TD2.105:
C37.6:CT	Regulations, rules, and instructions. Later TD2.106:

C37.6/2:CT	Handbooks, manuals, guides (unnumbered) Earlier C37.6: Later TD2.108:
C37.7:CT	President's Highway Safety Conference. Earlier FW2.18:
C37.7/a:CT	___ separates
C37.8:v.nos	Public roads, journal of highway research (bimonthly) Earlier GS3.8: Later TD2.109:
C37.8/a:CT	___ separates. Later TD2.109/a:
C37.9:date	Traffic volume trends (monthly) Proc. Earlier GS3.7:
C37.9/2:date	Traffic speed trends. Later TD2.115:
C37.10:v.nos.&nos.	Highways, current literature (weekly) Proc. Earlier FW2.8: Later TD2.112:
C37.11:CT	Transportation maps. Earlier FW2.13:
C37.12:v.nos	Planning, current literature (weekly) Proc. Earlier FW1.15:
C37.12/2:v.nos.&nos.	Urban transportation research and planning, current literature. Later TD2.112/2:
C37.13:CT	Maps (miscellaneous) Earlier FW2.12: Later TD2.116:
C37.14:	Releases
C37.14/2:nos	Ninth Pan American Highway Congress, Inaugural tours Inter-American Highway news
C37.15:v.nos.&nos.	Administration and management, current literature (biweekly)
C37.16:v.nos.&nos.	News in public roads (monthly)
C37.17:date	Highway statistics (annual) Earlier C37.2:H53 Later TD2.110:
C37.17/2:date	Highway statistics, summaries. Earlier FW2.2:H53/8 Later TD2.110/2:
C37.18:date	Highway finance (annual)
C37.19:date	Receipts for State administered highways. Annual. Proc. Official distribution
C37.19/2:date	Disbursements for State administered highways. Annual; Proc.
C37.19/3:date	Receipts for toll road and crossing facilities. Annual. Proc.
C37.19/4:date	Disbursements for toll road and crossing facilities. Annual. Proc.

C37.20:nos	Electronic computer program library memorandum. Proc.
C37.21:CT	Addresses. Later TD2.119:
C37.22:date	Price trends for Federal-aid highway construction. quarterly. Earlier C37.2:H53/5 Official use.
C37.23:nos	Hydraulic design series. Later TD2.127:
C37.24:nos	Highway research newsletter. Official use.
C37.25:nos	Highway construction contracts awarded by State highway departments. For official distribution. Earlier FW2.19:
C37.26:nos	Highway planning notes (irregular) Later TD2.111:
C37.27:nos	Highway planning technical reports. Later TD2.120:
C37.28:CT	Bibliographies and lists of publications
C37.29:nos	Public roads round-up. weekly. Official distribution. Later TD2.9:
C37.30:CT	Highway research and development studies Later TD2.113:
C37.31:v.nos.&nos.	BPR emergency readiness newsletter. Official distribution. Later TD2.114:
C37.32:nos	BPR program (series) Later TD2.117:
C37.33:CT	Posters

The Public Roads Bureau was transferred from the Commerce Department to the Federal Highway Administration, Transportation Department by Public law 89-670, approved Oct. 15, 1916.

C38 Industry Cooperation Office

Established in the Office of the Secretary of Commerce in January 1948

C38.1:date	Annual reports
C38.2:CT	General publications

C39 Maritime Administration

The Maritime Administration was created by Reorganization Plan 21, of 1950, effective May 24, 1950, as an agency in the Department of Commerce. These classes later appear under C39.200.

C39.1:date	Annual reports. Earlier MC1.1:
C39.2:CT	General publications. Earlier MC1.2:
C39.5:CT	Laws. Earlier MC1.5:
C39.6:CT	Regulations, rules, and instructions. Earlier MC1.6:

C39.101   Federal Maritime Board

The Federal Maritime Board was established as an agency within the Department of Commerce by Reorganization plan 21 of 1950, effective May 24, 1950.

C39.101:date Annual reports

C39.102:CT General publications

C39.106:CT Regulations, rules, and instructions.

C39.106/2:date Index of current regulations of Federal Maritime Board, Maritime Administration, National Shipping Authority. Later C39.206/4:

C39.108:v.nos Federal Maritime Board reports, decisions (bound volumes) Earlier MC1.22: Later FMC1.10:

C39.108/a:nos ___ separates. Earlier MC1.22/a: Later FMC1.10/a:

C39.109:dt.&nos Federal Maritime Board and Maritime Administration releases NR (series) Proc. Later C39.207:

C39.109/2:nos Federal Maritime Board, Maritime Administration releases SP [speeches] Proc. Later C39.210/2:

Reorganization Plan 7, effective Aug. 12, 1961, abolished the Board and transferred its regulatory functions to the Federal Maritime Commission, and functions relating to subsidization of merchant marine to Secretary of Commerce.

C39.200   Maritime Administration

Created by Reorganization Plan 21 of 1950, effective May.24,1950, as an agency in the Department of Commerce.

C39.201:date	Annual reports. Earlier MC1.1:
C39.202:CT	General publications. Earlier MC1.2:
C39.205:CT	Laws. Earlier MC1.5:
C39.206:CT	Regulations, rules, and instructions. Earlier MC1.6:
C39.206/2:nos	NSA orders (National Shipping Authority)
C39.206/3:CT	Handbooks, manuals, guides
C39.206/4:date	Index of current regulations of Maritime Administration, Maritime Subsidy Board, National Shipping Authority (annual) Earlier C39.106/2:
C39.207:date	Releases. Earlier C39.109:
C39.208:date	Employment of United States merchant fleet as of (date), Seagoing vessels 1,000 gross tons and over.
C39.209:	National Shipping Authority: Safety bulletin (quarterly)
C39.209/2:	Safety bulletins
C39.210:CT	Addresses
C39.210/2:nos	MA SP (series) Earlier C39.109/2:
C39.211:date	Merchant ships built in United States and other countries in Employment report of United States flag merchant seagoing vessels, 1,000 gross tons and over.
C39.212:date	Merchant fleets of world, seagoing steam and motor ships of 1,000 gross tons and over. Proc.
C39.212/2:date	New ship deliveries, calendar year
C39.212/3:date	New ship construction, oceangoing ships of 1,000 gross tons and over in United States and foreign shipyards (annual)

C39.213:date	Dry cargo service and area report, United States dry cargo shipping companies by ships owned and/or chartered by type of service and area operated. Proc. Earlier C39.202:D84
C39.214:date	United States and Canadian Great Lakes fleets, steam and motor ships of 1,000 gross tons and over. Proc.
C39.215:date	Charter report, Government-owned dry-cargo vessels operated by bareboat charters and/or agents of Maritime Administration. Monthly. Proc.
C39.216:nos	Shipbuilding progress report for month ending. Proc. Official distribution
C39.216/2:date	Relative cost of shipbuilding in various coastal districts of United States (annual)
C39.217:date	Vessel inventory report, United States Flag dry cargo and tanker fleets, 1,000 gross tons and over (semiannual)
C39.218:date	Handbook of merchant shipping statistics (annual)
C39.219:nos	Reserve fleet safety review
C39.220:nos	Value engineering information letters. Official use.
C39.221:date	Participation of principal national flags in United States oceanborne foreign trade (annual)
C39.222:date	Domestic oceanborne and Great Lakes Commerce of United States. Earlier C39.202:D71/date
C39.223:CT	Port series
C39.223/2:date/nos	Highlights of MarAd port activities
C39.224:date	Statistical analysis of world's merchant fleets (biennial) Earlier C39.202:
C39.225:date	Course of instruction at Merchant Marine Academy
C39.226:v.nos	Decisions of Maritime Subsidy Board, Maritime Administration
C39.227:CT	Bibliographies and lists of publications
C39.228:date	Ships registered under Liberian, Panamanian, and Honduran flags deemed by Navy Department to be under effective U.S. control (quarterly)
C39.229:date	Oceangoing merchant ships of 1,000 gross tons and over lost and scrapped during calendar year.

C39.230:date	Oceangoing foreign flag merchant type ships of 1,000 gross tons and over owned by United States parent companies (semiannual)
C39.231:date	Containerships under construction and on order (including conversions) in United States and foreign shipyards, oceangoing ships of 1,000 gross tons and over (semiannual)
C39.232:date	United States flag containerships and United States flag ships with partial capacities for containers and/or vehicles (semiannual)
C39.233:date	Foreign oceanborne trade of United States containerized cargo summary, selected trade routes (quarterly)
C39.234:v/nos	MARAD personnel newsletter
C39.235:date	Maritime manpower report: Seafaring, **longshore**, and shipyard employment. Earlier C39.202:Sel/2/date
C39.236:date	Seaword, developments in American flag shipping [quarterly]
C39.237:date	Inventory of American intermodal equipment **(annual)** Earlier similar C39.202: C76/2/973
C39.238:date	Merchant Marine data sheet (monthly)
C39.239:CT	Environmental impact statements

C40 National Production Authority

Established in Commerce Department by notice of the Secretary, filed Sept. 13, 1950, to carry out the functions assigned to the Secretary of Commerce by Executive order 10161, delegating certain functions of the President under the Defense Production Act.

C40.1:date	Annual report
C40.2:CT	General publications
C40.6:CT	Regulations, rules, and instructions
C40.6/2:nos	NPA regulations. Later C41.6/2:
C40.6/3:nos	NPA delegations. Later C41.6/3:
C40.6/4:le-nos	NPA orders. Later C41.6/4:
C40.6/5:nos	CMP regulations
C40.6/6:nos	Designation of scarce materials
C40.6/7:nos	NPA organization statements
C40.6/8:date	NPA regulatory material and forms, digest (monthly with weekly supplements in intervening weeks).
C40.6/9:nos	DMS [Defense materials system] regulations. Later C41.6/6:
C40.6/10:	Suspension orders
C40.7:nos	Business information service: Defense production aids. Proc.
C40.7/2:nos	___ Small business aids (series) Proc. Earlier C18.268:
C40.8:nos	Releases. Proc.
C40.9:nos	NPA notices. Later C41.6/5:
C40.10:v.nos	Construction and building materials, monthly industry report. Earlier C18.233: Later C41.30:

C40.11:v.nos.&nos.   Pulp, paper and board industry report (quarterly) Earlier C18.229: Later C41.32:

C40.12:v.nos   Containers and packaging industry reports (quarterly) Earlier C18.242: Later C41.33:

C40.13:nos   Questions and answers on controlled materials plan, Q & A (series)

C40.14:date   United States consumption of rubber (monthly) Proc. Later C41.31:

C40.15:date   NPA production series, quarterly indexes of shipments for products of metalworking industries. Proc.

C40.16:   Minutes of [meetings of committees of various industries]

C40.17:CT   Materials survey reports. See also A13.2:L97/16 and I28.97: Later C41.38:

C40.18:nos   Historical reports on defense production. Official use only.

The National Production Authority was abolished by Department order 152 issued by the Secretary of Commerce Oct.1,1953, effective Oct.1,1953.

Domestic Commerce Bureau

C41 Business and Defense Services Administration

Established as a primary organization unit of the Department of Commerce by Department order 152 issued by the Secretary of Commerce Oct. 1, 1953, effective Oct. 1, 1953.

C41.BDCOT	Official texts. Earlier C41.BDSAOT
C41:BDSAOT	(Official texts) Earlier C41.6/2:, C41.6/3:, C41.6/4:, C41.6/5:, C41.6/6:C41.6/8:
C41.1:date	Annual reports. Later C57.301:
C41.2:CT	General publications. Later C57.302:
C41.3:nos	Business service bulletin BSB (series) (Issued irregularly) Proc.
C41.3/2:v.nos.&nos.	BDSA bulletins, information of interest to employees. Official use.
C41.3/3:nos	Bulletin. National Defense Executive Reserve. Administrative.
C41.4:	
C41.5:CT	Laws
C41.6:CT	Regulations, rules, and instructions.
C41.6/2:nos	BDSA regulations. Formerly NPA regulations C40.6/2: Later C41.BDSAOT:
C41.6/2-2:nos	DPS regulations (numbered)
C41.6/3:nos	BDSA delegations. Formerly NPA delegations C40.6/3: Later C41.BDSAOT:
C41.6/3-2:nos	BDSA reporting delegations
C41.6/4:le-nos	BDSA orders. Formerly NPA orders C40.6/4: Later C41.6/4-2: BDSAOT
C41.6/4-2:nos	DMS orders. Formerly BDSA orders, C41.6/4:
C41.6/5:nos	BDSA notices. Formerly NPA notices C40.9: Later C41.BDSAOT:
C41.6/5-2:nos	BDC notices
C41.6/6:nos	DMS regulations. Earlier C40.6/9: Later C41.BDSAOT
C41.6/7:date	Background to industrial mobilization, manual for executive reservists.
C41.6/7a:nos	___ separates
C41.6/8:nos	BDSA emergency delegations. Later C41.BDSAOT

C41.6/9:CT	Handbooks, manuals, guides Later C57.508:
C41.6/10:CT	Industrial marketing guides
C41.6/11:nos	Rules of practice
C41.6/12:CT	Industrial civil defense handbooks
C41.7:	Releases
C41.8:CT	Business information service. **Proc. Earlier** C18.228: Later title, Business report, general publications
C41.8/2:nos	___ Area and industrial development aids. **Proc. Earlier** C18.228:
C41.8/3:CT/date	___ ___ Annual surveys. Earlier C18.228:
C41.9:nos	Synopsis of U.S. Government proposed procurement and contract awards (daily Monday thru Friday except Federal legal holidays) Earlier C18.284: Later title, Commerce business daily. Later C57.20:
C41.9/2:nos	Bulletin CBD-S (series)
C41.10:v.nos.&nos.	Bulletin of commerce (weekly) **Proc.** Earlier C18.269:
C41.11:v.nos.&nos.	Distribution data guide listing publications & reports containing basic information & statistics for use in market research, merchandising, sales promotion, advertising (monthly) **Proc.** Later title:Marketing information guide.
C41.12:CT	Bibliographies and lists of publications
C41.13:nos	Biweekly review, News and information of interest to field offices
C41.14:CT	Establishing and operating [businesses] Formerly in C18.255: and C18.271:
C41.15:CT	Addresses
C41.16:CT	Motion pictures abroad
C41.17:date	World motor vehicle registration (annual) Earlier C41.2:M85 Later C57.21:
C41.18:nos	Economic summary, printing and publishing and allied industries (monthly) Proc. Earlier issues classified C41.18: Later C57.311:
C41.19:date	Confectionery sales and distribution (annual) Earlier C41.8:C76/date Later C57.13:
C41.20:nos	Simplified practice recommendations. Earlier C18.277:
C41.21:v.nos	Bibliography of technical reports (monthly) Earlier C35.7/2: Later title, U.S. Government research reports
C41.21/a:CT	___ separates

C41.21/2:nos	Technical reports news letters (monthly) Earlier C35.7/2:
C41.21/3:nos	Catalog of technical reports CTR (series) [issued separately. Proc.] Earlier C35.11/3:
C41.21/4:date	New research and development reports available to industry. Official use.
C41.21/5:v.nos.&nos.	Keywords index to U.S. Government technical reports (permuted title index) (semimonthly)
C41.22:CT	Technical Services Office general publications. Earlier C35.2:
C41.23:nos	Bibliography of motion pictures and film strips, FB (series) Proc. Earlier C35.11/2:
C41.23/2:nos	Bibliography of reports IB (series) Earlier C35.11:
C41.23/3:nos	Selected industrial films SIF (series) Proc.
C41.23/4:CT	Bibliographies and lists of publications, Technical Services Office. Later C51.11:
C41.24:date	Technical digest service (monthly) Proc.
C41.25:nos	Commercial standard CS (series) Earlier C18.276: Later C13.20:
C41.26:nos	Technical division report, TAS (series) Proc. Earlier C35.13:
C41.26/2:nos	___ IR (series) Proc. Earlier C35.13/2:
C41.27:v.nos.&nos.	Area development **bulletin** (bimonthly) Later C49.5:, C46.9:
C41.27/2:nos	Federal reference material for State and economic development agencies
C41.28:nos	Technical Services Office releases
C41.28/2:date	Special announcement concerning research reports from Dept. of Commerce. OTS Later C51.7/3:
C41.29:nos	Atomic Energy Commission research reports for sale by Office of Technical Services. Earlier Y3.At7:15
C41.30:v.nos	Industry report: Construction and building materials (monthly) Earlier C41.10:
C41.30/2:CT	Construction & building materials, statistical supplements, Replaced by C41.30/4:

C41.30/3:v.nos	Construction review (monthly) Replaces C41.30: and L2.22: Later C57.310:
C41.30/3a:CT	___ separates
C41.30/4:CT	Construction review, statistical supplements. Replaces C41.30/2:
C41.30/5:date	Quarterly summary for future construction abroad
C41.31:date	United States consumption of rubber (monthly) Proc. Earlier C40.14:
C41.32:v.nos.&nos.	Pulp, paper and board industry report (quarterly) Earlier C40.11: Later C57.313:
C41.32/a:CT	___ separates
C41.33:v.nos	Industry report: Containers and packaging (quarterly) Earlier C40.12: Later C57.314:
C41.34:v.nos	Industry report: Copper (quarterly) Later C57.312:
C41.34/2:nos	Copper industry report, annuals
C41.35:v.nos	Industry report: Chemicals and rubber (monthly)
C41.36:v.nos	Industry report: International iron and steel (quarterly)
C41.37:nos	Month-end summary of domestic trade services rendered by Field Offices
C41.38:CT	Materials surveys. Earlier C40.17:
C41.39:date	Monthly motor truck production report. Proc.
C41.40:nos	Soviet bloc International geophysical year information (weekly) Proc. Published from Feb.14,1958 to Jan.2,1959. Later Y3.J66:14
C41.41:v.nos	Technical translations (semimonthly)
C41.41/a:CT	___ separates
C41.42:nos	Economic report ER- (series) Proc.
C41.42/2:nos	[Midyear review] MR- (series)
C41.42/3:date	U.S. industrial outlook (annual) Replaced by C41.42/4:
C41.42/4:date	Industrial outlook and economy at midyear (semiannual) Replaces C41.2:Ec7/dt. and C41.42/3: Later C57.309:
C41.43:nos	Automatics. Desig. PB 141095T

342

C41.43/2:nos	Automatics & telemechanics abstracts (monthly) Desig. PB 141096T
C41.44:nos	Automobile industry [abstracts] (monthly) Proc. Desig. PB 141 110 T
C41.45:nos	Exploration and conservation of natural resources [abstracts] (monthly) Proc. Desig. PB 141 135 T.
C41.46:nos	Geochemistry [abstracts] (monthly) [Proc.] Desig. PB 141 002T
C41.46/2:nos	Bulletin of Moscow Society of Naturalists, Geological division [abstracts] (bimonthly) Desig. PB 141 000T
C41.46/3:nos	Geodesy and cartography [abstracts] (monthly) Proc. Desig. PB 141 001T
C41.46/4:nos	News of Academy of Sciences of USSR, geography series [abstracts] (bimonthly) Desig. PB 141 004 T
C41.46/5:nos	News of Academy of Sciences of USSR, geology series [abstracts] (monthly) Proc. Desig. PB 141 106T
C41.46/6:nos	News of All-Union geographical society [abstracts] (Bimonthly) Desig. PB 141 006T
C41.47:nos	Hydraulic and engineering construction [abstracts] (monthly) Proc. Desig. PB 141 091T
C41.47/2:nos	Mechanization of construction [abstracts] (monthly) Proc. Desig. PB 141 093T
C41.47/3:nos	Hydraulic engineering and soil improvement [abstracts] (monthly) Desig. PB 141 092T
C41.48:nos	Journal of acoustics [abstracts] (quarterly) Proc. Desig. PB 141 039T
C41.49:nos	Radio engineering [abstracts] (monthly) Proc. Desig. PB 141 105T
C41.49/2:nos	Radio engineering and electronics [abstracts] (monthly) Desig. PB 141 106T
C41.49/3:nos	Radio [abstracts] Designated PB 141 104T
C41.50:nos	Reports of Academy of Sciences of USSR [abstracts] (3 times a month) Desig. PB 141 015T
C41.50/2:nos	Reports of Academy of Sciences USSR [abstracts] (monthly) Proc. Desig. PB 141 016T
C41.50/3:nos	News of Academy of Sciences of USSR, Department of Technical Services [abstracts] (monthly) Proc. Desig. PB 141 019T

C41.50/4:nos	Herald of Academy of Sciences of U.S.S.R. [abstracts] Monthly. Desig. PB 141 025T
C41.50/5:nos	News of Academy of Sciences of Estonia SSR, technical & physiomathematical sciences series [abstracts] (quarterly) Proc. Desig. PB 141 018T
C41.50/6:nos	Herald of Moscow University, physio-mathematical and natural sciences series [abstracts] (monthly) Proc. Desig. PB 141 051T
C41.50/7:nos	News of Academy of Sciences of Armenian SSR, physico-mathematical, natural and technical sciences series [abstracts] (monthly) Proc. Desig. PB 141 107T
C41.50/8:nos	Herald of Leningrad University, mathematics, mechanics, and astronomy series [abstracts] (quarterly) Desig. PB 141 037T
C41.50/9:nos	Herald of Academy of Sciences of Kazakh SSR [abstracts] (monthly) Desig. PB-141 026-T
C41.51:nos	Steel [abstracts] (monthly) Proc. Designated PB 141 136T
C41.52:nos	Progress of physical sciences [abstracts] (monthly) Proc. Desig. PB 141 049T
C41.52/2:nos	Journal of experimental and theoretical physics [abstracts] (monthly) Proc. Desig 141 052T
C41.52/3:nos	News of Academy of Sciences of USSR, Physics series [abstracts] (monthly) Desig. PB 141 041T
C41.52/4:nos	News of institutes of higher learning of Ministry of Higher Education, physics. [abstracts] (bimonthly) Proc. Desig. PB 141 043T
C41.52/5:nos	Herald of Leningrad University, physics and chemistry series [abstracts] (quarterly) Proc. Desig. PB 141 050T
C41.52/6:nos	Journal of technical physics [abstracts] (monthly) Proc. Desig. PB 141 053T
C41.52/7:nos	News of Academy of Sciences of USSR, geophysics series [abstracts] (monthly) Proc. Desig. PB 141 042T
C41.52/8:nos	Physics in school [abstracts] Designated PB 141 040
C41.53:nos	Journal of general chemistry [abstracts] (monthly) Proc. Desig. PB 141 075T
C41.53/2:nos	News of Acad. Sci. USSR, Dept. of Chemical Science [abstracts] (monthly) Desig. PB 141 055T
C41.53/3:nos	Progress of chemistry [abstracts] (monthly) Proc. Desig. PB 141 070T
C41.53/4:nos	Journal of inorganic chemistry [abstracts] (monthly) Proc. Desig. PB 140 074T

C41.53/5:nos	Journal of physical chemistry [abstracts] (monthly) Proc. Desig. PB 141 072T
C41.53/6:nos	Journal of analytical chemistry [abstracts] (bimonthly) Proc. Desig. PB 141 071T
C41.53/7:nos	Chemical industry [abstracts] (issued 8 times a year) Proc. Desig. PB 141 059T
C41.53/8:nos	News of institutes of higher learning, chemistry and chemistry technology [abstracts] (bimonthly) Proc. Desig. PB 141 056T
C41.53/9:nos	Scientific reports of higher schools, chemistry and chemical technology [abstracts] (quarterly) Proc. Desig. PB 141 066T
C41.53/10:nos	Chemical science and industry [abstracts] (monthly) Desig. PB 141 058T
C41.53/11:nos	Journal of applied chemistry [abstracts] (monthly) Desig. 141 076T
C41.54:nos	Nonferrous metals [abstracts] (monthly) Proc. Desig. PB 141 139T
C41.54/2:nos	Physics of metals and metallography [abstracts] (bimonthly) Proc. Desig. PB 141 126T
C41.54/3:nos	Metallurgist [abstracts] (monthly) Desig. PB 141 132T
C41.54/4:nos	Scientific reports of higher schools, metallurgy [abstracts] (quarterly) Proc. Desig. PB 141 133T
C41.54/5:nos	Mining journal [abstracts] Monthly. Desig. PB 141 127T
C41.54/6:nos	Automatic welding [abstracts] (monthly) Proc. Desig. PB 141 125T
C41.54/7:nos	Metallography and heat treatment of metals [abstracts] (monthly) Proc. Desig. PB 141 131T
C41.54/8:nos	Welding practice [abstracts] (monthly) Proc. Desig.PB 141 138T
C41.54/9:nos	Journal of abstracts, metallurgy [abstracts] (monthly) Proc. Desig. PB 141 140T
C41.54/10:nos	Foundry practice [abstracts] (monthly) Desig. PB 141 130T
C41.55:nos	Chemistry and technology of fuels and oils [abstracts] Desig. PB 141 060T
C41.55/2:nos	Petroleum worker [abstracts] (monthly) Desig. PB 141 085T
C41.55/3:nos	Petroleum economy [abstracts] (monthly) Desig. PB 141 086T

C41.55/4:nos	Petroleum and gas [abstracts] Designated PB 141 402T
C41.56:nos	Civil aviation [abstracts] (monthly) Desig. PB 141 078T
C41.56/2:nos	News of institutes of higher learning, aeronautical engineering [abstracts] (quarterly) Proc. Desig. PB 141 401T
C41.57:nos	Engineering for youth [abstracts] (monthly) Desig. PB 141 024T
C41.58:nos	Plant Laboratory [abstracts] (monthly) Desig. PB 141 027T
C41.59:nos	Herald of communications [abstracts] (monthly) Desig. PB 141 108T
C41.60:nos	Heat power engineering [abstracts] (monthly) Desig. PB 141 089T
C41.60/2:nos	Power engineer [abstracts] (monthly) Proc. Desig. PB 141 048T
C41.60/3:nos	Power engineering bulletin [abstracts] (monthly) Proc. Desig. PB 141 083T
C41.60/4:nos	Industrial power engineering [abstracts] (monthly) Desig. PB 141 078T
C41.61:nos	Applied mathematics and mechanics [abstracts] (bimonthly) Desig. PB 141 034T
C41.61/2:nos	News of institutes of higher learning of Ministry of Higher Education, USSR, Mathematics [abstracts] (bimonthly) Desig. PB 141 032T
C41.61/3:nos	Journal of abstracts, mathematics [abstracts] (monthly) Proc. Desig. PB 141 038T
C41.61/4:nos	Progress of mathematical sciences [abstracts] (bimonthly) Proc. Desig. PB 141 036T
C41.61/5:nos	News of Academy of Sciences of USSR, mathematics series [abstracts] (bimonthly) Proc. Desig. PB 141 031T
C41.61/6:nos	Mathematics symposium [abstracts] (monthly) Proc. Desig. PB 141 033T
C41.61/7:nos	Ukranian mathematics journal [abstracts] (quarterly) Proc. Desig. PB 141 035T
C41.61/8:nos	Theory of probability and its applications [abstracts] (quarterly) Desig. PB 141 048T
C41.62:nos	Vocational and technical education abstracts. Monthly. Desig. PB 141 022T
C41.63:nos	Optics and spectroscopy [abstracts] (monthly) Proc. Desig. PB 141 047T
C41.64:nos	Coke and chemistry [abstracts] (monthly) Proc. Desig. PB 141 063T
C41.65:nos	Machine builder [abstracts] (monthly) Proc. Desig. PB 141 116T
C41.65/2:nos	Machine tools and tools [abstracts] (monthly) Proc. Desig. PB 141 121T

C41.65/3:nos	Journal of abstracts, mechanics [abstracts] (monthly) Proc. Desig. PB 141 124T
C41.65/4:nos	Herald of machine building [abstracts] (monthly) Proc. Desig. PB 141 122T
C41.65/5:nos	Mechanization of labor and heavy work [abstracts] Desig. PB 141 117T
C41.65/6:nos	News of Institutes of higher learning, electromechanics [abstracts] (monthly) Desig. PB 141 110T
C41.65/7:nos	Scientific reports of higher schools, electro-mechanics and automation [abstracts] (quarterly) PB 141 102T
C41.65/8:nos	Scientific reports of higher education: Machine construction and instrument manufacture [abstracts] Desig. PB 141 118T
C41.66:nos	Electricity [abstracts] (monthly) Proc. Desig. PB 141 098T
C41.66/2:nos	Herald of electrical industry [abstracts] (monthly) Proc. Desig. PB 141 107T.
C41.66/3:nos	Journal of abstracts, electrical engineering [abstracts] (monthly) Proc. Desig. PB 141 109T
C41.66/4:nos	Electrical communications [abstracts] (monthly) Desig. PB 141 102T
C41.67:nos	Science & life [abstracts] (monthly) Proc. Desig. PB 141 020T
C41.68:nos	Glass and ceramics [abstracts] (monthly) Proc. Desig. PB 141 068T
C41.69:nos	Journal of scientific and applied photography and cinematography [Abstracts] (bi-monthly) Proc. Desig. PB 141 073T
C41.69/2:nos	News of institutes of higher learning of Ministry of Higher Education, USSR, geodesy & aerial photography [abstracts] (bimonthly) Proc. Desig. PB 141 007T
C41.70:nos	Raw and vulcanized rubber [abstracts] (monthly) Proc. Desig. PB 141 057T
C41.71:nos	Cement [abstracts] (bimonthly) Proc. Desig. PB 141 094T
C41.71/2:nos	Concrete and reinforced concrete [abstracts] (monthly) Proc. Desig. PB 141 090T
C41.72:nos	Standardization [abstracts] (bimonthly) Desig. PB 141 023T
C41.73:nos	Astronomical journal [abstracts] (bimonthly) Proc. Desig. PB 141 028T
C41.74:nos	Atomic energy [abstracts] (monthly) Proc. Desig. PB 141 082T

C41.75:nos	Measurement techniques [abstracts] (bimonthly) Proc. Desig. PB 141 112T
C41.76:nos	Refractories [abstracts] (monthly) Proc. Desig. PB 141 134T
C41.77:nos	Instruments and experimental techniques [abstracts] (bimonthly) Desig. PB 141 120T
C41.77/2:nos	Instrument manufacture [abstracts] (monthly) Proc. Desig. PB 141 119T
C41.78:nos	Meteorology and hydrology [abstracts] (monthly) Proc. Desig. PB 141 045T
C41.79:nos	Crystallography [abstracts] (bimonthly) Proc. Desig. PB 141 065T
C41.80:nos	Oxygen [abstracts] (bimonthly) Proc. Desig. PB 141 062T
C41.81:nos	Colloid journal [abstracts] (bimonthly) Desig. PB 141 064T
C41.82:nos	Bulletin on inventions [abstracts] (monthly) Desig. PB 141 014T
C41.83:nos	Refrigeration engineering [abstracts] (quarterly) Desig. PB 141 061T
C41.84:nos	English abstracts of selected articles from Soviet bloc and mainland China technical journals: Series 1, Physics, geophysics, astrophysics, astronomy, astronautics, and applied mathematics (monthly) Desig. 61-11,140.
C41.84/2:nos	___ Series 2, Chemistry, chemicals, and chemical products (monthly) Desig. 61-11,141.
C41.84/3:nos	___ Series 3, Metallurgy, metals, metal products, and nonmetallic minerals (monthly) Designated 61-11,142.
C41.84/4:nos	___ series 4, Engineering (mechanical), electrical aeronautical, nuclear, Petroleum, structural, and civil, machinery and equipment (general and special purpose) (monthly) Designated 61-11,143.
C41.84/5:nos	___ Series 5, Communications, transportation, navigation, electrical and electronic equipment, systems and devices, including aircraft and missile equipment (monthly) 61-11,144.
C41.84/6:nos	___ Series 6, General science and miscellaneous, including meteorology, oceanography, biology, astrobiology, botany, zoology, medical science, aeromedicine, education, fuel, fuel products, and power (monthly) 61-11,145
C41.84/7:nos	___ Series 7, Geophysics and astronomy. Desig. 62-11703
C41.85:date	Translated Swiss patents (first claim only) Earlier C41.22:Sw6/date
C41.85/2:date	Translated Polish patents (first claim only). Earlier C41.22:P75/date

C41.86:

C41.87:

C41.88:date   Salad dressing, mayonnaise, and related products (annual)   Earlier C41.8/3:Sa3   Later C57.316:

C41.89:nos   Area development aid: Area trend series.   Earlier C45.13:

C41.90:nos   Industry trend series.   Earlier C45.8/2:

C41.90/2:nos   Industrial location series.   Earlier C45.8/3:

C41.90/3:CT   Industrial fact sheets.   Earlier C45.8:

C41.90/4:CT   BDS industry growth studies

C41.90/5:CT   Patterns of industrial growth (series)

C41.91:CT   World survey of agricultural machinery and equipment

C41.92:CT   Foreign trade information on instrumentation [by country]   Earlier in C41.3:

C41.93:CT   Selected United States marketing terms and definitions, English-[foreign language]

C41.94:nos   Current review of Soviet technical press

C41.95:date   Bureau of Ships, shop practice suggestions (semiannual)

C41.96:CT   World survey of civil aviation

C41.97:nos   Community development series

C41.98:CT   Market for U.S. leather and shoes in [various foreign countries]

C41.99:date   Value of prime contracts awarded by Federal agencies in areas of substantial labor surplus (quarterly)   Later C46.10:

C41.100:CT   Household and commercial pottery industry in [various countries]

C41.101:date   United States lumber exports (annual)   Earlier C41.2:L97/date   Later C41.101:

C41.101/2:date   United States lumber imports (annual)

C41.102:v.nos.&nos.   OTS Briefs

C41.103:CT   Market for selected U.S. electric housewares in [various countries]

C41.104:CT	Market for U.S. telecommunications equipment in [various countries]
C41.105:CT	Market for U.S. microwave, forward scatter, and other radio communications equipment and radar in [various countries]
C41.106:CT	Market for selected U.S. household and commercial gas appliances in [various countries]
C41.107:CT	BDSA export potential studies
C41.108:date	United States foreign trade in photographic goods (annual)
C41.109:CT	Foreign market surveys
C41.110:nos	Industrial civil defense newsletter
C41.111:CT	Facts about wholesaling (series)
C41.112:date	Aluminum imports and exports (monthly) Earlier C41.2:Al8/3 Later C57.14:
C41.112/2:date	United States exports of aluminum. Later C57.10:
C41.112/3:date	United States imports of aluminum. Later C57.10/2:
C41.112/4:date	Aluminum metal supply, and shipments of products to consumers (millions of pounds). Earlier C41.2:Al8/4/date
C41.113:nos	**Executive reservist, bulletin from Industrial Mobilization, for members of National Defense Executive Reserve**
C41.114:date	Steel import data (monthly)

Functions transferred to the Domestic and International Business Administration, effective Nov. 17, 1972.

International Commerce Bureau

C42   Foreign Commerce Bureau

The Bureau of Foreign Commerce was established as a primary organization unit of the Department of Commerce by Department order 153, issued by the Secretary of Commerce Oct. 9, 1953, effective Oct. 12, 1953.

C42.1:date	Annual reports. Later C57.101:
C42.2:CT	General publications Later C57.102:
C42.3/2:nos	Investment opportunities abroad, bulletins (semimonthly) Proc.
C42.6:CT	Regulations, rules, and instructions
C42.6/2:CT	Handbooks, manuals, guides Later C57.108:
C42.6/3:CT	Export market guides
C42.7:nos	Releases
C42.8:v.nos	Foreign commerce weekly. Earlier C18.5/1: Later title International commerce. Later C1.58:
C42.8/a:CT	___ separates. Earlier C18.5/1a:
C42.8/2:CT	International commerce, supplements
C42.8/3:date	International commerce, quarterly index
C42.9:CT	Business information service. Proc. Earlier C18.228:
C42.9/2:nos	___ World trade series. Proc. Earlier C18.228:W89
C42.9/3:CT	___ International trade statistics series. Proc. Earlier C18.228:T67
C42.10:CT	Trade lists. Proc. Earlier C18.153: Later C57.22:
C42.10/2:date	Trade list catalog
C42.11:date	Comprehensive export schedule (annual) Earlier C18.267: Later C49.208:, C57.409:
C42.11/a:CT	___ separates. Later C49.208/2:, C42.11/a:

C42.11/2:nos	Current export bulletins [Supplements Comprehensive export schedule]. Earlier C18.266: Later C49.208/2: , C42.11/2:
C42.11/2a:CT	___ separates
C42.11/3:nos	Export control bulletin, supplement to Export control regulations. Later C59.409/2:
C42.12:date	Foreign commerce yearbook. Earlier C18.26/2: [none issued]
C42.13:date	Index to world trade information service reports. Replaces C42.9:, C42.9/2:, C42.9/3:
C42.13/1:nos	World trade information service. Pt.1. Economic reports. Replaces C42.9: Later C49.8/1:
C42.13/2:nos	World trade information service: Pt.2. Operations reports. Replaces C42.9: Later C49.8/2:
C42.13/3:nos	World trade information service: Pt.3, Statistical reports. Replaces C42.9: Later C49.8/3:
C42.13/4:nos	World trade information service: Pt.4. Utilities abroad Replaces C42.9:
C42.13/5:nos	World trade information service: pt.5, Fairs & exhibitions
C42.14:CT	Country-by-commodity series. Proc. Later C49.12:
C42.14/2:CT	Value series
C42.15:CT	Bibliographies and lists of publications Later C57.115:
C42.15/2:nos	Foreign market reports service listing
C42.15/3:nos	Foreign market reports, accession list (monthly) Later C57.110:
C42.15/3-2:date	Index to foreign production and commercial reports (cumulative)
C42.15/3-3:CT	Foreign production and commercial reports, cumulative indexes [by subject].
C42.16:CT	Doing business with [various countries]
C42.17:nos	Information sources on international travel. Proc.
C42.18:CT	Addresses
C42.19:CT	Reports of United States trade missions. Later C48.9:

The Secretary of Commerce, on August 8, 1961, established the Bureau of International Business Operations and the Bureau of International Programs under the direct supervision of the Assistant Secretary of Commerce for International Affairs. These two bureaus replace the Bureau of Foreign Commerce.

The Bureau of International Business Operations and the Bureau of International Programs have been merged into the Bureau of International Commerce under the Assistant Secretary for Domestic and International Business. Publications will be assigned C42 class numbers formerly assigned to publications of the Bureau of Foreign Commerce. [MC Feb. 1963]

C42.20:nos	Overseas business reports. Replaces C49.8/1: to C49.8/3: Later C1.50:
C42.20/2:CT	Market for U.S. products [by country]
C42.21:date	Export licenses approved and reexportation authorized (daily except Saturdays, Sundays, and holidays). Earlier C49.209: Later C57.410:
C42.22:nos	Reports prepared by Foreign Service of United States, listings.
C42.23:date	Export success story
C42.23/2:CT	Export sales promotions announcements
C42.24:date	International conference calendar, Administrative
C42.25:CT	Investment opportunity information
C42.26:date	Trends in U.S. foreign trade. Earlier C42.2:F76/3 Later C57.23:
C42.27:nos	Paris Air Show newsletter
C42.27/2:nos	Paris Air Show newsfillers
C42.28:CT	State export-origin series, exports from [various countries]
C42.29:CT	Kennedy round, special report
C42.30:nos	Economic trends and their implications for the United States. Later title, Foreign economic trends... Later C57.111:
C42.31:nos	International marketing information service, IMIS (series) Later C57.116:
C42.31/2:CT	International Marketing Information Service: Country market survey
C42.31/3:date	Market share report catalog
C42.31/4:nos	Export marketing digest, EMD (series) Later C57.112:
C42.32:date	Research on U.S. international trade

C42.33:CT   Global market survey   Later C57.109:

C42.34:date   International economic indicators, quarterly report Later C57.19:

Functions transferred to Domestic and International Business Administration. Effective Nov.12,1972.

C43 Business Economics Office

The Office of Business Economics was designated as a primary unit of the Department of Commerce by Department order 15 (amended) issued by the Secretary of Commerce, Dec.1,1953, effective Dec. 1,1953.

C43.1:date	Annual reports. Later C56.101:
C43.2:CT	General publications Later C56.102:
C43.7:nos	Business news reports and releases, OBE (series) Proc. Earlier C18.281: Later C56.107:
C43.8:v.nos	Survey of current business (monthly) Earlier C18.35: Later C56.109:
C43.8/a:CT	___ separates. Earlier C18.35/a:
C43.8/2:date	___ weekly supplement. Earlier C18.36: Later C56.109/2:
C43.8/3:CT	Supplements (special) to Survey of Current business. Earlier C18.35/2: Later C56.109/4:
C43.8/4:date	Business statistics, statistical supplement (biennial) Earlier C18.37: Earlier C43.8/4:
C43.9:date	Industry survey, manufacturers' sales, inventories, new and unfilled orders (monthly) Proc. Earlier C18.224:
C43.10:nos	Economic report to the Secretary of Commerce. Official use
C43.11:date	Foreign grants and credits by the United States Government. Earlier C18.279: Official use
C43.11/2:date	Foreign credits by United States Government, status of active foreign credits of the United States Government and of international organizations (semiannual) Later T1.45:
C43.12:date	Guide to current business data (weekly)
C43.13:CT	Addresses

C43.14:nos   Staff papers

Renamed Office of Economic Analysis and on Jan.1,1972 became a part of the Social and Economic Statistics Administration.

C44 International Trade Fairs Office

Established by Dept. order 159, Jan. 27, 1955 [F.R. 20:905]

C44.1:date	Annual reports. Later C48.101:
C44.2:CT	General publications Later C48.2:
C44.7:nos	Releases. Later C48.107:
C44.8:v.nos.&nos.	Fair facts, information for American industry (quarterly)
C44.9:CT	Addresses. Later C48.109:

Later subordinate to International Business Operations Bureau established August 8, 1961.

C45 Area Development Office

The Office of Area Development was established as a primary organization unit of the Department of Commerce by Department order 164 of Aug. 10, 1956.

C45.1:date	Annual reports
C45.2:CT	General publications
C45.7:nos	Releases
C45.8:CT	Industrial fact sheets. Proc. Later C41.90/3:
C45.8/2:nos	Area development aid, industry trend series. Proc. Later C41.90:

C45.8/3:nos	Area development aid: Industrial location series. Proc. Later C41.90/2:
C45.9:v.nos	Area development bulletin (bimonthly) Earlier C41.27: Later C46.9:
C45.10:date	Staff papers
C45.11:date	Conference of State planning and development officers with Federal officials, summaries (annual) Proc.
C45.12:CT	Addresses
C45.13:nos	Area trend series. Later C41.89:
C45.14:date	Area development memorandum for state planning and development offices.
C45.15:CT	Bibliographies and lists of publications.

1958 included in organization of Business and Defense Services Administration.

Economic Development Administration
C46   Area Redevelopment Administration

The Area Redevelopment Administration was established within the Department of Commerce by Public law 87-27 of the 87th Congress, 1st Session, approved May 1, 1961.
Functions, personnel, and property transferred to Economic Development Administration by Department order 4-A, effective Sept. 1, 1965.

C46.1:date   Annual reports

C46.2:CT   General publications

C46.6:CT   Regulations, rules and instructions

C46.7:nos   Press releases

C46.7/2:date   Industrial news

C46.8:CT   Handbooks, manuals, guides

C46.8/2:CT   Area redevelopment bookshelf of community aids

C46.9:v.nos.&nos   Area development bulletin (bimonthly) Earlier C41.27:

C46.9/2:v.nos.&nos. Redevelopment (monthly) Replaces C46.9: later title Economic development
C46.9/3:date   Economic development USA
C46.10:date   Value of prime contracts awarded by Federal agencies in areas of substantial labor surplus (quarterly) Earlier C41.99:

C46.11:CT   Addresses

C46.12:CT   State officers analyzer sheets. Official use.

C46.13:nos   Information news service. Administrative.

C46.14:nos   Area designation status reports

C46.15:date   ARA information memo

C46.16:CT   Q & A (series)

C46.17:CT   Maps and charts, Qualified areas [title varies]

C46.18:CT	Bibliographies and lists of publications
C46.19:date	Accelerated public works program, directory of approved projects (monthly)
C46.19/2:date	Directory of approved projects (monthly)
C46.20:nos	ARA case book
C46.21:nos	Monthly OEDP status report
C46.22:CT	ARA field reports
C46.22/2:CT	ARA staff studies
C46.23:date	Quarterly cumulative report of technical assistance
C46.24:CT	Economic redevelopment research
C46.25:nos	Qualified areas under Public works and economic development act of 1965. Public law 89-136, reports.
C46.25/2:pt.nos	Areas eligible for financial assistance designated under Public works and economic development act of 1965, reports (numbered)
C46.26:date	Research review
C46.27:CT	Urban business profiles (series)
C46.28:date	EDA news clips
C46.29:CT	Research reports

C.47 United States Travel Service

The United States Travel Service was established in the Department of Commerce by Public law 87-63, 87th Congress, 1st session, approved June 29, 1961. (75 Stat. 129)

C47.1:date	Semiannual reports
C47.2:CT	General publications
C47.7:nos	Press releases
C47.8:nos	Information sources on international travel. Earlier C42.17:
C47.9:CT	Addresses
C47.10:CT	Posters
C47.10/2:nos.-les.	U.S.T.S. [poster series]
C47.11:CT	Maps
C47.12:CT	Handbooks, manuals, guides
C47.13:CT	Bibliographies and lists of publications
C47.14:v./nos	Newsletter
C47.15:date	Statistical summary and analysis of foreign visitor arrivals, U.S. citizen and non-U.S. citizen departures (monthly) Earlier issue entitled Travel and travel dollar flow into and out of United States.
C47.15/a:date	___ separates
C47.15/2:date	Pleasure and business visitors to U.S. by port of entry and mode of travel Earlier C47.2:V82/date
C47.15/3:date	Major metropolitan market areas (quarterly)
C47.15/4:date	Arrivals and departures by selected ports (semi-annual)

C47.15/5:date	Annual summary, International travelers to U.S.
C47.16:nos	[Travel folders] USTS (series) Earlier in C47.2:
C47.17:date	Festival USA (annual) Earlier C47.2:F42

C48 International Business Operations Bureau

The Secretary of Commerce, on August 8, 1961, established the Bureau of International Business Operations and the Bureau of International Programs under the direct supervision of the Assistant Secretary of Commerce for International Affairs. These two bureaus replace the Bureau of Foreign Commerce.

C48.1:date   Annual reports

C48.2:CT   General publications

C48.8:CT   Addresses

C48.9:CT   Reports of United States trade misssion. Earlier C42.19:

C48.10:CT   Handbooks, manuals, guides.

Abolished by Departmental Order 182 of Feb. 1, 1963 which established the Bureau of International Commerce.

C48.101 International Trade Fairs Office

C48.101:date   Annual reports   Earlier C44.1:
C48.102:CT   General publications. Earlier C44.2:

C48.107:nos   Press releases. Earlier C44.7:
C48.108:nos   OITF policy statements
C48.109:CT   Addresses. Earlier C44.9:

C48.200:   Trade Promotion Office

C48.201:date   Annual reports
C48.202:CT   General publications

C48.300:   Commercial Services Office

Office of Foreign Commercial Services (Commerce) Established by the Secretary on Feb.1, 1963 and operated under Department Organization Order 40-4.

C48.301:date   Annual reports

C48.302:CT   General publications

Abolished on Sept.15,1970, by Department organization order 40-2A and functions transferred to Bureau of International Commerce.

C48.400:   International Investment Office

C48.401:date   Annual reports

C48.402:CT   General publications

C49 International Programs Bureau

The Secretary of Commerce, on August 8, 1961, established the Bureau of International Business Operations and the Bureau of International Programs under the direct supervision of the Assistant Secretary of Commerce for International Affairs. These two bureaus replace the Bureau of Foreign Commerce.

C49.1:date	Annual reports
C49.2:CT	General publications
C49.8/1:nos	World trade information service, part 1, Economic reports. Earlier C42.13/1: Replaced by C42.20:
C49.8/2:nos	World trade information service, part 2, Operations reports. Earlier C42.13/2: Replaced by C42.20:
C49.8/3:nos	World trade information service, part 3, Statistical reports. Earlier C42.13/3: Replaced by C42.20:
C49.9:CT	Sending gift packages to various countries. Earlier C42.2:
C49.10:CT	Bibliographies and lists of publications
C49.11:CT	Information for United States businessmen [by country]
C49.12:CT	Country-by-commodity series. Earlier C42.14:
C49.13:CT	Addresses

Abolished by Departmental order 182 of Feb.1, 1963 which established the Bureau of International Commerce.

C49.100:   Regional Economics Office

Established by the Secretary of Commerce on Jan. 6, 1966 pursuant to the Public Works and Economic Development Act of 1965 (79 Stat. 552).

C49.101:date   Annual report

C49.102:CT   General publications

Abolished by Department order 5A, Dec. 22, 1966 and functions vested in the Economic Development Administration.

C49.200:   Export Control Office

The Office of Export Control is an organization unit in the Bureau of International Programs which was established in the Department of Commerce by Dept. order 173 of August 25, 1961.

C49.201:date   Annual report

C49.202:CT   General publications

C49.206:CT   Regulations, rules, and instructions

C49.208:date   Comprehensive export schedule.   Earlier C42.11:   Later C42.11:

C49.208/a:CT   ___ separates.   Earlier C42.11/a: Later C42.11/a:

C49.208/2:nos   Current export bulletins.   Earlier C42.11:date and C42.11/2:nos   Later C42.11/2:

C49.209:date   Export licenses approved and reexportations authorized.   Daily, Mon.-Fri. except Federal legal holidays.   Later C42.21:

C49.300 International Economics Programs Office

The Office of International Economics Programs is an organization unit in the Bureau of International Programs, which was established in the Department of Commerce by Dept. order 173 of Aug. 8, 1961.

C49.301:date   Annual reports

C49.302:CT   General publications

C49.309:CT   Addresses

C50 Community Relations Service

The Community Relations Service was established in the Department of Commerce by Public law 352, 88th Congress, 2d session, approved July 3, 1964.

C50.1:date	Annual report. Later J23.1:
C50.2:CT	General publications. Later J23.2:
C50.3/2:nos	National Citizens Committee bulletin
C50.7:date	Press releases
C50.7/2:date	CRS media relations, newspapers, magazines, radio, television. Later J23.7:
C50.8:CT	Handbooks, manuals, guides. Later J23.8:
C50.9:CT	Addresses. Later J23.9:

Transferred to the Department of Justice by Reorganization Plan 1 of 1966, effective April 22, 1966.

National Technical Information Service

C 51   Clearinghouse for Federal Scientific and Technical
Information

The Clearinghouse for Federal Scientific and Technical Information was established in 1965.
The Clearinghouse was superseded on ept. 2, 1970 by the National Technical Information Service.

C51.1:date   Annual reports

C51.2:CT   General publications

C51.7/2:nos   Fast announcements

C51.7/3:nos   Special announcements. Earlier C41.28/2:

C41.7/4:nos   CFSTI news (irregular)

C51.7/5:nos./date Clearinghouse announcements in science and technology.
C51.7/6:date   NTIS monthly marketing
C51.8:CT   Handbooks, manuals, guides

C51.9:v.nos   Government-wide index to Federal research and development reports (monthly)
                [later title] Government reports index

C51.9/2:v.nos. &nos. ___ index (quarterly cumulative)

C51.9/3:v.nos. &nos. U.S. Government research and development reports (semimonthly) Earlier
                C41.21: [later title] Government reports announcements

C51.9/4:date   Government reports index (annual)

C51.9/5:nos   Weekly government abstracts, WGA-(series): Building technology

C51.9/6:nos   ___ Management practices & research

C51.9/7:nos   ___ Materials sciences

C51.9/8:nos   ___ Computers, control & information theory

C51.9/9:nos   ___ Transportation

C51.9/10:nos	Weekly government abstracts, WGA-(series): Building technology
C51.9/11:nos	___ NASA earth resources survey program
C51.9/12:nos	___ Behavior,
C51.9/13:nos	___ Biomedical technology & engineering
C51.9/14:nos	___ Urban technology
C51.9/15:nos	___ Library & information sciences
C51.9/16:nos	___ Industrial engineering
C51.9/17:nos	___ Business & economics
C51.9/18:nos	___ Energy
C51.9/19:nos	___ Agriculture and food, WGA-98 (series)
C51.9/20:nos	___ Chemistry
C51.9/21:nos	___ Civil & structural engineering, WGA-50 (series)
C51.9/22:nos	___ Electrotechnology, WGA-49 (series)
C51.9/23:nos	___ Government inventions for licensing, WGA-90 (series)
C51.9/24:nos	___ Medicine & biology, WGA-57 (series)
C51.9/25:nos	___ Natural resources
C51.9/26:nos	___ Ocean technology and engineering
C51.9/27:nos	___ Transportation
C51.9/28:nos	___ Communications
C51.9/29:nos	___ : Health planning, WGA-44 (series)
C51.9/30:nos	Government abstracts: Problem-solving technology for State & local governments.

C51.10:date	Monthly progress report. Official use.
C51.11:CT	Bibliographies and lists of publications. Earlier C41.23/4:
C51.11/2:date	Directory of computerized data files and related software available from Federal agencies (annual)
C51.11/3:date	Selected reports (monthly) Title varies
C51.12:CT	Special Foreign Currency Science Information Program, list of translations in process for fiscal year.

C52 Environmental Science Services Administration

Reorganization Plan no. 2, Effective July 13, 1965, consolidates the Coast and Geodetic Survey and the Weather Bureau to form a new agency in the Department of Commerce to be known as the Environmental Science Services Administration

C52.1:date	Annual reports
C52.2:CT	General publications
C52.3/2:date	Environmental data bulletin Later C55.203:
C52.6:CT	Regulations, rules, and instructions Later C55.106:
C52.7:nos	Press releases
C52.7/2:date	Radio-television news
C52.7/3:nos	Publications announcements
C52.7/4:v.nos.&nos.	ESSA news
C52.8:CT	Handbooks, manuals, guides
C52.8/2:nos	ESSA Research Laboratories technical manuals
C52.9:v.nos.&nos	Radio science (monthly) Replaces Sec.D of Journal of Research C13.22/sec.D:
C52.10:nos	Ionospheric predictions (monthly) Earlier C13.31/3: Later C1.59:
C52.11:CT	Climatic maps of United States
C52.11/2:date	Daily weather maps, weekly series. Earlier C30.12: Later C55.213:
C52.12:CT	Addresses
C52.13:nos	Monographs
C52.14:date	Essa world (quarterly) Replaced by C55.14:
C52.15:les-nos	ESSA Technical reports Later C55.13:
C52.15/2:nos	ESSA technical memorandums Later C55.13/2:

C52.16:v.nos	Data report, meteorological rocket network firings (monthly) Later C55.280:
C52.16/2:nos	Upper Atmosphere Geophysics, report UAG (series) Later C55.220:
C52.17:date	Federal plan for meteorological services and supporting research (annual) Later C55.16/2:
C52.18:nos	Solar-geophysical data, IER-FB-(series) (monthly) Later C55.215:
C52.19:nos	Atmospheric Sciences Library: Accession list
C52.20:nos	ESSA professional papers Later C55.25:
C52.21:nos	WB/BC-(series) Earlier C30.17/3:C61/2(nos)
C52.21/2:nos	WB/TA-(series) Earlier C30.17/3:So8/nos
C52.21/3:CT	Bibliographies and lists of publications
C52.21/4:date	Scientific and technical publications of ESSA Research Laboratories
C52.21/4-2:date	___: Earth Sciences Laboratories
C52.21/5:date	Management information on ERL's scientific and technical publications (annual)
C52.22:letters-nos	ESSA operational data reports
C52.23:date	Collected reprints, ESSA Institute for Oceanography (annual) Later C55.612:
C52.24:nos	Bomex bulletin Later C55.18:
C52.25:date	ESSA science and engineering (biennial) Earlier C52.2:Sci2

The Administration was abolished by Reorganization Plan No. 4 of 1970, effective Oct. 3, 1970, and its functions transferred to the National Oceanic and Atmospheric Administration.

C53 Regional Economic Development Office

The Office of Regional Economic Development was established by the Secretary of Commerce, by Department order 6-A of January 6,1966, pursuant to authority vested in the Secretary of Commerce by the Public works and economic development act of 1965 (79 Stat. 552; 42 U.S.C. 3121)

C53.1:date   Annual report

C53.2:CT   General publications

C53.7:date   Press releases

C53.9:CT   Bibliographies and lists of publications.

Abolished by Department order 5A, Dec. 22,1966, and functions vested in the Economic Development Administration.

C54 Foreign Direct Investments Office

The Office of Foreign Direct Investments was established by Departmental Order 184A on January 2 1968, pursuant to the authority vested in the Secretary of Commerce by Executive Order 11387 of January 1, 1968.

C54.1:date   Annual report

C54.2:CT   General publications

C54.6:CT   Regulations, rules, and instructions

C54.7:nos   Press releases

C54.9:CT   Addresses

C55   National Oceanic and Atmospheric Administration

The National Oceanic and Atmospheric Administration was established within the Department of Commerce by Reorganization plan 4 of 1970, effective Oct. 3, 1970.

C55.1:date	Annual report
C55.2:CT	General publications
C55.6:CT	Regulations, rules and instructions
C55.7:nos	Press releases
C55.8:CT	Handbooks, manuals, guides
C55.8/2:nos	NOAA handbooks (numbered)
C55.9:v./nos	NOAA week
C55.10:	[not used]
C55.11:v.nos.&nos.	Monthly weather review. Earlier C30.14:
C55.11/a:CT	___ separates. Earlier C30.14/a:
C55.12:nos	Federal Coordinator for Meteorological Services and Supporting Research, FCM (series)
C55.13:les-nos	NOAA technical reports. Earlier C52.15:
C55.13/2:les-nos	NOAA technical memorandums. Earlier C52.15/2:
C55.14:v.nos.&nos.	NOAA (quarterly) Replaces C52.14:
C55.14/a:CT	___ separates
C55.15:nos	NOAA program plans
C55.16:date	Federal plan for marine environmental prediction, fiscal year
C55.16/2:date	Federal plan for meteorological services and supporting research, fiscal year. Earlier C52.17:
C55.17:nos	NOAA publications announcements

C55.18:nos	BOMEX bulletin Earlier C52.24:
C55.19:nos	NOAA photoessays (numbered)
C55.20:nos	Natural disaster survey reports (numbered)
C55.21:nos	International Field year for Great Lakes: IFYGL bulletin
C55.21/2:date	___ News release
C55.21/3:date	___ IFYGL symposium, Annual meeting of the American Geophysical Union
C55.21/4:nos	___ Technical manual series
C55.22:nos	NOAA Atlases (numbered)
C55.23:	Atmospheric sciences and Marine and Earth Sciences: Library accession list.
C55.24:CT	Addresses
C55.25:nos	NOAA professional papers. Earlier C52.20:
C55.26:CT	Bibliographies and lists of publications
C55.27:date	Summary report, weather modification, fiscal year Earlier NS1.21:
C55.27/2:date	Weather modification activity reports, calendar year
C55.28:nos	Hydrometeorological report. Earlier C30.44:
C55.29:date	Manned undersea science and technology, fiscal year reports
C55.30:v.nos./nos	Data buoy technical bulletin (quarterly)
C55.31:date	Report to Congress on ocean dumping and other man-induced changes to ocean ecosystems (annual)
C55.32:date	Coastal zone management annual report for fiscal year
C55.33:date	National Environmental Communications summary plan
C55.34:CT	Draft environmental impact statements
C55.34/2:CT	Final environmental impact statements
C55.35:nos	NOAA dumpsite evaluation reports (numbered)

C55.70:date   National Oceanographic Instrumentation Center: Tests in progress sheets
                     (quarterly) Earlier D203.32:
C55.71:nos   Instrument fact sheet, IFS-(series) Earlier D203.32/2:

C55.72:CT   National Oceanic Instrumentation Center publications

C55.73:letters/nos   Technical bulletins   Earlier D203.32/3:

C55.100 National Weather Service

The National Weather Service was established within the National Oceanic and Atmospheric Administration of the Dept. of Commerce, by Dept. organization order 25-5A, effective Oct. 9, 1970.

C55.101:date	Annual report
C55.102:CT	General publications
C55.106:CT	Regulations, rules, and instructions. Earlier C30.6:, C52.6:
C55.108:CT	Handbooks, manuals, guides. Earlier C30.6/2:
C55.108/2:nos	Weather Service observing handbooks. Earlier C30.6/6:
C55.108/3:nos	Forecasters handbook. Earlier C30.6/4:
C55.108/4:nos	National Weather Service communications handbooks
C55.109:v.nos.&nos.	Average monthly weather outlook. Earlier C30.46:
C55.110:date	Ohio river summary and forecasts. Earlier C30.54/17:
C55.110/2:date	River summary and forecasts [Memphis, Tenn. area]. Earlier C30.54/7:
C55.110/2-2:date	___ New Orleans, Louisiana [area] Later C55.110/7:
C55.110/3:date	Missouri-Mississippi river summary & forecasts. Earlier C30.54:
C55.110/4:nos	Daily weather and river bulletin, Albuquerque, New Mexico. Earlier C30.54/4:
C55.110/5:date	Daily weather and river bulletin, New Orleans, La. Earlier C30.54/10:
C55.110/6:date	Daily weather and river bulletin, Shreveport, La. Earlier C30.54/12:
C55.110/7:date	River summary and forecasts. Published at Slidell, La. Replaces C55.110/2-2: and C55.110/2:
C55.111:date	Operations of National Weather Service. Earlier C30.83:

C55.112:CT	Marine Weather services charts. Earlier C30.22/6:
C55.113:v.nos.&nos.	Water supply outlook for western United States, water year. Earlier C30.85:
C55.113/2:v.nos.&nos.	Water supply outlook for northeastern United States (monthly)
C55.114:date	Pacific Northwest monthly precipitation and temperature. Earlier C30.62/3:
C55.115:date	Numerical weather prediction activities, National Meteorological Center. Earlier C30.2:N91/970
C55.116:nos	Engineering bits and fax. Issued by the Engineering Division
C55.117:v.nos	Daily river stages. Earlier C30.24:
C55.117/2:nos	River forecasts provided by National Weather Service. Later C55.285:
C55.118:v./nos	Cooperative observer regional newsletter
C55.118/2:v./nos	Cooperative observer, regional newsletter, Southern region
C55.118/3:v.nos.&nos.	Cooperative observer, regional newsletter, Central region
C55.119:date	Weather services of merchant shipping. Earlier C30.79:
C55.120:	[not used]
C55.121:nos	Training papers (numbered)
C55.122:CT	Maps and charts. Earlier C30.22:
C55.123:v.nos.&nos.	Gulf stream (monthly) Supersedes D203.29:

National Meteorological Center

C55.190:CT   National Meteorological Center publications

C55.200 Environmental Data Service

The Environmental Data Service was established within National Oceanic and Atmospheric Admin. of the Dept. of Commerce by Dept. organization order 25-5A, sec. 11, effective Oct. 9, 1970.

C55.201:date   Annual report

C55.202:CT   General publications

C55.203:date   Environmental data bulletin   Earlier C52.3/2:   Replaced by C55.222:

C55.208:CT   Handbooks, manuals, guides

C55.209:v.nos.&nos.   Weekly weather & crop bulletin.   Earlier C30.11:

C55.210:v.nos.&nos.   Mariners weather log (bimonthly)   Earlier C30.72:

C55.210/a:CT   ___ separates

C55.211:v.nos.&nos   Monthly climatic data for the world.   Earlier C30.50:

C55.212:v.nos.&nos   Storm data (monthly)   Earlier C30.74:

C55.213:date/nos   Daily weather maps, weekly series.   Earlier C52.11/2:

C55.213/2:date   Daily series, synoptic weather maps: pt.1, Northern Hemisphere sea level and 500 millibar charts (monthly)   Earlier C30.49:

C55.214:v.nos.&nos.   Climatological data: National summary.   Earlier C30.51:

C55.214/2:v.nos.&nos.   Climatological data: Alabama.   Earlier C30.18/3:

C55.214/3:v.nos.&nos.   Climatological data: Alaska.   Earlier C30.21:

C55.214/4:v.nos.&nos.   Climatological data: Arizona.   Earlier C30.18/4:

C55. 214/ 5: v. nos. &nos. Climatological data: Arkansas. Earlier C30.18/ 5:

C55. 214/ 6: v. nos. &nos. Climatological data: California. Earlier C30.18/ 6:

C55. 214/ 7: v. nos. &nos. Climatological data: Colorado. Earlier C30.18/ 7:

C55. 214/ 8: v. nos. &nos. Climatological data: Florida. Earlier C30.18/ 8:

C55. 214/ 9: v. nos. &nos. Climatological data: Georgia. Earlier C30.18/ 9:

C55. 214/ 10: v. nos. &nos. Climatological data: Hawaii. Earlier C30.19:

C55. 214/ 11: v. nos. &nos. Climatological data: Idaho. Earlier C30.18/ 10:

C55. 214/ 12: v. nos. &nos. Climatological data: Illinois. Earlier C30.18/ 11:

C55. 214/ 13: v. nos. &nos. Climatological data: Indiana. Earlier C30.18/ 12:

C55. 214/ 14: v. nos. &nos. Climatological data: Iowa. Earlier C30.18/ 13:

C55. 214/ 15: v. nos. &nos. Climatological data: Kansas. Earlier C30.18/ 14:

C55. 214/ 16: v. nos. &nos. Climatological data: Kentucky. Earlier C30.18/ 15:

C55. 214/ 17: v. nos. &nos. Climatological data: Louisiana. Earlier C30.18/ 16:

C55. 214/ 18: v. nos. &nos. Climatological data: Maryland and Delaware. Earlier C30.18/ 17:

C55. 214/ 19: v. nos. &nos. Climatological data: Michigan. Earlier C30.18/ 18:

C55. 214/ 20: v. nos. &nos. Climatological data: Minnesota. Earlier C30.18/ 19:

C55. 214/ 21: v. nos. &nos. Climatological data: Mississippi. Earlier C30.18/ 20:

C55. 214/ 22: v. nos. &nos. Climatological data: Missouri. Earlier C30.18/ 21:

C55. 214/ 23: v. nos. &nos. Climatological data: Montana. Earlier C30.18/ 22:

C55. 214/ 24: v. nos. &nos. Climatological data: Nebraska. Earlier C30.18/ 23:

C55. 214/ 25: v. nos. &nos. Climatological data: Nevada. Earlier C30.18/ 24:

C55. 214/ 26: v. nos. &nos. Climatological data: New England. Earlier C30.18/ 25:

C55. 214/ 27: v. nos. &nos. Climatological data: New Jersey. Earlier C30.18/ 26:

C55. 214/ 28: v. nos. &nos. Climatological data: New Mexico. Earlier C30.18/ 27:

C55. 214/ 29: v. nos. &nos. Climatological data: New York. Earlier C30.18/ 28:

C55. 214/30:v.nos.&nos. Climatological data: North Carolina. Earlier C30.18/29:

C55. 214/31:v.nos.&nos. Climatological data: North Dakota. Earlier C30.18/30:

C55. 214/32:v.nos.&nos. Climatological data: Ohio. Earlier C30.18/31:

C55. 214/33:v.nos.&nos. Climatological data: Oklahoma. Earlier C30.18/32:

C55. 214/34:v.nos.&nos. Climatological data: Oregon. Earlier C30.18/33:

C55. 214/35:v.nos.&nos. Climatological data: Pacific. Earlier C30.19/2:

C55. 214/36:v.nos.&nos. Climatological data: Pennsylvania. Earlier C30.18/34:

C55. 214/37:v.nos.&nos. Climatological data: Puerto Rico and Virgin Islands. Earlier C30. 20/

C55. 214/38:v.nos.&nos. Climatological data: South Carolina. Earlier C30.18/35:

C55. 214/39:v.nos.&nos. Climatological data: South Dakota. Earlier C30.18/36:

C55. 214/40:v.nos.&nos. Climatological data: Tennessee. Earlier C30.18/37:

C55. 214/41:v.nos.&nos. Climatological data: Texas. Earlier C30.18/38:

C55. 214/42:v.nos.&nos. Climatological data: Utah. Earlier C30.18/39:

C55. 214/43:v.nos.&nos. Climatological data: Virginia. Earlier C30.18/40:

C55. 214/44:v.nos.&nos. Climatological data: Washington. Earlier C30.18/41:

C55. 214/45:v.nos.&nos. Climatological data: West Virginia. Earlier C30.18/42:

C55. 214/46:v.nos.&nos. Climatological data: Wisconsin. Earlier C30.18/43:

C55. 214/47:v.nos.&nos. Climatological data: Wyoming. Earlier C30.18/44:

C55. 214/48:v.nos.&nos. Climatological data: West Indies and Caribbean

C55. 214/49:v.nos. &nos. Climatological data: for Arctic stations Earlier C30.21/2:

C55. 214/50:nos Climatological data for Antarctic stations. Earlier C30. 21/3:

C55. 215:nos Solar-geophysical data [reports] Earlier C52.18:

C55. 216:v.nos.&nos. Hourly precipitation data: Alabama. Earlier C30.59:

C55. 216/2:v.nos.&nos. Hourly precipitation data: Arizona. Earlier C30.59/3:

C55. 216/3:v.nos.&nos. Hourly precipitation data: Arkansas. Earlier C30.59/4:

C55. 216/4:v. nos. &nos.   Hourly precipitation data: California. Earlier C30.59/5:

C55. 216/5:v. nos. &nos.   Hourly precipitation data: Colorado. Earlier C30.59/6:

C55. 216/6:v. nos. &nos.   Hourly precipitation data: Florida. Earlier C30.59/7:

C55. 216/7:v. nos. &nos.   Hourly precipitation data. Georgia. Earlier C30.59/8:

C55. 216/8:v. nos. &nos.   Hourly precipitation data: Hawaii. Earlier C30.59/46:

C55. 216/9:v. nos. &nos.   Hourly precipitation data: Idaho. Earlier C30.59/9:

C55. 216/10:v. nos. &nos. Hourly precipitation data: Illinois. Earlier C30.59/10:

C55. 216/11:v. nos. &nos. Hourly precipitation data: Indiana. Earlier C30.59/11:

C55. 216/12:v. nos. &nos. Hourly precipitation data: Iowa. Earlier C30.59/12:

C55. 216/13:v. nos. &nos. Hourly precipitation data: Kansas. Earlier C30.59/13:

C55. 216/14:v. nos. &nos. Hourly precipitation data: Kentucky. Earlier C30.59/14:

C55. 216/15:v. nos. &nos. Hourly precipitation data: Louisiana. Earlier C30.59/15:

C55. 216/16:v. nos. &nos. Hourly precipitation data: Maryland and Delaware. Earlier C30.59/16:

C55. 216/17:v. nos. &nos. Hourly precipitation data: Michigan. Earlier C30.59/17:

C55. 216/18:v. nos. &nos. Hourly precipitation data: Minnesota. Earlier C30.59/18:

C55. 216/19:v. nos. &nos. Hourly precipitation data: Mississippi. Earlier C30.59/19:

C55. 216/20:v. nos. &nos. Hourly precipitation data: Missouri. Earlier C30.59/20:

C55. 216/21:v. nos. &nos. Hourly precipitation data: Montana. Earlier C30.59/21:

C55. 216/22:v. nos. &nos. Hourly precipitation data: Nebraksa. Earlier C30.59/22:

C55. 216/23:v. nos. &nos. Hourly precipitation data: Nevada. Earlier C30.59/23:

C55. 216/24:v. nos. &nos. Hourly precipitation data: New England. Earlier C30.59/24:

C55. 216/25:v. nos. &nos. Hourly precipitation data: New Jersey. Earlier C30.59/25:

C55. 216/26:v. nos. &nos. Hourly precipitation data: New Mexico. Earlier C30.59/26:

C55. 216/27:v. nos. &nos. Hourly precipitation data: New York. Earlier C30.59/27:

C55.216/28:v.nos.&nos. Hourly precipitation data: North Carolina. Earlier C30.59/28:

C55.216/29:v.nos.&nos. Hourly precipitation data: North Dakota. Earlier C30.59/29:

C55.216/30:v.nos.&nos. Hourly precipitation data: Ohio. Earlier C30.59/30:

C55.216/31:v.nos.&nos. Hourly precipitation data: Oklahoma. Earlier C30.59/31:

C55.216/32:v.nos.&nos. Hourly precipitation data: Oregon. Earlier C30.59/32:

C55.216/33:v.nos.&nos. Hourly precipitation data: Pennsylvania. Earlier C30.59/33:

C55.216/34:v.nos.&nos. Hourly precipitation data: South Carolina. Earlier C30.59/34:

C55.216/35:v.nos.&nos. Hourly precipitation data: South Dakota. Earlier C30.59/35:

C55.216/36:v.nos.&nos. Hourly precipitation data: Tennessee. Earlier C30.59/36:

C55.216/37:v.nos.&nos. Hourly precipitation data: Texas. Earlier C30.59/37:

C55.216/38:v.nos.&nos. Hourly precipitation data: Utah. Earlier C30.59/38:

C55.216/39:v.nos.&nos. Hourly precipitation data: Virginia. Earlier C30.59/39:

C55.216/40:v.nos.&nos. Hourly precipitation data: Washington. Earlier C30.59/40:

C55.216/41:v.nos.&nos. Hourly precipitation data: West Virginia. Earlier C30.59/41:

C55.216/42:v.nos.&nos. Hourly precipitation data: Wisconsin. Earlier C30.59/42:

C55.216/43:v.nos.&nos. Hourly precipitation data: Wyoming. Earlier C30.59/43:

C55.216/44:v.nos.&nos. Hourly precipitation data: Puerto Rico

C55.217:date   Local climatological data. Earlier C30.56:

C55.217/2:date   Local climatological data, Washington, D.C., Dulles International Airport

C55.217:date/nos   Ionospheric data (monthly)

C55.219:nos   Key to meteorological records documentation [miscellaneous reports] Earlier C30.66/2:

C55.219/2:nos   Key to geophysical records documentation

C55.219/3:nos   Key to oceanographic records documentation (series)

C55.219/4:date   Key to meteorological records documentation no.5.4. Environmental satellite imagery

C55.219/5:nos	Key to oceanic and atmospheric information sources
C55.220:nos	World Data Center A: Upper atmosphere geophysics, report UAG-(series) Earlier C52.16/2:
C55.220/2:date	World Data Center A: Oceanography, catalogue of accessioned Soviet publications
C55.220/3:date	World Data Center A: Oceanography, oceanographic data exchange. Earlier NS1.32:
C55.220/4:CT	World Data Center A, Oceanography: Publications (unnumbered)
C55.220/5:v./nos	World Data Center A: Meteorology data report
C55.221:nos	Climatography of United States: Climates of the States. Earlier C30.71/3:
C55.221/2:nos	Decennial census of U.S. climate. Earlier C30.71/5:
C55.222:date	Environmental Data Service (bimonthly) Replaces C55.290: and C55.203:
C55.223:nos	Abstracts of earthquake reports for United States, MSA-(series) Earlier C55.417: Later I19.69:
C55.224:date	Interim lists of periodicals in collection of Atmospheric Science Library and Marine and Earth Science Library
C55.225:v.nos	Storage-gage precipitation data for western United States
C55.226:date	United States earthquakes. Earlier C55.417/2:
C55.227:nos	International decade of ocean exploration, Progress reports
C55.228:nos	Publications (numbered) see, for similar class C55.419:

National Climatic Center

C55.280:v/nos	Data report, high altitude meteorological data. Earlier C52.16:
C55.280/2:v.nos	Data report, high altitude meteorological data, international delayed data issue
C55.281:CT	National Climatic Center publications
C55.282:v.nos	Marine climatological summaries (annual)
C55.283:letters-nos	Environmental information summaries
C55.284:date	Atmospheric turbidity and precipitation chemistry data for the world
C55.285:v.nos	River forecasts provided by National Weather Service (annual) Earlier C55.117/2:

National Oceanographic Data Center

C55.290: nos	Newsletter. Earlier D203.24/2: Later C55.222:
C55.291:date	Highlights. Earlier D203.24/3:N21
C55.292:CT	National Oceanographic Data Center publications. Earlier D203.24/3:

C55.300   National Marine Fisheries Service

The National Marine Fisheries Service was established within the National Oceanic and Atmospheric Administration of the Department of Commerce by Dept. organization order 25-A, effective Oct. 9, 1970.

C55.301:date   Annual report

C55.302:CT   General publications

C55.304:nos   Circulars

C55.308:CT   Handbooks, manuals, guides

C55.308/2:nos   Handbooks (numbered)

C55.309:date   Frozen fish report (preliminary) Earlier I49.8/3:

C55.309/2:nos   Current fishery statistics CFS (series) Earlier I49.8/2:

C55.309/3:nos   Industrial fishery products, situation and outlook, current economic analysis I (series) Earlier I49.8/9:

C55.309/4:nos   Shellfish situation and outlook, CEA-S (series) Earlier I49.8/8:

C55.309/5:nos   Foodfish situation and outlook, CEA-F (series) Earlier I49.8/6:
C55.309/6:nos   Food fish facts
C55.310:v.nos.&nos.   Commercial fisheries review (monthly) [later title] Marine fisheries review. Earlier I49.10:

C55.310/2:v.nos.&nos. Commercial fisheries abstracts (monthly) Earlier I49.40:

C55.311:v.nos.&nos.   Fishery industrial research. Earlier I49.26/2:

C55.312:nos   Special scientific reports: Fisheries. Earlier I49.15/2: Later C55.13:NMFS-SSRF-nos

C55.313:v.nos.&nos.   Fishery bulletin. Earlier I49.27:

C55.314:nos   Fishery leaflets. Earlier I49.28:

C55.314/2:nos	Foreign fisheries leaflets
C55.315:CT	Posters
C55.316:nos	Statistical digest. Earlier I49.32:
C55.317:nos	Resource report
C55.318:CT	Market news service regional publications Earlier I49.52/2:
C55.319:nos	Fishing information
C55.320:nos	Fishery market development (series) Earlier I49.49/2:
C55.321:nos	Test kitchen series. Earlier I49.39:
C55.322:nos	Fishery facts, FSHFA- (series)
C55.323:date	Grant-in-aid for fisheries program activities (annual)
C55.324:nos	Data reports. Earlier I49.59:
C55.325:nos	Translated tables of contents of current foreign fisheries, oceanographic, and atmospheric publications.

C55.400 National Ocean Survey

The National Ocean Survey was established within the National Oceanic and Atmospheric Administration of the Department of Commerce pursuant to Reorganization Plan no. 4 of 1970, effective October 3, 1970 to succeed the Coast and Geodetic Survey.

C55.401:date   Annual report

C55.402:CT   General publications

C55.408:CT   Handbooks, manuals, guides   Earlier C4.12/5:

C55.408/2:nos   NOS Technical manuals. Continuation of C&GS technical manual series C4.12/5:

C55.409:date   Dates of latest editions, aeronautical charts. Earlier C4.9/13:

C55.410:v./nos   Earthquake information bulletin (bimonthly) Earlier C4.54: Later C55.611:

C55.411:date   Instrument approach procedure charts (bimonthly) Earlier C4.9/18:

C55.411/2:date   Instrument approach procedure charts [Alaska, Hawaii, U.S. Pacific Islands]. Earlier C4.9/18-2:

C55.411/3:date   Airport construction charts (bimonthly)

C55.412:date   Preliminary determination of epicenters, monthly listing. Earlier C4.36/2-2: Later C55.690:

C55.413:CT   Bibliographies and lists of publications

C55.414:nos   Antarctic seismological bulletin. Earlier C4.36: Later C55.610:

C55.415:nos   Press releases

C55.416:date   Flight information publication: Supplement, Alaska

C55.417:nos   Abstracts of earthquake reports for United States MSA -(series) Earlier C4.42: Later C55.223:

C55.417/2:date	United States earthquakes (annual) Earlier C4.25/2: Later C55.226:
C55.418:nos/date	Nautical chart catalogs. Earlier C4.5:
C55.418/2:date	National Ocean survey catalog of aeronautical charts and related publications
C55.418/3:date	Latest editions of U.S. Air Force aeronautical charts. Earlier C4.9/13-2:
C55.418/4:date	Military fields United States, instrument approach procedure charts, dates of latest editions. Earlier C4.9/22:
C55.419:nos	NOS publications (numbered) Earlier C4.19/2:
C55.420:date	Great Lakes pilot (annual) Earlier D103.203:
C55.420/2:date	Great Lakes water levels. Earlier C55.402:G79
C55.421:date	Tide tables, high and low water predictions, west coast of North and South America including Hawaiian Islands. Earlier C4.15/5:
C55.421/2:date	___ East coast... including Greenland. Earlier C4.15/4:
C55.421/3:date	___ Europe and West coast of Africa, including the Mediterranean sea. Earlier C4.15/7:
C55.421/4:date	___ Central and Western Pacific Ocean and Indian Ocean. Earlier C4.15/6:
C55.422:nos	United States coast pilots. Earlier C4.6/1:, C4.6/2:, C4.6/3:, C4.6/4:, C4.7/1:, C4.7/2:, C4.7/3:
C55.423:date	Ship operations report (annual)
C55.424:CT	Tidal current charts. Earlier C4.29:
C55.425:date	Tidal current tables, Atlantic Coast of North America. Earlier C4.22:
C55.425/2:date	Tidal current tables, Pacific Coast of North America. Earlier C4.23:
C55.426:nos	EDR [Earthquake data report] series
C55.427:date	Government flight information publication: Pacific Chart supplement. Earlier TD4.16:

C55.500　National Environmental Satellite Service

C55.501:date　　Annual report

C55.502:CT　　General publications

C55.600 Environmental Research Laboratories

C55.601:date   Annual report

C55.602:CT   General publications

C55.609:nos   Hurricane research progress reports

C55.610:nos   Antarctic seismological bulletin, MSI-(series) Earlier C55.414:

C55.611:v./nos   Earthquake information bulletin. Earlier C55.410: Later I19.65:

C55.612:date   Collected reprints, Institute for Oceanography (annual) Earlier C52.23:

C55.612/2:date   Collected reprints of Wave Propagation Laboratory

C55.612/3:date   Collected reprints: Atmospheric Physics and Chemistry Laboratory

C55.613:

C55.613/2:date   Administrative bulletin

C55.614:CT   Addresses

C55.615:nos   ERL program plan

C55.616:CT   Bibliographies and lists of publications

C55.617:nos   MESA, Marine Ecosystems Analysis Programs, Reports

C55.618:nos   Geophysical monitoring for climatic change

National Earthquake Information Center

C55.690:date	Preliminary determination of epicenters, monthly listing. Earlier C55.412:
C55.691:CT	Publications

C56   Social and Economic Statistics Administration

The Social and Economic Statistics Administration was established on January 1, 1972 by the Secretary of Commerce.

C56.1:date   Annual report

C56.2:CT   General publications

C56.9:v./nos   Library notes. Earlier C3.207:

Terminated by Department of Commerce Organization Order 10-2, effective Aug. 4, 1975.

C56.100   Economic Analysis Bureau

The Economic Analysis Bureau was established within the Social and Economic Statistics Administration of the Commerce Department, effective Jan. 1, 1972

C56.101:date   Annual report. Earlier C43.1:   Later C59.1:

C56.102:CT   General publications. Earlier C43.2:   Later C59.2:

C56.107:nos   Press releases. Earlier C43.7:

C56.109:v./nos   Survey of current business. Earlier C43.8: Later C59.11:

C56.109/a:CT   ___ separates

C56.109/2:date   Business statistics, weekly supplement to Survey of current business. Earlier C43.8/2: Later C59.11/2:

C56.109/3:date   Business statistics, biennial supplement to Survey of current business. Earlier C43.8/4: Later C59.11/3:

C56.109/4:CT   Supplements to Survey of Current Business. Earlier C43.8/3: Later C59.11/4:

C56.110:date   Defense indicators (monthly) Earlier C3.241: Later C59.10:

C56.111:date   Business conditions digest (monthly) Earlier C3.226: Later C59.9:

C56.111/2:date   Advance BCD- Business conditions digest. Earlier C3.226/3: Later C59.9/2:

C56.112:P-nos/nos International population statistics report series P-(numbers) Earlier C3.205:P-90/nos

C56.112/2:P-nos/nos International population reports series. Earlier C3.186:

C56.113:nos   Bureau of Economic Analysis Staff paper BEA-SP (series)

C56.114:v.nos/nos SESA inquiries. Admin.

Bureau of Economic Analysis restored as a primary operating unit of Department of Commerce, Organization orders 35-1A, effective Aug. 4, 1975.

C56.200 Census Bureau

January 1, 1972 the Bureau of the Census became a part of the Social and Economic Statistics Administration.

C56.201:date   Annual report. Earlier C3.1: Later C3.1:

C56.202:CT   General publications. Earlier C3.2: Later C3.2:

C 56.206:CT	Regulations, rules and instructions. Earlier C3.6: Later C3.6:
C56.207:dt.-nos	Press releases. Earlier C3.209:
C56.208:CT	Handbooks, manuals, guides. Earlier C3.6/2: Later C3.6/2:
C56.209:dt/nos	Government finances GF (series) Earlier C3.191/2: Later C3.191/2:
C56.209/2:nos	Government employment, GE (series) Earlier C3.140/2: Later C3.140/2:
C56.210:nos	U.S. foreign trade FT-(series) Earlier C3.164: Later C3.164:
C56.210/2:date	Guide to foreign trade statistics (annual) Earlier C3.6/2:F76/date
C56.210/3:date	U.S. Foreign trade: Schedules. Earlier C3.150: Later C3.150:
C56.210/4:nos	U.S. General imports [various commodities] Earlier C3.164/2-2; -3; -4, -5, -6, -7; and -8:
C56.211:nos	Construction reports: Housing completions, C22(series) Earlier C3.215/13:
C56.211/2:nos	Construction reports: New one-family homes sold and for sale, C-25- (series) Earlier C3.215/9: Later C3.215/9:
C56.211/2-2:nos	Construction reports: Price index of new one-family houses sold C-27 (series) Later C3.215/9-2:
C56.211/3:nos	Construction reports: Housing starts, C20-(series) Earlier C3.215/2: Later C3.215/2:
C56.211/4:nos	Construction reports: Housing authorized by building permits and public contracts C40-(series) Earlier C3.215/4:
C56.211/5:nos	Construction reports: Value of new construction put in place, C30-(series) Earlier C3.215/3:C30-(nos) Later C3.215/3:C30-
C56.211/6:nos	Construction reports: Authorized construction, Washington, D.C. area, C41-(series) Earlier C3.215/15:
C56.211/7:nos	Construction reports: Residential aletrations and repairs, expenditures on residential alterations, maintenance and repairs and replacements, C50-(series) Earlier C3.215/8:
C56.211/8:date	Construction reports:C-45. Housing units authorized for demolition in permit issuing places. Earlier C3.215/12:
C56.212:nos	Data access description: Collection, evaluation and processing series CEP-(nos) Earlier C3.240/5: Later C3.240/5:

C56.212/2:dt/nos	Census users bulletins
C56.212/3:nos	Data access description: Computer tape series CT Earlier C3.240/3: Later C3.240/3:
C56.212/4:nos	Data access descriptions: Economic censuses printed reports series ECPR
C56.212/5:nos	Data access descriptions: Collection, evaluation, and processing series CEP. Earlier C3.240/6: Later C3.240/6:
C56.212/6:CT	Data access description [Miscellaneous]
C56.213:nos	Congressional district data, CDD-(series) Earlier C3.134/4: Later C3.134/4:
C56.213/2:date	Congressional district atlas. Earlier C3.62/5:
C56.213/3:nos	Congressional district data, computer profile
C56.214:nos	Current housing reports: Housing vacancies, series H-111 (quarterly) Earlier C3.215:H-111 Later C3.215:
C56.214/2:nos	Current housing reports, series H-150 Later C3.215/4:
C56.215:nos	Technical notes. Earlier C3.212/2: Later C3.212/2:
C56.215/2:nos	Technical papers. Earlier C3.212: Later C3.212:
C56.216:letters-nos	Current industrial reports. Earlier C3.158: Later C56.216:
C56.217:v.nos.&nos.	Small-area data notes. Earlier C3.238: Later C3.238:
C56.217/2:nos	Small-area statistics papers, series GE-41 Later C3.238/2:
C56.218:P-nos.&nos	Current population reports, series P-(nos)&(nos) Earlier C3.186: Later C3.186:
C56.218/2:nos	County demographic profiles, ISP-30 (series)
C56.219:nos	Current business reports: Monthly wholesale trade, sales and inventories BW-(series) Earlier C3.236: Later C3.236:
C56.219/2:nos	Current business reports: Green coffee inventories, imports, roastings, BG (series) Earlier C3.236: Later C3.236:
C56.219/3:nos	Special current business reports: Monthly Department store sales in selected areas, BD-(series) Earlier C3.211/5:BD-(nos)

C56.219/4:nos   Current business reports: Monthly retail trade sales and accounts receivable, BR- (series)   Earlier C3.138/3:   Later C3.138/3:

C56.219/4-2:date   ___: Annual retail trade.   Earlier C3.138/3-2:

C56.219/5:nos   Current business reports: Monthly selected service receipts, BS-(series)   Earlier C3.239:   Later C3.239:

C56.219/6:nos   Current business reports: Advance monthly retail sales, CG- (series)   Earlier C3.138/4:

C56.219/7:nos   Current business reports: Weekly retail sales, CB-(series)   Earlier C3.138/5:

C56.219/8:nos   Current business reports: Canned food, stock, pack, shipments B-1 (series)   Earlier C3.189:   Later C3.189:

C56.220:CT   Census use studies.   Earlier C3.244:   Later C3.244:

C56.220/2:date   Census use study research notes

C56.221:letters-nos Annual survey of manufactures M(date) (AS) (series)   Earlier C3.24/9:   Later C3.24/9:

C56.221/2:date   ___: Annual volumes.   Earlier C3.24/9-2:   Later C3.24/9-2:

C56.222:date   Bureau of Census catalog.   Earlier C3.163/3:   Later C3.163/3:

C56.222/a:CT   ___ separates

C56.222/2:date   Bureau of Census catalog, monthly supplement.   Earlier C3.163/2:   Later C3.163/2:

C56.222/2-2:date   Bureau of Census catalog of publications (historical compilation)   See for earlier class C3.2:P96/8/790-1945

C56.222/3:CT   Bibliographies and lists of publications.   Earlier C3.163/4:   Later C3.163/4:

C56.224/4:date   Indexes

C56.223:nos   Construction expenditures of State and local governments, GC (series) (quarterly)   Earlier C3.215/10:

C56.244:nos   Holdings of selected public employee retirement systems, quarterly report, GR (series)   Earlier C3.242:

C56.225:   [not used]

C56.226:nos.&nos.	Series ISP, International Statistics Program Office. Earlier C3.205/3: Later C3.205/3:
C56.226/2:nos	International research documents. Later C3.205/6:
C56.227:date	Census of agriculture: Area reports. Earlier C3.31/4:
C56.227/2:date	Census of agriculture: Special reports. Earlier C3.31/5:
C56.227/3:date	Census of agriculture: Final volumes [other than Area reports and Special reports]. Earlier C3.31/12:
C56.227/3a:CT	___ separates. Earlier C3.31/9a:
C56.227/4:nos	___ Preliminary and/or advance reports. Earlier C3.31/7:
C56.227/5:CT	___, publications. Earlier in C3.2:
C56.228:nos	Enterprise statistics, series ES- (nos) Earlier C3.230:
C56.229:nos	Working papers (numbered) Earlier C3.214: Later C3.214:
C56.230:date	Housing reports: Market absorption of apartments, H-130 (series) (quarterly)
C56.231:nos	State and local government special studies. Earlier C3.145: Later C3.145:
C56.231/2:date	Quarterly summary of State and local tax revenue, GT (series) Earlier C3.145/6: Later C3.145/6:
C56.232:nos	U.S. commodity exports and imports as related to output, series ES2. Earlier C3.229: Later C3.229:
C56.233:nos	County business patterns, CBP-(series) Earlier C3.204: Later C3.204:
C56.234:nos	We the Americans (series)
C56.235:nos	Census tract papers, GE-40 (series) Earlier C3.227/2:, Later C3.227/2:
C56.235/2:nos	Census tract memo. Earlier C3.227: Later C3.227:
C56.236:CT	Census of mineral industries: publications
C56.236/2:	___ Preliminary reports. Earlier C3.216/5:

C56.236/3:dt./nos Census of mineral industries: Industry series. Earlier C3.216:

C56.236/4:dt./nos ___ Area series. Earlier C3.216/2:

C56.236/5:dt./nos ___ Subject series. Earlier C3.216/4:

C56.237:nos Computerized geographic coding series GE60. Earlier C3.246: Later C3.246:

C56.238:date Foreign statistical publications, accessions list (quarterly) Earlier C3.199:

C56.239:nos Cotton ginnings, report on cotton ginnings by counties, A20- (series) Earlier C3..20/3: Later C3.20/3:

C56.239/2:date Cotton ginnings in U.S.

C56.239/3:date Cotton ginnings, Report on cotton ginnings, (by States) A10- (series) Earlier C3.20: Later C3.20:

C56.240:nos Employment and population changes, Special economic reports, Series ES 20

C56.241:nos DAUList (series) Earlier C3.247:

C56.242:nos United States maps, GE-50 (series) Earlier C3.62/4: Later C3.62/4:

C56.242/2:nos United States maps, GE-70 (series) Later C3.62/8:

C56.242/3:CT Maps (miscellaneous) Earlier C3.62/2:

C56.242/4:nos Urban atlas, tract data for standard metropolitan statistical areas, GE80 (series) Later C3.62/7:

C56.243:date Statistical abstract of United States. Earlier C3.134: Later C3.134:

C56.243/a:CT ___ separates.. Earlier C3.134/a: Later C3.134/a:

C56.243/2:CT ___ Supplements. Earlier C3.134/2: Later C3.134/2:

C56.243/3:date Pocket data book. Earlier C3.134/3: Later C3.134/3:

C56.244:v.nos Census of manufactures. Final volumes. Earlier C3.24/1:

C56.244/2:CT ___ General publications. Earlier C3.24/2:

C56.244/3:dt/nos ___ Special reports. Earlier C3.24/15:

C56.244/4:date ___, announcements and order forms. Earlier C3.24/10:

C56.244/5:dt/nos ___. Preliminary reports MC72(P) series. Earlier C3.24/8:

C56.244/6:dt./nos Census of manufactures. Industry series. Earlier C3.24/4: Later C3.24/4:

C56.244/7:dt./nos ___ Area series. Earlier C3.24/3: Later C3.24/3:

C56.244/8:dt./nos ___ Subject series. Earlier C3.24/12: Later C3.24/12:

C56.245:nos Manufacturers' shipments, inventories, and orders series, M3. Earlier C3.231: Later C3.231:

C56.246:CT Census of transportation: General publications. Earlier C3.233:

C56.246/2:nos Census of transportation: Final reports. Earlier C3.233/3:

C56.246/3:dt./v. ___ [By volume numbers] Earlier C3.233/2:

C56.247:dt./nos Census of governments: Preliminary reports. Earlier C3.145/5:

C56.247/2:dt/v.&nos Census of governments. Earlier C3.145/4:

C56.248:nos Research documents

C56.249:date Boundary and annexation survey (annual)

C56.250: [not used]

C56.251:CT Census of retail trade: General publications. Earlier C3.202:

C56.251/2:dt.&nos ___ area series Earlier C3.202/2:

C56.251/3:dt.&nos ___ Subject reports. Earlier C3.202/6:

C56.251/4:dt.&nos ___ Retail merchandise line sales service. Earlier C3.202/19:

C56.251/5:dt.&nos ___ Major retail centers. Earlier C3.202/13:

C56.251/6:dt.&nos ___ Final volumes. Earlier C3.202/5:

C56.251/7:letter/nos ___ Preliminary area reports. Earlier C3.202/12-2:

C56.252:CT Census of wholesale trade: General publications

C56.252/2:Le/nos ___ Preliminary reports. Earlier C3.202/12-2:

C56.252/3:dt./nos ___ Area statistics series. Earlier C3.202/3:

C56.252/4:dt/nos ___ Subject reports. Earlier C3.202/8:

C56.252/5:dt./nos ___ Final volumes. Earlier C3.202/5:

C56.253:CT   Census of selected service industries: General publications

C56.253/2:les/nos ___ Preliminary area reports. Earlier C3.202/12-2:

C56.253/3:dt./nos ___ Area statistics. Earlier C3.202/4:

C56.253/4:dt./nos ___ Subject reports. Earlier C3.202/7:

C56.253/5:dt/v.nos ___ Final volumes. Earlier C3.202/5:

C56.254:CT   Census of construction industries: General publications

C56.254/2:dt./nos ___ Preliminary reports, CC-(P) series

C56.254/3:les/nos ___ Industry series. Earlier C3.245/3:

C56.254/4:les/nos ___ area statistics. Earlier C3.245/3:

C56.254/5:nos   ___ Special report. Earlier C3.245/5:

C56.254/6:dt/v.nos ___ Final volumes. Earlier C3.245/3:

C56.255:CT   Geographic base (DIME) file, CUE, correction-update-extension. Earlier C56.202:G29   Later C3.249:, C3.249/2:

C56.256:nos   Methodological research documentation, quarterly list.

C56.257:CT   Addresses. Earlier C3.132:

C56.258:nos   Census portraits [various States] CP-(series)

C56.259:dt./nos   Economic censuses of outlying areas OAC (series) See for Earlier similar C3.24/11: and C3.202/15:

C56.260:dt./nos   Survey of minority-owned business enterprises MB (series)

The Bureau of the Census was restored as a primary operating unit of the Department of Commerce, organization order 2A effective Aug. 4, 1975.

C57   Domestic and International Business Administration

The Domestic and International Business Administration was established within the Department of Commerce by Department Organization Order 40-1, effective November 17, 1972.

C57.1:date   Annual reports

C57.2:CT   General publications

C57.7:nos   Press releases

C57.8:CT   Handbooks, manuals, guides

C57.9:CT   Addresses

C57.10:date   United States exports of aluminum (annual)   Earlier C41.112/2:

C57.10/2:date   United States imports of aluminum (annual)   Earlier C41.112/3:

C57.11:nos   Overseas business reports.   Earlier C1.50:

C57.12:date   Overseas promotions calendar.   Later title, Overseas export promotion calendar (quarterly)   Later C57.117:Ov2/date

C57.13:date   Confectionery sales and distribution (annual)   Earlier C41.9:

C57.14:date   Aluminum imports and exports (monthly)   Earlier C41.112:

C57.15:CT   Bibliographies and lists of publications

C57.16:date   Franchise opportunities handbook.   Earlier C41.6/9:F84/972

C57.17:CT   Trade data [various items]

C57.18:date   U.S. industrial outlook.   Earlier C57.309:

C57.19:date   International economic indicators, quarterly report   Earlier C42.34:

C57.19/2:v.nos./nos   International economic indicators and competitive trends (quarterly)

C57.20:date	Commerce business daily. Earlier C41.9:
C57.21:date	World motor vehicle and trailer production & registration (annual) Earlier C41.17:
C57.22:CT	Trade lists. Earlier C42.10:
C57.23:date	Trends in U.S. foreign trade (monthly) Earlier C42.26:
C57.24:date	U.S. Lumber exports. Earlier C41.101:

C57.100   International Commerce Bureau

November 17, 1972, by Department organization order 40-1

C57.101: date   Annual reports. Earlier C42.1:

C57.102: CT   General publications. Earlier C42.2:

C57.108:CT   Handbooks, manuals, guides   Earlier C42.6/2:

C57.109: CT   Global market survey. Earlier C42.33:

C57.110:date   Index to foreign production and commercial reports. Earlier C42.15/3:   Later title Index to foreign market reports

C57.111:nos   Foreign economic trends and their implications for United States. Earlier C42.30:

C57.112:nos   Country market survey, CMS (series) Earlier C42.31/4:

C57.113:date   Quarterly summary of future construction aborad. Earlier C41.30/5:

C57.114:nos   Commercial news for the Foreign Service (bimonthly)

C57.115:CT   Bibliographies and lists of publications. Earlier C42.15:

C57.116:CT   International Marketing Information series. Earlier C42.31:

C57.117:CT   International marketing events (series)

C57.118:CT   Consumer goods research

C57.119:CT   Country market sectoral surveys

C57.200 Resources and Trade Assistance Bureau

November 17,1972, by Department organization order 10-3 and 40-1.

C57.201:date   Annual reports

C57.202:CT   General publications

C57.208:CT   Handbooks, manuals, guides

C57.209:date   Steel import data, shipments from exporting countries in calendar year. Earlier similar C41.114:

C57.210:CT   Bibliographies and lists of publications

C57.300 Competitive Assessment and Business Policy Bureau

The Competitive Assessment and Business Policy Bureau was established within the Domestic and International Business Administration, by Dept. Organization order 40-1, effective Nov. 17, 1972.

C57.301:date   Annual reports. Earlier C41.1:

C57.302:CT   General publications. Earlier C41.2:   Later C57.502:

C57.309:date   U.S. Industrial outlook. Earlier C41.42/4:   Later C57.18:

C57.310:v. nos   Construction review. Earlier C41.30/3:   Later C57.509:

C57.311:v. nos   Printing and publishing. Earlier C41.18:   Later C57.510:

C57.312:v. nos. &nos.   Copper, quarterly industry report. Earlier C41.34:   Later C57.512:

C57.312/2:nos   Copper industry reports, annual. Earlier C41.34/2:   Later C57.512/2:

C57.313:v. nos. &nos.   Pulp, paper and board, quarterly industry report. Earlier C41.32:   Later C57.511:

C57.314:v. nos   Containers and packaging. Earlier C41.33:   Later C57.513:

C57.315:date   Notice to trade [various commodities]

C57.316:date   Mayonnaise, salad dressings, and related products (annual) Earlier C41.88:   Later C57.514:

C57.400 East-West Trade Bureau

The East-West Trade Bureau has been established within the Domestic and International Business Administration of the Department of Commerce by Dept. Organization Order 40-1, **effective Nov. 17, 1972.**

C57.401: date   Annual reports

C57.402:CT   General publications

C57.409:date   Export control regulations. Earlier C42.11:

C57.409/2:nos   Export control bulletin. Earlier C42.11/3: Later title, Export administration bulletin

C57.410:date   Export licenses approved and reexports authorized. Earlier C42.21:

C57.411:date   Export Administration. Earlier C1.26:

C57.412:CT   Market assessments for (various countries)

C57.500   Domestic Commerce Bureau

C57.501:date   Annual report

C57.502:CT   General publications. Earlier C57.302:

C57.508:CT   Handbooks, manuals, guides. Earlier C41.6/9:

C57.509:v.nos.&nos. Construction review, Monthly industry report. Earlier C57.310:

C57.510:v.nos.&nos. Printing and publishing. Earlier C57.311:

C57.511:v.nos.&nos. Pulp, paper and board. Earlier C57.313:

C57.512:v.nos.&nos. Copper, Quarterly industry report. Earlier C57.312:

C57.512/2:nos   Copper industry report, Annual. Earlier C57.312/2:

C57.513:v.nos   Containers and packaging, Quarterly industry reports. Earlier C57.314:

C57.514:date   Mayonnaise, salad dressings, and related products (annual) Earlier C57.316:

C58   National Fire Prevention and Control Administration

The National Fire Prevention and Control Administration (NFPCA) was established by the Federal Fire Prevention and Control Act of 1974 of October 29, 1974 (88 Stat. 1535; 15 U.S.C. 2201).

C58.1:date   Annual report

C58.2:CT   General publications

C58.7:nos   Press releases

C58.8:CT   Handbooks, manuals, guides

C58.9:CT   Addresses

C58.10:date   Fireword, a bulletin from the National Fire Prevention and Control Administration (irregular)

C59 Economic Analysis Bureau

C59.1:date   Annual report   Earlier C56.101:

C59.2:CT   General publications. Earlier C56.102:

C59.9:date   Business conditions digest (monthly) Earlier C56.111:

C59.9/2:date   Advance BCD (monthly) Earlier C56.111/2:

C59.10:date   Defense indicators (monthly) Earlier C56.110:

C59.11:v.nos.&nos. Survey of current business (monthly) Earlier C56.109:

C59.11/2:date   Business statistics, weekly supplement to Survey of current business. Earlier C56.109/2:

C59.11/3:date   Business statistics, biennial supplement to Survey of current business. Earlier C56.109/3:

C59.11/4:CT   Supplements [special] to Survey of current business. Earlier C56.109/4:

C59.12:nos   Foreign economic reports

CA   Civil Aeronautics Authority

June 23, 1938 (52 Stat. 980)

CA1.1:date	Annual reports. Later C31.1:
CA1.2:CT	General publications. Later C31.2:
CA1.3:nos	Civil Aeronautics bulletins. Later C31.103:
CA1.6:serial nos.	Regulations. Proc. Earlier C23.6/3: and CA1.14: Later C31.206:
CA1.7:vol	Weekly notices to airmen. Proc. Earlier C23.15: Later C31.9:
CA1.7/2:dt. &nos	Special notices to airmen. Proc. Later C31.10:
CA1.8:vol	Air Commerce bulletins. Monthly. Earlier C23.12: Superseded by CA1.17:
CA1.9:date	Tabulation of air navigation radio aids. Monthly. Proc. Earlier C23.18: Later C31.8:
CA1.10:nos	Manuals (numbered) Lettered-numbers - Sept.1939- Supersedes Instruction bulletins C23.16: Later C31.107:
CA1.11:nos	Planning and development reports. Proc. Earlier C23.19:
CA1.12:serial nos	Orders. Proc. Earlier CA1.14: Later C31.207:
CA1.13:CT	Maps. Later C31.115:
CA1.14:date	Rules of practice under title 4, Regulations and orders. Proc. Later regulations CA1.6: Later orders CA1.12:
CA1.15:chap. &pt. nos.	Manual of operations. Proc. Earlier C23.6/5: Later C31.116:
CA1.16:nos	Special tariff permission. Proc. Later C31.210:
CA1.17:vol	Civil aeronautics journal. Semimonthly. Supersedes CA1.8: Later C31.7:
CA1.18:date	Weekly summary of orders and regulations issued by the Authority. Proc. Later C31.208:
CA1.19:pt. nos	Civil air regulations. Earlier C23.6/3: Later C31.209:
CA1.20:nos	Technical development reports. Later C31.11:, C31.119:

CA1.21:nos   Certificate and inspection division releases. Later C31.111:

CA1.22:date   Domestic air carrier operation statistics (monthly) Proc. Earlier C23.20: Later C31.112:

CA1.23:vol   Civil aeronautics authority reports. Later C31.211:

CA1.24:   Maintenance instruction bulletins. Admin.

Transferred to Department of Commerce by section 7 of Reorganization plan IV, effective June 30, 1940.

CC Federal Communications Commission

Communications act of 1934, 48 Stat. 1064.

CC1.1:date	Annual reports. Earlier RC1.1:
CC1.1/2:date	Summary of activities, in fiscal [year]
CC1.2:CT	General publications. Earlier RC1.2:
CC1.3:	Bulletins
CC1.3/2:nos	ADM bulletins. Proc.
CC1.3/3:nos	INF bulletins
CC1.4:	Circulars
CC1.5:CT	Federal laws
CC1.6:CT	Regulations, rules and instructions. Includes handbooks and manuals.
CC1.6/a:CT	___ separates
CC1.6/1-10:date	Rules and regulations, v.1-10.
CC1.7:nos	Federal rules and regulations (in parts)
CC1.7/2:nos	___ amendments
CC1.7/3:nos	___ correction sheets
CC1.7/4:CT	Handbooks, manuals, guides
CC1.8:CT	Posters. Federal, maps.
CC1.9:CT	Papers in re. Earlier RC1.7:
CC1.10:date	List of radio broadcast stations. Mimeo. Earlier RC1.9: Call letters assigned excepting amateurs. Wkly. Proc. Earlier CC2.7:
CC1.11:CT	Examiner's reports, Broadcast division. Proc.
CC1.11/2:CT	Examiner's reports, Telegraph division. Proc.
CC1.11/3:CT	Examiner's reports, Telephone division. Proc.
CC1.12:vol.	Federal Communications Commission reports. Contains decisions, reports and orders.

CC1.12/a1:CT	Federal Communications Commission reports. Separates. Decisions, Broadcast division. Proc.
CC1.12/a2:CT	___ separates. Decisions, Telegraph division. Proc.
CC1.12/a3:CT	___ separates. Decisions, Telephone division. Proc.
CC1.12/a4:CT	___ separates. Commission orders. Proc.
CC1.12/a5:CT	___ separates. Broadcast division orders. Proc. Later CC1.12/a4:
CC1.12/a6:CT	___ separates. Telegraph division orders. Proc. Later CC1.12/a4:
CC1.12/a7:CT	___ separates. Telephone division orders. Proc. Later CC1.12/a4:
CC1.12/a8:nos	Memorandum opinions and orders, initial decisions, etc. (irregular)
CC1.12/a9:v.nos	___ separates. Selected decisions and reports (weekly)
CC1.12/2:v.nos	Federal Communications Commission reports, selected decisions, reports and other documents of Federal Communications Commission of United States (2d series)
CC1.12/2a:CT	___ separates
CC1.13:date	Operating data from monthly reports of telegraph carriers. Monthly. Later title added -cable & radiotelegraph carriers
CC1.14:date	Summary of monthly reports of large telephone carriers in U.S. Monthly. Later title, Operating data from ... Earlier IC1 telp.6:
CC1.14/2:date	Statistics of class A telephone carriers reporting annually to Commission. Proc. Earlier CC1.2:T236/11
CC1.15:CT	Addresses. Proc.
CC1.16:nos	Tariff circulars
CC1.17:nos	Telegraph accounting circulars. Proc.
CC1.18:nos	Telephone accounting circulars. Proc.
CC1.19:nos	Applications pending in Commission for exemption from radio provisions of International convention for safety of life at sea convention, London, 1929, title 3, pt.2 of Communications act of 1934, etc., Reports. Proc.
CC1.20:nos	Decisions; reports [of action taken]. Proc.

CC1.20/2:nos	Actions of Commission, reports (broadcast) Proc. Earlier CC1.20: Later title: Broadcast actions by Commission, reports (broadcast)
CC1.20/3:nos	Actions of Commission, reports (telephone and telegraph) Proc. Earlier CC1.20: Later title, Telephone and telegraph actions by Commission, reports.
CC1.21:date	List of radio broadcast stations, alphabetically by call letters. Annual. Proc. Earlier CC2.10:
CC1.22:date	List of radio broadcast stations by frequency. Annual. Proc. Prior to 1938 see CC2.11:
CC1.23:date	List of radio broadcast stations by State and City. Annual. Proc. Prior to 1938 see CC2.12:
CC1.24:date	Radio broadcast stations in United States, containing alterations and corrections. Monthly. Proc. Prior to 1938 see CC2.13:
CC1.25:nos	Radio service bulletins. Semi-monthly. Proc. Earlier CC2.3:
CC1.26:nos	Reports of applications received in radio broadcast stations. Earlier CC2.8:
CC1.26/2:nos	Standard broadcast applications ready and available for processing pursuant to sec.1.354(c) of Commission's rules, lists. (irregular)
CC1.27:nos	Reports of applications received in telegraph section
CC1.28:nos	Reports of applications received in telephone section. Earlier CC4.7:
CC1.29:nos	Reports of construction permits retired to closed files, etc. Monthly. Proc. Earlier CC3.9:
CC1.30:letters	Selected financial and operating data from annual reports. Proc.
CC1.31:date	Relay broadcast stations. Proc.
CC1.32:nos	Actions on motions, reports. Proc.
CC1.33:nos	Action in docket cases, reports. Proc.
CC1.33/2:nos	Commission instructions in docket cases. Proc.
CC1.34:dt.&nos	Applications [for permits] etc. Proc.
CC1.35:date	Statistics of communications industry in United States. Later title, Statistics of communications common carriers
CC1.35/a:CT	___ separates

CC1.36:nos	Common carrier services, public notices
CC1.36/2:nos	Common carrier actions, reports, public notices
CC1.36/3:nos	Common carrier tariff filings, reports, public notices
CC1.36/4:nos	Overseas common carrier section 214 applications accepted for filing, public notices
CC1.37:nos	Public notices. Proc.
CC1.37/2:nos	General information [releases]
CC1.37/3:nos	Experimental actions, reports, public notices
CC1.38:	Public notices: Petitions for rule making filed. Proc.
CC1.39:nos	Public notices: Safety & special radio services, report (wkly.) Proc.
CC1.39/2:nos	Safety and special actions, reports, public notices
CC1.39/3:nos	Safety and special radio services bulletins
CC1.40:nos	Fixed public service applications received for filing during past week, public notices (weekly) Proc.
CC1.41:date	Statistics of principal domestic and international telegraph carriers reporting annually to Commission (annual) Proc. Earlier CC1.2:T235/6
CC1.42:date	Hearings calendar (irregular)
CC1.43:date	Final TV broadcast financial data (annual)
CC1.43/2:date	AM-FM broadcast financial data. Earlier CC1.2:B78/25
CC1.44:nos	Request for new or modified broadcast call signs
CC1.45:nos	CATV requests filed pursuant to sec. 74.1107(a) of the rules, public notice
CC1.45/2:nos	CATV actions reports
CC1.46:nos	Report of Office of Chief Engineer- Research Division, R- (series)
CC1.47:nos	Cables television service applications, reports, public notices
CC1.47/2:nos	Cable television relay service (car) applications, reports, public notices
CC1.48:nos	Type approval actions, reports, public notices

CC1.48/2:nos   Equipment certification and type acceptance actions, reports, public notices

CC1.49:v.nos.&nos. FCC actions alert (weekly)

CC2 Broadcast Division

CC2.1:date   Annual reports

CC2.2:CT   General publications

CC2.3:nos   Radio service bulletins, Semi-monthly. Proc. Earlier RC1.3: Later CC1.25:

CC2.7:date   Call letters assigned (usually wkly.) July-Sept.1935 title Call signals assigned

CC2.8:nos   Reports of applications received. Proc. Slightly varying title

CC2.9:nos   Reports [of action taken] Usually wkly. Proc.

CC2.10:date   List of radio broadcast stations, alphabetically by call letters. Proc. For alterations and corrections see CC2.13: Earlier RC1.9: Later CC1.21:

CC2.11:date   List of radio broadcast stations, by frequency. Proc. For alterations and corrections see CC2.13: Earlier RC1.9: Later CC1.22:

CC2.12:date   List of radio broadcast stations, by zone and State. Proc. For alterations and corrections see CC2.13: Earlier RC1.9: Later CC1.23:

CC2.13:date   Radio broadcast stations in U.S., containing alterations and corrections. Proc.

Divisions of the F.C.C. are dissolved and abolished as of Nov.15,1937.

CC3 Telegraph Division

CC3.1:date   Annual reports

CC3.2:CT   General publications

CC3.7:nos   Reports of applications received. Proc. Title varies slightly.

CC3.8:nos   Reports [of action taken] Usually wkly. Proc.

CC3.9:nos   Reports of construction permits retired to closed files. Proc. Later CC1.29:

Divisions of the FCC are dissolved and abolished as of Nov.15,1937.

                CC4   Telephone Division

CC4.1:date   Annual reports

CC4.2:CT   General publications

CC4.7:nos   Reports of applications received. Proc. Slightly varying titles. Later CC1.28:

CC4.8:nos   Release [of action taken] Proc. Prior to Jan. 22,1936, Reports.

CC4.9:nos   Reports of construction permits retired to closed files. Proc.

Divisions of the FCC are dissolved and abolished as of Nov.15,1937.

CR   Civil Rights Commission

The Commission on Civil Rights was created in the executive branch of the Government by Public law 315, 85th Congress, 1st session, approved Sept. 9, 1957.

CR1.1:date	Reports
CR1.2:CT	General publications
CR1.6:CT	Regulations, rules, and instructions
CR1.6/2:CT	Handbooks, manuals, guides
CR1.7:date	Press releases
CR1.8:CT	Hearings and conferences before Commission on Civil Rights
CR1.9:CT	Bibliographies and lists of publications
CR1.10:nos	CCR special publications, later title CCR clearinghouse publication
CR1.11:CT	Urban studies
CR1.11/2:nos	Clearinghouse publication: Urban series
CR1.12:date	Civil rights digest (quarterly)

CS   Civil Service Commission

Organized 1883.

CS1.1:date	Annual reports
CS1.1/a:CT	___ separates
CS1.2:CT	General publications
CS1.2/a:CT	___ separates
CS1.3:nos	Bulletins
CS1.4:nos	Circulars
CS1.5:nos	Circular letter, miscellaneous, numbered. See for numbered circular letters 4th Civil Service Region, CS1.50:
CS1.6:CT	Instructions and information for applicants and for boards of examiners. See also CS1.26:
CS1.7:date	Laws, rules and regulations
CS1.7/2:CT	Laws, rules and regulations (Special)
CS1.7/3:nos	Organization and policy manual letters. (Admin.)
CS1.7/4:CT	Handbooks, manuals, guides. Earlier in CS1.7/2:
CS1.7/5:date	Federal fund-raising manual
CS1.8:date	Manual of examinations
CS1.9:date	Instructions to applicants, 1st district, Boston, Massachusetts.
CS1.10:date	___ 2d district, New York City
CS1.11:date	___ 3d district, Philadelphia, Pa.
CS1.12:date	___ 4th district, Washington, D.C.
CS1.13:date	___ 5th district, Atlanta, Georgia
CS1.14:date	___ 6th district, Cincinnati, Ohio
CS1.15:date	___ 7th district, Chicago, Illinois.
CS1.16:date	___ 8th district, St. Paul, Minn.

CS1.17:date	Instructions to applicants, 9th district, St. Louis, Mo.
CS1.18:date	___ 10th district, New Orleans, La.
CS1.19:date	___ 11th district. Seattle, Washington. Reorganized July 1, 1910 to include Washington, Oregon, Montana, Idaho
CS1.20:date	___ 12th district, San Francisco, California.
CS1.21:date	___ 13th district, Denver, Colorado
CS1.22:date	Information concerning transfers
CS1.23:date	Information concerning reinstatements
CS1.24:date	Information concerning removals, reducations, suspensions and furloughs.
CS1.25:date	Information concerning temporary appointments
CS1.26/1:dt. &nos.	Announcements and postponements of examinations. Annual series.
CS1.26/2:CT	Posters
CS1.26/3:nos	Announcements of examinations, 4th district. Proc.
CS1.26/4:nos	Announcements of examinations, field and local.
CS1.27:CT	Schedule of examinations for 4th-class postmasters (by States)
CS1.28:form nos.	Announcements of examinations (general series)
CS1.29:nos	Retirement circulars. Mim.
CS1.29/2:date	Retirement report, fiscal year, C.S. retirement act, Panama Canal annuity act. Earlier CS1.2:R31
CS1.29/3:date	Report, Civil Service retirement, Federal employees' group life insurance, Federal employee health benefits, fy.
CS1.30:date	Veteran preference (in appointment to civil offices under U.S. government - Form 1481)
CS1.31:date	Official register of the U.S. Earlier in S1.11:, I1.25:, C3.10:
CS1.32:date	Civil employment and pay rolls in Executive branch of U.S. **government**. Monthly. Proc. Later title, Monthly report of employment. Later CS1.32/2:

CS1.32/2:date	Monthly report of Federal employment. Proc. Replaces CS1.32: Later CS1.55/2:
CS1.33:date	Personnel statistics reports. Semi-annual. Proc. Varying titles.
CS1.34:date	Political activity and political assessments of Federal office-holders and employees. Changed from CS1.2:P75/1-15
CS1.35:nos	Recruiting circulars, 4th civil service district. Proc.
CS1.35/2:nos	Recruiting circulars, 4th civil service region (1944-) Proc.
CS1.36:CT	Class specifications. Preliminary drafts. Proc.
CS1.37:nos	Transfer circulars
CS1.38:nos	Departmental circulars, occupational deferment series.
CS1.39:date	Class specifications and statements of allocation standards for positions subject to classification act of 1923, as amended (monthly) Later title, Position classification standards for positions subject to classification act of 1949
CS1.39/a:letters-nos ___ separates	
CS1.39/2:GS-nos	[Position classification standards concerning positions in one agency.]
CS1.39/3:CT	Position classification plans for [various cities or districts]
CS1.40:letter-nos	P.C.D. manuals
CS1.41:nos	Federal personnel manual, transmittal sheets
CS1.41/a:CT	___ separates
CS1.41/2:trans.sh.nos. ___ special reprint	
CS1.41/3:nos	Federal personnel manual system issuances
CS1.41/4:nos	[Federal personnel manual] FPM supplements
CS1.42:nos	Equipment maintenance series, bulletins
CS1.43:date	Best Federal job opportunities, (bimonthly)
CS1.43/2:date	Best bets for returning veterans in Washington, D.C. area. Earlier CS1.2:V64/8
CS1.44:date	Handbook of occupational groups and series of classes established under Federal position-classification plan

CS1.45:le.-nos	Civil service handbook
CS1.46:nos	Examining circulars
CS1.46/2:nos	Examining circulars, 4th Civil Service Region
CS1.47:nos	Special bulletins. Proc.
CS1.48:nos	Pamphlets
CS1.48/2:nos	BEM pamphlets
CS1.49:nos	General displacement notices. Proc.
CS1.50:nos	Circular letters, 4th Civil Service Region. Proc.
CS1.51:nos	Bulletins, 4th Civil Service Region. Proc.
CS1.52:nos	Recruiting bulletin
CS1.53:nos	Recruiting authority circulars
CS1.54:nos	Personnel management series
CS1.55:date	Federal employment statistics bulletin (monthly) Proc.
CS1.55/2:date	Monthly release [of] Federal civilian manpower statistics. Formerly CS1.55: and CS1.32/2:
CS1.56:nos	How Federal agencies develop management talent, management staff development series reports
CS1.57:date	Press releases
CS1.58:nos	Personnel methods series
CS1.58/2:nos	Evaluation methods series (numbered)
CS1.59:nos	Federal employee facts
CS1.60:CT	Addresses
CS1.61:CT	Bibliographies and lists of publications
CS1.61/2:date	Dissertations and theses relating to personnel administration. Earlier CS1.61:P53
CS1.61/3:nos	Personnel bibliography series

CS1.61/4:date	Index to Civil Service Commission information (quarterly)
CS1.62:v.nos.&nos.	Personnel literature (monthly) Proc.
CS1.63:date	Organizations designated under E.O.10450, consolidated list (SCS form 385)
CS1.64:date	President's awards for distinguished federal civilian service (annual)
CS1.65:date	Interagency training programs. Issued twice yearly
CS1.65/2:date	Directory of ADP training services and sources of information. Earlier PrEx2.12/2:
CS1.65/3:date	Executive Seminar Centers [programs] Earlier CS1.2:Ex3/6/date
CS1.65/4:date	Interagency training courses, calendar (quarterly)
CS1.65/5:date	The General Management Training Center [report] (fiscal year) Earlier CS1.2: M31/4/date
CS1.66:v.nos.	Civil service journal (quarterly)
CS1.66/a:CT	___ separates
CS1.67:nos	Commission letters
CS1.68:nos	Civil service recruiter. Published periodically between Sept. and June
CS1.69:nos	Federal news clip sheet
CS1.70:date	University-Federal Agency Conference on Career Development, conference reports
CS1.71:nos	Personnel measurement research and development center. Technical series. Administrative.
CS1.71/2:nos	___ Professional series
CS1.71/3:nos	___ Technical study
CS1.71/4:nos	___ Technical memorandum
CS1.72:date	Current Federal workforce data (semiannual)
CS1.72/2:date	Federal workforce outlook
CS1.73:nos	Salary tables: Executive branch of the Government. Earlier GA1.10:
CS1.74:date	Federal employment of women (quarterly)

CS1.74/2:v.nos.&nos.   Women in action, an information summary for the Federal women's program.

CS1.75:date   Coordinator's scoreboard, review of what's new in placement of the handicapped.   Earlier CS1.2:C78

CS1.76:v.nos.&nos.   Equal opportunity in Federal employment newsletter (bimonthly)

CS1.76/2:nos   EEO for State and Local governments (series)

CS1.77:v.nos.&nos.   Congressional record digest

CS1.78:nos   Merit system methods   Earlier FS1.25:

CS1.79:v/nos   Administrator's alert

CS1.80:nos   Federal labor-management consultant (biweekly)

CS1.80/2:nos   Labor management relations issues in State and local governments (irregular)

CS1.81:date   State salary ranges of selected classes of positions in employment security-public welfare-public health-mental health-civil defense-vocational rehabilitation   Earlier HE1.22:

CS1.82:nos   Personnel advisory series

CS1.83:nos   Incentive awards notes.   Issued by Incentive System Office

CS1.84:nos   Federal trainer, Information exchange for the Federal training community

CS1.85:nos   Executive manpower management technical assistance papers. Prepared by Executive Manpower Management Technical Assistance Center.

CS1.86:date   Intergovernmental personnel notes (bimonthly)

CS1.87:date   Annual report of the Interagency Advisory Group

CS1.88:date   Telephone directory.   Earlier CS1.2:T23/974

CS1.89:CT   Posters

CS1.90:v.nos.&nos.   Occupational health reporter

CS1.91:v.nos.&nos.   The first line (bimonthly)

CSA Community Services Administration

The Community Services Administration was established by the Headstart, Economic Opportunity, and Community Partnership Act of 1974 (88 Stat. 2291; 42 U.S.C. 2701 note) as the successor to the Office of Economic Opportunity.

CSA1.1:date	Annual report
CSA1.2:CT	General publications
CSA1.8:CT	Handbooks, manuals, guides
CSA1.8/2:nos	CSA manuals (numbered) Earlier PrEx10.8/5:
CSA1.9:nos	CSA pamphlets (numbered) Earlier PrEx10.23:

Panama Canal Company and Canal Zone Government
CZ   Canal Zone Government

Pursuant to Public law 841, 81st Congress, approved Sept. 26,1950, the independent agency of the United States known as the Panama Canal was renamed Canal Zone Government by Executive order 10263 of June 29,1951, effective July 1,1951.

CZ1.1:date   Annual reports.   Earlier PaC1.1:

CZ1.2:CT   General publications.   Earlier PaC1.2:

CZ1.6:CT   Regulations, rules, and instructions

CZ1.7:   Releases

CZ1.8:v.nos   Panama Canal review (monthly) Earlier PaC1.11:

CZ1.9:date   Annual report of insurance business transacted in Canal Zone. Earlier PaC1.10:

CZ1.10:   Schedule of rates for supplies and services furnished at the Panama Canal and supplements. Admin.

CZ1.11: v.nos.&nos. Panama Canal spillway (weekly)

D   DEFENSE DEPARTMENT

The Department of Defense was established as an executive department of the Government by Public law 216, 81st Congress, approved Aug.10,1949. The law provides that there shall be within the Department of Defense (1) the Department of the Army, the Department of the Navy, and the Department of the Air Force, and each such department shall be military departments in lieu of their prior status as executive departments, and (2) all other agencies created under title 2 of the National security act of 1947.

D1.1:date	Annual reports. Earlier M1.1:
D1.1/2:CT	Annual reports of assistants to Secretary of Defense. Proc.
D1.1/3:date	Annual report of Secretary of Defense on Reserve Forces
D1.2:CT	General publications Earlier M1.2:
D1.3/2:v.nos.&nos.	Defense industry bulletin (monthly)
D1.5:CT	Laws
D1.6:CT	Regulations, rules, and instructions. Earlier M1.6:
D1.6/2:CT	Handbooks, manuals, guides
D1.6/3:date	Speakers' guide for service spokesmen, power for peace, Armed Forces Day (annual)
D1.6/4:date	Joint travel regulations, v.1. Members of the uniformed services. Earlier D212.6:T69
D1.6/5:date	Joint travel regulations, v.2, Department of Defense civilian personnel
D1.6/6:nos	LCC [life cycle costing]-(series)
D1.7:date	Telephone directory. Earlier M1.7:
D1.8:date	Military negotiation regulations. Later RnB1.6/4:
D1.9:date	Armed services catalog of medical matériel
D1.9/2:date	___ standard price supplement. Proc.
D1.9/3:nos	___ change bulletins

D1.9/4:date	Armed services catalog of medical matériel. Alphabetical index.
D1.9/5:date	___ component parts supplement
D1.10:nos	Education manuals. Earlier M1.9:
D1.10/2:date	USAFI information letter Proc.
D1.10/3:date	USAFI supply notice. Proc.
D1.10/4:date	USAFI catalog
D1.10/5:v.nos.&nos.	Dialog, for the Service Education Officer
D1.10/6:date	USAFI correspondence courses offered by participating colleges and universities (PC&U) through United States Armed Forces Institute. Earlier editions numbered with DOD pamphlets (D2.14:nos).
D1.11:v.nos	United States armed forces medical journal (monthly) Replaces D104.3: and D206.3:
D1.11/a:CT	___ separates
D1.11/2:v.nos	Medical technicians bulletin, supplement to U.S. Armed Forces medical journal (bimonthly) Replaces Hospital Corps Quarterly (M203.3/2:).
D1.11/2a:CT	___ separates
D1.12:1e-nos	Military specifications. Earlier M213.8:
D1.12/2:1e-nos	Military specifications. Temporary.
D1.12/3:1e-nos	Interim military specifications
D1.13:date	Armed services procurement regulations. Earlier M1.8:
D1.13/2:nos	Armed services procurement regulation, revision. Earlier M1.8/2:
D1.13/2-2:nos	Armed services procurement regulation supplements ASPS-(series)
D1.13/3:nos	Defense procurement circulars
D1.13/4:nos	Armed services procurement manual ASPM (series)
D1.14:date	Armed forces song folio (monthly) Earlier D202.10:
D1.15:date	Manual for courts-martial, United States. See for earlier issues of Manual for courts-martial, Air Force M301.6:C83/date and, Army M107.7:

D1.15/2:date	Manual for courts-martial, Army supplement. Formerly classified in D1.15:
D1.15/3:date	Manual for courts-martial, Air Force supplement. Formerly classified in D1.15:
D1.15/4:date	Manual for courts-martial, Navy supplement.
D1.16:sec.nos.&fasc.nos.	Atlas of tumor pathology
D1.16/2:CT	Medical Museum of Armed Forces Institute of Pathology publications
D1.16/3:fascile nos.	Atlas of tumor pathology, 2d series
D1.16/4:CT	Armed Forces Institute of Pathology: Publications
D1.17:nos	Qualified products lists Desig. QPL-nos. Proc. Official use only
D1.18:v.nos	Digest of opinions, Judge Advocate General of Armed Forces (quarterly)
D1.18/2:v.nos	___ (annual compilation)
D1.19:date	Annual report of Court of Military Appeals and Judge Advocates General of Armed Forces pursuant to Uniform code of military justice
D1.19/2:CT	United States Court of Military Appeals, publications (other than annual reports)
D1.19/3:date	Digest, annotated and digested opinions, U.S. Court of Military Appeals
D1.20:v.nos	Current list of medical literature (monthly) Earlier D104.7: CHANGED TO D8.8:
D1.21:date	Digest of decisions of Armed Services Board of Contract Appeals. Earlier D108.2:C76/942-50
D1.22:v.nos	Arctic bibliography
D1.23:CT	Headquarters European Command, publications
D1.23/2:v.nos.&nos.	Historical Division, Special studies series
D1.24:CT	General headquarters, Far East Command, General publications
D1.24/2:nos	Military History Section: Japanese operational monograph series
D1.25:CT	National Security Agency publications
D1.25/2:nos	___ [training program] TP (series) Proc.
D1.26:date	Feature sections of journals in NWC Library (annual) Proc. Issued by Periodicals and Documents Section, National War College Library

D1.26/2:date	List of periodicals in NWC Library (annual) Proc.
D1.26/3:v.nos.&nos.	Periodical literature bulletins, National War College Library
D1.26/4:v.nos.&nos.	Book news, National War College Library. Admin.
D1.27:v.nos	Emergency management of national economy. Issued by Industrial College of Armed Forces.
D1.27/2:CT	Economic mobilization studies
D1.28:date	Annual report of Army-Air Force Wage Board. Earlier D101.2:W12
D1.29:v.nos	Court-martial reports, holdings and decisions of Judge Advocates General Boards of Review and United States Courts of Military Appeals
D1.30:nos	Armed Services Medical Procurement Agency: Memorandum reports
D1.31:date	COBOL (common business oriented language)
D1.32:CT	U.S. Antarctic projects officer. Publications. Later D201.15/2:
D1.32/2:v.nos.&nos.	U.S. Antarctic projects officer. Bulletin
D1.33:CT	Bibliographies and lists of publications
D1.34:v.nos.&nos.	CD news feature page. Earlier PrEx4.7/4: Later D13.17:
D1.34/2:v.nos.&nos.	CD newspictures. Earlier PrEx4.7/3: Later D13.17/2:
D1.35:nos	Joint Military Packaging Training Center, course outlines
D1.36:date	Brief of the organization and functions, Secretary of Defense, Deputy Secretary of Defense, etc.
D1.37:nos	FTG TIF (series) CANCELLED Replaced by D301.45/31-4:
D1.38:date	Department of Defense cost reduction program, annual progress report
D1.38/2:date	Cost reduction report (irregular) Later Cost reduction journal
D1.39:nos	National communications system memoranda Official use
D1.39/2:nos	National Communications System instructions. official use.
D1.39/3:nos	National Communications System circulars. Official use.
D1.40:CT	Country law studies
D1.41:v.nos.&nos.	High School News Service report (monthly during school year)

D1.41/2:date	High School News Service report, basic fact edition, school year.
D1.42:nos	Shock and vibration monograph series
D1.43:nos	Selected economic indicators (monthly). Superseded by Defense indicators (monthly) C3.241:
D1.44:CT	Resource management monographs
D1.45:date	Defense management education and training catalog
D1.46:nos	Defense Contract Audit Agency DCAAP (series)
D1.46/2:nos	DCAAM (Defense Contract Audit Agency Manual) (numbered)
D1.47:nos	Electromagnetic Compatibility Analysis Cener, ECAP-PR-(series)
D1.48:date	Procurement from small and other business firms
D1.49:les-nos	Operational navigation charts, ONC (series)
D1.50:nos	Manpower development research program, Report MR (series)
D1.50/2:nos	Manpower research report, MA- (series)
D1.51:date	Military-civilian occupational source book
D1.52:date	Manpower requirements report (annual)

Office of Information for Armed Forces
Armed Forces Information Service
D 2 Armed Forces Information and Education Division

The Division was made a part of the Department of Defense by the National Security Act amendments of 1949 (61 Stat. 499 as amended).

D2.1:date	Annual reports
D2.2:CT	General publications
D2.3/2:nos	Voting information bulletin
D2.6:CT	Regulations, rules, and instructions
D2.7:nos	Armed forces talk. Earlier M104.7:
D2.7/2:nos	Armed forces information pamphlets
D2.8:CT	Pocket guides. Earlier W109.215:
D2.9:nos	Posters Desig. AFIED-P-nos.
D2.10:nos	Fact sheets, DOD fact sheets
D2.11:nos	You and your USA information kits
D2.11/2:nos	You and your U.S.A. series
D2.12:nos	Research reports
D2.12/2:nos	Attitude Research Branch: Reports
D2.13:nos	Know your communist enemy series
D2.14:nos	DOD pamphlets (irregular)
D2.15:v.nos.&nos.	For commanders, this changing world (semimonthly)
D2.15/2:v.nos.&nos.	Commanders digest (semiweekly)
D2.15/2-2:nos	___ indexes

444

D2.16:nos   Alert (series)

D2.17:nos   Information guidance series (irregular)

D3   Munitions Board

The Munitions Board, formerly subordinate to the National Military Establishment, was made a part of the Department of Defense by Public law 216, 81st Congress, approved Aug.10,1949.

D3.1:date	Annual reports Earlier M5.1:	
D3.2:CT	General publications Earlier M5.2:	
D3.5:CT	Laws	
D3.6:CT	Regulations, rules, and instructions	
D3.6/2:	Manual of policies and procedure for military specifications. Proc.	
D3.6/3:CT	Handbooks, manuals, guides relating to industrial mobilization and security	
D3.7:nos	Military standards. Earlier M5.8: Later D7.10:	
D3.8:nos	Munitions Board manuals	
D3.9:nos	ANC bulletins and documents. Earlier M5.9:	
D3.10:date	Index of military specifications and standards, military index, v.1(semi-annual) Superseded by D7.14:	
D3.11:letters	Industrial security poster PIN (series)	
D3.11/2:	[Industrial security statements]	
D3.11/3:	[Industrial security cartoons]	
D3.11/4:nos	Industrial security letter	
D3.11/5:nos	Posters	
D3.12:nos	Industrial personnel security review program, annual reports	
D3.13:nos	Manpower awareness series	

D4 Research and Development Board

The Research and Development Board, National Military Establishment, was made subordinate to the Department of Defense, under provisions of Public law 216, 81st Congress, approved Aug. 10, 1949.

D4.1:date   Annual reports. Earlier M6.1:

D4.2:CT   General publications. Earlier M6.2:

Abolished and functions vested in the Secretary of Defense by Reorganization Plan 6 of 1953.

D4.8:CT   Bibliographies and lists of publications. Issued by Office of Director of Defense Research and Development.

D4.9:nos   Parts specification management for reliability, PSMR-nos.

D4.10:CT   Handbooks, manuals, guides relating to research and development.

D4.11:nos   Plastics Technical Evaluation Center: PLASTEC reports

D4.11/2:nos   Plastics Technical Evaluation Center; PLASTEC notes

D4.12:nos   The Shock and vibration bulletin

D4.12/2:v.nos.&nos. Shock and vibration digest

D5 Joint Chiefs of Staff

The Joint Chiefs of Staff was established within the Department of Defense by Public law 216, 81st Congress, approved Aug. 10, 1949.

D5.1:date	Annual reports
D5.2:CT	General publications
D5.8:nos	JANP (series) Joint Army-Navy-Air Force publications
D5.9:date	National resources conference conducted by Industrial College of Armed Forces (annual) Earlier D5.2:R31/date Later title: National Security Seminar...
D5.9/2:date	National security seminar, presentation outlines and reading lists
D5.9/3:date	National security management instructional material of Industrial College of Armed Forces
D5.9/4:CT	Monograph series
D5.10:nos	[Monograph] M-nos. Industrial College of the Armed Forces
D5.10/2:nos	[Lectures] L-(series) Industrial College of the Armed Forces
D5.10/3:nos	Industrial College of Armed Forces: Monograph publication R (series)
D5.10/4:nos	Student Committee report SR-(series) Industrial College of Armed Forces
D5.10/5:nos	[Correspondence course textbooks] Vol.-(series) Industrial College of Armed Forces
D5.11:date	Industrial College of Armed Forces catalog
D5.12:nos	JCS publications (numbered)
D5.13:CT	Industrial College of the Armed Forces: Publications

D5.13/2:nos	Industrial College of Armed Forces. Information circulars.
D5.14:nos	Defense Atomic Support Agency: Technical analysis report DASA (series)
D5.14/2:nos	DASIAC [Defense Atomic Support Agency Information and Analysis Center] special reports
D5.15:CT	Bibliographies and lists of publications
D5.16:date	Industrial College of the Armed Forces: Perspectives in defense management.
D5.17:CT	National War College publications
D5.18:CT	Addresses

D5.100 Defense Communications Agency

The Defense Communications Agency was established on May 12, 1960, as an agency of the Defense Department under the direction, authority, and control of the Secretary of Defense. The Director is responsible to the Secretary of Defense through the Joint Chiefs of Staff.

D5.104:nos   DCA circulars

D5.109:CT   National Military Command Systems Information Processing System 360

D5.110:nos   Technical memorandum (series)

D5.111:date   AUTOVON, automatic global voice network, defense communications system directory (issued 5 times a year)

D5.200 Defense Intelligence Agency

The Defense Intelligence Agency was established as an agency of the Department of Defense by DOD Directive 5105.21, dated August 1, 1961, under provisions of National Security Act of 1947, as amended.

D5.201:date   Annual report

D5.202:CT   General publications

D5.203:date   DoD aeronautical chart bulletins Earlier D301.59:

D5.208:date   DoD aeronautical chart updating manual (CHUM) (monthly) Earlier D301.59/4:

D5.300 Defense Mapping Agency

The Defense Mapping Agency was established as an agency of the Department of Defense on January 1, 1972, under the provisions of the National Security Act of 1947, as amended to operate under the direction and authority and control of the Secretary of defense.

D5.301:date   Annual report

D5.302:CT   General publications

D5.315:dt./nos   Notice to mariners (weekly) Earlier D203.8:

D5.315/2:date   Summary of chart corrections

D5.316:dt./nos   Memorandum for aviators. Earlier D203.11:

D5.317:nos   Publications (numbered) Earlier D203.22:

D6 Public Information Office

The public relations activities of the three Departments are being coordinated thru the Office of Public Information. - 1st Annual report of the Secretary of Defense. 1948.

D6.1:date   Annual reports

D6.2:CT   General publications

D6.6:CT   Regulations, rules, and instructions

D6.7:dt.&nos   Releases

D6.7/2:dt.&nos   Addresses S (series)

D6.8:v.nos   Speakers guide for service spokesmen. Proc.

Defense Supply Agency

D7 Defense Supply Management Agency

The Defense Supply Management Agency was established within the Department of Defense by Public law 436, 82d Congress, approved July 1, 1952.

D7.1:date	Reports (semiannual)
D7.1/2:date	Annual historical summary: Defense Logistics Service Center, Battle Creek, Mich.
D7.1/3:date	Annual historical summary: Defense Industrial Plant Equipment Center
D7.1/4:CT	Annual historical summary: Defense Contract Administration Services [by regions]
D7.1/5:date	Annual historical summary: Defense Electronics Supply Center
D7.1/6:date	Annual historical summary: Defense Fuel Supply Center
D7.1/7:CT/date	Annual historical summary: Defense Depots
D7.1/8:date	Annual historical summary: Defense General Supply Center
D7.1/9:date	Annual historical summary: Defense Construction Supply Center
D7.1/10:date	Annual historical summary: Defense Documentation Center
D7.1/11:date	Annual historical summary: Defense Industrial Supply Center
D7.1/12:date	Annual historical summary: Defense Production Support Office
D7.1/13:date	Annual management report of the Defense Supply Agency
D7.2:CT	General publications
D7.6:CT	Regulations, rules, and instructions
D7.6/2:nos	Handbook DSMA H (series)
D7.6/3:chap.nos	Federal manual for supply cataloging

D7.6/4:CT	Handbooks, manuals, guides (relating to supply and logistics)
D7.6/5:date	Defense supply procurement regulations
D7.6/6:nos	Defense Supply Agency regulations DSAR (series)
D7.6/7:nos	Defense Supply Agency handbooks DSAH (series)
D7.6/8:nos	Defense Supply Agency manual DSAM (series)
D7.6/9:nos	HQM (series)
D7.6/10:nos	DSA-DLSC handbooks. Issued by Defense Supply Agency Defense Logistics Services Center, Battle Creek, Mich.
D7.6/10-2:nos	DSA-DLSC manuals
D7.6/11:nos	Quality and reliability assurance handbooks
D7.6/12:pt/dt	DOD activity address directory (DoDAAD) (Microfiche only)
D7.8:pt.nos	Federal item identification guides for supply cataloging
D7.9:group nos	Federal supply catalog, Department of Defense section
D7.10:nos	Military standard MIL-STD (series) Earlier D3.7:
D7.10/2:nos	Military standards (preliminary)
D7.11:date	Alphabetical listing register of planned mobilization procedures, manufactures of war material registered under Production allocation program (annual)
D7.11/2:date	Register of planned emergency procedures
D7.12:date	Active standardization projects, standards, specifications, studies and handbooks (quarterly) Later title, Standardization projects reported
D7.13:nos	Standardization directory
D7.13/2:date	Defense standardization program, directory of points of interest (quarterly)
D7.13/3:nos	Production equipment directory D (series)

D7.14:date	Department of Defense index of specifications and standards. Earlier D101.34:, D212.10:, D301.28:
D7.14/2:date	Federal supply classification listing of DOD standardization documents. Formerly pt. 3 of D7.14:
D7.15:nos	Quality control and reliability technical reports. Earlier D7.2:M42 and D7.6/4:T28
D7.16:CT	Bibliographies and lists of publications issued by Defense Supply Management Agency
D7.17:date	DCSC fiscal year procurement estimates catalog
D7.18:date	Small business report. Official use
D7.19:nos	DSA poster series
D7.20:date	Consolidated master cross reference list, C-RL-1
D7.20/2:	___ Microfiche edition
D7.21:date	Annual report to Congress on national industrial reserve under Public law 883, 80th Congress
D7.22:date	DCAS manufacturing cost control digest (annual) [Defense Contract Administration Services]
D7.23:nos	Quality assurance QA reporter (quarterly) Admin.

D8 Armed Forces Medical Library

The Army Medical Library was redesignated Armed Forces Medical Library, a joint agency of the Army, the Navy, and the Air Force, by General order 49 of the Department of the Army dated May 9, 1952, pursuant to authority vested in the Secretary of Defense by the National security act of 1947, as amended.

D8.1:date   Annual reports

D8.2:CT   General publications

D8.8:v.nos.&nos.   Current list of medical literature (monthly) **Earlier D104.7:** D1.20 has been cancelled. Later FS2.208:

D8.9:nos   Index catalogue of Armed Forces Medical Library. Earlier M102.8: The new class D104.8: not used. Earlier D104.8:   Later FS2.210:

D8.10:CT   [Bibliographies]   Later FS2.209:

The National Library of Medicine Act, approved August 3, 1956 (70 Stat. 960; 42 U.S.C. 275), established the National Library of Medicine in the Public Health Service and transferred to it all civilian personnel, property and funds of the Armed Forces Medical Library.

North Atlantic Treaty Organization
D9 Supreme Allied Commander in Europe

D9.1:   Reports

D9.8:CT   Supreme Allied Commander in Europe publications

Defense Documentation Center for Scientific and Technical
Information
D10   Armed Services Technical Information Agency

Established by a directive of the Secretary of Defense, effective May 14, 1951, as a joint project under the policy direction of the Research and Development Board, and the management control of the Department of the Air Force with the responsibility of providing an integrated program of scientific and technical report services for the Department of Defense and its contractors.

D10.1:date   Annual reports

D10.2:CT   General publications

D10.3/2:nos   Technical abstracts bulletins
D10.3/3:nos   ___ indexes
D10.3/4:nos   ___ quarterly indexes

D10.6:CT   Regulations, rules, and instructions

D10.8:nos   Title announcement bulletin [Issued irregularly. Proc.]

D10.8/2:nos   ___ AD numerical index. Proc.

D10.9:CT   Bibliographies and lists of publications.

D10.10:nos   Keywords in context title index

D10.11:nos   Defense Documentation Center digest

D11   Armed Services Petroleum Purchasing Agency

D11.1:date   Annual report

D11.2:CT   General publications

D11.3:nos   Oil contract bulletin IFB (series)

458

D12 National Guard Bureau

Established in the Defense Department as a joint bureau of the Department of the Army and the Department of the Air Force by the Department of Defense reorganization act of 1958 (Public law 599), 85th Congress, 2d session, approved August 6, 1958).

D12.1:date	Annual reports. Earlier D112.1:
D12.2:CT	General publications. Earlier D112.2: and D301.2:
D12.3:v.nos.&nos	National Guard Bureau bulletins. Admin.
D12.6:nos	Regulations. Earlier D112.6:
D12.8:nos	Pamphlets
D12.8/2:nos	Technical personnel pamphlets
D12.9:date	Official Army National Guard register. Earlier D112.8:
D12.9/2:date	Air National Guard register. Earlier D112.8/2:
D12.10:CT	Handbooks, manuals, guides (unnumbered)

D13 Civil Defense Office

The Office of Civil Defense was established in the Department of Defense, effective August 1, 1961, pursuant to Executive order 10952 of July 20, 1961.

D13.1:date	Annual reports. Later D119.1:
D13.1/2:date	Annual statistical report. Earlier PrEx4.1/2: Later D119.1/2:
D13.2:CT	General publications Later D119.2:
D13.3/2:nos	Information bulletin. Earlier PrEx4.3/3: Later D119.3/2:
D13.3/3:nos	Surplus property bulletin. Earlier PrEx4.3/5:
D13.8:CT	Handbooks, manuals, guides. Earlier PrEx4.12: Later D119.8:
D13.8/2:nos	Pocket manuals PM (series) Earlier PrEx4.12/6:
D13.8/3:nos	[Handbook] H (series) Earlier Pr34.761/2: and PrEx4.12/3: Later D119.8/2:
D13.8/4:nos	[National plan for civil defense] NP-nos Earlier PrEx4.6/7:
D13.8/5:nos	Student manuals SM (series) Earlier Pr34.761/7: Later D119.8/8:
D13.8/6:nos	Professional guide PSD-PG (series) Issued by Protective Structures Division
D13.8/7:nos	Instructor's guide IG (series) Earlier PrEx4.12/5: Later D119.8/7:
D13.8/8:1e-nos	Federal guidance for State and local civil defense, FG (series) Later D119.8/3:
D13.8/9:pt.(les.)	Federal civil defense guide. Later D119.8/4:
D13.8/10:nos	Technical manuals. Earlier PrEx4.12/4: Later similar D14.8/7:
D13.9:nos	Miscellaneous publications MP (series) Earlier Pr34.759: and PrEx4.14: Later D119.11:
D13.10:nos	Leaflet L (series) Earlier PrEx4.13: Later D119.13:

D13.11:nos   Public booklet PB (series)   Earlier Pr34.764:

D13.12:nos   Technical report TR (series)   Earlier Pr34.763:   Later D119.9:

D13.13:nos   Protective Structures Division, technical memorandums. Administrative

D13.14:CT   Addresses.   Later D119.12:

D13.15:les-nos   Protective structures, shelter design series

D13.16:date   Western Training Center, catalogs and schedule of courses

D13.17:v.nos.&nos.   CD news feature page.   Earlier D1.34:

D13.17/2:v.nos.&nos.   CD newspictures.   Earlier D1.34/2:   Later D119.10:

D13.18:nos   Region eight news

March 31, 1964 the Secretary of Defense assigned civil defense responsibilities delegated to him by Executive order 10952 to the Secretary of the Army.

D14 Defense Civil Preparedness Agency

The Defense Civil Preparedness Agency was established by direction of the Secretary of Defense and began operations May 5, 1972.

D14.1:date	Annual report. Earlier D119.1:
D14.1/2:date	Annual statistical report. Earlier D119.1/2:
D14.2:CT	General publications Earlier D119.2:
D14.8:CT	Handbooks, manuals, guides. Earlier D119.8:
D14.8/2:nos	Student manual SM (series) Earlier D119.8/8:
D14.8/3:nos	Handbook H-(series) Earlier D119.8/2:
D14.8/4:nos	Instructor's guide IG (series) Earlier D119.8/7:
D14.8/5:nos	FG-series. Earlier D119.8/3:
D14.8/6:nos	CPG Series Earlier in D14.2: and D14.8:
D14.8/7:nos	TM (series) Earlier similar D13.8/10:
D14.9:nos	Technical reports. Earlier D119.9:
D14.10:nos	Miscellaneous publications MP (series) Earlier D119.11:
D14.11:nos	HS-(series) Earlier D119.15:
D14.12:nos	Leaflets. Earlier D119.13:
D14.13:v. nos. &nos.	Survival [newsletter]
D14.13/2:	Information bulletin. Earlier D119.3/2:
D14.14:v. nos. &nos.	Foresight (bimonthly)
D14.15:	K-(series) Earlier in D14.2:
D14.16:nos	Buildings with environmental protection, design case studies. Earlier D119.14:

D101 Army Department

The Department of the Army was made a military department within the Department of Defense in lieu of its prior status as an executive department by Public law 216, 81st Congress, approved Aug. 10, 1949.

D101.1:date	Annual reports. Earlier M101.1:
D101.2:CT	General publications. Earlier M101.2:
D101.3:dt.&nos	Joint Army and Air Force bulletins. Earlier M101.3:
D101.3/2:nos	Military traffic management bulletins. Administrative.
D101.3/3:nos	Army Audit Agency bulletins
D101.3/3-2:nos	Army Audit Agency pamphlets Continuation of D101.3/3:
D101.3/4:nos	Advance Planning Procurement Information bulletin, APPI (series)
D101.3/5:date	Army Materiel Command: Employment bulletin. Earlier D101.2:Em7/3
D101.4:dt.&nos	Circulars. Earlier M101.4:
D101.6:CT	Regulations, rules, and instructions
D101.6/2:nos	Civilian personnel regulations Earlier W1.42:
D101.6/3:nos	Civilian personnel procedures manual
D101.6/4:date	Army procurement procedure. Earlier D101.6:P94
D101.6/5:CT	Handbooks, manuals, guides
D101.6/6:CT	Area handbooks
D101.7:dt.&nos	General orders. Earlier M101.7:
D101.8:dt.&nos	Special orders. Earlier M101.18:
D101.9:nos	Army regulations. Earlier M101.9:
D101.9/2:nos	Army Materiel Command regulations, AMCR (series)
D101.9/3:nos	Supply and Maintenance Command regulations SMCR (series)
D101.10:nos	Special regulations. Earlier M101.32:

D101.11:nos	Technical manuals. Earlier M101.18:
D101.11/2:nos	Strategic Communications Command: Technical manuals, CCTM-(series)
D101.12:v.nos	Army information digest (monthly) Earlier M101.10:
D101.13:dt.&nos	Civilian personnel and payroll letters. Proc. Earlier M101.19: Later D101.26:
D101.14:dt.&nos	General court-martial orders. Earlier M101.14:
D101.15:nos	Supply bulletins. Earlier M101.27:
D101.16:sec.nos.&le.nos.	Supply catalogs. Earlier M101.12:
D101.16/2:nos	Department of Army supply manual SM (series)
D101.17:v.nos.&nos.	Officers' call (monthly) Earlier M101.33:
D101.18:nos	Reduction tables. Earlier M101.31:
D101.19:nos	Tables of organization and equipment. Pubs.desig. TO&E nos. Earlier M101.2:
D101.20:nos	Field manuals. Earlier M101.17:
D101.21:nos	Graphic training aids. Earlier W1.53:
D101.22:nos	Pamphlets. Earlier M101.25:
D101.22/2:nos	IG pamphlets. Administrative.
D101.22/3:nos	Army Materiel Command, AMC pamphlets
D101.22/4:nos	United States Army, Alaska, pamphlets
D101.22/5:nos	Supply and Maintenance Command, SMC pamphlets
D101.22/6:nos	MTMTS [Military Traffic Management and Technical Service] pamphlets
D101.23:nos	Table of allowances. Earlier M101.29:
D101.24:dt.&nos	Training circulars. Earlier M101.22:
D101.25:le-nos	Technical bulletins. Earlier M101.13:
D101.26:dt.&nos	Civilian personnel circulars. Earlier M101.20: and replaces D101.13:

D101.27:date	United States Army index of specifications, including military (MIL and JAN) standards. Published annually with monthly supplements. Earlier M101.23: Later D101.34:
D101.28:nos	U.S. Army specifications. Earlier M101.26:
D101.29:sec.&le-nos	Modification work orders. Earlier W1.56:
D101.30:nos.	Army-Navy-Air Force, list of products qualified under military specifications
D101.31:dt.&nos	Special court-martial orders. Earlier M101.2:Sp3
D101.32:nos	Memorandums. Proc. and ptd. Earlier M101.24:
D101.33:nos	Joint Army and Air Force procurement circulars
D101.33/2:dt.&nos.	Army procurement circulars
D101.33/3:dt.&nos.	Procurement legal service circulars
D101.34:date	Index of specifications and standards used by Department of Army, military index, v.2 (semiannual) Earlier D101.27: Later D7.14:
D101.35:nos	Posters. Earlier M101.34:
D101.36:date	Department of Army chiefs and executives [organization chart] (bimonthly) Proc. Later D102.23:
D101.37:nos	Civilian personnel pamphlets. Earlier M101.35:
D101.38:nos	Armed Services Electro Standards Agency, lists Desig. AESEA list (nos)
D101.39:dt.&nos	Civilian personnel news letter (monthly) Superseded by D101.39/2:
D101.39/2:nos	Army personnel newsletter. Supersedes D101.39:
D101.40:date	United States army occupational handbook
D101.41:	Inspection guides
D101.41/2:	IG notes. Admin.
D101.42:CT	Headquarters, U.S. Army, Europe, publications
D101.42/2:CT	Historical Division publications
D101.42/3:v.nos.&nos.	Medical bulletin of U.S. Army, Europe

D101.43:v.nos   Army reservist (monthly) Replaces D107.7:

D101.44:nos   Psychological warfare school special texts   Admin.

D101.45:CT   Addresses

D101.46:   [not used]

D101.46/2:CT   Human Research Unit no. 2, Office, Chief of Army Field Forces, Fort Ord, Calif., Publications. Proc.

D101.46/3:CT   Human Research Unit no. 3, Office, Chief of Army Field Forces, Fort Benning, Ga., publications. Proc.

D101.47:v.nos.&nos. Army aviation digest (monthly) Published by Army Aviation School, Camp Rucker, Alabama.

D101.47/2:nos   Army Aviation School, Fort Rucker, Ala.; Special bibliography

D101.48:nos   ROTC manuals

D101.49:nos   Special bibliography, Artillery & Guided Missile School Library.

D101.50:date   Progress, United States Army reports (annual) Earlier D101.2:P94/2

D101.51:date   Joint Military-Industry Packaging and Materials Handling Symposium

D101.52:nos   United States Army research and development series

D101.52/2:date   Army research task summaries (annual)

D101.52/3:v.nos.&nos. Army research and development (monthly)

D101.52/4:date/v.no. U.S. Army research and development program guide. Earlier D101.6:R31/v.nos

D101.52/5:date   Research in progress, U.S. Army Research Office (Durham) (annual)

D101.52/5-2:nos   Army Research Office (Durham) Historical Summary

D101.52/5-3:date   U.S. Army Research Office - Durham. Engineering Sciences Division Engineering projects accomplishments

D101.52/6:date   United States Army human factors research & development, annual conference

D101.52/7:nos   Army Research Office, Durham: Reports. Designated ARO-D- reports

D101.53:v.nos.&nos. Infantry School quarterly

D101.54:nos   ARO [Army Research Office] reports

D101.55:nos   United States Army Service Center for the Armed Forces: Pamphlets. Desig. USASCAF pamphlet (nos)

D101.56:CT   Bibliographies and lists of publications

D101.57:CT   Dictionaries, glossaries, etc.

D101.58:nos   Firing tables. Earlier W34.34:

D101.59:nos   Army subject schedules

D101.60:nos   Army Personnel Research Office: APRO technical research notes. Earlier D102.27: Later title: Research Institute for the Behavioral and Social Sciences: Technical papers.

D101.60/2:nos   Army Personnel Research Office: Technical research reports. Earlier D101.27/2:

D101.61:date   Official bulletins, national trophy matches

D101.62:CT   Army Audit Agency publications. See D101.3/3: for Army Audit Agency bulletins

D101.63:date   Management improvement program, Plowback, improvements reported (semiannual)

D101.64:CT   Army Language School, Presidio of Monterey, Calif., publications

D101.65:nos   AMC historical studies

D101.66:v.nos.&nos. Transportation proceedings (monthly) Replaced by D101.66/2:

D101.66/2:nos.&nos. Translog (monthly) Replaces D101.66:

D101.67:nos   Behavioral Sciences Research Laboratory: Technical reports

D101.67/2:date   BESRL [Behavioral Science Research Laboratory] work program (annual)

D101.68:v.nos.&nos. Hallmark (monthly)

D101.69:v.nos.&nos. Army logistican (bimonthly)

D101.70:date   Army Materiel Command coordinated recruitment program annual progress report

D101.71:date   Arrowhead (monthly) Issued by Army Combat Developments Command, Fort Belvoir, Va.

D101.72:v./nos	Parameters, journal of Army War College
D101.73:v.nos.&nos.	Military chaplains' review (quarterly)
D101.74:CT	Vietnam studies
D101.75:nos	General information series/ General information leaflets. Issued by Public Information Office, 3d U.S. Infantry (The Old Guard), Fort Myer, Va.
D101.76:nos	Special bibliography, U.S. Army command and general staff college, Library Division, Ft. Leavenworth, Kansas.
D101.77:date	Air defense trends (quarterly)
D101.78:nos	Subcourse, correspondence course of the U.S. Army Armor School
D101.79:CT	U.S. Army Foreign Science and Technology Center: Publications
D101.80:nos	AMMRC [Army Materials and Mechanics Research Center] TR-nos
D101.81:CT	Army Scientific Advisory Panel: Publications

D102 Adjutant General's Office

The Adjutant General's Department is subordinate to the Department of the Army, which was made a military department within the Department of Defense in lieu of its prior status as an executive department within the National Military Establishment, by Public law 216, 81st Congress, approved Aug. 10, 1949.

D102.1:date	Annual reports. Earlier M108.1:
D102.2:CT	General publications. Earlier M108.2:
D102.6:CT	Regulations, rules and instructions
D102.6/2:CT	Handbooks, manuals, guides
D102.7:nos	Consolidated report of accessions; Monthly. Proc. Earlier M108.9:
D102.8:v.nos	Trials of war criminals before Nuremberg military tribunals
D102.9:date	Official Army register (annual) Earlier M108.8:
D102.10:date	Army hit kit of popular songs (monthly) Earlier M117.7: Later D1.14:
D102.11:CT	Supreme Commander for Allied Powers, publications. Earlier W1.84:
D102.11/2:date	Exports and imports (monthly) Proc.
D102.11/3:date	Report of Japan's export shipments and import receipts stated by areas and countries of destination and origin, with value expressed in United States dollars (monthly) Proc.
D102.11/4:date	Monthly Japanese foreign trade statistics. Proc.
D102.12:nos	Natural Resources Section weekly summary. Proc.
D102.13:nos	Weekly report on Japan. Proc. Earlier M105.22:
D102.14:nos	Memorandum for Japanese Government. Proc. Earlier M105.23:
D102.15:nos	Science and technology in Japan, reports. Proc. Earlier M105.24:
D102.16:nos	Official gazette [Japanese] English edition

D102.17:nos	[Memorandum of information.] Proc. Pubs. desig. MI-nos
D102.18:nos. &sec. nos.	Supreme Commander for Allied Powers: Japanese economic statistics bulletin (monthly) Proc. Earlier M105.28:
D102.19:nos	Military Government of Ryukyu Islands: Ryukyu statistical bulletin (monthly)
D102.19/2:nos	United States civil administration of Ryukyu Islands: Special bulletins. Proc.
D102.19/3:nos	Civil affairs activities in Ryukyu Islands (semiannual)
D102.19/4:date	Ryukyu Islands, Annual report to Food and Agriculture Organization of the United Nations
D102.20:nos	Supreme Commander for Allied Powers: Natural Resources Section reports. Earlier W1.80:, M105.25:
D102.20/2:nos	Natural Resources Section. Preliminary study. Earlier W1.80/2:
D102.21:nos	Technical papers. Proc.
D102.22:nos	Gazette of the Allied Commission for Austria (monthly) Earlier M105.26:
D102.23:date	Department of Army chiefs and executives (organization chart) (quarterly) Proc. Earlier D101.36:
D102.24:nos	Army Forces Far East, AFFE pamphlets
D102.25:CT	Adjutant General's School, Fort Benjamin Harrison, Indiana, reports and publications
D102.26:CT	Posters
D102.27:nos	PRB technical research notes. Proc. Later D101.60:
D102.27/2:nos	PRB technical research reports. Proc. Later D101.60/2:
D102.27/3:nos	PRB reports
D102.28:nos	Special bibliographies
D102.28/2:CT	Bibliographies and lists of publications
D102.28/3:nos	Selected current acquisitions, lists
D102.28/4:nos	Special lists. Issued by Army Library.
D102.28/5:nos	Selected periodical literature, lists

D102.29:nos   Special studies

Recruiting Publicity Bureau

D102.75:CT   Recruiting Publicity Bureau publications. Earlier M108.75:

D102.76:v.nos   Recruiting journal (monthly) Earlier M108.80: Later D118.9:

D102.77:v.nos   Life of soldier and airman (monthly) Earlier M108.77:

D102.78:nos   Recruiting Publicity Bureau posters   Earlier M108.78:

D102.79:nos   PRS nos. Published by Personnel Research Section

D102.80:date   TIPS (quarterly)

D102.81:v.nos.&nos. Army host (bimonthly)

Engineers' Corps

D103 Engineer Department

The Engineer Department, Army Department, was made subordinate to the Department of Defense, under provisions of Public law 216, 81st Congress, approved Aug. 10, 1949.

D103.1:date	Annual reports. Earlier M110.1:
D103.1/a:CT	___ separates. Earlier M110.1/a:
D103.1/2:dt.&pt. nos.	Water-borne commerce of United States (annual) Formerly pt. 2 of Annual report.
D103.1/3:date	Great Lakes-St. Lawrence Seaway Winter Navigation Board: Annual report
D103.2:CT	General publications Earlier M110.2:
D103.4:nos	Circulars
D103.6:CT	Regulations, rules, and instructions. Earlier M110.6:
D103.6/2:chap. nos.	Orders and regulations. Earlier W7.8/3:
D103.6/3:nos	Manual EM (series)
D103.6/4:nos	Regulations ER (series)
D103.6/5:CT	Handbooks, manuals, guides
D103.7:dt.&nos.	General orders. Earlier M110.14:
D103.8:nos	Port series. Earlier M110.11:
D103.9:pt. nos.&chap. nos.	Engineering manual for military construction. Earlier M110.13:
D103.9/2:nos	Guide specifications for military construction
D103.9/3:nos	Guide specifications for civil works construction
D103.10:nos	Transportation series. Earlier M110.17:
D103.11:nos	Miscellaneous series. Earlier M110.12:
D103.12:date	Index of specifications used by Corps of Engineers. Earlier M110.9:
D103.13:date	Statistical report of marine commerce of Duluth-Superior Harbor, Minn. and Wis. Proc. Earlier M110.2:D88

D103.14:pt.nos.&chap.nos.	Engineering manual, civil works construction. Earlier M110.7:
D103.15:nos	Technical reports of Beach Erosion Board. Earlier M110.307: Later D103.42/5:
D103.15/2:nos	Beach Erosion Board: Miscellaneous papers. Later D103.42/2:
D103.16:v.nos.&nos.	Bulletin of Beach Erosion Board (quarterly) Earlier M110.303: Later D103.42/3:
D103.17:date	St.Marys Falls Canal, Mich., statistical report of lake commerce passing through canals at Sault Ste.Marie, Mich., and Ontario. Earlier M110.16:
D103.17/2:date	Statistical report of commerce passing through canals at Sault Ste.Marie, Mich., and Ontario, salt water ship movements for season
D103.18:nos	Lake series. Earlier W7.25:
D103.19:nos	Technical memorandum of Beach Erosion Board. Proc. Earlier M110.308:
D103.20:CT	Army Map Service, publications. Earlier W7.33:
D103.20/2:nos	AMS technical manuals. Earlier W7.33/2:
D103.20/3:nos	Army Map Service Bulletins. Earlier M110.20:
D103.20/4:nos	Army Map Service: Technical reports
D103.21:chap.nos.	Engineering manual for emergency construction. Proc.
D103.21/2:nos	Guide specifications for emergency-type military construction. Desig. CE-E-nos
D103.22:CT	Engineer reports (pertaining to creeks, rivers, harbors, wharfs, etc.)
D103.22/2:date	Projects recommended for deauthorization, annual report
D103.23:CT	Board of Engineers for Rivers and Harbors, report of hearings
D103.24:nos	Waterways Experiment Station: Bulletins. Proc. Earlier M110.19:
D103.24/2:nos	___Technical memorandums. Later title, Technical reports Earlier M110.18:
D103.24/3:nos	___Translations. Proc.
D103.24/4:nos	___Miscellaneous papers. Proc.
D103.24/5:nos	___Research reports
D103.24/6:date	___List of publications. Earlier D103.2:W31

D103.24/7:nos	Waterways Experiment Station: Instruction reports
D103.24/8:nos	Annual summary of investigations in support of civil works program for calendar year
D103.24/9:nos	Waterways Experiment Station: Contract reports
D103.24/10:CT	Waterways Experiment Station capabilities
D103.24/11:nos	Waterways Experiment Station, EERO Technical report. [Explosives Excavation Research Office
D103.24/12:nos	PSTIAC reports. Pavements and Soil Trafficability Information Analysis Center
D103.24/13:nos	Aquatic Plant Control Program. Technical report
D103.25:nos	Engineer Research and Development Laboratoties reports. Proc.
D103.25/2:nos	___ Technical report TR (series)
D103.26:nos	SIPRE reports [Snow, Ice, and Permafrost Research Establishment]
D103.27:date	Annual report, passage of fish over Bonneville Dam, Columbia River, Oregon and Washington
D103.27/2:nos	Bonneville Hydraulic Laboratory, reports
D103.28:nos	Reports of Committee on Tidal Hydraulics
D103.28/2:nos	Technical bulletin of Committee on Tidal Hydraulics
D103.29:nos	Engineer intelligence notes. Proc.
D103.30:nos	Releases. Engineer Research & Development Laboratories. Proc.
D103.30/2:nos	Books & Notes, Technical Reference Library, Engineer Research & Development Labs. Admin.
D103.30/3:date	Press release: Arkansas Water Basin news
D103.31:nos	Arctic Construction and Frost Effects Laboratory. Technical reports
D103.31/2:nos	___ Miscellaneous papers. Proc.
D103.31/3:nos	___ Translations
D103.32:nos	Military hydrology bulletins

D103.33:nos	Army Snow, Ice, and Permafrost Research Establishment [Later, Cold Regions Research and Engineering Laboratory] Technical reports
D103.33/2:nos	___ Special reports
D103.33/3:nos	___ Research reports
D103.33/4:nos	___ Translations
D103.33/5:CT	___ General publications
D103.33/6:date	___ List of publications
D103.33/7:nos	___ Cold regions science and engineering
D103.33/8:date	___ CRREL in Alaska, annual report
D103.33/9:date	___ Quarterly progress report
D103.33/10:date	___ Experimental Engineering Division. Quarterly progress report
D103.33/11:date	Cold Regions Research and Engineering Laboratory: R & D notes
D103.33/12:nos	Cold Regions Research and Engineering Laboratory: CRREL reports
D103.34:nos	Recruitment announcements. Admin.
D103.35:CT	Water resources development by Corps of Engineers by area. Earlier D103.2:W29
D103.36:v.nos	Digest of decisions of Corps of Engineers Board of Contract Appeals
D103.37:CT	Army Polar Research and Development Center, Fort Belvoir, Va., General publications
D103.37/2:nos	___ Report
D103.38:nos	Ohio River Division Laboratories: Technical reports
D103.38/2:nos	___ Miscellaneous papers
D103.38/3:nos	___ Technical memorandums
D103.39:CT	Bibliographies and lists of publications
D103.40:CT/dt	Military geology (series)
D103.41:nos	Missouri River Division: M.R.D. sediment series

D103.41/2:date	Missouri River main stem reservoirs, annual operating plan and summary of actual operation
D103.42:nos	Coastal Engineering Research Center: Technical memorandum
D103.42/2:nos	___ Miscellaneous papers. Earlier D103.15/2:
D103.42/3:date	___ CERC bulletin and summary report of research progress for fiscal year Earlier D103.16:
D103.42/4:nos	___ Reprints
D103.42/5:nos	___ Technical reports. Earlier D103.15:
D103.42/6:nos	___ Special reports
D103.42/7:nos	GITE [General Investigation of Tidal Inlets] reports
D103.43:nos	Pamphlet EP (series)
D103.44:nos	U.S. Army Engineer Division, North Pacific: Technical reports
D103.45:date	Stages and discharges of Mississippi River and tributaries in Vicksburg District (annual) Formerly in D103.309:
D103.45/2:date	Stages and discharges of Mississippi River and tributaries in Memphis District (annual) Formerly in D103.309:
D103.45/3:date	Stages and discharges of Mississippi River and tributaries in St. Louis District (annual) Formerly in D103.309:
D103.45/4:date	Stages and discharges of Mississippi River and tributaries and other watersheds in New Orleans District (annual) Formerly included in D103.309:
D103.46:nos	Potamology investigations
D103.47:CT	Flood plain investigation
D103.47/2:CT	Floods in ... how to avoid damage (folders)
D103.48:v.nos.&nos.	Water spectrum (quarterly)
D103.49:nos	Resources atlas project--Thailand atlases
D103.50:nos	EARI [Engineer Agency for Resources Inventories] Development research series reports
D103.51:nos	Honolulu District: Technical reports (numbered)

D103.52:nos	Contract report
D103.53:nos	Construction Engineering Research Laboratories: Technical reports
D103.53/2:nos	Construction Engineering Research Laboratory, Champaign, Ill., Technical manuscript
D103.53/3:let/nos	Construction Engineering Research Labs. Preliminary report
D103.53/4:let/nos	Construction Engineering Research Labs., Conference proceedings
D103.53/5:let/nos	Construction Engineering Research Labs., Interim report
D103.53/6:let/nos	Construction Engineering Research Lab., Technical information pamphlets
D103.54:nos	NCG [Nuclear Cratering Group] technical report
D103.55:nos	Hydraulic Engineering Center: Technical papers
D103.55/2:CT	Hydraulic Engineering Center: General publications
D103.55/3:date	Hydraulic Engineering Center: Annual report
D103.55/4:nos	Hydraulic Engineering Center: Research notes
D103.56:CT	Press releases
D103.57:nos	IWR reports. [Army Engineers Institute for Water Research]
D103.57/2:nos	Center for Economic Studies, Institute for Water Resources: Center papers
D103.57/3:date	Institute for Water Resources. Annual report
D103.57/4:nos	IWR pamphlets
D103.58:date	List of Illinois River terminals, docks, mooring locations & warehouses. Issued by St.Louis Districts, St.Louis, Mo.
D103.58/2:date	List of Mississippi River terminals, docks, mooring locations and warehouses
D103.59:nos	U.S. Army Engineer District, Los Angeles, Reports (numbered)
D103.60:nos	Wastewater management reports
D103.61:date	Columbia River water management report for water year

D103.62:CT	Environmental impact statement [by area]
D103.63:dt./nos	Lake Erie water quality newsletter (quarterly)
D103.64:nos	Committee on Channel Stabilization. Technical report
D103.65:CT	Final environmental impact statements CLASS CANCELLED
D103.66:CT	Navigation charts: Missouri River
D103.66/2:CT	Navigation charts: Ohio River
D103.66/3:nos	Navigation charts: (Numbered river)
D103.66/4:CT	Navigation charts: Allegheny & Monongahela Rivers

D103.100   Engineer School, Fort Belvoir, Va.

D103.101:date   Annual reports. Earlier M110.401:

D103.102:CT   General publications. Earlier M110.402:

D103.107:nos   Engineer School Library bulletin. Earlier M110.407:

D103.108:nos   Weekly periodical index. Earlier M110.408:

D103.109:nos   Engineer School special text, ST (series)

D103.109/2:CT   Programmed texts

D103.110:CT   Master lesson plans. Prepared for use at Engineer school only.

D103.111:nos   Courses, Engineer School, Ft.Belvoir, Va. Admin.

D103.111/2:nos   Correspondence course program, subcourses.

D103.112:nos   Conference notes. Official use.

D103.112/2:nos   Student material for use with conference notes. Proc.

D103.112/3:nos   Industrial material to accompany conference notes. Proc.

D103.113:nos   USAR training bulletin. Monthly. Proc.

D103.114:CT   Bibliographies and lists of publications, Engineer School, Formerly in D103.102:

D103.115:v.nos.&nos.   Engineer (quarterly) Issued by U.S. Army Engineer School, Fort Belvoir, Va.

D103.200 Lake Survey Office

D103.201:date	Annual reports. Earlier M110.101:
D103.202:CT	General publications. Earlier M110.102:
D103.203:nos	Bulletins. Earlier M110.103: Later title, Great Lakes pilot Later C55.402:
D103.203/2:nos	Bulletins, B (series)
D103.208:date	Catalog of charts of the Great Lakes and connecting waters, also Lake Champlain, New York Canals, Minnesota-Ontario border lakes (annual) Earlier D103.2:C38/3
D103.209:nos	Research reports
D103.210:nos	Miscellaneous papers
D103.211:nos	Basic data reports

D103.300 Mississippi River Commission

The Mississippi River Commission is subordinate to the Department of the Army, which was made a military department within the Department of Defense by Public law 216, 81st Congress, approved Aug.10,1949.

D103.301:date   Annual reports. Earlier M110.201:

D103.302:CT   General publications. Earlier M110.202:

D103.307:CT   Maps. Earlier M110.208:

D103.308:CT   Topographic quadrangle maps of alluvial valley of lower Mississippi River. Earlier W31.9:

D103.308/2:date   Index of topographic quadrangle maps of alluvial valley of lower Mississippi River. Earlier W31.9/2:

D103.309:date   Stages and discharges, Mississippi River and its outlets and tributaries (annual) Earlier M110.207:   Later D103.45:, D103.45/2

D103.309/2:date   Annual maximum, minimum, and mean discharges of Mississippi River and its outlets and tributaries.

Army Medical Department 1968-

Army Medical Service 1950-

D104 Medical Department

D104.1:date	Annual reports. Earlier M102.1:
D104.2:CT	General publications. Earlier M102.2:
D104.3:v.nos	Bulletin of Army Medical Department (monthly) Earlier M102.3: Later see D1.11:
D104.6/2:CT	Handbooks, manuals, and guides
D104.7:v.nos	Current list of medical literature (weekly) Earlier M102.7: Later D8.8:
D104.8:vol	Index-catalogue of Library of Surgeon General's Office, 4th series. Earlier M102.8: Later D8.9:
D104.9:nos	Medical Department equipment list. Earlier M102.9:
D104.10:CT	Army Medical Library bibliographies. Proc.
D104.10/2:CT	Bibliographies and lists of publications
D104.11:CT	Medical Department of the Army in World War II
D104.12:date	Medical Research and Development Board, Research progress report (annual)
D104.12/2:nos	Medical Research and Development Board, Research progress report (quarterly)
D104.13:nos	Medical sciences publications
D104.14:nos	Army Medical Research Laboratory reports. Proc.
D104.15:nos	Walter Reed Army Institute of Research, research reports WRAIR series. Internal use only.
D104.15/2:nos	Walter Reed Army Medical Center. Army Prosthetics Research Laboratory. Technical reports.
D104.15/3:date	Walter Reed Army Medical Center. Annual progress report.

D104.15/4:nos   Walter Reed Army Institute for Research, Walter Reed Army Medical Center: Health data publications

D104.15/5:v.nos.&nos. Walter Reed General Hospital: Progress notes, Department of Medicine (monthly)

D104.16:date   Dependents' medical care program, annual report

D104.17:nos   Army Medical Nutrition Laboratory, Fitzsimmons Army Hospital, reports.

D104.18:nos   Armed Services Research and development report on insects and rodent control (quarterly) Administrative only.

D104.18/2:date   Armed Forces Pest Control Board. Annual reports

D104.19:date   Army medical research & nutrition laboratory. Report of activities

D104.20:v.nos   Health of the Army

D104.20/a:CT   ___ separates

D104.21:nos   Aeromedical Research Unit, Fort Rucker, Ala.; USAARU reports

D104.22:date   Surgical Research Unit, Brooke Army Medical Center, Fort Sam Houston, Tex.: Annual research progress report

D104.23:date   Abstracts from annual and technical reports submitted by USAMRDC contractors/grantees (quarterly)

D104.23/2:date   Advanced abstracts of scientific and technical papers submitted for publication and presentation (quarterly)

D104.24:v.nos.&nos. Newsletter of U.S. Army Medical Department

D104.25:nos   Biomedical reports of the 406 Medical Laboratory

D104.26:v.nos.&nos. AMED Spectrum [Army Media Department]

D104.27:date   United States Army Medical Research Institute of Infectious Diseases, annual progress report

D104.28:v.nos&nos Perspectives (monthly)

D104.29:nos   Letterman Army Institute of Research: Institute reports

Ordnance Corps
D105   Ordnance Department

D105.1:date	Annual reports. Earlier M111.1:
D105.2:CT	General publications. Earlier M111.2:
D105.3:nos	Ordnance Corps bulletin. Admin. Earlier W34.3:
D105.6:CT	Regulations, rules & instructions. Earlier W34.12/1:, W34.12/2:
D105.6/2:nos	Ordnance Corps manual ORD M (series)
D105.6/3:CT	Handbooks, manuals, guides
D105.7:v.nos	Ordnance Department Safety bulletin. Proc. Earlier M111.7:
D105.8:dt.&nos	Ordnance Department orders. Earlier M111.8:
D105.9:nos	Ordnance Corps pamphlet ORDP (series)
D105.10:nos	Ballistics Research Laboratories: BRL memorandum reports. Proc.
D105.10/2:nos	___ reports
D105.10/3:nos	___ Technical notes
D105.10/4:nos	Ordnance computer research reports
D105.11:CT	Rock Island Arsenal Laboratory, technical reports. Proc.
D105.11/2:CT	___, reports
D105.12:nos	Picatinny Arsenal, Dover, N.J., technical reports. Proc.
D105.12/2:nos	___ technical notes
D105.12/3:nos	Feltman Research Laboratories, Picatinny Arsenal, Dover, N.J., Technical report FRL-TR (series)
D105.12/4:nos	Feltman Research Laboratories, Picatinny Arsenal, Dover, N.J., Technical notes FRL-TN (series)
D105.12/5:nos	Feltman Research Laboratories, Picatinny Arsenal, Dover, N.J., Technical memorandums

D105.13:nos	Rodman Process Laboratory, Watertown Arsenal, reports. Proc.
D105.13/2:nos	Watertown Arsenal Laboratory, report WAL (series)
D105.13/2-2:nos	Watertown Arsenal Laboratory: Technical report (series)
D105.13/2-3:nos	Watertown Arsenal: Technical report WARD-TR **(series)**
D105.13/2-4:nos	Metallurgical Advisory Committee on Titanium information bulletins
D105.13/3:nos	Ordnance Materials Research Offices, Watertown Arsenal, OMRO publications
D105.14:nos	Diamond Ordnance Fuze Laboratories [Later, Harry Diamond Laboratories] Technical report TR (series)
D105.14/2:v.nos	___ Technical review.
D105.14/3:nos	Harry Diamond Laboratories, Washington, D.C. TM-
D105.14/4:nos	HDL [Harry Diamond Laboratories] technical disclosure bulletin
D105.15:nos	Army Ballistic Missile Agency, research reports. Proc.
D105.15/2:nos	U.S. Army Ballistic Missile Agency, DG-TR (series)
D105.16:nos	Coating and Chemical Laboratory, Aberdeen Proving Ground, Md., report CCL (series) Proc.
D105.17:1e-nos	Frankford Arsenal reports. Proc.
D105.17/2:nos	Frankford Arsenal memorandum report MR (series) Proc.
D105.17/3:nos	Frankford Arsenal: Technical memorandums.
D105.18:nos	Detroit Arsenal, reports
D105.18/2:nos	Ordnance Tank-Automotive Command, Detroit Arsenal, Land Locomotion Laboratory: Reports
D105.19:nos	Springfield Armory: Technical report SA-TR (series)
D105.20:nos	Watervliet Arsenal report WVTRI (series)
D105.21:nos	Missile purchase description, MPD (series) Administrative.
D105.22:nos	Army Ordnance Missile Command RE-TR (series)

D105.22/2:nos	Army Missile Command: Report RT-TR (series)
D105.22/2-2:nos	Army Missile Command: Report RG-TR (series)
D105.22/3:nos	Army Missile Command. Redstone Scientific Information Center, Redstone Arsenal, Alabama, RSIC-(series)
D105.23:nos	White Sands Missile Range, N.Mex., Inter-Range Instrumentation Group. IRIG documents.
D105.24:nos	Human Engineering Laboratories, Aberdeen Proving Ground, Md.; Technical Memorandums.
D105.25:nos	Army Ordnance School, Aberdeen Proving Ground, Md. Special text ST (series)
D105.26:nos	Army Materials Research Agency: Technical report AMRA CR (series)
D105.27:nos	Army Ordnance Center and School, Aberdeen Proving Ground, Md.: OSPAM (series)

D106 Quartermaster General of Army

The Quartermaster General of the Army is subordinate to the Department of the Army, which was made a military department within the Department of Defense in lieu of its prior status as an executive department within the National Military Establishment by Public law 216, 81st Congress, approved Aug. 10, 1949.

D106.1:date	Annual reports. Earlier M112.1:
D106.2:CT	General publications. Earlier M112.2:
D106.3/2:nos	Quartermaster Food and Container Institute for Armed Forces: Library bulletin
D106.3/3:nos	___ , supplements
D106.4:	QMC circulars. Admin.
D106.6:CT	Regulations, rules, and instructions. Earlier M112.6:
D106.6/2:nos	Quartermaster Corps manual QMC (series) **Earlier M112.8:**
D106.7:v.nos	Depot and market center operations (bimonthly) Proc. Restricted. Earlier M112.7:
D106.8:nos	Q.M.C. Historical studies Earlier M112.9:
D106.8/2:date	Q.M.C. Historical studies, series II
D106.8/3:CT	Historical publications (unnumbered)
D106.9:nos	Footwear and leather series reports. Proc. Later, Clothing and Organic Materials Lab., F & L (series) Later D106.21:
D106.9/2:nos	Textile series reports. Proc.
D106.9/2-2:nos	Textile Engineering Laboratory reports
D106.9/3:nos	Environmental Protection Division reports
D106.9/4:nos	Environmental Protection Division, technical report EP (series)
D106.9/5:nos	Chemical and Plastics Division, technical report CP (series)

D106.10:nos	Technical library bibliographic series. Proc. Earlier M112.10:
D106.10/2:CT	Bibliographies and lists of publications (unnumbered)
D106.10/3:nos	Bibliographic series
D106.11:date	Index Quartermaster Corps specifications (quarterly) Proc.
D106.12:date	Statistical yearbook of Quartermaster Corps. Earlier D106.2:St2
D106.13:nos	QMC pamphlets. Earlier D106.2:C18
D106.14:date	Index, coordinated purchase descriptions.
D106.15:CT	Addresses.
D106.16:nos	QMFCIAF reports. Issued by Quartermaster Food and Container Institute for Armed Forces.
D106.17:nos	Earth Sciences Division: Technical report ES (series) Later D106.21:
D106.17/2:nos	Earth Sciences Division: Special report S (series)
D106.18:v.nos.Qtr.nos.	Activities report
D106.19:nos	Operation studies
D106.20:nos	U.S. Army Natick Laboratories. Food Division, Natick, Mass. Technical report FD-
D106.21:nos	Natick Laboratories, Natick, Mass.: Technical reports. This series consists of reports numbered in one series, which were formerly numbered in separate series. Earlier D106.9: and D106.17:
D106.22:nos	Army Quartermaster School correspondence subcourse, QM (series)

D107　Troop Information and Education Division

D107.1:date   Annual reports. Earlier M104.1:
D107.2:CT   General publications. Earlier M104.2:

D107.7:v.nos   Report to Army (semimonthly). Earlier M104.8:   Later replaced by D101.43:

Judge Advocate General's Office

D108 Judge Advocate General's Department

D108.1:date	Annual reports. Earlier M107.1:
D108.2:CT	General publications. Earlier M107.2:
D108.3:v.nos	Bulletin of Judge Advocate General of Army (quarterly) Earlier M107.3:
D108.5:CT	Laws
D108.5/2:date	Military laws of United States (Army) Earlier W1.8/1:
D108.7:date	Manual for courts martial, Army
D108.8:date	Memorandum of opinions of Judge Advocate General of the Army. Earlier W10.7:-W10.9:
D108.9:nos	Special text of Judge Advocate General's School
D108.9/2:date	Judge Advocate General's School: Commandant's annual report
D108.10:CT	Handbooks, manuals, guides
D108.11:v.nos.&nos.	Army lawyer

D109 Military Academy, West Point

The Military Academy is subordinate to the Department of the Army which was made a military department within the Department of Defense by Public law 216, 81st Congress, approved Aug. 10, 1949.

D109.1:date	Annual reports. Earlier M109.1:
D109.2:CT	General publications. Earlier M109.2:
D109.6:CT	Regulations, rules, and instructions. Earlier M109.6:
D109.6/2:date	Regulations for United States Corps of Cadets prescribed by Commandant of cadets. Earlier M109.6/2:
D109.7:date	Official register of officers and cadets. Earlier M109.11:
D109.8:date	Catalog of information (annual) Earlier M109.2:M59
D109.9:date	Student Conference on United States Affairs (annual) Proc.
D109.10:nos	USMA library bulletin
D109.11:CT	Maps (miscellaneous)

D110   Command and General Staff College, Fort Leavenworth

D110.1:date   Annual reports. Earlier M119.1:

D110.2:CT   General publications. Earlier M119.2:

D110.7:v.nos&nos. Military review (monthly) Earlier M119.7:

D110.7/a:CT   ___ separates

D110.8:nos   Special orders. Earlier W28.6:

D111 Signal Corps

The Signal Corps, Army Department, was made subordinate to the Department of Defense, under provisions of Public law 216, 81st Congress, approved Aug. 10, 1949.

D111.1:date	Annual reports. Earlier W42.1:
D111.2:CT	General publications. Earlier W42.2:
D111.6:CT	Regulations, rules and instructions
D111.7:v.nos	MARS bulletin
D111.8:date	Index of Signal Corps specifications and standards. Proc.
D111.9:nos	Technical memorandums, Signal Corps Engineering Laboratories, Ft. Monmouth, N.J.
D111.9/2:nos	Engineering reports, Signal Corps Engineering Laboratories, Ft. Monmouth, N.J. Proc.
D111.9/3:nos	Technical reports of Army Signal Research and Development Laboratory, Fort Monmouth, N.J.
D111.9/4:nos	AELRDL TR Army Electronics Research and Development Laboratories, Fort Monmouth, New Jersey, Technical report. [later title] Research and development technical report. ECOM (series)
D111.10:nos	[Publications] SIG (nos)
D111.11:CT	Handbooks, manuals, guides
D111.12:nos	U.S. Army Electronic Proving Ground, USAEPG-SIG (series)
D111.13:CT	Bibliographies and lists of publications

D112 National Guard Bureau

The National Guard Bureau is subordinate to the Department of the Army, which was made a military department within the Department of Defense by Public law 216, 81st Congress, approved Aug. 10, 1949.

D112.1:date	Annual reports. Earlier M114.1: Later D12.1:
D112.2:CT	General publications. Earlier M114.2: Later D12.2:
D112.4:dt.&nos	NGB circulars. Earlier M114.4:
D112.6:nos	National Guard regulations. Earlier M114.6: Later D12.6:
D112.6/2:CT	Regulations, rules, and instructions
D112.7:nos	National Guard Bureau manual. Earlier W70.8:
D112.7/2:CT	Jet propulsion manual. Restricted.
D112.8:date	Official National Guard register. Earlier W70.5: Later D12.9:
D112.8/2:date	Air National Guard register. Later D12.9/2:

Established in the Defense Department as a joint bureau of the Department of the Army and the Department of the Air Force by Department of Defense Reorganization act of 1958 (Public law 599) 85th Congress, 2d session, approved August 6, 1958.

D113 Panama Canal

D113.1:date	Annual reports. Earlier M115.1: Later PAC1.1:
D113.2:CT	General publications Earlier M115.2: Later PAC1.2:

Dl13.7:date   Tide tables, Balboa and Cristobal, Canal Zone. Earlier Ml15.7: Later PaCl.7:

Dl13.8:nos   Canal Zone Junior College catalogues. Earlier Ml15.9: Later PaCl.8:

Dl13.9:CT   Panama Railroad Company publications. Later PaCl.9:

Dl13.10:date   Annual report of insurance business transacted in Canal Zone. Earlier Ml15.10: Later PaCl.10:

Sept. 26, 1950. Proclamation 2902.

D114 Historical Division

August 10, 1949 the Department of the Army was made a military department within the Department of Defense.

D114.1:date	Annual reports. Earlier M103.1:
D114.2:CT	General publications. Earlier M103.2:
D114.7:CT	United States Army in World War II. Earlier M103.7:
D114.7/2:nos	United States Army in World War II: Master index, reader's guide
D114.8:	World War I (1917-19) publications. Earlier M103.9:
D114.9:	Armed Forces in Action (series) Earlier M103.8: [Class originally reserved for but never used]
D114.10:date	Order of Battle of United States Land Forces [Class originally reserved for but never used]
D114.10:date	Publications of Office, Chief of Military History
D114.10/2:date	Army historical program, fiscal year
D114.11:v.nos	Army lineage series
D114.12:CT	Handbooks, manuals, guides
D114.13:CT	Posters
D114.14:nos	U.S. Army Military Research Collection, Special bibliography series
D114.14/2:v.nos.&nos.	U.S. Army Military Research Collection, Carlisle Barracks, Pa., Perspectives in military history
D114.15:date	Department of the Army historical summary
D114.16:dt.&nos	Army museum newsletter (irregular)

Dl14.17:CT   Special studies series

D115 Public Information Division   Earlier M118
[made for classified list 7-20-50]

D115.1:date   Annual reports. Earlier M118.1:

D115.2:CT   General publications. Earlier M118.2:

D116 Chemical Corps

D116.1:date	Annual reports
D116.2:CT	General publications
D116.8:date	Index of Chemical Corps specifications. Later title, List of chemical-biological-radiological specifications and standards
D116.9:date	Alphabetical list of CMIC directives. Proc. Admin.
D116.9/2:date	Index to CMLC directives. Admin.
D116.10:nos	Chemical Corps purchase description. Admin.
D116.11:date	Index of Chemical Corps drawings. Official use.
D116.12:date	Proceedings of annual statistical engineering symposium. Proc.
D116.13:nos	Chemical Warfare Laboratories: CWL special publications
D116.14:nos	Engineering Command report, ENCR (series)
D116.15:nos	Army Chemical Research and Development Laboratories: CRDL special publications
D116.15/2:nos	Chemical Research and Development Laboratories: Technical report SRDLR (series)
D116.16:date	Index of instruction manuals for inspection aids (annual)

D117 Transportation, Office of Chief of

D117.1:date   Annual reports. Earlier W109.301:

D117.2:CT   General publications. Earlier W109.302:

D117.7:v.nos/nos   Technical progress reports, research and development. Earlier M120.7:

D117.8:nos   Transportation Research and Development Command: Research technical memorandums. Proc.

D117.8/2:nos   Transportation Research Command, Fort Eustis, Va., TREC technical reports

D117.8/3:nos   Army Transportation Research Command: Interim reports

D117.8/4:nos   USAAMRDL technical notes

D117.8/5:nos   USAMRDL series

D117.9:nos   TC in the current national emergency, Historical report no.

D117.9/2:CT   TC in the current national emergency: The post Korean experience

D117.10:nos   TREC reports

D117.11:nos   Army Transportation Engineering Agency: USATEA reports

D118 Personnel Operations Office

D118.1:date   Annual reports

D118.2:CT   General publications

D118.9:v.nos.&nos. Recruiting & career counseling journal (monthly) Earlier D102.76:

D119 Civil Defense Office

March 31, 1964 the Secretary of Defense assigned civil defense responsibilities delegated to him by Executive order 10952 to the Secretary of the Army.

D119.1:date	Annual report.	Earlier D13.1: Later D14.1:
D119.1/2:date	Annual statistical report.	Earlier D13.1/2: Later D14.1/2:
D119.2:CT	General publications.	Earlier D13.2: Later D14.2:
D119.3/2:nos	Information bulletin.	Earlier D13.3/2: Later D14.3/2:
D119.3/3:CT	FG (series)	
D119.8:CT	Handbooks, manuals, guides.	Earlier D13.8: Later D14.8:
D119.8/2:nos	[Handbook] H (series)	Earlier D13.8/3: Later D14.8/3:
D119.8/3:nos	FG (series)	Earlier D13.8/8: Later D14.8/5:
D119.8/4:pt.nos	Federal civil defense guide.	Earlier D13.8/9:
D119.8/5:nos	Technical memorandums	
D119.8/6:nos	Professional manuals PM (series)	
D119.8/7:nos	Instructor guides.	Earlier D13.8/7: Later D14.8/4:
D119.8/8:nos	Student manuals.	Earlier D13.8/5: Later D14.8/2:
D119.9:nos	Technical reports.	Earlier D13.12: Later D14.9:
D119.10:v.nos.&nos.	CD newspictures.	Earlier D13.17/2:
D119.11:nos	Miscellaneous publications MP (series)	Earlier D13.9: Later D14.10:
D119.12:CT	Addresses.	Earlier D13.14:
D119.13:nos	Leaflets.	Earlier D13.10:

D119.14:nos   Buildings with fallout protection, design case studies (numbered)
               Later D14.16:
D119.15:nos   HS-(series) Later D14.11:

Superseded by the Defense Civil Preparedness Agency, established by the Secretary of Defense, which began operations May 5, 1972.

D120 Provost Marshal General, Office of (Army)

The Provost Marshal General has staff responsibility for the broad functions of protective services, preserving law and order, and of crime prevention applicable Army-wide. [MC August 1969]

D120.1:date	Annual reports
D120.2:CT	General publications
D120.8:CT	Handbooks, manuals, guides

D201   Navy Department

The Navy Department was made a military **department** within the Department of Defense in lieu of its prior status as an executive department by Public law 216, 81st Congress, approved Aug. 10, 1949.

D201.1:date	Annual report. Earlier M201.1:
D201.1/2:date	Financial report, fiscal year, Office of Comptroller. Replaces D212.8:
D201.2:CT	General publications. Earlier M201.2:
D201.5:CT	Navy contract law
D201.5:date	Laws. Earlier M201.10:
D201.6:CT	Regulations, rules, and instructions. Earlier N1.19:
D201.6/2:v.nos	Navy comptroller manual. Supersedes D212.6:Su7/949 and N20.13:Su7/2/946
D201.6/3:	Navy Comptroller manual, advance changes
D201.6/4:	NavCompt instruction nos.
D201.6/5:	NAVCOMP notice
D201.6/6:date	Office equipment handbook. Proc.
D201.6/7:index nos.	Office equipment guide. Proc.
D201.6/8:index nos.	Office equipment news. Proc.
D201.6/9:nos	Navy Property redistribution and disposal regulations
D201.6/10:date	Navy procurement directives. Earlier D201.6:P94
D201.6/10-2:nos	___ supplements
D201.6/11:date	Index to Navy procurement information. Earlier D201.2:P94/3
D201.6/12:CT	Handbooks, manuals, guides. Formerly in D201.6:
D201.6/13:dt.&nos.	Navy current procurement directives, NCPD (series)
D201.6/14:date	Survey of procurement statistics (quarterly)

D201.7:date	Telephone directory. Earlier M201.8:
D201.7/2:date	Naval Material Command telephone directory
D201.8:dt.&nos	Court-martial orders. Earlier M201.9:
D201.9:series nos.	Your navy, from the viewpoint of the Nation's finest artists [lithographic prints, announcement and order form].
D201.10:	[not used]
D201.11:date	Navy regulations. Earlier M201.11:
D201.12:CT	Potomac River Naval Command publications, later title Naval District, Washington, D.C., publications
D201.13:nos	Military standard MIL-STD (Navy) series
D201.14:v. nos.&nos.	Navy management review (monthly)
D201.15:date	United States Antarctic programs, annual report
D201.15/2:CT	Naval Support Force, Antarctica, publications. Earlier D1.32:
D201.15/3:nos	___: Monograph (series)
D201.16:CT	Addresses
D201.17:date	Direction, **guidelines** in public information for commanders and public information officers (monthly)
D201.18:v. nos.&nos.	Civilian manpower management, journal of Navy and civilian personnel management (quarterly) CLASS CANCELLED SEE D204.9:
D201.19:CT	Posters
D201.20:nos	MC reports (numbered) Sponsored by Maury Center for Ocean Science
D201.21:nos	Naval Weapons Laboratory, Dahlgren, Va.: NWL technical report TR- (series) Earlier D215.14:
D201.21/2:nos	Naval Weapons Laboratory, Dahlgren, Va.: NWL administrative report AR- (series)
D201.22:nos	NADC - Naval Air Development Center, NADC-CS (series)
D201.23:nos	Naval Weapons Center, China Lake, Calif.:NWC technical publication TP (series)

D201.24:date   NAVNEWS, A NAVYNEWS service

D201.25:date   Navy wifeline (quarterly)

Naval Air Systems Command, May 1, 1966-
D202   Aeronautics Bureau

The Aeronautics Bureau is subordinate to the Department of the Navy, which was made a military department within the Department of Defense, in lieu of its prior status as an executive department within the National Military Establishment by Public law 216, 91st Congress, approved Aug. 10, 1949.

D202.1:date	Annual reports. Earlier M208.1:
D202.2:CT	General publications. Earlier M208.2:
D202.6:CT	Regulations, rules, and instructions. Earlier M208.6:
D202.6/2:date	Bureau of Aeronautics manual. Earlier N28.7:
D202.6/3:	BUAER instructions. Administrative.
D202.6/4:	BUAER instruction NAVAER. Admin.
D202.6/5:	BUAER notice. Admin.
D202.6/6:	BUAER notice NAVAER. Admin.
D202.6/7:CT	Handbooks, manuals, guides. Earlier in D202.6:
D202.6/8:nos	[Language guides] PT- (series)
D202.7:dt. &nos	Technical notes. Earlier M208.10:
D202.8:dt. &nos	Technical orders. Earlier M208.7:
D202.9:nos	Naval aviation news. Changed from D207.7: Later D217.8:
D202.9/2:nos	Naval aviation news (monthly) Restricted. Changed from D207.7/2:
D202.10:dt. &nos	Flight safety bulletins. Proc. Earlier M207.8:
D202.11:	Military standard (designs) Desig. MS-nos
D202.12:letter	Aviation circular letter Earlier M208.8:
D202.13:v.nos	Approach, U.S. Naval aviation safety review (monthly) Later D217.10:

D202.14:nos   Naval Air Development Center, Johnsville, Pa., Aeronautical Electronic and Electrical Laboratory, report NADC-EL (series) Later D217.19:

D202.15:CT   Charts and posters

D202.16:nos   Buaer reports

Abolished by act approved August 18, 1959 (73 Stat. 395) and functions transferred with those of Bureau of Ordnance to the Bureau of Naval Weapons, effective not later than July 1, 1960.
The Naval Air Systems Command was established May 1, 1966 in the reorganization of the Navy Department. The Naval Weapons Bureau was disestablished on the same date and some of its field activities and employees assigned to the Naval Air Systems Command.

D202.17:date   Employment opportunities. Earlier D217.9:

D202.18:nos   What's happening in the personnel field   Earlier D217.13:

D202.19:date   Mech (quarterly)   Earlier D202.2:M46/967

D202.20:v.nos.&nos. Fathom (quarterly)

Naval Oceanographic Office (July 10, 1962 (76 Stat. 154)

D 203   Hydrographic Office

The Hydrographic Office is subordinate to the Department of the Navy, which was made a military department within the Department of Defense, in lieu of its prior status as an executive department within the National Military Establishment by Public law 216, 91st Congress, approved Aug. 10, 1949.

D203.1:date	Annual reports. Earlier M202.1:
D203.2:CT	General publications. Earlier M202.2:
D203.3:nos	Hydrographic bulletins (weekly) Earlier M202.3:
D203.3/2:nos	Bi-weekly information bulletin
D203.3/3:nos	The bulletin. Admin.
D203.4:nos	Circulars. Earlier M202.4:
D203.7:dt. &nos	Notice to aviators (biweekly) Earlier M202.7:
D203.8:dt. &nos	Notice to mariners (weekly) Earlier M202.8:, D203.10: Later D5.315:
D203.8/2:dt. &nos	Notice to mariners (semimonthly) Restricted. Earlier M202.8/2:
D203.8/3:date	Special notice to mariners
D203.9:dt. &nos	Notice to mariners relating to Great Lakes and tributary waters west of Montreal (weekly) Proc. Earlier M202.9: Later T47.20:
D203.9/2:nos	Local hydrographic memorandum for aviators
D203.10:dt. &nos	Notice to mariners, North American-Caribbean edition (weekly) Earlier M202.10: Later D203.8:
D203.11:dt. &nos	Memorandum for aviators. Proc. Earlier M202.11:
D203.12:date	Tide, moon and sun calendar, Baltimore, Md. (monthly) Proc.Earlier M202.12:
D203.13:date	Tide calendar for Hampton Roads (Sewalls Pt.) Va. (monthly) Earlier M202.13:
D203.14:date	Tide calendar, Savannah, Ga.; Monthly. Proc. Earlier M202.14:
D203.14/2:date	Sun and moon tables for Cleveland, Ohio. (monthly) Proc.
D203.15:date	Pilot chart of Central American waters; no. 3500 (monthly) Earlier M202.15:

D203.16:date	Pilot chart of Indian Ocean; no. 2603 (monthly) Earlier M202.16:
D203.17:date	Pilot chart of north Atlantic Ocean; no.1400 (monthly) Earlier M202.17:
D203.18:date	Pilot chart of south Atlantic Ocean; no. 2600 (quarterly) Earlier M202.18:
D203.19:date	Pilot chart of north Pacific Ocean; no.1401 (monthly) Earlier M202.19:
D203.20:date	Pilot chart of south Pacific Ocean; no. 2601 (quarterly) Earlier M202.20:
D203.21:nos	Maps and charts. Earlier M202.21:
D203.21/2:date	Chart correction list. Earlier D203.8:date/corr list
D203.21/3:date	Hydrographic office chart, correction list, arranged according to consecutive numbers
D203.22:nos	Hydrographic office publications (numbered) Earlier M202.23: Later D5.317:
D203.22/2:date & serial nos.	Monthly corrections affecting portfolio chart list and Index-catalog of nautical charts and publications. Restricted.
D203.22/3:nos	Special publications
D203.23:nos.	Hydro notice
D203.24:nos	National Oceanographic Data Center publications (numbered)
D203.24/2:nos	National Oceanographic Data Center newsletter. Later C55.290:
D203.24/3:CT	National Oceanographic Data Center publications (unnumbered) Later C55.292:
D203.24/4:date	National Oceanographic Data Center announcements
D203.24/5:date	National Oceanographic Data Center: List of fully processed oceanographic cruises. Earlier D203.24/3:C88
D203.24/6:v.nos.&nos.	NODC quarterly accessions
D203.25:nos	Translations
D203.26:nos	Technical report TR-
D203.26/2:nos	Informal reports
D203.27:CT	Posters
D203.28:v.nos	Naval oceanographic newsletter

D203.29:v.nos.&nos.   Monthly summary, the Gulf Stream   Later C55.123:

D203.29/2:nos   ___, supplements

D203.30:nos   News releases

D203.31:v.nos   Global ocean floor analysis and research data series

D203.32:date   National Oceanographic Instrumentation Center: Tests in progress sheet (quarterly)   Later C55.70:

D203.32/2:nos   National Oceanographic Instrumentation Center: Instrument fact sheet, IFS- (series)   Later C55.71:

D203.32/3:letters-nos ___ Technical bulletin   Later C55.73:

Civilian Manpower Management Office (June 22, 1966-)

D204 Industrial Relations Office

Activated Sept. 14, 1945.

D204.1:date   Annual reports. Earlier M204.1:

D204.2:CT   General publications. Earlier M204.2:

D204.6:CT   Regulations, rules, and instructions

D204.6/2:CT   Handbooks, manuals, guides

D204.7:v.nos   Safety review (monthly) Earlier M204.7:

D204.8:v.nos   Personnel of Naval Shore Establishment (quarterly) Restricted. Earlier M204.8:

D204.9:v.nos.&nos. Civilian manpower management, journal of Navy and civil **personnel management** (quarterly)

514

D205 Judge Advocate General

August 10, 1949, Public law 216, 81st Congress Navy Department is in the Department of Defense.

D205.1:date	Annual reports. Earlier M214.1:
D205.2:CT	General publications. Earlier M214.2:
D205.6:CT	Regulations, rules, and instructions.
D205.6/2:CT	Handbooks, manuals, guides
D205.7:date	JAG journal (monthly) Earlier M214.7:
D205.8:date	Laws relating to Navy, annotated. Earlier M214.8:
D205.9:date	Federal income tax information. Earlier D202.2:In2

D206 Medicine and Surgery Bureau

August 10, 1949, Public law 216, 81st Congress, Navy Department is in the Department of Defense.

D206.1:date	Annual reports. Earlier M203.1:
D206.2:CT	General publications. Earlier M203.2:
D206.3:v.nos	Naval medical bulletin (bimonthly) Earlier M203.3: Replaced by D1.11:
D206.3/a:CT	___ separates
D206.6:CT	Regulations, rules, and instructions. Earlier M203.6:
D206.6/2:	BUMED instructions. Admin.
D206.6/3:CT	Handbooks, manuals, guides. Formerly in D206.6:
D206.7:v.nos	Medical news letter (biweekly) Proc. Earlier M203.7:
D206.8:chap.nos	Manual of Medical Department, Navy. Earlier M203.12:
D206.8/2:date	Manual of Medical Department, Navy. (complete volume)
D206.9:project nos. &rp.nos.	Naval Medical Institute reports. Earlier M203.8:
D206.10:nos	Medical Research Laboratory report. Proc. Earlier M203.13:
D206.10/2:nos	U.S. Naval Submarine Medical Center, Submarine Base, Groton, Conn: Memorandum reports
D206.10/3:nos	U.S. Naval Submarine Medical Center: Special reports
D206.11:date	Medical statistics, U.S. Navy. Earlier editions entitled, Statistics of diseases and injuries in Navy. Earlier M203.10:
D206.12:nos	History of Medical Department of Navy in World War II.
D206.12/2:date	History of Medical Department of United States Navy
D206.13:nos	BUMED circular letter
D206.14:nos	Naval Medical Research Institute: Lecture and review series. Proc.

D206.15:v.nos.&nos.	Statistics of Navy medicine, monthly highlights of trends and facts.
D206.16:CT	Naval School of Aviation Medicine. Research reports.
D206.17:date	Summaries of research reported on during calendar year. Earlier D206.2:R31
D206.18:nos	Naval Aerospace Medical Institute, NAMI (series)
D206.19:v.nos.&nos.	Naval Medical Field Research Laboratory, Camp Lejeune, N.C. [reports]
D206.20:CT	Bibliographies and lists of publications
D206.21:nos	Neuropsychiatric Research Unit, San Diego, Calif.: Reports
D206.21/2:date	Neuropsychiatric Research Unit, San Diego, Calif. Abstracts of completed research.

D207 Naval Operations Office

August 10, 1949, Public law 216, 81st Congress, Navy Department is in the Department of Defense.

D207.1:date   Annual reports. Earlier M207.1:

D207.2:CT   General publications. Earlier M207.2:

D207.6:CT   Regulations, rules, and instructions. Earlier M207.6:

D207.6/2:CT   Handbooks, manuals, guides

D207.6/3:letters-nos   NATOPS manual

D207.7:nos   Naval aviation news (monthlh) Earlier M207.7: Changed to D202.9:

D207.7/2:nos   Naval aviation news (monthly) Restricted. Earlier M207.7/2: Changed to D202.9/2:

D207.8:   O & NAV instructions. Proc. Admin.

D207.9:nos   Naval warfare publications. Desig. NWP-nos

D207.10:v.nos   Dictionary of American naval fighting ships

D207.10/2:CT   Historical publications

D207.11:CT   Bibliographies and lists of publications

D207.12:v.nos   Naval documents of the American revolution

D207.13:date   Shipbuilding and conversion program (annual) Earlier D207.2:Sh6/2

D207.14:CT   Excerpts from slide presentations by Office of Chief of Naval Operations

D207.15:v.nos.&nos.   Lifeline, the Naval safety journal (bimonthly) Issued by Naval Safety Center, Norfolk, Va.

D207.16:CT   Posters

D207.17:nos All hands (monthly) Earlier D208.3:

D207.18:v.nos.&nos. Surface warfare (bimonthly)

D207.101 Naval Technical Training Command

The Naval Technical Training Command was established Aug. 1, 1971, and operates under the direction of Chief of Naval Operations.

D207.101:date   Annual report

D207.102:CT   General publications

D207.108:CT   Handbooks, manuals, guides

D207.109:nos   Modular individualized learning for electronics

Naval Education and Training Command
D207.200 Naval Training Command

The Naval Training Command was established July 1, 1972, and operates under the direction of Chief of Naval Operations.

D207.201:date	Annual reports
D207.202:CT	General publications
D207.208:CT	Handbooks, manuals, guides
D207.208/2:CT	Rate training manuals. Earlier D208.11/2: , D208.11:
D207.208/3:CT	Personnel qualification standards
D207.208/4:CT	Navy training text material. Earlier D208.11/2:
D207.209:date	Campus, Navy education and training (monthly) Earlier D208.7:

D208   Naval Personnel Bureau

The Naval Personnel Bureau is subordinate to the Department of the Navy, which was made a military department within the Department of Defense, in lieu of its prior status as an executive department within the National Military Establishment by PL 81-216, approved August 10, 1949.

D208.1:date	Annual reports. Earlier M206.1:
D208.2:CT	General publications. Earlier M206.2:
D208.3:nos	All hands, Bureau of Naval Personnel information bulletin (monthly) Earlier M206.3: Later D207.17:
D208.3/a:CT	___ separates
D208.3/2:date	Navy chaplains bulletin (quarterly)
D208.6:CT	Regulations, rules, and instructions. Earlier M206.6:
D208.6/2:date	Bureau of naval personnel manual. Admin.
D208.6/3:CT	Handbooks, manuals, buides. Earlier in D208.6:
D208.7:nos	U.S. naval training bulletin (monthly) Earlier M206.7: Later D207.209:
D208.8:nos	Sea clipper (weekly) Earlier M206.8:
D208.9:CT	Instructor's training aids guide
D208.10:date	Naval reservist (monthly) Earlier M206.9:
D208.11:CT	Navy training courses. Earlier N17.25: Later D207.208/2:
D208.11/2:CT	Navy training text material. Later D207.208/2:, D207.208/4:
D208.11/3:CT	Navy life, reading and writing for success in the Navy
D208.12:date	Register of commissioned and warrant officers of United States Navy and Marine Corps. Earlier M206.10:
D208.12/2:date	Register of commissioned and warrant officers of Naval Reserve. Earlier M206.2:R 26/949, N17.38:, and N25.6:
D208.12/3:date	___, regular and reserve, of the Navy and Marine Corps

D208.13:pt.nos	Case instruction, cases. Earlier N17.31:
D208.14:nos	U.S. Naval Postgraduate School. Technical reports
D208.14/2:nos	___ Research papers
D208.14/3:nos	___ Reprints
D208.14/4:date	___ Catalogue
D208.14/5:CT	___ Theses
D208.14/6:CT	___ Publications (unnumbered)
D208.15:CT	Bibliographies and lists of publications
D208.16:v.nos.&nos.	Navy recruiter
D208.17:v.nos.&nos.	Naval history, supplements. Admin.
D208.18:nos	Technical bulletins
D208.19:date	Link, enlisted personnel distribution bulletin (quarterly)
D208.20:CT	Final environmental impact statement

D208.100   Naval Academy

August 10, 1949, Public law 216, 81st Congress, Navy Department is in the Department of Defense.

D208.101:date   Report of board of visitors to Naval Academy (annual)   Earlier M206.101:

D208.102:CT   General publications. Earlier M206.102:

D208.107:date   Annual register of Naval Academy. Earlier M206.107:

D208.108:date   Regulations governing admission of candidates into Naval Academy as midshipmen and sample examination questions (annual) Earlier M206.108:

D208.109:date   Catalogue of information. Earlier D208.2:In3/date

D208.110:date   United States Naval Academy, superintendent's statement to Board of Visitors (annual)

D208.111:date   Trident scholars (annual)

D208.200   Naval War College, Newport

August 10, 1949, Public law 216, 81st Congress, Navy Department is in the Department of Defense.

D208.201:date   Annual reports.   Earlier M206.201:

D208.202:CT   General publications.   Earlier M206.202:

D208.207:v.nos   International law documents.   Earlier M206.207:

D208.207/2:   ___ Indexes

D208.209:date   Naval War College Review (monthly)

D208.210:v.nos   Historical monograph series

Naval Facilities Engineering Command (May 1966-)

D209   Yards and Docks Bureau

August 10, 1949, Public law 216, 81st Congress, Navy Department is in the Department of Defense.

D209.1:date	Annual reports. Earlier M205.1:
D209.1/2:date	Progress report, fiscal year
D209.2:CT	General publications. Earlier M205.2:
D209.7:v.nos	U.S. Navy Civil Engineer Corps bulletin (monthly) Earlier M205.7:
D209.8:nos	Technical digest (monthly) Earlier M205.8: Later combined with D209.7: to form D209.13:
D209.9:date	Register of Civil Engineer Corps commissioned and warrant officers of United States Navy and Naval Reserve on active duty (quarterly) Proc.
D209.10:les-nos	Technical publications NAVDOCKS TP (series) Proc.
D209.11:nos.&le	Specifications. Earlier N21.10:
D209.12:le-nos	U.S. Naval Civil Engineering Research and Evaluation Laboratory, Port Hueneme, Calif., Technical Memorandums
D209.12/2:nos	___ Technical reports.
D209.12/3:nos	___ Technical notes
D209.13:v.nos.&nos.	Navy civil engineer (monthly)
D209.13/a:CT	___ separates
D209.14:CT	Handbooks, manuals, guides
D209.14/2:nos	Design manuals
D209.15:CT	Index of Bureau of Yards and Docks publications
D209.16:nos	NAVFAC Technical Training Center: NTTC courses

D210 Naval Research Office

August 10, 1949, Public law 216, 81st Congress, Navy Department is in the Department of Defense.

D210.1:date	Annual reports. Earlier M216.1:
D210.2:CT	General publications. Earlier M216.2:
D210.5:1e-nos	ONR symposium reports
D210.6:CT	Regulations, rules, and instructions
D210.6/2:CT	Handbooks, manuals, guides
D210.7:date	Scientific personnel bulletin (annual)
D210.8:nos	NRL reports (Naval Research Laboratory) Earlier M216.7:
D210.8/2:nos	NRL memorandum report (series) Proc.
D210.8/3:nos	Technical reports
D210.8/3-2:nos	ONR technical report RLT (series)
D210.9:dt.&nos	NRL reprints
D210.10:nos	Daily upper air bulletin Earlier C30.57:
D210.11:date	Research reviews (monthly)
D210.11/a:CT	___ separates
D210.12:v.nos	Naval research logistics quarterly
D210.12/a:CT	___ separates
D210.13:nos	Bibliographies. Proc.
D210.13/2:CT	Bibliographies and lists of publications
D210.14:nos	Special Devices Center, Port Washington, N.Y., technical report SPECDEVCEN (series) Proc. Naval Training Device Center-NAVTRADEVCEN (series)
D210.14/2:CT	___ publications

D210.14/3:nos	Human engineering report
D210.14/4:v.nos.&nos.	Training device developments
D210.14/5:device nos.	Survival plant recognition cards. Issued by Naval Training Device Center.
D210.15:le-nos	ONR symposium report, ACR - series
D210.16:nos	Technical reports. Naval Research Office, London. Issued by U.S. Embassy, London
D210.16/2:nos	European scientific notes. Issued by U.S. Embassy, London
D210.17:date	Report of NRL Progress (monthly)
D210.17/2:date	Annual report, Naval Research Laboratory
D210.18:v.nos.&nos.	Science education program (semiannual)
D210.19:date	Symposium on naval hydrodynamics
D210.20:date	Naval research task summary (annual)
D210.21:date	Naval Research Laboratory quarterly on nuclear science and technology progress reports. Limited distribution
D210.22:nos	Underwater Sound Reference Laboratory: USRL research reports
D210.23:date	Direct energy conversion literature abstracts. Earlier title Thermoelectricity abstracts. Earlier D210.2:En2/2
D210.24:v.nos.&nos.	Digital computer newsletter
D210.25:nos	Test and evaluation reports
D210.26:dt/nos	Navy scientific and technical information program, newsletter

Naval Ship Systems Command, May 1, 1966-

    D 211   Ships Bureau

August 10, 1949, Public law 216, 81st Congress, Navy Department is the Department of Defense.

D211.1:date	Annual reports. Earlier M210.1:
D211.2:CT	General publications. Earlier M210.2:
D211.3:nos	Bulletin of information (quarterly) Earlier M210.3:
D211.3/2:v.nos.&nos.	Bulletin. Admin.
D211.6:CT	Regulations, rules, and instructions
D211.6/2:CT	Handbooks, manuals, guides. Formerly in D211.6:
D211.7:chap.nos	Bureau of Ships manual. Earlier M210.8: Later D211.7/3:
D211.7/2:nos	___ changes. Earlier M210.8/2:
D211.7/3:nos./date	Bureau of Ships technical manual. Formerly D211.7:
D211.8:v.nos.&nos.	Bureau of Ships journal (monthly) Later title, Naval ship systems command technical news
D211.8/a:CT	___ separates
D211.9:nos	David W. Taylor Model Basin reports. Later title, Naval Ship Research and Development Center reports. Center formed in March 1967 by merging the David W. Taylor Model Basin at Carderock, Md. and the Marine Engineering Lab at Annapolis, Md.
D211.9/2:nos	David W. Taylor Model Basin report R - (series)
D211.9/3:nos	David W. Taylor Model Basin Aero reports
D211.9/4:nos	David Taylor Model Basin: Translations
D211.10:nos	Industrial notes
D211.11:nos	Navy Electronics Laboratory reports. Proc.
D211.11/2:CT	Navy Electronics Lab., San Diego, Calif., publications (misc.)

D211.12:nos	Pamphlet NBS (series) NBS- Navy Bureau of Ships
D211.13:nos	U.S. Naval Radiological Defense Laboratory, Research and Development report USNRDL (series) Proc.
D211.13/2:nos	U.S. Naval Radiological Defense Laboratory: Research and Development technical report, USNRDL-TR (series)
D211.13/3:nos	U.S. Naval Radiological Defense Laboratory: Reviews and lectures R & L (series)
D211.13/4:nos	U.S. Naval Radiological Defense Laboratory: Evaluation report ER (series)
D211.14:nos	Bureau of Ships translations
D211.15:nos	Naval Engineering Experiment Station, Annapolis, Md., report E.E.S. (series)
D211.16:nos	Rubber Laboratory, Mare Island Naval Shipyard, Vallejo, Calif., reports. Proc.
D211.17:nos	Boston Naval Shipyard: Materials Laboratory, Evaluation reports
D211.18:CT	New York Naval Shipyard, Brooklyn, N.Y., Publications
D211.19:nos	Materials Laboratories, Puget Sound Naval Shipyard: Evaluation reports
D211.20:date	Directory
D211.21:nos	U.S. Navy Underwater Sound Laboratory, New London, Conn., USL reports
D211.22:v.nos.&nos.	Faceplate (quarterly)
D211.23:CT	Naval Torpedo Station, Keyport, Washington: Publications

Naval Supply System Command, May 1, 1966-

D 212   Supplies and Accounts Bureau

The Bureau of Supplies and Accounts is subordinate to the Department of the Navy, which was made a military department within the Department of Defense in lieu of its prior status as an executive department within the National Military Establishment, by Public law 216, 81st Congress, approved August 10, 1949.

D212.1:date	Annual reports. Earlier M213.1:
D212.2:CT	General publications. Earlier M213.2:
D212.6:CT	Regulations, rules, and instructions. Earlier M213.6:
D212.6/2:nos	Instruction memorandum
D212.6/3:CT	Handbooks, manuals, guides. Earlier in D212.6:
D212.7:dt. &pt. nos.	Index of specifications used by Navy Department. Earlier M213.9:
D212.8:date	Naval expenditures. Earlier M213.10: Replaced by D201.1/2:
D212.9:nos	Navy Department specifications. Earlier M213.7:
D212.10:date	Index of specifications and standards used by Department of the Navy, military index, v.3 (semiannual) Later D7.14:
D212.10/2:date	___ v.3, specifications cancelled or superseded (annual) Proc.
D212.11:nos	Instruction memorandum. Earlier N20.13:2
D212.11/2:nos	Afloat accounting instruction memorandum
D212.11/3:nos	BUSANDAINST [Bureau of Supplies and Accounts instructions.) Official use
D212.12:nos	Research and Development Division reports
D212.13:nos	BUSANDA notice. Admin.
D212.14:v. nos. &nos.	Newsletter, magazine of Navy Supply Corps. Admin.
D212.15:CT	Bibliographies and lists of publications

531

D213 Naval Observatory

The Naval Observatory is subordinate to the Department of the Navy, which was made a military department within the Department of Defense, by Public law 216, 81st Congress, approved Aug. 10, 1949.

D213.1:date	Annual reports. Earlier M212.1:
D213.2:CT	General publications. Earlier M212.2:
D213.4:nos	Circulars. Proc.
D213.7:date	American air almanac. Earlier M212.7:
D213.8:date	American ephemeris and nautical almanac. Earlier M212.8:
D213.8/2:date	Improved lunar ephemeris
D213.8/3:date	Astronomical phenomena (annual) Earlier D213.2:As8
D213.9:v.nos.&pt.nos.	Astronomical papers prepared for use of American ephemeris and nautical almanac. Earlier N11.7:
D213.10:v.nos	Publications of Naval Observatory, 2d series. Earlier M212.10:
D213.11:date	American nautical almanac. Earlier M212.9:
D213.12:nos	Ephemeris of sun, polaris, and other selected stars. Earlier I53.8:

D214 Marine Corps

August 10, 1949, Public law 216, 81st Congress, Navy Department is in the Department of Defense

D214.1:date	Annual reports. Earlier M201.9:
D214.2:CT	General publications. Earlier M209.2:
D214.6:CT	Regulations, rules, and instructions
D214.7:nos	Manuscript register series (Marine Corps Museum, Quantico, Va.)
D214.9:date	Marine Corps manual. Earlier M209.9:
D214.9/2:CT	Miscellaneous manuals
D214.9/3:1e/nos	Technical manual TM (series)
D214.9/4:nos	Fleet Marine Force manuals FMFM (series)
D214.10:dt.&nos	Reserve marine (monthly)
D214.11:date	Combined lineal list of officers on active duty in Marine Corps (annual) Earlier D214.2:Of3/4
D214.11/2:date	Lineal list of commissioned and warrant officers of Marine Corps Reserve. Earlier D214.2:Of3/3
D214.12:CT	[Regimental and squadron histories]
D214.13:CT	Historical publications. Includes Marine Corps monographs
D214.14:nos	Marine Corps historical reference series
D214.14/2:CT	Marine Corps historical reference pamphlets
D214.15:nos	Marine Corps historical bibliographies
D214.16:CT	Lithographs
D214.16/2:letters	Marine Corps photographs set

D214.17:nos   Museum manuscript register series

D214.18:v.nos./nos. College marine (monthly during school year. Admin.)

D214.9:nos   Marine Corps papers series

D214.20:v.nos/nos Fortudine, newsletter of Marine Corps Historical Program

D214.21:v.nos./nos Marine Corps Gazette

D214.22:date   Food service information bulletin (irregular)

D215 Ordnance Bureau

August 10, 1949, Public law 216, 81st Congress, Navy Department is in the Department of Defense.

D215.1:date	Annual reports. Earlier M211.1:
D215.2:CT	General publications. Earlier M211.2:
D215.6:CT	Regulations, rules, and instructions. Earlier M211.6:
D215.6/2:CT	Handbooks, manuals, guides
D215.7:nos	NavOrd reports. Later D217.18:
D215.8:date	Employment opportunities (bimonthly) Proc. Later D217.9:
D215.9:nos	Ordnance pamphlets. Earlier N18.7: Later D217.2:
D215.10:nos	Technical report NGF (series) Engineering Research and Evaluation Division, Engineering Department, Naval Gun Factory.)
D215.11:nos	U.S. Naval Ordnance Test Station, Inyokern, Technical memorandums. Proc.
D215.12:CT	U.S. Naval Propellant Plant publications. Later D217.15:
D215.13:nos	Naval Ordnance Laboratory, Corona, Calif.: Reports. Later D217.20:
D215.14:nos	Naval Weapons Lab., Dahlgren, Va., NWL technical report TR.

Abolished by act of August 18, 1959 (73 Stat. 395) and functions transferred with those of Bureau of Aeronautics to the Bureau of Naval Weapons, effective not later than July 1, 1960.

Naval Ordnance Systems Command

The Naval Ordnance Systems Command was established May 1, 1966 in the reorganization of the Navy Department.

D215.14:nos	NWL technical report TR -(series) Earlier D217.17:

Military Sealift Command

D216 Military Sea Transportation Service

Established on October 1, 1949.

D216.1:date   Annual reports

D216.2:CT   General publications

D216.6:CT   Regulations, rules, and instructions

D216.8:v.nos.&nos. Sealift magazine (monthly) Formerly Military Sea Transportation magazine

D216.9:date/pt.nos.&nos. Financial aid statistical report

Air, Electronic, and Ordnance Systems Commands, (May 1966-)
D 217   Naval Weapons Bureau

The Bureau of Naval Weapons was established by Public law 174, 86th Congress, 1st session, approved Aug. 18, 1959. The Bureaus of Aeronautics and Ordnance abolished on or before July 1, 1960 and their functions transferred to the Bureau of Naval Weapons. Abolished by Department of Defense Reorg. order of Mar. 9, 1966, effective May 1, 1966 and functions transferred to Secretary of the Navy (31 F.R. 7188). Air, Electronic, and Ordnance Systems Command.

D217.1:date	Annual reports
D217.2:CT	General publications
D217.4/2:nos	Engineering circulars
D217.6/2:	[Bureau of Naval weapons instructions] BUWEPSINST (series)
D217.8:date	Naval aviation news (monthly) Earlier D202.9:
D217.9:date	Employment opportunities (bimonthly) Earlier D215.8: Later D202.17:
D217.10:v.nos. &nos.	Approach, Naval aviation safety review (monthly) Earlier D202.13:
D217.10/a:CT	___ separates
D217.11:nos	U.S. Naval Avionics Facility, Indianapolis, Ind., NAFI-TP (series)
D217.12:nos	Ordnance pamphlets, OP (series) Earlier D215.9:
D217.13:nos	What's happening in the personnel field. Later D202.18:
D217.14:CT	Handbooks, manuals, guides
D217.15:CT	U.S. Naval Propellant Plant, publications Earlier D215.12:
D217.16:1e-nos	Standards Laboratory cross-check procedure, Department of Navy, BUWEPS-BUSHIPS calibration program
D217.16/2:1e-nos	Standards Laboratory Instrument calibration procedure, Department of Navy, BUWEPS-BUSHIPS calibration program
D217.16/2-2:date	Calibration procedure change notice book

D217.16/3:le-nos	Standards Laboratory measurements system operation procedure, Department of Navy, BUWEPS-BUSHIPS calibration program.
D217.16/4:le-nos	Technical manuals, Department of Navy, BUWEPS-BUSHIPS calibration program.
D217.16/4-2:le-nos	Technical manual, Navy Calibration program, measurement systems operation procedure
D217.16/5:le-nos	Fabrication instructions, Department of Navy, BUWEPS-BUSHIPS calibration program.
D217.16/6:nos	Modification instructions
D217.16/7:le-nos	Standards Laboratory instrument calibration technique
D217.16/8:nos	Technical manual: Cross-check procedure
D217.17:nos	Naval Weapons Laboratory, NWL reports Later D215.14:
D217.17/2:nos	Naval Weapons Laboratory, Dahlgren, Va.: Technical memorandums
D217.18:nos	NavWeps reports. Formerly NavOrd reports, D215.7:
D217.19:nos	U.S. Naval Air Development Center, Johnsville, Pa., Aeronautical Electronic and Electrical Laboratory, report NADC-EL (series) Earlier D202.14:
D217.20:nos	Naval Ordnance Laboratory, Corona, Calif., NOLC reports. Earlier D215.13:
D217.21:nos	Naval Air Material Center, Philadelphia, Pa., Aeronautical Engine Laboratory, NAMC-AEL (series)
D217.22:dt.-nos	United States Naval Ordnance Laboratory, White Oak, Md., Technical reports NOLTR (series)
D217.22/2:nos	___ News for release
D217.23:nos	Naval Ordnance Test Station, China Lake, Calif.: Technical publications NOTS TP (series)
D217.24:	Daylighter. Issued by U.S. Navy Weather Research Facility, Naval Air Station, Norfolk, Va.
D217.25:date	Bureau of Naval Weapons directory, organizational listing and correspondence designations
D217.26:nos	Naval Missile Center: NMC-MP (series)

D217.26/2:nos	Pacific Missile Range, Point Mugu, Calif.: Technical memorandum PMR-TR (series)
D217.26/3:nos	Pacific Missile Range, Point Mugu, Calif.; Technical report PMR-TR (series)
D217.27:nos	Naval Air Test Center, Patuxent River, Md.: Technical reports

The Naval Weapons Bureau was disestablished May 1, 1966.

D218 Oceanographer of Navy, Office of

The Office of the Oceanographer of the Navy was recently established by instructions from the Secretary of the Navy and the Chief of Naval Operations. [MC September 1967]

D218.1:date   Annual report

D218.2:CT   General Publications

D218.9:nos   Pamphlets. (numbered) Earlier PrEx12.9:

Naval Electronic Systems Command
D 219   Electronic Systems Command

The Electronic Systems Command was established May 1, 1966, in the reorganization of the Navy Department.

D219.1:date   Annual report

D219.2:CT   General publications

D219.8:CT   Handbooks, manuals, guides.

D220 Naval Weather Service Command

Under the command of the Chief of Naval Operations, the Commander, Naval Weather Service Command insures the fulfilment of Department of the Navy meteorological requirements and Department of Defense requirements for oceanographic analyses/forecasts, and provides technical guidance in meteorological matters throughout the naval service.

D220.1:date	Annual reports
D220.2:CT	General publications
D220.8:CT	Handbooks, manuals, guides
D220.9:date	Project Stormfury annual report
D220.10:CT	Summary of synoptic meteorological observations
D220.11:date	Annual typhoon report. Issued by Fleet Weather Central/Joint Typhoon Warning Center.

D301 Air Force Department

The Department of the Air Force was made a military Department within the Department of Defense in lieu of its prior status as an executive department, by Public law 216, 81st Congress, approved Aug. 10, 1949.

D301.1:date	Annual reports. Earlier M301.1:
D301.2:CT	General publications. Earlier M301.2:
D301.3:dt.&nos	Air Force bulletins. Proc.
D301.6:nos	AFR regulations. Proc. and printed. Earlier M301.6:
D301.6/2:CT	Regulations, rules and instructions. Earlier M301.6:
D301.6/3:nos	MATS regulations
D301.6/4:date	Air Force procurement instructions. Earlier D301.6/2: Superseded by D1.13/2-3:
D301.6/5:CT	Handbooks, manuals (unnumbered), guides
D301.6/6:nos	Civil Air Patrol regulations. Admin.
D301.7:nos	Air Force manual. Earlier M301.18:
D301.7/2:nos	AFTRC manuals
D301.7/3:nos	ConAC manuals
D301.7/4:nos	Civil Air Patrol manual CAPM (series)
D301.7/5:nos	AACS manuals
D301.7/6:nos	MATS manual MM (series)
D301.7/7:nos	ATRC manual
D301.8:date	Air Reserve Forces review (monthly)
D301.9:date	United States Air Force radio facility charts, Europe, Africa, Middle East. Proc. Earlier M301.7: Later title, [United States Air Force and Navy] flight information publication, enroute-low altitude (RFC), Europe (new title)

D301.9/2:v.nos. &nos. Military aviation notices (weekly) Proc. Earlier M301.17/2:

D301.9/3:date Special notices, supplement to Radio facility charts and in-flight data, Europe (monthly) Proc.

D301.9/4:date Flight information publication: Enroute high altitude, Europe (monthly) Later title... Europe and N.Africa.

D301.9/5:v.nos. &nos. Military aviation notices, corrections to FLIP enroute Europe and North Africa.

D301.10:date United States Air Force radio facility charts, Caribbean and South America area (bimonthly) Proc. Later title [U.S.Air Force and Navy] flight information publication, enroute-low altitude, Caribbean and South America. Earlier M301.19:

D301.10/2:nos Military aviation notices, corrections to FLIP publications, Caribbean and South America. Earlier M301.19:

D301.11:date United States Air Force, United States Navy radio facility charts, North Atlantic area. Proc. Earlier M301.15: Later title adds .. and East Canada. Replaced by D301.13/3:

D301.11/2:v.nos Military aviation notices, North Atlantic and East Canada. Proc.

D301.12:date United States Air Force and United States Navy radio facility charts, central Pacific-Far East (monthly) Proc. Earlier M301.16: Later title, USAF/USN flight information publication, enroute-low altitude Pacific and Southeast Asia.

D301.12/2:dt. &nos. Military aviation notices, Pacific. Proc. Later title, Military aviation notices, corrections to flight information publications, Enroute, Pacific and Southeast Asia.

D301.12/3:date Flight information publication: Terminal, low altitude, Pacific and Southeast Asia (monthly)

D301.12/4:date ___ Terminal, high altitude, Pacific and Southeast Asia (monthly)

D301.13:date United States Air Force, United States Navy and Royal Canadian Air Force radio facility charts, West Canada and Alaska (bimonthly) Proc. Earlier M301.14: Replaced by D301.13/3:

D301.13/2:dt. &nos. Military aviation notices, West Canada and Alaska. Proc.

D301.13/3:date United States Air Force, Navy, Royal Canadian Air Force and Royal Canadian Navy radio facility charts and in-flight data, Alaska, Canada and North Atlantic (monthly) Proc. Replaces D301.11: and D301.13: Later title, Flight information publication; Enroute, Alaska.

D301.13/4:v.nos.&nos. Military aviation notices, corrections to Enroute-low altitude - Alaska.

D301.13/5:date/M-nos Flight information publication: Enroute intermediate altitude, United States. Issued every four weeks. Issued in 4 sections, M1 and M-2, and M-3 and M-4, M-5 and M-6, M-7 and M-8.

D301.13/6:date ___ Terminal, low altitude, Africa and Southwest Asia (monthly)

D301.14:v.nos.&nos. CADO technical data digest. Proc. Earlier M301.9:

D301.15:date Alphabetical list, U.S. Air Force and Air Force-Navy aeronautical standard drawings (semiannual) Proc. Earlier **M301.11:** Replaced by D301.16/2:

D301.16:date Numerical list of U.S. Air Force and Air Force-Navy aeronautical standard drawings. Proc. (monthly) Earlier M301.12: Later D301.16/2:

D301.16/2:date Index of U.S. Air Force, Air Force-Navy aeronautical and military **(MS)** standards (sheet form) (semiannual) Replaces D301.15: and D301.16:

D301.17:dt.&nos Numerical index of technical publications. Restricted. Proc. Earlier M301.13:

D301.17/2:nos Technical orders. Designated TO- nos.

D301.18:date Index of specifications and bulletins approved for U.S. Air Force procurement. Later D301.28:

D301.19:nos Specifications bulletins. Earlier M301.2:Sh6

D301.20:nos Technical publications for Air Force technical libraries, Book lists. Proc. Earlier M301.8:

D301.21: [not used]

D301.22:nos Qualified products list. Desig. AFQPL-nos.

D301.22/2:nos Preferred parts lists. Desig. PPL-nos. Official use only.

D301.23:nos Air National Guard manuals. Desig. ANG-nos.

D301.23/2:nos Air National Guard regulations

D301.24:nos Air Force letters. Proc. Pubs.desig. AFL-nos

D301.24/2:nos Air Force policy letters for commanders from Office of Secretary of Air Force. Admin.

D301.24/3:nos ___ Supplements.

D301. 25:dt.&nos   Headquarters, Air Force [organization chart] (monthly) Earlier D301. 2:Ai7/

D301. 26:v. nos. &nos. Air University quarterly review

D301. 26/ 2:v. nos   Air University periodical index (quarterly) Proc.

D301. 26/ 3:CT   Air University documentary research study, publications. Proc.

D301. 26/ 4:date   USAF extension course catalog. Proc.

D301. 26/ 5:v. nos. &nos. ECI letter

D301. 26/ 6:CT   Air University publications

D301. 26/ 7:nos   Air University, Human Resources Research Institute, Research memorandum.

D301. 26/ 8:nos   ADTIC publications. Proc.

D301. 26/ 9:date   ECI clip sheet (monthly) Proc.

D301. 26/10:nos   Technical research reports pub. by Air Force Personnel and Training Center. Air Research and Development Command.

D301. 26/11:nos   Special bibliography

D301. 26/12:CT   Air University, AFROTC [text books]

D301. 26/13:   Research reports BUT cancelled SEE D301. 26/13-2:

D301. 26/13-2:nos   Air University, School of Aviation Medicine: [Publications]

D301. 26/13-3:date   Publications of School of Aviation Medicine, index, fiscal year

D301. 26/13-4:nos   Aeromedical reviews

D301. 26/13-5:CT   School of Aviation Medicine: General publications

D301. 26/13-6:nos   School of Aerospace Medicine: Technical documentary report SAM-TDR (series)

D301. 26/14:v. nos. &nos. Contact. Admin.

D301. 26/15:date   Research and special studies progress report (annual)

D301. 26/16:date   Air University catalog

D301. 26/16-2:date   Guide to Air University

D301.26/17:nos   ECI courses

D301.26/18:v.nos.&nos. Air Force Institute of Technology, Air University, U.S. Air Force catalogue.

D301.26/19:nos   USAF historical studies

D301.26/20:v.nos   Air University abstracts of research reports (annual)

D301.26/21:v.nos.&nos. Air University Library selected documents accession list (weekly)

D301.26/22:v.nos.&nos. Air University Library selected acquisitions (monthly)

D301.27:nos   Air Weather Service manual. Earlier M301.21:

D301.27/2:les-nos   Air Weather Service pamphlet, AWSP (series)

D301.28:date   Index of specifications and related publications used by Air Force, military index, v.4 (semiannual) Later D7.14:

D301.29:nos   Air Force-Navy aeronautical design standards Desig. AND-nos

D301.30:nos   Air Force-Navy aeronautical standards   Desig. AN-nos

D301.31:nos   U.S. Air Force standards

D301.32:nos   Notices

D301.33:nos   ANA notice (weekly)

D301.34:nos   ANA bulletin

D301.35:nos   Air Force pamphlet AFP (series) Proc.

D301.35/2:nos   Civil Air Patrol pamphlet CAPP (series)

D301.35/3:nos   Air Force Systems Command pamphlets

D301.36:nos   Air Training Command, Human Resources Research Center: List of publications

D301.36/2:nos   ___ Technical reports

D301.36/3:nos   ___ Research bulletins

D301.36/4:nos   ___ Research reviews

D301.36/5:CT   ___ Information bulletins. Proc.

D301.36/6:nos	Research report AFPTRC-TN (series) Proc.
D301.36/7:nos	Development report AFPTRC-TN (series)
D301.36/8:nos	[Crew Research Laboratory] Technical memorandums CRL-TM-nos. Official use only.
D301.36/9:nos	___ Laboratory notes, CRL-IN-nos. [unpublished draft]
D301.36/10:CT	Bibliographies and lists of publications, Operational Applications Office
D301.37:nos	CADO reclassification bulletin. Proc.
D301.38:v.nos.&nos.	Air training (monthly)
D301.38/2:v.nos.&nos.	Training analysis and development, informational bulletins Later title, Air Training Command instructor's journal
D301.38/2a:CT	___ separates
D301.38/3:CT	Air Training Command, Miscellaneous publications.
D301.38/4:v.nos.&nos.	Aircraft observer (quarterly) Later title, Navigator
D301.38/5:date	On the job training program, JP series Desig. JA, JB, JP etc.
D301.38/6:nos	ATC Pamphlet. Air Training Command.
D301.38/7:v.nos.&nos.	Instructors' journal (quarterly) Issued by Air Training Command
D301.39:nos	Air Weather Service: Training guides. Proc.
D301.40:nos	Air Weather Service. Technical reports. Proc. Earlier M301.22:
D301.40/2:nos	Environmental Technical Applications Center. Technical Notes
D301.41:	This class changed to D301.26/3:
D301.42:nos	Air Weather Service: Bibliography. Proc.
D301.42/2:nos	Aerospace sciences review. AWS recurring publication 105-2.
D301.43:date	Radio facility charts and supplementary information, United States, LF/MF edition.
D301.43/2:date	Radio facility charts, United States, VOR edition. Official use only.
D301.43/3:date	Flight information publication: Enroute-high altitude, United States, Northeast [and Southeast] issued every four weeks.

D301.43/3-2:date	Flight information publication: Enroute-high altitude, United States, Northwest [and Southwest] Issued every four weeks.
D301.44:nos	Flying safety (monthly) **Later title,** Flying safety
D301.45:CT	Air Research and Development Command publications Later title Air Force Systems Command
D301.45/2:nos	Geophysical research papers. Proc.
D301.45/3:nos	Releases. Air Research and Development Command. Proc. , Later ARDC news
D301.45/4:nos	Air Force Cambridge Research Center: AFCRC technical reports. Proc.
D301.45/4-2:nos	AFCRC technical notes TN (series)
D301.45/4-3:nos	AFCRL (series)
D301.45/5:nos	WADC technical reports
D301.45/6:nos	AF technical reports, Wright Air Development Center. Proc.
D301.45/7:nos	HFORL memorandum TN (series) Issued by Human Factors Operations Research Laboratories, Air Research & Development Command, Bolling Air Force Base, Washington, D.C.
D301.45/8:nos	HFORL technical report TR (series)
D301.45/9:nos	Air Force surveys in geophysics
D301.45/10:nos	Instrumentation for geophysical research series. Issued by Geophysics Research Directorage, Air Force Cambridge Research Center.
D301.45/11:date	New shop techniques and development of Research Services Division, annual report
D301.45/12:date	[Electronic Research Directorate technical memorandum] ERD-CRRK-TM (series)
D301.45/12-2:nos	___ Technical note ERD-TN (series)
D301.45/13:nos	WADC technical notes
D301.45/14:nos	ARDC manuals Later title, AFSC manuals
D301.45/14-2:nos	AFSCR [Air Force Systems Command Regulations] (series) ,
D301.45/15:date	Quarterly index of technical documentary reports. Proc. Later title, OAR indexes of research results
D301.45/16:nos	GRD research notes, Geophysics Research Directorate, Air Force Cambridge Research center.

D301.45/16-2:nos	Geophysics Research Directorate: Technical notes, GRD-TN (series)
D301.45/16-3:nos	GRD [Geophysics Research Directorate] technical report TR (series)
D301.45/16-4:date	Geophysics Research Directorate, annual report
D301.45/17:nos	Air Force Missile Development Center technical reports
D301.45/17-2:nos	Air Force Missile Development Center Technical notes, AFMDC-TN (series)
D301.45/18:nos	Air Force Office of Scientific Research, technical notes. Desig. AFOSR-TN
D301.45/19:nos	Air Force Office of Scientific Research: Technical reports AFOSR-TR
D301.45/19-2:nos	___ AFOSR (series)
D301.45/19-3:nos	___ AFOSR technical documents
D301.45/19-4:nos	___ Directorate of Research Analysis, AFOSR/DRA (series)
D301.45/20:nos	Air Force Special Weapons Center: Technical reports, Desig. AFSWC-TR
D301.45/20-2:nos	Air Force Special Weapons Center: Technical notes, AFSWC-TN
D301.45/20-3:nos	___ Technical documentary report AFSWC-TDR (series)
D301.45/21:nos	Air Research and Development Command: Technical reports, ARDC-TR-
D301.45/22:1e-nos	Wright aeronautical serial reports
D301.45/23:nos	Air Force Missile Test Center: Technical reports, AFMTC TR-(series)
D301.45/23-2:nos	AFMTCP - Air Force Missile Test Center
D301.45/24:nos	Air Force Command and Control Development Division: Technical notes AFCCDD-TN (nos)
D301.45/25:nos	ARL technical reports
D301.45/26:nos	Aeronautical Systems Division: ASD technical note TN (series)
D301.45/26-2:nos	___ ASD technical report TR (series)
D301.45/26-3:nos	___ Technical documentary report ASD-TDR (series)
D301.45/27:nos	Personnel Research Laboratory: Technical documentary report PRL-TDR (series) Later Air Force Human Resources Lab. AFHRL-TR

D301.45/27-2:nos   Air Force Human Resources Laboratory: AFHRL(TT)-TRM (series)

D301.45/27-3:nos   Air Force Human Resources Laboratory: Technical report analysis condensation evaluation (TRACE)

D301.45/28:nos   Electronic Systems Division: Technical reports, ESD-TR (series)

D301.45/28-2:nos   ___ Technical documentary report ESD-TDR (series)

D301.45/29:nos   Air Force Systems Command, Andrews Air Force Base: Press releases

D301.45/29-2:CT   ___ Addresses

D301.45/30:nos   Arctic Aeromedical Laboratory: Technical reports AAL TR (series)

D301.45/30-2:nos   Arctic Aeromedical Laboratory: Technical documentary report AAL-TDR- (series)

D301.45/30-3:nos   ___ Technical note AAL-TN (series)

D301.45/31:nos   Air Force Flight Test Center: AFFTC technical reports

D301.45/31-2:nos   ___ Technical documentary report FTC-TDR (series)

D301.45/31-3:nos   ___ Technical information memorandum FTC-TM (series)

D301.45/31-4:nos   ___ Technical information handbook FTC-TIH (series)

D301.45/32:nos   Aerospace Medical Research Laboratories: Technical documentary report MRL-TDR (series), AMRL-TDR

D301.45/32-2:nos   ___ AMRL memorandums

D301.45/32-3:nos   ___ Technical reports AMRL-TR (series)

D301.45/33:nos   Arnold Engineering Development Center, AEDC-TR

D301.45/33-2:nos   ___ AEDC-TDR (series)

D301.45/33-3:nos   ___ AEDC-TN (series)

D301.45/34:v.nos.&nos.   Research and Technology Division. RTD technology briefs

D301.45/34-2:nos   ___ Technical documentary report RTD-TDR (series)

D301.45/34-3:nos   Air Force Weapons Laboratory: Technical report AFWL-TR (series)

D301.45/35:nos   Air Force Weapons Laboratory. Research and Technology Division, AFWL-TDR (series) CANCELLED   See D301.45/34-2:

D301.45/36:nos	Ballistic Systems Division. Technical documentary report BSD-TDR
D301.45/37:nos	Operational Applications Laboratory. Air Force Cambridge Research Center, OAL-TM (series)
D301.45/38:date	Air Force Systems Command annual report
D301.45/39:nos	Environmental research papers
D301.45/40:nos	Physical sciences research papers
D301.45/41:date	Cyrogenic materials data handbook, yearly summary reports. (Contractor report by non-govt. organization) Earlier C13.6/3:
D301.45/42:nos	Special reports, Issued by Air Force Cambridge Research Laboratories
D301.45/43:nos	Geophysics and space data bulletin
D301.45/44:nos	Air Force Institute of Technology: New books in Library
D301.45/45:nos	AF Avionics Laboratory: Technical documentary report AL TDR (series)
D301.45/46:nos	Air Flight Dynamics Laboratory, Research and Technology Division, Air Force Systems Command, Wright-Patterson Air Force Base, Ohio. Technical documentary report FDL-TDR
D301.45/46-2:nos	___ AFFDL-TR
D301.45/47:nos	AF Materials Laboratory. Research and Technology Division, Air Force Systems Command, Wright-Patterson Air Force Base, Ohio. Technical documentary report ML-TDR
D301.45/47-2:nos	___ Technical report AFML-TR
D301.45/48:nos	Systems Engineering Group. Research and Technology Division, Air Force Systems Command, Wright-Patterson Air Force Base, Ohio. Technical documentary report no. SEG-TDR
D301.45/48-2:nos	Systems Engineering Group: Technical reports SEG-TM (series)
D301.45/49:nos	ARDC Technical program planning document AF ARPD (Formerly AF TPPD)
D301.45/50:nos	Air Proving Ground Center, Elgin Air Force Base, Fla., Technical notes APGC-TN
D301.45/50-2:nos	Air Proving Ground Center, Elgin Air Force Base, Fla., APGC-TR (series)
D301.45/50-3:nos	Air Proving Ground Center, PGN documents

D301.45/51:nos   Air Force Aero Propulsion Laboratory: Technical documentary report, APL-TDR (series)

D301.45/51-2:nos Air Force Aero Propulsion Laboratory: Technical report AFAPL-TR (series)

D301.45/52:nos   Aerospace Medical Division: Technical report AMD-TR (series)

D301.45/52-2:nos Aeromedical Research Laboratory: Technical documentary report ARL-TDR (series)

D301.45/53:nos   Maintenance Laboratory. Air Force Personnel Training Research Center ML-TM (series)

D301.45/54:date   Research and technology briefs

D301.45/55:nos   SAMSO-TR-(series)

D301.46:v.nos.&nos. Air Force information policy letter for commanders

D301.46/2:nos   ___ supplements

D301.47:v.nos.&nos. Aircraft flash (monthly) Published by Ground Observer Corps

D301.48:date   United States Air Force, Navy, Royal Canadian Air Force, and Royal Canadian Navy, supplementary flight information, North American area (excluding Mexico and Caribbean area) Proc. Replaced by D301.52:

D301.48/2:dt./nos Military aviation notices, corrections (monthly) Proc. Replaced by D301.52:

D301.49:date   United States Air Force and Navy supplementary flight information, Europe, Africa, and Middle East. Replaced by D301.52:

D301.49/2:dt.&nos Military aviation notices, corrections to Supplementary flight information, Europe, Africa and Middle East (monthly) Proc. Replaced by D301.52:

D301.49/3:v.nos   Aeronautical chart & information bulletin, Europe, Africa and Middle East, new editions of aeronautical charts published (monthly) Proc. Later NAS1.43/3:

D301.49/4:letters-nos. Lunar charts and mosaics series. Later NAS1.43/3:

D301.50:date   United States Air Force and Navy supplementary flight information documents, Pacific and Far East. Replaced by D301.52:

D301.50/2:dt.&nos Military aviation notices, corrections to Supplementary flight information document, Pacific and Far East. Proc. Replaced by D301.52:

D301.51:date   Supplementary flight information document, Caribbean and South America. Proc. Replaced by D301.52:

D301.51/2:dt.&nos. USAF military aviation notices, amending SFID, Caribbean and South America. Replaced by D301.52:

D301.52:date   U.S. Air Force and U.S. Navy flight planning document. Replaces D301.48 through D301.51/2:

D301.52/2:date   Quarterly check list, USAF/USN Flight information publications, Planning. Proc.

D301.52/3:nos   Military aviation notices: corrections to Flight information publications

D301.53:nos   Ground accident abstracts

D301.53/2:date   Ground accident abstracts. Monthly. Proc. Official use.

D301.54:nos   Information services fact sheets

D301.55:nos   Air Force visual aid series. Desig. AFVA-nos

D301.56:v.nos   MATS flyer (monthly) Later title MAC flyer

D301.56/2:date   MATS quarterly schedule

D301.56/3:date   Military Airlift Command: Airlift Service management report (annual)

D301.57:nos   Rome Air Development Center, technical report RADC-TR (series) Proc.

D301.57/2:nos   ___ RADC-TN (series)

D301.57/3:nos   ___ Technical documentary report RADC-TDR (series)

D301.58:v.nos.&nos. Aircraft accident and maintenance review. Later Comptroller news. Later D306.8:

D301.58/a:CT   ___ separates

D301.59:nos   Aeronautical Chart & Information Center bulletins (semimonthly) Official use. Later D5.203:

D301.59/2:nos   ACIC technical reports. Proc.

D301.59/3:v.nos.&nos. Aeronautical Chart and Information Squadron bulletin. Official use

D301.59/4:date   Chart updating manual (CHUM) (monthly) Later D5.208:

D301.59/5:date   Aeronautical Chart & Information Center bulletin digest (semiannual)

D301.60:v.nos./nos   Airman (monthly)

D301.61:nos   Planning Division processes and procedures. Proc. Admin.

D301.62:CT   PACAF [Pacific Air Forces] basic bibliographies. Proc.

D301.62/2:CT   Bibliographies and lists of publications

D301.63:CT   Air Force Reserve Officer Training Corps. [textbooks]

D301.64:CT   Translations. Earlier in D301.2:

D301.65:v.nos.&nos. Air Force civil engineer (quarterly) Later title, Air Force engineering and services

D301.66:nos   Alaskan Air Command, Arctic Aeromedical Laboratory: Technical notes

D301.67:nos   Air Materiel Command: Technical reports. Desig. AMC technical reports

D301.68:CT   Air Force Ballistic Missile Division, publications

D301.69:nos   OAR news. Office of Aerospace Research

D301.69/2:nos   Aeronautical Research Laboratory, Office of Aerospace Research, ARL (series)

D301.69/3:nos   Office of Aerospace Research, OAR (series)

D301.69/4:date   In-house list of publications, Aeronautical Research Laboratory, Office of Aerospace Research

D301.69/5:CT   Office of Aerospace Research publications

D301.69/6:v.nos   OAR Research review. Later D301.69/6-2:

D301.69/6-2:date/nos Air Force research review. Formerly D301.69/6:

D301.69/7:date   List of OAR research efforts (quarterly)

D301.69/8:date   OAR quarterly index of current research results. Earlier D301.69/3:64-5

D301.69/9:date   Office of Aerospace Research: Annual reports

D301.69/10:nos   Monographs

D301.70:v.nos.&nos. Interceptor. Published by Chief of Safety, Air Development Command

D301.71:nos   Space Systems Division: Technical documentary report TDR (series)

D301.72:v.nos.&nos. Driver, automotive magazine of the U.S. Air Force (monthly)

D301.72/a:CT   ___ separates

D301.73:v.nos.&nos. Air Force Comptroller (quarterly)

D301.74:v.nos.&nos. Accounting and finance tech. digest (biweekly) Official use

D301.75:nos   Aerospace speech series. Official use

D301.75/2:nos   Air Force fact sheets. Official use. Superseded by D301.75/2-2:

D301.75/2-2:nos   Background information (series) Supersedes D301.75/2:

D301.75/3:CT   Air Force information series

D301.76:nos   Lithograph series

D301.76/2:nos   Historical aircraft photopackage

D301.76/3:date   Lithograph series catalog

D301.77:nos   Air Force Machinability Data Center - AFMDC - (series)

D301.78:date   Proceedings of Military History symposium (biennial) Issued by Office of Air Force History

D301.79:nos   Soviet military thought series

D301.80:nos   Community College of the Air Force: General catalog

D301.81:v.nos.&nos. Combat crew (monthly)

D301.82:CT   Army Air Forces in World War II   Earlier D114.7:Ai71

D301.83:date   Air Force budget (annual)

D301.84:v/nos   Maintenance (quarterly)

D301.85:v.nos   Studies in communist affairs (series)

D301.86:v.nos.&nos. USAF Southeast Asia monograph series

D302 Judge Advocate General of the Air Force

D302.1:date   Annual reports

D302.2:CT   General publications

D302.6:nos   Regulations, rules, and instructions.

D302.7:v.nos.&nos. Digest of Judge Advocate General of the Air Force (quarterly) Superseded by D1.18:

D302.8:CT   Handbooks, manuals, guides Earlier in D302.6:

D302.9:v.nos.&nos. USAF JAG law review (bimonthly) Later title, Air Force law review

D302.10:v./nos   LITE newsletter: A computerized information retrieval system for legal research. (quarterly)

Administrative Services

D303   Air Adjutant General's Office

D303.1:date	Annual reports. Earlier M302.1:
D303.2:CT	General publications Earlier M302.2:
D303.7:date	Air Force Register. Earlier M302.7:
D303.8:date	Activities serviced by headquarters USAF mail center (monthly)
D303.9:date	Air Force writing (quarterly) Air Force recurring publication 10-1

D304 Air Force Medical Service

Established by Department of Air Force general order 35, dated June 8, 1949, effective July 1, 1949.

D304.1:date   Annual reports

D304.2:CT   General publications

D304.7:date   Releases

D304.8:v.nos.&nos. U.S. Air Force medical service digest (monthly)

D305 Air Force Academy, Colorado Springs

The United States Air Force Academy was established in the Department of the Air Force by Public law 325, 83d Congress, approved Apr.1,1954.

D305.1:date	Annual reports
D305.2:CT	General publications
D305.8:date	Air Force Academy catalogue. (annual)
D305.9:date	Report of Board of Visitors
D305.10:nos	Harmon memorial lectures in military history (annual)
D305.11:date	Final reports of Air Force Academy Assembly (annual)
D305.12:nos	Special bibliography series
D305.13:	Proceedings of Military History Symposium See also (preferred number) D301.78:
D305.14:nos	Research reports

D306 Inspector General (Air Force)

D306.1:date — Annual reports
D306.2:CT — General publications

D306.8:v.nos.&nos. Aircraft accident and maintenance review (monthly) Earlier D301.58:

DC DISTRICT OF COLUMBIA

1874

DC1 Commissioners

DC1.1:date	Annual reports
DC1.1/a:date	___ separates
DC1.1/a:CT	___ separates. Miscellaneous.
DC1.2:CT	General publications
DC1.2/a:CT	___ separates
DC1.3:nos	Bulletins [none issued]
DC1.4:nos	Circulars [none issued]
DC1.5:Cong.	Acts affecting District of Columbia
DC1.6:date	District of Columbia real estate tax
DC1.7:CT	Specifications
DC1.8:CT	Regulations, rules, and instructions. Includes handbooks and manuals and codes. Changed from DC1.2:
DC1.9:nos	Do you know (monthly)
DC1.10:date	State of the Nation's Capital (annual)

DC2   Asphalt and Cement Inspector

1881

DC2.1:date   Annual reports

DC2.2:CT   General publications [none issued]

DC2.3:nos   Bulletins [none issued]

DC2.4:nos   Circulars [none issued]

1875   DC3   Assessor

DC3.1:date   Annual reports

DC3.2:CT   General publications [none issued]

DC3.3:nos   Bulletins [none issued]

DC3.4:nos   Circulars [none issued]

Incorporated in Finances of District of Columbia embracing annual reports of Auditor, Assessor and Collector of Taxes for which see DC4.1: from 1921.

                  Collector of Taxes **(1921-)**
           DC4   Auditor

1874

DC4.1:date   Annual reports

DC4.2:CT   General publications [none issued]

DC4.3:nos   Bulletins [none issued]

DC4.4:nos   Circulars [none issued]

1877   DC5   Building Inspector

DC5.1:date   Annual reports

DC5.2:CT   General publications

DC6   Central Dispensary and Emergency Hospital

1st report to Commissioners 1881

DC6.1:date	Annual reports
DC6.2:CT	General publications [none issued]
DC6.3:nos	Bulletins [none issued]
DC6.4:nos	Circulars [none issued]

DC7   Charities Board

Office created under District appropriation act of Aug. 6, 1890.

DC7.1:date	Annual reports
DC7.1/a:date	___ separates
DC7.2:CT	General publications
DC7.3:nos	Bulletins [none issued]
DC7.4:nos	Circulars [none issued]

Board abolished and work taken over by Public Welfare Board, DC52, (Public 47, 69C, app. March 16, 1926).

DC8   Children's Guardians Board

Constituted by act of Congress approved July 26, 1892.

DC8.1:date	Annual reports
DC8.2:CT	General publications [none issued]
DC8.3:nos	Bulletins [none issued]
DC8.4:nos	Circulars [none issued]

Board abolished and work taken over by Public Welfare Board, DC52. (Public 47, 69C, app. March 16, 1926).

DC9 Court of Appeals

Feb. 9, 1893 (Stat. L. 27:434)

DC9.1:date	Annual reports [none issued]
DC9.2:CT	General publications
DC9.3:nos	Bulletins [none issued]
DC9.4:nos	Circulars [none issued]
DC9.5:CT	Papers in re
DC9.6:date	Calendars
DC9.7:date	Rules

DC10 Engineer Department

Organized by Act of June 20, 1874.

DC10.1:date	Annual reports
DC10.2:CT	General publications
DC10.3:nos	Bulletins [none issued]
DC10.4:nos	Circulars [none issued]
DC10.5:CT	Maps
DC10.6:CT	Regulations, rules, and instructions. Includes handbooks and manuals.

DC11 Excise Board

Established by act of Mar. 3, 1893.

DC11.1:date	Annual reports
DC11.2:CT	General publications [none issued]
DC11.3:nos	Bulletins [none issued]
DC11.4:nos	Circulars [none issued]

DC12   Fire Department

1874

DC12.1:date   Annual reports

DC12.2:CT   General publications

DC12.3:nos   Bulletins [none issued]

DC12.4:nos   Circulars [none issued]

DC13   Reform School for Girls of District of Columbia

SEE J9

DC14   Health Department

1872

DC14.1:date   Annual report

DC14.1/a:CT   ___ separates

DC14.2:CT   General publications

DC14.3:nos   Bulletins

DC14.4:nos   Circulars

DC14.5:date   [Monthly] milk reports. Later title, Milk and ice cream report.

DC15   Industrial Home School

Established 1867.

DC15.1:date   Annual reports

DC15.2:CT   General publications

DC15.3:nos   Bulletins [none issued]

DC15.4:nos   Circulars [none issued]

DC16 Metropolitan Police Department

1861

DC16.1:date	Annual reports
DC16.2:CT	General publications
DC16.3:nos	Bulletins [none issued]
DC16.4:nos	Circulars [none issued]
DC16.5:dt.&nos.	Special orders
DC16.6:dt.&nos.	General orders

DC17 Public Library

Established by act of June 3, 1896.

DC17.1:date	Annual reports
DC17.2:CT	General publications
DC17.3:nos	Bulletins [none issued]
DC17.4:nos	Circulars [none issued]
DC17.5:nos	Reference lists
DC17.6:v.nos	Monthly bulletins
DC17.7:v.nos	Your library (monthly)
DC17.8:nos	Informational educational opportunities in Washington
DC17.9:date	Technology book news. Monthly.
DC17.10:date	Monthly list of selected books. Proc.

DC18   Education Board

1845

DC18.1:date	Annual reports
DC18.1/a:CT	___ separates
DC18.2:CT	General publications
DC18.3:nos	Bulletins [none issued]
DC18.4:nos	Circulars [none issued]
DC18.5:dt.&nos.	School documents
DC18.6:CT	Regulations, rules, and instructions

DC19   National Training School for Boys

May 3, 1876 (19 Stat. 49)

DC19.1:date   Annual reports. Later J8.1:

Transferred to Justice Department by Reorganization Plan II, pt.1, sec. 3b, effective July 1, 1939.

DC20   Street Cleaning Department

Became an independent Department of the District of Columbia, Sept. 30, 1890.

DC20.1:date	Annual reports
DC20.2:CT	General publications [none issued]
DC20.3:nos	Bulletins [none issued]
DC20.4:nos	Circulars [none issued]

DC 21   District Court of United States for District of Columbia
                        Name changed- P.L. 796, 74 C. June 25, 1936.
          DC 21   Supreme Court

Mar. 3, 1901, (Stat. L, v. 31, sec. 63p. 1199)

DC21.1:date   Annual reports

DC21.2:CT   General publications

DC21.3:nos   Bulletins [none issued]

DC21.4:nos   Circulars [none issued]

DC21.5:CT   Briefs

DC21.6:date   Star route trials

DC21.6/a:CT   ___ separates

DC21.6/7:date   Trial calendars

DC21.8:v.nos   Reports

DC21.9:date   List of legal investments for trust funds in District of Columbia (semiannual)
                 Earlier DC21.2:T77/3

          DC 22   Collector of Taxes

1874

DC22.1:date   Annual reports

DC22.2:CT   General publications

DC22.3:nos   Bulletins [none issued]

DC22.4:nos   Circulars [none issued]

DC 23 Telegraph and Telephone Service

1882

DC23.1:date	Annual reports
DC23.2:CT	General publications
DC23.3:nos	Bulletins [none issued]
DC23.4:nos	Circulars [none issued]

By orders of Commissioners of District of Columbia, July 15, 1898 and April 17, 1890, this service became a part of the Electrical Department (DC25).

DC 24 Washington Asylum

1874.

DC24.1:date	Annual reports
DC24.2:CT	General publications
DC24.3:CT	Bulletins [none issued]
DC24.4:nos	Circulars [none issued]

Washington Asylum Hospital shall be discontinued as a separate institution during fiscal year ending June 30, 1923 and merged into Gallinger Municipal Hospital (DC54) (Stat. L42, pt. 1: 702).

DC 25 Electrical Department

Organized July 15, 1898.

DC25.1:date	Annual reports
DC25.2:CT	General publications
DC25.3:nos	Bulletins [none issued]
DC25.4:nos	Circulars [none issued]

DC 26 Women's Christian Association

1882

DC 26.1:date   Annual reports

DC 26.2:CT   General publications

DC 26.3:nos   Bulletins [none issued]

DC 26.4:nos   Circulars [none issued]

DC 27 Children's Hospital

1871

DC 27.1:date   Annual reports

DC 27.2:CT   General publications [none issued]

DC 27.3:nos   Bulletins [none issued]

DC 27.4:nos   Circulars [none issued]

DC 28 Criminal Court

DC 28.1:date   Annual reports [none issued]

DC 28.2:CT   General publications

DC 28.2/a:CT   ___ separates

DC 28.3:nos   Bulletins [none issued]

DC 28.4:nos   Circulars [none issued]

About 1874 (?) the Supreme Court of the District of Columbia (DC 21) was authorized to hold criminal terms.

DC29   Columbia Hospital for Women

Established by act of June 1, 1866.

DC29.1:date	Annual report
DC29.2:CT	General publications
DC29.3:nos	Bulletins [none issued]
DC29.4:nos	Circulars [none issued]

DC30   Bathing Beach

1892

DC30.1:date	Annual reports
DC30.2:CT	General publications [none issued]
DC30.4:nos	Circulars [none issued]

DC31   Insurance Department

Created by act of Mar. 3, 1901, to take effect January 1, 1902.

DC31.1:date	Annual reports
DC31.1/a:date	___ separates
DC31.2:CT	General publications
DC31.3:nos	Bulletins [none issued]
DC31.4:nos	Circulars [none issued]

DC32   Medical Supervisors Board

Organized Board of Medical Supervisors, July 2, 1896.

DC32.1:date	Annual reports
DC32.2:CT	General publications [none issued]

DC33 Gas and Meters Inspector

Office created by act of June 23, 1874.

DC33.1:date   Annual reports

DC33.2:CT   General publications

DC33.3:nos   Bulletins [none issued]

DC33.4:nos   Circulars [none issued]

Became subordinate to Public Utilities Commission in accordance with section 8 of D.C. appropriation act, app. Mar. 4, 1913.

DC34 Eastern Dispensary and Casualty Hospital

Incorporated under laws of District of Columbia, Apr. 13, 1888.

DC34.1:date   Annual reports

DC34.2:CT   General publications [none issued]

DC34.3:nos   Bulletins [none issued]

DC34.4:nos   Circulars [none issued]

DC35 Home for Aged and Infirm

Formerly a part of the Washington Asylum (see DC24). Reorganized as a separate institution under act of June 27, 1906 (Stat. L 34, pt. 1:509).

DC35.1:date   Annual reports

DC35.2:CT   General publications

DC35.3:nos   Bulletins [none issued]

DC35.4:nos   Circulars [none issued]

DC36   Aid Association for the Blind

Organized Dec. 8, 1897. Incorporated Apr. 13, 1899.

DC36.1:date   Annual reports

DC36.2:CT   General publications   [none issued]

DC36.3:nos   Bulletins   [none issued]

DC36.4:nos   Circulars   [none issued]

DC37   Industrial Home School for Colored Children

Organized July 1, 1907.

DC37.1:date   Annual reports

DC37.2:CT   General publications   [none issued]

DC37.3:nos   Bulletins   [none issued]

DC37.4:nos   Circulars   [none issued]

DC38   Washington Home for Foundlings

Act of Mar. 3, 1909 provides that reports shall be made to D.C. Commissioners and not to Secretary of the Interior.

DC38.1:date   Annual reports

DC38.2:CT   General publications   [none issued]

DC38.3:nos   Bulletins   [none issued]

DC38.4:nos   Circulars   [none issued]

DC39   Tuberculosis Hospital

June 27, 1906 (Stat. L34:pt. 1:511)

DC39.1:date   Annual reports

DC39.2:CT   General publications   [none issued]

DC40 Workhouse

DC40.1:date   Annual reports

DC40.2:CT   General publications

DC40.3:nos   Bulletins

DC40.4:nos   Circulars

DC41 George Washington University Hospital

DC41.1:date   Annual reports

DC41.2:CT   General publications

DC41.3:nos   Bulletins

DC41.4:nos   Circulars

Public Service Commission
DC43 Public Utilities Commission

Created by sec. 8 of D.C. appropriation act for 1914.

DC43.1:date   Annual reports

DC43.1/a:date   ___ separates

DC43.2:CT   General publications

DC43.3:   Bulletins

DC43.4:   Circulars

DC43.5:CT   Opinions and orders

DC44 Weights, Measures and Markets Department

DC44.1:date   Annual reports

DC44.2:CT   General publications

DC44.3:nos   Bulletins

DC44.4:   Circulars

DC45   Rock Creek Park Control Board

DC45.1:date   Annual reports

DC45.2:CT   General publications

DC45.3:   Bulletins

DC45.4:   Circulars

DC46   Playgrounds Department

DC46.1:date   Annual reports

DC46.2:CT   General publications

DC46.3:   Bulletins

DC46.4:   Circulars

DC47   Reformatory

DC47.1:date   Annual reports

DC47.2:CT   General publications

DC47.3:   Bulletins

DC47.4:   Circulars

DC48   License Bureau

Created July 1, 1917 by act making appropriations for District of Columbia for fiscal year 1918.

DC48.1:date   Annual reports

DC48.2:CT   General publications

DC48.3:   Bulletins

DC48.4:   Circulars

DC49   District Council of Defense

Organization effected June 9, 1917.

DC49.1:date   Annual reports

DC49.2:CT   General publications

DC49.3:   Bulletins

DC49.4:   Circulars

DC50   Minimum Wage Board

Appointed October 19, 1918.

DC50.1:date   Annual reports

DC50.2:CT   General publications

DC50.3:nos   Bulletins

DC50.4:   Circulars

DC50.5:nos   M.W.B. orders.

DC51   Traffic Director

Authorized by Public 68-2, Stat. L43, pt.1:119-26, Mar. 3, 1925.

DC51.1:date   Annual reports

DC51.2:CT   General publications

DC51.3:   Bulletins

DC51.4:   Circulars

DC51.5:date   Regulations

Department of Public Welfare
DC52 Public Welfare Board

Created by Public 47, 69 C. app. Mar. 16, 1926.

DC52.1:date	Annual reports
DC52.2:CT	General publications.
DC52.3:	Bulletins
DC52.4:	Circulars

DC53 Highways Department

DC53.1:date	Annual reports
DC53.2:CT	General publications
DC53.3:	Bulletins
DC53.4:	Circulars

DC54 Gallinger Municipal Hospital

June 29, 1922 (Stat. L 42, pt. 1:702).

DC54.1:date	Annual reports
DC54.2:CT	General publications
DC54.3:	Bulletins
DC54.4:	Circulars
DC54.5:CT	Laws
DC54.6/1:date	Regulations (general)
DC54.6/2:CT	Regulations (miscellaneous)

DC55 Recorder of Deeds

DC55.1:date   Annual reports

DC55.2:CT   General publications

DC55.5:CT   Laws

DC56 Works Progress Administration
(The District of Columbia WPA)

DC56.1:date   Annual reports

DC56.2:CT   General publications

DC56.6:CT   Regulations, rules, and instructions. Includes handbooks and manuals.

DC56.7:vol   Work, journal of progress. Monthly. Proc.

National Capital Housing Authority
Capital Housing Authority, June 1, 1943-
DC57 Alley Dwelling Authority

Public 307, 73d Congress, June 12, 1934; Executive order 6868, Oct. 9, 1934.

DC57.1:date   Annual reports

DC57.2:CT   General publications

DC58 Unemployment Compensation Board

Public 386, 74th Congress, August 28, 1935.

DC58.1:date   Annual reports

DC58.2:CT   General publications

DC58.6:CT   Regulations, rules, and instructions.

DC59 District of Columbia Auditorium Commission

Created by act of July 1, 1955 (69 Stat. 243)

DC59.1:date   Reports

DC59.2:CT   General publications

Submitted final report to Congress Jan. 31, 1957, pursuant to act of Apr. 27, 1956 (70 Stat. 115)

DM Defense Materials Procurement Agency

Created by Executive order 10281 of Aug. 28, 1951.

DM1.1:date   Annual reports

DM1.2:CT   General publications

DM1.6:CT   Regulations, rules, and instructions

DM1.6/2:nos   Delegations. Irregular. Proc.

DM1.6/3:nos   Mineral orders MO (series)

DM1.6/4:nos   Operating procedures. Proc. Admin.

DM1.6/5:nos   Compliance and security memorandums. Admin.

DM1.7:nos   Releases. Proc.

Abolished by Executive order 10480 of August 14, 1953, and functions transferred to General Services Administration, where it functions as Materials Division under Emergency Procurement Service.

DP Defense Production Administration

The Defense Production Administration was established by Executive Order 10200 of Jan. 2, 1951, pursuant to the Defense Production Act of 1950 (64 Stat. 798).

DP1.1:date	Annual reports. Changed from Pr33.1101:
DP1.2:CT	General publications. Changed from Pr33.1102:
DP1.6:CT	Regulations, rules, and instructions
DP1.6/2:nos	Delegations
DP1.6/3:nos	Regulations DPA (series)
DP1.7:nos	Releases. Changed from Pr33.107:
DP1.8:v.nos	Defense production record (weekly)
DP1.9:nos	List of basic materials and alternates
DP1.10:	Defense production notes. Irregular. Proc.
DP1.11:	Defense production briefs. Proc.
DP1.12:	Summary of DPA-NPA operations.

Executive Order 10433, of Feb. 4, 1953, abolished the Defense Production Administration and transferred its **functions** to the Office of Defense Mobilization.

EB   Efficiency Bureau

Feb. 28, 1916 made an independent bureau. Formerly (since Mar. 25, 1913) Efficiency Division of the Civil Service Commission.

EB1.1:date	Annual reports
EB1.2:CT	General publications
EB1.2/a:CT	___ separates
EB1.3:	Bulletins
EB1.4:	Circulars
EB1.5:nos	General circulars

Abolished June 1933. Functions transferred to Bureau of the Budget.

EC   Employees' Compensation Commission

Created by an act of Sept. 7, 1916.

EC1.1:date	Annual reports. Later FS13.301:
EC1.1/a:CT	___ separates. Later FS13.302:
EC1.2:CT	General publications
EC1.3:	Bulletins
EC1.3/2:nos	Special bulletins. Proc.
EC1.4:	Circulars
EC1.5:date	Regulations (general)
EC1.5/2:nos	Regulations. Proc.
EC1.5/3:nos	Rules and regulations
EC1.6:CT	Rules, regulations and instructions
EC1.7:	Opinions
EC1.7/a:nos	___ separates
EC1.8:nos	Accident prevention series; bulletins
EC1.9:vol	Safety bulletins. Monthly. Proc. Later FS13.307:

Functions transferred to the Federal Security Administrator by Reorganization plan no. 2, effective July 16, 1946.

EP1   Environmental Protection Agency

The Environmental Protection Agency was established by Reorganization plan 3 of 1970, effective December 2, 1970.

EP1.1:date	Annual report
EP1.1/2:date	Annual report of the activities of the Effluent Standards Water Quality Information Advisory Committee
EP1.2:CT	General publications
EP1.3:date	EPA bulletin (biweekly)
EP1.3/2:date	EPA citizens bulletin
EP1.5:CT	Laws
EP1.5/2:CT	Environmental law series
EP1.5/3:CT	Legal compilation, statutes and legislative history, Executive orders, regulations, guidelines and reports
EP1.5/3-2:nos	Legal compilation supplements
EP1.5/3-3:date	___ Indexes
EP1.5/4:date	Index of EPA legal authority, statutes & legislative history, executive orders, regulations
EP1.6:CT	Regulations, rules and instructions
EP1.6/2:CT	Background document for noise emission regulations
EP1.6/3:CT	Noise emission standards for construction equipment, Background document for [various items]
EP1.7:date	Press releases
EP1.7/2:date	Environmental news
EP1.7/3:date	Safety management information
EP1.7/4:nos	Environment news
EP1.7/5:date	EPA technical notes

EP1.7/6:date	EPAlert, to alert you to important events (Region 3, Philadelphia, Pa.)
EP1.7/7:date	Environmental news summary
EP1.8:CT	Handbooks, manuals, guides
EP1.8/2:trans.no.	Grants administration manual
EP1.8/3:CT	Development document for effluent limitations guidelines and new source performance standards
EP1.8/4:CT	Economic analysis of proposed effluent guidelines
EP1.8/5:CT	Background information for standards of performance: [various industries]
EP1.8/6:nos	OAQPS guidelines series. Office of Air Quality Planning and Standards
EP1.8/7:nos	Stationary source emission series
EP1.8/8:CT	Water quality management guidance
EP1.9:date	Project register, projects approved, monthly summary Earlier I67.16/2:
EP1.9/2:date	Project register, waste water construction grants
EP1.10:CT	Addresses
EP1.11:date	Comprehensive studies of solid waste management, annual report. Earlier HE20.1402:C73
EP1.12:date	Telephone directory
EP1.13:date	Southwestern Radiological Health Laboratory. Monthly Activities report
EP1.14:date	Western Environmental Research Laboratory. Monthly activities report
EP1.14/2:date	Western Environmental Research Laboratory. Annual report
EP1.15:date	No nonsense
EP1.16:nos.&letters	Water pollution control research series Earlier EP2.10:
EP1.16/2:CT	Conference in matters of pollution of navigable waters, proceedings Earlier in EP2.2:
EP1.17:nos	Solid waste management series, SW-nos. Earlier EP3 classes

EP1.17/2:CT	Reducing waste at its source (series)
EP1.17/3:v.nos.&nos.	Solid waste management, monthly abstracts bulletin
EP1.18:v.nos.&nos.	Accession bulletin, solid waste information retrieval system. Earlier EP3.3/2:
EP1.19:date	Pacific Northwest Water Laboratory: Quarterly report. Earlier EP2.22:
EP1.20:	Environmental input (bi-weekly) Region VII, Kansas City, Missouri. Admin.
EP1.21:CT	Bibliographies and lists of publications
EP1.21/2:date	Monthly translations list and current contents
EP1.21/3:date	Current awareness of translations (monthly)
EP1.21/4:nos	Summaries of Foreign Government environmental reports (monthly)
EP1.21/5:nos	Air pollution aspects of emission sources: [various subjects], a bibliography with abstracts. Earlier publications classed in Publication, AP-(series), EP4.9:
EP1.21/6:date	ORD publications summary (quarterly)
EP1.21/7:date	EPA reports bibliography (quarterly)
EP1.21/8:nos	Air pollution technical publications of the U.S. Environmental Protection Agency, quarterly bulletin. Earlier EP1.21:Ai7
EP1.21/9:date	Research reports, National Environmental Research Center, Las Vegas [list]
EP1.22:nos	Alaska Water Laboratory, College, Alaska; Reports (numbered)
EP1.22/2:date	Alaska Water Laboratory quarterly research reports. Earlier publications issued by Federal Water Pollution Administration, Interior Department. Classified here to keep set together.
EP1.23:nos	Ecological research series, EPA-R3
EP1.23/2:nos	Environmental protection technology series, EPA-R2
EP1.23/3:dt.-nos	Socioeconomic environmental studies series EPA-R5
EP1.23/4:nos	Environmental health effects research series, EPA-R1
EP1.23/5:nos	Environmental monitoring series EPA-R4
EP1.23/6:nos	Miscellaneous series

EP1.23/7:nos	Scientific and technical assessment reports (STAR)
EP1.24:v./nos	EPA log (weekly)
EP1.25:date	Oil pollution research newsletter. Issued by Edison Water Quality Research Laboratory, National Environmental Research Center, Edison, N.J.
EP1.26:CT	Policies and trends in municipal waste treatment
EP1.27:v./nos	Youth Advisory Board newsletter
EP1.28:	not used yet
EP1.28/2:	not used yet
EP1.28/3:	not used yet
EP1.28/4:	not used yet
EP1.28/5:date	Region 5 public reports Later EP1.28/7:
EP1.28/6:CT	Environmental Midwest together (annual)
EP1.28/7:date	Environment Midwest (monthly) Earlier EP1.28/5:
EP1.29:CT	Water quality standards summary [for various States]
EP1.29/2:CT	Water quality standards criteria digest, compilation of Federal/State criteria on [various subjects]
EP1.30:date	Noise facts digest
EP1.31:date	Journal holdings report
EP1.32:date	EXPRO, a listing of extramural projects to be funded in fiscal year
EP1.33:date	Digests of State air programs, fiscal year
EP1.34:date	Life--pass it on. President's environmental merit awards program. Earlier EP1.2:L62
EP1.34/2:nos	Life--pass it on, PAO-(series) Issued by the Rocky Mountain Prairie Region, Denver, Colorado
EP1.35:date	Quarterly awards listing, grants assistance programs. Earlier EP1.2: Awl/date

EP1.36:date	Inside EPA, publication for employees
EP1.37:date	Coastal pollution research highlights. Issued by Pacific Northwest Environmental Research Laboratory
EP1.37/2:nos	Pacific Northwest Environmental Research Laboratory: PNERL working papers
EP1.37/3:date	Pollution identification research highlights. Issued by Southeast Environmental Research Lab.
EP1.38:nos	EPA orders
EP1.39:date	Quarterly calendar of environmental meetings
EP1.40:date	Monthly status report
EP1.41:date	Inventory of interstate carrier water supply systems
EP1.42:date/nos	Environmental facts (irregular)
EP1.43:date	Clean water, annual report to Congress
EP1.44:date	Environmental studies division, FY program
EP1.45:v.nos	Comprehensive planning series
EP1.46:date	National Environmental Research Center, Research Triangle Park, N.C., annual report
EP1.46/2:date	National Environmental Research Center, Cincinnati, Ohio. Annual report
EP1.46/3:date	National Environmental Research Center, Las Vegas, Report (quarterly)
EP1.46/4:date	Grosse Ile Laboratory, quarterly report
EP1.46/5:date	Control Systems Laboratory: Annual report. Name changed to Industrial Environmental Research Laboratory, RTP
EP1.47:date	National Air Monitoring Program: Air quality and emission trends, annual report
EP1.48:CT	Posters
EP1.49:CT	News of environment research in Cincinnati. Issued by National Environmental Research Center, Cincinnati, Ohio
EP1.50:nos	United States LPPSD technical information exchange documents. Later ER1.16:
EP1.51:nos	Surveillance and Analysis Division, Region 9, San Francisco, Calif.;Technical report

EP1.51/2:nos	Annapolis Field Office, Middle Atlantic Region 3, Philadelphia, Pa., Technical reports
EP1.51/3:nos	Surveillance and Analysis Division, Region 8, Denver, Colorado, Technical Support Branch: SA/TSB- (series)
EP1.51/4:nos	Surveillance and Analysis Division, Region 8, Technical Investigation Branch SA/TIB- (series)
EP1.52:date	State air pollution implementation plan progress report (semi-annual)
EP1.53:date	Air quality data, statistics.
EP1.54:date	Lifecycle (monthly)
EP1.55:CT	National emissions inventory of sources of emissions
EP1.56:nos	Wastewater treatment construction grants data base, Public law 92-500, project records, grants assistance program (monthly)
EP1.56/2:date	Project register, waste water treatment construction grants (monthly)
EP1.56/3:nos	State municipal project priority lists, grants assistance programs
EP1.57:CT	Final environmental impact statement for proposed waste treatment facilities [various locations]
EP1.57/2:	Final environmental impact statement for waste water facilities [various locations]
EP1.57/3:CT	Final environmental impact statements
EP1.57/4:CT	Draft environmental impact statements
EP1.57/5:CT	Standards support and environmental impact statements
EP1.58:nos	Implementation plan review for [various States] as required by the Energy supply and environmental coordination act
EP1.59:date	Monitoring and air quality trends report (annual)
EP1.60:date	Southeast Environmental Research Laboratory quarterly summary
EP1.61:CT	Evaluation of [various States] water supply program
EP1.62:date	The cost of clean air, annual report of the administrator of Environmental Protection Agency to the Congress of the United States in compliance with Public law 91-604. Earlier HE1.35: (FS1.35:)

EP1.63:v.nos	Collection of legal opinions
EP1.64:date	National emissions report (annual)
EP1.65:date	Semi-annual list of reports prepared for or by the Office of Toxic Substances
EP1.66:v.nos	Decisions of the Administrator and decisions of the General Counsel
EP1.67:v.nos.&nos.	EPA journal (monthly)

Water Programs Office

EP2 Water Quality Office

The Federal Water Quality Administration has been transferred from the Interior Department to the Environmental Protection Agency, and renamed the Water Quality Office.

EP2.1:date	Annual reports. Earlier I67.1:
EP2.2:CT	General publications. Earlier I67.2:
EP2.3/2:letters/nos	Technical bulletins
EP2.5:CT	Laws
EP2.8:CT	Handbooks, manuals, guides. Earlier I67.8:
EP2.9:nos	Selected summaries of water research. Earlier I67.12:
EP2.10:nos	Water pollution control research series. Earlier I67.13/4: Later EP1.16:
EP2.11:letters-nos	Oil and hazardous material program series
EP2.12:date	Research, development, and demonstration projects, grants and contract awards
EP2.13:date	Project register, projects approved under sec. 8, of Federal water pollution control act (Pub. law 660, 84th Cong.), as amended and sec. 3, of Public works acceleration act (Publc law 658, 87th Cong.) Earlier I67.16:
EP2.14:date	Cost of clean water [annual report to Congress]. Earlier I67.1/2:
EP2.15:date	Northwest shellfish sanitation research planning conference, proceedings. Earlier FS2.2:Sh4/6
EP2.16:nos	Analytical reference service reports (numbered) Earlier HE20.113:, HE20.1700:
EP2.17:date	Inventory municipal waste facilities in United States. Earlier I67.22:
EP2.17/2:date/v	National water quality inventory, Report to Congress

EP2.18:nos	TR - (series)
EP2.19:nos	Estuarine pollution study series. Earlier I67.21:
EP2.20:date	Sewage facilities construction [annual] Earlier I67.11:
EP2.21:date	Digest of State program plans, fy.
EP2.22:date	Pacific Northwest Water Laboratory: Quarterly report. Later EP1.19:
EP2.23:nos	Working papers (numbered) Earlier I67.23:
EP2.24:date	Fish kills caused by pollution (annual) Earlier I67.9:
EP2.25:nos	Pesticide study series
EP2.26:nos	Technical studies report, TS (series)
EP2.27:CT	Bibliographies and lists of publications Earlier I67.14:
EP2.28:nos	MCD [Municipal Construction Division] series

EP3 Solid Waste Management Office

The Office of Solid Waste Management was transferred from the Department of Health, Education & Welfare and placed within the Environmental Protection Agency by Reorganization Plan 3 of 1970, effective Dec. 2, 1970.

EP3.1:date	Annual report Earlier HE20.1401:
EP3.2:CT	General publications Earlier HE20.1402:
EP3.3/2:v.nos.&nos.	Accession bulletin, solid waste information retrieval system (monthly) Later EP1.18:
EP3.5:CT	Laws
EP3.8:CT	Handbooks, manuals, guides **Earlier HE20.1408:**
EP3.9:CT	Bibliographies and lists of publications.
EP3.10:date	State solid waste planning grants, agencies, and progress, report of activities Earlier similar FS2.2:So4/12/969 and FS2.2:So4/13/969
EP3.11:CT	Posters
EP3.12:date	Solid waste management training bulletin of courses.

Air and Water Programs Office
Air Programs Office
EP4   Air Pollution Control Office

The functions of the National Air Pollution Control Administration have been transferred to Air Pollution Control Office, Environmental Protection Agency, by Reorganization plan 2 of 1970.

EP4.1:date   Annual report. Earlier HE20.1301:

EP4.2:CT   General publication. Earlier HE20.1302:

EP4.8:CT   Handbooks, manuals, guides. Earlier HE20.1308:

EP4.9:nos   Air Pollution Control Office publications, AP-(series) Earlier HE20.1309:

EP4.9/a:CT   ___ separates.

EP4.9/2:nos   Air Pollution Control Office publication APTD-(series) Earlier HE20.1309/2:

EP4.10:CT   Air Pollution report, Federal facilities, air quality control regions. Earlier HE20.1310/2:

EP4.11:v.nos.&nos. Air pollution abstracts. Earlier HE20.1303/3:

EP4.12:CT   Addresses. Earlier HE20.1312:

EP4.13:date   Air pollution training courses and university training programs (fiscal year) Earlier HE20.1303/4:

EP4.14:CT   Descriptions of [various] courses

EP4.14/2:date   Chronological schedule, Institute for Air Pollution Training courses

EP4.15:CT   Real property owned by the Federal Government in [various States].

EP4.16:date   Progress in prevention and control of air pollution, Report to Congress.

Pesticides Programs Office
EP5 Pesticides Office

Established by Reorganization plan 3 of 1970, effective Dec. 2, 1970.

EP5.1:date	Annual report
EP5.2:CT	General publications
EP5.6:	Regulations, rules and instructions
EP5.8:CT	Handbooks, manuals and guides.
EP5.9:v.nos. &nos.	Health aspects of pesticides, abstract bulletin. Earlier HE20.4011:
EP5.10:	Addresses
EP5.11/1: date	EPA compendium of registered pesticides, volume 1, Herbicides and plant regulators (monthly)
EP5.11/2:date	EPA compendium of registered pesticides, volume 2, Fungicides and nematicides (monthly)
EP5.11/3:date	EPA compendium of registered pesticides, volume 3. Insecticides, acaricides, molluscicides, and antifouling compounds (monthly)
EP5.11/4:date	EPA compendium of registered pesticides, volume 4. Rodenticides and mammals, birds and fish toxicants. (quarterly)
EP5.11/5: date	EPA compendium of registered pesticides, volume 5
EP5.12:CT	Bibliographies and lists of publications
EP5.13:nos	Substitute chemical program, initial scientific and minieconomic review of [various chemicals]
EP5.14:CT	Environmental impact statements

Radiation Programs Office
EP6 Radiation Office

Reorganization Plan 3 of 1970, effective Dec. 3, 1970.

EP6.1:date	Annual report. Earlier HE20.1501:
EP6.1/2:date	EPA review of radiation protection activities (annual)
EP6.2:CT	General publications. Earlier HE20.1502:
EP6.8:CT	Handbooks, manuals, guides
EP6.9:v.nos.&nos.	Radiological health data and reports (monthly) Earlier HE20.1509:
EP6.10:nos	RO/EERL [Eastern Environmental Radiation Laboratory] (series)
EP6.10/2:nos	ORP/SID [Surveillance and Inspection Division] (series) Earlier FS2.314/3:
EP6.10/3:nos	ORP/CSD [Criteria and Standards Division] (series)
EP6.10/4:nos	EPA/ORP (series)
EP6.11:date	Radiological quality of the environment (annual)

EP7 Technology Transfer

Established as part of Environmental Protection Agency in Sept. 1971

- EP7.1:date   Annual report
- EP7.2:CT   General publications

- EP7.8:CT   Handbooks, manuals, guides
- EP7.8/2:CT   Processing design annual for [various subjects]
- EP7.9:date   Technology Transfer, the bridge between research and use
- EP7.10:nos   EPA Technology Transfer seminar publications
- EP7.11:nos   EPA technology transfer capsule reports

ER Energy Research and Development Administration

The Energy Research and Development Administration (ERDA) was established by the Energy Reorganization Act of 1974 (88 Stat.1233; 3 U.S.C. 301).

ER1.1:date   Annual report

ER1.2:CT   General publications

ER1.7:nos   News releases

ER1.8:CT   Handbooks, manuals, guides

ER1.9:v.nos. &nos.   Energy abstracts for policy analysis (monthly) Earlier Y3.At7:59

ER1.10:v.nos. &nos.   Nuclear science abstracts (semimonthly) Earlier Y3.At7:16

ER1.10/2:v.nos. &pt.nos.   ___ indexes. Earlier Y3.At7:16-5

ER1.11:letters & nos.   Research and development reports. Earlier Y3.At7:22

ER1.12:v.nos/nos   Information from ERDA, weekly announcements Replaces Y3.At7:32-2
ER1.12/2:date   Information from ERDA
ER1.13:nos   Materials and components in fossil energy applications and ERDA newsletter

ER1.14:CT   ERDA critical review series

ER1.15:date   ERDA research abstracts (monthly) Later title ERDA energy research abstracts

ER1.16:nos   United States LPPSD Technical Information Exchange documents. Earlier EP1.50:

ER1.17:date   Telephone directory

ER1.18:nos   USERDA translation lists. Earlier Y3.At7:44-2

ER1.19:date   Journals available in the ERDA Library (semiannual)

ER1.20:CT   Addresses

ER1.21:CT   Maps, charts and posters

ER1.22:CT   Program approval documents, executive summaries

ES   Economic Stabilization Agency

Established pursuant to the Defense Production Act of 1950 (Public law 774, 81st Congress) and Executive order 10161.

ES1.1:date	Annual reports
ES1.2:CT	General publications
ES1.6:CT	Regulations, rules and instructions
ES1.6/2:	Regulations. Includes: Ceiling price regulations, General regulations, Wage procedure regulations.
ES1.6/3:nos	General orders. Proc. Admin.
ES1.7/1:nos	Releases. Desig. GPE-nos. Proc. Later ES3.7/1:
ES1.7/2:nos	Speeches. Desig. GPE-S-nos

Terminated April 30, 1953, pursuant to Executive order 10434 of February 6, 1953. Liquidation completed October 31, 1953, pursuant to Executive order 10480 of August 14, 1953.

ES2   Wage Stabilization Board

Established in the Economic Stabilization Agency by Executive order 10161 of Sept. 9, 1950.

ES2.1:date	Annual reports
ES2.2:CT	General publications
ES2.6:CT	Regulations, rules, and instructions
ES2.6/2:nos	General regulations

ES2.6/3:nos	General wage regulations
ES2.6/4:nos	Construction Industry Stabilization Commission regulations
ES2.6/5:nos	Resolutions
ES2.7/1:1e-nos	Releases. Desig. WSB-nos.
ES2.7/2:nos	Wage Stabilization Committee releases, WSC (series) Proc.
ES2.8:nos	Interpretation bulletins

Terminated April 30, 1953, pursuant to Executive order 10434 of February 6, 1953, and provisions of the Defense Production Act amendments of 1952 & 1953. (66 Stat. 296, 67 Stat. 131.)

ES3   Price Stabilization Office

Established in the Economic Stabilization Agency by Executive order 10161 of Sept. 9, 1950.

ES3.1:date	Annual reports
ES3.2:CT	General publications
ES3.5:CT	Laws
ES3.6:CT	Regulations, rules, and instructions
ES3.6/2:nos	Administrative orders
ES3.6/3:nos	Distribution orders
ES3.6/4:nos	General ceiling price regulations
ES3.6/5:nos	Ceiling price regulations
ES3.6/6:nos	Enforcement and procedure regulations
ES3.6/7:nos	OPS guides Desig. OPSG nos.
ES3.6/8:nos	Distribution regulations
ES3.6/9:nos	General overriding regulations

ES3.6/10:nos	Summary of orders
ES3.6/10-2:nos	Combined summary of orders
ES3.6/11:nos	Delegations of authority
ES3.6/12:nos	PI-M (series)
ES3.6/13:nos	OPS trade guide TP (series)
ES3.6/14:nos	General interpretations
ES3.6/15:nos	OPS trade aide TA (series)
ES3.6/16:date	Abstracts of price regulations
ES3.6/17:	General disallowance orders
ES3.6/18:	Price procedural regulations
ES3.7/1:nos	General press releases Earlier ES1.7/1:
ES3.7/2:nos	Speeches. Designated S-nos.
ES3.7/3:nos	Releases relating to orders. Proc. or ptd. Designated O-nos
ES3.7/4:nos	[Releases relating to questions on price regulations and orders] TP (series)
ES3.8:nos	Addresses. Designated OPSA-nos. Beginning with no. 4, desig. PI-nos.
ES3.9:CT	OPS trade bulletins
ES3.10:date	Directory of commodities and services
ES3.10/2:date	Directory of commodities and services exempted or suspended from price control.
ES3.11:nos	PI-H (series)

Terminated April 30, 1953, pursuant to Executive order 10434 of February 6, 1953, and provisions of the Defense Production Act amendments of 1952 and 1953 (66 Stat. 296, 67 Stat. 131).

ES4 Salary Stabilization Board

Established by the Economic Stabilization Administrator on May 10, 1950

ES4.1:date	Annual reports

ES4. 2:CT	General publications
ES4. 6:CT	Regulations, rules, and instructions
ES4. 6/2:nos	General salary stabilization regulations GSSR (series)
ES4. 6/3:nos	General salary orders
ES4. 6/4:nos	Interpretations
ES4. 6/5:nos	Salary procedural regulations
ES4. 7:	Releases

Terminated April 30, 1953 pursuant to Executive order 10434 of February 6, 1953, and provisions of Defense Production act amendments of 1952 and 1953 (66 Stat. 296) 67 Stat. 131).

ES5 Rent Stabilization Office

Established by General order 9 of Economic Stabilization Administrator on July 31, 1951.

ES5. 1:date	Annual reports
ES5. 2:CT	General publications
ES5. 5:CT	Laws
ES5. 6:CT	Regulations, rules, and instructions
ES5. 7:nos	Releases
ES5. 7/2:CT	Questions and answers on rent control. Proc.

Abolished by Executive order 10475 of July 31, 1953 and **functions transferred to Office of Defense Mobilization.**

ES6 National Enforcement Commission

The National Enforcement Commission was established within the Economic Stabilization Agency by General order 18 of the Economic Stabilization Administrator, effective July 30, 1952.

ES6.1:date   Annual reports

ES6.2:CT   General publications

ES6.7:nos   Releases

Functions transferred to Attorney General by Executive order 10494 of October 14, 1953.

FA Fine Arts Commission

Created by act of Congress May 17, 1910 (36 Stat. 371)

FA1.1:date	Annual reports
FA1.1/a:CT	___ separates
FA1.2:CT	General publications
FA1.2/a:CT	___ separates
FA1.3:	Bulletins
FA1.4:	Circulars
FA1.5:CT	Laws

FAA   Federal Aviation Agency

The Federal Aviation Agency was established by the Federal aviation act of 1958 (Public law 726, 85th Congress, 1st session, approved Aug. 23, 1958).

FAA1.1:date	Semiannual reports. Later TD4.1:
FAA1.2:CT	General publications. Later TD4.2:
FAA1.4/2:nos	Advisory circular. Admin.
FAA1.5:CT	Laws. Later TD4.5:
FAA1.6:CT	Regulations, rules, and instructions. Later TD4.6/2:
FAA1.6/2:nos	Special civil air regulations. Earlier C31.206/3:
FAA1.6/3:nos	Maintenance Operations Division instructions. Earlier C31.106/4: Admin.
FAA1.6/4:nos	Regulations of administrator. Earlier C31.140: Replaced by FAA1.6/8:
FAA1.6/5:nos	Civil air regulations draft releases. Earlier C31.209/2: Preliminary. Published in Federal Register
FAA1.6/6:pt.nos	Civil air regulations. Earlier C31.209: Replaced by FAA1.6/8:
FAA1.6/7:nos	Systems Maintenance Division instructions. Administrative.
FAA1.6/8:pt.nos	Federal aviation regulations. Replaces FAA1.6/6: and FAA1.6/4: Later TD4.6:
FAA1.6/9:date	Rules of flight (annual)
FAA1.7:nos	Releases
FAA1.7/2:nos	Press releases T (series)
FAA1.7/3:nos	FAA news [Dulles International Airport] DIA -(series)
FAA1.7/4:date	News features from Federal Aviation Agency
FAA1.8:CT	Handbooks, manuals, guides Later TD4.8:
FAA1.8/2:les.&nos.	FAA handbooks (numbered) Later TD4.8/2:

FAA1.9:CT　　　　　　Dictionaries, glossaries, etc.

FAA1.10:date　　　　List of FAA publications.　Earlier C31.162:　Later TD4.17:

FAA1.10/2:nos　　　Bibliographies of technical reports, information retrieval lists. Later TD4.17/3:

FAA1.10/3:nos　　　Bibliographic list.　Later TD4.17/3:

FAA1.11:v.nos.&nos.　Fly-by, official employee publication of Federal Aviation Agency

FAA1.12:CT　　　　　Addresses　Later TD4.29:

FAA1.13:nos　　　　　Federal Aviation Agency specification.　Earlier C31.120:　Admin.

FAA1.14:date　　　　Summary of supplemental type certificates and approved replacement parts.　Later FAA5.12:

FAA1.15:date　　　　General aviation accidents (non-air carrier), statistical analysis, calendar year.　Earlier C31.160/2:

FAA1.16:CT　　　　　Maps and charts.　Later TD4.27:

FAA1.17:cl.nos.　　　FAA National supply catalog.　Admin.

FAA1.18:date　　　　Status of Civil air regulations and Civil aeronautics manuals.　Earlier C31.151:　Later TD4.13:

FAA1.19:v.nos.&nos.　Management services notices.　Monthly.　Admin.

FAA1.20:v.nos　　　　Flight information manual.　Earlier C31.128:　Later FAA3.13/2:

FAA1.21:v.nos　　　　Alaska flight information manual.　Earlier C31.134:

FAA1.22:v.nos　　　　International flight information manual.　Earlier C31.139:　Later FAA3.13:

FAA1.23:v.nos.&nos.　Airman's guide (biweekly)　Earlier C31.127:　Later FAA1.45:

FAA1.23/2:date　　　Directory of airports and seaplane bases, Airman's guide supplement (quarterly)　Later FAA1.45:

FAA1.24:v.nos.&nos.　Alaska airman's guide, notices to airmen (biweekly)　Earlier C31.135:

FAA1.25:v.nos.&nos.　Airman's guide and flight information manual, Pacific supplement (semiannual) Proc.　Earlier C31.136:　Later FAA1.25/3:, FAA1.25/4:

FAA1.25/2:date　　　Airman's guide and flight information manual.

FAA1.25/3:v.nos.&nos.   Airman's guide, Pacific supplement (semimonthly) Formerly in FAA1.25: Replaced by FAA1.25/5:

FAA1.25/4:v.nos   Flight information manual, Pacific supplement, Formerly in FAA1.25:

FAA1.25/5:v.nos.&nos.   Pacific Airman's guide and chart supplement. (monthly) Replaces FAA1.25/3: Later TD4.16:

FAA1.26:v.nos.&nos.   International notams (weekly) Earlier C31.133: Later TD4.11:

FAA1.27:date   FAA air traffic activity (annual) Earlier C31.158: Later TD4.19:

FAA1.27/2:date   Activities at air traffic control facilities, fiscal year

FAA1.27/3:date   Air traffic patterns for VFR general aviation, fiscal year

FAA1.27/4:date   Air traffic patterns for IFR and VFR aviation, calendar year Later TD4.19/2:

FAA1.28:nos   FAA airworthiness directives (biweekly) Proc. Earlier C31.147/2: Later TD4.10:

FAA1.28/2:date   Summary of airworthiness directives for small aircraft. Later TD4.10/2:

FAA1.28/3:date   Summary of airworthiness directives for large aircraft. Later TD4.10/3:

FAA1.29:date   Aircraft specifications. Earlier C31.120/2: Later TD4.15:

FAA1.29/2:date   Engine & propeller specifications. Earlier C31.120/3: Later TD4.15/2:

FAA1.30:date   Annual report of operations under Federal airport act. Earlier C31.145/3: Later TD4.22:

FAA1.31:date   General maintenance inspection aids summary and supplements. Earlier C3.163: Later TD4.409:

FAA1.31/2:nos   General maintenance alert bulletins. Earlier C31.163/2:

FAA1.32:date   FAA statistical handbook of aviation. Earlier C31.144: Later TD4.20:

FAA1.32/2:date   Statistical study of U.S. civil aircraft (annual) Earlier C31.160: Replaced by FAA1.35/2:

FAA1.33:date   Aircraft in agriculture (annual) Earlier FAA1.2:Ag8

FAA1.34/1-8:nos   Civil aeronautics manuals (numbered 1-8) Earlier C31.107/2:

FAA1.35:date   United States active civil aircraft by State and County. Earlier C31.132/2:

FAA1.35/2:date   Census of U.S. civil aircraft. Replaces FAA1.32/2: and FAA1.35: Later TD4.18:

FAA1.35/3:date   United States civil aircraft register (semiannual) Earlier FAA5.14:Later TD4.18/2

617

FAA1.36:nos   Jet age planning progress reports. Earlier C31.168:

FAA1.37:date   FAA plan for air navigation and air traffic control systems. Earlier C31.167:

FAA1.38:nos   Technical standards orders. Earlier C31.143:

FAA1.39:date   General aviation aircraft use

FAA1.40:date   Aircraft instrument approaches, fiscal year

FAA1.41:v.nos.&nos. Aviation news (monthly)

FAA1.41/2:v.nos.&nos. FAA aviation news (monthly) Continuation of Aviation news, FAA1.41: Later TD4.9:

FAA1.42:date   Aviation forecasts, fiscal years

FAA1.43:date   Field facility directory (quarterly) Later TD4.21:

FAA1.44:nos   Security reminder. Official use.

FAA1.45:nos   Technical reports   Earlier FAA3.13/2:

Functions transferred to the Federal Aviation Administration in the Department of Transportation by the Department of Transportation Act of Oct.15,1966 (80 Stat. 931).

FAA2   Systems Research and Development Service

The Aviation Research and Development Service was redesignated, with changes, as the Systems Research and Development Service by FAA order of May 16,1962.

FAA2   Research and Development Bureau

The Bureau of Research and Development was established within the Federal Aviation Agency by Administrative order 1 of the Administrator, Federal Aviation Agency, dated Nov.1,1958. It absorbed the functions of the Airways Modernization Board which was transferred to the Federal Aviation Agency by Executive order 10786 of Nov.1,1958. A later name for this agency was Aviation Research and Development Service.

FAA2.1:date   Program and progress report. Later TD4.501:

FAA2.2:CT   General publications   Later TD4.502:

FAA2.7:date   Releases

FAA2.8:nos   Technical development reports. Earlier C31.119:

FAA2.8/2:nos   Reports

FAA2.9:date   Annual international aviation research and development symposium, report of proceedings

FAA2.10:date   Design for national airspace utilization system. Class cancelled Jan.1964. SEE FAA2.2:Ai7/5

FAA2.11:v.nos   Consolidated abstracts of technical reports

FAA2.11/2:v.nos   Consolidated abstracts of technical reports: General distribution

Public law 89-670, transferred to Transportation Department.

Air Traffic Service
FAA3   Air Traffic Management Bureau

The Air Traffic Management Bureau was established in the Federal Aviation Agency pursuant to the Federal Aviation Act of 1958 (Public law 726, 85th Congress, 2d session, approved Aug. 23, 1958.)

FAA3.1:date   Annual reports   Later TD4.301:

FAA3.2:CT   General publications   Later TD4.302:

FAA3.6:CT   ATS manuals

FAA3.6/2:nos   ATM directives

FAA3.8:CT   ATM manuals   Later title ATS manuals

FAA3.8/2:CT   Handbooks, manuals, guides   Later TD4.308:

FAA3.9:date   Air traffic control procedures. Formerly entitled ANC procedures for control of air traffic C31.106/2:

FAA3.9/2:date   Communications procedures, ATM-2-B. Later title, Aeronautical communications and pilot services.

FAA3.10:date   Location identifiers. Earlier C31.157: Later TD4.310:

FAA3.11:date   Enroute IFR air traffic survey. Earlier C31.165: Later TD4.19/3:

FAA3.11/2:date   IFR altitude usage peak day

FAA3.11/3:date   Enroute IFR peak day charts, fiscal year   Later TD4.313:

FAA3.12:CT   Maps. Earlier C31.115:

FAA3.13:v.nos   International flight information manual. Earlier FAA1.22: Later TD4.309:

FAA3.13/2:v.nos   Flight information manual. Earlier FAA1.20:   Later FAA1.45:

FAA3.13/3:sec.nos/date   Airman's information manual. Later TD4.12:

FAA3.14:date   ATS fact book (quarterly)

The Federal Aviation Administration was established in the Transportation Department by Public law 89-670, approved Oct.15,1966. Functions, powers and duties of the Federal Aviation Agency and offices thereof are transferred to and vested in the Secretary of Transportation.

FAA4   Facilities Bureau

The Facilities Bureau was established in the Federal Aviation Agency pursuant to the Federal Aviation Act of 1958 (Public law 726, 85th Congress, 2d session, approved August 23, 1958)

FAA4.1:date   Annual reports

FAA4.2:CT   General publications

FAA4.8:date   National airport plan. Earlier C31.145/2: Later FAA8.11·

FAA4.9:nos	Bureau of Facilities manual of operations. Earlier C31.116/3:
FAA4.9/2:CT	Handbooks, manuals, guides
FAA4.9/3:date	Airport design manual
FAA4.10:date	Standard specifications for construction of airports. Earlier C31.120:Ai7/date Later TD4.24:
FAA4.11:date	Air commerce traffic pattern, calendar year. Earlier C31.153: Later FAA8.9:
FAA4.12:nos	Planning series. Note--Some publications carry title, Planning guide

The Federal Aviation Administration was established in the Transportation Department by Public law 89-670, approved Oct.15,1966. Functions, powers and duties of the Federal Aviation Agency and offices thereof are transferred to and vested in the Secretary of Transportation.

FAA5 Flight Standards Bureau

The Bureau of Flight Standards was established in the Federal Aviation Agency pursuant to the Federal aviation act of 1958 (Public law 726, 85th Congress, 2d session, approved Aug. 23,1958).

FAA5.1:date	Annual reports. Later TD4.401:
FAA5.2:CT	General publications. Later TD4.402:
FAA5.7:nos	Bureau of Flight Standards releases. Earlier C31.111:
FAA5.8:nos	Technical manuals. Earlier C31.138:
FAA5.8/2:CT	Handbooks, manuals, guides. Later TD4.408:
FAA5.9:date	United States standard facilities flight check manual. Earlier C31.163/3:
FAA5.10:nos	Bureau practice. Administrative.
FAA5.11:nos	Quality control digests. Earlier C31.166:
FAA5.12:date	**Summary of supplemental type certificates** approved replacement parts. Earlier FAA1.14: Later TD4.36:

FAA5.13:   Standard instrument approach procedure [by type]   Official use.

FAA5.14:date   United States civil aircraft register (semiannual)   Later FAA1.35/3:

FAA5.15:date   Acceptable methods, techniques, and practices: Aircraft inspection and repair.   Later TD4.28/2:

FAA5.16:date   Acceptable methods, techniques, and practices: Aircraft alterations. Later TD4.28:

The Federal Aviation Administration was established in the Transportation Department by Public law 89-670, approved Oct.15,1966.

FAA6   National Capital Airports Bureau

The Bureau of National Capital Airports was established in June 1959 to provide management responsibility for Washington National Airport and Dulles International Airport.

FAA6.1:date   Annual report

FAA6.2:CT   General publications.

The Federal Aviation Administration was established in the Transportation Department by Public law 89-670, approved Oct.15,1966.

FAA7   Aviation Medicine Bureau

In March 1960 the Federal Aviation Agency established the Bureau of Aviation Medicine to replace the former Office of the Chief Air Surgeon.

FAA7.1:date   Annual reports.   Later TD4.201:

FAA7.2:CT   General publications.   Later TD4.202:

FAA7.3/2:nos   Federal Air Surgeon's bulletin.   Internal use only.

FAA7.8:date   List of aviation medical examiners (semiannual)   Later TD4.211:

FAA7.9:CT   Handbooks, manuals, guides. Later TD4.208:

FAA7.10:nos   FAA aviation medical research reports

FAA7.10/2:nos   Civil Aeromedical Research Institute: Technical publications

FAA7.11:v.nos.&nos. Medical newsletter (monthly)

FAA7.12:nos   [Aviation medical reports] AM (series) Later TD4.210:

FAA7.13:nos   Aviation medical education series. Later TD4.209:

The Federal Aviation Administration was established in the Transportation Department by Public law 89-670, approved October 15, 1966.

FAA8   Airports Service

The Airports Service was established effective November 6, 1961, by Federal Aviation Agency order 23. Agency order 23 also abolished the Airports Division of the Aviation Facilities Service and transferred its personnel, records, etc. to the Airports Service.

FAA8.1:date   Annual reports. Later TD4.101:

FAA8.2:CT   General publications. Later TD4.102:

FAA8.8:CT   Handbooks, manuals, guides. Later TD4.108:

FAA8.9:date   Air commerce traffic pattern (scheduled carriers), fiscal year. Earlier FAA4.11: Later combined in C31.251:

FAA8.10:CT   Federal-aid airport program publications.

FAA8.11:date   National airport plan, fiscal years. Earlier FAA4.8: Later TD4.109.

The Federal Aviation Administration was established in the Transportation Department by

Public law 89-670, approved Oct. 15, 1966. Functions, powers and duties of the Federal Aviation Agency and offices thereof are transferred to and vested in the Secretary of Transportation.

FC Fish Commission

Established by Joint resolution of Congress, Feb. 9, 1871.

FC1.1:pt. nos	Annual reports
FC1.1/a:date	___ separates. Commissioners' report
FC1.1/a:CT	___ separates. Miscellaneous
FC1.2:CT	General publications
FC1.2/a:CT	___ separates
FC1.3:v. nos	Bulletins. Later C6.3:
FC1.3/a:CT	___ separates
FC1.4:nos	Circulars
FC1.5:nos	Statistical bulletins. Later C6.5:
FC1.6:sec. nos	Fisheries and fishing industries
FC1.6/a:CT	___ separates
FC1.7:CT	Special bulletins.

Transferred to Commerce and Labor Department, July 1, 1903 (C6.)

FCA Farm Credit Administration

March 27, 1933.

FCA1.1:date	Annual reports. Later A72.1:, FCA1.1:
FCA1.2:CT	General publications. Later A72.2:, FCA1.2:
FCA1.2/a:CT	___ separates
FCA1.3:nos	Bulletins. Later A72.3:, FCA1.3:
FCA1.4:nos	Circulars. Later A72.4:, FCA1.4:
FCA1.4/2:le.	Circulars (lettered) Later A72.4:letter-nos, FCA1.4/2:
FCA1.4/3:le-nos	Circulars on cooperative marketing. Later A72.4:C-nos
FCA1.5:	Laws
FCA1.6:CT	Regulations, rules and instructions, etc. Later A72.6:
FCA1.7:date	Statement of condition of Federal land banks, joint stock land banks, etc. Earlier T48.6:
FCA1.7:vol	Farm credit quarterly. Continuation of FCA1.7:date Later A72.15:
FCA1.7/2:date	Statements of condition of joint stock land banks. Earlier in FCA1.7: Later A72.16:
FCA1.8:nos	Posters
FCA1.8/2:nos	Charts
FCA1.9:CT	Addresses (usually mimeographed) Later A72.11:
FCA1.10:vol	News for farmer cooperatives. Monthly. Mim. Later A72.10:
FCA1.10/a:CT	___ separates. Later A72.10/a:
FCA1.11:vol	Farm credit notes. Monthly. Multigraphed.
FCA1.12:date	Monthly report on loans and discounts. (Rotaprinted) Later quarterly. Later A72.12:
FCA1.12/2:date	Loans and discounts of lending institutions supervised by Farm Credit Administration, semiannual report. Proc. Earlier A72.12:
FCA1.13:nos	Miscellaneous reports. Proc. Later A72.8:

FCA1.14:vol	Cooperative savings with Federal credit unions. Monthly. Proc.
FCA1.14/2:vol	Cooperative savings with Federal credit unions. Bimonthly. Later A72.13:
FCA1.15:date	Federal credit unions. Monthly. Proc. Later A72.14:
FCA1.16:date	Federal credit unions, report on operations. Quarterly, semiannual and annual. Proc. Later A72.19:
FCA1.17:nos	Lecture notes for film strip. Proc.
FCA1.18:nos	Summary of cases relating to Farmers cooperative associations. Proc. Later A72.18:
FCA1.19:CT	Farmer cooperatives (by States) Later A72.17:
FCA1.20:CT	Publications, Lists of. Later A72.21:
FCA1.21:nos	Special reports. Later A72.9:

Transferred to Department of Agriculture, Reorganization plan I, April 25, 1939.

The Farm Credit Administration, formerly in the Department of Agriculture was made an independent agency in the Executive branch of the Government by Public law 202, 83d Congress, approved Aug. 6, 1953, effective Dec. 4, 1935. The Library of the Division of Public Documents will classify publications of this newly established independent agency in the FCA1. classes assigned to the independent agency of the same name between May 27, 1933 and June 30, 1939.

FCA1.22:date	Production credit associations, summary of operations (annual) Proc. Earlier A72.25:
FCA1.23:date	Report to national farm loan associations (annual) Earlier FCA1.2:N21f
FCA1.24:date	Farm and credit outlook for [year]

FCD   Federal Civil Defense Administration

The Federal Civil Defense Administration was established originally in the Executive Office of the President by Executive order 10186 of Dec. 1, 1950. It was established as an independent agency by Public law 920, 81st Congress, approved Jan. 12, 1951.

FCD1.1:date	Annual reports. Earlier Pr33.801: Later Pr34.701:
FCD1.1/2:date	Annual statistical report. Later Pr34.751/2:
FCD1.1/2-2:dt.&nos.	Progress reports. Later Pr34.751:
FCD1.2:CT	General publications. Earlier Pr33.802: Later Pr34.702:
FCD1.3:nos	Technical bulletins. Later Pr34.753:
FCD1.3/2:nos	Advisory bulletins. Later Pr34.753/3:
FCD1.6:CT	Regulations, rules, and instructions
FCD1.6/2:nos	Administrative guides, AG (series) Later Pr34.761/6:
FCD1.6/3:nos	Technical manual TM (series) Later Pr34.761/3:
FCD1.6/4:nos	Handbook H (series) Later Pr34.761/2:
FCD1.6/5:nos	Instructor's guide IG (series) Desig. IG-nos. Later Pr34.761/4:
FCD1.6/5-2:CT	Interim instructor's guides. Later PrEx4.12/5-2:
FCD1.6/6:nos	Manuals. Designated M-nos.
FCD1.6/7:nos	Program guide PG (series)
FCD1.6/8:nos	Pocket manual PM (series) Later Pr34.761/5:
FCD1.7:	Releases
FCD1.7/2:nos	Special promotion [releases] SP-series. Later Pr34.757/3:
FCD1.7/3:nos	Leader's guide, special bulletin series in support of annual National civil defense week. Proc. **Earlier FCD1.6:L46/dt/supp.** Later Pr34.757/4:
FCD1.8:v.nos	Civil defense alert (monthly)

FCD1.9:nos	Training and education bulletin TEB (series) Desig. TEB-nos.
FCD1.9/2:nos	Training bulletin, Training officer series. (unnumbered publications in this series are CT)
FCD1.9/3:nos	Training bulletin, School series
FCD1.10:nos	Volunteer manpower booklet VM (series)
FCD1.11:nos	Poster series
FCD1.11/2:1e-nos	[Photographs of A-Bomb test, Operation Doorstep, Yucca Flat, Nevada, Mar.17,1953]
FCD1.12:v.nos	Impact of air attack in World War II, selected data for civil defense planning (Stanford Research Institute reports); Division 1, Physical damage to structures, facilities, and persons
FCD1.12/2:v.nos	___ Division 2, Effects on general economy
FCD1.12/3:v.nos	___ Division 3, Social organization, behavior, and morale under stress
FCD1.12/4:CT	Stanford Research Institute, final reports
FCD1.13:nos	Public affairs PA (series) Proc. Designated FTI-nos. Earlier PA-nos.
FCD1.13/2:nos	Technical advisory services, Health Office, for your information, TAS (series) Proc. Replaced by FCD1.13/11:
FCD1.13/3:nos	Office of Administrator, for your information, AD (series) Proc. Replaced by FCD1.13/11:
FCD1.13/4:nos	Operations Control Services, for your information, OC (series) Irregular. Proc. Replaced by FCD1.13/11:
FCD1.13/5:nos	Education Services, for your information [Issued irregularly. Proc.] Replaced by FCD1.13/11:
FCD1.13/6:nos	Office of Executive Assistant Administrator, for your information [Issued irregularly] Proc. Replaced by FCD1.13/11:
FCD1.13/7:nos	Office of General Counsel, for your information [Issued irregularly] Proc. Replaced by FCD1.13/11:
FCD1.13/8:nos	Planning Staff, for your information [releases] Replaced by FCD1.13/11:
FCD1.13/9:nos	Industrial survival, for your information [releases] Proc. Replaced by FCD1.13/11:

FCD1.13/10:nos	Survival series, for your information [releases] Proc. Replaced by FCD1.13/11:
FCD1.13/11:nos	Information bulletins. Replaces FCD1.13/2: to FCD1.13/10: Later Pr34.753/2:
FCD1.14:nos	Technical report TR (series) Later Pr34.763:
FCD1.15:v.nos	FCDA public affairs newsletter (monthly)
FCD1.16:v.nos.&nos.	News features (monthly) Later Pr34.760/2:
FCD1.16/2:v.nos.&nos.	Newspictures. Later Pr34.760:
FCD1.17:nos	[Public affairs flyer] PA-F (series) Later Pr34.764/2:
FCD1.17/2:nos	[Public affairs] booklet PA-B (series) Later Pr34.764:
FCD1.18:date	Report on Washington Conference of Mayors and Other Local Government Executives on National Security (annual) Earlier FCD1.2:C74/2
FCD1.18/2:date	Report on Washington Conference of national Women's Advisory Committee on FCDA (annual) Earlier FCD1.2:C74/4
FCD1.19:date	Federal Civil Defense Administration directory. Earlier FCD1.2:D62
FCD1.20:nos	[Leaflets] L-(series) Later Pr34.758:
FCD1.21:date	Civil defense publications available from Superintendent of Documents. Earlier FCD1.2:P96
FCD1.21/2:date	Index to Federal Civil Defense Administration publications (annual) Earlier FCD1.2:In2
FCD1.22:nos	Miscellaneous publications, MP series. Later Pr34.759:
FCD1.23:date	National Civil Defense Week publications. Earlier FCD1.2: Later Pr34.762:
FCD1.24:nos	Newsletter, by, for, and about women in civil defense (irregular)

Reorganization plan no.1 of 1958, effective July 1, 1958, consolidated the Office of Defense Mobilization and the Federal Civil Defense Administration to form the Office of Defense and Civilian Mobilization.

FE Federal Energy Administration

Established by the Federal Energy Administration Act of 1974 (88 Stat. 96) effective June 28, 1974.

FE1.1:date	Annual reports	Earlier similar PrEx21.1:
FE1.2:CT	General publications	Earlier similar PrEx21.2:

FE1.7:date	Press releases. Earlier similar PrEx21.7:
FE1.8:CT	Handbooks, manuals, guides Earlier similar PrEx21.8:
FE1.8/2:CT	Energy handbook for small business
FE1.8/3:v./date	Federal energy guidelines, basic volumes
FE1.8/4:v./date	Federal energy guidelines, exceptions and appeals (basic volumes)
FE1.8/5:nos	Federal energy guidelines, transmittals
FE1.9:date	Petroleum situation report (weekly) Earlier PrEx21.9:
FE1.9/2:date	Petroleum imports reporting system (weekly) Earlier PrEx21.13:
FE1.9/3:date	Weekly petroleum statistics reports
FE1.9/4:date	Monthly petroleum statistics report. Replaces FE1.9: and FE1.9/3:
FE1.10:CT	Addresses Earlier similar PrEx21.10:
FE1.11:nos	Decision list
FE1.12:date	Petroleum market shares (monthly)
FE1.13:date	Telephone directory Earlier similar PrEx21.11:
FE1.14:date	Monthly energy indicators
FE1.15:date	Energy information reported to Congress as required by Public law 93-319, quarterly report.
FE1.15/2:date	Report to Congress on the economic impact of energy actions as required by public law 93-275, section 18(d) (semiannual)
FE1.16:date	Federal energy management program annual reports
FE1.17:date	Monthly energy review

FE1.18:CT	Project independence blueprint final task force reports
FE1.19:date	Energy reporter, Federal Energy Administration citizen newsletter (monthly)
FE1.20:nos	Technical reports
FE1.21:nos	Draft environmental impact statements
FE1.22:nos	Conservation papers
FE1.23:CT	Bibliographies and lists of publications
FE1.24:date	Energy information in the Federal Government, a directory of energy sources identified by the Interagency Task Force on Energy Information (annual)

FF Federal Farm Board

Established by act of Congress approved June 15, 1929.

FF1.1:date	Annual reports
FF1.2:CT	General publications
FF1.3:nos	Bulletins
FF1.4:nos	Circulars
FF1.5:	Laws
FF1.6:	Regulations
FF1.7:vol.nos	Agricultural cooperation. Fortnightly. Mim. Earlier A36.12:
FF1.8:date	Federal Farm Board. Report of activities.
FF1.Z:nos	News releases
FF1.Z/2:nos	Information Division releases

Executive order 6084 of March 27, 1933, effective May 27, 1933, changed name to Farm Credit Administration.

FHL   Federal Home Loan Bank Board

Pursuant to the Housing Amendments of 1955, Public law 345, approved August 11, 1955, the Home Loan Bank Board was redesignated the Federal Home Loan Bank Board and made an independent agency in the Executive branch of the Government. Prior to this legislation the Board was a constituent agency of the Housing and Home Finance Agency.

FHL1.1:date	Annual reports. Earlier HH4.1:
FHL1.2:CT	General publications. Earlier HH4.2:
FHL1.6:CT	Regulations, rules, and instructions. Earlier HH4.6:
FHL1.6/2:CT	Handbooks, manuals, guides
FHL1.7:date	Releases. Earlier HH4.8:
FHL1.7/2:date	Flow of savings in savings and loan associations (monthly) Proc. Earlier HH4.8/2:
FHL1.7/3:date	Mortgage lending activity of savings and loan associations (monthly) Proc. Earlier HH4.8/3:
FHL1.8:date	Nonfarm real estate foreclosure report (quarterly) Proc. Earlier HH4.7: Replaced by FHL1.8/2:
FHL1.8/2:date	Real estate foreclosure report (quarterly) Replaces FHL1.8:
FHL1.9:date	Mortgage recording letter (monthly) Proc. Earlier HH4.9:
FHL1.10:date	Savings, mortgage financing and housing data (monthly) Proc. Earlier HH4.10: Replaced by FHL1.20:
FHL1.11:date	Savings and home financing source book (annual) Proc. Earlier HH4.2:So8 Later in FHL1.12:
FHL1.11/2:nos	Savings and home financing chart book
FHL1.12:date	Combined financial statements, members of Federal Home Loan Bank System (annual) Proc. Earlier HH4.2:F49/2 Later FHL1.12/2:
FHL1.12/2:date	FHLB system S & LA's combined financial statements; Savings and home financing source book. Earlier FHL1.12:

FHL1.13:date   Investments of individuals in savings accounts, U.S. savings bonds and life insurance reserves (annual) Proc. Earlier HH4.2:In9

FHL1.14:v.nos.&nos. Federal Home Loan Bank Board digest (monthly) Proc.

FHL1.15:date   Trends in savings and loan field. Earlier HH4.2:Sa9/2

FHL1.16:date   Estimated home mortgage debt and financing activity (quarterly) Proc.

FHL1.17:date   Participation loan transactions. Earlier FHL1.2:L78

FHL1.18:date   Nonfarm mortgage investments of life insurance companies (annual)

FHL1.19:date   Conventional loans made in excess of 80 percent of property appraisal by Federal savings and loan associations (quarterly)

FHL1.20:date   All operating savings and loan associations, selected balance sheet data [and flow of savings and mortgage lending activity] (monthly) Replaces Savings, mortgage financing and housing data FHL1.10:

FHL1.20/2:date   FSLIC insured savings and loan associations, savings and mortgage activity, selected balance sheet items (monthly)

FHL1.21:date   Insured savings and loan associations, average annual dividend rates paid (annual) Earlier FHL1.2:In7/2

FHL1.22:date   Conventional loans made to finance acquisition and development of land, Federal savings and loan associations (quarterly)

FHL1.23:CT   Addresses

FHL1.24:date   Mortgage interest rates on conventional loans, largest insured savings and loan associations (monthly)

FHL1.25:date   Home mortgage interest rates and terms (monthly)

FHL1.26:date   Number of foreclosures [and Rates of foreclosure] by FSLIC insured savings and loan associations (quarterly)

FHL1.27:v.nos.&nos. Journal of Federal Home Loan Bank Board (monthly)

FHL1.28:date   Economic briefs

FIS   Federal Interdepartmental Safety Council

Established by Executive order 8071 of March 21, 1939.

FIS1.1:date   Annual reports. Proc. Later L30.1:

FIS1.2:CT   General publications. Later L30.2:

FIS1.7:CT   Addresses. Proc.

FIS1.8:v.nos   Federal safety news (bimonthly) Proc. Replaced by Safety Standards, L16.34:

The Federal Safety Council was established in the Department of Labor by Executive order 10194 of Dec. 19, 1950.

FL   Federal Loan Agency

Created by President's Reorganization Plan I, of April 25, 1939.

FL1.1:date   Annual reports

FL1.2:CT   General publications

FL1.7:CT   Addresses. Proc.

FL1.8:v.nos   Federal loan agency news. Biweekly.

By act of Congress, approved June 30, 1947, (61 Stat. 202) the Agency was abolished and its functions transferred to the Reconstruction Finance Corporation.

FL2   Federal Housing Administration

Formerly an independent agency. Transferred to the newly created Federal Loan Agency July 1, 1939.

FL2.1:date   Annual reports. Earlier Y3.F31/11:1 Later NHA2.1:

FL2.2:CT   General publications. Earlier Y3.F31/11:2 Later NHA2.2:

FL2.3:   Bulletins

FL2.4:   Circulars. Earlier Y3.F31/11:4

FL2.5:CT   Laws. Earlier Y3.F31/11:5

FL2.6:CT   Regulations, rules and instructions. Earlier Y3.F31/11: Later NHA2.6:

FL2.7:vol   Clip sheets. Wkly. Earlier Y3.F31/11:14 Later NHA2.10:

FL2.8:nos   Magazine digest. Wkly. Proc. Earlier Y3.F31/11:21

FL2.9:nos   Press digest. (Daily except Sat. and Sun.) Proc. Earlier Y3.F31/11:38 Later NHA2.9:

FL2.10:nos   Advertising digest. Wkly. Proc. Earlier Y3.F31/11:39

FL2.11:CT   Minimum construction requirements for new dwellings. Earlier
                   Y3.F31/11:2 D96/2-60

FL2.12:vol   Insured mortgage portfolio. Monthly. Earlier Y3.F31/11:32   Later
                   NHA2.8:

FL2.12/a:CT   ___ separates. Earlier Y3.F31/11:32a   Later NHA2.8/a:

FL2.13:date   Amortization achedules. Earlier Y3.F31/11:36

FL2.14:nos   General orders. Proc. Earlier Y3.F31/11:16

FL2.15:nos   Technical bulletins. Earlier Y3.F31/11:19

FL2.16:nos   Land planning bulletins. Later HH2.7:

FL2.17:nos   Technical circulars. Proc. Earlier Y3.F31/11:40   Later NHA2.12:

FL2.18:CT   Addresses. Proc. Earlier Y3.F31/11:10

FL2.19:nos   Comptroller [circular letters] Proc. Earlier Y3.F31/11:37   Later NHA2.11:

FL2.20:nos   Architectural bulletins. Proc.

FL2.21:nos   Technical letters.

February 24, 1942 the Federal Housing Administration was made a unit of the National Housing Agency. NHA2.

FL3   Federal Home Loan Bank Board

Formerly an independent agency (Y3.F31/3:). Transferred to Federal Loan Agency by the President's Reorganization Plan 1, effective July 1, 1939 (Public 19, 76th Cong. 1st sess.) pursuant to provisions of Reorganization act of 1939, approved April 3, 1939.

FL3.1:date   Annual reports. Earlier Y3.F31/3:1   Later NHA3.1:

FL3.2:CT   General publications. Earlier Y3.F31/3:2   Later NHA3.2:

FL3.5:CT   Laws. Later NHA3.5:

FL3.6:CT   Regulations, rules, and instructions. Earlier Y3.F31/3:7   Later NHA3.6:

FL3. 7:v. nos   Federal home loan bank review. Monthly. Earlier Y3.F31/3:9 Later NHA3. 8:

FL3. 8:date   Non-farm real estate foreclosures. Monthly. Proc. Earlier Y3.F31/3:10 Later NHA3. 9:

FL3. 9:CT   Home Owners' Loan Corporation publications. Earlier Y3.F31/3:8

February 24, 1942 made a unit of National Housing Agency (NHA3.) by Executive order 9070, Feb. 24, 1942.

FL4   Electric Home and Farm Authority

Formerly an independent agency (Y3.El2/2:) Transferred to Federal Loan Agency by the President's Reorganization plan I, effective July 1, 1939.

FL4. 1:date   Annual reports. Earlier Y3.El2/2:1

FL4. 2:CT   General publications. Earlier Y3.El2/2:2

FL4. 4:nos   Circulars. Earlier Y3.El2/2:4

Executive order 9071 of February 24, 1942 transferred functions to Department of Commerce. Terminated by Executive order 9256 of October 13, 1942.

FL5   Reconstruction Finance Corporation

Formerly an independent agency (Y3.R24:). Transferred to Federal Loan Agency by the President's Reorganization plan I, effective July 1, 1939.

FL5. 1:date   Annual reports. Earlier Y3.R24:Ac85 Later C33.1:, FL5.1:, Y3.R24:1

FL5. 2:CT   General publications. Earlier Y3.R24:2 Later C33. 2:, FL5. 2:, Y3.R24:2

FL5. 4:nos   Circulars. Earlier Y3.R24:4 Later C33. 4:, FL5. 4:, Y3.R24:4

FL5. 5:CT   Laws. Earlier Y3.R24:5 Later C33. 5:, FL5. 5:, Y3.R24:5

FL5. 6:CT   Regulations, rules, and instructions

FL5. 7:date   Quarterly reports. Earlier Y3.R24:7 Later C33. 7:, FL5. 7:

FL5.8:date   Reports. Monthly. Proc. and printed. When Congress is in session these reports are issued as House documents. Earlier Y3.R24:11

FL5.9:CT   Addresses. Proc. Earlier Y3.R24:12 Later C33.10:

FL5.10:CT   Papers in re. Earlier Y3.R24:10 Later C33.8:, FL5.10:

Transferred to Department of Commerce by Executive Order 9071 of February 24, 1942. Returned to the Federal Loan Agency by Public law 4, 79th Congress, approved Feb. 24, 1945.

FL5.11:date   Summary of surplus property (semimonthly) Proc. Earlier C33.11: Later Pr33.210:

FL5.12:date   RFC surplus property news. Later Pr33.207:

FL5.13:nos   Surplus Government property special listings. Later Pr33.209:

FL5.14:nos   Surplus reporter. Later Pr33.208:

FL5.15:date   RFC small business activities (bimonthly) Proc. Earlier Pr32.4825: (Smaller War Plants Corporation program and progress report)

FL5.16:CT   Federal National Mortgage Association information circulars. Proc. Earlier Y3.R24:13, Later Y3.R24:13

FL5.17:date   Federal National Mortgage Association semiannual report. Proc./ Printed for official use. Later Y3.R24:2F31n

The act approved June 30, 1947 (Sec. 204, 61 Stat. 202; 12 U.S.C. sup. 1801 note) abolished the Federal Loan Agency and all functions were assumed by the Reconstruction Finance Corporation.

FM   Federal Mediation and Conciliation Service

Created by Public law 101, 80th Congress, effective Aug. 22, 1947.

FM1.1:date   Annual reports. Earlier L19.1:

FM1.2:CT   General publications. Earlier L19.2:

FM1.7:date   Press releases

FM1.8:CT   Addresses

FMC Federal Maritime Commission

The Federal Maritime Commission was established by Reorganization plan 7 of 1961, effective August 12, 1961.

FMC1.1:date	Annual reports
FMC1.2:CT	General publications
FMC1.6:CT	Regulations, rules, and instructions
FMC1.6/2:CT	Handbooks, manuals, guides
FMC1.7:nos	News releases, NR (series)
FMC1.9:nos	FMC SP (series)
FMC1.9/2:CT	Addresses
FMC1.10:v.nos	Decisions. Earlier MC1.22:
FMC1.10/a:v.nos.&page nos.	___ separates. Earlier C39.108/a:
FMC1.10/a2:date	[Orders, notices, rulings and decisions]
FMC1.11:date	Approved conference, rate and interconference agreements of steamship lines in foreign commerce of United States

FO   Foreign Operations Office

Established by Reorganization plan no. 7 of 1953, effective Aug. 1, 1953.

FO1. 1:date	Annual reports. Later S17.1:
FO1.1/2:nos	Semiannual report on operations under Mutual defense assistance control act of 1951. Earlier Pr33.901/2: Later S17.1/2:
FO1.1/3:date	Report to President on Foreign Operations Administration
FO1. 2:CT	General publications. Later S17. 2:
FO1. 3:nos	Procurement information bulletins. Replaced by S17. 3:
FO1. 3/2:nos	Technical bulletins. Proc. Later S17. 3/2:
FO1. 5:CT	Laws
FO1. 6:CT	Regulations, rules, and instructions. Later S17. 6:
FO1. 6/2:nos	Regulations (numbered)
FO1. 7:	Releases
FO1. 8:date	Procurement authorizations and allotments, European and Far East programs (monthly) Proc. Earlier Pr33.908: Later information appears in FO1. 9/2:
FO1. 9:date	Paid shipments, European and Far East program. (monthly) Proc. Earlier Pr33.909: Later information appears in FO1. 9/2:
FO1. 9/2:date	Allotments, authorizations, & paid shipments, data (monthly) Proc. Consolidation of FO1. 8: and FO1. 9:
FO1. 10:date	Monthly report on European and Far East programs. Earlier Pr33.910: Later S17.10:
FO1. 11:date	European program, local currency counterpart funds (monthly) Proc. Earlier Pr33.911: Beginning with Sept. 30, 1954 issue this is combined with FO1.11/2: and new class is FO1.11/3:
FO1. 11/2:date	Far East program, local currency counterpart funds (monthly) Proc. Earlier Pr33.911/2: Later in FO1.11/3:
FO1. 11/3:date	Counterpart funds and FOA foreign currency accounts, a consolidation of FO1. 11: and FO1. 11/2: Later S17.11/3:

FO1.12:

FO1.13: Small business circular FOA/SBC (series) Earlier Pr33.913: Later S17.13:

FO1.13/2: Small business circular TCA/SBC (series) Earlier Pr33.913/2:

FO1.14: Small business memo FOA/SBM (series) Earlier Pr33.914:, Pr33.914/2: Later S17.14:

FO1.15:

FO1.16:nos Contact clearinghouse service CCHS summary. Earlier Pr33.916:

FO1.17:nos Small business weekly summary, trade opportunities and information for American suppliers. Earlier Pr33.917:

FO1.18:date Industrial projects bulletin (monthly) Proc. Later S17.18:

FO1.19:

FO1.20:

FO1.21:

FO1.22:date Report of commodities and funds for relief and rehabilitation by American agencies registered with Advisory Committee on Voluntary Foreign Aid as shown on their monthly schedule C200 reports of experts [and Summary statement of income and expenditures of voluntary relief agencies registered with Advisory Committee on Voluntary Foreign Aid as shown in their Schedule C 100 reports]. (quarterly) Earlier S1.99/3: Later S17.22:

FO1.23:CT SRE special pub.

FO1.23/2:CT Special Representative in Europe publications.

FO1.24:nos FOA fact sheets. Irregular.

FO1.25:CT FOA country series. Proc. Earlier MSA country series, Pr33.919: Later S17.25:

FO1.26:nos FOA financed awards. Later S17.26:

FO1.27:CT Mutual Security Mission to China, publications. Earlier Pr33.921:

FO1.28:CT Plant requirements reports (series) Later S17.28:

FO1. 29:CT   Training films. Later S17. 29/1:

FO1. 30:   Economic forces in United States in facts and figures. Later S17. 8:

FO1. 31:   Newsletter on community development in technical cooperation. Later S17. 31:

FO1. 32:CT   Bibliographies and lists of publications.

Executive order 10610 of May 9, 1966, effective at close of June 30, 1955, transfers to the Department of State all offices of the Foreign Operations Administration exclusive of the Office of the Director. The administration and the Office of the Director are abolished.

FP   Federal Power Commission

Created by act approved June 10, 1920 (Public 280, 66th Congress).

FP1.1:date	Annual reports
FP1.1/a:CT	___ separates: Opinions
FP1.2:CT	General publications
FP1.3:	Bulletins
FP1.4:	Circulars
FP1.5:CT	Laws
FP1.6:date	Rules and regulations (general)
FP1.6/2:CT	Rate series, 1938
FP1.7:CT	Rules and regulations (miscellaneous)
FP1.7/2:date	Uniform system of accounts prescribed for natural gas companies (Class A and B, D, and D)(FPC A-102) Earlier FP1.7:G21/date, FP1.7:G21/4/date, and FP1.7:G21/5/date
FP1.7/3:date	Uniform system of accounts prescribed for public utilities and licensees. Earlier FP1.7:Ac2/3, FP1.7:Ac2/4 and FP1.7:Ac2/5
FP1.7/4:nos	Staff reports, FPC/OCE- (series)
FP1.8:date	Rules of practice
FP1.8/2:CT	Rules of practice
FP1.9:nos	Questionnaires
FP1.10:nos	Rate series. Pubs. desig. F.P.C.R.-nos
FP1.10/2:nos	Rate series 2, State reports
FP1.11:date	Production of electricity for public use in the U.S. Monthly. Proc. Earlier I19.33:
FP1.11/a:CT	___ separates
FP1.11/2:date & nos	Production and utilization of electric energy in United States (monthly) Proc. Earlier FP1.11: Later FP1.27:

FP1.11/3:dt.&nos	Consumption of fuel for production of electric energy (monthly) Proc. Later in FP1.27:
FP1.11/4:date	Stocks of coal and days' supply (monthly) Proc. Information previously included in FP1.11/3:
FP1.11/5:dt.&nos	Revenues and income of privately owned class A & B electric utilities in the U.S. (monthly) Proc. Later in FP1.27:
FP1.11/6:dt.&nos	Sales of electric energy to ultimate consumers (monthly) R-nos. Proc. Later in FP1.27:
FP1.11/7:date	Weekly electric output, United States. Proc. Later in FP1.25:
FP1.12:nos	Power series. Beginning with no.8 series designated F.P.C.-p-nos
FP1.12/a:CT	___ separates
FP1.13:CT	Maps
FP1.14:CT	Addresses. Proc.
FP1.15:letter	Rate series A. This is rate series 10.
FP1.16:CT	Rate series B (by States) This is rate series 11, 1937 series. See for 1938-39 series, FP1.16/2:
FP1.16/2:CT	Typical electric bills (by States)
FP1.16/3:CT(date)	Typical residential electric bills. Proc. Earlier (prior to 1942) FP1.16/2:
FP1.16/4:CT(date)	Typical commercial and industrial electric bills. Proc. Earlier in FP1.16/2:
FP1.17:CT	Papers in re
FP1.18:CT	National electric rate book (by States)
FP1.18/2:date	National electric rate book bulletin service, important rate changes. (monthly)
FP1.19:nos	Orders
FP1.20:vol	Opinions and decisions. Back title reads: Federal Power Commission reports
FP1.20/a:v.no./date-no	___ preliminary prints (monthly)

FP1.21:nos	[Statistical series] Pubs.desig. FPC S-no.
FP1.21/a:CT	___ separates
FP1.22:date	Statement of taxes, dividends, salaries and wages, class A and class B privately owned electric utilities in U.S. (quarterly) Proc.
FP1.23:date	Effect of income tax law revision on electric taxes and income (quarterly) Proc.
FP1.24:date	Electric utility system loads (monthly) Later in FP1.27:
FP1.25:v.nos/nos	Daily news digest. Proc.
FP1.25/2:nos	Release for publication (series)
FP1.25/3:v./nos	FPC news
FP1.25/4:nos	Press releases
FP1.26:date	Forms and publications, list and order blank. Irregular. Proc. Earlier FP1.2: P96/2
FP1.27:date	Electric power statistics. Consolidation of FP1.11/2:, FP1.11/3:, FP1.11/5:, FP1.11/6:, FP1.24:
FP1.28:date	List of electric power suppliers with annual operating **revenues of $2,500,000** or more classified as public utilities under Federal power act
FP1.29:CT	Planning status report
FP1.30:date	Cost of pipeline and compressor station construction under non-budget type of certificate authorizations as reported by pipeline companies (annual)
FP1.31:CT	Evaluation report, water resources appraisal for hydroelectric licensing
FP1.32:date	Monthly report of cost and quality of fuels for steam-electric plant (FPC form 423), staff report (quarterly)
FP1.33:CT	Environmental impact statements

FPI   Federal Prison Industries, Inc.

Created by Executive Order 6917 of December 11, 1934.

FPI1.1:date   Annual reports. Later J16.51:

FPI1.2:CT   General publications. Later J16.52:

FPI1.7:CT   Price lists. Proc. Earlier in J16.2:

Transferred to Justice Department and made subordinate to Prisons Bureau (J16.) by the President's Reorganization Plan 2, effective July 1, 1939.

Federal Reserve System

FR Federal Reserve Board

December 23, 1913 (38 Stat. 251)

FR1.1:date	Annual report
FR1.1/a:date	___ separates: Report of Board
FR1.1/a:CT	___ separates
FR1.2:CT	General publications
FR1.3/1:v./nos	Federal reserve bulletin
FR1.3/a:CT	___ separates
FR1.3/2:vol	Federal reserve bulletin
FR1.3/a:CT	___ separates
FR1.3/2:vol	Federal reserve bulletin (brief edition)
FR1.3/3:v. nos	Index-digest, Federal Reserve Bulletin
FR1.4:dt.&nos	Circulars. See for Circulars 1-2, RB1.4:1-2
FR1.5:nos	Regulations
FR1.6:letters	Regulations (lettered)
FR1.7:CT	Papers in re
FR1.8:dt.&nos	Instruction, special
FR1.8/2:CT	Rules, regulations, and instructions, Miscellaneous
FR1.8/3:CT	Handbooks, manuals, guides
FR1.9:date	Federal reserve inter-district collection system, list of banks upon which items will be received by Federal reserve banks for collection and credit. Replaced by FR1.9/2:
FR1.9/2:date	Federal Reserve system memorandum on exchange charges (monthly) Replaces FR1.9:

FR1.10:date	Digest and index of opinions of counsel, informal rulings of Federal Reserve Board and matter relating thereto, from Federal reserve bulletin
FR1.11:nos	Abstract of condition reports of member banks. Later titles, Member bank call report, condition of member banks, Summary report, assets and liabilities of member banks
FR1.11/2:date	Member bank loans. Key number E.2.4. Proc. Later title, All member bank (irregular)
FR1.11/3:date	Member bank earnings (semiannual) Key no. E.5. Proc. Later title Member bank income (annual)
FR1.11/4:date	Deposits, reserves, and borrowings of member banks (semimonthly) Key no. J.1
FR1.11/5:date	State member banks of Federal Reserve System and nonmember banks that maintain clearing accounts with Federal Reserve Banks (annual with monthly supplements. Proc.
FR1.11/6:date	Distribution of bank deposits by countries and Standard metropolitan areas (biennial) Proc. Earlier FR1.2:D44
FR1.12:incl. dates.	Digest of rulings
FR1.13:date	Federal reserve act, as amended (compilations)
FR1.13/2:CT	Laws
FR1.14:date	Bank debits. Wkly. Proc. See for monthly issue FR1.17:
FR1.15:date	Condition of Federal Reserve Banks. Wkly. Proc. Later title, Factors affecting bank reserves and condition statement of Federal Reserve Banks
FR1.15/2:date	Reserve positions of major reserve city banks (weekly) Key no. H.5.
FR1.15/3:date	Aggregate reserves and member bank deposits (weekly) Key no. H.3
FR1.16:date	Condition of weekly reporting member banks in large cities. Proc. Key no. FR1.14:
FR1.16/2:date	Condition of weekly reporting member banks in central reserve cities. Key no. H.4.3. Proc.
FR1.17:date	Monthly statement of debits to individual accounts by banks in reporting centers. See for weekly issue FR1.14:

FR1.17/2:date	Bank debits to demand deposit accounts except interbank and Government accounts. (annual) Earlier FR1.2:D35/4
FR1.17/3:date	Debits, demand deposits, and turnover at 233 individual centers (monthly)
FR1.18:date	Report of finishers of cotton fabrics. Monthly. Proc.
FR1.19:date	Business indexes. Monthly. Proc.
FR1.19/2:date	National summary of business conditions (monthly) Key no. G.12.2. Proc.
FR1.19/3:date	Industrial production (G.12.3) (monthly) Replaces FR1.19/2:
FR1.20:date	Department store sales, preliminary reports, Monthly. Proc. Early issues read Retail trade in U.S.
FR1.21:date	Wholesale trade in U.S. (monthly) Proc.
FR1.22:date	Weekly review of periodicals. Proc. Includes quarterly supplement
FR1.22/2:date	Selected list of additions to research library. Key no. K.11. Proc. CLASS CANCELLED Publications classified FR1.29:
FR1.23:CT	Addresses
FR1.24:nos (later date)	Weekly department store sales, R & S wrt-nos
FR1.24/2:date	Department store sales, by cities (weekly) Key no. H.11, later H.8b. Proc.
FR1.24/3:date	Department store sales. Proc. Key number G.7.2
FR1.24/4:date	Department store stocks (monthly) Key no. G.7.4. Proc.
FR1.24/5:date	Department store sales and stocks by major departments (monthly) Key no. G.7.3. Proc.
FR1.24/6:date	Department store merchandising data (monthly) Key no. G.7.4.1. Proc.
FR1.24/7:date	Department store trade, United States distribution of sales by months (annual) Key number C.7.3.1. Proc. Earlier FR1.2:D44/3
FR1.24/8:date	Department store trade, United States distribution of sales by months (annual) Key number C.7.3.2. Proc. Earlier FR1.2:D44/3
FR1.24/9:date	Department store trade, United States Departmental sales indexes, without seasonal adjustment (annual) Key number C.7.3.3. Proc. Earlier FR1.2:D44/3

FR1.24/10:date	Department store trade, United States departmental stock indexes, without seasonal adjustment (annual) Key number C.7.3.4. Proc. Earlier FR1.2: D44/3
FR1.24/11:date	Department store trade, United States departmental stock-sales ratios (annual) Key number C.7.3.5. Earlier FR1.2:D44/3
FR1.25:nos	Federal reserve chart books. Later see FR1.30:
FR1.26:nos	Sales finance companies (monthly) Proc. Earlier C3.151: Pubs.desig. R&S sfc-nos. (Research and Statistics, sales finance companies)
FR1.27:nos	Postwar economic studies
FR1.28:date	Assets and liabilities of all banks in United States (monthly) Proc. Desig. G.7.
FR1.28/2:date	All banks in United States and possessions, principal assets and liabilities (semiannual) Key no.K.4. Proc.
FR1.28/3:date	Assets and liabilities of all member banks, by districts (monthly) Key number G.7.1
FR1.28/4:date	Assets and liabilities of all commercial banks in United States (wkly) Key number H.8.
FR1.29:dt./nos	Selected list of additions, Research Library (monthly) Proc. Later title, Research library, recent acquisitions
FR1.30:date	Federal reserve charts on bank credit, monthly rates and business (monthly) Earlier FR1.25:
FR1.30/2:date	Federal reserve charts on bank credit, money rates and business, historical supplement. Proc.
FR1.31:date	Releases. Proc.
FR1.31/2:date	Summary of equity security transactions and ownership of directors, officers, and principal stockholders of member State banks, as reported pursuant to sec.16(a) of Securities exchange act of 1934 (monthly)
FR1.32:date	Foreign exchange rate (for week) Key no.H.10. Proc.
FR1.32/2:date	Foreign exchange rates (monthly) Key no.G.5. Proc.
FR1.32/3:dt./nos	Selected interest & exchange rates for major counties of U.S., weekly series of charts. Key number H-13

FR1.32/4:date	Interest rates charged on selected types of bank loans. Key number G.10
FR1.32/5:date	Bank rates on short-term business loans (quarterly) Key number E.2
FR1.33:dt./nos	Changes in State bank membership, announcements (weekly) Key no. K3
FR1.33/2:date	Changes in status of banks and branches during month, name and location of banks and branches
FR1.34:date	Consumer installment loans of principal types of financial institutions (monthly) Key no. G.17.1. Proc.
FR1.34/2:date	Retail installment credit of furniture and household appliance stores (monthly) Key no. G.17.2
FR1.34/3:date	Department store credit (monthly) Key no. G.17.3. Proc.
FR1.34/4:date	Automobile installment credit developments. G.26.
FR1.34/5:date	Finance and other terms on new and used car installment credit contacts purchased from dealers by major auto finance companies (monthly) Key no. G.11
FR1.34/6:date	Automobile loans by major finance companies (monthly) Key no. G.25. Absorbed by FR1.34.4:
FR1.34/7:date	Finance rates and other terms on selected categories of consumer installment credit extended by finance companies. Key number J.3.
FR1.34/8:date	Automobile credit
FR1.35:date	Statement of Voluntary Credit Restraint Committee. Proc. These releases appear later in FR1.3/1:
FR1.35/2:nos	Bulletin of Voluntary Credit Restraint Committee. Proc. These releases appear later in FR1.3/1:
FR1.36:date	Consumer credit (monthly) Key no. G.19. Proc.
FR1.36/2:date	Consumer installment credits of commercial banks (monthly) Key no. G.18.1 Proc.
FR1.36/3:date	Consumer installment credits of industrial banks (monthly) Proc. Key no. G.18.2
FR1.36/4:date	Consumer installment credits of industrial loan companies (monthly) Key no. G.18.3. Proc.
FR1.36/5:date	Consumer installment credit extended and repaid (monthly) Key no. G.22. Proc.

FR1.36/6:date	Consumer finance companies, loans outstanding and volume of loans made (monthly) Key number G.21. Proc. Later title, Consumer loans made under effective State small loan laws
FR1.36/7:date	Consumer credit at consumer finance companies (monthly) Desig. G.22
FR1.37:date	Crop report, by Federal reserve districts (monthly during crop harvesting months, usually from July through November. Key no. G.10. Proc.
FR1.38:date	Index numbers of wholesale prices (monthly) Key no. G.8. Proc.
FR1.39:date	Changes in commercial and industrial loans, by industry and purpose (weekly) Key no. H.12. Proc.
FR1.40:date	Sales, profits, and dividends of large corporations (quarterly) Key no. E.6. Proc.
FR1.41:date	Retail furniture report (monthly) Key no. G.16. Proc.
FR1.42:date	Employment in nonagricultural establishments (monthly) Key no. G.12.4. Proc.
FR1.43:date	Interdistrict settlement fund [and Federal Reserve agents' fund], summary of transactions (monthly) Key no. G.15(a) and G.15(b). Proc.
FR1.44:date	Open-market money rates in New York City (monthly) Key no. G.13. Proc.
FR1.45:date	Federal Reserve Board publications. Earlier FR1.2:P96
FR1.45/2:nos	Current periodical articles (monthly) Key no. K13.
FR1.45/3:nos	Selected current articles and new publications of Federal Reserve System. Key no. K12.
FR1.45/4:CT	Bibliographies and lists of publications
FR1.46:date	List of stocks registered on national securities exchanges and of redeemable securities of certain investment companies (annual) Proc. Earlier FR1.2:St6
FR1.46/2:date	U.S. Government security yields and prices, calendar week. Desig. H.15.
FR1.46/3:date	U.S. Government security yields and prices **(yields in** per cent per annum) (monthly) Desig. G.14
FR1.47:date	Demand deposits, currency and related items. Issued twice a month.

FR1.48:nos	Applications to merge bank form or expand a bank holding company received by the Board, announcements (weekly)
FR1.49:nos	Review of foreign developments. Prepared for internal circulation. Key no. L.5.2
FR1.50:date	Official opening and closing hours of Board of Governors of Federal reserve banks and branches; also holidays during month. Desig. K.8
FR1.51:nos	Staff economic studies
FR1.52:date	Weekly summary of banking and credit measures. Federal reserve statistical release. H.9
FR1.53:date	Volume and composition of individual's savings (quarterly)
FR1.54:date	Maturity distribution of Euro-dollar deposits in foreign branches of U.S. banks (monthly) Key number G.17.
FR1.54/2:date	Maturity distribution of outstanding negotiable time certificates of deposit (monthly) Key number G.9.
FR1.55:date	Capacity utilization in manufacturing, quarterly averages, seasonally adjusted. Key number E.5.
FR1.56:date	Flow of funds, seasonally adjusted (quarterly) Earlier FR1.2:F96/3
FR1.56/2:date	Flow of funds, unadjusted (quarterly) Earlier FR1.2:F96/5/date Later in FR1.56:
FR1.57:date	Annual report to Congress on the Federal Trade Commission Improvement act for [calendar year]

Health, Education and Welfare Department

FS Federal Security Agency

Created by President's reorganization plan I, April 25, 1939.
The Department of Health, Education, and Welfare was created by Reorganization Plan 1 of 1953, under provisions of the act approved April 1, 1953 (67 Stat. 18:U.S.C. 623), effective April 11, 1953.

FS1.1:date	Annual reports. Later HE1.1:
FS1.1/a:CT	___ separates
FS1.2:CT	General publications. Later HE1.2:
FS1.3/2:	Personnel bulletins.
FS1.4:nos	Agency circulars
FS1.6:CT	Regulations, rules, and instructions
FS1.6/2:pt.nos	Agency manuals. Proc. Admin.
FS1.6/3:CT	Handbooks, manuals, guides. Later HE1.6/3:
FS1.6/4:nos	Emergency manual guides
FS1.6/5:date	Handbook on programs of Department of Health, Education and Welfare (annual)
FS1.6/6:date	Grants-in-aid and other financial assistance programs administered by Department of Health, Education, and Welfare. (annual) Supplement to FS1.6/5: Later title: Catalog of HEW assistance providing financial support and service to: States, communities, organizations, individuals
FS1.6/7:trans.nos.	Grants administration manual. Later HE1.6/7:
FS1.6/7-2:nos	Grants administration manual circulars
FS1.7:CT	Addresses. Proc. Later HE1.7:
FS1.8:nos	Here's your answer, programs
FS1.9:nos	I hear America singing (radio scripts; Wkly.) Proc.
FS1.10:nos	Training manuals. Later HE1.10:

FS1.11:v.nos.&nos.	Accession list, Library (biweekly) Proc.
FS1.12:nos	Supervision and management series.
FS1.13:date	Aging [issued about 3 times a year] Later FS14.9:
FS1.13/2:nos	Reports and guidelines from White House Conference on Aging (series)
FS1.13/3:nos	Pattern for progress in aging case studies. Later FS14.9/5:
FS1.13/4:date	Highlights of legislation on aging. Later FS14.9/2:
FS1.13/5:nos	Facts on aging. Later FS14.9/3:
FS1.14:nos	Agency orders
FS1.15:1e-nos	Releases. Proc. Later HE1.15:
FS1.16:nos	Regional and Field letter
FS1.17:date	Field directory (annual) Proc. Earlier FS1.2:F45 Later HE1.17:
FS1.17/2:date	Regional office directory, professional and administrative personnel (semiannual) Proc. Earlier FS1.2:R26
FS1.18:CT	Bibliographies and lists of publications. Earlier in FS1.2: Later HE1.18:
FS1.18/2:nos	Selected references on aging (numbered) Later FS14.9/4:
FS1.19:date	Health, education and welfare trends (annual) Later HE1.19:
FS1.20:date	Health, education and welfare indicators (monthly)
FS1.20/a:CT	___ separates
FS1.21:date	HEW facts and figures. Earlier FS1.2:H77/insert Later HE1.21:
FS1.22:date	State salary ranges, selected classes in employment security. Earlier FS1.2:SA3 Later HE1.22:
FS1.23:date	Mental retardation, fiscal year program of **Department of Health, Education and Welfare.** Earlier FS1.2:M52/3 Later HE1.23:
FS1.23/2:date	Fiscal year appropriations for mental retardation programs of Dept. of Health, Education and Welfare.
FS1.23/3:date	Mental retardation grants, fiscal year. Later HE1.23/3:
FS1.23/4:date	Mental retardation reports. Later title, Programs for the handicapped. Later HE1.23/4:

FS1.23/5:date   Mental retardation activities of Department of Health, Education, and Welfare, annual report. Earlier FS1.2:M52/2/965   Later HE1.23/5:

FS1.24:nos   Educational Television Facilities Program: Program bulletins.

FS1.24/2:nos   Educational Television Facilities Program: Public notices

FS1.25:nos   Merit system methods. Administrative.   Later CS1.78:

FS1.26:date   Education and training, annual report of Secretary of Health, Education and Welfare to Congress on training activities under Manpower development and training act. Earlier FS1.2:Ed8   Later HE1.26:

FS1.27:nos   HEW field letter

FS1.28:date   Telephone directory. Earlier FS1.2:T23/date   Later HE1.28:

FS1.29:date-nos Program analysis (series)   Later HE1.29:

FS1.30:v.nos.&nos. The Secretary's letter

FS1.31:date   Grants administration report   Later HE1.31:

FS1.32:CT   Task Force on Prescription drugs, publications

FS1.33:date   Reports of Career Service Board for Science   Later HE1.33:

FS1.34:date   HEW consumer newsletters.   Later HE1.34:

FS1.35:date   Cost of clean air, report of Secretary of Health, Education, and Welfare to Congress in compliance with Public law 90-148, Air quality act of 1967. Later HE1.35:

FS1.36:nos   Project Head Start (series)   Earlier PrEx10.12:

FS1.36/2:date   Child Development Office; Manuals (numbered)   Later HE21.8/2:

All Health, Education and Welfare Department publications received in the Division of Public Documents after December 15, 1969 are being classified under a new designation, HE.

FS2   Public Health Service

Transferred from Treasury Department to Federal Security Agency by reorganization plan I, part 2, series 201-205, effective July 1, 1939.

FS2.1:date   Annual reports. Earlier T27.1:   Later HE20.1:

FS2.1/a:CT   ___ separates.   Earlier T27.1/a:

FS2.2:CT	General publications. Earlier T27.2: Later HE20.2:, HE20.1002:, HE20.1302:, HE20.2002:, HE20.2012:, HE20.2402:, HE20.2502:, HE20.2552:, HE20.2602:, HE20.2652:, HE20.2702:
FS2.2/a:CT	___ separates
FS2.3:nos	Public health bulletins. Earlier T27.12:
FS2.3/2:nos	Information bulletin. Admin.
FS2.3/3:nos	Technical information bulletins
FS2.4:	Circulars
FS2.4/2:nos	Circular memos [Conference on State Sanitary Engineers]
FS2.5:CT	Laws Later HE20.5:
FS2.6:CT	Regulations, rules, and instructions. Proc. Earlier T27.14:
FS2.6/2:CT	Handbooks, manuals, guides. Earlier in FS2.6: Later HE20.1108:, HE20.1308:, HE20.2608:, HE20.2658:, HE20.1308: , HE20.8: HE20.3006:
FS2.6/3:CT	Film guides. Earlier FS2.211/2:
FS2.6/4:les-nos	Health mobilization course manual [sections] Admin.
FS2.6/5:CT	Air quality criteria
FS2.6/6:nos	PHS rehabilitation guide series
FS2.6/7:nos	BHS programmed instruction (series)
FS2.6/8:CT	Guidelines for [various health professionals and sub-professionals] in home health services.
FS2.7:vol	Public health reports. Wkly. Earlier T27.6/1: Later HE20.2010:
FS2.7/a:CT	___ separates
FS2.7/a:nos	___ reprints. Earlier T27.6/1a:
FS2.7/a2:nos	___ Tuberculosis control issues (monthly)
FS2.7/2:v.nos	___ [bound volumes]. Earlier T27.6:
FS2.7/3:v.nos	___ Tuberculosis control issues, index.

FS2.8:nos	Supplements to Public health reports. Earlier T27.6/2:
FS2.8/a:supp.nos.&nos.	___ separates
FS2.9:vol	Venereal disease information. Monthly. Earlier T27.26:
FS2.9/a:nos	___ reprints. Earlier T27.26/a:
FS2.10:nos	Supplements to Venereal disease information bulletin. Earlier T.27.26/2:
FS2.11:nos	Venereal disease bulletins. Earlier T27.20:
FS2.11/2:date	Current literature on venereal disease. irregular. Proc. Later HE20.2311:
FS2.11/3:nos	Statistical letter
FS2.11/4:nos	VD fact sheet. Annual. Proc. Later HE20.7018:
FS2.12:vol	Hospital news. Semi-monthly. Proc. Earlier T27.33:
FS2.12/2:CT	Hospital elements, planning and equipping for 50-, 100-, and 200-, bed general hospitals
FS2.13:vol	Public health engineering abstracts. Wkly. later monthly. Proc. Earlier T27.28:
FS2.14:nos	General circulars. Proc. Earlier T27.15/3:
FS2.15:vol	Health officer. Monthly. Proc. Earlier T27.34:
FS2.16:date	Shellfish shippers, list of. Proc. Earlier T27.2:Sh4, Later FS13.135:
FS2.16/2:date	Shellfish sanitation workshop, proceedings (biennial) Later HE20.4032:
FS2.17:nos	Hospital division circulars. Proc. Earlier T27.24:
FS2.17/2:nos	___ new series, Oct.1,1943- Proc.
FS2.18:nos	Hospital division similar letters. Proc. Earlier T27.27:
FS2.18/2:date	Division of Hospitals, annual statistical summary, fiscal year. Later HE20.2709:
FS2.19:vol	National Negro health news (quarterly) Proc. Earlier T27.30:
FS2.20:nos	Educational publications
FS2.21:nos	Public health bibliography series. Later HE20.11:

FS2.22:CT	National Institute of Health. General publications. Later HE20.3402:, HE20.2402:, HE20.3002:, HE20.3102:, HE20.3152:, HE20.3302:, HE20.3352:, HE20.3502:, HE20.3202:, HE20.3452: HE20.3702:
FS2.22/2:	N.I.H. record. Admin.
FS2.22/3:nos	Cancer control letter
FS2.22/4:nos	Reference guide (series)
FS2.22/5:date	Heart health news for health departments
FS2.22/6:date	National Institutes of Health, annual lectures. Earlier FS2.22:L49
FS2.22/7:date	Research grants and fellowships awarded by Public Health Service (annual) Earlier FS2.22:R31 Later HE20.3013:
FS2.22/7-2:date	Research grants index (annual) Later H E20.3013/2:
FS2.22/7-3:date	National Institutes of Health research grants Later HE20.3013/2-2:
FS2.22/7-4:date	Mental health training grant awards, fiscal year. Earlier FS2.22/7:dt/pt.1, supp.A.
FS2.22/7-5:date	National Institutes of Health training programs, fiscal year
FS2.22/8:date	Research and training grants and awards of Public Health Service (annual)
FS2.22/9:date	Papers approved for publication or presentation. Proc.
FS2.22/10:nos	Progress reports. Admin.
FS2.22/11:date	Highlights of heart progress (annual) Earlier FS2.22:H35/4
FS2.22/11-2:date	Public Health Service support of cardiovascular research, training and community programs (annual) Earlier FS2.22:C17/4
FS2.22/12:date	Highlights of progress in research on neurologic disorders (annual)
FS2.22/13:CT	Bibliographies and lists of publications Later HE20.2417: Later HE20.3012:, HE20.3113:
FS2.22/13-2:date	Recent translations, selected list (monthly) Issued by NIH Library Later HE20.3009/2:
FS2.22/13-3:date	Periodicals currently received in NIH library (annual) Later HE20.3009/3:

FS2.22/13-4:v.nos.&nos. International bibliography on crime and delinquency. Later title, Crime and delinquency abstracts. Later HE20.2420:

FS2.22/13-5:v.nos.&nos. Artificial kidney bibliography (quarterly) Later HE20.3311:

FS2.22/13-6:date Fibrinolysis, thrombolysis, and blood clotting bibliography Later HE20.3209:

FS2.22/13-7:nos Reports on reproduction and population research (series)

FS2.22/13-8:date Scientific directory and annual bibliography. Earlier FS2.21:75 Later HE20.3017:

FS2.22/13-9:date NIH quarterly publications list Later HE20.3009:

FS2.22/14:date Highlights of progress in research on cancer (annual)

FS2.22/14-2:date Progress against cancer, report by National Advisory Cancer Council. Earlier FS2.22:C16/29 Later HE20.3024:, HE20.3163:

FS2.22/15:CT Handbooks, manuals, guides. Earlier in FS2.22: Later HE20.3008:, HE20.3208:, HE20.3408:

FS2.22/16:date Highlights of progress in mental health research

FS2.22/16-2:date Research project summaries, National Institute of Mental Health (annual)

FS2.22/17:date Highlights of research progress in allergy and infectious diseases (annual)

FS2.22/18:nos National Cancer Institute monographs Later HE20.3162:

FS2.22/18a:CT ___ separates

FS2.22/19:CT Russian Scientific Translation Program publications

FS2.22/19-2:nos Bulletin of translations from Russian medical sciences. Issued by Russian scientific translation program. Internal use only.

FS2.22/19-3:CT Translations for National Institutes of Health

FS2.22/20:date Highlights of research progress in general medical sciences (annual)

FS2.22/21:date Highlights of research progress in arthritis and metabolic diseases (annual)

FS2.22/22:date Members of advisory councils, study sections, and committees of National Institutes of Health (annual) Earlier FS2.22:Ad9 Later HE20.3018/2:

FS2.22/22-2:date NIH public advisory groups, authority, structure, functions. Later HE20.3018:

FS2.22/23:date Highlights of progress in research on oral diseases (annual)

FS2.22/24:date	Plant safety branch handbooks
FS2.22/25:date	Research highlights in aging (annual)
FS2.22/25-2:date	Research programs in aging. Earlier FS2.22:Ag4/2
FS2.22/25-3:nos	Adult development and aging abstracts. Later HE20.3359:
FS2.22/26:date	Activities of the National Institutes of Health in the field of gerontology (annual) Earlier FS2.22:G31
FS2.22/27:nos	NIMH analyses series
FS2.22/28:date	Research highlights, National Institutes of Health. Earlier FS2.22:R31/5
FS2.22/29:v.nos	Psychopharmacology service center bulletins. Later Psychopharmacology bulletin. Later HE20.2409:
FS2.22/29-2:v.nos.&nos.	Psychopharmacology abstracts Later HE20.2409/2:
FS2.22/30:nos	Cancer chemotherapy reports Later HE20.3160:
FS2.22/30-2:v.nos.&nos.	Cancer chemotherapy abstracts Later HE20.3160/4:
FS2.22/30-3:v.nos.&nos.	Cancer chemotherapy reports part 2. Later HE20.3160/2:
FS2.22/30-4:v.nos.&nos.	Cancer chemotherapy reports part 3, Program information Later HE20.3160/3:
FS2.22/31:nos	Mental health monographs
FS2.22/32:nos	National Cancer Institute research reports.
FS2.22/32-2:CT	National Cancer Institute research reports (unnumbered) Later HE20.3166:
FS2.22/33:nos	Resources for medical research reports. Later HE20.3014:
FS2.22/34:nos	Heart research news
FS2.22/35:nos	Resources analysis memos Later HE20.3014/2:
FS2.22/36:date	National Institutes of Health organization handbook (annual)
FS2.22/37:date	Proceedings, annual conference of Model Reporting Areas for Blindness Statistics. Later HE20.3759/2:
FS2.22/37-2:date	Statistical report, annual tabulations of Model Reporting Area for Blindness Statistics Later HE20.3759:
FS2.22/38:date	Data on patients of outpatient psychiatric clinics in United States

FS2.22/38-2:date   Data on staff and man-hours, outpatient psychiatric clinics in United States

FS2.22/38-3:date   Outpatient psychiatric clinics, community service activities

FS2.22/38-4:date   Directory of outpatient psychiatric clinics, psychiatric day-night services and other mental health resources in United States and territories. Earlier FS2.22: P95/5

FS2.22/39:v.nos.&nos. Carcinogenesis abstracts (monthly) Later HE20.3159:

FS2.22/40:CT   Special statistical reports [and tables]

FS2.22/41:CT   Research and utilization series

FS2.22/42:date   National Institute of Mental Health training grant program, fiscal year

FS2.22/43:nos   Research profiles   Later HE20.3152:

FS2.22/44:date   Annual Conference of Model Reporting Area for Mental Hospital Statistics, proceedings, panel presentations, etc.

FS2.22/45:date   Proceedings of annual conference, mental health career development program

FS2.22/46:date   Patient movement data, State and county mental hospitals (annual) Earlier FS2.22:M52/39

FS2.22/47:v.nos.&nos. Arthritis and rheumatic diseases abstracts (monthly) Later HE20.3312:

FS2.22/48:nos   Androgenic and myogenic endocrine bioassay data (irregular)

FS2.22/48-2:v.nos.&nos. Endocrinology index   Later HE20.3309:

FS2.22/49:date   Mental health directory   Later HE20.2418:

FS2.22/50:CT   National Clearinghouse for Mental Health Information: Conference report series

FS2.22/50-2:date   Drug dependence and abuse notes

FS2.22/50-3:date   Occupational mental health notes   Later HE20.2411:

FS2.22/50-4:date   Mental health program reports   Later HE20.2419:

FS2.22/50-5:date   Mental health digest.   Later HE20.2410:

FS2.22/50-6:nos   Bulletin of suicidology. Earlier FS2.22:Su3 Later HE20.2413:

FS2.22/50-7:date   Drug dependence

FS2.22/51:v.nos   Current projects in prevention, control and treatment of crime and delinquency (semiannual)

FS2.22/52:v.nos.&nos.   Mental retardation abstracts (quarterly)   Later FS17.113:

FS2.22/53:v.nos.&nos.   Diabetes literature index (monthly)   Later HE20.3310:

FS2.22/53-2:date   ___ annual index issue.   Later HE20.3310/2:

FS2.22/54:v.nos   Gastroenterology abstracts and citations (monthly)   Later HE20.3313:

FS2.22/55:nos   NINIM monographs.   Later HE20.3510:

FS2.22/55a:CT   ___ separates

FS2.22/56:v.nos   Reading guide to cancer virology literature

FS2.22/57:CT   Nutrition surveys [by country]   Earlier Y3.In8/13:3

FS2.22/58:CT   National Institutes of Health: Addresses.   Later HE20.3019:

FS2.22/59:v.nos.&nos.   Epilepsy abstracts (monthly)   Later HE20.3509:

FS2.22/59-2:date   ___ (compilations)   Later HE20.3509/2:

FS2.22/60:CT   Nursing clinical conference presented by Nursing Department of Clinical Center.   Later HE20.3021:

FS2.22/61:nos   Current population research reports   Later HE20.3362:

FS2.22/62:date   National Institute of General Medical Sciences, annual report

FS2.22/63:CT   Chemotherapy fact sheets.   Later HE20.3164:

FS2.22/64:nos   Computer Research and Technology Division: Technical reports   Later HE20.3011:

FS2.23:nos   National Institute of Health. Bulletins.   Earlier T27.3:

FS2.24:CT   Bibliographies.   Earlier T27.40:

FS2.24/2:date   Publications issued by Public Health Service   Later HE20.2012:, HE20.9:

FS2.24/3:nos   Selective listing of radiological health documents, lists.

FS2.24/4:date   Smoking and health bibliographical bulletin (monthly)   Later HE20.2609:

FS2.25:nos   Folders.   Earlier T27.43:   Transfer to FS2.32:

FS2.26:CT   Posters.   Earlier T27.19:   Later FS2.26/2:

FS2.26/2:nos   Public Health Service Posters.   Earlier FS2.26:

FS2.27:nos	Posters. VD. Earlier T27.19:Sy7, no.1-6
FS2.28:date	Chronological list of official orders to commissioned and other officers. Proc. Earlier T27.13:
FS2.29:nos	Miscellaneous publications. Earlier T27.17:
FS2.30:CT	Addresses. Proc. Earlier T27.31: Later HE20.1312:
FS2.31:v.nos	National Cancer Institute. Journal of (bi-monthly) Later HE20.3161:
FS2.31/a:nos	___ separates
FS2.32:nos	VD folders. Earlier T27.43:
FS2.33:nos	Workers' health series
FS2.34:date	Conference of State and Territorial Health officers with United States Public Health Service, Transactions. Proc. Earlier T27.32:
FS2.35:nos	Community health series
FS2.35/2:CT	Portraits in community health
FS2.36:nos	[Film advertisements]. Pubs.desig. F.A.no.
FS2.36/2:date	Public Health Service film catalog. Earlier FS2.2:F48/2 Later HE20.3608/4:
FS2.37:CT	Health leaflets. **(see for leaflets numbered series)** T27.35/2:
FS2.38:nos	Special VD education circulars. Proc.
FS2.39:nos	VD education circulars. Proc.
FS2.40:nos	Letters relative to current developments in medical and science and medical military information (semimonthly) Proc.
FS2.41:nos	Malaria folders
FS2.42:nos	T.B. folders
FS2.42/2:date	Newly reported tuberculosis cases and tuberculosis deaths, United States and territories (annual) Proc.
FS2.42/3:date	Reported tuberculosis data (annual) Earlier FS2.2:T79/9 Later HE20.2313:
FS2.43:nos	National Institute of Health, Special study series
FS2.44:nos	V.D. war letters

FS2.45:vol	Industrial hygiene news letters (monthly) Proc.
FS2.45/2:nos	IH-activities. Issued by Division of Occupational Health
FS2.46:nos	[Nursing education] leaflets. Publications desig. N.E. leaflets
FS2.47:nos	Trade names index
FS2.48:v.nos.&nos.	Cadet Nurse Corps news
FS2.49:nos	Employees' health service folders
FS2.50:nos	Health education series. Later title Health information series. Proc. Later HE20.10:
FS2.50/2:CT	Don't gamble with your health (series)
FS2.50/3:nos	Federal employee health series Later HE20.5410:
FS2.51:CT	Recruitment ideas. Proc.
FS2.52:date	Compilation of Public Health Service regulations
FS2.53:nos	Mental health series
FS2.53/2:le-nos	Mental health statistics, current reports. Proc. Changed from FS2.11:5 Later HE20.2415/2:
FS2.53/2-2:letter/nos	Mental health statistics Later HE20.2415:
FS2.53/3:nos	Mental health manpower, current statistical and activities report
FS2.54:date	Freedmen's Hospital. Annual reports. Earlier I1.12/1:
FS2.54/2:CT	___ General publications. Earlier I1.12/2:
FS2.54/3:date	___ Bulletin. School of Nursing, announcements. Earlier FS2.54/2:N93/2
FS2.55:v.nos	For a healthier world (monthly) Proc.
FS2.56:nos	Studies on household sewage disposal system.
FS2.56/2:date	Public sewage treatment plant construction (annual) Earlier FS2.2:Se8 Later title, Sewage and water works construction. Later I67.11:
FS2.56/3:date	Sewage treatment works contract awards
FS2.56/4:date	Water and sewer bond sales in United States. Later I67.10:

FS2.57:nos   Cancer series

FS2.58:v.nos.&nos. CDC bulletin (monthly)

FS2.58/a:CT   ___ separates. Proc.

FS2.59:date   Patients in mental institutions. Earlier C3.59/2:

FS2.60:date   Communicable Disease Center, activities

FS2.60/2:CT   Communicable Disease Center publications   Later HE20.2302:

FS2.60/3:nos   Communicable Disease Center, Technical Development Services, summary of activities (quarterly)

FS2.60/4:date   Quarterly report, Training Branch. Proc.

FS2.60/5:nos   CDC Technology branch. Summary of investigations. Semiannual. Proc. Admin.

FS2.60/6:date   Communicable Disease Center releases.

FS2.60/7:CT   Communicable Disease Center: Handbooks, manuals, guides. Earlier in FS2.60/2:   Later HE20.2308:

FS2.60/8:date   CDC training program bulletin (annual)

FS2.60/9:v.nos   Morbidity and mortality weekly report. Earlier FS2.107/2:   Later HE20.2310:

FS2.60/10:date   Film reference guide for medicine and allied sciences (annual) Earlier FS2.211: Later FS2.202:F48

FS2.60/11:nos   Library horizons

FS2.60/12:nos   National Communicable Disease Center salmonella surveillance reports. Earlier FS2.60/2:Sa3/3/rp.(nos)   Later HE20.2309:

FS2.60/12-2:date   ___ annual summary   Later HE20.2309/2:

FS2.60/13:nos   National Communicable Disease Center hepatitis surveillance reports. Later HE20.2309/5:

FS2.60/14:CT   National Communicable Disease Center neurotropic viral disease surveillance [reports] Later HE20.2309/8:

FS2.60/15:CT   National Communicable Disease Center zoonoses surveillance [reports] Later HE20.2309/9:

FS2.60/16:nos   National Communicable Disease Center shigella surveillance reports. Later HE20.2309/3:

FS2.60/17:nos	National Communicable Disease Center rubella surveillance [reports] Later HE20.2309/7:
FS2.60/18:date	National Communicable Disease Center foodborne outbreaks annual summary Later HE20.2309/6:
FS2.60/19:date	CDC [Communicable Disease Center] veterinary public health notes. Later HE20.2312:
FS2.61:nos	Cancer morbidity series
FS2.62:nos	Public health technical monographs. Later title, Public health monographs
FS2.63:date	United States National Committee on Vital and Health Statistics, Annual reports. Later FS2.120:
FS2.63/2:CT	___ General publications
FS2.64:nos	Water pollution publications
FS2.64/2:date	Water supply and pollution control, research inventory, active projects (annual)
FS2.64/3:CT	National Conference on Water Pollution, publications
FS2.64/4:CT	___ addresses, papers, etc.
FS2.64/5:nos	Clean water, announcements [for radio and television]
FS2.64/6:date	Building for clean water, progress report on Federal incentive grants for municipal waste treatment, fiscal year. Earlier FS2.2:W29/29 Later FS16.9:
FS2.64/7:date	Water pollution control research and training grants, list of awards, research grants, research fellowships, training grants, demonstration grants. Earlier FS2.2:W29/47 Later I67.13:
FS2.64/8:date	Selected summaries of water research. Later I67.12:
FS2.65:date	National mental health program progress reports. [Irregular]
FS2.66:nos	Commissioned Officers Travel Committee, memoranda
FS2.66/2:nos	DCO circulars
FS2.67:nos	Administrative bulletins
FS2.68:nos	National Heart Institute circulars
FS2.69:date	Index of hospitals and sanatoria with tuberculosis beds in United States and territories (annual)

FS2.70:nos	Field memorandum, Division of Foreign Quarantine
FS2.71:CT	Industrial waste guide series. Later I67.8/2:
FS2.71/2:dt/v.	Inventory, municipal and industrial waste facilities. Later I67.22:
FS2.72:dt.&nos	Map and chart series. Proc.
FS2.72/2:date	Tuberculosis chart series
FS2.73:nos	Special information bulletins
FS2.73/2:date	New health and hospital projects authorized for construction under controlled materials plan (monthly) Proc.
FS2.74:date	Hill-Burton project register, hospital and medical facility projects approved. Monthly. Later HE20.2509:
FS2.74/2:date	Hospital and mental facilities construction program under Title 6 of Public Health Services act, semiannual analysis of projects approved for Federal Aid. Earlier FS2.2:H79/19
FS2.74/3:le-nos	Hospital and medical facilities series under Hill-Burton program. Desig. PHS pub. 930-letter-nos. Later HE20.2511:
FS2.74/4:nos	Hospital and medical facilities series, health professions education
FS2.74/5:le-nos	Hospital and medical facilities series: Facilities for mentally retarded
FS2.74/6:date	Representative construction cost of Hill-Burton hospitals and related health facilities (biannual) Later HE20.2510:
FS2.75:	Official classification of ... watering points
FS2.76:nos	Sources of morbidity data Superseded by FS2.76/2:
FS2.76/2:date	Health economics studies information exchange. Supersedes FS2.76:
FS2.77:date	Directory of full-time local health units (annual) Earlier FS2.2:L78
FS2.77/2:date	Directory of State and Territorial health authorities (annual) Earlier FS2.2: H34/5 Later HE20.2015/2:
FS2.78:date	List of acceptable interstate carrier equipment having sanitation significances (semiannual) Proc.
FS2.79:date	Medical supply catalog (irregular) Earlier FS2.2:M46/3
FS2.80:date	Organization and staffing for full-time local health services (annual) Earlier FS2.2:Or3

FS2.81:date	Census of nurses employed for public health work in United States, in Territories of Alaska and Hawaii, and in Puerto Rico and Virgin Islands (biennial) Proc. Later HE20.3110:
FS2.82:date	Salaries of State public health workers. Earlier FS2.2:Sa3/2:
FS2.83:date	Proceedings of annual conferences of surgeon general, Public Health Service, and chief, Children's Bureau with State and Territorial health officers, etc. Earlier FS2.2:C76/2
FS2.83/2:date	Proceedings biennial conference of State and territorial dental directors with Public Health Service and Children's bureau
FS2.83/3:date	Annual conference, surgeon general, Public Health Service, with State and Territorial mental health authorities, proceedings
FS2.83/4:date	Conference of State sanitary engineers, report of proceedings. Later HE20.1010:
FS2.84:date	Municipal water facilities, communities of 25,000 population and over, continental United States and territorial possessions (annual)
FS2.84/2:date	National water quality network, annual compilation of data
FS2.84/3:date	Municipal water facilities inventory [serving places having population of 100 or more]
FS2.84/4:CT	Digest of water pollution control legislation (by States)
FS2.84/5:nos	PHS water pollution surveillance system applications and development reports. Formerly titled National water quality network applications and development reports.
FS2.85:1e-nos	U.S. national health survey reports
FS2.85/2:nos	Vital and health statistics. Later HE20.2210:
FS2.85/3:v.nos.&nos.	Life tables Later HE20.6215:
FS2.85/4:v.nos.&nos.	Life tables (bound volumes)
FS2.86:CT	Indians on Federal reservations in United States [by area]
FS2.86/2:date	Report on Indian health (quarterly)
FS2.86/3:date	Dental services for Indians, annual report, fiscal year Later HE20.2659
FS2.86/4:date	To the first Americans, annual report of Indian health program. Earlier FS2.2:Am3 Later HE20.2014/2:

FS2.86/5:CT/date   Indian vital statistics

FS2.86/6:date   Annual statistical review, hospital and medical services. Issued by Division of Indian Health. Earlier FS2.2:In25/17

FS2.86/7:date   Division of Indian Health, annual discharge summary.

FS2.87:nos   DP pamphlets

FS2.88:CT   Dictionaries, glossaries, etc.

FS2.89:date   Medical internships in Public Health Service hospitals. Earlier FS2.2:In85/2

FS2.89/2:date   Dental internships in Public Health Service hospitals. Earlier FS2.2:D43/4

FS2.89/3:date   Pharmacy internships in Public Health Service hospitals

FS2.89/4:date   Dietetic internship, Public Service Hospital, Staten Island, N.Y.

FS2.90:nos   Radiological health data, monthly report   Later HE20.1110:

FS2.90/a:CT   ___ separates

FS2.91:CT   Announcements [of examinations for appointment of officers in Public Health Service]

FS2.92:nos   Robert A. Taft Sanitary Engineering Center: Technical reports

FS2.92/2:date   Environmental **sciences and** engineering training program bulletin

FS2.92/3:date   Bulletin of courses, training program, National Center for Air Pollution Control

FS2.92/4:date   Training Institute of Environmental Control Administration, bulletin of courses (annual)

FS2.93:date   Digest of State air pollution laws. Earlier FS2.2:Ai7/11

FS2.93/2:nos   Air pollution announcements

FS2.93/3:nos   National **Pollution** Control Administration publication AP (series)   Later HE20.1309:

FS2.93/3-2:nos   National Air Pollution Control Administration publications APTD (series) Later HE20.1309/2:

FS2.93/4:date   Federal research & development planning & programming: Sulfur oxides pollution control (annual)

FS2.93/5:CT   Reports for consultation on air quality control regions   Later HE20.1310:

FS2.93/6:v.nos.&nos. APTIC [Air Pollution Technical Information Center] bulletin Later HE20.1303/2:

FS2.94:date   Pollution-caused fish kills (annual) Later I67.9:

FS2.95:date   Hill-Burton program, progress report (annual) Later HE20.2509/2:

FS2.96:date   National Clearinghouse for Poison Control Centers, bulletins Later HE20.1203/2:

FS2.96/a:CT   ___ separates

FS2.97:nos   Today's health problems, series for teachers

FS2.98:CT   National Conference on Air Pollution, publications, addresses, etc.

FS2.98/2:nos   National Conference on Air Pollution, papers (numbered)

FS2.98/3:date   National Conference on Air Pollution: Communicator (irregular)

FS2.99:nos   Health economics series

FS2.100   National Office of Vital Statistics

The National Office of Vital Statistics in the Office of the Surgeon General, Public Health Service, was formerly the Division of Vital Statistics in the Bureau of the Census, Department of Commerce. Under Reorganization plan no. 2, effective July 16, 1946, the functions of the Bureau of the Census with respect to vital statistics were transferred to the Federal Security Agency for administration by the Public Health Service.

FS2.101:date   Activities reports. Later HE20.2201:

FS2.102:CT   General publications. Later HE20.2202:

FS2.102/a:CT   ___ separates

FS2.106:CT   Regulations, rules and instructions. Later HE20.2206:

FS2.106/2:CT   Handbooks, manuals, guides relating to vital statistics. Later HE20.2208:

FS2.107:v. nos	Weekly mortality index. Proc. Earlier C3.41:
FS2.107/2:v. nos	Morbidity and mortality weekly reports. Later FS2.60/9:
FS2.108:v. nos	Current mortality analysis (monthly) Proc. Earlier C3.152: Replaced by FS2.116:
FS2.109:v. nos	Vital statistics, special reports. Earlier C3.67:
FS2.110:v. nos	Vital statistics bulletin; Monthly. Earlier C3.127: Replaced by FS2.116:
FS2.111:v. nos	The registrar (monthly) Proc. Earlier C3.126: Later HE20.2216:
FS2.112:date	Vital statistics of United States. Earlier C3.139: Later HE20.2212:
FS2.112/a:date/sec.nos	___ separates by sections. Later HE20.6210:
FS2.113:v. nos	Marriage report; Quarterly. Proc. See for similar statistics for earlier date, C3.186:PM-nos. &nos.
FS2.114:v. nos	Marriage report; Monthly Proc. Earlier C3.186:PM-4 + nos.
FS2.115:le-nos	Mental health statistics: Current reports. Changed to FS2.53/2:
FS2.116:v. nos	Monthly vital statistics report. Replaces Current mortality analysis, FS2.108:, Monthly marriage report FS2.114:, and Monthly vital statistics bulletin, FS2.110: Later HE20.2209:
FS2.117:date	Communicable **disease summary** (weekly) Proc.
FS2.118:CT	Addresses
FS2.119:nos	Comparison deck nos. Proc. Admin.
FS2.120:date	Annual report of United States National Committee on Vital and Health Statistics, fiscal year. Proc. Earlier FS2.63: Later HE20.2211:
FS2.121:CT	Bibliographies and lists of publications. Later HE20.2213:
FS2.122:date	Proceedings of National meeting of public health conference on records and statistics. Later HE20.2214:
FS2.123:date	Health resources statistics (annual) Later HE20.2215:

FS2.200 National Library of Medicine

Established in the Public Health Service by Public law 941, 84th Congress, approved Aug. 3, 1956. (70 Stat. 960)

FS2.201:date   Annual reports.   Later HE20.3601:

FS2.202:CT   General publications   Later HE20.3602:

FS2.208:v.nos   Current list of medical literature (monthly)   Earlier D8.8:   Later see FS2.208/2:

FS2.208/2:v.nos.&nos.   Index medicus.   Replaces FS2.208:   Later HE20.3612:

FS2.208/3:date   List of journals indexed in Index medicus.   Later HE20.3612/4:

FS2.208/4:v.nos   Cumulated index medicus (annual)   Later HE20.3612/3:

FS2.208/5:v.nos.&nos.   Abridged index medicus (monthly)   Later HE20.3612/2:

FS2.209:CT   Bibliographies.   Earlier D8.10:   **Later HE20.3614:**

FS2.209/2:v.nos   Bibliography of medical reviews.   Later HE20.3610/2:

FS2.209/2-2:v.nos.&nos.   Bibliography of medical reviews (monthly)   Later HE20.3610:

FS2.209/3:v.nos.&nos.   Bibliography of medical translations (semimonthly)   Earlier FS2.209: T68, which is considered v.1 of this series.

FS2.209/4:nos   Bibliography of the history of medicine (annual, cumulated every five years)   Later HE20.3615:

FS2.210:v.nos   Index catalogue of library of Surgeon General's Office   Earlier D8.9:

FS2.211:date   Film reference guide for medicine and allied sciences (annual)   Earlier FS2.202:F48   Later FS2.60/10:, FS2.211:, HE20.3608/2:

FS2.211/2:CT   Motion picture guides (miscellaneous)   Later FS2.6/3:

FS2.211/3:CT   Selected list of audiovisuals

FS2.212:date   Medical subject headings

FS2.213:v.nos.&nos. National Library of Medicine News. Monthly. Admin. Later HE20.3619:

FS2.214:CT   Scientific Translation Program publications

FS2.215:v.nos.&nos. Notes for medical catalogers (irregular) Later HE20.3611:

FS2.216:date   National Library of Medicine current catalog (biweekly) Supersedes LC30.13: Later HE20.3609:

FS2.216/2:date   National Library of Medicine current catalog quarterly cumulation. Later HE20.3609/2:

FS2.216/3:date   ___ Annual cumulation. Later HE20.3609/3:

FS2.217:CT   Handbooks, manuals, guides. Later HE20.3608:

FS2.218:v.nos.&nos. Toxicity bibliography (quarterly) Later HE20.3613:

FS2.300:1es-nos   Environmental health series   Later HE20.1011:

FS2.300/2:v.nos   Environmental health factors, nursing homes

FS2.300/3:date   Research grants, environmental engineering and food protection, fiscal year

FS2.300/4:nos   Urban environmental health planning advisory (series)

FS2.300/5:nos   Analytical Reference Service studies. Earlier FS2.300:UIH 8, UIH-10, UIH-11 and WP-26   Later HE20.1113:

FS2.301:CT   Technical memoranda for municipal, industrial and domestic water supplies, pollution abatement, public health. [Southeast river basins]

FS2.302:1es-nos   Health mobilization series   Later HE20.2013:

FS2.303:date   Activities report, Basic and Applied Sciences Branch, Division of Water Supply and Pollution Control (annual)

FS2.304:date   Fluoridation census (annual) Earlier FS2.2:F67/8/date   Later HE20.3112:

FS2.305:nos   Office of Solid Wastes Information series SW (nos)

FS2.306:year/nos Foreign epidemiological summary

FS2.307:date	Air quality data from national air sampling networks and contributing State and local networks (annual)
FS2.308:nos	CCPM pamphlets Later HE20.13:
FS2.309:date	Health consequences of smoking, Public Health Service review
FS2.310:nos	Workshop series of Pharmacology Section, N.I.M.H.
FS2.311:nos	Studies in medical care administration
FS2.312:nos	Rheumatic fever memo
FS2.313:date	Progress report, regional medical program for heart disease, cancer, stroke, and related diseases. Earlier FS2.22:H35/13 Later HE20.2610:
FS2.314:nos	MORP [Medical and Occupational Radiation Program] (series) Later HE20.1516:
FS2.314/2:nos	DMRE [Division of Medical Radiation Exposure] (series) Later HE20.1516:
FS2.314/3:nos	DER [Division of Environmental Radiation] (series) Later EP6.10/2:
FS2.315:date	Calendar of National meetings (quarterly) Later HE20.2009:
FS2.316:nos	Injury Control Research Laboratory: Research report, ICRL-RR (series) Later HE20.1116:
FS2.317:date	Grants-in-aid and other financial assistance programs, Health Services and Mental Health Administration. Later HE20.2016:
FS2.318:nos	National Center for Health Services Research and Development Digest, Later Focus, HE20.2109:
FS2.319:date	Partnership for health news Later HE20.2559:
FS2.320:nos	Emergency health services digest. Later HE20.2013:
FS2.321:date	Health Services and Mental Health Administration public advisory committees: Authority, structure, functions Later HE20.2011:
FS2.321/2:v.nos	Health Services and Mental Health Administration public advisory committee: Roster of members. Later HE20.2011/2:

FS3 Social Security Board

Formerly an independent agency; transferred to the newly created Federal Security Agency July 1, 1939.

FS3.1:date	Annual reports. Earlier SS1.1: Later HE3.1:
FS3.1/a:CT	___ separates
FS3.2:CT	General publications. Earlier SS1.2: Later HE3.2:
FS3.3:vol	Social security bulletin. Monthly. Earlier SS1.25: Later HE3.3:
FS3.3/a:CT	___ separates. Misc. Earlier SS1.25/a4:
FS3.3/a2:date	Public assistance. Monthly. (Preprinted from Social Security Bulletin) Earlier SS1.25/a1:
FS3.3/a3:date	Employment security program, operations of; etc. Monthly.
FS3.3/2:date	Social security yearbook
FS3.3/2a:CT	___ separates
FS3.3/2a:nos	Public assistance reports. Preprints from Social Security yearbook.
FS3.3/3:date	Social security bulletin, annual statistical supplements. Issued as part of bulletin for September from 1950 to 1955. Later HE3.3/3:
FS3.3/4:nos	Commissioner's bulletin
FS3.4:nos	Circulars. Earlier SS1.4: Later HE3.4:
FS3.5:CT	Laws. Earlier SS1.5: Later HE3.5:
FS3.6:CT	Regulations, rules, and instructions (miscellaneous) Earlier SS1.6: Later HE3.6:
FS3.6/2:issue nos.	Regulations no. 4, Old-age and survivors insurance (loose-leaf edition)
FS3.6/3:CT	Handbooks, manuals, guides Later HE3.6/3:
FS3.6/4:nos	Health insurance for the aged, HIM-(series) Later HE3.6/4:
FS3.7:vol	Law accession list (of) library. Proc. Earlier SS1.22:
FS3.8:vol	Weekly accession list (of) library. Proc. Earlier SS1.17:
FS3.9:nos	Bureau reports. Research and statistics bureau. Earlier SS1.30:
FS3.10:CT	Addresses. Earlier SS1.8:CT

FS3.11:nos	Bureau memorandum. Proc. Earlier SS1.27:
FS3.11/a:CT	___ separates
FS3.12:nos	Research memorandum. Proc. Later title: Public Assistance research memorandum.
FS3.13:nos	Public assistance reports. [Note.-Sent through as FS3.2a:9/nos in D.I.no.1705, Dec.1941] Later FS14.213:
FS3.13/2:nos	[Public assistance information] PAI-(series) Later FS14.213/2:
FS3.13/3:date	Public assistance (annual)
FS3.14:nos	Bureau circulars (Public assistance bureau). Proc.
FS3.14/2:date	Advance release of statistics on public assistance. Proc. Later FS14.209:
FS3.14/3:date	Financial statistics for public assistance, calendar year
FS3.14/4:date	Money payments to recipients under State-Federal assistance programs. annual release. Proc.
FS3.15:v.	Review of operations (monthly) Proc. Earlier SS1.33:
FS3.16:date	Comparative statistics of general assistance operations of public agencies in selected large cities (monthly)
FS3.17:date	Public Assistance Bureau. Applications: Old-age assistance, aid to dependent children, aid to the blind [and] general assistance (monthly)
FS3.18:nos	Pleasantdale folks. 2d series. Proc.
FS3.19:nos	Actuarial studies. Proc. Earlier SS1.34: Later H E3.19:
FS3.19/2:nos	Actuarial notes. Later HE3.19/2:
FS3.20:nos	Illustrations from State public assistance agencies, current practices in staff training.
FS3.21:nos	Fact sheets. Proc.
FS3.22:CT	Posters
FS3.23:v.nos	Case records in public assistance.
FS3.24:date	Digest of rulings (old-age and survivors insurance)
FS3.24/2:nos	Digest of rulings (OASI) transmittal sheets
FS3.25:nos	Your new social security, fact sheets

FS3. 25/2:dt.&nos. Amendments to Social security law [fact sheets] Desig. OASI-dt-nos   Later HE3. 25/2:

FS3. 26:v.nos.&nos. Daily press digest

FS3. 27:nos   Fiscal letters

FS3. 28:nos   Research and statistics letters

FS3. 28/2:nos   Research and statistics notes   Later HE3. 28/2:

FS3. 28/3:dt./nos Research and statistics legislative notes

FS3. 28/4:nos   Health insurance statistics, CMS (series)   Later HE3. 28/4:

FS3. 28/5:nos   Health insurance statistics, HI (series)   Later HE3. 28/5:

FS3. 28/6:dt.&nos Monthly benefit statistics.   Later HE3. 28/6:

FS3. 28/6-2:date   Monthly benefit statistics: Calendar year benefit data.   Later HE3. 28/6-2:

FS3. 28/6-3:date   Monthly benefit statistics: Fiscal year benefit data.   Later HE3. 28/6-3:

FS3. 29:nos   Unemployment compensation program letters

FS3. 30:nos   Administrative orders

FS3. 31:nos   State letters

FS3. 32:nos   Adjudication instructions

FS3. 33:nos   International technical cooperation series.   Later HE3. 33:

FS3. 34:   Informational letters

FS3. 35:nos   OASI (series)

FS3. 36:v.nos.&nos. Oasis (monthly)

FS3. 36/a:CT   ___ separates

FS3. 37:CT   How they do it, illustrations of practice in administration of public assistance programs. Proc.   Later HE17. 408/2:

FS3. 38:CT   Bibliographies and lists of publications.   Later HE3. 38:

FS3. 39:date   Characteristics of families receiving aid to dependent children (biennial)

FS3. 39/2:date   Aid to dependent children of unemployed parents (monthly)   Earlier FS3. 2:C43/4   Later FS14. 210:

FS3.39/3:date	Statistical summary of aid to dependent children of unemployed parents. Later title: Annual statistics of workers under Social Security.
FS3.40:date	Handbook of old-age and survivors insurance statistics. Earlier FS3.2:Oℓ1/3 Later HE3.40:
FS3.41:date	Report of Advisory Council on Social Security Financing Later HE3.41:
FS3.42:nos	Employee publications. Official use
FS3.43:date	Current Social security program operations. Monthly. Administrative.
FS3.44:dt.&nos	Social security rulings on Federal old-age, survivors, and disability insurance (quarterly) Later HE3.44:
FS3.44/2:date	Social security rulings, cumulative bulletins. Later HE3.44/2:
FS3.45:date	Reasons for opening and closing public assistance cases. Earlier FS3.2: P96/22 Later FS14.214:
FS3.46:nos	Beneficiary studies notes
FS3.47:nos	Analytical notes
FS3.48:nos	National survey of old-age and survivors insurance beneficiaries: Highlight reports.
FS3.49:nos	Research reports Later HE3.49:
FS3.49/2:date	Index to Research reports and Research and statistics notes
FS3.50:nos	Public information notes FIS (series)
FS3.51:date	Directory of providers of services: Home health agencies
FS3.51/2:date	___ Hospitals
FS3.51/3:date	___ Extended care facilities
FS3.51/4:date	Directory of suppliers of services: Independent laboratories
FS3.51/5:date	Directory [of] Medicare providers and suppliers of services
FS3.52:nos	Social security information SSI-(series) Later HE3.52:
FS3.52/2:nos	TIB (series) Later HE3.52/2:
FS3.53:nos	Medicare newsletter
FS3.54:series/nos	Disability studies notes

FS3.54/2:nos   From the Social security survey of the disabled, reports   Later HE3.54/2:

FS3.55:nos   HIR (series)

FS3.100 Employment Security Bureau

Functions of United States Employment Service consolidated with unemployment compensation functions of Social Security Board in Bureau of Employment Security and transferred to Federal Security Agency as provided in Reorganization Plan I, effective July 1, 1939.

FS3.101:date   Annual reports

FS3.102:CT   General publications

FS3.105:CT   Laws

FS3.106:CT   Regulations, rules, and instructions

FS3.107:vol   Employment service news. Monthly. Earlier L7.14: Later Pr32.5209:

FS3.107/a:CT   ___ separates. Earlier L7.14/a: Later Pr32.5209/a:

FS3.108:vol   Unemployment compensation interpretation service, benefit series. Monthly. Later L7.37:

FS3.109:vol   Unemployment compensation interpretation service. State series (quarterly) Earlier SS1.21:

FS3.110:nos   Employment security memorandum. Printed and proc.

FS3.111:nos   Administrative standards bulletins. Proc. and printed.

FS3.112:nos., vol.nos. &pt.nos. Industrial classification code, State operations bulletins. Proc. Earlier SS1.27:23   Later FS3.112/2:

FS3.112/2:vol   Industrial classification code. 3d. ed. Earlier FS3.112:

FS3.113:date   Labor market developments (monthly) Proc. Later FS3.113/2:

FS3.113/2:date   Labor market (monthly) Earlier FS3.113:   Later Pr32.5211:

FS3.114:date   Employment security activities: Summary of. Monthly. Proc. Later L7.40:

FS3.115:date	Employment security operations; Preliminary reports of. Monthly. Proc.
FS3.116:date	Labor supply and demand in selected defense occupations, as reported by public employment offices. bi-monthly. Proc. Later title, Labor supply and demand in selected war occupations.
FS3.117:date	Labor supply available at public employment offices in selected defense occupations (monthly) Proc.
FS3.118:date & nos	Benefit payments, Duration of. Proc.
FS13.119:date & nos	Vocational training activities of public employment offices (monthly) Proc.
FS3.120:date	Farm labor market conditions. Proc.
FS3.121:date	Employers' estimates of labor needs in selected defense industries (bi-monthly) Proc.
FS3.122:date	Employment and wages of workers covered by State unemployment compensation laws: Estimated. (quarterly)
FS3.123:date	National Conference Veterans' Employment Representatives. Proc. Earlier L7.2:V64 Later Pr32.5202:V64/5
FS3.124:letter-nos	Job family series. Later Pr32.5212:
FS3.125:nos	Legislative reports (monthly) Proc.
FS3.126:nos	Agricultural reports: Summary of. wkly. Later Pr32.5210:
FS3.127:CT	Addresses. Proc.
FS3.128:v.nos	Insured unemployment (weekly) Proc. Later L7.38:, L7.37:
FS3.129:v.nos	Unemployment insurance claims (weekly) Proc. Later L7.39:
FS3.130:v.nos	Employment Service Review (monthly) Earlier L7.18:
FS3.131:date	Labor market information industry series: Current supplements (monthly) Earlier L7.23/2:
FS3.131/2:nos	___ Basic statements. Earlier L7.23:
FS3.132:date	Labor market information area series, current supplements (monthly) Earlier L7.22/2:
FS3.133:CT	Occupational guide series: Job descriptions. Earlier L7.32:, Pr32.5228:, L7.16: Later L7.16:

694

FS3.133/2:CT   Occupational guide series: Labor market information. Earlier L7.32/2:
                    Later L7.32/2:

FS3.134:CT   Labor market survey (by States)

FS3.135:   Veterans Employment Service Newsletter

EO 9247 of Sept. 17, 1942, transferred U.S. Employment Service from Social Security Board to War Manpower Commission.

                FS3.200   Children's Bureau

Transferred from the Labor Department by Reorganization plan 2, July 16, 1946.

FS3.201:date   Annual reports. Earlier L5.1: Later FS14.101:

FS3.202:CT   General publications. Earlier L5.2: Later FS14.102:

FS3.205:CT   Laws

FS3.206:

FS3.206/2:CT   Handbooks, manuals, guides. Later FS14.108:

FS3.207:v.nos   The child (monthly) Earlier L5.35: Superseded by FS3.207/2:

FS3.207/a:CT   ___ separates. Earlier L5.35/a:

FS3.207/2:v.nos   Children (bimonthly) Supersedes FS3.207: Later FS14.109:

FS3.207/2a:CT   ___ separates

FS3.208:date   Preliminary monthly statistical report on EMIC program. Proc. Earlier L5.50:

FS3.209:nos   Publications. Earlier L5.20: Later FS14.111:

FS3.210:nos   Folders. Earlier L5.22: Later FS14.118:

FS3.211:nos   Child guidance leaflets, series on eating, for parents. Earlier L5.51:

FS3.212:nos   Our Nation's children. Earlier L5.49:

FS3.213:date   Publications of Children's Bureau. Earlier L5.24:

FS3.213/2:CT   Bibliographies and lists of publications. Later FS14.112:

FS3.214:nos   Statistical series. Later FS14.113:

FS3.215:nos   Child welfare reports. Earlier L5.52: Later FS14.121:

FS3.216:nos   MCH information circulars. Printed and processed.

FS3.217:nos   Midcentury White House Conference on Children and Youth, progress bulletins.

FS3.218:   CC information circulars   CC: Crippled children

FS3.219:date   News notes on juvenile delinquency. Issued irregularly.

FS3.220:nos   Research relating to children, inventory of studies in progress. Changed from FS3.202:R31   Later FS14.114:

FS3.220/2:nos   Research relating to special groups of children. Later FS14.114/2:

FS3.221:CT   Posters. Earlier L5.14:

FS3.222:date/nos   Juvenile delinquency, facts, facets. Later FS14.115:

FS3.223:nos   Work with children coming before courts (series) Later FS14.116:

FS3.224:nos   Headliner series. Later FS14.117:

FS3.225:CT   Addresses. Later FS14.110:

Reassigned to a newly created Welfare Administration by Department reorganization on Jan. 28, 1963.

FS3.300   Federal Credit Union Bureau

Established by Public law 813, 80 C. approved June 29, 1948, effective July 29, 1948.

FS3.301:date   Annual reports. Earlier Y3.F31/8:14   Later HE3.301:

FS3.302:CT   General publications. Later HE3.302:

FS3.303:v.nos.&nos. BFCU bulletin. Later HE3.303:

FS3.305:CT   Laws   Later HE3.305:

FS3.306:CT   Regulations, rules, and instructions

696

FS3.306/2:CT   Handbooks, manuals, guides. Later HE3.306/2:, NCU1.8:

FS3.307:date   New Federal credit union charters, quarterly report of organization. Earlier Y3.F31/8:13

FS3.308:CT   Maps and charts

FS3.309:nos   Research reports   Later HE3.309:

FS3.310:v.nos.&nos. Credit union statistics (monthly)

FS4   Civilian Conservation Corps

Formerly an independent agency (Y3.C49:), transferred to Federal Security Agency by the President's Reorganization Plan 1, effective July 1, 1939.

FS4.1:date   Annual reports. Earlier Y3.C49:1

FS4.2:CT   General publications. Earlier Y3.C49:2

FS4.5:   Laws

FS4.7:nos   Forestry publications. Earlier Y3.Em3:7/nos and Y3.C49:9/nos

FS4.8:date   Safety bulletins. Proc. Earlier Y3.C49:7

FS4.9:nos   [Project training series]. Pubs.desig. PT.series no. Earlier I1.71:

FS4.10:nos   Camp life arithmetic workbooks.

July 2, 1942 (56 Stat. 569) provided for the liquidation of the CCC not later than June 30, 1943.

FS5   Education Office

Transferred from Interior Dept. (I16.) by the President's Reorganization plan 1, effective July 1, 1939

FS5.1:date   Annual reports. Earlier I16.1:   Later HE5.1:

FS5.1/2:nos   Annual report of commissioner ... concerning administration of Public laws 874 and 851 (81st Congress)   Later HE5.222:22003

FS5.2:CT	General publications. Earlier I16.2: Later HE5.2:
FS5.3:dt.&nos	Bulletins. Earlier I16.3:
FS5.3/a:CT	___ separates
FS5.3/2:nos	School assignments in Federally affected areas, bulletins. Admin.
FS5.3/3:nos	Commissioner's bulletins. Admin.
FS5.3/4:series no.&no.	Financial management bulletin.
FS5.4:nos	Circulars. Proc. Earlier I16.4:
FS5.4/2:nos	Loose-leaf circulars. Proc.
FS5.5:CT	Laws
FS5.6:CT	Regulations, rules and instructions. Later HE5.6:
FS5.6/2:CT	Handbooks, manuals, guides. Earlier in FS5.6:
FS5.7:vol	School life. (monthly except Aug. and Sept.) Earlier I16.26: Replaced by Education for Victory (FS5.26:) for duration of war, 1942-1945.
FS5.7/a:CT	___ separates. Earlier I16.26/1a:
FS5.7/a2:nos	___ Pan-American club news. Earlier FS5.26/a2:
FS5.8:CT	Addresses. Earlier I16.55: Later HE5.8:
FS5.9:date	Publications (general lists) Proc. Earlier I16.14/1:
FS5.10:CT	Publications (miscellaneous lists) Earlier I16.14/2: Later HE5.10:
FS5.10/2:CT	School facilities services (lists & references) Proc.
FS5.10/3:date	General catalogs of educational films (annual) Earlier FS5.2:F48/5
FS5.10/4:CT	References on local school administration. Proc.
FS5.10/5:date	Clearinghouse exchange of publications of State departments of education [elementary education personnel]
FS5.10/6:date	___ [secondary education personnel]
FS5.11:nos	[Miscellaneous series] Proc. Earlier I16.54/5: Pubs.desig. Misc.no.
FS5.12:nos	Language usage series. Earlier I16.75:

FS5.13/1:nos	Democracy in action (radio scripts: wkly.) Earlier I16.74:
FS5.13/2:nos	Democracy in action: Public health series (radio scripts; wkly.) Proc.
FS5.13/3:nos	Democracy in action; [Social security] (radio scripts; weekly) Proc.
FS5.13/4:nos	Democracy in action: [For Labor's welfare] (radio scripts; wkly) Proc.
FS5.13/5:nos	Democracy in action: Census (radio script)
FS5.13/6:nos	Democracy in action: Roof over America (radio script)
FS5.14/1:nos	The world is yours (radio scripts) wkly. Proc. Earlier I16.56/2:
FS5.14/2:vol	___ supplements. Published weekly for 26 consecutive weeks beginning in Oct. 1939 by Columbia University Press, N.Y.
FS5.15:nos	Gallant American women (radio scripts; weekly) Proc.
FS5.16:nos	Bibliographies (numbered) See prior to July 1,1939, I16.46:
FS5.16/2:nos	Bibliographies, Guidance and Student Personnel Section.
FS5.17:nos	Pamphlets. Earlier I16.43:
FS5.18:nos	Leaflets. Includes Guidance leaflets. Earlier I16.44:
FS5.18/2:CT	Guidance leaflets. Issued by Guidance and Student Personnel Section
FS5.19:nos	March of education. Proc. Earlier I16.26/3:
FS5.20:CT	Posters. Earlier I16.27: Later HE5.20:
FS5.21:nos	Vocational Rehabilitation Division, Leaflets. Earlier I16.54/8:
FS5.22:nos	Education and national defense series pamphlets
FS5.23:dt.&vol.nos.&chap.nos.	Biennial survey of education in United States. Formerly issued in Bulletin series, I16.3:dt.&nos. and FS5.3:dt.&nos.
FS5.24:nos	Service bulletins on defense training in vocational schools. Proc.
FS5.25:nos	Educational directory. Earlier issues included in FS5.3: Later HE5.25:
FS5.26:vol	Education for victory (biweekly) Replaces School Life, FS5.7: for duration of the war
FS5.26/a:CT	___ separates
FS5.26/a2:nos	___ Pan-American club news. Earlier FS5.35: Later FS5.7/a2:

FS5.27:date	Freedom's people, radio scripts. At intervals of about a (month) Proc.
FS5.28:nos	Vocational rehabilitation series, bulletins. Earlier issues included in I16.54/3: Later FS10.7:
FS5.29:nos	Victory Corps series pamphlets
FS5.30:nos	[Bulletins] misc. Earlier I16.71:
FS5.30/a:CT	___ separates
FS5.31:nos	Inter-American education demonstration centers. Proc.
FS5.31/2:CT	___ (misc.) Proc.
FS5.32:nos	School children and the war series. Leaflets.
FS5.33:nos	Adjustments of college curriculum to wartime conditions and needs. Reports. Proc.
FS5.34:nos	Nutrition education series pamphlets
FS5.35:nos	Pan American club news. Later FS5.26/a2:
FS5.36:nos, later dt.	News exchange, extended school services for children of working mothers, letters. Proc.
FS5.37:vol	Higher education
FS5.37/a:CT	___ separates
FS5.38:nos	Family contributions to war and post-war morale
FS5.39:CT	Statistical circulars. Printed and processed. Earlier I16.39:
FS5.40:CT	Publications of Howard University. Earlier I1.18:
FS5.41:nos	Special series
FS5.42:nos	Adult education ideas. Proc.
FS5.43:nos	Selected references. Proc.
FS5.44:nos	Education briefs. Proc.
FS5.45:dt.&nos.	Defense information bulletins. Proc.
FS5.45/2:nos	Civil defense education project, information sheets (irregular) Proc.
FS5.45/3:nos	Civil defense education project, classroom practices. Proc.

FS5.46:nos	Progress report of school facilities survey. Later title, School facilities survey reports.
FS5.47:nos	Scientific manpower series.
FS5.47/2:nos	Information bulletins (National Scientific Register) Ptd. & Proc.
FS5.48:	Circular letters. Earlier I16.76:
FS5.49:nos	Adult education references. Proc.
FS5.49/2:date	Adult education in American Education Week. Title varies. Earlier FS5.2:Ad9
FS5.50:nos	Spotlight on organization and supervision in large high schools
FS5.51:nos	Special publications
FS5.52:CT	Teaching aids for developing international understanding. Proc.
FS5.53:date	Secondary education (irregular)
FS5.54:nos	Guide lines, guidance & pupil personnel services. Proc.
FS5.55:CT	Aviation education series. Irregular. Proc.
FS5.56:nos	Fact sheet, education (irregular)
FS5.56/2:date	Education fact sheet (monthly) Proc.
FS5.57:date	Newsnotes on education around the world. Later FS5.214:14035-nos.
FS5.57/2:nos	Information on education around the world
FS5.58:date	Conference on elementary education reports (annual) Proc. Earlier FS5.2:El2/3
FS5.58/2:date	Conference for supervisors of elementary education in large cities (annual) Proc. Earlier FS5.2:El2/4
FS5.59:CT	Studies in comparative education
FS5.60:date	Audiovisual education directors in State Departments of education and in large city school systems (annual) Proc. Later FS5.60/2:
FS5.60/2:date	Key audiovisual personnel in public schools and library systems in States and large cities and in large public colleges and universities. See for earlier directories FS5.2:Au2/3/date and FS5.60:
FS5.61:date	Undergraduate engineering curricula accredited by Engineers' Council for Professional Development (annual) Earlier FS5.2:En3/7

FS5.62:date	Progress of public education in United States of America (annual) Earlier FS5.2:Ed8/2
FS5.63:nos	Scholarships and fellowship information. Proc.
FS5.64:date	Teacher exchange opportunities under International educational exchange program (annual) Earlier FS5.2:Ex2/4
FS5.64/2:date	Teacher exchange opportunities abroad, teaching, summer seminars under International Educational Exchange Program of Department of State [announcements] Proc. Earlier FS5.2:Ex2/6
FS5.64/3:date	Opportunities for teachers of French language and literature (annual) Earlier FS5.2:T22/12
FS5.64/4:date	Opportunities for teachers of Spanish and Portuguese. Proc.
FS5.65:v.nos.&nos.	Case book, education beyond high school, practices underway to meet the problems of the day
FS5.66:date	Report on principal bills introduced into Congress affecting education either directly or indirectly (annual) Proc. Earlier FS5.2:Ed8/3
FS5.67:nos	Citizen leaflets. Proc.
FS5.68:CT	Local school administration briefs. Proc.
FS5.69:date	Cooperative research program: Projects under contract
FS5.70:nos	Bulletin on National defense education act, Public law 85-864. Admin.
FS5.71:nos	Program activity reports, Public Law 85-864
FS5.72:date	Business and public administration notes
FS5.73:CT/date	Public school finance program [by State]
FS5.73/2:date	Public school finance program [compilations] Later HE5.73/2:
FS5.74:v.nos.&nos.	HE instruction in agriculture, programs, activities, developments
FS5.75:v.nos.&nos.	American education Later HE5.75:
FS5.75/a:CT	___ separates Later HE5.75/a:
FS5.76:date	Manpower development and training, projects approved
FS5.77:nos	Research in education (monthly) Later HE5.77:

FS5.78:v.nos.&nos. Community service and continuing education, Title 1, Higher education act of 1965.

FS5.79:date Title I, Elementary and secondary education act of 1965, States report (annual) Later HE5.79:

FS5.80:nos Status of compliance, Public school districts, 17 southern and border States, reports (monthly) Later HE5.80:

FS5.81:date Higher education reports Later HE5.81:

FS5.82:date Report on cooperative research to improve the Nation's schools (annual) Later HE5.82:

FS5.83:date Composite list of eligible institutions for guaranteed loans for college students, Higher education act of 1965. Later HE5.83:

FS5.83/2:date Composite list of eligible institutions under National vocational student loan insurance act of 1965. Later HE5.83/2:

FS5.84:CT Institute programs for advanced studies. Later HE5.84:

FS5.85:date National Advisory Council on Vocational Education annual report. Later HE5.85:

FS5.86:date Better education for handicapped children, annual report. Later HE5.86:

FS5.100 Federal Radio Education Committee

Appointed by the Federal Communications Commission

FS5.101:date Annual reports

FS5.102:CT General publications

FS5.103:nos Bulletins of Federal Radio Education Committee. Proc.

FS5.106:CT Regulations, rules, and instructions

FS5.107:v.nos Service bulletins. Monthly.

FS5.121 Vocational Division

FS5.121:date	Annual reports. Earlier in I16.1:
FS5.122:CT	General publications Earlier I16.54/2:
FS5.123:nos	Bulletins. Earlier I16.54/3:
FS5.126:CT	Regulations, rules, and instructions.
FS5.127:nos	Vocational Division [Miscellaneous] circulars. Proc. Earlier I16.54/7: Pubs. desig. Misc. circular. no.
FS5.128:nos	Vocational Division, Monographs. Earlier I16.54/9:
FS5.129:nos	Vocational Division, Leaflets. Earlier I16.54/8:
FS5.130:nos	Defense training leaflets
FS5.130/2:	Vocational training for defense (war production) workers. Preemployment and refresher courses.
FS5.131:date	Digest of annual reports of State boards for vocational education to Office of Education, Vocational Division, Earlier issued in Misc. series. FS5.11:
FS5.132:CT	Addresses, Division of Vocational Education
FS5.133:date	Basic preparatory programs for practical nurses by States and changes in number of programs. Earlier FS5.122:N93
FS5.210:nos	Miscellaneous: General, OE 10,000-10,999 Later HE5.210:
FS5.211:nos	___: Publications about OE and HEW, OE 11,000-11,999 Later HE5.211:
FS5.212:nos	___: Research, OE 12,000-12,999 Later HE5.212:
FS5.213:nos	___: Adult education, OE 13,000-13,999 Later HE5.213:
FS5.214:nos	___: International education, OE 14,000-14,999 Later HE5.214:
FS5.215:nos	___: Library services, OE 15,000-15,999 Later HE5.215:

FS5.216:nos	___: Nursery schools and kindergartens, OE 16,000-16,999 Later HE5.216:
FS5.220:nos	Elementary & Secondary education: Misc., general statistics, OE 20,000-20,999 Later HE5.220:
FS5.221:nos	___: Buildings, equipment, OE 21,000-21,999 Later HE5.221:
FS5.222:nos	___: Finances, receipts, expenditures, OE 22,000-22,999 Later HE5.222:
FS5.223:nos	___: Administration, faculties, salaries, OE 23,000-23,999 Later HE5.223:
FS5.224:nos	___: Enrollment, retention, graduates, OE 24,000-24,999 Later HE5.224:
FS5.225:nos	___: Guidance, testing, counseling, OE 25,000-25,999 Later HE5.225:
FS5.226:nos	___: Careers, OE 26,000-26,000 Later HE5.226:
FS5.227:nos	___: Foreign languages, OE 27,000-27,999 Later HE5.227:
FS5.228:nos	___: Health, physical education, recreation, OE 28,000-28,999 Later HE5.228:
FS5.229:nos	___: Mathematics, science, OE 29,000-29,999 Later HE5.229:
FS5.230:nos	___: Language arts, reading, writing, speaking, OE 30,000-30,999 Later HE5.230:
FS5.231:nos	___: Social studies, OE 31,000-31,999 Later HE5.231:
FS5.232:nos	___: Curriculums, subjects, activities (elementary only), OE 32,000-32,999 Later HE5.232:
FS5.233:nos	___: Curriculums, subjects, activities (secondary and elementary-secondary) OE 33,000-33,999 Later HE5.233:
FS5.234:nos	___: Audiovisual, OE 34,000-34,999 Later HE5.234:
FS5.235:nos	___: Special education, exceptional children, OE 35,000-35,999 Later HE5.345:
FS5.236:nos	___: Rural schools, rural education, OE 36,000-36,999 Later HE5.236:
FS5.237:nos	___: Education of the disadvantaged, OE 37,000-37,999 Later HE5.237:
FS5.238:nos	___: Equal educational opportunities, OE 38,000-38,999 Later HE5.238:

FS5.250:nos   Higher education: Miscellaneous, general statistics, OE 50,000-50,999 Later HE5.250:

FS5.251:nos   ___: Buildings, equipment, OE 51,000-51,999   Later HE5.251:

FS5.252:nos   ___: Finances, receipts, expenditures, OE 52,000-52,999   Later HE5.252:

FS5.253:nos   ___: Administration, faculties, salaries, OE 53,000-53,999 Later HE5.253:

FS5.254:nos   ___: Admission, enrollment, retention, degrees, graduates, OE 54,000-54,999   Later HE5.254:

FS5.255:nos   ___: Student financial assistance, OE 55,000-55,999   Later HE5.255:

FS5.256:nos   ___: Courses of study, subjects, OE 56,000-56,999   Later HE5.256:

FS5.257:nos   ___: Junior Colleges, community colleges, post high school courses, OE 57,000-57,999   Later HE5.257:

FS5.258:nos   ___: Teacher education, OE 58,000-58,999   Later HE5.258:

FS5.280:nos   Vocational education: Miscellaneous, OE 80,000-80,999   Later HE5.280:

FS5.281:nos   ___: Agricultural education, OE 81,000-81,999   Later HE5.281:

FS5.282:nos   ___: Distributive education, OE 82,000-82,999   Later HE5.282:

FS5.283:nos   ___: Home economics education, OE 83,000-83,999   Later HE5.283:

FS5.284:nos   ___: Trade & Industrial education, OE 84,000-84,999   Later HE5.284:

FS5.285:nos   ___: Practical nurse education, OE 85,000-85,999   Later HE5.285:

FS5.286:nos   ___: Business education, OE 86,000-86k999   Later HE5.286:

FS5.287:nos   ___: Manpower development and training, OE 87,000-87,999   Later HE5.287:

FS6 National Youth Administration

Formerly an agency Y3.N21/14:0 within Works Progress Administration (Y3.W89/2:). Transferred to Federal Security Agency by the President's Reorganization plan 1, effective July 1, 1939.

FS6.1:date	Annual reports. Earlier Y3.N21/14:1 Later Pr32.5251:
FS6.2:CT	General publications. Earlier Y3.N21/14:2 Later Pr32.5252:
FS6.4:nos	Circulars. Proc. Earlier Y3.N21/14:4
FS6.6:CT	Regulations, rules, and instructions.
FS6.7:nos	Letters (To State youth administrators) Proc. Earlier Y3.N21/14:7
FS6.8:nos	Information exchange bulletins. Proc.
FS6.9:nos	Related training letters. Proc.
FS6.10:CT	Tomorrow's work (by industries)
FS6.11:nos	Modern world at work.
FS6.12:nos	Handbook of procedures memorandum. Later Pr32.5257:
FS6.13:nos	Editorial comment on National Youth Administration, Weekly summaries of. Proc. Pubs.design. EC-no.
FS6.14:nos	Technical information circulars. Proc. Earlier Y3.N21/14:11
FS6.15:CT	Addresses. Proc.
FS6.16:nos	Safety bulletins. Proc.
FS6.17:nos	Manual of finance and statistics memorandum. Later Pr32.5258:

Transferred to War Manpower Commission by Executive Order 9247 of September 17, 1942.

FS7 Food and Drug Administration

Food and Drug Administration, Agriculture Department (A46.) and its functions except those functions relating to the administration of the Insecticide act of 1910 and Naval stores act are transferred to Federal Security Agency, by the President's reorganization plan 4, effective June 30, 1940.

FS7.1:date	Annual reports. Earlier A46.1: Later FS13.101:
FS7.2:CT	General publications. Earlier A46.2:CT Later FS13.102:
FS7.4:nos	Food and drug circulars.
FS7.6:CT	Regulations, rules, and instructions. Later FS13.106:
FS7.7:vol	Food and drug review. Earlier A46.5: [Confidential] Later FS13.107:
FS7.8:nos	Service and regulatory announcements, Food, drug and cosmetic. Earlier A46.19: Later FS13.115:
FS7.9:nos	Notices of judgment under caustic poison act. Earlier A46.9: Later FS13.112:
FS7.10:nos	Notices of judgment under Federal food, drug and cosmetic act, Foods. Earlier A46.20: Later FS13.109:
FS7.11:nos	Notices of judgment under food and drugs act. Earlier A46.6:
FS7.12:nos	Notices of judgment under Federal Food, drug, and cosmetic act: Drugs and devices. Earlier A46.22: Later FS13.108:
FS7.13:nos	Notices of judgment under Federal food, drug, and cosmetic act:Cosmetics. Earlier A46.21: Later FS13.113:
FS7.14:nos	Service and regulatory announcements, Tea. Earlier A46.14:
FS7.15:nos	Miscellaneous publications. Later FS13.111:
FS7.16:nos	Microanalytical Division publications. Proc. Earlier A46.17:
FS7.17:nos	Notices of judgment summarizing judicial **review of orders** under sec. 701(F) of Federal food, drug and cosmetic act. Later FS13.116:

Made a part of the Special Services Division July 16, 1946.

FS8   Coordinator of Health, Welfare, and Related
        Defense Activities Office

Established November 28, 1940 by the Council of National Defense.

FS8.1:date   Annual reports. Later Pr32.4501:

FS8.2:CT   General publications. Later Pr32.4502:

FS8.7:CT   Addresses. Proc. Later Pr32.4507:

FS8.8:nos   Recreation bulletins. Proc. Later Pr32.4509:

FS8.9:nos   Family security confidential bulletins. Proc. Later Pr32.4510:

FS8.10:   News letter. Admin.

Superseded by Defense Health and Welfare Services Office, within the Emergency Management Office. Sept. 3, 1941. (Pr32.4501)

FS9   Community War Services Office

The establishment of the Office of Community War Services by the Federal Security Administrator was authorized by Executive order 9338, dated Apr. 29, 1943. The order abolished the Office of Defense Health and Welfare Services in the Office for Emergency Management and transferred the functions, duties, powers, etc. of the abolished office to the Federal Security Agency.

FS9.1:date   Annual reports. Earlier Pr32.4501:

FS9.2:CT   General publications. Earlier Pr32.4502:

FS9.6:CT   Regulations, **rules and instructions**. Includes handbooks and manuals. Earlier Pr32.4506:

FS9.7:CT   Recreation bulletins. Proc. Earlier Pr32.4509:

FS9.8:CT   Addresses. Proc.

FS9.9:nos   [Contact reports] Proc.

Terminated December 31,1946, pursuant to Act of July 26,1946 (60 Stat. 695)

FS10 Vocational Rehabilitation Office

Established by Federal Security Agency order 3 (rev. July 1,1940) supp.1, Sept. 4,1943.

FS10.1:date   Annual reports. Later FS13.201:

FS10.2:CT   General publications. Later FS13.202:

FS10.6:CT   Regulations, rules, and instructions. Later FS13.206:

FS10.7:nos   Vocational rehabilitation series, bulletins. Earlier FS5.28:

FS10.8:CT   Addresses. Later FS13.208:

Made a part of the Special Services Office July 16,1946.

FS11 St.Elizabeth's Hospital

Transferred from the Department of the Interior under the provisions of the President's Reorganization plan no. 4, effective June 30,1940.

FS11.1:date   Annual reports. Earlier I1.14/1:

FS11.2:CT   General publications Earlier I1.14/2:   Later HE20.2422:

FS12 Physical Fitness Committee

Established under Executive order 9338, April 29, 1943, and a Federal Security Agency order implementing it.

FS12.1:date   Annual reports

FS12.2:CT   General publications

FS12.6:CT   Regulations, rules, and instructions.

Terminated June 30, 1945.

FS13 Special Services Office

The Office of Special Services was established under the Federal Security Agency through Reorganization plan no. 2, effective July 16, 1946. The Office includes the Food and Drug Administration and the Office of Vocational Rehabilitation which formerly were directly subordinate to the Federal Security Agency

FS13.1:date   Annual reports

FS13.2:CT   General publications

FS13.100 Food and Drug Administration

Included in the Special Services Office established through Reorganization plan no. 2, effective July 16, 1946.

FS13.101:date   Annual reports. Earlier FS7.1: Later HE20.1201:

FS13.102:CT   General publications. Earlier FS7.2: Later HE20.1202:

FS13.103/2:nos   Food and Drug technical bulletin

FS13.104/2:nos   Investigational drug circulars

FS13.105:CT	Laws Later HE20.1205:
FS13.106:CT	Regulations, rules and instructions. Earlier FS7.6: Later HE20.1206:
FS13.106/2:pt.nos.	F.D.C. regulations (by part numbers) Earlier desig. Service & regulatory announcements and classified FS13.115:
FS13.107:v.nos	Food and drug review (monthly) Proc. Confidential. Earlier FS7.7:
FS13.108:nos	Notices of judgment under Federal food, drug and cosmetic act: Drugs and devices. Earlier FS7.12:
FS13.109:nos	Notices of judgment under Federal food, drug, and cosmetic act: Foods. Earlier FS7.10:
FS13.110:nos	Service and regulatory announcements, Caustic poison. Earlier A46.13:
FS13.111:nos	Miscellaneous publications. **Earlier FS7.15:** Later HE20.4015:
FS13.112:nos	Notices of judgment under caustic poison act. Earlier FS7.9:
FS13.112/2:nos	Notices of judgment under Federal hazardous substances labeling act.
FS13.113:nos	Notices of judgment under Federal food, drug, and cosmetic act: Cosmetics. Earlier FS7.13:
FS13.114:nos	Service and regulatory announcements, Import milk. Earlier A46.11:
FS13.115:nos	Service and regulatory announcements: Food, drug, and cosmetic. Earlier FS7.8: Later publications designated F.D.C.Regs. and classified FS3.106/2:
FS13.116:nos	Notices of judgment summarizing judicial review of orders under sec. 701(F) of Federal food, drug, and cosmetic act. Earlier FS7.17:
FS13.117:nos	Leaflets
FS13.118:date	Report on enforcement and compliance (monthly)
FS13.119:CT	Handbooks, manuals, guides. Later HE20.1208:
FS13.120:date	Report of import detentions Later HE20.1212:
FS13.121:nos	FDA memo for consumers, CM (series)
FS13.122:nos	Student reference sheet, SR (series)
FS13.123:	Monthly report on adverse reactions to drugs and therapeutic devices. Official use only.

FS13.124:date   Radio-TV packet

FS13.125:CT   Bibliographies and lists of publications   Later HE20.1214:

FS13.126:v.nos.&nos. Interbureau bylines. Official use. Later HE20.4025:

FS13.127:nos   FDA poster (series)

FS13.128:v.nos.&nos. FDA papers (monthly) Later HE20.1210:

FS13.128/a:CT   ___ separates. Later HE20.4010/a:

FS13.129:CT   FDA's life protection series

FS13.130:nos   Bureau of Drug Abuse and Control: Fact sheets   Later J24.10:

FS13.130/2:date   BDAC bulletin

FS13.131:CT   Addresses

FS13.132:v.nos.&nos. FDA clinical experience abstracts (biweekly)

FS13.133:v.nos.&nos. Health aspects of pesticides, abstract bulletin. Later HE20.1209:

FS13.134:date   National drug code directory. Later HE20.4012:

FS13.135:date   Interstate shellfish shippers list (monthly) Earlier FS2.16: Later HE20.1213:

FS13.200   Vocational Rehabilitation Office

Included in Special Services Office established through Reorganization plan no. 2, effective July 16, 1946.

FS13.201:date   Annual reports. Earlier FS10.1: Later FS17.101:

FS13.202:CT   General publications. Earlier FS10.2: Later FS17.102:

FS13.204:nos   VR-ISC [Information service circular] (series)

FS13.205:CT   Laws

FS13.206:CT   Regulations, rules and instructions. Earlier FS10.6: Later FS17.106:

FS13.207:nos   Rehabilitation service series. Later FS17.110/3:

FS13.208:CT   Addresses. Proc. Earlier FS10.8:

FS13.209:nos   Rehabilitation standards memorandum

FS13.210:v.nos   Selected rehabilitation abstracts (bimonthly) Proc. (This is Rehabilitation services series no. 26. See for other numbers in the Rehabilitation service series, FS13.207:)

FS13.211:nos   Information service series. Proc. Later FS17.110/2:

FS13.212:nos   Administrative service series. Proc. Later FS17.110:

FS13.213:nos   State exchange service item series. Admin.

FS13.214:nos   Director's letters. Admin.

FS13.215:nos   GPT [guidance, training, and placement] bulletins

FS13.216:v.nos.&nos Rehabilitation record (bimonthly) Later FS17.109:

FS13.216/a:CT   ___ separates. Later FS17.109/a:

FS13.217:date   Handbook on programs of Office of Vocational Rehabilitation

FS13.217/2:CT   Handbooks, manuals, guides   Later FS17.108:

FS13.218:CT   Bibliographies and lists of publications   Later FS17.112:

FS13.219:nos   Program administration review, PAR (nos) (biennial)

FS13.220:nos   Publicity pointers for State rehabilitation directors, letters.

FS13.221:v.nos.&nos. VRA bulletin board. Earlier L5.14:

The Vocational Rehabilitation Administration was disestablished on August 15, 1967.

FS13.300 Employees Compensation Commission

FS13.301:date   Annual reports Earlier EC1.1: Later L26.1:

FS13.302:CT   General publications. Earlier EC1.2: Later L26.2:

FS13.305:CT   Laws. Later L26.5:
FS13.307:v.nos.   Safety bulletin (monthly) Earlier EC1.9: Later L26.7:

Transferred to Department of Labor by Reorganization plan 19, of 1950, effective May 24, 195

714

FS14 Welfare Administration

The Welfare Administration was established in the Department of Health, Education, and Welfare by the Secretary, effective Jan. 28, 1963.

FS14.1:date	Annual reports
FS14.2:CT	General publications
FS14.8:CT	Handbooks, manuals, guides
FS14.9:nos	Aging (monthly) Earlier FS1.13: Later FS15.10:
FS14.9/a:CT	___ separates Later FS17.309/a:
FS14.9/2:date	Highlights of legislation on aging. Earlier FS1.13/4:
FS14.9/3:nos	Facts on aging. Earlier FS13.5:
FS14.9/4:CT	Selected references on aging. Earlier FS1.18/2: Later FS15.12/2:
FS14.9/5:nos	Patterns for progress in aging, case studies. Earlier FS1.13/3: Later FS15.11:
FS14.10:v.nos.&nos.	Welfare in review (monthly) Later FS17.9:
FS14.10/a:CT	___ separates Later HE17.9/a:
FS14.10/2:date	Welfare in review, statistical supplement
FS14.11:CT	Addresses
FS14.12:CT	Federal assistance for projects in aging
FS14.13:CT	Bibliographies and lists of publications Later similar class FS17.17:
FS14.14:nos	Welfare research reports
FS14.15:date	Resettlement recap, periodic report from Cuban Refugee Center. Administrative.

FS14.16:nos	Public information communicator (series)
FS14.17:CT	Parole series Later FS17.16:
FS14.17/2:CT	Correction series Later FS17.16/2:
FS14.17/3:CT	Legal series Later FS17.16/3:
FS14.17/4:CT	Studies in delinquency Later FS17.16/4:

The Welfare Administration was disestablished on August 15,1967 upon the establishment of the Social and Rehabilitation Service, by the Secretary of the Department of Health, Education and Welfare.

FS14.100   Children's Bureau

Reassigned to a newly created Welfare Administration by Departmental reorganization on Jan. 28, 1963.

FS14.101:date	Annual report. Earlier FS3.201: Later FS17.201:
FS14.102:CT	General publications. Earlier FS3.202: Later FS17.202:
FS14.108:CT	Handbooks, manuals, guides. Earlier FS3.206/2: Later FS17.208:
FS14.109:v.nos.&nos.	Children, interdisciplinary journal for professions serving children (bimonthly) Earlier FS3.207/2: Later FS17.209:
FS14.109/a:CT	___ separates. Later FS17.209/a:
FS14.110:CT	Addresses. Earlier FS3.225: Later FS17.217:
FS14.110/2:CT	Jessie M. Bierman annual lectures in maternal and child health
FS14.111:nos	Publications (numbered) Earlier FS3.209: Later FS17.210:

FS14.112:CT	Bibliographies and lists of publications. Earlier FS3.213/2: Later FS17.212:
FS14.113:nos	Statistical series. Earlier FS3.214: Later FS17.213:
FS14.114:nos	Research relating to children. Earlier FS3.220: Later FS17.211:
FS14.114/2:nos	Research relating to special groups of children. Earlier FS3.220/2: Later FS17.211/2:
FS14.115:nos	Juvenile delinquency, facts, facets. Earlier FS3.222:
FS14.116:nos	Work with children coming before courts. Earlier FS3.223:
FS14.117:nos	Headliner series. Earlier FS3.224: Later FS17.216:
FS14.118:nos	Folders. Earlier FS3.210: Later FS17.215:
FS14.119:CT	Facts about children
FS14.120:date	Project on cost analysis in children's institutions. Earlier FS14.102:In7
FS14.121:nos	Child welfare report. Earlier FS3.215:

The Children's Bureau has been assigned to the Social and Rehabilitation Service which was established August 15, 1967, by the Secretary of the Department of Health, Education, and Welfare in a major realignment of Federal welfare rehabilitation and social welfare service programs.

FS14.200 Family Services Bureau

Assigned to Welfare Administration by Secretary's reorganization of January 28, 1963.

FS14.201:date	Annual reports.
FS14.202:CT	General publications. Formerly in FS3.2:
FS14.208:CT	Handbooks, manuals, guides.

FS14.208/2:CT	Medical care in public assistance, guides and recommended standards. Earlier FS3.6/3:M46 and M46/2:
FS14.208/3:CT	Mental health in public assistance (series)
FS14.208/4:CT	Staff development series
FS14.209:date	Advance release of statistics on public assistance (monthly) Earlier FS3.14/2: Later FS17.10:
FS14.210:date	Unemployed-parent segment of aid to families with dependent children (monthly) Earlier FS3.39/2: Later FS17.11:
FS14.211:date	State maximums and other methods of limiting monthly payments to recipients of special types of public assistance, annual release. Later FS17.2:P96/966 and FS17.626:
FS14.212:date	Public assistance, annual statistical data, calendar year Later FS17.13:
FS14.213:nos	Public assistance reports. Earlier FS3.13: Later FS17.19:
FS14.213/2:nos	Public assistance information PAI (series) Earlier FS3.13/2:
FS14.214:date	Reasons for opening and closing public assistance cases. Earlier FS3.45: Later FS17.411:
FS14.215:date	Source of funds expended for public assistance payments. Earlier FS14.202:P96/2 Later FS17.631:
FS14.216:CT	Addresses
FS14.217:CT	Bibliographies and lists of publications
FS14.218:date	Medical assistance for the aged, fact sheet (semiannual)
FS14.219:date	Impact on public assistance caseloads of (a) **Training programs under** Manpower development and training act and Area redevelopment Act and (b)Public assistance work and training program (quarterly) Earlier FS14.202:P96/6/963-64 Later FS17.409:
FS14.220:date	Progress report on staff development (annual) Later FS17.2:M46/2
FS14.221:date	Public assistance, vendor payments for medical care by type of service, fiscal and calendar years. Earlier FS14.202:M46 Later FS17.617:

Functions redelegated to the Social and Rehabilitation Service by Secretary's reorganization act of Aug.15,1967.

FS15 Aging Administration

The Administration on Aging was established within the Department of Health, Education, and Welfare by Public Law 89-73, approved July 14, 1965 (79 Stat. 226)

FS15.1:date   Annual report   Later FS17.301:

FS15.2:CT   General report   Later FS17.302:

FS15.8:CT   Handbooks, manuals, guides.   Later FS17.308:

FS15.9:CT   Addresses   Later FS17.312:

FS15.10:nos   Aging. Earlier FS14.9:   Later FS17.309:

FS15.11:nos   Patterns for progress in aging.   Earlier FS14.9/5:   Later HE17.313:

FS15.12:CT   Bibliographies and lists of publications   Later FS17.311:

FS15.12/2:CT   Selected references on aging.   Earlier FS14.9/4:   Later HE1.18/2:

FS15.13:CT   Federal financial assistance for projects in aging.   Later FS17.310/2:

The Administration on Aging has been assigned to the Social and Rehabilitation Service which was established August 15, 1967, by the Secretary of the Department of Health, Education, and Welfare in a major realignment of Federal welfare rehabilitation and social welfare service programs.

FS16 Federal Water Pollution Control Administration

The Federal Water Pollution Control Administration was created within the Department of Health, Education, and Welfare by Public law 89-234, approved Oct. 2, 1965, effective 90 days after enactment of the act.

FS16.1:date   Annual report   Later I67.1:

FS16.2:CT   General publications   Later I67.2:

FS16.5:CT   Laws   Later I67.5:

FS16.9:date   Building for clean water, report on Federal incentive grants for municipal waste treatment. Earlier FS2.64/6:   Later I67.15:

The Federal Water Pollution Control Administration was transferred from the Department of Health, Education and Welfare to the Department of the Interior by Reorganization Plan no. 2 of 1966, effective May 10,1966.

FS17   Social and Rehabilitation Service

Established August 15,1967 by the Secretary of the Department of Health, Education and Welfare in a major realignment of Federal welfare rehabilitation and social welfare service programs.

FS17.1:date   Annual report   Later HE17.1:

FS17.2:CT   General publications   Later HE17.2:

FS17.6:CT   Rules, regulations and instructions.   Later HE17.6:

FS17.8:CT   Handbooks, manuals, guides   Later HE17.8:

FS17.8/2:CT   Manuals for volunteer probation programs   Later HE17.8/2:

FS17.9:v.nos.&nos.   Welfare in review. Earlier FS14.10:   Later HE17.8:

FS17.9/a:CT   ___ separates. Earlier FS14.10/a:

FS17.10:date   Advance release of statistics on public assistance (monthly)   Earlier FS14.209:   Later FS17.610:

FS17.11:date   Unemployed-parent segment of aid to families with dependent children (monthly) Earlier FS14.210:   Later FS17.611:

FS17.12:date   Statistical report on social services, Form FS-2069, quarter ended. Earlier FS14.202:Sol/4/date   Later FS17.626:

FS17.13:date   Public assistance, annual statistical data. Earlier FS14.212:   Later FS17.615:

FS17.13/2:date   Public welfare personnel, annual statistical data. Earlier FS14.202:P96/13 Later FS17.629:

FS17.14:CT   Addresses. Later HE17.14:

FS17.15:date   Social and Rehabilitation Service research and demonstration projects. Earlier FS13.202:R31/3/date   Later HE17.15:

FS17.16:CT   Parole decision making, parole series. Earlier FS14.17:   Later HE17.16:

FS17.16/2:CT   Correction series. Earlier FS14.17/2:   Later HE17.16/2:

FS17.17:CT   Bibliographies and lists of publications. Earlier FS14.13:   Later HE17.17:

FS17.16/3:CT   Legal series. Earlier FS14.17/3:   Later HE17.16/3:

FS17.16/4:CT   Studies in delinquency. Earlier FS14.17/4:   Later HE17.16/4:

FS17.17:CT   Bibliographies and lists of publications. Earlier FS14.13:   Later HE17.17:

FS17.18:v.nos.&nos. Research briefs. Later HE17.18:

FS17.19:nos   Public assistance reports. Earlier FS14.213:   Later HE17.19:

FS17.100   Rehabilitation Services Administration

August 15,1967, in a major realignment of Federal welfare rehabilitation and social welfare service programs, the Rehabilitation Services Admin. is assigned to Social and Rehabilitation Service.

FS17.101:date   Annual reports. Earlier FS13.201:   Later HE17.101:

FS17.102:CT   General publications. Earlier FS13.202:   Later HE17.102:

FS17.106:CT   Regulations, rules and instructions. Earlier FS13.206: Later HE17.106:

FS17.108:CT   Handbooks, manuals, guides. Earlier FS13.217/2: Later HE17.108:

FS17.109:v.nos.&nos. Rehabilitation record. Earlier FS13.216: Later HE17.109:

FS17.109/a:CT   ___ separates. Earlier FS13.216/a:

FS17.110:nos   Administrative service series. Earlier FS13.212:

FS17.110/2:nos   Information service series. Earlier FS13.211:

FS17.110/3:nos   Rehabilitation service series. Earlier FS13.207: Later HE17.110/3:

FS17.111:date   Caseload statistics, State vocational rehabilitation agencies, fiscal year. Earlier FS13.202:C26/date Later HE17.111:

FS17.112:CT   Bibliographies and lists of publications. Earlier FS13.218: Later HE17.112:

FS17.113:v.nos.&nos. Mental retardation abstracts. (quarterly) Earlier FS2.22/52: Later HE17.113:

FS17.200   Children's Bureau

The Children's Bureau has been assigned to the Social and Rehabilitation Service which was established August 15, 1967, by the Secretary of the Department of Health, Education, and Welfare in a major realignment of Federal welfare rehabilitation and social welfare service programs. The Welfare Administration was disestablished on the same date.

FS17.201:date   Annual report. Earlier FS14.101:

FS17.202:CT   General publications. Earlier FS14.102: Later HE21.2: and HE21.102:

FS17.208:CT   Handbooks, manuals, guides. Earlier FS14.108: Later HE21.108:

FS17.209:v.nos.&nos. Children. Earlier FS14.109: Later HE21.9:

FS17.209/a:CT   ___ separates. Earlier FS14.109/a: Later HE21.9/a:

FS17.210:nos   Publications (numbered) Earlier FS14.111: Later HE21.110:

FS17.211:nos   Research relating to children. Earlier FS1.114: Later HE21.112:

FS17.212:CT   Bibliographies and lists of publications. Earlier FS14.112: Later HE21.113:

FS17.213:nos   Statistical series. Earlier FS14.113: Later HE17.23:

FS17.214:nos   Research reports

FS17.215:nos   Folders. Earlier FS14.118: Later HE21.111:

FS17.216:nos   Headliner series. Earlier FS14.117: Later HE21.114:

FS17.217:CT   Addresses. Earlier FS14.110:

FS17.300: Aging Administration

The Administration on Aging has been assigned to the Social and Rehabilitation Service which was established August 15, 1967, by the Secretary of the Department of Health, Education, and Welfare in a major realignment of Federal welfare rehabilitation and social welfare service programs.

FS17.301:date   Annual report. Earlier FS15.1: Later HE17.301:

FS17.302:CT   General publications. Earlier FS15.2: Later HE17.302:

FS17.308:CT   Handbooks, manuals, guides. Earlier FS15.8: Later HE17.308:

FS17.309:nos   Aging. Earlier FS15.10: Later HE17.309:

FS17.309/a:CT   ___ separates. Earlier FS14.9/a: Later HE17.309/a:

FS17.310:CT   Designs for action for older Americans (series) Later HE17.310:

FS17.310/2:CT   Federal financial assistance for projects in aging. Earlier FS15.13:

FS17.311:CT   Bibliographies and lists of publications. Earlier FS15.12: Later HE17.311:

FS17.312:CT   Addresses. Earlier FS15.9: Later HE17.312:

FS17.400:   Assistance Payments Administration

The Assistance Payments Administration has been assigned to the Social and Rehabilitation Service which was established August 15, 1967, by the Secretary of the Department of Health, Education, and Welfare in a major realignment of Federal welfare rehabilitation and social welfare service programs.

FS17.401:date   Annual report. Later HE17.401:

FS17.402:CT   General publications   Later HE17.402:

FS17.408:CT   Handbooks, manuals, guides   Later HE17.408:

FS17.409:date   Impact on public assistance caseloads of: (a) Public assistance work and training programs, and (b) Training programs under Manpower development and training act (quarterly) Earlier FS14.219   Later FS17.635:

FS17.410:nos   Trend report, graphic presentation of public assistance and related data (annual)   Later FS17.612:

FS17.411:date   Reasons for opening and closing public assistance cases (semiannual) Earlier FS14.214:   Later FS17.613:

FS17.500 Medical Services Administration

The Medical Services Administration, formerly the Mental Retardation Division of the Bureau of Health Services, Public Health Service, has been assigned to the Social and Rehabilitation Service which was established August 15, 1967, by the Secretary of the Department, of Health, Education, and welfare in a major realignment of Federal welfare rehabilitation and social welfare service programs.

FS17.501:date	Annual report	Later HE17.501:
FS17.502:CT	General publications	Later HE17.502:

FS17.600: National Center for Social Statistics

The National Center for Social Statistics was established as part of Social and Rehabilitation Service to provide staff coordination, direction, and advice for all statistical activities and programs for Social and Rehabilitation Service.

FS17.601:date   Annual report. Later HE17.601:

FS17.602:CT   General publications   Later HE17.602:

FS17.609:date   Child care arrangements of AFDC recipients under the work incentive program. NCSS Report E-4.   Later HE17.609:

FS17.610:date   Advance release of statistics on public assistance and appendix on work experience and training programs under title 5 of Economic opportunity act as amended, NCSS report A-2 (monthly)   Earlier FS17.10:   Later HE17.610:

FS17.611:date   Unemployed-parent segment of aid to families with dependent children, NCSS report A-3 (monthly)   Earlier FS17.11:   Later HE17.611:

FS17.612:nos   Trend report: graphic presentation of public assistance and related data, NCSS report A-4.   Earlier FS17.410:   Later HE17.612:

FS17.613:date   Reasons for opening and closing public assistance cases, NCSS report A-5 (semiannual)   Earlier FS17.411:   Later HE17.613:

FS17.614:nos   Program facts on federally aided public assistance income maintenance program. NCSS report A-6. Later HE17.614:

FS17.615:date   Public assistance, annual statistical data, NCSS report A-7. Earlier FS17.13:   Later HE17.615:

FS17.616:date   Medical assistance financed under public assistance titles of Social security act. NCSS report B-1. Earlier FS17.2:M46/2 Later HE17.616:

FS17.617:date   Public assistance, vendor payments for medical care by type of service calendar year, NCSS report B-2. Earlier FS14.221: Later HE17.617:

FS17.618:   Reserved

FS17.619:   Reserved

FS17.620:date   Medicaid, fiscal year, NCSS report B-5. Later HE17.620:

FS17.621:date   Medicaid and other medical care financed from public assistance funds. NCSS report B-6. Later HE17.621:

FS17.622:   [not used]

FS17.623:   [not used]

FS17.624:   [not used]

FS17.625:date   OAA and AFDC, cost standards for basic needs and percent of such standards met for specified types of cases, NCSS report D-2. Earlier FS17.2:Oℓ1   Later HE17.625:

FS17.626:date   State maximums and other methods of limiting money payments to recipients of special types of public assistance, NCSS **report D-3**. Earlier FS14.211: and FS17.2:P96/966   Later HE17.626:

FS17.627:date   Money payments to recipients of special types of public assistance, NCSS report D-1. Earlier FS14.202:P96/4/date   Later HE17.627:

FS17.628:date   Statistical report on social services, Form FS-2069, quarter ended, NCSS report E-1. Earlier FS17.12: Later HE17.628:

FS17.629:date   Public welfare personnel, annual statistical data, NCSS report E-2. Earlier FS17.13/2:   Later HE17.629:

FS17.630:date   Progress report on staff development for fiscal year, NCSS report E-3. Earlier FS17.2:Stl/date   Later HE17.630:

FS17.631:date   Source of funds expended for public assistance payments, fiscal year. Earlier FS14.215: Later HE17.631:

FS17.632:   [not used]

FS17.633:date   Public assistanae, costs of State and local administration, services and training, fiscal year, NCSS report F-3. Earlier FS14.202:P96/7/date. Later HE17.633:

FS17.634:date   Source of funds expended for public assistance payments and for cost of Administration, service, and training, fiscal year, NCSS report F-2. Later HE17.634:

FS17.635:date   Impact on public assistance caseloads of (a) Public assistance work and training programs, and (b) Training programs under Manpower development and training act, NCSS G-1 (quarterly) Earlier FS17.409: Later HE17.635:

FS17.636:date   Concurrent receipt of public assistance money payments and old-age, survivors, and disability insurance cash benefits by persons aged 65 or over. Earlier FS17.402:P96/date Later HE17.636:

FS17.637:   [not used]

FS17.638:date   Child welfare statistics, NCSS report CW-1 Later HE17.638:

FST Freedman's Savings and Trust Company

A banking institution chartered under act of March 3, 1865 for the benefit of freed slaves.

FST1.1:date   Annual reports

FST1.2:CT   General publications

FST1.3:nos   Bulletins [none issued]

FST1.4:nos   Circulars [none issued]

By act of February 21, 1881 the comptroller of the currency was made sole commissioner to finish the liquidation which was begun after 1874.

FT Federal Trade Commission

Federal Trade Commission act of September 26, 1914 (38 Stat. 717:15)

FT1.1:date	Annual reports
FT1.1/a:CT	___ separates
FT1.2:CT	General publications
FT1.2/a:CT	___ separates
FT1.3:nos	Bulletins
FT1.3/2:nos	Consumer bulletins
FT1.4:nos	Circulars
FT1.5:CT	Papers in re
FT1.5:L-CT	Laws
FT1.6:nos	Conference rulings bulletins
FT1.7:date	Rules of practice
FT1.8:CT	Rules, regulations, and instructions (miscellaneous)
FT1.8/2:CT	Handbooks, manuals, guides
FT1.8/3:nos	Consumer survey handbooks
FT1.1.8/4:nos	Buyer's guides
FT1.9:nos	Foreign trade series
FT1.10:CT	Cost reports
FT1.11:v.nos	Decisions
FT1.11/a:v.nos	___ separates. T.P., Ind. table of cases & commodities
FT1.11/a2:nos	___ separates. Report of findings and order of commission
FT1.11/a3:CT	___ separates. Decisions of courts on orders of commission
FT1.11/2:date	Federal Trade Commission decisions (monthly)
FT1.11/3:nos	Stipulations

FT1.12/2:nos	Advisory opinion digests
FT1.13:incl.dt.	Statutes and decisions
FT1.13/2:date	Statutes and court decisions, supplements
FT1.14:CT	Addresses. Mimeographed
FT1.15:date	Monthly summary of work. Proc. Slightly varying titles.
FT1.16:CT	Trade practice rules (by industries) Proc.
FT1.16:date	Trade practice rules (compilations)
FT1.16/2:CT	Proposed trade practice rules (irregular) Proc.
FT1.17:CT	Industrial corporation reports (by industries) Proc.
FT1.18:date	Industrial financial report series for all United States manufacturing corporations; Quarterly.
FT1.19:date	Releases. Proc.
FT1.19/2:nos	Clip sheets. [Issued irregularly] Proc. Later title, News summary
FT1.20:date	Quarterly financial report, United States retail and wholesale corporations. Proc. Previously classified FT1.2:R31/6/date
FT1.21:date	Report of Federal Trade Commission on rates of return (after taxes) for identical companies in selected manufacturing industries. Proc. Earlier FT1.2:R18
FT1.22:date	List of publications (annual) Proc. Earlier FT1.2:P96/3
FT1.22/2:nos	Special reference lists
FT1.23:nos	Dockets [Circuit Court of Appeals]
FT1.24:date/nos	Advertising alert (irregular)
FT1.24/2:v.nos.&nos.	Consumer alert
FT1.25:date	Calendar
FT1.26:nos	FTC packets
FT1.27:CT	Background information [on various subjects]
FT1.28:nos	Statistical Reports (numbered)

FTZ Foreign-Trade Zones Board

June 18, 1934 (48 Stat. 998)

FTZ1.1:date   Annual reports

FTZ1.2:CT   General reports

FTZ1.5:CT   Laws

FTZ1.7:nos   News bulletins. Proc.

FTZ1.8:nos   General description of foreign-trade zones. Proc.

FTZ1.9:CT   Addresses. Proc.

FW Federal Works Agency

Created by President's Reorganization Plan I, April 25, 1939.

FW1.1:date   Annual reports

FW1.2:CT   General publications

FW1.5:CT   Laws

FW1.6:CT   Regulations, rules, and instructions

FW1.6/2:nos   Field operations instructions

FW1.7:CT   Addresses. Proc.

FW1.8:nos   Special orders. Proc. Pubs. desig. P.WA-nos.

FW1.9:nos   General circulars. Proc.

FW1.10:nos   General orders. Proc.

FW1.11:v.nos.   Library accessions (bi-weekly) Proc.   Earlier FW4.11:

FW1.12:nos   Training bulletins.

FW1.13:nos   Defense housing construction bulletins (wkly) Proc.

FW1.14:nos   Transmittal letters, Manual of regulations and procedure

FW1.15:v.nos   Planning, current literature (weekly) Proc.   Later C37.12:

FW1.16:nos   Construction materials (monthly) Proc.   Earlier Pr32.4827:   Later GS1.7:

FW1.17:   Staff memorandum. Proc. Admin.

FW1.18:   Administrator's memorandums. Proc. Admin.

FW1.19:   Field memorandum. Proc. Admin.

FW1.20:   Chief Engineer, Office of. Circular letter. Proc. Admin.

FW1.21:   Administrative procedure memorandum. Admin.

FW1.22:nos   Administrative orders. Proc. Admin.

Abolished by act approved June 30,1949 (63 Stat. 378) and functions transferred to General Services Administration.

FW2   Public Roads Administration

Formerly in Department of Agriculture. Transferred to Federal Works Agency July 1,1939.

FW2.1:date   Annual reports. Earlier A22.1: Later GS3.1:

FW2.2:CT   General publications. Earlier A22.2: Later GS3.2:

FW2.5:CT   Laws. Later C37.5:

FW2.6:CT   Regulations, rules and instructions. Includes handbooks and manuals.

FW2.7:v.nos.   Public roads, journal of highway research. Monthly. Earlier A22.6: Later GS3.8:

FW2.7/a:CT   ___ separates

FW2.8:v.nos   Highways, current literature. Wkly. Proc. Earlier A22.10: Later C37.10:

FW2.9:nos   Planning survey memorandum. Proc. Earlier A22.12:

FW2.10:nos   Statewide highway planning surveys; news bulletins. Proc. Earlier A22.13:

FW2.11:date   Traffic volume trends (monthly) Proc. Earlier A22.15: Later FW2.14:

FW2.12:CT   Maps, Progress. Earlier A22.9: Later C37.13:

FW2.13:CT   Maps, Transportation. Earlier A22.9/2: Later C37.11:

FW2.14:date   Traffic volume trends. Monthly. Proc. Earlier FW2.11: <u>Transfer to FW2.16:</u>

FW2.15:CT   Addresses

736

FW2.16:nos   Traffic volume trends. Monthly. Proc. Prior to June 1948 entitled Information memorandum, traffic volume trends. Later GS3.7:

FW2.17:nos   Automobile registration characteristics. Proc.

FW2.18:CT   President's Highway Safety Conference publications. Later C37.7:

FW2.19:CA-nos&date. Highway construction contracts awarded by State highway departments, tables. Proc. Later C37.25:

By provisions of Public law 152, 81st Congress, 1st session, effective July 1, 1949, the Public Roads Administration was transferred from the Federal Works Agency to the General Services Administration and its name changed to the Public Roads Bureau.

FW3   Housing Authority

Transferred from Interior Department (I40.) by the President's Reorganization plan 1, effective July 1, 1939.

FW3.1:date   Annual reports. Earlier I40.1: Later NHA4.1:

FW3.2:CT   General publications. Earlier I40.2: Later NHA4.2:

FW3.5:CT   Laws. Earlier I40.6:

FW3.7:vol.   Public housing. Wkly. Later NHA4.8:

FW3.7/a:CT   ___ separates. Later NHA4.8/a:

FW3.8:CT   Addresses. Proc. Earlier I40.8:

FW3.9:nos   Bulletins on policy and procedure. Earlier I40.10:

FW3.10:nos   Management experience notes.

FW3.11:nos   Technical information notes. Proc. Earlier I40.11:

Feb. 24, 1942 made a unit of National Housing Authority NHA4.

737

FW4 Work Projects Administration

Reorganization plan I, July 1, 1939 provided for the consolidation of Works Progress Administration into the Federal Works Agency as Work Projects Administration.

FW4.1:date	Annual reports. Earlier Y3.W89/2:1
FW4.2:CT	General publications. Earlier Y3.W89/2:2
FW4.6:CT	Regulations, rules, and instructions. Earlier Y3.W89/2:6
FW4.7:letter-nos	National research project, Reports. Proc. Earlier Y3.W89/2:42
FW4.8:nos	Operating procedure memorandum. Proc. Earlier Y3.W89/2:30
FW4.9:nos	Handbook of procedures letters. Proc. Earlier Y3.W89/2:29
FW4.10:nos	Digest of procedures. Monthly. Proc. Earlier Y3.W89/2:10
FW4.11:vol.	Library accessions. Wkly. Proc. Earlier Y3.W89/2:41
FW4.12:nos	General letters. Proc. Earlier Y3.W89/2:23
FW4.13:date	Statistical bulletins. Monthly. Proc. Earlier Y3.W89/2:58
FW4.14:CT	Historical records survey. Proc. Earlier Y3.W89/2:43
FW4.15:nos	Information service letters. Proc. Earlier Y3.W89/2:39
FW4.16:nos	General orders. Proc.
FW4.17:nos	Technical series: Research and records project circulars. Laboratory circulars. Proc. Earlier Y3.W89/2:59
FW4.18:nos	Technical series: Research and records projects circulars. Proc.
FW4.19:nos	Social problems. Earlier Y3.W89/2:57
FW4.20:nos	Safety bulletins. Proc. Earlier Y3.W89/2:11
FW4.21:nos	Technical series: Recreation circulars. Earlier Y3.W89/2:38

FW4.22:nos	Technical series: Research, statistical and survey projects circulars. Proc. Earlier Y3.W89/2:52
FW4.23:nos	Technical series. Research and records projects bibliographies.
FW4.24:nos	Technical series: Workers' service circulars. Proc.
FW4.25:CT	Addresses. Earlier Y3.W89/2:54
FW4.26:nos	Technical series: Community service circulars. Proc.
FW4.27:nos	Technical series: Library. Proc.
FW4.28:CT	Writers' publications. Proc. and ptd. Earlier Y3.W89/2:24
FW4.29:pt.nos	Bibliography of aeronautics. Proc. Non-Government. Earlier Y3.W89/2:60
FW4.30:vol	Manual of rules and regulations, Transmittal letters. Proc.
FW4.31:CT	Projects operated by Work Projects Administration, Accomplishments on. Proc. (by States)
FW4.32:date	Federal work programs and public assistance (monthly) Proc.
FW4.33:date	Federal work and construction projects (monthly) Proc. Earlier Y3.W89/2:61
FW4.34:nos	Technical series: Art circulars. Proc. Earlier Y3.W89/2:48
FW4.35:nos	Research monographs. Earlier Y3.W89/2:17
FW4.36:vol	Marketing laws survey [publications] See also C18.227:
FW4.37:nos	WPA week in national defense. Proc.
FW4.38:nos	Technical series: Welfare circulars. Proc.
FW4.39:nos	Commissioner's letters. Proc.
FW4.40:CT	Posters
FW4.41:	Community service letters. Proc. Admin.

Letter of President to the Federal Works Administration, Dec.4,1942 authorized its liquidation.

FW5 Public Works Administration

Formerly an independent agency. The President's Reorganization plan I, effective July 1, 1939 consolidated the Federal Emergency Administration of Public Works into the Federal Works Agency to be administered as the Public Works Administration.

FW5.1 :date	Annual reports. Earlier Y3.F31/4:1	
FW5.2:CT	General publications. Earlier Y3.F31/4:2	
FW5.5:CT	Laws. Earlier Y3.F31/4:5	
FW5.7:CT	Addresses. Proc. Earlier Y3.F31/4:9	
FW5.8:nos	Administrative orders. Proc. Earlier Y3.F31/4:22	
FW5.9:	General orders. <u>Cancelled.</u>	
FW5.10:	Accounting Division orders. Proc.	
FW5.11:	Engineering Division orders. Proc. Admin.	
FW5.12:	Letters of instructions. Admin.	

Executive order 9357 of June 30, 1943 transferred functions to the office of the Federal Works Administrator.

FW6 Public Buildings Administration

Public buildings of the Procurement division (T58.) and its functions, the Branch of buildings management of the National Park Service (I29.) and its functions except those relating to monuments and memorials) and the functions of the National Park Service in the District of Columbia in connection with the general assignment of space, the selection of sites for public buildings, and the determination of the priority in which the construction or enlargement of public buildings shall be undertaken shall be administered by the Public Buildings Administration December 1939.

FW6.1:date	Annual reports. Later GS6.1:	
FW6.2:CT	General publications. Later GS6.2:	

FW6.6:CT   Regulations, rules, and instructions. Later GS6.6:

FW6.7:nos   Bulletins, Section of fine arts. Proc. Earlier T58.16:

FW6.8:date   Telephone directory, Republic 7500 (monthly, later bimonthly) Later GS6.7:

FW6.9:CT   President's Conference on Fire Prevention publications

FW6.10:nos   Accident and fire prevention news (bimonthly) Proc. Nos.1-6 entitled Safety news. The first 9 numbers were issued monthly.

Abolished by act approved June 30, 1949 (63 Stat. 378) and functions transferred to General Services Administration.

FW7 Community Facilities Bureau

The Bureau of Community Facilities was established Jan.1, 1945, by administrative order of the Federal Works Administrator.

FW7.1:date   Annual reports   Later HH5.1:

FW7.2:CT   General publications   Later HH5.2:

FW7.6:CT   Regulations, rules, and instructions.

FW7.7:date   Report on plan preparation of State and local public works (semiannual)

Transferred to General Services Administration by act approved June 30, 1949. (63 Stat. 378) where it functioned as Community Facilities Service.

GA   General Accounting Office

The General Accounting Office is vested with all the powers... of the former Comptroller of the Treasury and the six auditors of the Treasury Dept. and others as imposed by the Budget and Accounting Act of June 10, 1921.

GA1.1:date	Annual reports
GA1.2:CT	General publications
GA1.3:nos	Bulletins
GA1.4:nos	Circulars
GA1.5:v.nos	Decisions of Comptroller General. Earlier T15.5:
GA1.5/a:v.nos	___ separates. Monthly. Earlier T15.5/a:
GA1.5/2:year & month	___separates. irregular. mimeographed.
GA1.5/3:date	Index to published decisions of Accounting officers of United States
GA1.5/4:date	Daily synopses of published decisions. Proc. Later title, Digest of published decisions of Comptroller General
GA1.5/5:v.nos. &nos.	Quarterly digest of **unpublished** decisions of Comptroller General of United States: Civilian personnel
GA1.5/6:v.nos. &nos.	___: Pay and allocations of uniformed service
GA1.5/7:v.nos. &nos.	___: Contracts
GA1.5/8:v.nos. &nos.	___: Transportation
GA1.5/9:v.nos. &nos.	___: Appropriations and miscellaneous subjects (quarterly)
GA1.5/10:v.nos. &nos.	___: Procurement law
GA1.5/11:v.nos. &nos.	___: Personnel law, Military personnel
GA1.5/12:v.nos. &nos.	Digests of unpublished decisions of the Comptroller General of the United States: General government matters, appropriations and miscellaneous (semiannual)
GA1.6:nos	General regulations
GA1.6/1:date/trans.nos.	GAO manual for guidance of federal agencies, title 1, United States General Accounting Office, transmittal sheet nos.
GA1.6/2:date	___ Title 2, Accounting principles and standards and internal auditing guidelines

GA1.6/3:date	___ Title 3, Audit
GA1.6/4:	
GA1.6/5:date	___ Title 5. Transportation
GA1.6/6:	
GA1.6/7:date	___ Title 7, Standardized fiscal procedure
GA1.6/8:	
GA1.6/9:	
GA1.6/10:date	General Accounting Office policy and procedures manual for guidance of Federal agencies, titles 1-9.
GA1.7:CT	Special regulations
GA1.7:nos	Comptroller general's special regulations. Proc.
GA1.8:nos	General office orders
GA1.9:CT	Papers in re
GA1.10:nos	General Accounting Office salary tables. Later CS1.73:
GA1.11:nos	Accounting systems memorandum. Proc.
GA1.11/2:nos	Accounting principles memorandum. Proc.
GA1.12:nos	Progress under joint program to improve accounting in Federal Government (annual) Later title, Joint financial management improvement program, annual report
GA1.12/2:date	Federal financial management directory (annual)
GA1.13:CT later letters-nos.	Reports to Congress on audits, reviews, and examinations
GA1.14:CT	Handbooks, manuals, guides
GA1.15:date	GAO review (quarterly)
GA1.16:CT	Bibliographies and lists of publications
GA1.16/2:v.nos.&nos.	List of GAO publications (semiannual) Earlier GA1.16:P96
GA1.16/3:v.nos.&nos.	Monthly list of GAO reports
GA1.17:date	Consolidated list of persons or firms currently debarred for violations of various public contracts acts incorporating labor standards provisions

GA1.18:CT   Addresses

GA1.19:nos   Audit standards, Supplement series (numbered)

GA1.20:date   Alphabetical listing of Presidential campaign receipts, Federal election campaign act of 1971 (P.L. 92-225)

GB   Geographic Board

Created by Executive order, Sept. 4, 1890.

GB1.1:date	Annual reports
GB1.2:CT	General publications
GB1.3:nos	Bulletins
GB1.4:nos	Circulars [none issued]
GB1.5:nos	Decisions Later I33.5:
GB1.5/a:	___ separates
GB1.5/2:nos	Decisions. Oct.1,1930. Later I33.5:
GB1.6:date	Index to reports and supplements

Transferred to Interior Department by Executive Order 6680, of April 17, 1934.

GP   GOVERNMENT PRINTING OFFICE

June 23, 1860.
GP1   Public Printer

GP1.1:date	Annual reports
GP1.1/a:CT	___ separates
GP1.2:CT	General publications
GP1.2/a:CT	___ separates
GP1.3:nos	Bulletins [none issued]
GP1.3/2:nos	Engineering bulletins
GP1.4:nos	Circulars [none issued]
GP1.5:date	Alphabetical list of employees
GP1.6:date	General orders
GP1.7:CT	Specifications, proposals, and advertisements
GP1.8:nos	Division of stores, circular advertisements of sale
GP1.9:nos	Technical bulletins
GP1.10:nos	Apprentice series
GP1.10/a:CT	___ separates
GP1.11:CT	Posters
GP1.12:Cong. &Sess	Dated publications. [For official use only] Later title: List of open jackets and current work
GP1.13:nos	Apprentice lectures
GP1.14:v.nos	AGPO
GP1.15:CT	Addresses
GP1.16:nos	Administrative orders
GP1.17:v.nos	Recreation and welfare news
GP1.18:nos	Safety pamphlets
GP1.19:v.nos	G.P.O. bulletin. Employee newspaper
GP1.20:nos	Personnel bulletins

GP1.21:nos	Purchase circulars
GP1.22:date	Dated periodical schedules.
GP1.23:CT	Regulations, rules, and instructions
GP1.23/2:nos	Security procedures. Official use.
GP1.23/3:nos	Planning Division, instruction and procedure. Administrative.
GP1.23/4:CT	Handbooks, manuals, guides
GP1.24:nos	Safety bulletins. Proc.
GP1.25:letter-nos.	GPO-PIA joint research bulletins
GP1.26:CT	Apprentice training series
GP1.27:v.nos	General management series
GP1.27/2:v.nos	Office management series
GP1.27/3:v.nos.	Management Review [non-Govt.-American Management Association]
GP1.27/4:v.nos.	International management series [non-Govt. - American Management Ass'n]
GP1.27/5:v.nos	Financial management series [non-Govt. - American Management Ass'n.]
GP1.27/6:v.nos	Personnel [bi-monthly] [non-Govt. - American Management Association]
GP1.27/7:v.nos	Personnel series [non-Govt. - American Management Association]
GP1.27/8:v.nos	Insurance series [non-Govt. - American Management Association]
GP1.27/9:nos	Manufacturing series [non-Govt. - American Management Association]
GP1.27/10:nos	Marketing series [non-Govt. - American Management Association]
GP1.27/11:nos	Packaging series [non-Govt. - American Management Association]
GP1.27/12:nos	Production series [non-Govt. - American Management Association]
GP1.28:nos	Circular letters
GP1.29:nos	Current work, new publications
GP1.30:nos	Employee letters
GP1.31:nos	Tests and Technical Control Division: Information bulletins

GP1.32:CT	Bibliographies and lists of publications
GP1.33:date	United States Government Printing Office paper catalog
GP1.34:v.nos.&nos.	GPO newsletter

GP2 Library

Established by act approved July 19, 1897 (Stat. L. v. 30, p. 135).

GP2.1:date	Annual reports
GP2.2:CT	General publications
GP2.3:nos	Bulletins [none issued]
GP2.4:nos	Circulars [none issued]
GP2.5:date	Lists of books in library.

Abolished by act approved Mar. 4, 1909 (Stat. L, v. 35, pt. 1, p. 1024)

Assistant Public Printer (Superintendent of Documents)
Public Documents Division (Department)
GP3 Documents Office

Created in accordance with printing act of Jan. 12, 1895 (Stat. L, v. 28, p. 601)

GP3.1:date	Annual reports
GP3.1/2:date	___, original sheet [including] Record of publications distributed
GP3.2:CT	General publications
GP3.3:nos	Bulletins
GP3.4:nos	Circulars
GP3.5:nos	Bibliographies
GP3.6:nos	Document catalog
GP3.7:nos	Document index. Superseded by GP3.7/2:
GP3.7/2:C&S	Numerical list and schedule of volumes. Supersedes GP3.7:
GP3.8:date	Monthly catalog
GP3.8/a:date	___ separates
GP3.8/2:date	Monthly catalog index. quarterly.

GP3.8/3:date	United States Government publications monthly catalog decennial cumulative index.
GP3.9:nos	Price lists
GP3.10:nos	Bibliography of United States public documents. Department lists.
GP3.11:nos	Schedule of volumes (for document index)
GP3.12:nos	Free lists
GP3.13:nos	Leaflets
GP3.14:CT	Advance sheets of 3d edition of Checklist United States public documents
GP3.15:nos	Numerical tables and schedule of volumes (for Document index)
GP3.16:nos	Depository invoices. Monthly.
GP3.16/2:nos	Geological invoices, Depository libraries
GP3.17:date	Weekly list of selected U.S. government publications. Later title, Selected United States government publications
GP3.17/2:CT	Selected United States Government publications. Later GP3.22:
GP3.17/3:nos	Periodic supplement, Selected United States Government publications. Irregular.
GP3.17/4:date	Selected U.S. Government publications, supplements
GP3.18:date	Information governing distribution of government publications and price lists. Changed from GP3.2:
GP3.19:date	Price lists of Government publications
GP3.20:nos	Division memorandums. Proc.
GP3.20/2:nos	Division procedures
GP3.21:CT	[Advertising circulars] Later [Publications announcements]
GP3.22:CT	List of publications (miscellaneous) Earlier GP3.17/2:
GP3.22/2:nos	SB [Subject bibliography]
GP3.23:nos.&date	Checklist C (series)

GP3.24:date   List of classes in 1950 revision of classified list of United States Government publications by departments and bureaus. Irregular. Later title, List of classes of United States Government publications available for selection by depository libraries

GP3.25:v.nos.&nos. Newsletter to sales agents. Administrative.

GP3.26:CT   Regulations, rules, and instructions

GP3.27:v.nos.&nos. Public Documents highlights

GS General Supply Committee

Created by Executive Order 1071, May 13, 1909.

GS1.1:date   Annual reports

GS1.2:CT   General publications [none issued]

GS1.3:nos   Bulletins [none issued]

GS1.4:nos   Circulars [none issued]

GS1.5/1:CT   General schedule of supplies, fiscal year 1910.

GS1.5/2:form letters or class nos. General schedule of supplies, fiscal year 1911.

GS1.6:date   List of awards showing contractors and prices for material and supplies contained in general schedule, fiscal year..

Act of June 7, 1910 (36 Stat. 531) established a general supply committee in the Treasury Dept.

GS General Services Administration

Under provisions of Public law 152, 81st Congress, 1st session, effective July 1, 1949, the General Services Administration was established as an agency in the executive branch of the Government. The functions of the Bureau of Federal Supply, the Office of Contract Settlement, the Federal Works Agency and of all agencies thereof, and the National Archives Establishment were transferred to the newly created agency.

GS1.1:date	Annual reports
GS1.2:date	Annual report on the management improvement program
GS1.2:CT	General publications
GS1.4/2:letters-nos	General Services Administration circular
GS1.4/3:nos	Federal management circular (numbered)
GS1.5:CT	Laws
GS1.6:CT	Regulations, rules, and instructions
GS1.6/2:CT	[Special regulations]
GS1.6/3:nos	General regulations
GS1.6/4:trans.le.nos.	Regulations of General Services Administration
GS1.6/5:nos	Federal procurement regulations FRP circulars
GS1.6/5-2:nos	Federal procurement regulations, FRP notices
GS1.6/5-3:nos	GSA bulletin FPR, Federal procurement
GS1.6/6:CT	Handbooks, manuals, guides
GS1.6/6-2:nos	Counseling guides (numbered)
GS1.6/7:nos	Defense materials regulations
GS1.6/8:letters-nos	Federal property management regulations, temporary regulations
GS1.6/8-2:letters-nos	GSA bulletin, FPMR (series)
GS1.7:nos	Public construction (monthly) Proc. Earlier FW1.16:
GS1.8:nos	Administrative orders. Proc.
GS1.9:nos	Specifications. Proc.

GS1.10:nos	Federal specifications announcements
GS1.11:date	Telephone directory, General Services Administration and Defense materials procurement agency (quarterly) Later GS12.12:
GS1.12:nos	Releases
GS1.13:nos	Accident and fire prevention bulletin (monthly)
GS1.14:date	Federal Fire Council, Annual reports
GS1.14/2:date	___ Fire loss to Government property (annual) Proc.
GS1.14/3:date	___ Minutes of meetings. Proc.
GS1.14/4:date	___ Federal Fire Council news letter. Admin.
GS1.14/5:CT	___ Publications
GS1.14/6:date	___ Library material received (monthly)
GS1.14/7:nos	___ Recommended practices RP (series)
GS1.14/8:date	___ Fire safety activities [list] Administrative.
GS1.14/9:nos	___ Construction problems relating to fire protection. Official use
GS1.14/10:CT	___ Addresses
GS1.14/11:nos	___ Significant fire writeup
GS1.14/12:nos	___ Research report digest. Admin.
GS1.14/13:nos	___ Pamphlets
GS1.15:date	Inventory report on real property owned by United States throughout the world.
GS1.15/2:date	Inventory report on real property leased to United States
GS1.15/3:date	Inventory report on legislative jurisdiction
GS1.16:date	Disabling injuries, report for year
GS1.17:CT	Bibliographies and lists of publications
GS1.18:CT	Addresses
GS1.19:nos	Consumer information series THIS CLASS WAS CANCELLED
GS1.20:date	GSA news (bimonthly) Admin.

GS1.21:P-nos	GSA stockpile information
GS1.22:date	Stockpile report to the Congress (semiannual) Earlier PrEx4.9:
GS1.23:date	Management report
GS1.24:date	Annual report of the Public Buildings Service value engineering program
GS1.25:CT	Environmental impact statements

GS2 Federal Supply Bureau

Under provisions of Public law 152, 81st Congress, 1st session, effective July 1, 1949 the functions of the Federal Supply Bureau were transferred from the Treasury Department to the General Services Administration.

GS2.1:date	Annual reports. Earlier T58.1:
GS2.2:CT	General publications. Earlier T58.2:
GS2.4:nos	Federal supply circular. Proc. Material later issued as Personal property management regulations GS1.6/2:P945/nos
GS2.4/2:nos	Circular DC-nos. Washington Store. Proc.
GS2.4/3:nos	Excess personal property available for transfer, Circulars [Proc.] Earlier GS2.2:P43/list nos.
GS2.4/3-2:nos	Department of Defense list of excess personal property available for transfer to Federal civil agencies. Proc. Supersedes GS2.4/3:
GS2.4/4:nos	Circular letter A (series) Earlier T58.11/2:
GS2.4/5:nos	Circular letter E (series) Earlier T58.11/3:
GS2.6:CT	Regulations, rules and instructions
GS2.6/2:nos	Federal handbook HB (series)
GS2.6/3:CT	Handbooks, manuals, guides (unnumbered) Earlier in GS2.6:
GS2.6/4:CT	Scientific inventory management series
GS2.7:class nos.&date.	Federal supply schedule. Printed and Proc. Earlier T58.8: Later GS2.7/4:
GS2.7/2:nos	___ amendments. Earlier T58.8/4: Later GS2.7:amdts.
GS2.7/3:date	___ check list (quarterly) Proc.
GS2.7/4:group nos.&date.	Federal supply schedule (by groups). Earlier GS2.7:
GS2.8:1e-nos	Federal standard stock catalog. Federal specifications. Earlier T58.10/3:
GS2.8/2:date	Federal specifications, index. Earlier T58.10/3:
GS2.8/3:nos	Federal standards. Earlier T58.2:St2/2, no.1

GS2.8/4:1e-nos	Federal standard stock catalog: sec. 4, pt. 5, Emergency Federal specifications
GS2.8/5:1e-nos	Interim federal specifications. Proc.
GS2.8/6:les-nos	Proposed federal specifications. Preliminary.
GS2.8/7:nos	Federal test method standards
GS2.9:nos	Traffic service letters. Proc. Earlier T58.20:
GS2.10:date	Store stock catalog, General Services Administration, zone price lists, zone 1 (quarterly) Earlier T58.2:St6/3/date, zone.
GS2.10/2:date	Stores stock catalog (semiannual) Earlier GS2.2:St7/date Later GS2.10/6:
GS2.10/2-2:date	General stores stock catalog, hand tool section. Earlier GS2.2:H19, v. 1-2. Later GS2.10/6:pt. 3/date
GS2.10/3:date	Stores stock catalog, price lists. Region 3. Official use.
GS2.10/4:date	Standard forms catalog. Earlier in GS2.10/2: Later GS2.10/6:pt. 2/dt.
GS2.10/5:date	Federal stock number reference catalog
GS2.10/6:pt.nos/date	GSA stock catalog. Earlier GS2.10/2:, GS2.10/2-2: and GS2.10/4:
GS2.10/6-2:date	Special supplement to stock catalog
GS2.10/7:date	Federal Supply catalog: National supplier change index (quarterly) Replaces GS2.10/6:pt.1/date/supp.nos.
GS2.11:	Department of defense exchange sale of personal property available for transfer to Federal agencies. Proc. Admin.
GS2.12:nos	Term contracts, TC- (series)
GS2.13:date	The supplier. Official use.
GS2.14:date	Annual motor vehicle report for fiscal year Later GS8.9:
GS2.15:date	Inventory of automatic data processing equipment in United States Government, fiscal year. Earlier PrEx2.12: Later GS12.10:
GS2.16:nos	Consumer information series
GS2.17:date	Marketips (monthly)

GS2.18:date   Federal motor vehicle fleet reports

GS3 Public Roads Bureau

By provisions of Public law 152, 81st Congress, 1st session, effective July 1, 1949, the Public Roads Administration was transferred from the Federal Works Agency to the General Services Administration and its name changed to the Public Roads Bureau.

GS3.1:date   Annual reports. Earlier FW2.1: Later C37.1:

GS3.2:CT   General publications. Earlier FW2.2: Later C37.2:

GS3.7:date   Traffic volume trends (monthly) Earlier FW2.16: Later C37.9:

GS3.8:v.nos.&nos. Public roads, journal of highway research. Earlier FW2.7: Later C37.8:

Transferred to the Department of Commerce by Reorganization plan no. 7 of 1949, effective Aug. 20, 1949.

National Archives and Records Service

GS4 National Archives

Under provisions of Public law 152, 81st Congress, 1st session, effective July 1, 1949, the National Archives Establishment and its functions, personnel, etc., were transferred to the General Services Administration.

GS4.1:date	Annual reports. Earlier AE1.1:
GS4.2:CT	General publications. Earlier AE1.2:
GS4.3:nos	Bulletins of National Archives. Earlier AE1.3:
GS4.4/2:nos	National Archives and Records Service circular
GS4.6:CT	Regulations, rules, and instructions. Earlier AE1.6:
GS4.6/2:CT	Handbooks, manuals, guides. Earlier in GS4.6:
GS4.7:nos	Special list. Proc. Earlier AE1.11:
GS4.8:nos	National archives accessions (quarterly) Proc. Earlier AE1.7:
GS4.9:date	Franklin D. Roosevelt Library, annual report of archivist of United States. Earlier AE1.8:
GS4.10:nos	Preliminary inventory. Proc. and ptd. Earlier AE1.10:
GS4.10/2:nos	National archives inventory series
GS4.11:nos	Facsimiles. Earlier AE1.21:
GS4.11/2:CT	Facsimilies (unnumbered)
GS4.12:nos	Staff information circulars. Proc. Earlier in AE1.9: Later title: Staff information papers
GS4.13:nos	Territorial papers of United States. Earlier S1.36:
GS4.14:CT	National Historical Publications Commission. [Publications]
GS4.14/2:date	Annotation, the newsletter of the National Historical Publications and Records Commission (quarterly)

GS4.15:nos	National Archives reference information papers. Earlier AE1.12:
GS4.16:dt.&nos.	Interagency Records Administration Conference, reports of meetings
GS4.17:date	Publications of National Archives and Records Service. Earlier GS4.2:P96
GS4.17/2:date	List of National Archives microfilm publications. Earlier GS4.2:M58/date
GS4.17/2a:CT	___ separates from Catalog of National Archives microfilm...
GS4.17/3:CT	Bibliographies and lists of publications
GS4.17/4:nos	Microfilm lists
GS4.18:nos	Guides to German records microfilmed at Alexandria, Virginia
GS4.19:date	List of record groups in National Archives and Federal records centers
GS4.20:nos	National archives microfilm publications, pamphlet accompanying microcopy
GS4.20/2:nos	Contents and price list for microfilm publications
GS4.21:v.nos/fascile nos.	Military operations of Civil War, guide-index to official records of Union and Confederate armies, 1861-65. Earlier Y3.C49/2:9
GS4.22:nos	General information leaflets
GS4.23:v.nos.&nos.	Prologue, journal of the National Archives
GS4.24:date	Directory of U.S. Government audiovisual personnel
GS4.25:date	News notes (irregular)

GS4.101 Federal Register Division

GS4.101:date — Annual reports. Earlier AE2.1:

GS4.102:CT — General publications. Earlier AE2.2:

GS4.107:v.nos.&nos. Federal register (daily) Earlier AE2.7:

GS4.107/a:CT — ___ separates

GS4.108:title nos — Code of Federal regulations. Earlier AE2.12:

GS4.108/2:date — ___ Title 3, supplements. (annual)

GS4.108/3:date — ___ List of CFR sections affected

GS4.108/4:date — ___ finding aids series

GS4.109:date — United States Government organization manual. Earlier AE2.11:

GS4.109/2:CT — Government organization handbooks

GS4.110/1:Cong.,sess.&nos. Slip laws: Public laws. Earlier S7.5/1:

GS4.110/2:Cong.,sess.&nos. Public resolutions. Earlier S7.5/2:

GS4.110/3:Cong.,sess.&nos. Private laws. Earlier S7.5/3:

GS4.111:v.nos./pt.nos. Statutes at large. Earlier S7.9:

GS4.111/2:v.nos — Statutes at large, tables of laws affected

GS4.112:v.nos.&nos. Abstracts of defense regulations (monthly)

GS4.113:date — Public papers of the Presidents of United States

GS4.113/2:CT — Proclamations and Executive orders

GS4.114:v.nos.&nos. Weekly compilation of Presidential documents

GS 5 Contract Settlement Office

Under provisions of Public law 152, 81st Congress, 1st session, effective July 1, 1949, the functions of the Contract Settlement Office were transferred from the Treasury Department to the General Services Administration.

GS5.1:date   Annual reports. Earlier T67.1:

GS5.2:CT   General publications. Earlier T67.2:

GS5.7:v.nos   Decisions of Appeal Board (bound volumes) Earlier T67.8/2:

GS5.7/a:v.nos.&print nos. ___ Appeal Board proceedings, prints. Earlier T67.8/2a:

Abolished by act approved July 14,1;952 (66 Stat. 627; 41 U.S.C. 113 note)

Service
GS6 Public Buildings Administration

Established December 11, 1949 by the Administrator of General Services to supersede the Public Buildings Administration.

GS6.1:date	Annual reports. Earlier FW6.1:
GS6.2:CT	General publications. Earlier FW6.2:
GS6.4:nos	Circulars. Proc. Later issued as Real property management regulations, GS1.6/2:R 229/nos
GS6.6:CT	Regulations, rules, and instructions. Earlier FW6.6:
GS6.6/2:CT	Handbooks, manuals, guides
GS6.7:date	Telephone directory, REpublic 7500, Executive 6300, District 0525 (quarterly) Earlier FW6.8:
GS6.8:nos	Historical studies (numbered)
GS6.9:CT	Environmental impact statements

GS7 Federal Facilities Corporation

Executive order 10720 of July 11, 1957 directed that the Corporation be under the supervision of a Director to be appointed by and subject to direction of Administrator of General Services.

GS7.1:date   Annual reports. Earlier T69.1:

GS7.2:CT   General publications. Earlier T69.2:

Dissolved by act of Aug. 30, 1961 (75 Stat. 418: 50 U.S.C. 1929 note), and records documents, property, assets, and liabilities transferred to Administrator of General Services.

GS8 Communications Service / Transportation and Public Utilities Service

Established July 1, 1955, by the Administrator of General Services under authority delegated by the Federal Property and Administrative Services act of 1949, as amended.

GS8.1:date   Annual reports

GS8.2:CT   General publications

GS8.6:CT   Regulations, rules, and instructions

GS8.6/2:CT   Handbooks, manuals, guides.

GS8.8:CT   Public utility schedules

GS8.9:date   Annual motor vehicle report. Earlier GS2.14:

Abolished by administrative order, effective July 15, 1972.

GS9 Utilization and Disposal Service

Established on July 1, 1961 by the Administrator of General Services.

GS9.1:date   Annual report

GS9.2:CT   General publications

GS9.3/2:nos   Excess property bulletins

GS9.9:nos   Excess property catalog

On July 29, 1966 functions transferred to Property Management and Disposal Service.

GS10 Property Management and Disposal Service

The Property Management and Disposal Service was established on July 29, 1966 by the Administrator of General Services. Transferred to the Service were functions formerly assigned to the Defense Materials Service and the Utilization and Disposal Service.

GS10.1:date   Annual report

GS10.2:CT   General publications

GS10.7/2:nos   Stockpile information

Abolished on July 1, 1973 and functions transferred to the Federal Supply Service, Public Buildings Service and the Office of Stockpile Disposal.

GS11 Consumer Product Information Coordinating Center

The Consumer Product Information Coordinating Center was established within the General Services Administration by Executive order 11566, approved Oct. 26, 1970.

GS11.1:date   Annual report

GS11.2:CT   General publications

GS11.9:date   Consumer product information, index of selected federal publications of consumer interest.

GS11.9/2:nos   New for consumers, highlights of new federal consumer publications

GS12 Automated Data and Telecommunications Service

The Automated Data and Telecommunications Service was established within the General Services Administration, August 1972.

GS12.1:date	Annual report
GS12.2:CT	General publications
GS12.9:date	Summary of Federal ADP activities for fiscal year
GS12.10:date	Inventory of automatic data processing equipment in United States Government, fiscal year. Earlier GS2.15:
GS12.11:CT	New way of saving (series)
GS12.12:date	Telephone directory, central office and region 3. Earlier GS1.11:

INDEX

Accident investigation division	IC1 acci
Accident prevention conference	C1.17
Accidents and deposits commissioner	T60
Accounts and disbursements division	A2
Accounts bureau (Post office)	P22
Accounts bureau (Treasury)	T63.101
Accounts committee. House	Y4.Ac2
Accounts division	IC1 acco
Acquisitions department (office)	LC27
ACTION	AA
Adams, John, Pres. U.S. 1797-1890	Pr2
Adams, John Q., Pres. U.S. 1825-1829	Pr6
Adjutant general's department (office)	W3, M108, D102
Administrative conference of United States	Y3.Ad6
Administrative management office	A91
Administrative office of United States courts	Ju10
Administrative services	D303
Administrator of veterans affairs office	VA1
Admiral of navy	N3
Advisory commission on information	Y3.Ad9/7
Advisory commission on intergovernmental relations	Y3.Ad9/8
Advisory commission on international educational and cultural affairs	Y3.Ad9/9
Advisory commission on universal training	Y3.Ad9/5
Advisory commission to council of national defense	Y3.C831:101
Advisory committee on education	Y3.Ad9/2
Advisory committee on fiscal relations study	Y3.Ad9
Advisory committee on intergovernmental policy	Y3.P43/2
Advisory committee on the arts	Y3.Ad9/10
Advisory committee on voluntary foreign aid	Y3.Ad9/4
Advisory committee on weather control	Y3.Ad9/6
Advisory council on historic preservation	Y3.H62
Advisory council on woman's educational programs	Y3.Ed8/6
Aeronautical and space sciences committee. Senate	Y4.Ae8
Aeronautical chart and information center	D301.59:
Aeronautical research laboratory	D301.69
Aeronautical systems division	D301.26
Aeronautics and space exploration, Select committee on. House	Y4.A58
Aeronautics board	Y3.Ae8
Aeronautics bureau	N28, M208, D202
Aeronautics division	LC15
Aerospace information division	LC38
Aerospace medical research laboratories	D301.45/32
AF Avionics laboratory	D301.45/45
AF Flight dynamics laboratory	D301.45/46
AF Materials laboratory	D301.45/47
Aging administration	FS15, FS17.300, HE17.300, HE1.200
Aging, Select committee. House	Y4.Ag4/2
Aging, Special committee on. Senate	Y4.Ag4
Agricultural adjustment administration (agency)	A55, A76.401, A79.401, A80.2101, A80.601, A83, A82.100
Agricultural and industrial chemistry bureau	A77.100
Agricultural chemistry and engineering bureau	A70, A77.100
Agricultural conservation and adjustment administration	A76

Agricultural conservation program services	A90
Agricultural credits in Europe, Commission to investigate and study	Y3.Ag8/1
Agricultural defense relations office	A74
Agricultural economics bureau	A36
Agricultural engineering bureau	A53
Agricultural inquiry joint commission	Y3.Ag8/2
Agricultural instruction office	A45
Agricultural marketing administration	A75
Agricultural marketing service	A66
Agricultural marketing service	A88
Agricultural research administration (service)	A77
Agricultural soils division	A26
Agricultural stabilization and conservation service	A82
Agriculture and forestry committee. Senate	Y4.Ag8/2
Agriculture committee. House	Y4.Ag8/1
Agriculture department	A
Agriculture department graduate school	A1.42
Agrostology division	A3
Air adjutant general's office	M302, D303
Air and water programs office	EP4
Air commerce bureau	C23
Air coordinating committee	Y3.Ai7/3
Air corps	W87
Air, electronics and ordnance systems command	D217
Air Force academy, Colorado Springs	D305
Air Force aero propulsion laboratory	D301.45/51
Air Force cambridge research center	D301.45/4
Air Force command and control development division	D301.45/24
Air Force department	M301, D301
Air Force flight test center	D301.45/31
Air Force medical service	D304
Air Force missile development center	D301.45/17
Air Force missile test center	D301.45/23
Air Force office of scientific research	D301.45/18, 19
Air Force special weapons center	D301.45/20
Air Force systems command	D301.45/38, D301.45/29
Air Force weapons laboratory	D301.45/35
Air information division	LC38
Air mail and ocean mail contracts, Special committee on investigation of, Senate	Y4.Ai7/2
Air-mail carriers division	IC1 air
Air-mail service	P20
Air materiel command	D301.67
Air pollution control office (programs)	EP4
Air proving ground center	D301.45/50
Air research and development center	D301.45/21
Air research and development command	D301.45
Air service	W87, W108.101
Air service (A.E.F.)	W95.21
Air services, Select committee of inquiry into operation of	Y4.Ai7
Air traffic management bureau (service)	FAA3, TD4.300
Air training command	D301.38
Air training command, Human resources research center	D301.36
Air university	D301.26

Aircraft board	Y3.Ai7
Airports joint commission	Y3.Ai7/2
Airports service	FAA8, TD4.100
Airways modernization board	Y3.Ai7/4
Alabama claims, Court of commissioners of	Y3.Aℓ1
Alaska	I1.5, I35.10
Alaska agricultural experiment station	A10.10, A77.440
Alaska commissioner for Department of agriculture	A50
Alaska, Department of	W71
Alaska division	I16.11
Alaska fisheries service	C6.8
Alaska forest experiment station	A13.73
Alaska game commission	A5.10
Alaska international rail and highway commission	Y3.Aℓ1s
Alaska power administration	I68
Alaska railroad	I1.59
Alaska road commission	W74, I35.10/21
Alaskan air command, Arctic aeromedical laboratory	D301.66
Alaskan fisheries division	C2
Alcatraz Island, Commission on disposition of	Y3.Aℓ16
Alcohol, drug abuse, and mental administration	HE20.8000
Alcohol in manufactures and arts, Joint select committee on	Y3.Aℓ1/1
Alcohol, tobacco and firearms bureau	T70
Alexander Hamilton bicentennial commission	Y3.Hl8
Alien property bureau	J19
Alien property custodian	Y3.Aℓ4, J19, Pr32.5701
Alien property office	J22
Alley dwelling authority	DC57
American battle monuments commission	Y3.Am3
American commission for protection and salvage of artistic and historical monuments in war areas	Y3.Am3/4
American ethnology bureau	SI2
American expeditionary forces	W95
American historical association	SI4
American marine standards committee	C13.19
American merchant marine, Special committee to investigate	Y3.Am3/4
American national red cross	W102, Y3.Am3/5
American relief administration	Y3.Am3/3
American republics bureau	AR
American retail federation, Committee on investigation. House	Y3.Am3/3
American revolution bicentennial commission	Y3.Am3/6
American Samoan commission	Y3.Am3/2
American shipbuilding commission	Y3.Sh6/2
American ship-building committee. House	Y4.Am3/1
American small business, Special committee to study problems of. Senate	Y4.Am3/5
American sugar refining company, Special committee on investigation	Y4.Am3/2
Americanization division	I16.30
Anglo-American Caribbean commission	S5.47
Animal and plant health(inspection)service	A101
Animal industry bureau	A4, A77.201
Anthracite coal commission	Y3.An8/2
Antitrust division	J20
Appalachian forest experiment station	A13.63

Appalachian regional commission	Y3.Ap4/2
Applied mathematics panel	Pr32.413/8
Appointment clerk	A30
Appointment division	C17
Appointments division	T2
Appraisers	T20
Apprentice training service	L23
Apprenticeship and training bureau	L23, L37.100
Appropriations committee. House	Y4.Ap6/1
Appropriations committee. Senate	Y4.Ap6/2
Arbitrations under treaty of Washington	S3.13
Architect of capitol	I1.7:1-2, Y3.Ar2
Architect, Supervising	T39
Arctic aeronautical laboratory	D301.45/30, D301.66
Arctic construction and frost effects laboratory	D103.31
Area development office	C45
Area redevelopment administration	C46
Arizona, Department of	W65
Arizona, Governor	I1.6
Arkansas-white-Red-Basins Interagency committee	Y3.F31/13-2
Arlington memorial amphitheater commission	Y3.Ar5
Arlington memorial bridge commission	Y3.Ar5/2
Armed forces information and education (service) division	D2
Armed forces institute of pathology	D1.16
Armed forces medical library	D8
Armed forces pest control board	D104.18/2
Armed services committee. House	Y4.Ar5/2
Armed services committee. Senate	Y4.Ar5/3
Armed services medical procurement agency	D1.30
Armed services petroleum purchasing agency	D11
Armed services technical information agency	D10
Armor plant, Special committee to investigate cost of	Y4.Ar5
Arms control and disarmament agency	S1.117, AC
Army-Air force wage board	D1.28
Army air forces	W108
Army air forces, Army air corps	W108.101
Army audit agency	D101.3/3, D101.62
Army aviation school	D101.47
Army ballistic missile agency	D105.15
Army chemical research and development laboratories	D116.16
Army corps areas and departments	W99
Army department	M101, D101
Army electronics research and development laboratories	D111
Army industrial college	W104
Army map service	W7.33, D103.20
Army materials research agency	D105.26
Army medical department	D104
Army medical nutrition laboratory	D104.17, 18
Army medical research laboratory	D104.14
Army medical school	W44.6
Army medical service	D104
Army missile command	D105.22
Army-Navy civil committee on aircraft design criteria	Y3.Ar5/3
Army Navy explosives safety board	M3

Army ordnance missile command	D105.22
Army personnel research office	D101.60
Army polar research and development center, Ft.Belvoir	D103.37
Army research office	D101.52
Army school of nursing, Walter Reed General Hospital	W44.23
Army service forces	W87.100, W109
Army service schools	W28
Army signal research and development laboratory	D111.9/3
Army snow, ice and permafrost research establishment	D103.26
Army transportation engineering agency	D117.11
Army war college	W55
Arnold engineering development center	D301.45/33
Arthur, Chester Alan, Pres. U.S., 1881-1885	Pr21
Asiatic division	LC17
Assistance payments administration	FS17.400, HE17.400
Assistant public printer (Superintendent of documents)	GP3
Assistant secretary of war	W1.24
Astrophysical observatory	SI1.12
Atlantic division	W64
Atlantic-Pacific Interoceanic canal study commission	Y3.At7
Atomic energy commission	Y3.At7
Atomic energy joint committee	Y4.At7/2
Atomic energy, Special committee on. Senate	Y4.At7
Attorney General	J1
Attorney-general, Assistant for court of claims	J2
Attorney-general, Assistant for customs matters	J12
Attorney-general, Assistant for Indian depredation claims	J3
Attorney-general, Assistant for Post office department	P6
Attorney-general, Assistant for Spanish treaty claims commission	J10
Attorney general, Select committee on investigation of	Y4.At8
Auditor for Interior department	T5
Auditor for Navy department	T6
Auditor for Post office department	T9
Auditor for State and other departments	T7
Auditor for Treasury department	T3
Auditor for War department	T4
Automated data & telecommunications service	GS12
Aviation advisory commission	Y3.Av5
Aviation medicine bureau	FAA7
Aviation medicine office	FAA7, TD4.200

B

Ballistic research laboratories	D105.10
Ballistic systems division	D301.45/36
Baltic States, Incorporation into U.S.S.R., Select committee to investigate. House	Y4.B21
Banking and currency committee. House	Y4.B22/1
Banking and currency committee. Senate	Y4.B22/3
Banking and receivership proceedings in U.S. courts, Special committee to investigate, Senate	Y4.B22/4
Banking, currency and housing committee	Y4.B22/1
Banking, housing and urban affairs committee. Senate	Y4.B22/3
Bankruptcy laws commission	Y3.B22
Banks, National, failed, Select committee on	Y4.B22/2

Battle of Lake Erie sesquicentennial celebration commission	Y4.B32/2
Battle of New Orleans sesquicentennial celebration commission	Y3.B32
Beach erosion board	M110.301, D103.15, I6
Bergdoll, Grover Cleveland, general prisoner, Select committee to investigate escape of. House	Y4.B45/2
Berger, Victor L., Special committee appointed under H.Res.6 concerning	Y4.B45
Bering sea claims commission	S3.7/2
Berlin silver commission	Y3.B54
Bibliography division	LC2
Biological survey bureau	A5, I47
Bituminous coal commission	Y3.B54
Bituminous coal consumers' counsel	Y3.B54/2
Bituminous coal division	I46
Blind and physically handicapped, Division for	LC19
Blind-made products, Commission on purchase of	Y3.B61
Block signal and train control board	IC1 blo
Board for international broadcasting	Y3.B78
Board of officers considering relief of Lieut. Greely and party at Lady Franklin Bay	Y3.G81
Bonneville dam	D103.27
Bonneville power administration	I44
Bookkeeping and warrants division	T9
Books for the adult blind	LC19
Boston national historic sites commission	Y3.B65
Botany division	A6
Broadcast division	CC2
Buchanan, James, Pres. U.S. 1857-1861	Pr15
Budget and finance office	A58
Budget bureau	T51, Pr32.100, Pr33.100, Pr34.100 PrEx2
Budget committee. House	Y4.B85/3
Budget committee. Senate	Y4.B85/2
Budget, national committee for consideration of. Senate	Y4.B86/2
Budget select committee. House	Y4.B86/1
Building operations and supplies division	P23
Bureau of controller	P25
Business advisory(and planning)council	C28
Business and defense services administration	C41
Business economics office	C43

C

Cabinet committee on opportunity for the Spanish speaking	Y3.Sp2/7
California debris commission	W50
California, Department of	W13
California forest and range experiment station	A13.62
Campaign expenditures, Special committee to investigate. House	Y4.C15
Canada, relations with, Committee on	Y4.C16
Canadian-American fisheries commission	S3.26
Canal zone	W79
Canal zone government	CZ
Capital building, Joint commission on plans for extension and completion	Y3.C17
Capital buildings and grounds, Superintendent	I1.7
Capital, Centennial celebration of laying of corner	Y4.C17
Capital issues committee	Y3.C17/2

Capital, United States, Commission for extension of	Y4.C17/2
Card division	LC28
Carlisle Indian School	I20.16
Catalog division	LC9
Censorship office	Y3.C33/6
Censure charges, Select committee to study. Senate	Y3.C33/4
Census, 1st-12th	I2-I13
Census bureau	C3, C56.200, C3
Census committee, House	Y4.C33/1
Census committee, Senate	Y4.C33/2
Census of partial employment, unemployment and occupations	Y3.C33/5
Census office	I14
Center for disease control	HE20.2300, HE20.7000
Center for population research	HE20.3362
Center for studies of crime and delinquency	in HE20.3800, HE20.8114/2
Central American peace conference	S5.12
Central and South American commission	Y3.C33
Central department	W78
Central housing commission	Y3.C33/3
Central intelligence agency	Y3.N21/17:101 Pr33.650, Pr34.611 PrEx3.10
Central States forest experiment station	A13.68
Central statistical board	Y3.C33/2
Central statistical commission	Y3.C33/4
Central translating office	S16
Centralization of heavy industry in United States	Y3.C33/3
Chemical and plastics division	D106.9/5
Chemical corps (Army)	D116
Chemical warfare laboratories	D116.13
Chemical warfare service	W91
Chemistry and soils bureau	A47
Chemistry bureau	A7
Chicago strike commission	Y3.C43
Chickamauga and Chattanooga national military park commission	W4
Chickamauga and Chattanooga national military park commission, National committee on	Y3.C43
Chief clerk	A31
Chief clerk and superintendent	T10
Chief coordinator for general supply	T51.7
Child development office (services bureau)	HE21, HE1.400
Children's bureau	C19, L5, FS3.200, FS14.100, FS17.100 HE21.100, HE1.450, HE1.480
China, United States court for	S14
Circuit courts	Ju1
Citizens food committee	Pr33.11
Citizenship training division	L6.7
Civil aeronautics administration	C31.100
Civil aeronautics authority	CA, C31
Civil aeronautics board	C31.201
Civil affairs division, Army department	M105
Civil and defense mobilization office	Pr34.700, PrEx4
Civil defense office	Pr34.700, PrEx4, D13, D119
Civil defense planning office	M4

Civil rights commission	CR
Civil service commission	CS
Civil service committee. House	Y4.C49/1
Civil service committee. Senate	Y4.C49/2
Civil war centennial commission	Y3.C49/2
Civilian conservation corps	Y3.C49, I42, FS4
Civilian defense office	Pr32.4400
Civilian manpower office	D204
Civilian production administration	Pr32.4800
Claims commissioners	Y3.C52
Claims committee. House	Y4.C52/1
Claims committee. Senate	Y4.C52/2
Clearinghouse for federal scientific and technical information	C51
Cleveland, Grover, Pres. U.S., 1893-1897	Pr22, Pr24
Coal commission, 1922	Y3.C63
Coal research office	I63
Coast and geodetic survey	T11, C4
Coast and insular committee. Senate	Y4.C63
Coast artillery office	W53
Coast artillery school	W29
Coast guard	T47, N24, T47, TD5
Coastal engineering research center	D103.42
Coastal plains regional commission	Y3.C63/2
Coating and chemical laboratory	D105.16
Coinage, weights and measures committee. House	Y4.C66
Cold regions research and engineering laboratory	D103.33
Colorado, Department of the	W14
Colorado river interstate governmental commission	Y3.C71
Columbia basin inter-agency committee	Y3.C72
Columbia, Department of the	W15
Columbia institution for instruction of deaf and dumb	I1.8:
Combined production and resources board, United States, Great Britain and Canada	Y3.C73/3
Combined raw materials board, United States and Great Britain	Y3.C73/2
Command and General Staff (School) College, Fort Leavenworth	W28, M119, D110
Commerce committee. House	Y4.C73/1
Commerce committee. Senate	Y3.C73/2
Commerce court	Ju8
Commerce department	C
Commerce, Select committee on. House	Y4.C73/6
Commercial economy board	Y3.C83/11
Commercial services office	C48.300
Commission on organization of executive branch of the government	Y3.Or3, Y3.Or3/2
Commission on renovation of the executive mansion	Y3.R29/2
Commission to revise statutes relating to patents, trade, other marks and trade and commercial names	Y3.P27
Commissioner of customs	T16
Committee for preservation of White House	Y3.W58/10
Committee on channel stabilization	D103.64
Committee on tidal hydraulics	D103.28
Commodity credit corporation	Y3.C73, A71, A80.400 A82.300
Commodity exchange administration	A59
Commodity exchange authority	A85
Commodity futures trading commission	Y3.C73/5

Commodity stabilization service	A82
Commodity transaction, Select committee to investigate. House	Y4.C73/4
Communicable disease center	FS2.60
Communication office	A21
Communist aggression, Select committee on. House	Y4.C73/5
Communist propaganda in United States, Special committee to investigate	Y4.C73/3
Community development office	HH9
Community environmental management bureau	HE20.1800, HE20.2850
Community facilities administration	HH5
Community facilities bureau	FW7
Community health service	HE20.2550
Community health services bureau	HE20.5100
Community relations service	C50, J23
Community services administration	CSA
Community war services office	FS9
Competitive assessment and business policy bureau	C57.300
Comprehensive health planning service	HE20.2580
Comptroller, 1st	T13
Comptroller, 2d	T14
Comptroller general	GA
Comptroller of currency	T12
Comptroller of the Treasury	T15
Conciliation service	L19
Conduct of the war, Joint committee on	Y4.C75
Conference committees, House and Senate	Y4.C76/1
Conference on Central American affairs	S5.22
Conference on limitation of armament	S3.29
Conference on oil pollution of navigable waters	S5.24
Congress. Bills and resolutions	Y2
Congress. Committees	Y4
Congress. Contested elections	Y5
Congress, Joint committee on organization of	Y4.C76/3
Congress, Miscellaneous publications	Y1
Congress, Proceedings of	X
Congress, Special committee on organization of. Senate	Y4.C76/6
Congressional budget office	Y10
Congressional operations joint committee	Y4.C76/7
Congressional research service	LC14
Construction and repair bureau	N4
Construction bureau	SB11
Construction division	W92
Construction engineering research laboratory	D103.53
Construction industry collective bargaining commission	Y3.C76
Construction industry stabilization commission	ES2.6/4
Construction of building for Museum of History and Technology for Smithsonian, Joint Committee	Y4.C76/5
Consumer affairs office	PrEx16
Consumer affairs office	HE1.500
Consumer and marketing service	A88
Consumer product information coordinating center	GS11
Consumer product safety commission	Y3.C76/3
Consumer protection and environmental health service	HE20.1000
Consumer services administration	HE17.700
Consumers' counsel division	A75.100

Consumers' counsel division	I48.51
Consumers' counsel of National bituminous coal commission	I39
Consumers' division	L17
Contract labor, convicts and paupers, Select committee on importation of. House	Y4.C76/2
Contract settlement office	Y3.W19/7:100, T67, GS5
Contributions select committee. Senate	Y4.C76/4
Coolidge, Calvin, Pres. U.S., 1923-1929	Pr30
Cooperative cataloging and classification service	LC22
Cooperative enterprise in Europe committee	Y3.C78/2
Cooperative extension work office	A43.5
Cooperative State experiment station service	A94
Cooperative state research service	A94
Coordinator for health, welfare, and related defense activities	FS8
Coordinator for industrial cooperation	Y3.C78
Coordinator of information	Y3.C78/3
Coordinator of inter-American affairs office	Pr32.4600
Copyright office	LC3
Corporations bureau	C5
Corrupt combinations of members of Congress, Alleged, Select committee to investigate. House	Y4.C81/1
Corruptions in government, Alleged, Select committee to investigate	Y4.C81/2
Cost accounting standards bureau	Y3.C82
Cost of living council	PrEx17
Council of economic advisers	PrEx6
Council of national defense	Y3.C83
Council of national defense, 1940	Y3.C831
Council on environmental quality	PrEx14
Council on wage and price stability	PrEx22
Court of appeals	Ju2
Court of claims	Ju3
Court of customs and patent appeals	Ju7
Court of private land claims	Ju5
Credit mobilier bribery, Alleged, Select committee to investigate	Y4.C86
Crime, organized, in interstate commerce, Special committee to investigate. Senate	Y4.C86/2
Crime, Select committee on. House	Y4.C86/3
Criminal identification bureau	J15
Crop estimates bureau	A27
Crop insurance, select committee. Senate	Y4.C88
Crop production loan office	A54
Cuba and Porto Rico, Special commissioner	T1.16
Cuba, Division of	W25
Cuba, Posts department	P1.17
Cuba, Provisional governor	W1.16:
Cuba relations committee. Senate	Y4.C89
Cuba, Western, Department of	W60
Cuban census office	W47
Cultural relations division	S15
Customs bureau	T17
Customs court	T20, Ju9

D

Dairying bureau (Dairy industry bureau)	A44, A77.600
Dakota, Department of	W16

Dakota, Governor	I1.10
Daughters of American revolution	SI5
David W. Taylor model basin	D211.9
Dead letters division	P7
Decimal classification office	LC37
Defense civil preparedness agency	D14
Defense communications agency	D5.100
Defense contract audit agency	D1.46
Defense department	D
Defense documentation center	D10
Defense electric power administration	I56
Defense fisheries administration	I54
Defense health and welfare services office	Pr32.4500
Defense housing coordination division	Pr32.4300
Defense intelligence agency	D5.200
Defense manpower commission	Y3.D 36
Defense manpower office	L27
Defense mapping agency	D5.300
Defense materials procurement agency	DM
Defense minerals administration	I55
Defense minerals exploration administration	I55
Defense mobilization office	Pr33.1000, Pr34.200
Defense power administration	I56
Defense production administration	Pr33.1100, DP
Defense production joint committee	Y3.D36
Defense savings staff	T1.101
Defense solid fuels administration	I57
Defense supply agency	D7
Defense supply management agency	D7
Defense transport administration	IC1 def
Defense transportation office	Pr32.4900
Delaware river commission	Y3.D37/2
Department of Washington	W52
Departmental methods committee	Y3.D44
Dependency benefits office	W97.100
Descriptive cataloging division	LC9
Detroit arsenal	D105.18
Development loan fund	Y3.D49
Diabetes mellitus coordinating committee	HE30.3317
Diamond ordnance fuze laboratories	D105.14:
Dirigible disasters, Joint committee to investigate	Y4.D62
Disarmament administration	S1.117
Displaced persons commission	Y3.D63/2
Distribution office	A78
District court of United States for District of Columbia	DC21
District courts	Ju4
District of Columbia	DC
District of Columbia and United States, Joint committee on fiscal relations between	Y4.D63/5
District of Columbia and United States, Select committee to investigate fiscal relations between	Y4.D63/7
District of Columbia auditorium commission	DC59
District of Columbia, Commission to investigate title or United States to lands in	Y3.D63
District of Columbia, Committee on the, House	Y4.D63/1

District of Columbia, Committee on the, Senate	Y4.D63/2
District of Columbia excise board, Special Committee to investigate	Y4.D63/4
District of Columbia, Joint Select committee to investigate	Y4.D63/3
District of Columbia, Select committee to investigate public school system of	Y3.D63/6
Division of the blind and physically handicapped	LC19
Documents division	LC7
Documents office	GP3
Domestic and international business administration	C57
Domestic commerce bureau	C41, C57.500
Domestic commerce office	C36
Domestic council	PrEx15
Dominican customs receivership	W6.13, I35.14
Drug abuse and control bureau	FS13.130
Drug enforcement administration	J24

E

Earth sciences division	D106.20
East, Department of the	W17
East-West foreign trade board	Y3.T67
East west trade bureau	C57.400
Economic advisers council	PrEx6
Economic analysis bureau	C56.100, C59
Economic cooperation administration	Y3.Ec74/3
Economic development administration	C46
Economic joint committee	Y4.Ec7
Economic opportunity office	PrEx10
Economic report joint committee	Y4.Ec7
Economic research service	A93
Economic security committee	Y3.Ec74
Economic stabilization agency	ES
Economic stabilization office	Pr32.6000
Economic warfare board	Y3.Ec74/2
Economy and efficiency commission	Y3.Ec7
Education and labor committee. House	Y4.Ed8/1
Education and labor committee. Senate	Y4.Ed8/3
Education and special training committee	W26.17
Education committee. House	Y4.Ed8/2
Education division	HE19
Education office	I16, FS5, HE5, HE19.100
Educational extension division	I16.31
Efficiency bureau	EB
Eight hour commission	Y3.Ei4
Eisenhower, Dwight D., Pres.U.S., 1953-1960	Pr34
Election of President, Vice President, and Representatives committee. House	Y4.El2
Electric home and farm authority	Y3.El2/2, FL4
Electric railways	IC1 eler
Electrical commission	S5.17
Electronic research directorate	D301.45/12
Electronic systems command	D219
Electronic systems division	D301.45/28
Emergency boards (National railway labor panel)	NMB
Emergency conservation work	Y3.Em3
Emergency court of appeals	Ju12

Emergency loan guarantee board	Y3.Em3/2
Emergency management office	Pr32.401
Emergency planning office	PrEx4
Emergency preparedness office	PrEx4
Employees compensation appeals board	L22
Employees' compensation commission (bureau)	EC, FS13.300, L26
Employers' liability and workman's compensation commission	Y3.Em7
Employment and training administration	L37
Employment security bureau	FS3.101
Employment service	L7
Employment standards administration	L36
Energy research and development administration	ER
Engineer corps	D103
Engineer department (Corps (Army))	W7, M110, D103
Engineer research and development laboratories	D103.25
Engineer school, Fort Belvoir, Virginia	W7.16, M110.401, D103.101
Engineering bureau	N19
Engraving and printing bureau	T18
Entomological commission	I26, A8
Entomology and plant quarantine bureau	A56, A77.300
Entomology bureau	A9
Environmental control administration	HE20.1100
Environmental data service	C55.200
Environmental protection agency	EP
Environmental protection division	D106.9/3-4
Environmental research laboratories	C55.600
Environmental science services administration	C52
Epidemic diseases committee. Senate	Y4.Ep4/2
Epidemic diseases, Select committee on origin, introduction and prevention of. House	Y4.Ep4/1
Equal employment opportunity commission	Y3.Eq2
Equipment bureau	N5
Ericsson memorial commission	Y3.Er4
Ether discovery, Select committee on. House	Y4.Et3/1
Ether discovery, Select committee on. Senate	Y4.Et3/2
Ethnology bureau	SI2
European affairs division	LC31
Examiners board	T19
Execution without trial in France, Special committee to investigate charges of	Y4.Ex3
Executive agencies of government, Select committee on investigation of	Y4.Ex3/3
Executive agencies, Special committee to investigate. House	Y4.Ex3/4
Executive council	Y3.Ex3/2
Executive departments, joint commission on laws organizing	Y3.Ex3/2
Executive office of the President	PrEx
Executive papers, Committee on disposition of. House	Y4.Ex3/2
Exhibits office	A40
Expenditures in Department of Agriculture committee. House	Y4.Ex7/1
Expenditures in Department of commerce and labor committee House	Y4.Ex7/2
Expenditures in Department of justice committee. House	Y4.Ex7/4
Expenditures in Interior department committee. House	Y4.Ex7/3
Expenditures in Navy department committee. House	Y4.Ex7/5
Expenditures in Post-office department committee. House	Y4.Ex7/6

Expenditures in Public buildings committee. House	Y4.Ex7/7
Expenditures in Senatorial primary and general elections. Senate	Y4.Ex7/12
Expenditures in State department committee, House	Y4.Ex7/8
Expenditures in the executive departments, Committee on. House	Y4.Ex7/13
Expenditures in the executive departments. Committee on. Senate	Y4.Ex7/14
Expenditures in Treasury department committee. House	Y4.Ex7/9
Expenditures in War department, Committee. House	Y4.Ex7/10
Expenditures in War department, Select committee. House	Y4.Ex7/11
Experiment stations office	A10, A77.401
Export-import bank of the United States	Y3.Ex7/3
Export-import bank of Washington	Y3.Ex7/3
Export control administrator	Y3.Ex7/2
Export (control) office	Y3.Ec74/2:100
Export control office	C49.200
Export control, Select committee on. House	Y4.Ex7/15
Export marketing service	A99
Exports bureau	WT3
Exports control committee	Y3.Ex7
Express companies	IC1 exp
Extension service	A43, A80.300, A43

F

Facilities bureau	FAA4
Facilities engineering and construction agency	HE1.100
Facts and figures office	Pr32.4700
Family services bureau	FS14.200
Famine emergency committee	A1.70
Farm credit administration	FCA, A72, FCA
Farm labor conditions in the West. Special committee to investigate. Senate	Y4.F22
Farm labor division	L7.12
Farm management and farm economics office	A37
Farm security administration	A61, A80.700, A61
Farm tenancy special committee	Y3.F22
Farmer cooperative service	A89
Farmers' home administration	A84
Farmers' seed loan office	A51
Federal aid in construction of post roads, Joint committee on	Y4.F31
Federal alcohol administration	Y3.F31/10, T59
Federal aviation administration	TD4
Federal aviation agency	FAA
Federal board for vocational education	VE
Federal board of surveys and maps	Y3.Su7
Federal bureau of investigation	J1.14
Federal civil defense administration	Pr33.800, FCD
Federal civil works administration	Y3.F31/7
Federal committee on apprentice training	Y3.F31/12
Federal committee on pest control	Y3.F31/18
Federal committee on research natural areas	Y3.F31/19
Federal communications commission	CC
Federal communications commission, Select committee to investigate. House	Y3.F31/4
Federal coordinator of transportation	Y3.F31/6
Federal council for science and technology	Y3.F31/16
Federal council on aging	Y3.F31/15
Federal credit union bureau	FS3.300, HE3.300

Federal crop insurance corporation	A62, A76.101, A79.301, A80.900, A82.200, A62
Federal deposit insurance corporation	Y3.F31/8
Federal development planning committee for Appalachia	Y3.Ap4
Federal election commission	Y3.El2/3
Federal electric railways commission	Y3.F31
Federal emergency administration of public works	Y3.F31/4
Federal emergency relief administration	Y3.F31/5
Federal employees compensation office	L36.300
Federal employment stabilization board	C26
Federal energy administration	FE
Federal energy office	PrEx21
Federal executive board	Y3.F31/20
Federal extension service	A43
Federal facilities corporation	T69, GS7
Federal farm board	FF
Federal farm loan bureau	T48
Federal fire council	GS1.14
Federal fuel distributor	Y3.F31/2
Federal health programs service	HE20.2700, HE20.5200
Federal highway administration	TD2
Federal home loan bank board (administration)	Y3.F31/3, FL3, NHA3, HH4, FHL
Federal horticultural board	A35
Federal housing administration	Y3.F31/11, FL2, NHA2, HH2
Federal insurance administration	HH1.10, HH10
Federal interagency committee on education	Y3.Ed8
Federal inter-agency committee on recreation	Y3.F31/14
Federal inter-agency river basin committee	I1.81, Y3.F31/13
Federal interdepartmental safety council	FIS
Federal judicial center	Ju13
Federal labor relations council	Y3.F31/21
Federal library committee	LC1.32
Federal loan agency	FL
Federal maritime board	C39.101
Federal maritime commission	FMC
Federal mediation and conciliation service	FM
Federal narcotics control board	T53
Federal national mortgage association	HH6
Federal oil conservation board	I1.67
Federal power commission	FP
Federal prison industries, inc.	FPI, J16.51
Federal prisoners, Joint committee to determine what employment may be furnished	Y4.F31/2
Federal public housing authority	NHA4
Federal radiation commission	RC
Federal radiation council	Y3.F31/17
Federal radio education committee	FS5.101
Federal railroad administration	TD3
Federal reconstruction and development planning commission for Alaska	Y3.Al1s/3
Federal register division (office)	AE2, GS4.100
Federal reserve system, Board of governors	FR
Federal safety council	L30
Federal security agency	FS

Federal services impasses panel	Y3.F31/21
Federal supply bureau (service)	T58, GS2
Federal surplus commodities corporation	A69
Federal surplus relief corporation	Y3.F31/9
Federal tariff board	T51.10
Federal trade commission	FT
Federal water pollution control administration	FS16, I67
Federal water quality administration	I67
Federal working group on pest management	Y3.P43
Federal works agency	FW
Fiber investigations office	A11
Field artillery office	W96
Field division, Council of national defense	Y3.C83:81
Field service branch	A82.101
Fillmore, Milard, Pres. U.S., 1850-53	Pr13
Finance and administration bureau	P4
Finance bureau	SB10
Finance, Committee on. Senate	Y4.F49
Finance department	W97, M116
Fine arts commission	FA
Fine arts division	LC25
First assistant postmaster general	P2
Fiscal director's office	W97
Fiscal service	T63
Fish and wildlife service	I49
Fish commission	FC
Fisheries bureau	C6, I45
Fisheries committee. Senate	Y4.F53
Five civilized tribes commissioner	I1.11
Five civilized tribes superintendent	I20.21
Fixed nitrogen research laboratory	A38
Flight standards bureau (service)	FAA5, TD4.400
Flood control committee. House	Y4.F65
Food administration	Y3.F73
Food and drug administration	FS17, FS13.100, HE20.1200,HE20.4000
Food and drug inspection board	A32
Food and feed conservation office	A86
Food and nutrition service	A98
Food distribution service	A78, A80.100
Food, drug and insecticide administration	A46
Food production administration	A79, A80.201
Food products, Select committee to investigate use of chemicals in	Y4.F73/2
Food shortages, Special committee to investigate. House	Y4.F73
Foreign affairs committee. House	Y4.F76/1
Foreign agricultural relations office	A67
Foreign agricultural service	A64
Foreign agricultural service	A67
Foreign aid program, Special committee to study. Senate	Y4.F76/6
Foreign aid, Select committee on. House	Y4.F76/5
Foreign and domestic commerce bureau	C18
Foreign broadcast information service	Pr34.651, PrEx7
Foreign claims settlement commission	Y3.F76/3
Foreign commerce bureau	S4

Foreign commerce bureau	C42
Foreign direct investment office	C54
Foreign economic administration	Pr32.5801
Foreign economic development service	A100
Foreign economic policy commission	Y3.F76/2
Foreign funds control	T65
Foreign mail service	P8
Foreign markets division	A12
Foreign operations office	FO
Foreign relations committee. Senate	Y4.F76/2
Foreign scholarships board	Y3.F76/4
Foreign service institute	S1.114
Foreign trade, Special adviser to the President on	Y3.F76
Foreign trade zones board	FTZ
Forest products laboratory, Madison, Wisconsin	A13.27
Forest reservations and protection of game committee. Senate	Y4.F76/3
Forest service	A13
Forestry, Joint committee on	Y4.F76/4
Fortifications and other defenses board	Y3.F77
Four corners regional commission	Y3.F82
Fourth assistant postmaster general	P5
Frankford arsenal	D105.17
Franklin Delano Roosevelt memorial commission	Y3.R67
Free delivery division	P13
Freedman's hospital	FST
Freedman's savings and trust company	I1.12, FS2.54
Freer gallery of art	S17
French and American claims commission	S3.6
French spoilation claims commission	S3.5
Fuel administration	Y3.F95
Fuel situation in the middle west, Special committee to investigate. Senate	Y4.F49
Fur seal arbitration	S3.7

G

Garden and grounds division	A14
Garfield, James Abram, Pres. U.S., 1881	Pr20
Gas corporations	IC1 gas
Gasoline and fuel oil shortages, Special committee to investigate. Senate	Y4.G21
General accounting office	GA
General counsel of Dept. of agriculture	A33
General land office	I21
General reference and bibliography division	LC2
General service schools	W28
General services administration	GS
General staff corps	W2, M113
General supply committee	GS, T45
Geographic board	GB
Geographical and geological survey of the Rocky Mountain Region (Powell)	I17
Geographical names board	I33
Geographical surveys west of 100th meridian (Wheeler)	W8
Geography and map division	LC5
Geological and geographical survey of the territories (Hayden)	I18
Geological survey	I19
Geophysics research directorate	D301.45/10, 16

George Rogers Clark sesquicentennial commission	Y3.G29
George Washington bicentennial commission	Y3.W27/2
Gettysburg national military park commission	W46
Goddard space flight center	NAS1.28
Gold and silver inquiry commission. Senate	Y4.G56
Government actuary	T50
Government financial operations bureau	T63.100
Government hospital for the insane	I1.14, FS11
Government hospital for the insane, Special committee on investigation of	Y4.G74
Government operations committee. House	Y4.G74/7
Government operations committee. Senate	Y4.G74/6
Government operations with respect to intelligence activities Select committee to study. Senate	Y4.In8/17
Government organization, Joint committee on	Y4.G74/4
Government organization, Select committee on. House	Y4.G74/3
Government organization, Select committee on. Senate	Y4.G74/5
Government patents board	Y3.G74
Government printing office	GP
Government procurement commission	Y4.G74/4
Government reports office	Pr32.201, Pr33.401
Government research, Select committee on. House	Y4.G74/8
Government security commission	Y3.G74/2
Grades and salaries committee	Y3.G75
Grain corporation	Y3.W56:11
Grain futures administration	A41
Grant, Ulysses Simpson, Pres. U.S., 1869-1877	Pr18
Grant memorial commission	Y3.G73
Grazing division	I38
Great Lakes basin commission	Y3.G79/3
Great Lakes pilotage administration	C1.47
Great plains committee	Y3.G79/2
Great plains drought area committee	Y3.G79
Guam agricultural experiment station	A10.22
Guam territories office	I35.15
Gulf, Department of the	W18
Gun foundry board	Y3.G95

H

Haiti and Santo Domingo committee. Senate	Y4.H12
Haitian customs receivership	W6.15
Hampton normal and agricultural institute	I20.17
Harding, Warren Gamaliel, Pres. U.S., 1921-1923	Pr29
Harpers Ferry invasion, Select committee. Senate	Y4.H23
Harriman geographic code system, Select joint committee on	Y4.H23/2
Harrison, Benjamin, Pres. U.S., 1889-1893	Pr23
Harrison, William Henry, Pres., U.S. 1841	Pr9
Harry Diamond laboratories	D105.14
Hatch, Davis, Select committee appointed to investigate memorial of	Y4.H28
Havana and Pinar del Rio, Department of the	W57
Hawaii	I1.41, I35.11
Hawaii agricultural experiment station	A10.9
Hawaii, Department	W81
Hawaii, Joint committee	Y4.H31
Hawaiian commission	Y3.H31

Hawaiian volcano observatory	I19.28, 29
Hayes, Rutherford Birchard, Pres. U.S., 1877-1881	Pr19
Head start and child development bureau	HE21.2u0
Health care facilities service	HE20.2500, HE20.6400
Health, education, and welfare department	FS, HE
Health education division	I16.29
Health facilities planning and construction service	HE20.2500
Health insurance benefits advisory council	HE20.17
Health maintenance organization service	HE20.2050
Health manpower bureau	HE20.6600
Health manpower education bureau	
Health professions education and manpower training bureau	HE20.3100
Health resources administration	HE20.6000
Health resources development bureau	HE20.6100
Health services administration	HE20.5000
Health services and mental health administration	HE20.2000
Health services research (and evaluation) bureau	HE20.6500
Heavy ordnance and projectile board	Y3.H352
Highways transport committee	Y3.C83:21
Hispanic foundation	LC24
Historical branch, War plans division	W26.15
Historical division (Army)	W110, M103, D114
Home economics bureau	A42, A77.700
Homes administration	Y3.H75
Hoover, Herbert, Pres. U.S., 1929-1933	Pr31
Hot Springs reservation	I1.17
Hours of service division	IC1 hou
House administration committee. House	Y4.H81/3
House committee on printing	Y4.P93/2
House of representatives	Y1.2
House of Representatives, Commission to supervise construction of building for offices for	Y4.H81
House resolution 1, Select committee pursuant to	Y4.H81/5
House restaurant, Select committee on. House	Y4.H81/6
House restaurant, Special committee to investigate management and control of	Y4.H81/2
House rooms distribution select committee. House	Y4.H81
Housing and home finance agency	HH
Housing and urban development department	HH
Housing assistance administration	HH3
Housing authority	I40, FW3
Housing corporation	L8
Housing expediter office	Y3.H81/2
Housing joint committee	Y4.H81/4
Howard university	I1.18
Hudson-Champlain celebration commission	Y3.H86
Human engineering laboratories, Aberdeen proving ground	D105.24
Human factors operations research laboratories	D301.45/7
Human nutrition and home economics bureau	A77.701
Human resources research center	D301.26
Hydraulic engineering center	D103.55
Hydrographic office	N6, M202, D203
Hygenic laboratory	T27.3

I

Idaho, Governor	I1.19

Immigration and naturalization bureau	T21, C7
Immigration and naturalization committee. House	Y4.Im6/1
Immigration and naturalization service	L15, J21
Immigration bureau	L3
Immigration commission	Y3.Im6
Immigration committee. Senate	Y4.Im6/2
Impeachments	Y6
Imports bureau	WT4
Improper activities in labor management field, Select committee on. Senate	Y4.Im7
Incentive system office	CS1.83
Increased industrial use of agricultural products commission	Y3.In2/7
Indian affairs bureau	I20
Indian affairs committee. House	Y4.In2/1
Indian affairs committee. Senate	Y4.In2/2
Indian affairs, Joint committee to investigate	Y3.In2/3
Indian affairs office	I20
Indian bureau, Joint committee on transfer of	Y4.In2/3
Indian claims commission	Y3.In2/6
Indian currency commission (Great Britain)	Y3.In2/1
Indian depredations committee. Senate	Y4.In2/4
Indian health service	HE20.2650,
Indian service investigation committee	Y4.In2/9
Indian territory, Select committee to investigate matters connected with affairs in. Senate	Y4.In2/5
Indian tribes, Joint special committee on condition of	Y4.In2/6
Industrial alcohol bureau	T54
Industrial analysis committee	Y3.In2/5
Industrial arts and expositions committee. House	Y4.In2/7
Industrial college of armed forces	in D5
Industrial commission	Y3.In2/2
Industrial expositions committee. Senate	Y4.In2/8
Industrial housing and transportation bureau	L8
Industrial relations commission	Y3.In2/4
Industrial relations office	M204, D204
Industry cooperation office	C38
Information and education division	W111
Information and education service	L9
Information division	I43
Information office	A21
Inland and coastwise waterways service	W101
Inland waterways corporation	W103, C29
Insecticide and fungicide board	A34
Inspector general (Air Force)	D306
Inspector general's department	W9
Institute of tropical forestry	A13.64
Insular affairs bureau	W6
Insular affairs committee	Y4.In7/1
Insurrectionary States, Late, Joint select committee to inquire into the condition of affairs in	Y4.In7/2
Intelligence division, Army department	M106
Intelligence. Select committee on. House	Y4.In8/18
Interagency advisory group	CS1.87
Interagency committee on agricultural surplus disposal	Y3.In8/11
Interagency committee on automatic data processing	Y3.In8/16
Interagency committee on export expansion	Y3.In8/22

Interagency committee on foreign shipments	Y3.W19/7:9
Interagency committee on international athletics	Y3.In8/20
Interagency committee on Mexican American affairs	Y3.In8/23
Interagency committee on oceanography	Y3.F31/16:9
Interagency committee on water resources	Y3.In8/8
Interagency land acquisitions conference	Y3.L22
Inter-agency policy committee on rubber	Y3.W19/7
Interagency racial data committee	Y3.R11
Inter-American affairs office	Pr32.4600
Inter-American conference for maintenance of peace	S5.38
Inter-American conference on agriculture, forestry, and animal industry	S5.32
Inter-American defense board	S5.45
Inter-American development commission	S5.43
Inter-American technical aviation conference	S5.40
Interbureau committee on post-war program	A1.63
Interdepartmental board of contracts and adjustments	T51.9
Interdepartmental board on simplified office procedure	T51.11
Interdepartmental committee for study of jurisdiction over federal areas within the States	Y3.In8/10
Interdepartmental committee on children and youth	Y3.In8/6
Interdepartmental committee on civilian compensation	Y3.In8/14
Interdepartmental committee on internal security	Pr33.608
Interdepartmental committee on narcotics	Y3.In8/9
Interdepartmental committee on nutrition for national defense	Y3.In8/13
Interdepartmental committee on radiation preservation of food	Y3.In8/12
Interdepartmental committee on scientific research and development	Y3.In8/4
Interdepartmental committee on status of women	Y3.In8/21
Interdepartmental committee to coordinate federal urban area assistance programs	Y3.In8/17
Interdepartmental committee to coordinate health and welfare activities	Y3.In8/3
Interdepartmental council to coordinate all Federal juvenile programs	Y3.J98
Interdepartmental federal tort claims committee	Y3.In8/19
Interdepartmental highway safety board	Y3.In8/18
Interdepartmental intelligence conference	Pr33.609
Interdepartmental social hygiene board	Y3.In8/2
Intergovernmental relations commission	Y3.In8/7
Interim compliance board (panel)	Y3.C73/4
Interior and insular affairs committee. House	Y4.In8/14
Interior and insular affairs committee. Senate	Y4.In8/13
Interior Department	I
Interior Department and Forestry service, Joint committee to investigate	Y4.In8/8
Intermountain forest and range experiment station	A13.65
Internal improvements select committee. House	Y4.In8/7
Internal revenue bureau	T22
Internal revenue bureau, Select committee on investigation of	Y4.In8/10
Internal revenue frauds, Select committee on. House	Y4.In8/2
Internal revenue office (service)	T22
Internal revenue taxation, Joint committee of	Y4.In8/11
Internal security committee. House	Y4.In8/15
International agricultural development service	A95
International American conference(s)	S5.9
International bank for reconstruction and development	S5.51

International business operations bureau	C48
International civil aeronautics conference	S5.28
International civil aviation organization	S1.70.5:In85, S5.52
International commerce bureau	C42, C57.100
International commission for air navigation	S5.42
International commission of inquiry into existence of slavery and forced labor in Republic of Liberia	S5.33
International commission on large dams of world power conference	S5.37
International conference for revision of convention of 1914 for safety of life at sea	S5.29
International congress of military medicine and pharmacy	S5.39
International congresses, conferences and commissions	S5
International cooperation administration	S17
International development advisory board	Y3.In8/5
International development agency	S18
International economic programs office	C49.300
International exchange commission	Y3.In8
International exhibitions and expositions	S6
International field year for the Great Lakes	C55.21
International fisheries commission	S5.39
International geograpnic congress	S5.6
International geologic congress	I19.34
International geological congress	S5.7
International high commission	T1.23
International investment office	C48.400
International labor affairs office	L29
International labor conference, 1st	L1.10
International marine conference	S5.10
International monetary fund and international bank for reconstruction and development	S5.46
International postal service division	P8
International prison commission	S5.18/2
International prison congress	S5.18/1
International programs bureau	C49
International radiotelegraph conference	S5.25, S5.26
International railway commission	S5.8
International relations committee. House	Y4.In8/16
International rules of judicial procedure commission	Y3.In8/15
International sanitary conference	S5.11
International statistical congress	S5.5
International telecommunications union	S5.50
International telegraph conference	S5.27
International trade fairs office	C44, C48.100
International trade operations office	C34
International waterways commission	W68
Interoceanic canal committee. Senate	Y4.In8/1
Interoceanic canal congress	S5.15
Interstate and foreign commerce committee. House	Y4.In8/4
Interstate commerce acts	IC1 act
Interstate commerce commission	IC
Interstate commerce committee. Senate	Y4.In8/3
Interstate commerce joint subcommittee	Y4.In8/9
Interstate commission on the Potomac River basin	Y3.In8/24
Interstate migration of destitute citizens, Select committee. House	Y4.In8/12
Invalid pensions committee. House	Y4.In8/5

Investment and entrenchment committee. Senate	Y4.In8/6
Iron, steel and other metals, Board for testing	Y3.Ir6
Irrigation and reclamation committee. House	Y4.Ir7/2
Irrigation and reclamation committee. Senate	Y4.Ir7/1
Irrigation inquiry office	A15
Irrigation of San Joaquin, Tulare and Sacramento Valleys, California, Board of Commissioners	Y3.Ir7
Isthmian canal commission	Y3.Is7:, W73

J

Jackson, Andrew, Pres. U.S., 1829-1837	Pr7
James Madison memorial commission	Y3.M26
Jamestown-Williamsburg-Yorktown celebration commission	Y3.J23
Jefferson, Thomas, Pres. U.S., 1801-1809	Pr3
John E. Fogarty international center for advanced study in the health sciences	HE20.3700
John Marshall bicentennial celebration commission	Y3.M35
Johnson, Andrew, Pres. U.S., 1865-1869	Pr17
Johnson, Lyndon B., Pres. U.S., 1963-1969	Pr36
Joint chiefs of staff	D5
Joint committee on reorganization of the administrative branch of the government	Y4.R29
Joint publications research service	Y3.J66
Joint special committee to investigate Chinese immigration	Y4.C44
Joint study committee on budget control	Y4.B85
Judge advocate general (Army)	W10, M107, D108
Judge-advocate general, Navy	N7, M214, D205
Judge-advocate general of the air force	D302
Judge advocate general's department (office)	W10, M107, D108
Judiciary	Ju
Judiciary committee. House	Y4.J89/1
Judiciary committee. Senate	Y4.J89/2
Justice department	J
Juvenile justice and delinquency prevention office	J1.47

K

Kansas investigating special committee. House	Y4.K13
Katyn forest massacre. Select committee to conduct investigation	Y4.K15
Kennedy, John F., Pres. U.S. 1961-1963	Pr35
Kindergarten division	I16.18

L

Labor and public welfare committee. Senate	Y4.L11/2
Labor bureau	La, C8
Labor committee	Y3.C83:31
Labor committee. House	Y4.L11
Labor department	L
Labor employment board	A16
Labor management relations joint committee	Y4.L11/3
Labor-management reports bureau	L31
Labor standards division	L16
Labor statistics bureau	L2
Lake states forest experiment station	A13.61
Lake survey office. Army department	M110, D103.200
Lakes, Department of the	W19
Land and facilities development administration	HH5
Land and water policies of United States, Special committee on survey of	Y4.L22
Land management bureau	I53

Language service division	S16
Law bureau	SB8
Law enforcement assistance administration	in J1
Law library	LC10
Laws, Committee on revision of. House	Y4.L44/2
Laws of United States	S7
Laws of the United States, Commission to revise	Y3.L44
Laws, Special joint committee on revision of	Y4.L44/1
Legislative budget joint committee	Y4.L52
Legislative reference service	LC14
Lend-lease administrative office	Pr32.5500
Library (Agriculture department)	A17
Library (Documents office)	GP2
Library (Interior department)	I22
Library (Justice department)	J4
Library (Treasury)	T23
Library (War)	W11
Library and naval war records office	N16
Library buildings and grounds superintendent	LC8
Library committee. House	Y4.L61/1
Library committee. Senate	Y4.L61/3
Library joint committee	Y4.L61/2
Library of Congress	LC
Life saving appliance board	T24.8, T47.12
Life saving service	T24
Lighthouse board (Bureau)	T25, C9
Lilley, George L., Select committee on investigation of charges made against	Y4.L61
Lincoln, Abraham, Pres. U.S., 1861-1865	Pr16
Lincoln sesquicentennial commission	Y3.L66
Loans and currency division	T26
Lobby investigation select committee. House	Y4.L78
Lobbying activities, Select committee on. House	Y4.L78/3
Lobbying activities, Special committee to investigate. Senate	Y4.L78/2
Locomotive inspection bureau	IC1 ℓoc
Lorimer, William, Committee to investigate election of. Senate	Y4.L89
Luzon, Department of	W56

M

McKinley, William, Pres. U.S., 1897-1901	Pr25
Madison, James, Pres. U.S., 1809-1817	Pr4
Management and budget office	PrEx2
Manufactures bureau	C10
Manufactures committee. House	Y4.M31/1
Manufactures committee. Senate	Y4.M31/2
Manuscript division	LC4
Maps and charts division	LC5
Marihuana and drug abuse commission	Y3.M33/2
Marine and dock industrial relations division	SB4
Marine corps	N9, M209, D214
Marine inspection and navigation bureau	C25
Maritime administration	C39.200
Maritime advisory committee	Y3.M33
Maritime commission	MC
Maritime labor board	ML
Marketing and marketing agreements division	A65

A-24

Marketing services office	A80.800, A81
Markets and crop estimates bureau	A36
Matanzas and Santa Clara, Department of	W58
Maternal and child health service	HE20.2750
Mediation and conciliation board	MCB
Mediation board	MB
Mediation commission	Y3.M46
Medical department, Army	W44, M102, D104
Medical field services school, Carlisle Barracks, Pa.	W44.21
Medical research and development board	D104.12
Medical section, Council of National defense	Y3.C83:41
Medical services administration	FS17.500, HE17.500
Medical services bureau	HE20.5400
Medicine and surgery bureau	N10, M203, D206
Members of Congress, Select committee to investigate alleged charges against	Y4.M51
Memorial addresses and addresses on acceptance of statues	Y7
Mental health service	HE20.2450
Merchant marine and fisheries committee. House	Y4.M53
Merchant marine commission	Y3.M53
Messages and documents	Y8
Mexico, Select committee on proceedings of boards of commissions on claims against	Y4.M59
Microscopy division	Y4.M58
Migratory bird conservation commission	Y3.M58
Military academy. West Point	W12, M109, D109
Military academy, West Point, Commission to examine	Y3.M59
Military affairs committee. House	Y4.M59/1
Military affairs committee. Senate	Y4.M59/2
Military Government of Germany	W1.72
Military history, Office of Chief of	D114
Military information division	W26
Military intelligence division	W100
Military prison, Fort Leavenworth	W27
Military sea transportation service	D216
Militia committee. House	Y4.M59/3
Mindanao, Department of	W72
Minerals and solid fuels office	I60
Minerals exploration office	I55
Minerals mobilization office	I60
Mines and mining committee. House	Y4.M66/1
Mines and mining committee. Senate	Y4.M66/2
Mines bureau	I28
Mining enforcement and safety administration	I69
Mint bureau	T28
Miscellaneous division	T42
Missing persons in southeast Asia, Select committee on. House	Y4.M69/3
Mississippi river commission	W31, M110.200, D103.300
Mississippi river, Committee on levees and improvement of. House	Y4.M69/2
Mississippi. Select committee to inquire into alleged frauds in recent elections in	Y4.M69/1
Missouri basin inter-agency committee	Y3.M69
Missouri, Department of the	W20
Missouri river basin commission	Y3.M69/2
Missouri river basin inter-agency committee	I1.78-80, Y3.M69

Missouri river commission	W32
Mixed claims commission, United States and Germany	S3.31
Mixed claims commission, United States and Mexico	S3.34
Monetary conference	S5.13
Monetary or silver commission of U.S., 1876	Y4.M74
Money orders division	P9
Monroe, James, Pres. U.S., 1817-1825	Pr8
Montana, Governor	I1.22
Morale services division	W109.200
Motion pictures division	I37
Motor carrier safety bureau	TD2.300
Motor carriers division	IC1 mot
Motor transport corps	W88
Motor vehicle service division	P21
Mounted service school	W30
Municipal construction division	EP2.28
Munitions board	M5, D3
Munitions industry, Special committee investigating. Senate	Y4.M92
Muscle shoals commission	Y3.M97
Muscle shoals joint committee	Y4.M97
Music division	LC12
Mutual security agency	Pr33.900

N

Narcotics and dangerous drugs bureau	J24
Narcotics bureau	T56
National academy of sciences	NA
National advisory commission on criminal justice standards and goals	Y3.C86
National advisory committee on aeronautics	Y3.N21/5
National advisory committee on education of the deaf	HE5.289
National advisory committee on oceans and atmospheres	Y3.Oc2
National advisory committee on the handicapped	HE5.86, HE19.117
National advisory council for career education	HE19.116
National advisory council for drug abuse prevention	Y3.D84
National advisory council on adult education	Y3.Ed8/4
National advisory council on child nutrition	Y3.C43/2
National advisory council on extension and continuing education	Y3.Ex8
National advisory council on Indian education	Y3.In2/10
National advisory council on international monetary and financial	Y3.N21/16
National advisory council on vocational education	Y3.V85
National advisory loan committee	A52
National aeronautics and space administration	NAS
National aeronautics and space council	PrEx5
National agricultural library	A17
National air museum	SI9
National air pollution control administration	HE20.1300
National archives and records service	GS4
National archives (establishment)	AE, GS4
National bituminous coal commission	I34
National board for promotion of rifle practice	W82
National board of health	T29
National bureau of standards	T41, C13
National business council for consumer affairs	Y3.N21/27
National cancer institute	in FS2, HE20.3150

National capital airports bureau	FAA6
National capital housing authority	DC57
National capital park and planning commission	NC
National capital planning commission	NC2
National capital regional planning council	NC3
National capital sesquicentennial commission	Y3.N21/20
National capital transportation agency	Y3.N21/21
National cartographic information center	I19.71
National center for education statistics	HE19.300
National center for family planning services	HE20.2900
National center for health services research (and development)	HE20.2100
National center for health statistics	HE20.2200
National center for social statistics	FS17.600, HE17.600
National clearinghouse for drug abuse information	PrEx13, HE20.8215
National clearinghouse for mental health information	FS2.22/50
National clearinghouse for poison control centers	FS2.96
National climatic center	C55.280
National coast defense board	Y3.N21/4
National collection of fine arts	S16
National commission for industrial peace	Y3.In2/11
National commission for manpower policy	Y3.M31
National commission for review of Federal and State laws relating to wiretapping and electronic surveillance	Y3.W74/2
National commission for the protection of human subjects of biomedical and behavioral research	Y3.H88
National commission for United Nations educational, scientific and cultural organization	S5.48
National commission on consumer finance	Y3.C76/2
National commission on finance of postsecondary education	Y3.Ed8/5
National commission on fire prevention and control	Y3.F51
National commission on food marketing	Y3.N21/22
National commission on law observance and enforcement	Y3.N21/7
National commission on libraries and information science	Y3.L61
National commission on materials policy	Y3.M41
National commission on product safety	Y3.N21/25
National commission on reform of Federal criminal laws	Y3.N21/26
National commission on State workmen's compensation laws	Y3.W89/3
National commission on technology, automation and economic progress	Y3.T22
National commission on the observance of international woman's year	Y3.W84
National commission on water quality	Y3.W29.2
National committee on wood utilization	C1.14
National communicable disease center	HE20.2300
National conference on air pollution	FS2.98
National conference on water pollution	FS2.64
National council on Indian opportunity	Y3.In2/9
National council on marine resources and engineering development	PrEx12
National council on the arts	PrEx11
National credit union administration	NCU
National criminal justice reference service	J1.42/3
National cultural center	SI10
National defense migration, Select committee investigating. House	Y4.N21/5
National defense program in its relation to small business, Select committee to conduct study and survey of. House	Y4.N21/7
National defense program, Special committee investigating. Senate	Y4.N21/6
National disabled soldiers league, Inc., Select committee to investigate	Y4.N21/3

National earthquake information center	C55.690
National emergency council	Y3.N21/9
National emergency, Termination of the, Special committee. Senate	Y4.N21/9
National endowment for the arts	NF2
National endowment for the humanities	NF3
National enforcement commission	ES6
national environmental research center(s)	EP1.46
National environmental satellite service	C55.500
National export expansion council	C1.42/3
National eye institute	HE20.3750
National fire prevention and control administration	C58
National forest reservation commission	Y3.N21/6
National foundation on the arts and the humanities	NF
National gallery of art	SI8
National guard bureau	W70, M114, D112, D12
National heart and lung institute	HE20.3200
National herbarium	SI3.8
National highway safety bureau	TD2.200, TD8
National highway traffic safety administration	TD8
National home for disabled volunteer soldiers	NH1
National housing agency	NHA
National industrial pollution control council	Y3.In2/8
National information center for the handicapped	HE19.119
National institute for child health and human development	HE20.3350
National institute for occupational safety and health	HE20.2800, HE20.7100
National institute of allergy and infectious diseases	HE20.3250
National institute of arthritis and metabolic diseases	HE20.3300
National institute of child health and human development	HE20.3350
National institute of dental research	HE20.3400
National institute of education	HE18, HE19.200
National institute of environmental health sciences	HE20.3550
National institute of general medical sciences	HE20.3450
National institute of law enforcement and criminal justice	in J1
National institute of mental health	in FS2.22:, HE20.2400 HE20.3800, HE20.8100
National institute of neurological diseases and stroke	HE20.3500
National institute of occupational safety and health	HE20.2800
National institute on aging	HE20.3850
National institute on alcohol abuse and alcoholism	HE20.8300
National institute on drug abuse	HE20.8200
National institute on law enforcement and criminal justice	in J1
National institutes of health	FS2.22:, HE20.3000
National interregional highway committee	Y3.N21/15
National inventors council	C32
National labor board	Y3.N21/10
National labor relations board	Y3.N21/13, LR
National land use planning committee	A1.39
National library of medicine	FS2.200, HE20.3600
National marine fisheries service	C55.300
National mediation board	NMB
National meteorological center	C55.190
National military establishment	M
National monetary commission	Y3.N21/2
National munitions control board	NMC

National museum	SI3
National naval medical center, Bethesda	N10.100
National ocean survey	C55.500
National oceanic and atmospheric administration	C55
National oceanographic data center	D103.24, C55.290
National oceanographic instrumentation center	D203.32/ , C55.70
National office of vital statistics	FS2.100
National park service	I29
National portrait gallery	SI11
National production authority	C40
National railroad adjustment board	RA
National recovery administration	Y3.N21/8
National recovery review board	Y3.N21/11
National research council	NA2
National resources committee	Y3.N21/12
National resources, Committee on conservation of. Senate	Y4.N21/l
National resources planning board	Pr32.301
National science foundation	NS
National screw thread commission	C13.23
National security council	Y3.N21/17, Pr33.600 PrEx3
National security league, Special committee to investigate. House	Y4.N21/2
National security resources board	Y3.N21/18, Pr33.700
National security training commission	Y3.N21/19
National society of Daughters of American revolution	SI5
National student volunteer program	AA3
National technical information service	C51
National tourism resources review commission	Y3.T64
National training school for boys	DC19, J8
National transportation safety board	TD1.i00
National visitor center study commission	Y3.N21/13
National war labor board	L10, Pr32.5101
National war savings committee	T1.26
National water commission	Y3.N21/24
National water resources, Select committee on. Senate	Y4.N21/8
National waterways commission	Y3.N21/3
National weather service	C55.100
National woman's liberty loan committee	T1.27/11
National youth administration	Y3.N21/14, FS6, Pr32.5250
Naturalization bureau	C7.10, L6
Naturalization commission	Y3.N21/1
Nautical almanac office	N11
Navajo-Hopi Indian administration joint committee	Y4.N22/4
Naval academy	N12, M206.100, D208.100
Naval affairs committee. House	Y4.N22/1
Naval affairs committee. Senate	Y4.N22/2
Naval affairs joint committee	Y4.N22/3
Naval air development center. Aeronautical, electronic and electrical laboratory	D202.14, D217.19
Naval air materiel center, Philadelphia	D217.21
Naval air systems command	D202
Naval air test station, Patuxent River, Md.	D217.27
Naval consulting board	N1.29

Naval education and training command	D207.200
Naval electronic systems command	D219
Naval facilities engineering command	D209
Naval intelligence office	N13
Naval medical research institute	in M203, D206
Naval medical school, Bethesda	N10.10, N10.200
Naval militia affairs division	N23
Naval militia office	N1.27
Naval observatory	N14, M212, D213
Naval oceanographic office	D203
Naval operations office	N27, M207, D207
Naval ordnance laboratory, Corona, California	D215.43, D217.20
Naval ordnance systems command	D215
Naval personnel bureau	N17, M206, D208
Naval research laboratory	in D210
Naval research office	N32, M216, D210
Naval reserve force division	N25
Naval sea systems command	D211
Naval ship research and development center	D211.9
Naval ship systems command	D211
Naval supply system command	D212
Naval support force, Antarctica	D201.50
Naval technical training command	D207.101
Naval torpedo station, Keyport, Washington	D211.23
Naval training command	D207.200
Naval training device center	D210.14
Naval training support command	D208
Naval war college	N15, M206,200, D208.200
Naval weapons bureau	D217
Naval weapons center, China Lake, California	D201.23
Naval weapons center, Dahlgren, Virginia	D217.17, D215.14, D201.21
Naval weather service command	D220
Navigation and steamboat inspection bureau	C25
Navigation bureau	T30, C11
Navigation bureau	N17
Navy department	N, M201, D201
Navy electronics laboratory, San Diego	D211.11
Near East relief	Y3.N27
Negro economics division	L1.8
New England regional commission	Y3.N42/2
New England river basins commissions	Y3.N42/3
New Jersey tercentenary celebration commission	Y3.N42
New Mexico	I1.24
New Orleans riots select committee. House	Y4.N42/1
New York election frauds, alleged, Select committee on. House	Y4.N42/2
Newburgh, N.Y., Monument and centennial celebration of 1883, Joint select committee on	Y4.N42/3
Nicarauga canal commission	Y3.N51
Nine foot channel from Great Lakes to the Gulf, Select committee on. Senate	Y4.N62
NLRB Special committee to investigate. House	Y4.N21/4
North Atlantic Regional water resources study coordinating committee	Y3.N81/3
North Carolina tercentenary celebration commission	Y3.N81/2

North Central forest experiment station	A13.82
Northeastern boundary arbitration	S3.10
Northeastern department	W86
Northeastern forest experiment station	A13.67, A13.^2
Northern and northwestern lakes survey	W33
Northern division, Army	W62
Northern forest experiment station	A13.73
Northern Pacific railroad land grants, Joint committee on investigation	Y4.N81
Northern Rocky Mountain forest and range experiment station	A13.30
Northwest territory celebration commission	Y3.N81
Nuclear regulatory commission	Y3.N88
Nutrition and human needs, Select committee	Y4.N95

O

Oak Ridge associated universities	Y3.At7:25
Oak Ridge institute of nuclear studies	Y3.At7:25
Obscenity and poronography commission	Y3.Ob7
Occupational safety and health administration	L35
Occupational safety and health bureau	HE20.1600
Occupational safety and health review commission	Y3.Oc1
Oceanograpner of the Navy, Office	D218
Office of exports	Y3.Ec74/2:101
Office of information for armed forces	D2
Office of internal revenue	T22
Office of juvenile justice and delinquency prevention	J1.47
Office of management and budget	PrEx2
Office of saline water	in I1
Ohio River division laboratories	D103.33
Oil and gas office	I64
Oil cases, Special counsel for United States in	Y3.Oi5
Oil import administration	I61
Oil import appeals board	I62
Oklahoma	I1.26
Oklahoma, Select committee to investigate Indian contracts in	Y4.Ok4
Old age pension plans, Select committee to investigate. House	Y4.Oℓ1
Old-age pension system, Special committee to investigate.Senate	Y4.Oℓ1/2
Older Americans volunteer program	AA2
Oliver Wendell Holmes device permanent committee	Y3.H73
Operational applications laboratory	D301.45/37
Operations bureau	SB9
Order division	LC13
Ordnance and ammunition, Select committee on investigation	Y4.Or2/4
Ordnance and fortification board	W35
Ordnance and war-ships Select committee. Senate	Y4.Or2/2
Ordnance bureau	N18, M211, D215
Ordnance department	W34, M111, D105
Ordnance, Heavy, and projectiles, Select committee on. Senate	Y4.Or2/1
Ordnance, Joint select committee on	Y4.Or2/3
Organization of executive branch of the government commission	Y3.Or3/2
Organization of the government for the conduct of foreign policy commission	Y3.F76/5
Orientalia division	LC17
Ornithology and mammology division	A4
Outdoor recreation bureau	I66
Outdoor recreation resources review commission	Y3.Ou8

Outer continental shelf research management advisory board	I1.99
Outrages in Southern States, alleged, Selected committee on investigation	Y4.Ou8
Overseas private investment corporation	OP
Ozarks regional commission	Y3.Oz1

P

Pacific Coast naval base, Joint committee	Y4.P11/4
Pacific, Department of the	W21
Pacific division	W51
Pacific islands and Porto Rico committee. Senate	Y4.P11/1
Pacific northwest environmental research laboratory	EP1.37
Pacific northwest forest and range experiment station	A13.66
Pacific northwest regional commission	Y3.P11/5
Pacific northwest river basins commission	Y4.P11/4
Pacific railroad committee. House	Y4.P11/3
Pacific railroad committee. Senate	Y4.P11/2
Pacific railway commission	Y3.P11
Pacific Southwest Federal inter-agency technical committee	Y3.P11/3
Pacific Southwest forest and range experiment station	A13.62
Packers and stockyards administration	A39, A96
Pan American congress of highways	S5.23
Pan American financial conference	T1.22
Pan-American medical congress	S5.16
Pan American sanitary bureau	PAS
Pan American scientific congress(es)	S5.14
Pan American union	AR, PA
Pan Pacific Conference on education, rehabilitation, reclamation and recreation	I1.61
Pan-Pacific educational conference	S5.21/2
Pan-Pacific scientific conference	S5.21
Panama canal	W79, M115, D113, PaC
Panama canal company and canal zone government	CZ
Parcel post, General, Joint committee to investigate	Y4.P21
Patent and trade mark laws commission	Y3.P27
Patent and trade mark office	C21
Patent office	I23, C21
Patents committee. House	Y4.P27/1
Patents committee. Senate	Y4.P27/2
Pay department	W36
Paymaster general	W36
Peace conference, Paris, 1919	S3.28
Peace corps	S19, AA4
Pearl harbor attack, Joint committee investigating	Y4.P31
Penitentiary, Atlanta, Georgia	J14
Penitentiary, Fort Leavenworth	J6
Penitentiary, McNeill Island	J13
Pennsylvania avenue development corporation	Y3.P38
Pension benefit guaranty corporation	Y3.P38/2
Pension bureau	I24, VA2
Pensions, bounty, and back pay, Select committee on payment of	Y4.P38/3
Pensions committee. House	Y4.P38/1
Pensions committee. Senate	Y4.P38/2
Periodical division, Library of Congress	LC6
Permanent conference on printing	T51.8
Permanent court of arbitration	S3.18

Permanent international association of road congresses	S5.31
Perry's victory memorial commission	I1.62
Personnel (and business administration) office	A49
Personnel classification board	PC
Personnel operations office	D118
Personnel research branch	D102.27
Personnel research laboratory	D301.45/27
Pesticide programs office	EP5
Pesticides office	EP5
Petroleum administration for defense	I58
Petroleum administration for war	Y3.P44
Petroleum administrative board	I32
Petroleum conservation division	I41
Petroleum coordinator for war office	I50
Petroleum resources, Special committee investigating. Senate	Y4.P44
Philippine alien property administration	Pr33.501
Philippine commission 1899-1900 (Schurman commission)	Y3.P53
Philippine Islands	W49
Philippine Islands President	W106
Philippine Islands, U.S. High commissioner to	W105
Philippine war damage commission	Y3.P53/2
Philippines committee. Senate	Y4.P54
Philippines division	W21
Phosphate resources of the United States, Joint committee to investigate	Y4.P56
Physical fitness committee	FS12
Picatinny arsenal, Dover, N.J.	D105.12
Pierce, Franklin, Pres. U.S., 1853-1857	Pr14
Pipeline companies division	IC1 pip
Planning and statistics division	SB5
Plant and operations office	A60
Plant industry bureau	A19
Plant industry, soils and agricultural engineering bureau	A19, A77.500
Plant quarantine and control administration	A48
Platte, Department of the	W22
Pneumatic tube commission	P17
Pneumatic tube mail service joint commission	Y3.P74/2
Pneumatic tubes, Joint commission on government purchase of	Y3.P74
Political activities, lobbying and campaign contributions, Special commission	Y4.P75
Political activity of government personnel commission	Y3.P75
Polk, James Knox, Pres. U.S., 1845-1849	Pr11
Pomology division	A20
Population growth and the American future, Commission on	Y3.P81
Pornographic materials, current, Select committee on. House	Y4.P82
Port facilities commission	SB6
Porto Rico SEE Puerto Rico	
Post office and civil service committee. House	Y4.P84/10
Post office and civil service committee. Senate	Y4.P84/11
Post office and post roads committee. House	Y4.P84/1
Post office and post roads committee. Senate	Y4.P84/2
Post office department, Select committee on relations of members with. House	Y4.P84/3
Post office inspectors division	P14
Post office leases, Senate committee	Y4.P84/6
Post office operations bureau	P24

Post war economy policy and planning, Special committee on. Senate	Y4.P84/7
Post-war military policy, Select committee on. House	Y4.P84/9
Postage on 2d class matter and compensation for transportation of mails, Joint committee	Y4.P84/4
Postal commission 1906-07	Y3.P84/2
Postal rate commission	Y3.P84/4
Postal salaries joint commission	Y4.P84/5
Postal savings division	P19
Postal savings system	PS
Postal service commission to investigate, 1898-1901	Y3.P84/1
Postal service joint commission	Y3.P84/3
Postmaster general	P1
Potomac river naval command	D201.12
Precious metals, Royal [British] commission appointed to inquire into recent changes in relative value of	Y3.P91
President of United States	Pr
Presidential and senatorial campaign expenditures, Special committee on investigation of	Y4.P92/2
Presidential campaign activities. Select committee on	Y4.P92/4
Presidential campaign expenditures, Special committee investigating	Y4.P92
Presidential, Vice presidential, and senatorial campaign expenditures, 1944, Special committee to investigate. Senate	Y4.P92/3
President's committee on administrative management	Y3.P92/3
President's committee on civil service improvement	Y3.P92/4
President's committee on crop insurance	Y3.P92/2
President's committee on religion and welfare in armed forces	Y3.P92/5
President's organization on unemployment relief	C1.15:
Press intelligence division	PI
Price administration and civilian supply office	Pr32.4200
Price administration and civilian supply office, consumer division	Pr32.5350
Price administration office	Pr32.4200
Price commission	Y3.P93/4
Price stabilization office	ES3
Printing and publications division	C16
Printing and stationery division	T36
Printing committee. Senate	Y4.P93/3
Printing investigation commission	Y3.P93
Printing, Joint committee	Y4.P93/1
Printing, Public, Select committee to investigate	Y4.P93/4
Prints and photographs division	LC25
Prints division	LC11
Priority in transportation commissioner	Y3.P93/2
Prison industries reorganization administration	Y3.P93/3
Prisons bureau	J16
Private land claims committee. House	Y4.P93/5
Privileges and elections committee. Senate	Y4.P93/6
Processing department	LC30
Processing tax board of review	T61
Procurement and materiel office	N30
Procurement division	T58
Production and marketing administration	A82
Production management office	Pr32.4001
Prohibition bureau	J17
Project, Books for the blind	LC19

Property management and disposal service	GS10
Provost marshal general	W37, D120
Public assistance bureau	SS
Public buildings administration (service)	FW6, GS6
Public buildings and grounds committee. House	Y4.P96/6
Public buildings and grounds committee. Senate	Y4.P96/7
Public buildings and grounds office	W38
Public buildings and public parks of national capital office	PB
Public buildings commission	Y3.P96/4
Public contracts division	L18
Public debt bureau	T57, T63.201
Public documents division	I15
Public documents division	GP3
Public domain, Committee on conservation and administration	Y3.P96/5
Public expenditures committee. House	Y4.P96/5
Public health and national quarantine committee. Senate	Y4.P96/9
Public health, Select committee. House	Y4.P96/8
Public health service	T27, FS2, HE20
Public housing administration	HH3
Public information committee	Y3.P96/3
Public information division, Army dept.	M118
Public information office	D6
Public land commission 1879-80	Y3.P96/1
Public land commission 1903-05	Y3.P96/2
Public land law review commission	Y3.P96/7
Public moneys division	T31
Public printer	GP1
Public relations bureau	W107
Public relations office	N31, M215
Public roads (bureau, office) administration	A22, FW2, GS3, C37 TD2.100
Public sector labor relations information exchange	L1.66
Public service commission	DC43
Public works administration	FW5
Public works and transportation committee. House	Y4.P96/11
Public works committee. House	Y4.P96/11
Public works committee. Senate	Y4.P96/10
Publication board	Y3.P96/6
Publications and supplies division	L4
Publications division	A21
Publicity bureau, Liberty loan of 1917	T1.25
Publicity bureau, War loan organization	T1.27/21
Puerto Rico	I1.39-40, S10, W75, I35.12
Puerto Rico agricultural experiment station	A10.12, A77.461
Puerto Rico attorney general	J7
Puerto Rico auditor	T43, W75.6
Puerto Rico census office	W48
Puerto Rico commission to revise laws	Y3.P83
Puerto Rico, Department of	W23
Puerto Rico laws commission	Y3.P83
Puerto Rico reconstruction administration	I36
Purchase of products and services of the blind and other severely handicapped committee	Y3.P97
Purchase, storage and traffic division	W89
Purchasing agent	P15

Q

Quality assurance bureau	HE20.5500
Quartermaster corps	W77, M112, D106
Quartermaster department	W39
Quartermaster general of army	D106

R

Radiation (programs) office	EP6
Radio commission, Federal	RC
Radio service	N22
Radiological health bureau	HE20.4100
Radiological health service	HE20.1500
Railroad administration	Y3.R13/2
Railroad labor board	RL
Railroad retirement board	RR
Railroad retirement commission	Y3.R13/3
Railroad retirement legislation joint committee	Y4.R13/3
Railroad safety bureau	TD3.100
Railroad securities commission	Y3.R13
Railroads commissioner	I25
Railroads committee. Senate	Y3.R13/2
Railway mail service	P10
Railways and canals committee. House	Y4.R13
Rare book collections (division)	LC23
Rate section	IC1 rat
Readjustment of service pay, Special joint committee. House	Y4.R22/2
Readjustment service pay, Select committee	Y4.R22
Real estate bondholders' reorganizations, Select committee on investigation of. House	Y4.R22/3
Real estate service	W94
Reclamation (service) bureau	I19.17, I27
Reclassification of salaries, Joint commission	Y4.R24/2
Reconstruction and production select committee. Senate	Y4.R24/3
Reconstruction finance corporation	Y3.R24, FL5, C33
Reconstruction joint committee	Y4.R24
Reconstruction research division	Y3.C83:91
Record and pension office	W40
Recruiting publicity bureau	M108, D102.75
Recruiting service	SB3
Reduction of non essential federal expenditures	Y4.R24/4
Reference department	LC29
Reforestation, Select committee. Senate	Y4.R25
Reform school for girls of District of Columbia	DC13, J9
Refugees, freedmen and abandoned lands bureau	W41
Regional economic development office	C53
Regional economics office	C49.100
Regional medical programs service	HE20.2600, HE20.6300
Register of treasury	T32
Rehabilitation services administration	FS17.100, HE17.100, HE1.600
Renegotiation board	RnB
Renewal assistance administration	HH7
Renovation of executive mansion committee	Y3.R29/2
Rent commission of District of Columbia	Y3.R29
Rent stabilization office	ES5
Reorganization of courts of United States and reform judicial procedure, Special committee to study. Senate	Y4.R29/2

Research and development board	M6, D4
Research and development board	FAA2
Research and marketing act, Office of administrator	A87, A77.8
Research and statistics division	T62
Research and technology division	D301.45/34
Research bureau	WT5
Research bureau	SB7
Reserve bank organization committee	RB1
Resettlement administration	Y3.R31, A61
Resources and trade assistance bureau	C57.200
Retraining and reemployment administration	L24
Retrenchment committee. Senate	Y3.R31/1
Retrenchment joint select committee	Y3.R31/2
Revenue commission	T1.18
Revenue cutter service	T33
Review of the National policy toward gambling commission	Y3.G14
Revision of Federal court of appellate system commission	Y3.Ap4/3
Revision of statutes commission	Y3.R32
Rivers and harbors committee. House	Y4.R52
Roads and canals committee. Senate	Y4.R53
Roads committee. House	Y4.R53/2
Robert A. Taft Sanitary Engineering Center	in FS2
Rock Island arsenal laboratory	D105.11
Rocky mountain forest and range experiment station	A13.69
Rodman process laboratory. Watertown arsenal	D105.13
Rolls and library bureau	S8
Rome air development center	D301.57
Roosevelt, Franklin Delano, Pres. U.S., 1933-1945	Pr32
Roosevelt, Theodore, Pres. U.S., 1901-1909	Pr26
Rubber laboratory, Mare Island naval shipyard, Vallejo, Calif.	D211.16
Rubber producing facilities disposal commission	Y3.R82
Rules and administration committee. Senate	Y4.R86/2
Rules committee. House	Y4.R86/1
Rural community development service	A97
Rural credits, Joint committee	Y4.R88
Rural delivery division	P16
Rural development committee	Y3.R88/3
Rural development program committee	Y3.R66/2
Rural development service	A102
Rural electrification administration	Y3.R88, A68

S

Safety bureau	IC1 saf
Safety office	TD3.100
St. Augustine quadricentennial commission	Y3.Sa2/2
St. Elizabeth's hospital	I1.14, FS11
St. Lawrence seaway development corporation	Y3.Sa2, TD6
Salaries and allowances division	P12
Salary stabilization board	ES4
Sanitary commission	Y3.Sa58
Santiago and Puerto Principe, Dept. of	W59
Santo Domingo commission of inquiry to	Y3.Sa5
Savings bond division	T66
Savings system, War loan organization	T1.27/31
Science and astronautics committee. House	Y4.Sci2

Science and technology committee. House	Y4.Sci2
Science and technology division	LC33
Science and technology office	PrEx8
Science and technology project	LC32
Science, art and education division	S15
Science division	LC33
Science information council	NS3
Science information service office	NS2
Second assistant postmaster general	P3
Second section, general staff	W26
Secret service (division)	T34
Secretary of the treasury	T1
Securities and exchange commission	SE
Seed and plant introduction section	A23
Seed division	A24
Select and special committee, House	Y4.Se4/1
Select committee on investigation of Government printing office. Senate	Y4.G74/2
Select committee on investigation of illegal appointments in Civil Service	Y4.C49/3
Select committee to establish University of the United States	Y4.Un3/2
Select committee to investigate educational and training program under G.I.bill. House	Y4.Ed8/4
Selective service system	Y4.Se4, Pr32.5271, Y4.Se4
Semitic literature division	LC20
Senate	Y1.3
Senate contingent expenses committee to audit and control. Senate	Y4.Se5/3
Senatorial campaign expenditures, Select committee on. Senate	Y4.Se5/2
Serials division	LC6
Service for the blind	LC16
Services of supply	W109
Shiloah national military park commission	W63
Ship purchase lobby, alleged, Special committee to investigate. Senate	Y4.Sh6/2
Ship structure committee	Y3.Sh6
Ship subsidy, alleged. Select committee to investigate. House	Y4.Sh6
Shipping board	SB
Shipping board bureau	C27
Shipping board emergency fleet corporation	SB2
Shipping board emergency fleet corporation, Select committee. House	Y4.Sh4
Shipping board operations, Select committee. House	Y4.Sh6/3
Shipping commissioners	C12
Ships bureau	N29, M210, D211
Short time record credits joint committee	Y4.Sh8
Sickness and mortality on emigrant ships, Select committee of Senate on	Y4.Si1
Signal corps engineering laboratories	D111.9
Signal office (corps)	W42, D111
Signal school, Army, Fort Monmouth, New Jersey	W42.34
Signal service, Geological survey, Coast and geodetic survey and Hydrographic Office, Joint committee to consider present organization of	Y3.Si2
Silk section	A25
Silver, Special committee on the investigation	Y4.Si3
Slavic and East (Central) European division	LC35
Small business administration	SBA

Small business (Permanent) Select committee on. House	Y4.Sm1
Small business, Select Committee on. Senate	Y4.Sm1/2
Small defense plants administration	SDP
Smithsonian insitution	SI
Social and economic statistics administration	C56
Social and rehabilitation services	FS17, HE17
Social security board (administration)	SS, FS3, HE3
Soil conservation service	A57, A76.201, A79.201 A80.201, A80.501, A57
Soil erosion service	I30
Soils bureau	A26
Soldiers home	W43
Solicitor for Interior Department	I48
Solicitor for Labor Department	L21
Solicitor general	J11
Solicitor for Department of Agriculture	A33
Solicitor of the Navy Department	N8
Solicitor of Treasury	T44, J5
Solid fuels administration for war	I51
Solid waste management bureau	HE20.1400
Solid waste management office	EP3
Souris-Red-Rainy river basin commission	Y3.So8
South, Department of the and South, Division of the	W66
Southeastern department	W84
Southeastern district branch of predator and rodent control	I49.61
Southeastern forest experiment station	A13.63
Southeastern power administration	I65
Southern department	W83
Southern forest experiment station	A13.40
Southwestern division	W69
Southwestern forest experiment station	A13.43
Southwestern power administration	I59
Space and astronautics, Special committee on. Senate	Y4.Sp1
Space systems division	D301.71
Spanish treaty claims commission	Y3.Sp2
Special action office for drug abuse prevention	PrEx20
Special advisor to the President on foreign trade	Y3.F76
Special agents division	T35
Special committee on federal penal and reformatory institutions	Y4.F31/3
Special committee on termination of the national emergency. Senate	Y4.N21/9
Special committee to investigate administration and operation of civil service laws	Y4.C49/4
Special devices center	D210.14
Special representative for trade negotiations office	PrEx9
Special services division	W109.101, M117
Special services office	FS13
Speeches	Y9
Sport fisheries and wildlife bureau	I49
Springfield armory	D105.19
Stack and reader division	LC34
Standards and conduct, Select committee. Senate	Y4.St2/2
Standards bureau	C13
Standards of official conduct committee. House	Y4.St2/3
Standards, weights and measures committee. Senate	Y4.St2

State and local cooperation division	Pr32.4100
State councils section	Y3.C83:71
State department	S
State law index	LC21
State technical services office	C1.53
State, war and navy department building office	S12
States relations office	A10
Statistical reporting service	A92
Statistics bureau	A27
Statistics bureau	C14
Statistics bureau	T37
Steam engineering bureau	N19
Steam roads bureau	IC1 ste
Steamboat inspection service	T38, C15
Strategy council on drug abuse	Y3.St8
Subject cataloging division	LC26
Submarine defense school	W61
Subsistence department	W5
Subsistence homesteads division	I31
Subversive activities control board	Y3.Su1
Sugar agency	A76.300
Sugar division	A63
Sugar equalization board	Y3.Su3
Superintendent of documents	GP3
Supervising tea examiner	T46
Supplies and accounts bureau	N20, M213, D212
Supplies division	P18
Supply bureau	T52
Supply division	T55
Supreme allied commander in Europe	D9.8
Supreme commander for allied powers	W1.84, D102.11
Supreme court	Ju6
Surplus marketing administration	A73
Surplus property board	Y3.W19/7:200
Surplus property, Select committee to investigate deposition. House	Y4.Su7
Surplus war property administration	Y3.W19/7
Survivors benefits, Select committee on. House	Y4.Su7/2
Systems engineering group	D301.45/48
Systems research and development service	FAA2, TD4.500

T

Taft, William Howard, Pres. U.S. 1909-1913	Pr27
Tank corps	W90
Tariff board 1909-12	Y3.T17/2
Tariff commission	TC
Tariff commission, 1882	Y3.T17
Tariff commission, Select committee on investigation of	Y4.T17
Tax appeals board	Y3.T19
Tax court	Ju11
Tax evasion and avoidance, Joint committee on	Y4.T19
Tax-exempt foundations and comparable organizations, Special committee to investigate	Y4.T19/3
Tax research division	T64
Taxation of governmental securities and salaries, Special committee on. Senate	Y4.T19/2
Taylor and other systems of ship management, Special committee	Y4.T21

A-40

Taylor, Zachary, Pres. U.S., 1849-1850	Pr12
Technical information division	LC36
Technical services office	C35
Technical staff office	T68
Technology assessment and forecast office	C1.24
Technology assessment office	Y3.T22/2
Technology transfer	EP7
Telecommunications policy office	PrEx18
Telegraph companies division	IC1 telg
Telegraph division	CC3
Telephone division	CC4
Telephone division	IC1 telp
Temporary Alaska claims commission	Y3.Aℓ1s/2
*Temporary controls office	Pr33.300
Temporary national economic committee	Y3.T24
Tennessee valley authority	Y3.T25
Tennessee valley authority, Joint committee	Y4.T25
Territories and insular affairs committee. Senate	Y4.T27/2
Territories and island possessions division	I35
Territories committee. House	Y4.T27/1
Territories office	I35
Texas, Department of	W24
Textile engineering laboratory	D106.9/2-2
Third assistant postmaster general	P4
Thomas Jefferson memorial commission	Y3.T36
Tobacco commission	Y3.T53
Tonnage, American, Committee on causes of reduction of	Y4.T61
Topography division	P11
Trade promotion office	C48.200
Trade relations bureau	S11
Training and employment service	L34
Training camp activities commission	N26
Training camp activities commission	W85
Training service	L12
Transport economics and statistics bureau	IC1 ste
Transportation and communications service	GS8
Transportation and international services bureau	P10
Transportation and public utilities service	GS8
Transportation bureau	P10
Transportation bureau	WT2
Transportation department	TD
Transportation investigation and research bureau	Y3.T68
Transportation office	D117
Transportation, Office of Chief of	W109.300
Transportation research (and development) command	D117.8
Transportation routes, Seaboard, Select committee on	Y4.T68
Transportation service	W98
Treasurer of United States	T40, T63.300
Treasury department	T
Treaties	S9
Tripartite claims commissioner	S3.37
Troop information and education division	M104, D107
Tropical forest experiment station	A13.64
Truman, Harry S., Pres. U.S. 1945-1953	Pr33

A-41

Trust territory of Pacific islands	I35.17
Tuberculosis committee	Y3.T79
Tyler, John, Pres. U.S. 1841-1845	Pr10

U

Un American activities, Special committee on. House	Y4.Un1/2
Un American activities, Special committee on. Senate	Y4.Un1
Unemployment and relief, Special committee to investigate	Y4.Un2/2
Unemployment insurance. Committee. Senate	Y4.Un2
Unemployment insurance service	L33
Unemployment problems, Special committee on. Senate	Y4.Un2/3
Union catalog (division)	LC18
United Nations conference on food and agriculture	S5.41
United Nations conference on international organization	S5.44
United States and Mexican claims commission	S3.12
U.S. Antarctic projects officer	D1.32:
U.S. Army audit agency	D101.3
United States army medical research institute of infectious diseases	D104.27
U.S. Army Natick laboratories	in D106
United States constitution sesquicentennial commission	Y3.Un3
United States court for China	S14
United States court of military appeals	D1.19
United States grain corporation	Y3.W56
U.S. High commission for Austria	S1.88-89
U.S. High commissioner for Germany	S1.90-91
United States information agency	IA
United States international trade commission	TC
United States mission to the United Nations	S5.55
United States national committee for vital and health statistics	HE20.6211
United States national committee on vital and health statistics	FS2.63
U.S. Naval air development center	D217.19
U.S. Naval avionics facility, Indianapolis, Ind.	D217.11
U.S. Naval civil engineer corps	in D209
U.S. Naval civil engineering research and evaluation laboratory	D209.12
United States naval ordnance laboratory, White Oak, Md.	D217.22
United States naval ordnance test station, China Lake, Calif.	D215.11:, D217.23
U.S. Naval postgraduate school	D208.14
U.S. Naval propellant plant	D215.12, D217.15
U.S. Naval radiological defense laboratory	D213.13
United States postal service	P
United States-Puerto Rico Commission on the status of Puerto Rico	Y3.Un3/5
United States railway association	Y3.R13/4
United States school garden army	I16.28
United States study commission on Neches, Trinity, Brazos, and San Jacinto river basins and intervening area	Y3.Un3/2
United States study commission on Southeast river basins	Y3.Un3/4
United States travel bureau	I29.37
United States travel service	C47
Upper Great Lakes regional commission	Y3.Up6
Urban management assistance administration	HH8
Urban mass transportation administration	TD7
Urban renewal administration	HH7
Utah	I1.31, 32

Utilization and disposal service	GS9

V

Valuation bureau	IC1 val
Valuation division	IC1.69
Van Buren, Martin, Pres. U.S. 1837-1841	Pr8
Vegetable physiology and pathology division	A28
Venezuelan boundary commission	Y3.V55
Ventilation and acoustics, Committee on	Y4.V56
Veterans administration	VA
Veterans affairs committee. House	Y4.V64/3
Veterans affairs committee. Senate	Y4.V64/4
Veterans affairs, Joint committee on	Y4.V64/2
Veterans bureau	VB, VA3
Veterans bureau investigation select committee. Senate	Y4.V64
Veterans education appeals board	Y3.V64
Veterans reemployment rights division (office)	L25
Vicksburg national military park commission	W54
Virgin islands	I1.65, I35.13
Virgin islands agricultural experiment station	A10.26, A77.491
Virginia and North Carolina, Department of and James, Division of	W67
Visayas, Department of	W80
vocational division	I16.54, FS5.121
Vocational rehabilitation office	FS10, FS13.200
Volunteers in service to America	AA3.9

W

Wage and hour and public contracts division	L22
Wage and hour division	L36.200
Wage and hour division	L20
Wage stabilization board	ES2
Wages and prices. Select committee to investigate. Senate	Y4.W12
Walter Reed Army Institute of Research (medical center) (general hospital)	D104.15
War assets administration	Pr32.200, Y3.W19/8
War claims arbiter	Y3.W19/4
War claims commission	Y3.W19/9
War college division	W26
War communications board	Pr32.5600
War contracts price adjustment board	Y3.W19/6
War department	W
War department claims board	W93
War finance corporation	Y3.W19/3
War finance division	T66
War food administration	A80
War industries board	Y3.C83:51, Y3.W19/2
War information office	Pr32.5000
War investigating commission	Y3.W19
War labor policies board	L11
War labor policies board	Y3.W19/5
War loan organization	T1.27
War manpower commission	Pr32.5200
War mobilization and reconversion office	Y3.W19/7
War mobilization office	Pr32.5900
War plans division	W26
War policies commission	Y3.W19/5

War production board	Pr32.4800
War records office	W45
War relocation authority	Pr32.5400, I52
War risk insurance bureau	T49
War risk litigation bureau	J18
War shipping administration	Pr32.5300
War trade board	WT
War trade board section	S13
Ward, Montgomery & Co., Select committee to investigate seizure of	Y4.W21
Washington	I1.35
Washington, Department of	W52
Washington, George, Commission for celebrating 200th anniversary of	Y3.W27/2
Washington, George, Pres. U.S. 1789-1797	Pr1
Washington metropolitan problems joint committee	Y4.W27/2
Washington monument, Joint commission to complete	Y3.W27
Washington railway and elevated company, Special committee	Y4.W27
Waste reclamation service	C20
Water carriers division	IC1 wat
Water hygiene office	HE20.1700
Water power committee. House	Y4.W29
Water program(s) (operations) office	EP2
Water quality office	EP2
Water resources council	Y3.W29
Watertown arsenal	D105.13
Watervliet arsenal	D105.20
Waterways experiment station	D103.24
Ways and means committee. House	Y4.W36
Weather bureau	A29, C30
Welfare administration	FS14
Welfare and education of congressional pages, Select committee. House	Y4.W45
Western division and western department	W76
Western hemisphere immigration, Select committee on	Y3.W52
Wheat director	Y3.W56
Wheeler, Burton K., Select committee on investigation of charges against	Y4.W56
White County bridge commission, Select committee to conduct an investigation and study financial position of	Y4.W58
White House conference on aging	Y3.W58/4
White House conference on child health and protection	Y3.W58
White House conference on children	Y3.W58/3-2
White House conference on children and youth	Y3.W58/3
White House conference on conservation	Y3.W58/6
White House conference on education committee	Y3.W58/2
White House conference on equal employment opportunity	Y3.W58/13
White House conference on export expansion	Y3.W58/8
White House conference on food, nutrition and health	Y3.W58/16
White house conference on handicapped individuals	Y3.W58/18
White House conference on health	Y3.W58/14
White House conference on industrial world ahead	Y3.W58/17
White House conference on international cooperation	Y3.W58/11
White House conference on mental retardation	Y3.W58/9
White House conference on narcotic and drug abuse	Y3.W58/5
White House conference on national economic issues	Y3.W58/7
White House conference on natural beauty	Y3.W58/12

White House conference on youth	Y3.W58/3-3
White House conference "to fulfill these rights"	Y3.W58/15
White Sands missile range, N.Mex.	D105.23
Wickersham commission	Y3.N21/7
Wildlife conservation committee. House	Y4.W64/2
Wildlife research laboratory	I49.47
Wildlife resources, Special committee on. Senate	Y4.W64
Wilson, Woodrow, Pres. U.S. 1913-1921	Pr28
Wireless telegraphy, Inter-departmental board on	Y3.W74
Woman suffrage, Senate, Select committee on	Y4.W84
Woman's committee	Y3.C83:61
Women's bureau	L13, L36.100
Woodrow Wilson centennial celebration commission	Y3.W86
Woodrow Wilson international center for scholars	SI12
Woodrow Wilson memorial commission	Y3.W86/2
Woods Hole laboratory	I49.62
Wool, Special committee to investigate production, transportation and marketing of. Senate	Y4.W88
Work programs bureau	L32
Work projects administration	FW4
Workers compensation programs, Office of	L36.400
Working conditions service	L14
Workmen's compensation programs office	L36.400
Works progress administration	Y3.W89/2
World power conference	S5.36
World war foreign debt commission	Y3.W89
World war veterans legislation committee. House	Y4.W89
Wright air development center	D301.45/5
Wyoming	I1.36

Y

Yards and docks bureau	N21, M205, D209
Yorktown monument or centennial commission	Y3.Y8
Yorktown sesquicentennial commission	Y3.Y8/2
Youth development and delinquency prevention administration	HE17.800
Youth development office	HE1.300